SEE & CONTROL
Demons
&
Pains

رؤية الجن و الآلام
و السيطرة عليها

From My Eyes, Senses and Theories

في نظري، و إحساسي و نظرياتي

Book 2
الكتاب الثاني

By
Rizwan Qureshi

تأليف
رضوان قرشي

true information and incidents 100%
about Demons & Pains

معلومات و مواقف صحيحة 100 % عن الجن و الآلام

A TEXTBOOK ON DEMONS
كتاب عن الجن

My first book, See and Control Demons and Pains, I wrote sometime between the end of year 2010 and the beginning of year 2011. In book 2, even on some same topics, I will try to give better and more explanations with lots of new and more advance topics about demons and the rest of the invisible world.

لقد قمت بتأليف كتابي الأول، رؤية الجن و الآلام و السيطرة عليها، في الفترة ما بين عام 2010 و عام 2011. سأحاول في كتابي الثاني أن أذكر تفسيرات أكثر و بشكل أفضل، حتي في نفس المواضيع و سأذكر مواضيع كثيرة متقدمة عن الجن و باقي العالم الغير مرئي.

In dreams, pictures, novels, and movies, demons and ghosts are presented as really big and tall monsters with big long hairy black hands and legs, long ugly ears, big scary red and silver eyes, and sharp red blood teeth, etc. But in reality, they are not big at all. Demons do not look scary or bloody at all. They are really small flying objects, from very small size to a size of a small cockroach. They are either a smoky blackish color or a very light smoky black and clear color combination. Demons, even if they are very small and look very harmless when flying in the air, actually are extremely powerful and damaging creatures. Demons and pains are different from each other but still a lot similar. Demons have a lot of power to hurt and damage a living body physically and mentally. Demons can damage any part or any organ of a body by taking the possession of that body, including the brain, heart, and other major organs. Demons can very easily damage the physical brain and even thoughts, emotions, and temperament by possessing a body and by the use of powerful hypnotism. Demons are very sensible & intelligent objects or bodies. Demons are not parasites. Demons share our food in shape of energy sometimes during the time, they possessed our body. Pains are more damaging compared to demons because pains stay in our bodies for twenty-four hours. During their stay inside us to get food or energy, pains damage some tissues and joints. Demons are always in and out, so they do not damage us just to get some energy. Demons usually get their energy from the atmosphere. So demons are less damaging for our body and parts as compared to pains because demons live less inside our bodies.

يعرض الجن و الأشباح بالأحلام ،و الصور،و الروايات و الأفلام بشكل وحوش مخيفة حجمها و طولها كبير، أرجلهم و أيديهم كبيرة و طويلة، بها شعر أسود كثيف، ولها أذن طويلة و بشعة، وعيون حمراء و فضية مخيفة، و أسنان حادة مغطاة بالدم إلخ...لكنها في الحقيقة ما هي كبيرة،. الجن ما هم مخيفين ، هم مخلوقات صغيرة طائرة ، حجمها يتراوح ما بين الحجم الصغير جداً، إلي حجم الصرصار الصغير، لونها أسود حالك مثل الدخان، أوخليط من الأسود الخفيف و الأسود الشفاف... برغم إن الجن حجمهم صغير جداً و شكلهم غير ضار وهم يطيرون في الهواء، إلا أن لهم مخلوقات قوية و مدمرة جداً في الحقيقة. الجن و الآلام مختلفين عن بعضهم، لكن بينهم تشابه كبير. الجن لهم قدرة كبيرة علي إحداث الألم للكائن الحي جسدياً و عقلياً. الجن يقدروا يدمروا أي جزء أو عضو من الجسم بالسيطرة علي هذا الجسم، بما فيه من عقل و قلب و أعضاء رئيسية. الجن يمكن أن يدمروا المخ و حتي الأفكار ، و المشاعر و الأمزجة، بالسيطرة علي الجسم، و إستخدام التنويم المغناطيسي.الجن كائنات أو أجسام حساسة و ذكية جداً. الجن ما هم طفيليات. هم يشاركونا طعامنا في شكل طاقة خلال اليوم أحياناً، فهم يسيطرون علي أجسامنا. الآلام مدمرة أكثر من الجن، لأن الآلام تستمر في أجسامنا أربعة و عشرون ساعة وتدمر بعض الأنسجة و المفاصل في جسمنا أثناء و جود الجن بداخلنا ليحصلوا علي الطعام أو الطاقة.

1

SEE & CONTROL DEMONS & PAIN

Demons are the most intelligent and a major part of the invisible parallel world. In the invisible world, only demons have the tool or the language of hypnotism, unlike other creatures in the parallel invisible world. Not all demons live inside a living body because very limited numbers of living bodies are available as compared to the number of demons. Most demons live here and there and keep looking and fighting with each other to have a possession of a living body. Demons do not live in a dead body. Demons like to live on a same kind of breed or race instead of keep finding new breed once old living body died. But all demons are equally capable of possessing and controlling any living body. Almost each and every living body is possessed by a demon.

The population of the demons is so much even they live each and every living body like trees, insects, birds, animals, human, still for every 1000+, demons, and only one living body is available. If they cannot find a living body, usually demons live in an open atmosphere temporarily in the daytime and in relatively dark and unused places in our houses and offices in the night time. Pains are different from demons. Pains are not capable of hypnotizing any living body. Pains are 50 percent parasites as compared to diseases. Pains cannot live in an open atmosphere. Pains always need a medium to reside in. Pains usually do not leave a living body easily.

الجن يدخلون في أجسامنا و يخرجون منها ليحصلوا علي الطاقة فقط، كي لا يدمرونا. عادة الجن يحصلون علي الطاقة من الهواء، لهذا فالجن أقل تدميراً بالمقارنة بالآلام لأنهم يعيشون في أجسامنا مدة أقل. الجن أكثر المخلوقات ذكاءاً، وهي جزء من العالم الغير مرئي الموازي لعالمنا، ففي العالم الغير مرئي، يملك الجن وحدهم أدوات و لغة التنويم المغناطيسي، بالمخالفة للكائنات الأخري الموجودة بذلك العالم الموازي لعالمنا. لا يعيش الجن كلهم داخل الأجساد، لأن أعدادها محدودة بالنسبة لأعداد الجن.

يعيش معظم الجن هنا و هناك و يستمرون في البحث عن جسم حي للسيطرة عليه و يتصارعون من أجل هذا.لا يعيش الجن في جسم ميت. يحب الجن أن يعشوا علي نفس النوع من النسل أو العرق، بدلاً من البحث عن نسل جديد، بمجرد أن يموت الجسم الحي الإستحواذ و السيطرة علي أي جسم حي. تقريباً كل جسم حي يسيطر عليه جني.إن عدد الجن كثير لدرجة أنهم يعيشون في كل جسم حي، مثل الأشجار، و الحشرات و الطيور و الحيوانات والإنسان. يوجد حوالي أكثر من ألف جني في مقابل جسم حي واحد موجود. إذا لم يجد الجن جسم حي، فهم غالباً يعيشون في الجو المفتوح بالنهار وفي أماكن مظلمة و غير مستخدمة في بيوتنا و مكاتبنا بالليل. تختلف الآلام عن الجن. الآلام لا تقدر علي تنويم أي جسم حي، فهي عبارة عن طفيليات بنسبة 50% بالمقارنة بالأمراض. لا تقدر الآلام علي أن تعيش في الجو المفتوح، فهي تحتاج إلي وسط تعيش فيه، و لا تترك الجسم الحي بسهولة. تحتاج الآلام إلي بعض الطاقة لتنشيط نفسها، عند بقائها في الجسم الحي. الآلام لا تأكل أجسامنا أو أعضائنا مثل الأمراض.، لكن لابد أن تدمر جزء من أجسامنا من الداخل كي تحصل علي طعامها في شكل طاقة، فهم يمكنهم الحصول عليها عندما يحتاجونها.

During their stay in a living body, pains always need some energy to energize them. Pains don't eat our body or organs like diseases. But to get their food in the shape of energy, they damage a little bit of that source inside our body, where they can suck some energy whenever they need it. Usually pains make room between our joints, between our skull & brain, inside the muscles or backbone area, in some other areas from where they can feed or energize themselves easily. The minor damages created by these pains open a wide door for diseases/insects to attack damaged parts or organs, & eventually, those diseases/insects become the cause of major cancers and infections. Pains are not totally wild or insensible like diseases. Pains are sensible and able to understand our communications, but still pains are not as sensible as demons are. In figures, I can say, as compared to the demons, pains are 50 percent less sensible but at least 75 percent more responsible for physical damages. Pains also expand themselves like demons, but demons are not limited to any particular size; demons can expand themselves to possess any physical living body regardless of whether it's an elephant or a very small spider. Pains can only expand themselves usually to create a damaging block in our organs or to clog heart vessels, the kidney, the brain, or brain vessels, etc. Pains cannot expand themselves to all over the body.

عادة توجد اللآلام بين مفاصلنا، بين جماجمنا و أمخاخنا، داخل عضلاتنا، أو في عمودنا الفقري، و أيضاً في بعض المناطق التي يستطيعون أن يحصلوا علي غذائهم ليتزودوا بالطاقة بسهولة. تفتح الأضرار الكبيرة التي تسببها الآلام الباب أمام الأمراض/ الحشرات لتهاجم الأجزاء أو الأعضاء المصابة بالضرر، و في النهاية تكون هذه الأمراض / الحشرات سبباً رئيسياً في السرطانات و الإصابات. لا تعتبر الآلام فظيعة أو غير مدركة، لكنها تدرك و تفهم إتصالاتنا، لا تكون بقدر إدراك الجن. نقدر نقول بالأرقام إن الآلام أقل إدراكاً من الجن بنسبة 50%، لكنها تكون مسئولة أكثر عن الأضرار الجسمانية بنسبة 75% بالمقارنة بالجن. تمتد الآلام مثل الجن، لكن الجن لا ينحصرون في حيز معين، فهم قادرون علي نشر أو مد أنفسهم في أي جسم حي، سواء كان جسم فيل أو جسم عنكبوت صغير. تنتشر الآلام لتحدث كتلة ضارة في أعضائنا أو لتسد أوعية القلب، أو الكلي ، أو المخ، أو أوعية المخ، إلخ. لا تقدر الآلام علي نشر نفسها في الجسم كله.لا تقدر اللآلام علي السيطرة التامة علي الجسم الحي، فهي فقط تختار بعض الأماكن به. ترسل الآلام إشارات مؤلمة لأجزاء كثيرة من الجسم الحي أثناء الأكل أو الحصول علي الطاقة فالضغط المرتفع و المنخفض أو إنسداد أنابيب الإنزيمات تكون بسبب إنتشار اللآلام .تعتبر الأمراض حشرات صغيرة جداً بشكل أساسي ولا تري بالعين المجردة لأنها صغيرة جداً.لا تنتمي الأمراض إلي نفس الجنس أو الطبقة أو النسل مثل الجن و الآلام.

تعتبر هذه الأمراض أو الحشرات الصغيرة السبب الرئيسي للإصابات الكبيرة و السرطانات، حيث تأكل هذه الأعضاء و الأجزاء بإستمرار.

Pains cannot possess any living body completely; they just choose some areas of living bodies. During the process of feeding or getting energy, pains send hurtful signals to a lot of parts of the living body. High blood pressure, low blood pressure, or blockage of harmony or enzyme-delivery tubes is caused by the expansion quality of the pains. Diseases are basically very tiny insects. They are not visible to the naked eye because they are very small. Diseases do not belong to the same gender or class or breed like demons or pains. These diseases or tiny insects are the main causes of creating major infections and cancers by continuously eating those organs and the parts. Diseases cannot expand themselves. Diseases/insects do not have the quality of hypnotizing or possessing a living body. Diseases/ insects are 100 percent very dangerous parasites. Once diseases/ insects attack any organ or a part of the living body, they do not leave that body until they eat that part/body completely; even if that body dies, they do not leave until they eat that body completely. The attack of diseases/insects is continuous. Demons and pains do not live on dead bodies. They leave the body immediately once it dies. Demons do not stay in a body under attack or under some kind of extreme behavior; somehow most demons feel insecure and leave that body for some time. Usually regular demons start leaving a body during extreme and negative activity, like yelling, being angry, fighting, etc. The reason for this is during those conditions, living bodies start absorbing all kinds of insects, pains, and uncountable demons from the open atmosphere. This makes less brave demons come out from that insecure body. Usually they choose to stay either in an open atmosphere or any available living body temporarily until their permanent host body returns to a secure and normal level. Pains do not leave bodies easily. Even in an unusual or any extreme condition when, usually leave the insecure body, pains still stay there.

لا يمكن للأمراض/ الحشرات أن تنشر نفسها ، فهي لا تملك القدرة علي تنويم الجسم الحيمغناطيسياً أو إمتلاكه، وهي طفيليات خطيرة جداً 100%، فبمجرد أن تهاجم الأمراض / الحشرات أي عضو أو جزء من الجسم الحي، لا تتركه إلا بعد أن تأكل هذا الجزء/ الجسم تماماً، حتي لو مات هذا الجسم ، لا تتركه حتي تأكله تماماً. يظل هجوم الأمراض / الحشرات مستمراً. لا يعيش الجن و الآلام في الجسم الميت، فهم يتركون الجسم بعد موته مباشرةً. لا يبقي الجن في جسم يتعرض للهجوم أو لأي نوع من السلوك المتطرف، فمعظم الجن يشعرون بعدم الأمان نوعاً ما ويتركون الجسم بعض الوقت. عادة يترك الجن العاديون الجسم أثناء حدوث نشاط سلبي حاد ، مثل الصراخ، و الغضب و الصراع، إلخ...السبب في ذلك هو أن الأجسام الحية تمتص كل أنواع الحشرات و الآلام و العدد الذي لا يحصي من الجن من الجو أثناء حدوث كل هذه الظروف. و هذا يجعل الجن الأقل شجاعة يخرجون من هذا الجسم الغير آمن، فهم يختارون أن يبقوا إما في الجو، أو في أي جسم موجود مؤقتاً إلي أن يعود الجسم المضيف لمستوي طبيعي آمن.لا تترك اللاآلام الجسم بسهولة.، حتي في حالة تعرضه لأي ظروف حادة ، التي عادة ما يجب علي الآلام أن تترك الجسم الغير آمن فيها ، فإن الآلام تظل موجودة به. و لا تترك الجسم إلا في حالة موته. إن العلاج أو إجراء الجراحات تجعل الآلام تترك الجسم، لكن هذا يكون بشكل مؤقت.، فإما أن ترجع نفس الألم للجسم أو يبدأ ألم جديد في البقاء به. تعتبر الأمراض/ الحشرات الغير مرئية شيئ مختلف تماماً عن الجن. كل فعل تحدثه تلك الأمراض / الحشرات هو عبارة عن الأكل و التدمير و القتل بنسبة 100%.

Rizwan Qureshi	رؤية الجن و الآلام السيطرة عليها

Pains only leave a body once a body is dead. Some medical treatment or surgeries also make them leave, but this is very temporary; either the same pain comes back or another pain starts living in that body. Invisible diseases/insects are very different from demons. Each and every action of diseases/insects is 100 percent just eating, damaging, and killing.

The only solution is to kill these diseases/insects to get cure from major infections and all kind of cancers. Later on in this book, I will describe how we can secure our body from the attacks of these cancer diseases/insects and, if someone is already suffering from any cancer, how they can be cured from that cancer very easily by using my cancer cure procedures with the help and advice of their doctors. I do not think it will be difficult or expensive anymore to treat any cancer once my procedure is adopted properly by medical Science.On same topic, this is my second book. To understand a lot of things and theories, it will be very helpful for a reader to read book 1 first. A lot of things, terms, theories I am using or talking about, because, I just assumed that reader is already aware about it. It will be very difficult for a direct reader of book 2 to understand and absorb these unbelievable and mysterious information and knowledge.

لا يمكن للأمراض/ الحشرات أن تنشر نفسها ، فهي لا تملك القدرة علي تنويم الجسم الحيمغناطيسياً أو إمتلاكه، وهي طفيليات خطيرة جداً 100%، فبمجرد أن تهاجم الأمراض / الحشرات أي عضو أو جزء من الجسم الحي، لا تتركه إلا بعد أن تأكل هذا الجزء/ الجسم تماماً، حتي لو مات هذا الجسم ، لا تتركه حتي تأكله تماماً . يظل هجوم الأمراض / الحشرات مستمراً. لا يعيش الجن و الآلام في الجسم الميت، فهم يتركون الجسم بعد موته مباشرةً. لا يبقي الجن في جسم يتعرض للهجوم أو لأي نوع من السلوك المتطرف، فمعظم الجن يشعرون بعدم الأمان نوعاً ما ويتركون الجسم بعض الوقت. عادة يترك الجن العاديون الجسم أثناء حدوث نشاط سلبي حاد ، مثل الصراخ، و الغضب و الصراع، إلخ...السبب في ذلك هو أن الأجسام الحية تمتص كل أنواع الحشرات و الآلام و العدد الذي لا يحصي من الجن من الجو أثناء حدوث كل هذه الظروف. و هذا يجعل الجن الأقل شجاعة يخرجون من هذا الجسم الغير آمن، فهم يختارون أن يبقوا إما في الجو، أو في أي جسم موجود مؤقتاً إلي أن يعود الجسم المضيف لمستوي طبيعي آمن.لا تترك اللآلام الجسم بسهولة.، حتي في حالة تعرضه لأي ظروف حادة ، التي عادة ما يجب علي الآلام أن تترك الجسم الغير آمن فيها ، فإن الآلام تظل موجودة به. و لا تترك الجسم إلا في حالة موته. إن العلاج أو إجراء الجراحات تجعل الآلام تترك الجسم، لكن هذا يكون بشكل مؤقت.، فإما أن ترجع نفس الألم للجسم أو يبدأ ألم جديد في البقاء به. تعتبر الأمراض/ الحشرات الغير مرئية شيئ مختلف تماماً عن الجن. كل فعل تحدثه تلك الأمراض / الحشرات هو عبارة عن الأكل و التدمير و القتل بنسبة 100%.

SEE & CONTROL DEMONS & PAIN

It will be really difficult for a direct reader to understand a lot of ideas and theories in this book. So it is a very good idea to read book 1 first to understand and learn all the definitions, explanations, actions, reactions, incidents, and theories about the demons, pains, and diseases around us. Like book 1, I am also categorizing book 2 in three major parts related and is of concern to us, i.e., demons, pains, and diseases. Or in other words, those who bother and hurt us most. So demons are mainly responsible for hypnotizing and possessing our bodies, animals, trees, boards, reptiles, insects, etc., to create some good but mostly very bad situations for us, like anger, extreme behavior, too much crazy love or hate, unhealthy competition, anxiety and panic attacks, too much disappointment, suicidal tendencies, depression, etc. Second part is the pains. Pains are not as nice or friendly as demons are. But pains are not as cruel or bad or hurtful as diseases. Third are the diseases/invisible insects. They are completely 100 percent hunters, 100 percent parasites. They just eat our bodies continuously. The cruel actions of these diseases create all kinds of infections and cancers. Their cruel action of eating and killing externally/ internally equally hurts us, trees, animals, birds, etc. These diseases/ insects cannot hurt or kill or damage any of the demons or pains because of their electromagnetic structure.Demons and pains do not have any blood or meat in their bodies whatever these diseases/insects like to eat all the time by damaging and killing us.

رضوان قرشي

الجزء الثاني هو الآلام. إليست الآلام جيدة و ودودة مثل الجن، لكنها ليست بنفس قسوة و سوء و ألم الأمراض. ثالثاً الأمراض/ الحشرات الغير مرئية التي تعتبر مسببة للألم و طفيليات بنسبة100%.، وهي تأكل أجسامنا 100% بإستمرار.تسبب أفعال هذه الأمراض القاسية كل أنواع الإصابات و السرطانات. إن ما تفعله هذه الأمراض من أكل و قتل داخلياً/خارجياً، يتسبب في الألم لنا وللأشجار و الحيوانات و الطيور، إلخ...لا تقدر هذه الأمراض/الحشرات علي إصابة أو قتل أو تدمير أي جني من الجن أو الآلام، لأن لها تركيبة كهرومغناطيسية.

الجن و الآلام ليس لهما دم ولا لحم في أجسادهما. تأكل الأمراض/الحشرات عن طريق تدميرنا و قتلنا. لا يحبنا الجن أبداً، لكن لهم نظام أسر و إسلوب حياة مثلنا تماماً، قد يكون السبب الوحيد في هذا هو أنهم يحيطون بنا كثيراً. يختار الجن أركان و أماكن غير مستخدمة بكثرة، مثل تحت الأسرة، السندرات، وراء الأريكة، و الخزائن، و المخازن و الحمامات، والأشجار، و في كل تلك الأماكن التي لا نذهب إليها غالباً.يعيش الجن دائماً في مجموعة مثل الأسرة، و نحن الذين ندفع إيجار أو رهن البيت،وأيضاً ندفع التأمين وفاتورة الكهرباء و فاتورة المياه. نحن نقول ونظن أننا نملك البيت، لكن في الحقيقة الجن هم الأكثر سيطرة في بيوتنا و في أماكن أخري. فكر في الأمر بهذه الطريقة.

Demons do not look like us at all, but their living style and family system are exactly like ours. The only reason for this possibly is because demons stay around us so much. Demons choose really dark corners and least used places, like under beds, attics, behind a couch or sofa, behind cabinets, cupboards, backseats of cars, cabinets in restrooms, trees, and all those places and areas where we do not go frequently. Demons always live in a group as a family. We are the ones who pay the rent or the mortgage of the house. We are the ones who pay the insurance, electric bill, gas, and water bill. We say and think we are the owner of the house, but actually, these demons are more dominant in our houses and other places. Think of it this way—how long have you been living in your house? Now think how long the demons have been living in that house. How long do we usually live? Usually demons live several thousands of years. When I started cleaning my house for demons, I thought they were gone, but I was wrong. Once a demon cannot move freely in a particular place, they usually change places. So when I started removing them from some areas of my house and from my workplace, I thought they were all gone, but actually they never left my house or workplace. They were still there. Instead of flying everywhere, they limit themselves to those areas of my house I use least. They just move to all those corners of the house where usually I will never bother them.

رؤية الجن و الآلام السيطرة عليها

كم من الوقت كنت تعيش في المنزل؟ و كم من الوقت نعيش عادةً؟ . يعيش الجن عادة عدة آلاف من السنين.عندما بدأت أنظف بيتي ظننت أن الشياطين ذهبوا، لكنني كنت مخطئاً. بمجرد أن يصبح الجني غير قادر علي علي الحركة بحرية في مكان محدد، فإنه يغير أماكنه عادةً، فعندما بدأت أن أطردهم من بعض الأماكن في بيتي و في مكان عملي ظننت أنهم رحلوا جميعاً، لكنهم في الحقيقة لم يتركوا بيتي ولا مكان عملي أبداً، لقد ظلوا باقين هناك.و بدلاً من أن يطيروا هنا و هناك، حددوا إقامتهم في المناطق التي لا أستخدمها كثيراً. إنهم يتحركون في أركان البيت التي لا أضايقهم فيها أبداً. ربما حالتي غير عادية قليلاً، فليس من السهل مضايقة الجن. تعلمت من تجربتي أنه من الأفضل أن نترك لهم القليل من الأماكن بالبيت. لا تعتبر الصراع مع الجن فكرة جيدة، لهذا إتركهم يعيشون في بعض المناطق بالبيت و أن ترك لهم بعض الأماكن.بمجرد أن يعيش الجن في مكان ما لوقت طويل، لا يتركونه بسهولة بأي حال من الأحوال، لهذا فإن التصرف السليم هو عدم مضايقتهم كثيراً. يجب أن نتركهم و نتجنب الذهاب إلي هذه الأماكن من البيت حيث يعيشون، بقدر الإمكان. عادة ما تكون هذه الأماكن من البيت مظلمة معظم الوقت و لا تستخدمه كثيراً، فإذا لم تضايقهم عمداً، فلن يقوموا بمضايقتك أيضاً.

7

SEE & CONTROL DEMONS & PAIN	رضوان قرشي
Maybe my case is a little bit unusual; it is not easy to bother demons. From this experience, I learned that it is a better idea if we just leave a few places for them in the house. Honestly, it is not a good idea to pick a fight with demons, so let them live in some areas of house and leave a few places for them. Once demons live in a particular place for a long time, there is no way they will leave that place easily. So the better policy is not to bother them too much. Leave them alone, and avoid going to those areas of the house as much possible where they live. Usually these are places in your house stay dark most of the time and you do not use them as much. If you are not bothering them intentionally, chances are they will not bother you either. How will you know which areas of your house are totally occupied by the demons? Usually, when you go to those areas of the house, either you will get a headache, start vomiting, have hyper feelings, depression, or some kind of panic attack, etc. This will happen every time with anyone who goes in those areas. I hope these are enough signs for you. So be careful and do not take any risk; just leave them alone and stay in your areas only. It sounds wrong and bad, but trust me, you do not have too many choices. The worst thing you can do is go in those areas of your house, sit there, and eat your lunch or dinner there. I hope you will never make these kinds of mistakes.	كيف ستعرف المناطق التي يتواجد بها الجن في بيتك؟.عادةً عندما تذهب إلي تلك المناطق، إما ستشعر بصداع، أو ستتقيأ، أو ستشعر بشعور حاد،أو بإكتئاب، أو نوع من الرعب.، إلخ...سيحدث ذلك مع أي شخص يذهب إلي تلك المناطق. أتمني أن تكون هذه العلامات كافية بالنسبة لك، لهذا كن حريصاً ولا تغامر. عليك أن تبقي في المناطق المخصصة لك فقط. يبدو ذلك سيئ و خطأ لكن ثق بي، ليس لديك خيارات كثيرة.أسوأ ما يمكنك فعله هو أن تذهب إلي هذه المناطق في بيتك و تأكل غذائك أو عشائك بها. أتمني ألا تقوم أبداً بإرتكاب مثل هذه الأخطاء. ليس من الجيد ترك البيت تحت تصرف الجن. إنهم موجودون في كل مكان وفي كل بيت. بعضهم شرير و بعضهم في غاية الشر. أفضل طريقة للتعامل معهم هي أن تترك لهم بعض المناطق التي تشعر بوجود ضغط أو مشاكل من الجن. أنني أعتبر أن الشخص الذي يقرر أن يصارع الجن أو يهزمهم، شخص أحمق. إنها فكرة سيئة لأن الأشخاص العاديون لا يقدرون أن يروا الجن. يقدر الجن أن يسيطروا علي أذهان الأشخاص العاديون و علي تفكيرهم بنسبة 100%، بتنويمهم مغناطيسياً. لا يقدر أن يصارعهم أي شخص طبيعي. لا تفكر حتي في أن تهزمهم.إنها فكرة سيئة أن يعلمك شخص ما هذا. سأشرح في هذا الكتاب لاحقاً كيف يمكنك أن تجعل الجن أصدقائك و أن تطلب منهم البقاء في بيتك بدون أن يضايقونك أو يؤذونك.

It is not a good idea to leave the house due to them. They are everywhere. They are in every house. Some are bad & some are very bad. The best way to handle them is to just leave some areas for them, where you feel, more pressure or problems, due to demons. I will consider a normal person a fool and not smart if he decides to fight with demons or try to defeat demons. It is a very bad idea. They are invisible to normal people. Demons are 100 percent capable of controlling minds and thoughts by hypnotizing normal people. Nobody normal can fight with them. Do not even think about defeating them. Very bad idea if someone is teaching you this. Later on in this book, I will describe how to make them your friend and how to ask them to live in your house without bothering and hurting you. Demons live in groups in particular areas of our houses. Even if they are not paying for the house, they are still the owners of those places. People come and go from houses, but the same demons keep living in the same places. No doubt if you leave a house dark and vacant for long time, demons will have more control of that house or place. And later on, if someone tries to occupy that house, those demons will do their best to harass those people by scaring them through scary dreams, keeping them sick, by mental illness, etc. Later on in this book, I will describe what to do when you occupy or start living in an old or vacant place.

رؤية الجن و الآلام السيطرة عليها

يعيش الجن في مجموعات في مناطق معينة في بيوتنا. حتى لو لم يدفعوا مالاً من أجل المنزل، فهم مازالوا يملكون هذه الأماكن به. يجيئ و يرحل الناس من المنازل، لكن يبقى نفس الجن في نفس الأماكن. لاشك إذا تركت بيتك مظلماً و خالياً لفترة، سيسيطر الجن عليه أكثر.إ ذا حاول بعض الأشخص البقاء في البيت، سيبذل هؤلاء الجن ما في وسعهم لمضايقتهم بالأحلام المخيفة و أن بيقوهم مرضي بدنياً أو عقلياً إلخ...سأشرح لاحقاً كيف تسكن في بيت قديم أو خالي.

لا يمكن لآي شخص أن يحارب أو يهزم الجن السيئ أو الشرير. لا تفكر في ذلك أو تتعب نفسك إلا إذا تأثر أحد أفراد عائلتك بهم.لا يعتبر الصراع مع الجن صعباً، لكن فكرتي و نظريتي و سياستي هي أنك إذا لم تضايقهم لن يضايقونا، هكذا ببساطة. تذكر أننا نستطيع أن نؤذيهم أو نضايقهم بنسبة 1%، لكنهم يمكنهم أن يؤذوننا أو يضايقوننا بنسبة 99%، لذا مرة أخري الصراع معهم ليس فكرة جيدة، إنني أقول مراراً و تكراراً لا تتصارعوا معهم و لا تضايقونهم. إذا تم ذلك سيكون من السهل أن نجعلهم أصدقائك، و بمجرد أن يصبحوا أصدقائك لن يؤذوك ، لن يؤذوك كثيراً، بل سيقومون بحمايتك من الجن الآخرين. بمجرد أن يصبحوا أصدقائك سيساعدوك كثيراً. إنك تتسائل كيف لي أن أكتب مثل تلك الأشياء والمعلومات عن الجن؟. لا يحب الجن الماء و الأماكن المضيئة، إنهم موجودون في الهواء بالداخل و الخارج و في كل مكان. يسيطر أحد الجن علي أجسامنا من حين إلي آخر عادةً، لكن هذا لا يعني أن لدينا جني واحد في بيتنا.

Nobody can fight or defeat bad or very bad demons. Do not even think or bother about it, unless someone in your family is affected due to them. It is not difficult to fight with them. But my idea, theory, and policy is if you do not bother them, they do not need to bother us. Simple. Remember, we can hurt them or bother them only 1 percent, but they can hurt us or bother us 99 percent. So again, it is not a good idea to pick a fight with them. I am, again and again, saying do not fight with them and do not bother them. This way it is easier to make them friends. And once they become friends, they will not hurt you. They will not hurt you as much; they will protect you from other demons. And once they become friends, they are very helpful. You're thinking how come I am able to write so much stuff and information about demons? Demons do not like water and bright places; they are in the air inside, outside, and everywhere. At one time or another, one demon usually possesses our body. But it doesn't mean we have only one demon in our house. In an average house, inside and outside, you can expect more than five-hundred-plus demons easily. Now the best way to live in your house in peace is to the keep lights on most of the time and spray holy water toward the ceiling, everywhere, every day. But remember, when you spray holy water, it means you are bothering demons. So you need to make sure you leave some areas of house where you don't spray holy water and you do not go there.

من المتوقع أن تجد أكثر من خمسمائة جني داخل و خارج أي بيت عادي بسهولة. إن أفضل طريقة أن تعيش في بيتك بسلام هي أن تضيئ الأضواء معظم الوقت، و أن تقوم برش مياه مقدسة نحو السقف، و في كل مكان و كل يوم. تذكر أنك عندما ترش الماء المقدس، تضايق الجن، لهذا يجب أن تترك بعض المنطق في المنزل لا ترش بالماء، و لا تذهب إلي هناك، فهذا مفيد لك و هم سيكونون سعداء أيضاً. سأشرح لك كيف تقوم بتحضير الماء المقدس بنفسك لاحقاً في هذا الكتاب. لا يذهب الجن إلي العمل، ولايقومون بإدارة الأعمال و لا يدفعون الإيجار، ولا الرهان، ولا التأمين، و لكن الحكمة الحكيمة تقول أنهم مثلنا . لديهم قوي لا يمللكها الإنسان العادي، لهذا فهم لديهم فهم الفراغ و الكثير من الوقت للتدخل في حياتنا و شئوننا. أحياناً يكونون مرتبطين بحياتنا لدرجة أنهم يسيطرون عليها دون أن ندري مطلقاً. ما تعلمناه هو أننا عندما نقع تحت سيطرة الجني، نرفض سيطرته علينا. سأقول لك كيف تبعد الجن عنك لاحقاً في هذا الكتاب.

نفس الشيئ بنطبق علي الجن و الآلام و الأمراض، لكنني سأكتب الآن عن الآلام و الأمراض.

تنتشر الأمراض في كل مكان في الصيف أو الربيع، عندما لا يكون الجو بارداً جداً. تنتشر الأمراض في الداخل و الخارج ، في الأجسام ، و الأشجار، و الحيوانات، و الزواحف، و الحشرات، وفي كل مكان. إنها تستخدم الأجسام الحية كأوساط تعيش و تأكل فيها. الحيوانات، و الطيور و الزواحف و الحشرات كلها لديها حساسية أقل من البشر.

It is good for you, and they will be happy too. Later in this book, I will tell you how to prepare holy water by yourself. Demons do not go to work or run businesses or pay rent or mortgage or insurance. But wisdom wise they are same as us. They have all kinds of powers a normal human doesn't have. So demons are basically free and they have a lot of time to interfere with our life and our affairs. Sometimes they are so much involved in our lives that they control our lives and we are totally unaware of it. So one thing we learned is when we are under the influence of a demon, we can try to reject the control of the demon. I will tell you how you can keep them away from you later in this book.

The same principle applies to demons, pains, and diseases, but I am writing about pains and diseases right now.

In the summer or spring, when the weather isn't so cold, diseases live everywhere—inside, outside, bodies, trees, animals, reptiles, insects, everywhere. They use living bodies as mediums to live and eat. Trees, animals, reptiles, birds & insects all have less sense than people, so you can say they are unable to fight against these pains and diseases. Trees, animals, birds, reptiles, and insects can't go to doctors when they suffer from pains and diseases.

رؤية الجن و الآلام السيطرة عليها

تستطيع أن تقول أنهم لا يقدرون أن يصارعوا هذه الآلام و الأمراض، فالأشجار، والحيوانات، و الطيور، و الزواحف، و الحشرات لا يستطيعون الذهاب إلي الأطباء عندما يعانون من الآلام و الأمراض. عادة يساعد البشر القليل من الحيوانات، ويقدموا لهم العلاج، و لكن حتي هذا يحدث بشكل محدود. 99% من الحيوانات لا يكون لديهم إختيار آخر. إنهم فقط يعانون أو يظلون مصابين بالمرض أو يموتون بسبب هذه الآلام و الأمراض. لكن هذا الجن، و هذه الآلام و الأمراض لا يحبون الجو البارد. في الشتاء عندما تبقي الأشجار، و الطيور و الحيوانات و الزواحف و الحشرات في الجو البارد، يترك الجن و الآلام والأمراض هذه الأجسام الباردة، و تبحث عن جو دافئ و جسم دافئ. البشر يقدرون أن يحافظوا علي درجة حرارة أجسامهم و درجة حرارة الجو من حولهم. الأجسام البشرية تعتبر أفضل بيئة لهذه الآلام و الأمراض لتعيش فيها. يصارع البشر هذه الأمراض و الآلام بتناول الأدوية. لكن تظل هذه الآلام و الأمراض تتحرك من إنسان إلي آخر في موسم الشتاء. كلما تغيرت المواسم، تعيش هذه الأمراض مرة أخري في حيوانات أخري. لا يعيش الجن و الآلام في الأجسام الميتة، فهم يتركونها في الحال و يبحثون عن جسم آخر يعيشون فيه. لكن الأمراض تعيش في الأجسام الميتة حتي تأكلها تماما، و بمجرد ألا يتبقي لها ما تأكله، عن أجسام جديدة إن الجن و الآلام و الأمراض ثلاث أشياء غير مرئية ومختلفة، ولها تصرفات مختلفة:

1. إن تصرفات الجن مختلفة، و يمكنك السيطرة عليها بسهولة بإستخدام المياه المقدسة بشكل صحيح، (أو الكهرومغناطيسية في المستقبل، حين تكتشف العلوم الطبية إشعاعات الكثافة الصحيحة).

Usually, humans can help a few animals and provide medications, but even that is limited. Ninety-nine percent of animals have no choice. They just suffer and stay sick or die because of these pains and diseases. But like everybody else, these demons, pains, and diseases don't like cold weather. In the winter when trees, birds, animals, reptiles, and insects stay out in the open in the cold climate, these demons, pains, and diseases leave those cold bodies and look for a warm atmosphere and a warm body. Humans are able to maintain the temperature of their bodies and the atmosphere around them. In the winter season, human bodies make for better places for these pains and diseases to live. Humans fight against them by using medication, but these pains and diseases still move from one human to another for the winter season. Whenever seasons change, most of these diseases start living again in other animals. Demons and pains do not live in dead bodies. They immediately leave dead bodies and find another body in which to live. Diseases, however, live in dead bodies until they have completely eaten those bodies. Once there is nothing left for them to eat, they look for new bodies. Demons, pains, and diseases are three different invisible things with different actions.

1. The actions of demons are different, and you can control them easily by using holy water properly (or electromagnetism in the future, when medical science discovers the rays of proper intensity).

2-تؤثر الآلام في أعصابنا و مفاصلنا، وعضلاتنا إلخ...إنها تبقي في مكان معين من الجسم، و ترسل إشارات الألم لمختلف أجزاء الجسم، لتحدث ألم الصداع النصفي و آلام المفاصل، و التقيؤ، و الإسهال، أو ضغط الدم المرتفع أو المنخفض. يمكن السيطرة علي هذه الآلام بسهولة بإستخدام الكهرومغناطيسية، من خلال إستخدام الإشعاعات بطريقة سليمة، لكن لابد للعلوم الطبية أن تكتشف هذه الإشعاعات.

3. الآن سوف أقول لكم كيف تسيطرون علي المرض و الإصابة و السرطان و تهزمهم لقد قلت من قبل أن هذه الأمراض عبارة عن طفيليات. إنها حشرات غير مرئية، بلا رحمة، تنتشر في الشخص. إنها تهاجمنا من زاوية 90 درجة من سطح الجسم. أقول أن 90 % من الهجمات تأتي من جهة أفقية بالنسية لسطح جسمنا. إذا كان هناك شخص يعاني من سرطان الثدي، أو سرطان في الكبد ، أو سرطان البروتستاتا، أو مرض بالقلب، أو حرقان بالمعدة، أو إصابات الأمعاء، أو المعدة، أو مرض السكر، أو مرض الغدة الدرقية، أو إصابات الكلية، أو الإصابات الداخلية و الخارجية، أو أي نوع آخر من السرطانات, التي يحتاج الشخص عمل ما يلي للتعامل مع هذه الأمراض:

أ. لابد من تناول الكثير من أقراص المضادات الحيوية، و مضادا ت البكتيريا، و مضاد الإصابة، أو مضادات السرطان، يجب أخذ تلك الأقراص علي أساس منتظماً، حتي تهزم إصابة معينة أو تهزم السرطان تماماً. لكن تذكر أنه يجب عليك أكل الطعام المناسب قبل تناول أي قرص للتقليل من الآثار الجانبية. لا تتناول أي دواء أبداً و معدتك خالية. إن هذه الأدوية تساعدك فقط في الشفاء من العدوي أو السرطان.

Rizwan Qureshi

2. Pains work on our nerves, joints, muscles, etc. They stay in one particular part of the body and send pain signals to different body parts to create migraines, arthritis pain, vomiting, diarrhea, or high/low blood pressures.

These pains can be easily controlled with electromagnetism through the use of the proper rays; however, medical science still needs to discover those rays.

3. Now I am going to tell you how to control and defeat a disease, infection, or cancer. As I said before, these diseases are parasites. They are heartless, invisible insects that can swarm a person. Their direction of attack on us is from a ninety-degree angle to our body's surface. I will say that 90percent of attacks are from a horizontal direction to our body surface. If someone is suffering from breast cancer, liver cancer, prostate cancer, heart disease, heartburn, intestine or stomach infections, diabetes, thyroid disease, kidney infection, or internal/external infection, or other cancers, that person needs to do the following:

a. Take a lot of antibiotics, antibacterial, anti-infection, or anticancer tablets on a regular basis until you defeat a particular infection or cancer completely. But remember that you should always eat the proper food before you take any tablets to reduce the side effects. Do not ever take any medication on an empty stomach. These medications just help you heal the infection or cancer. As you start recovering, keep increasing the power or strength of your medication gradually, as per instructions of your physician/doctor. This healing medication is effective only if we stop continuous attacks of diseases or insects.

رؤية الجن و الآلام السيطرة عليها

أثناء تعافيك من المرض، لابد أن تزيد من قوة دوائك بالتدريج، حسب تعليمات طبيبك. يكون الدواء مؤثراً فقط ، إذا أوقفنا هجمات الأمراض و الحشرات

ب. الخطوة الثانية هي أن تستخدم مراهم مضادات العدوي، مراهم مضادات السرطان، مراهم المضادات الحوية، أو مراهم مضادات البكتيريا، التي تستخدم علي سطح الجسم، سواء كان التعامل مع العدوي أو السرطانات، و لابد أن ندهن هذه المراهم أربع مرات علي الأقل. يمكنك أن تزيد قوة المراهم تدريحياً إلي أن تهزم الإصابة أو السرطان تماما. تقوم الأقراص بعلاج الإصابة الداخلية في حالة سرطان الثدي أو سرطان البروتستاتا، و أيضاً إستخدام المراهم يقتل و ينظف و يطرد سيل الأمراض.

إن لم تفعل ذلك ستسمح للأمراض بأن تعيش في جلدك و بعد ذلك ستخترق جسمك و تظل تصيبك. لا تتباطأ أو تترك تناول المراهم المضادة للسرطان، أو المضادة للعدوي. إذا ظلت هذه الحشرات موجودة بجسمك، لن يفيد العلاج بالدواء مع وجود الهجمات المستمرة لهذه الحشرات. لابد أن نوقفهم ولا نسمح لهم بالبقاء علي جلدنا وأن يخترقوا أجسامنا. إن إستخدام المراهم المضادة للعدوي و المضادة للسرطان سيساعد كثيراً. إجلس علي الأرض أثناء إستخدامك للمرهم. يمكنك أن تضع أي جزء من جسمك علي أي معدن أو أرض صلبة، لتجعل ترك هذه الحشرات لجسمك سهلاً.

13

b. In the second step, you need to use anti-infection, anticancer, antibiotic, or antibacterial creams and ointments on the surface of your body, regardless of whether dealing with infections or cancers, at least four times a day. Keep gradually increasing the strength of the creams or ointments until you defeat the infection or cancer completely. In the case of breast cancer or prostate cancer, tablets will heal the internal injury, and the use of creams and ointments will kill, clean, and repel the stream of diseases.

Otherwise, you will allow them to live on your skin and then penetrate your body and keep infecting you. Do not slow down or give up the use of anticancer or anti-infection creams, because if these insects keep going inside your body, the healing medication will not be as helpful against the continuous attacks of these insects. We need to stop them and not allow them to stay on our skin or penetrate our bodies. The use of anti-infection or anticancer cream will help a lot. Always ground yourself when you are applying these creams to your body. You can ground any of your body parts to any metal or concrete floor to give these insects an easy path to leave your body.

ج. الآن الجزء الثالث، و الأكثر أهمية هو أن تتعلم كيف تعزل جسمك عن الهواء الطلق. يمكنك أن تستخدم عازل مطاطي، أو بلاستيكي، مريح و مرن و رقيق،و هذا يمثل عازل ممتاز ضد أي مادة. ستحتاج إلي أن تلبس هذا العازل لمدة أربعة و عشرون ساعة. ستغطي الملابس ذات الأكمام الكاملة من الرقبة إلي منطقة الورك. تأكد من عدم وجود ثقوب أو خياطات مفتوحة. ستبقي هذه الملابس المطاطية أو البلاستيكية الحشرات السرطانية بعيداً عن أجسامنا. تقوم معظم حشرات العدوي و السرطان بالهجوم من جهات أفقية، فبمجرد أن نلبس هذه الملابس البلاستيكية أو المطاطية، ستنقذنا من الحشرات السرطانية هذه. إذا كان جسمك أو جلدك به الكثير من حشرات الإصابة أو السرطان، فإن الإستخدام المستمر لمراهم و أقراص مضادات العدوي، أو مضادات البكتيريا، ستهزم هذه المراهم و الأقراص السرطان بسهولة. إذا ما توقفنا عن تناول هذه المراهم و الأقراص ستدمر هجمات الحشرات المستمرة الأعضاء الداخلية و الخارجية، لهذا من الجيد تغطية الجسم بالكامل بالملابس المطاطية أو البلاستيكية الرقيقة المعدة طبياً لإبعاد الحشرات السرطانية عن أجسادنا. يجب أن تستخدم مراهم الإصابة عدة مرات يومياً تحت الملابس المطاطية، إذا كت تعاني من سرطان الثدي، سرطان الكبد، أو سرطان الكلية، أو سرطان البروتستاتا، أو أي نوع من السرطان. إذا قمت بعمل ذلك، أنا متأكد 100% أنك ستهزم أي سرطان بسهولة.

c. Now the third and most important part is learning how to isolate your body from the open atmosphere. Simple, clear, comfortable, flexible, and thin but strong rubber or plastic can make for the perfect insulator against any substance. You'll need to wear this material for twenty four hours. Full sleeves should cover the neck to the hip area. Make sure there are no holes or open stitching. This plastic or rubber dress will keep cancer insects away from our bodies. Most infection or cancer insects attack from a horizontal directions. Once we wear this plastic or rubber clothing, we will be saved from these cancer insects. If you already have a lot of infection or cancer insects inside your body or on your skin, then the continuous use of anti-infection or antibacterial creams and tablets will be able to defeat cancer easily. If we stop, however, the continuous attacks of insects will damage the surface or internal organs. Hence, it is good to cover the entire body with medically prepared thin plastic or rubber dress to keep cancer insects away from our bodies. Plastic or rubber dress infection creams several times a day under this plastic dress if you are suffering from breast, liver, kidney, prostrate, or any other kind of cancer. If you adopt this behavior, I am 100 percent sure you will be able to defeat any cancer very easily. Companies can make clothing for regular people or normal use, such as jeans or shirts with inner plastic or comfortable rubber layers. Remember, even for normal people, it is not enough just to wear this plastic undergarment. It is very important to use antibiotic or anti infection ointments all the time. During this process, if you feel any movement of insects, just rub the area with as much pressure as you can without removing the protective rubber clothing.

تقوم الشركات بصنع الملابس للناس العاديين، أو للإستخدام العادي، مثل بنطلونات الجينز، أو قمصان بها طبقات بلاستيكية داخلية، أو مطاطية مريحة. تذكر أن بالنسبة للناس العاديين ليس كافياً أن يلبسوا هذه الملابس الداخلية. يجب إستخدام المضاد الحيوي ومراهم المضاد الحيوي دائماً. إذا شعرت أثناء ذلك بحركة الحشرات، ما عليك إلا أن تحك المنطقة بضغط بقدر الإمكان، بدون إزالة الغطاء المطاطي الوقائي.

بمجرد أن تلبس هذا الرداء الذي يغطي من الرقبة إلى القدم لمدة أربعة و عشرون ساعة، ستنقذ نفسك من الآثار الجانبية للأدوية، مثل التقيؤ، مشاكل القلب،، و إضطراب المعدة.

ستتعجب من تحسن صحتك، عندما لا تقدر الحشرات علي مهاجمة المناطق المغطاة.ستهاجم الحشرات المنطقة التي فوق الرقبة. سنحتاج مساعدة من العلوم الطبية لنحدد كيف نحمي رؤوسنا. الفكرة في منتهي الوضوح. من الصعب هزيمة السرطان، لكن إذا إستخدم الشخص الإجراءات التي ذكرناها سابقاً، سيتمكن الرجل أو المرأة من هزيمة أي نوع من السرطان بمنتهي السهولة. سأستخدم كلمة "سرطان الثدي " كثيراً لأن هذا النوع من السرطان من الموضوعات الرئيسية في هذه الأيام.

كما ذكرت في هذا الكتاب، يعيش المرض المسبب لسرطان الدم، عادةً في منطقة الصدر في جسمنا. المناطق الرئيسية التي أشعر فيها بمشاكل صحية عندما أعالج أي سرطان دم، هي إما في عظام الرقبة، إلتهاب اللثة، عظام الأنف، عظام الأذن ومحيطها، لكنني متأكد أن هذه الإجراءات ستسيطر ، أو تقلل، أو تعالج سرطان الدم، لكن ستحدد العلوم الطبية نسبة فعالية هذه الإجراءات.

SEE & CONTROL DEMONS & PAIN	رضوان قرشي

Once you start wearing this dress from neck to feet for twenty-four-hour periods, you will save yourself from the side effects of medication, such as vomiting, heart problems, and upset stomachs. You will be surprised with the improvement of your health condition. When these insects cannot attack your body at the covered areas, they will attack the areas above the neck. To determine how to protect our heads, we will need help from medical science. The concept is very clear. Cancer is very difficult to treat, but if someone uses all the above procedures, he or she will be able to defeat any cancer very easily. Because breast cancer is one major issue these days, I will use the words "breast cancer" frequently.

As I described somewhere in the book, the disease responsible for creating blood cancer usually lives or stays above the chest area of our body. Neck bone, gum sore bones nose or bones of nose, ear or bones around ear are main areas where I always feel problems whenever I treat any blood cancer. But I am sure these procedures will control, reduce, or cure the blood cancer also, but medical science needs to determine how much. I already attached two or three pages from book on how to use medications, ointments, and rubber/plastic insulation to a body suffering from breast cancer or any other cancer. Now I am going to describe what will happen and how to handle this procedure properly. Remember, do everything completely under the supervision of your physician or doctor.

لقد كرست صفحتين أو ثلاثة من هذا الكتاب لشرح كيفية إستخدام الأدوية، والمراهم،و العازل المطاطي/البلاستيكي في الجسم الذي يعاني من سرطان الثدي.أو أي نوع من السرطان. سأشرح الآن ماذا سيحدث، و كيف نستطيع أن نقوم يهذا الإجراء بشكل سليم.تذكر أن تفعل كل شيئ تحت إشراف لطبيب الخاص بك.

1.إذا كان الشخص لا يريد أن يرتدي الملابس (المطاطية العازلة) عل الجسم بالكامل، فإنه من المفيد أن يرتدي ملابس مطاطية، عازلة و مانعة للتسرب مشابهة لثوب السباحة، التي تغطي الأعضاء بشكل أساسي. لابد أن يقوم الشخص بتغطية مناطق الصدر، المعدة،الوسط و الخصر بشكل جيد. لابد أن تلبس هذه الملابس لمدة أربعة و عشرون ساعة، و تغير كل أربعة و عشرين ساعة. لابد أن يتم كل شيئ تحت إشراف الطبيب الخاص بك.

2.لابد أن يتم تغيير الملابس المطاطية / العازلة كل أربعة و عشرون ساعة.

3.لا تستخدم أبداً أي مرهم ضد الحكة تحتالملابس المطاطية.

4.لابد أن تستخدم مراهم المضاد الحيوي أو مضادات البكتيريا أو مضادات السرطان، ولا يستخدم الكريم. لابد أن يستخدم المرهم الذي يصفه لك الطبيب الخاص بك.

Rizwan Qureshi

1. If someone does not want to wear clothing (rubber, insulated) all over their body, then it will be helpful if they just wear a rubber, insulated, leak-free clothing similar to a swimsuit. That should cover mainly all the organs. One should cover his chest, stomach, waist, and hip area properly, The clothing should be worn for twenty-four hours and changed every twenty-four hours; everything should be done under the instruction of your physician or doctor.
2. Rubber, insulated dress/clothing should be changed every twenty-four hours.
3. Do not use any anti-itch cream under rubber clothing ever.
4. Only use antibiotic or antibacterial or anticancer ointments, not cream, prescribed and under the instructions of your physician or doctor.
5. Antibacterial tablet needs to be taken every day or every other day for a long time under the supervision of your doctor.
6. The rubber dress covering will keep you safe from heart problems; stomach, intestine, and bladder diseases; and other kinds of disease also if you wear it all the time.
7. Once you will take antibacterial tablets every day, ably antibacterial ointment every day and wear rubber clothing twenty-four hours, what will happen during that and what should you need to do with the help and instructions of your physician and doctor?
8. Insects or bugs that create infections or cancers mainly live inside our body or on our skin or in our bed, chairs, or sofa. They frequently move or travel in and out of our body all the time.

رؤية الجن و الآلام السيطرة عليها

5.لا بد من تناول الأقراص المضادة للبكتيريا كل يوم أو يوم بعد يوم لمدة طويلة تحت إشراف طبيبك.

6.ستقيك الملابس المطاطية التي تغطي جسمك، من مشاكل في القلب، و المعدة، و الأمعاء، و أمراض المرارة، و أي نوع من الأمراض الأخرى، إذا قمت بإرتدائه طوال الوقت.

7.ماذا يجب عليك فعله بمساعدة طبيبك و بتوجيهاته و ماذا سيحدث بمجرد أن تتناول الأقراص المضادة للبكتيريا و المراهم المضادة للبكتيريا يومياً، مع إرتداء الملابس المطاطية لمدة أربعة و عشرون ساعة؟.

8.قد تعيش الحشرات المسببة للإصابات أو السرطانات في جسمنا أو تحت جلدنا، أو تحت سريرنا، كراسينا، أو أريكتنا. إنها غالباً ما تتحرك داخل و خارجأجسادنا طوال الوقت.

9.لقد جربت ذلك على نفسي، لكنك تحتاج إلي إتباع تعليمات الطبيب الخاص بك. إنني أستخدم Enforcer Home Pest Control XII، التي أشتريته من متجر AL&M hardware. لابد أن ترش منه علي سريرك، و كراسيك، و أريكتك، و في كل مكان تجلس أو تستلقي أو تنام كل يوم. إذا قمت برش pest control كل يوم، سيقوم بقتل كل الحشرات المتسببة في إصابات فيروس نقص المناعة البشرية، و أنواع السرطانات المختلفة. لابد أن ترش منه كل يوم لتبعد أوتقتل الحشرات الموجودة في جسمك، أو في جلدك، أو داخل سريرك.

9. I already tested this on myself, but you need to follow your doctor's instructions. I use Enforcer Home Pest Control XII, which I buy from AL&M hardware store. You need to spray every day on your bed, chairs, sofa, couch, wherever you sit or lay down or sleep. If you spray pest control every day, it will kill all the insects responsible for creating HIV infections and different kinds of cancers. You need to spray every day so insects inside your body or on your skin or inside your bed will be killed or repelled.

Regular spray will reduce the number of insects everywhere. Eventually, it will be helpful in the fight against cancer or internal/external infections.

10. Now as I described, most of the insects attack our body in a horizontal direction. Right now I am not talking about demons and pains. I am just talking about the insects responsible of creating different kinds of cancers, infections, and diseases. Once we will wear rubber/plastic, very thin, insulated, leak free soft flexible, will protect us from the attacks of most of the cancers/infections insects. Insects still can sit on top of a rubber/plastic surface but will not be able to attack the skin. Remember, insects can attack uncovered parts of the body also.

10. إن الرش المنتظم سيقلل عدد الحشرات في كل مكان. في النهاية، سيكون مفيداً في محاربة السرطان أو الإصابات الداخلية و الخارجية. لقد شرحت في السابق أن معظم هجمات الحشرات علي جسمنا تأتي بشكل أفقي. الآن سأتكلم عن الجن و الآلام. أنني أتكلم عن الحشرات المتسببة في أنواع السرطانات المختلفة، و الإصابات، و الأمراض. بمجرد أن نرتدي الملابس المطاطية/البلاستيكية، الرقيقة، العازلة، المانعة للتسرب، ستحمينا هذه الملابس من هجمات معظم حشرات السرطانات/العدوي. تقدر هذه الحشرات أن تبقي علي سطح الملابس المطاطية/البلاستيكية، لكنهم لن يقدروا علي مهاجمة الجلد. تذكر أن الحشرات تقدر علي مهاجمة الأجزاء الغير مغطاة أيضاً، لهذا لابد أن تؤمن هذه الأجزء الغير مغطاه، و لابد أيضاً أن تتناول الأدوية حسب تعليمات الطبيب الخاص بك. بما أن الحشرات لا تستطيع الدخول إلي جسمنا/جلدنا، هذا يعني أن هذه الحشرات لن تستطيع الوصول إلي أعضائنا أو المناطق المدمرة أصلاً في جسمنا مثل القرحةأو السرطانات. هذه الملابس المطاطية/البلاستيكية ستوقف أو تقلل هجمات الحشرات علي جسمنا. سيقتل Pest control الحشرات الموجودة في سريرنا، أو كرسينا، أو أريكتنا، إلخ.. ناقش نصائح طبيبك و إتبعها قبل إستخدام أي دواء، أو كيماويات، أو الملابس المطاطية/البلاستيكية.

11. ولآن ماذا يحدث إذا تناولت أقراص المضاد الحيوي؟ ستدخل أدوية المضاد الحيوي هذه داخل جسمنا و ستبدأ في العلاج، وأثناء العلاج تموت حشرات الإصابة أو السرطان، أو ستهرب من جسمك لتنفذ نفسها، ومعني ذلك أن معظم الحشرات إما يموتوا بسبب الإستمرار في إستخدام المضادات الحيوية أو يهربوا من جسمنا.

So secure those uncovered body parts and take some medications as per the instructions of your doctor. Once these insects cannot go inside our body/skin, this means those insects will not be reaching our organs or the already-damaged areas of our body, like ulcers or cancers. This way rubber/plastic will stop or reduce the attacks of the insects to our body. Pest control will kill them when they are in our bed or chair or in our couch, etc. Discuss and follow your doctor's advice and instructions before you use any medication, chemical, or rubber/plastic clothing.

11. Now what will happen if you take antibiotic tablets? Those antibiotic medications will go inside our body and will start the healing process. During this, either those cancer/infection insects will die or will run from our body to save themselves. Most of the insects either will be killed due to the continuous use of antibiotic medications or they will run away from our body. If we wear rubber/plastic clothing and under this rubber clothing we are applying antibiotic ointment on our skin everywhere, those insects coming out from deep inside our body will not find any way out. Those insects coming out from deep inside the body will get stuck in the ointment at first, and second, the rubber/plastic will not allow those insects to breathe or go back to the atmosphere. This is my strategy of trapping and hunting the cancer/insects. Once these insects get stuck in the ointment trap, they will be dead within the next twenty-four hours.

إذا ما إرتدينا الملابس المطاطية/البلاستيكية، و قمنا بدهن مرهم مضاد حيوي علي جلدنا، لن تجد الحشرات الخارجة من جسمنا مكاناً تهرب منه، ستلتصق الحشرات بالمرهم أولاً،ثانياً لن تسمح الملابس المطاطية /البلاستيكية لهذه الحشرات بالتنفس أو العودة إلي الجو.هذه هي طريقتي لمحاصرة و صيد السرطان/الحشرات. بمجرد أن تنحصر الحشرات في المرهم ستموت في خلال أربعة و عشرون ساعة.

12.أثناء القيام بهذه الإجراءات، ستشعر بوضوح بحركة هذه الحشرات فوق جلدك، وتحت الملابس المطاطية/البلاستيكية. من فضلك لا تقوم بخلع أو إزالة الملابس البلاستيكية في هذه المرحلة، إذا فعلت ذلك، ستطير هذه الحشرات مرة أخري في الجو، و ستهاجمك أو ستهاجم شخص آخر. يمكنك حك هذه المنطقة المعينة فقط، لقتل هذه الحشرات، بدلاً من خلع هذه الملابس المطاطية. هذا الفعل سيساعد في قتل الكثير من الحشرات الموجودة علي جلدك.

13.ستري كل يوم بعض النتوءات تغطي جلدك، و أيضاً ستري بقعاً بنية علي الملابس البلاستيكية. تعتبر هذه النتوءات الصغيرة و البقع البنية هي في الحقيقة حشرات سرطان ميتة. قم بغسل جلدك كل أربعة و عشرين ساعة، أو كل ثمانية و أربعين ساعة، بعد ذلك قم بدهان طبقة جديدة من المرهمعلي جلدك، و قم بإرتداء الملابس المطاطية. سيكون من السهل إرتداء الملابس البلاستيكية أولاً، ثم قم بدهن المرهم. تحته.

14.هذه البقع البنية الموجودة علي الملابس البلاستيكية، هي حشرات ميتة، لذلك لا ترمي هذه الملابس هنا أو هناك. قم بربط الملابس ووضعها في كيس قمامة بلاستيكي، و قم بالتخلص منه بعيداً عن المنزل ، كي لا يصاب أي شخص بالعدوي من هذه الحشرات.

12. During this action, you will feel very clearly a lot of movement from these insects on top of your skin and under the rubber/plastic clothing. At this point, please do not remove or take off the plastic clothing; otherwise, all these insects will fly back in the atmosphere. After some time, they will attack you again or someone else. Instead of removing the rubber clothing, just rub over and over that particular area to kill these insects. This action will help kill more and more insects on top of your skin.

13. Every day you will see some very small bumps all over your skin; you will see some brown spots on the plastic clothing also. All these small bumps and brown spots on the plastic clothing are actually dead insects of cancer. Wash and clean your skin every twenty-four hours to forty-eight hours. Apply a new layer of antibiotic ointment on top of your skin and wear new rubber clothing. It will be easier to wear the plastic clothing first and then apply the ointment under it.

14. Those brown spots on the rubber clothing are actually dead insects. Please do not just throw away the rubber clothing's here and there. Seal them in a plastic trash bag and dispose of properly away from house so nobody else gets infected with those insects.

15. Regardless, if someone has breast cancer or prostate cancer or any other cancer, the use of these procedures will help cure their cancers in just a few weeks. We should adopt this procedure as an everyday routine.

15.بغض النظر عن ما ذكر، ستساعد هذه الإجراءات في علاج سرطان الأشخاص المصابين لسرطان الثدي، أو سرطان البروستاتا أو أي نوع من السرطان في أسابيع قليلة. لا بد أن نقوم بهذه الإجراءات كل يوم كجزء من الروتين اليومي.

16.بمجرد أن تهزم العدوي/السرطان، لا تترك إستخدام الملابس المطاطية، لكن يمكنك أن تستخدم المرهم كل ثلاثة أيام.

يقول صديقي المفضل الوحيد طوال الوقت:"أريد أن أعيش مائة سنة علي الأقل". هذا الشخص لم يعد موجوداً، لكني متأكد من أن إستخدام تقنياتي للعلاج و الحماية من الجو و الأمراض، من الممكن للناس أن يعيشوا بصحة أكثر، مائة سنة و أكثر.

لا تستخدم الكريم المضاد للحكة تحت الملابس البلاستيكية، لأنني عندما جربته وجدت أن حشرات العدوي/السرطان تقدر أن تعيش مع الكريم المضاد للحكة. أنا متأكد أنه يوماً ما ستقدم العلوم الطبية تفسيرات أكثر لذلك. لكنني عندما جربت مراهم المضادات الحيوية الثلاثية، وجدت أنها ممتازة. لابد أن تتبع تعليمات طبيبك لتص غلي أفضل طريقة لصيد و قتل حشرات السرطان/العدوي هذه. تعطيك نظرياتي فكرتين. الخطوة القلي هي عندما تخرج هذه الحشرات من جسمك لتهرب أو تتنفس، فإنها تلتصق بالمرهم، و نتيجة لإرتدائك الملابس البلاستيكية، فإنها لن تستطيع أن تعود إلي الجو. سيموتون في غضون أربعة وعشرون ساعة علي الأقل إلي ثمانية و أربعون ساعة.

رؤية الجن و الآلام السيطرة عليها

16. Once you defeat the infection/cancer, do not give up the use of rubber clothing, but you can use the ointment every three days.

My one and only best friend used to say all the time, "I want to live at least one hundred years." That person is not around anymore, but I am sure by using my techniques to get cured and protected from the atmosphere and the diseases, people will be able to live way longer than one hundred years and healthier.

Do not use anti-itch cream under the plastic clothing. Somehow, when I was experimenting, infection/cancer insects were able to survive with anti-itch cream. I am sure someday medical science will offer more explanations about it. But my experiments with the use of triple antibiotic ointments were perfect. You need to follow the instructions of your doctors to find the best ointment to hunt and kill these cancer/infection insects. My theory gives you two ideas. In first step, when these insects will come out of a body either to run away or to breathe, those insects will immerse or stuck with the ointment. Due to the plastic clothing, these insects will not be able to go back into the atmosphere. Give them some time, a minimum of twenty-four to forty-eight hours; all of them will be dead within that time limit. You will be able to see those dead cancer insects on top of your skin and plastic clothing. If you are a completely healthy person, you can do this procedure twice a week.

ستستطيع رؤية حشرات السرطان الميتة هذه علي جلدك و علي ملابسك البلاستيكية. إذا كنت شخصاً سليماً صحياً، ستستطيع القيام بهذا الإجراء مرتين في الإسبوع، أما إذا كنت تعاني من أي إصابة بسرطان/عدوي رئيسية، فإنك تحتاج إلي أن تفعل ذلك كل يوم. ليس من مطلوباً أن تغير الملابس البلاستيكية يومياً، لكنك لا يجب أن تعرض جسمك لحشرات جديدة، لهذا فإن أفضل فكرة هي أن تغسل و تطهر جسمك، و ترتدي ملابس بلاستيكية جديدة فوراً. كما نعلم، فإن الصحة ثروة، لهذا يجب أن تضحي قليلاً للحفاظ علي صحتك بإبقاء حشرات السرطان هذه بعيداً عن جسمك دائماً. إنه من الخطأ أن تقتل حشرات السرطان في ثمانية و أربعون ساعة، و تظن أن ترك جسمك بدون حماية شيئاً حسناً، لأن مجموعة من الحشرات الجديدة ستهاجم جسمك مرة أخري، ولهذا لا تستهين بالأمر. إذا كنت تريد أن تبقي في صحة جيدة و آمناً من هجمات هذه الحشرات كل لحظة، يجب أن تبقي جسمك محمياً من هجماتهم كل يوم. ثاني خطوة هي أنه لا يكفي إستخدام مرهم المضاد الحيوي بدون الملابس البلاستيكية، لأن الملابس البلاستيكية ستبقي الحشرات و تحصرهم في مرهم المضاد الحيوي الثلاثي لساعات قبل موتهم. لهذا فإن كلتا الخطوتين مهمتين. في كثير من الأحيان لا تحتاج حتي إلي تناول أي أقراص لقتل حشرات السرطان. إن الإستخدام الجيد و الدائم للملابس البلاستيكية و المرهم سيكون كافياً لصيد أو قتلهم كل لحظة و كل يوم.

صدقني، إذا قامت العلوم الطبية بعمل القليل من الأبحاث علي حشرات السرطان الميتة الموجودة علي جلدك و علي ملابسك البلاستيكية، ستكون قادرة علي إنتاج مراهم أكثر قوة لصيد و قتل حشرات السرطان.

If you are suffering from any cancer/major infection then do this every day. You do not need to change plastic clothing every day, but you do not need to open your body for new insects. So the best idea is to wash and cleanse your body and wear new plastic clothing again immediately. As we know, health is wealth, so sacrifice a little bit to maintain your health by keeping these cancer insects always away from your body. Otherwise, you will kill them in forty-eight hours and think it will be okay to leave your body unprotected after that; that will be a mistake, because a bunch of new insects will attack your body again. So do not take it easy. If you want to stay secure and healthy each and every second, please keep your body secure and protected from their attacks each and every second. Second thing is it is not enough just to use the antibiotic ointment without the plastic clothing because this plastic clothing will keep them or hold them in the triple action antibiotic ointment for hours before they die. So both steps are important. A lot of times you do not even need to take any tablets to kill cancer insects. Proper and permanent use of the plastic clothing and the ointment will be enough to hunt and kill them every second every day.

Trust me, if medical science did a little bit of research on those dead cancer insects on your skin and on top of your plastic clothing, they will be able to introduce more powerful ointments to hunt and kill cancer insects. According to my calculations, any cancer at any stage, including breast cancer, should be 100 percent cured within two months.

.يمكن علاج أي نوع من السرطان بما في ذلك سرطان الثدي، خلال شهرين بنسبة 100%،وفقاً لحساباتي. تذكر أنك عندما تكون جاهزاً لخلع الملابس البلاستيكية لإستبدالها بأخري جديدة، لا تعتقد أن البقع البنية الموجودة علي ملابسك البلاستيكية ألا وهي حشرات السرطان، لا تعتقد أنها ميتة حقاً ، إلا إذا قال لك الطبيب ذلك، فربما تكون قد علقت في الملابس البلاستيكية ولم تمت تماماً، فإذا رميت هذه الملابس في الهواء الطلق، قد تعود هذه الحشرات نشيطة مرة أخري، لهذا عليك التخلص من هذه الملابس بإستخدام أكياس قمامة بلاستيكية نظيفة، و قم بربطها جيداً، ثم قم بحرقها أو إلقائها في القمامة. المشكلة هي، لماذا لا يتم شفاء السلرطان، أو التقليل من حدته، حتي أن مرضي السرطان يتناولون أدوية قوية للعلاج من أي نوع من السرطان؟.مثلاً بعتير سرطان الثدي عدوي أو إصابة داخلية، لكن من المستحيل الشفاء منه إلا إذا تم إستنصال الجزء المصاب عن طريق الجراحة. إن الشفاء ممكن إذا ما تم إكتشاف المرض في مرحلة مبكرة، لكن صدقني ليس بعد ذلك. حالياً بالرغم من أن مريض السرطان يعالج علاجاً جيدا إلا، أن سيل الأمراض السرطانية و عدد حشرات السرطان مرتفع جداً، و هماتهم لا تتوقف. إن العلاج الحديث مؤثر و قوي جداً، لكن لا يوجد علاج، ويموت الناس في النهاية. اليبب في ذلك هو أن عندما يهاجم الدواء حشرات السرطان هذه، تقوم الحشرات بترك هذا المكان المعين في الجسم، و إما أن تبقي علي الجلد، أو تذهب في الهواء المحيط لساعات قليلة، و بعدها تهاجم هذه الحشرات أو حشرات سرطان جديدة المناطق المدمرة أصلاً من الجسم، بعد أن يقل مفعول الدواء. تأكل حشرات السرطان هذه أجزاء من جسمنا و أعضائنا و المناطق المصابة. هذا كل ما يستطيعون عمله، و كل مايفعلونه. تعتبر حشرات السرطان كائنات حية مثالنا، إنها ليست كالجن و الآلام.

Remember, when you're ready to remove the plastic clothing to replace it with a new one, do not ever think, until your doctor tells you, that those brown spots on the plastic clothing, i.e., the dead cancer insects, are really dead. Maybe they just got stuck there and are not completely dead. If you just throw away the plastic clothing in an open atmosphere, maybe those insects will get active again. So to avoid that risk, always use a clean plastic trash bag to dispose of those used plastic clothing; tie those trash bags properly before you burn them or trash them. Problem, why cancer is not curable or reducing even cancer patients take very powerful medication to get cured from any cancer?

For example, breast cancer is an internal infection, but it is impossible to cure it unless you remove the affected part through surgery. And it is curable by surgery only once it is detected at a very early stage. But trust me, not anymore. Right now even cancer patient is proper medication every day, but the stream of cancer diseases or the number of the cancer insects is extremely high and their attacks to our body is nonstop. Modern medication is very effective and powerful but there is still no cure, and eventually people are dying. The reason is when medication attacks the cancer disease/insects, those cancer insects leave that particular area of the body and either stay on the top of skin or go to the surrounding atmosphere for a few hours.

إنها أجسام كهرومغناطيسية، لهذا من السهل قتل هذه الحشرات. لا تستطيع حشرات السرطان أن تبني داخل الجسم لفترة طويلة، لابد لها أن تدخل جسمنا و تخرج منه للتنفس ايضاً. إن حشرات السرطان صغيرة الحجم جداً، لهذا فهي تستطيع إختراق جسمنا بعمق من خلال جلدنا.

يقدر عدد الحشرات بالملايين أو البلايين من حولنا، لذا ليس لدينا إختيار آخر، ولن نستطيع صيدهم يوماً ما و نظن أن المهمة إنتهت،لا، إنها معركة يومية الآن. ربما قد نهدأ بمرور الوقت بمجرد أن نستطيع أن نصيد معظم هذه الحشرات و نقتلها، لكن الآن من السهل القضاء عليهم بالأدوية الحديثة، و المراهم، و بإتباع إجراءاتي. ليس عليك فعل الكثير، فقط عليك تحمل إرتداء هذه الملابس البلاستيكية و وضع المراهم من تحتها ، و إرتدائها تحت ملابسك العادية. يعتبر الباقي عملية أتوماتيكية. حتى الأشخاص الذين لا يعانون من مشاكل صحية ظاهرة، وحتى لو كانت نتائج ضغط الدم لديهم جيدة، تبقي في أجسادهم و فوق جلودهم، و في أعضائهم من الداخل، أعداد لا تحصي من الأمراض/الحشرات، لهذا فإنني أقول لابد أن تجري فحوصات طبية. إستخدم إجراءاتي العلاجية لتري إذا كنت ستلاحظ بقعاً بنيةعلي جلدك.بعد ثمانية و أربعون ساعة. هذا لإقناعك أنت، لا أنا، لأني أعرف أنهسيكون لديك الكثير من الحشرات الميتة علي جلدك، و علي الملابس البلاستيكية بعد مرور ثمانية و أربعون ساعة. لا تستطيع الآلام و الجن إحداث أي نوع من السرطان. إنها تقوم بعمل فتحات صغيرة أو خسائر لحشرات السرطان هذه فقط. يستطيع الأشخاص الأصحاء إجراء هذا العلاج مرتين في الإسبوع علي الأقل، للإحتياط. أثناء العلاج، ستشعر بحركة هذه الحشرات تحت ملابسك البلاستيكية....

SEE & CONTROL DEMONS & PAIN	رضوان قرشي

After a few hours, when the effect of the medication is reduced, those insects or new cancer insects attack the already-damaged part of the body. These cancer insects just eat our body parts and organs and infected areas; that are all they can do and that's all they do. These cancer insects are living objects like us. They are not like demons or the pains, i.e., electromagnetic bodies. So it is very easy to kill these insects. These cancer insects cannot stay inside the body for a long time. They have to move in and out of our body to breathe also. These cancer insects are so little and tiny, and that's why they are able to penetrate deep inside our body from our skin.

Their numbers are in millions or billions around us. So we have no choice. We just cannot hunt them one day and think the job is done. No, this is an everyday fight right now. Maybe after some time, once we are be able to hunt and kill most of them, we can slow down; but right now, it is very easy to kill them with modern medications, ointments, and my procedures. You really do not have to do too much; you only just have to tolerate this plastic clothing and ointment under your regular clothes. The rest is an automatic process. Even when people have no visible or noticeable health issues, even if their blood results are very good, their bodies still, on their skin and deep inside their organs, carry uncountable diseases/insects.

لا تقلق بشأنهم، إتركهم، و إستمر في حك هذه المنطقة بالذات بقوة إلي أن تقتلهم بأسرع ما يمكن. لا تفتح الملابس البلاستيكية أو تخلعها في هذا الوقت، و إلا ستسمح لهم بالخروج إلي الجو. المشكلة معقدة، لأن حشرات السرطان متعطشة للقتل، و أعدادها كبيرة، لدرجة أن 5 % من هذه الحشرات موجودة في جسمنا، و تأكل جوج و عدوي السرطان بنا، لكن تظل نسبة 95 % من حشرات السرطان/العدوي هذه خارج جسمن، وتنتظر دورها، أو تكون قد أكلت ما يكفيها في يومها. و الآن قم بتغطية مريض السرطان، أو مريض نقص المناعة البشرية، بالملابس البلاستيكية و زمرهم المضاد الحيوي، ولآن يقتل هذا الشخص كل الحشرات الموجدة داخل جسمه، ولكن ما الذي يمكن أن يفعله هذا الشخص و أنت لحماية الآخرين أو حتي هذا المريض من نسبة الـ95 % من الحشرات؟. بمجرد أن يحمي مريض السرطان جسمه بإستخدام الملابس البلاستيكية، ستظل حشرات السرطان تهاجم من سطح الملابس البلاستيكية. لكن هذه الحشرات لن تجد أي طعام، ولن تستطيع أن تخترق الملابس البلاستيكية، إلي جسم مريض السرطان، فماذا تفعل هذه الحشرات؟.

ستهاجم حشرات السرطان هذه، إما الأجزاء الغير مغطاة من الشخص المريض بالسرطان، أ و الناس الموجودون حول مرضي السرطان. لابد أيضاً في أثناء صيدنا لحشرات السرطان الموجودة داخل الجسم و قتلها، أن نصيد و نقتل الـ95 % الباقية من الحشرات الموجودة في الجو. كيف لنا أن نفعل ذلك؟. تعتبر السجاجيد الموجودة بمنازلنا و مكاتبنا المصدر الرئيسي أو المأوي لهذه الحشرات، حيث يعيشون و يتكاثرون بسرعة كبيرة، لهذا يجب تجنب السجاجيد، إستخدام الأرض القابلة للتنظيف.

So I will say test yourself. Use my cure procedures and see if you notice brown spots on your skin after forty-eight hours. This is just to convince you, not to me, because, I already know you will have a lot of dead insects on top of your skin and on the plastic clothing after forty-eight hours. Pains and demons cannot create any cancer. They just create small openings or damages for these cancer insects. Extremely healthy people can use this cure procedure at least twice a month, just to stay on safe side. During treatment, you will be able to feel the movement of these insects under your rubber clothing. Do not worry about them; let them stay there. Keep rubbing hard over that particular area so you can kill them as fast as possible. Do not open or remove the plastic clothing at that time; otherwise you will let them go to the open atmosphere. The problem is very complicated. These cancer insects are hungry killers. Their numbers are so high even 5 percent of those insects are inside our body and eating our cancer wound or infections, but still 95 percent of these cancer/infection insects are outside our body and waiting for their turn or may be already eat enough for the day. Now cover a cancer or HIV infection patient with plastic clothing and antibiotic ointment. Now that person is killing all the insects inside his body, but what will he or you do to protect others and even that patient from the other 95 percent of insects? Once the cancer patient protects their bodies by using the plastic clothing, cancer insects still attack on the surface of the plastic clothing. But from that plastic surface, they cannot get any food and they cannot penetrate deep inside the body of that cancer patient, so what does those insects do?

لابد أن تنظف الأرض بالمطهرات الكيماوية لقتل حشرات السرطان هذه، و لوقف نموها. لابد من تغطية الكراسي، والأرائك، و الأسرة بغطاء بلاستيكي، لمنع حركة حشرات السرطان لتدخل أجسامنا. لابد أن نرش pest control chemicals فوق، و حول، و تحت الكراسي و الأرائك و الأسرة، يومياً. تساعد الحيوانات علي النمو السريع لحشرات السرطان.عليك أخذ كافة الإحتياطات لمنع نمو حشرات السرطان هذه. بمجرد أن تتبع العلاج بإرتداء الملابس البلاستيكية، ستقل تكاليف الدواء لمستوي مدهش. لن تحتاج إلي دهن المرهم أغلب الوقت تحت الملابس البلاستيكية.يكفي أحياناً أن تدهن المرهم جيداً ليقتل ملايين من حشرات السرطان هذه مرة واحدة في ثمانية وأربعون ساعة. إنها فقط مسألة وقت.

بمجرد أن تعرف بعد بضعة أسابيع أنك أصبحت في صحة جيدة، و خالي من الألم، لن تشعر بأي حمل علي صدرك.ستعمل كليتيك ، و أمعائك، وكبدك، و معدتك، و مناطق أخري، ستعمل بشكل جيد، و ستصبح أكثر صحةً. ستبدأ في إرتداء الملابس البلاستيكية طوال الوقت، وعندها ستبدأ حياتك الصحية فعلاً, حظ سعيد لك!

لقد عرفت كيف أستطيع القضاء علي الألم أو المرض، أو الجن القادم من شخص آخر. حدث ذلك منذ عدة سنوات. في البداية حقيقةً كان من الصعب معرقة ماذا سبب ألم ما أو مشكلة ما؟ من مسئول عن ألم معين؟حتي الآن، معظم الناس إما يعانون من مرض أو معاناة نتيجة لحدوث ألم ما. معظم المشاكل الصحية التي يسببها الألم.في المرحلة الأولي، و تحدث الأمراض/الحشرات في المرحلة الثانية.

Either those cancer insects attack the uncovered parts of the cancer patient or attack the people around those cancer patients. So while it is important to hunt and kill the cancer insects inside the body, it is equally important to hunt and kill the remaining 95 percent of insects in the atmosphere. So how do you hunt and kill the 95 percent of cancer insects in the living and growing in the atmosphere? Home and office carpets are the main source or residence of these insects. They live and grow there extremely rapidly. So if possible, avoid carpets. Use washable flooring. You need to wash floors frequently with antiseptic chemicals to kill and stop the growth of these cancer insects. Chairs, sofas, couches, beds, etc., should have a primary plastic covering to block the movement of the cancer insects toward our bodies. We need to spray pest control chemicals on top, around, and under them on a daily basis. Animals are very help full in the rapid growth of cancer insects. So use every possible precaution to prevent the growth of these cancer insects. Once you use plastic clothing treatment, medication cost will reduce to a surprisingly very low level. You do not need to apply ointment frequently under the plastic clothing. Sometimes once you apply one time thoroughly; it will be enough for forty-eight hours and will kill millions of those cancer insects just in one attempt. It is just a matter of time. Once you learn within a few weeks that you are healthy and pain free, you do not feel any load on your chest, your kidneys work good, your intestine, liver, stomach, and other areas are getting more healthier, you will start wearing plastic clothing all the time. And that will be the time when your true healthy life will start, Good luck to you!

تعتبر الأفعال/ ردود الأفعال التي يسببها جني واحد أو جن كثيرون ، عادةً جزء من شخصية الفرد، مثل العصبية التي تتوقف فجأة، التطرف، و عادات أخرى . لا أعتقد أن هناك أي شخص يحاول السيطرة علي أحلامه، أعتقد أن السبب هو عدم إدراكهم بالعالم الغير مرئي وقدراته. علي أي حال، النقطة التي أريد مناقشتها الآن بدايةً هي المرض و الآلام، و السبب في ذلك هو أن كلما تكلمت مع شخص ما، تجده إما أنه يعاني من مرض ما أو نوع من أنواع الألم أو الآلام. لقد تعلمت بمرور الوقت، أن الأمراض بصفة خاصة لا ترحم، و هي عبارة عن طفيليات. الأمراض لا إحساس ولا حكمة لها، إنها فقط مجرد حشرات قاسية كل ما تفعله هو الإتلاف. إنها تستطيع أن تتلف الجسم أو العضو عن طريق الإستمرار في أكله. لقد إستطعت أن أبعدهم عن الجسم أو العضو المصاب نوعاً ما، سواء كانت هذه الحشرات تمتص/تهاجم جسمي أو جسم أي شخص آخر. لن تترك الأمراض/ الحشرات صيد أجسامنا أو أعضائنا. علي أي حال، لقد صارعت ضدها لسنوات، لكن النتيجة كانت مؤقتة. لقد إستطعت تنظيف جسم أو عضو متضرر ومصاب، و إستطعت أن أحرره من الألم، لكن لفترة قصيرة، فبمجرد أن إتخذت طريقاً آخر بعيدً عن ذلك المكان، ولم أعد أتصل بذلك الشخص، هؤلاء الأشخاص تعرضوا لهجوم الأمراض و الحشرات الأخري ثانيةً. أنا متأكد من أن ليس كل الأشخاص يواجهون تلك المشكلة، لكن الأشخاص الذين لديهم عدوي/سرطان أو تلف أو ضررخطير في أجسامهم/أعضائهم، هم عرضة لهجوم هذه الأمراض أو الحشرات بعد أيام قليلة. لقد علمنا بمرور الوقت أن هذه الحشرات قاسية و لا ترحم. إن هذه الحشرات تبحث عن الطعام، و تعتبر أجسامنا و أعضائنا هي طعامها الأفضل و الأسهل. علمت أيضاً أن الجن و الآلام مختلفون عن الأمراض/الحشرات.

Several years ago, when I figured out that I was able to eliminate pain or disease or a demon from another person, honestly in beginning, when, it was difficult to figure out which pain or problem is caused by whom? Who is responsible for a particular pain? At that time, even now, most people either suffer from a disease or suffer due to some pains. Most of the health issues mainly caused by pains in the first step in the second diseases/insects are the cause..

Actions/ reactions due to the involvement of a demon or demons are usually considered a part of the person's personality, like having a short temperament, extremism, and so many other habits. I do not think anybody really tries to control their dreams; the reason is, I think, is their unawareness of a parallel invisible world and their unawareness about their capabilities. Anyway, my point of discussion, right now is, in beginning, I was more running behind disease and pains. The reason behind this is because whoever you talk to is either suffering from a disease or suffering from some kind of pain or pains. In time, I learned, especially about diseases, that diseases are heartless and are parasites. Diseases do not have any sense or wisdom.

They are just cruel insects and the only thing they can do is damage. They can do damage to a body or organ by eating them continuously. Somehow I was able to move them away from a damaged body or organ, but either they were absorbing/attacking my body or choosing someone else's body. Those diseases/insects will not give up hurting our bodies or organs. Anyway, I did that struggle for years, but the result was only temporary.

رؤية الجن و الآلام السيطرة عليها

إن الجن أذكياء و حساسون جداً، و الآلام حساسة بنسبة 50 %، بالمقارنة بالجن، أو ربما تكون أقل قليلاً. لكن المشكلة هي أن الآلام مسئولة عن بدء المرض. تبحث الآلام عن مكان تكمن فيه داخل جسمنا، مثل المفاصل، أو العضلات، أو أي عضو أو أي مكان داخل و خارج الجلد. تتلف الآلام جسمنا، أو أي عضو قليلاً، و لكن ليس بدرجة كبيرة. عادةً ما يكون ذلك بداية للأمراض. عندما يكمن الألم داخل جسمنا، فإنه يحدث أضرار أو تلف ليس خطيراً.

بغض النظر عن وجود بعض التلف في جسمنا، لن نشعر بالألم إلا إذا ذهب الألم إلي هذه المنطقة التالفة و يبدأ في إيلامنا. و الآن حتى لو لم يعد هناك ألم بالمرة، فإن هذه التلفيات البسيطة داخل أو خارج أجسامنا، ستكون دعوة مفتوحة للأمراض أو الحشرات الجائعة. تشن هذه الحشرات الجائعة سلسلة من الهجوم علي جسمنا و أعضائنا. هذه الحشرات موجودة في كل مكان، علي جلد، علي سريرك، علي كراسيك، علي السجادة، في الهواء،في الماء، في اللحم، وفي كل مكان.ببساطة فإن أجزاء و أعضاء جسمنا التالفة المتضررة، تعتبر طعام لهذه الأمراض.

ذهبت ذات يوم للقاء شخص يعالج من السرطان في المستشفى. لقد بقيت هناك لساعات قليلة فقط، لكني رأيت العالم الحقيقي في هذه الزيارة، وهناك رأيت التلف الحقيقي و الأضرار الحقيقية التي يتسبب فيها السرطان/الحشرات. لقد كانت صحتي جيدة تماماً، لكن حتى أن لم يكن لدي رغبة في أي شيئ لعدة أيام، ظللت أفكر في هؤلاء الأشخاص الذين إكتشفوا أن شخص ما يعاني من سرطان الدم، أو سرطان الثدي، إلخ....

I was able to clean one already-damaged body or organ and was able to make it pain free but not for a long time. As soon as I was weaving that place or not in contact with that person anymore, those people were again under attack of the other disease or insects. I am sure not everyone has that problem, but those people whose body/organ has some serious infection/cancers or damages were under attack again from these disease or insects after a few days. In time, I learned these diseases are cruel and heartless. These insects just look for food, and our bodies and organs are their favorite and the easiest available food. In time, I learned that demons and pains are different from diseases/insects. Demons are very intelligent and sensible. Pains are 50 percent sensible as compared to demons or maybe a little less. But the problem is a lot of times pains are responsible to start a disease. Usually, pains look for a place to reside in inside our body, like joints or muscles or any organ or anywhere inside or outside our skin. Pains damage our body or any organ a little bit but not too much. Usually that is the beginning of diseases. When pain is residing inside our body, for sure it creates some minor damages.

Now regardless of some damages inside our body, we will not feel any pain until the pain goes to that damaged part and starts hurting us. Now even if somehow the pain is not there anymore, those very minor damages inside or outside our body will be an open invitation for diseases or hungry insects. These hungry insects cast a continuous stream of attacks to our body and organs. These insects are everywhere—on top of our skin, on our bed, chairs, carpet, in the air, in the water, in meat, everywhere. Simply put, our damaged body parts or organs are food for these diseases.

ظللت أفكر لعدة أيام ما إذ كان في مقدوري إزالة الألم من أي جسم لأريحه من هجوم الألم و المرض،لكني ظللت أفكر أنه لا شيىء، لاشيئ، لا يكفي أن نعطي شخص ما علاجاً، أو أقول علاجاً دائماً. ولكنه يستغرق وقتاً طويلاً، ومليئ بالصراعات. أعرف بلا شك أن هذه نقطة تحول بالنسبة لي.أتذكر أنني ظللت أدعو لله كي يهديني إلى حل ما للسيطرة علي السرطان أو العدوي. أعتقد أن هذا إستغرق بعض الوقت، لكن شيئاً فشيئاً حصلت علي بعض الأفكار من مصادر غير مرئية، عن كيفية علاج السرطان.لا أستطيع ان أفصح عنها لكني قمت بإجراء عدة تجارب للتأكد منها. أنا الآن واثق من علاجي المقترح لعلاج السرطان و العدوي بنسبة 100 %. إنه يعتمد الآن علي العلوم الطبية و علي المدة التي يستغرقها للتأكد منه. إن إجراءات العلاج التي إقترحتها لعلاج السرطانات و العدوي، ستسمح لمرضي السرطان بإستخدامها. لا يوجد جديد في علاج االسرطان الذي إقترحته. هناك بعض العلاج الذي يجب إستخدامه بطريقتي، و الذي يتطلب إذن الطبيب الخاص بك. يمكن توفير الراحة من أمراض السرطان/الحشرات. لا تجعلهم يهربون إلي الجو، أو ينتقلوا لجسم آخر ليحدثوا به سرطان. لابد أن تقتل هذه الحشرات كل يوم. إذا تركتهم يهربون إلي الجو، سيهاجموك مرة أخري أو سيهاجمون شخصاً آخر.

إن أفضل طريقة لإقتلاع السرطان/الحشرات من جذورها، هي أن نقتلهم كل ثانية. لابد أن يتأكد مريض السرطان أنه قتل كل حشرة من السرطان، و مصادرها لتجنب المشاكل المستقبلية بالنسبة له و لغيره.

علي أي حال، عندما بدأت في الكتابة عن هذا الموضوع في البداية، قلت أنني أحاول أن أقدم المساعدة و أجد طرق أكثر لمحاربة الأمراض.

SEE & CONTROL DEMONS & PAIN

One time I went to meet someone at a cancer treatment hospital. I was there maybe for few hours only, but during that visit, I saw the real world. There I saw the real damages caused by these cancer diseases/insects. I was completely healthy, but even I didn't have any desire or anything for several days. I kept thinking about those people who just discovered that someone has blood cancer or someone has breast cancer, etc. For several days, I kept thinking, about my abilities to remove pain from a body just to release them from the attack of that pain and disease. But I kept thinking that it was nothing, it is nothing; it is not enough to really give a cure to someone or I will say a permanent cure to someone. It was possible but very time-consuming and full of struggles. I know, definitely, that was a turning point for me. I remember I kept praying to God continuously to get a clue or solution to control a cancer or infection. I think it took some time, but slowly and steadily, I was keep getting feeding from invisible sources day by day, how to cure a cancer. I cannot reveal what, but I did several experiments to verify it, and now I am 100 percent confident about my suggested cancer and infection treatment. Now it depends on medical science and how long they will take to verify. My procedures for the cure of cancers and infections will allow the cancer patients to use it. There is nothing new in my cancer treatments. Some medication/but need to use in my way with permission of your doctor. Rest of my cancer diseases/insects. Do not let them escape to the atmosphere or to transfer to another body to create cancer there. You need to kill these insects every second everyday. You let them escape in the atmosphere, they will attack you again or some other body.

رضوان قرشي

لم أتعرض كثيراً للجن، السبب في ذلك هو نفس السبب، لأن معظمنا لم يدرك متى سنعاني من تأثير الجن. إن علاج السرطان/العدوي الذي إقترحته، سيبعد الكثير من الأمراض عنهم. بالنسبة للألم، هو مثل الجن ليس من الحشرات. إنه يتنقل بالطريقة الكهرومغناطيسية. إنه حساس و ذكي. الألم أكثر قسوة و لا يرحم بالمقارنة بالجن. إذا تم حماية أجسامنا بملابس عازلة، سيساعد كثيراً ضد هذه الآلام. ستظل الآلام قادرة علي الدخول إلي جسمنا، لكنها لن تستمر في البقاء لفترة طويلة. الوضع سيكون غير مريح بالنسبة للآلام، لكن لا يستطيع أي شخص تحدي الألم. تذكر دائماً الطريقة التي صمم بها جسمنا، يستخدم الألم أعصابنا و يهاجمها ليجعلنا نشعر بشعور مؤلم. تجيد الآلام صيد/ضغط علي أعصابنا لنظل نشعر بالألم. مثلاً، إذا غطينا جسمنا بالملابس المطاطية/البلاستيكية، لكن لم نغطي ذراعنا جيداً بها، ستبحث الآلام عن أي عصب خلف ذراعنا، و سيرسل إشارات مؤلمة لكليتنا، و حتي لو لم يهاجم الألم كليتينا، سيبحث الألم مباشرةً عن أي جزء غير مغطي من جسمنا، و يضغط أو يؤلم أعصابنا، و يرسل إشارات لمناطق مختلقة من جسمنا. إن الآلام أجسام مادية و غير مرئية.تتنقل اللآلام بسهولة بطريقة كهرومغناطيسية في الجو.إن سرعة إنتقال الجن و الآلام بسرعة مذهلة مثل سرعة الصوت. تستجيب اللآلام لي بسهولة، إنني أصر علي شدها لتترك الجسم، أحياناً يستغرق ذلك بضعة دقائق، أحياناً أخري يستغرق مدة أطول. من السهل جداً أن تجعل الجني صديقاً لك، هذا من واقع تجربتي. المسألة مسألة وقت. إنهم يجعلون أوقاتي عصيبة. لكن الجن و الآلام كلاهما من أفضل الأصدقاء، بينما آلام الجن من أسوأ الأصدقاءعندما لم يكن جسمي مغطي بملابس عازلة، كنت أشعر عادةً بإشارات آلام يمكن إحتمالها في كل جسمي، في قلبي، و في معدتي، وفي كليتي، و في كل مكان، لكن منذ ذلك الوقت أغطي بعض أجزاء من جسمي بملابس عازلة مطاطية /بلاستيكية، و لا أشعر بأي ألم في هذه الأجزاء من جسمي...

Rizwan Qureshi

The best way to pull these cancer disease/insects from their roots is to kill them every second. Every cancer patient needs to make sure they kill each and every insect of cancer and their source to avoid future problems for them and for others.

Anyway, when I started writing about this topic in the beginning I was trying to say that I was more into helping and was trying to find more and more ways to fight diseases. I was less involved with demons. Same reason, because most of us even do not realize, when, we are suffering due to demon's affects. My cancer/infection cure will keep a lot of diseases away from them. As far as pain, like demons, they are not insects. They travel electromagnetically. They are very sensible and intelligent. Pains are way more cruel and heartless as compared to demons. Protecting our bodies with insulated clothing will help a lot against pains. Pains can still go inside our body, but pains will not stay there for long time. Somehow, it is an uncomfortable situation for them. But no one can challenge a pain; Pain cannot go inside our joints or muscles or organs when we are covered with rubber or plastic clothing. Always remember the way our body is designed; pains use or attack our nerves to give us painful feelings. Pains are very good in hurting/pinching our nerves to keep us in pain. For example, if our body is covered with rubber/ plastic clothing properly but our arms arc not covered with rubber/ plastic clothing, pains are very good in finding a nerve on the back side of our arm and will send a painful signal to our kidney. So even if pain is not attacking our kidneys directly pain can still choose some other uncovered area of our body and pinch or hurt our nerves to send a pain signal to different areas of our body.

رؤية الجن و الآلام السيطرة عليها

لقد أوصلني هذا إلى هذه النتيجة : عندما نرتدي الملابس المطاطية/البلاستيكية العازلة، حتى الآلام لا تضيع وقتها للذهاب إلى هذا الجزء من الجسم. تذكر أنك تستطيع تحدي أمراض وحشرات السرطان/العدوي المفتوحة و تصيدها وتقتلها. هذا جيد، لكن لا تفكر أبداً بإعتراض أو تحدي الجني أو الألم. تعتبر الجن و الآلام مخلوقات خارقة تعيش طويلاً. إنهما يستطيعا أن يتعاركا و يقتلا بعضهما البعض، ولكن هذا بعيد عن إدراكنا. يمكننا إبعاد الألم عن جسمنا، عندما يكتشف العلماء الطرق السليمة لإبعادهم. لماذا أقول هذا، لماذا أثق في إمكانية معالجة الألم بإستخدام الطرق السليمة لإبعاده عن طريق المسح أو الحك؟. لأني أفعل هذا طوال الوقت، كل يوم. إنني إستطعت أن أتواصل مع الآلام الجديدة، الموجودة في أشخاص جدد و غرباء، و إستطعت أن أقنعهم معظم الوقت بالتخاطر أن يتركوا جسم هذا الشخص. تستجيب الآلام لي دائماً، وفوراً أحياناً، و يستغرق ذلك بضعة دقائق في أحيان أخري. ما أود أن أقوله هو أن لدي عيني و عقلي طريقة ما للتواصل مع الألم، و تستجيب الآلام لي بالتواصل التخاطري، بدون الذهاب بالقرب من الجسم، لهذا هناك عدة طرق متاحة لإبعاد الآلام عن الجسم، يحتاج ذلك فقط إلي العلوم الطبية لتكتشفها و تستخدمها. أريد أن أتكلم مرة أخري عن الآلام و الجن بتفصيل أكثر. لا تعتقد أنك تستطيع قتل الألم أو الجن أو تسيطر عليهما، لا تتكلم بجنون، أو تقول كلام سيئ عنهم حتي لو كانوا يسببون الآلام لنا. لابد أن نفهم أنهم في غاية القوة، و مضايقتهم و جعلهم أعداء لنا ليست فكرة جيدة. سأكتب عن طرق كثيرة مختلفة لتحويلهم إلي أصدقاء، في مكان ما لاحقاً في هذا الكتاب، و أنا متأكد 100 % من أن الناس ستنجح في جعل الجن أصدقاء.

SEE & CONTROL DEMONS & PAIN

Pains are physical & invisible bodies. Pains travel very easily electromagnetically in the atmosphere. The speed of travel of demons and pains is incredible, like the speed of light. Most of the time pains listen to me very easily. I am able to insist or can pull them to leave a body also. Sometimes it takes few minutes; sometimes a little longer. It is extremely easy to make demon or pain your friend. This is my experience. Only is time, they give me hard time, after that both demons and pains, both are better friends than of that both demons, pains both one bitter friends than human as far as listening obeying and following your talk & instructions when, my body was not covered with insulated clothing, usually I was able to feel friendly pain signals all over my body. In my heart, stomach, kidney, anywhere, but since then, I am covering my some areas of body with an insulated rubber/plastic clothing, I do not get any even friendly pain signals in that part of body. This thing brings me to this conclusion: when we wear insulated rubber/plastic clothing, even pains do not waste their time to go inside that part of the body. Again remember, you can challenge open cancer/infection diseases or insects and hunt or kill them. It is okay, but do not ever think about challenging or defining a demon or a pain. Demons and pains are supernatural creatures that have long lives. They, demon or pains, can fight with each other, and they can kill each other but this is beyond our limit. We can very easily keep pain away from our body when scientists discover the proper ways to repel them. Why am I saying this and why am I so confident about the possible cure of pain by the use of proper ways to repel wiping? Because I do this all the time, every day.

رضوان قرشي

فيما يتعلق بالالام، لست متأكداً كيف بمكن للناس أن يسيطروا علي الآلم. لقد أصبح الجن و الآلام أصدقاء لي فقط، لأنهم رأوا أن بعض الصفات و القدرات بداخلي. إنهم لم يصبحوا أصدقاءً لي فوراً. بالنسبة للجن، فإنني أحتاج أربعة و عشرون ساعة لفهم و إختبار قدراتي و صلاحياتي. بمجرد أن يعرف الجن أنني أستطيع أن أراهم، وأشعر بهم، و أتواصل معهم، لا أعتقد أن لديهم سبب وجيه لمضايقتي أو تسبب الألم لي. بمجرد أن يصبحوا أصدقاء لي، فإني أستطيع أن أطلب منهم أن يفعلوا أي شيئ من أجلي. إنهم يستطيعون أن يفعلوا ما أشعر به. و هكذا، فإن تغطية أي جسم بملابس مطاطية/بلاستيكية عازلة، يبعد الآلم عنا دائماً. لكن لا أحد يستطيع قتل الآلام. لا تزال الآلام قادرة علي الذهاب إلي أي جزء من جسمنا، لكن من خلال تجربتي من عدة أشهر ماضية عرفت أنه إذا تم تغطية أي جسم بالملابس المطاطية/البلاستيكية، عادةً لا تذهب الآلام إلي هذه المنطقة. لقد إكتشفت علاج للمرض، عدوي الأمراض، و أمراض أخري منذ ذلك الوقت. الحشرات الغير مرئية تسبب المرض، وأنا أتواصل معهم بالتخاطر. إنني أتواصل مع الآلام و الجن لأني لست شخصاً إجتماعياً بالمرة، لهذا لم ألتقي بالكثير من الناس، و هذا لا يتيح لي التواصل مع آلام جديدة كل ساعة، لكن لا زلت أجد فرص قليلة مع أشخاص مختلفون يعانون من أنواع مختلفة من الآلام كل يوم، و هكذا أجد العديد من الفرص لمقابلة آلام أشخاص مختلفين و التواصل معها كل يوم.

في البداية لم أكن علي صلة بالكثير من الجن مثل صلتي بهم في هذه الأيام. يأتي جن جدد بالقرب مني و يحاولون السيطرة علي أو علي جسمي. ليس هذا الجن هو الجن الذي أخرجه من أجسام البشر الآخرين. هؤلاء الجن ليسوا ممن يعيشون من حولي أو بطريقتي.

32

Rizwan Qureshi

I communicate with new pains residing in totally new and strange people, and most of the time I'm able to convince them telepathically to leave the body of that person. Pains always listen to me—sometimes immediately, sometimes it take few minutes—but my point is my eyes or my mind has some kind of way to contact and communicate with pain. And pains listen to my telepathic communication, without toughing even most of the, without going close to a body. So there is a system of ways available to repel pains from a body; medical science only needs to discover it and start using it. Again, I want to write about pains and demons some more.

Do not think anyone can kill or control a pain or a demon. So do not talk crazy or say bad stuff about them even if they hurt us. We need to understand that they are extremely powerful, and it is not a good idea to upset them and make them our enemies. I will write a lot of different ways to turn them into friends somewhere later on in this book, and I am sure 100 percent of the people will be successful in making demons their friends. In the case of pains, I am not sure how many people will be able to control pain. Demons and pains became my friends only because they saw some different qualities and abilities in me. They did not become my friends immediately. For demons, I need twenty-four hours to understand and test my abilities and powers. Once the demons figure out I am able to see them, I am able to sense them, and I am able to communicate with them, I think they do not have any good reason to bother me or hurt me.

رؤية الجن و الآلام السيطرة عليها

أشعر أن يزورني من الجن حوالي من عشرين إلي ثلاثين جني جديد، أو يتجمعون حولي، أو علي الأقل يظلون علي إتصال بي. كما كتبت عدة مرات، أنني لا أتحمل وجود جني بداخلي أو بالقرب من جسمي، مثلي مثل أي شخص طبيعي. بمجرد أن يأتي جن جدد بالقرب مني، يجب أن أطلب منهم الخروج من جسمي في وجود القليل من الناس، حتي لو لم أرد ذلك.

لقد كانت عملية صعبة و طويلة منذ سنوات، لكن الآن يستمع إلي الجن فوراً معظم الوقت. عندما أكتشف وجود مرض سرطان/عدوي ليست صديقة لأي شخص، فإنني أجد طريقة ما لقتلهم أو إيلامهم. إني أقوم بذلك الآن، وقريباً جداً سيقوم بذلك كل الناس، و هكذا لن أضيع وقتي في التواصل مع الأمراض. يعتبر الألم البوابة الأولي للمرض.

تذهب الآلام داخل جسمنا و تحدث أضرار بسيطة و تلف بسيط في أماكن مختلفة من جسمنا أو أعضائنا. أخيراً تعتبر هذه العدوي دعوة مفتوحة للسرطان/عدوي الأمراض/ الحشرات. إذا غطينا جسمنا جيداً بالملابس المطاطية/البلاستيكية العازلة، و تناولنا الدواء والعلاج المناسب لصيد و قتل الأمراض/الحشرات المختلفة، بما فيها أمراض/حشرات السرطان. بهذا يستطيع الإنسان السيطرة علي الجو الغير صحي و المليئ بالمرض، حتي مع إستمرار وجود الآلام، السبب في ذلك هو صيد و قتل حشرات السرطان بشكل سليم، بمساعدة العلوم الطبية.

فيما بعد، عندما تكتشف العلوم الطبية نظام الإشعاع، سيمكن هذا من إبعاد الآلام من الجسم، و هكذا سيكون للإنسان و العلوم الطبية فرصة أفضل للسيطرة علي أنواع مختلفة من الآلام. يصعب علي العلوم الطبية إيجاد علاج لإبعاد الألم، لأنها لم تفكر في هذا الإتجاه.

Once they become friends, I can ask them to do anything for me, whatever I feel they are able to do. So a covered body with insulated rubber/plastic keeps pains also away from us. But no one can kill pains; pains can still go to any part of our body to hurt us, but in my experience in the last several months, if a body is covered with rubber/plastic, usually pains do not go in that section or area. Since I discovered the cure for cancer, infection diseases and other diseases. Sicknesses created by invisible insects, I just work on them telepathically. But still, I communicate with pains and demons because I am not a social person at all; that's why I do not get a chance to meet with too many people. When I do not meet with too many people, I am not getting too many chances to communicate with new pains every hour. But still, I get a few chances with different people suffering from different kinds of pains every day. And this way still, I am getting several chances to meet and communicate with different pains from different people every day.

Now since the beginning, I was not in contact with as many demons as I am in these days. Only brand-new demons come close to me or possess or try to possess my body. These demons are not those demons whatever; I snatch them from other human bodies. These are not those demons that live around me or in my way. I feel every day twenty to thirty new demons are visiting me and getting grouped around me or at least staying in contact with me. As I wrote several times, I do not have any tolerance for a demon inside or even close to my body, just like you or any normal person. Once new demons come close to me, even if I do not want to sometimes due to presence of few people, I have to tell the demons to come out of my body.

إذا إتجهت العلوم الطبية إلي التفكير في هذا الإتجاه اليوم، أنا متأكد أنهم سيجدون علاج للآلام غداً. أنا لا أتكلم عن الجن الآن. هذا مثال بسيط عن صداقة الألم. إن إبنتي طفلة طبيعية بنسبة 100%، إنها لا تعاني من أي مشاكل مثلي. إنها لا تري أي جني أو تشعر به أو تتصل به. إذا حدث ذلك مرة واحدة، سأقول أنها صدفة، لكن هذا حدث عدة مرات. كانت هناك فتاه بجوار إبنتي تعاني من صداع شديد، و آلام أخري، و حاولت إبنتي البحث عني في كل مكان، ولم تجدني، فحاولت التحدث مع الألم في جسم صديقتها.

لقد تواصلت فقط مع الألم بطريقة طبيعية، و تجاوب الألم معها و ترك جسد صديقتها. لقد تعجبت صديقتها من ذلك. لقد حدث ذلك عدة مرات، ما أود أن اشرحه هنا هو أنه بمجرد أن يصبح الجن و الآلام أصدقاء لنا، فإنهم سيتجاوبون معنا و يطيعوننا بكل سهولة. علي أي حال، أنا لا أعرف ما إذا كنت أقول لك هذا الآن، أم أنني أسألك سؤالاً. إنني أتواصل مع حوالي ثلاثين جني كل يوم، بدون دعوتهم أو التفاعل معهم. أعرف أن كل جني ينتمي إلي مجموعة كبيرة من الجن و يمثلهم، و أصبح هؤلاء الجن كلهم أصدقاء لي، فهم يستمعون لي و يطيعوني معظم الوقت. إذاً ماذا سأفعل في هذا الموضوع؟ ماذا يمكنك فعله بهذه الأنواع من القوي ؟

إن السرطان عبارة عن مجموعة من الآلام و أمراض/الحشرات. عادة ما تحدث الآلام تلفيات و أضرار في منطقة معينة من الجسم. حتي إذا ترك الألم هذا الجسم، إن التلفيات و الأضرار التي تحدث داخل الجسم أو داخل أي عضو، يدعو حشرات السرطان/عدوي الأمراض، و بمجرد أن تبدأ هذه الحشرات في الهجوم /أكل أي جزء من الجسم، لا تتركه إلا بعد أن تدمر هذا الجزء من الجسم أو العضو تماماً.

It used to be a difficult and long process a few years ago, but nowadays they listen to me immediately most of the time. Once, I figure out a cancer/infection disease is not a friend anyone, I find a way to kill them or hunt them. Now I am doing it; everybody else will start doing it pretty soon. Also this way, I am not wasting my time in contacting the diseases.

Now usually, pain is the first door to any disease. Pains go inside our bodies and create minor damages in different paths of our bodies or organs. Finally that minor damage is an open invitation for cancer/ infection diseases/insects. So if we cover our body properly with the insulated rubber/plastic and use and take proper medication to hunt and kill different disease/insects, including cancer disease/insects. And to total this, the role of the pains will reduce. Because pains can create some or more pains and minor damages only, pains cannot cause serious diseases or cancer by inviting cancer/infections insects. This way, even pains still exist, but due to proper hunting and killing of cancer diseases/insects, mankind can easily control unhealthy and sick atmosphere in this world, with the help of medical science. Later on when medical science discovers the rays system that will be capable of repelling pains from a body, mankind and medical science will have better control of different kinds of pains. It is only difficult for medical science to find a cure to repel pain because medical science is not thinking and trying in that direction. If medical science starts thinking and trying in that direction of cure today, I am sure they will find a cure for pains tomorrow.

حتي لو كان هناك آداة قوية و مؤثرة أو علاج للسيطرة علي الألم في الجسم، يجب علي العلوم الطبية أن تكتشف نظام إشعاعي طارد، لطرد الألم من جسم الإنسان. إذا نظمنا أنفسنا فقط لصيد و قتل حشرات السرطان/الأمراض المعدية، لصبدها و قتلها، سنستطيع عندها علاج مشاكل السرطان 100 %.

إن طبيعة و تركيبة الألم مشابهة للجن. إن حشرات السرطان/الأمراض المعدية/ عبارة عن مجموعات كبيرة من الحشرات في الغالب، و هي حشرات صغيرة جداً و غير مرئية للعين المجردة. تتحرك الآلام بطريقة كهرومغناطيسية. إن متوسط حجم الألم يساوي حجم ذبابة صغيرة أو بعوضة كبيرة، لكن الآلام ليست حشرات. إن آليتهم تشبه الكهرومغناطيسية و الإشعاعات. أنا واثق أن ليس هناك أمر شخصي، لكن الآلام تذهب داخل مفاصلنا، و عضلاتنا، و أعضائنا، و أجزاء أخري من الجسم لتبقي هناك فقط.

إن هذا تصرف شريرو مؤلم، بلا شك، لكنهم يفعلون ذلك طوال الوقت، لكن إلي حد ما إما تجيد الآلام فعل هذا، أو أن في مهاجمتهم و إيلامهم لنا، يهاجمون أعصابنا، و يحدث ذلك تلقائياً. لماذا تهاجم الآلام أعصابنا؟. إما أنهم يحبون ذلك، أو أن هناك شيئ ما يجذب الآلام لأعصابنا.

الشئ المشترك بين الآلام و بين أعصابنا هو الكهرباء، أو أن ترسل أعصابنا بعض الإشارات إلي أجزء من جسمنا و إلي مخنا طوال الوقت. تجيد الآلام إستخدام أعصابنا عن طريق الضغط عليها و إيلامها، لإرسال إشارة ألم إلي أجزاء مختلفة من جسمنا. وفقاً لنظريتي، المشكلة الرئيسية هي أن حشرات السرطان/العدوي، و حشرات الأمراض، كثيرة العدد، كثيرة العدد، وموجودة في كل مكان.

I am not talking about demons right now. This is a very simple example of a pain friendship. My daughter, she is a 100 percent normal child. She does not have any problems like me. She cannot see or sense or communicate with any demon. If it happened one time, I may say it was an accident, but it happened several times. Someone around my daughter was having some serious headache and some other pains. My daughter tried to look for me everywhere. When she was unable to find me, she decided to talk to the pain in the body of her friend.

She just communicated with the pain in a normal way, and the pain listened to her and left the body of her friend. Her friend was so surprised with that. It happened several times. So what I am trying to explain here is once demon and pains become our friends, they listen and obey us very easily. So anyway, I do not know if I am telling you this now or I am asking you a question. Without inviting them or any interaction, I am getting in contact with around thirty demons every day. And I know each demon belongs or represents a big group of demons, and all of these demons are becoming my friends. They listen to me and they obey me most of the time, so what will I do with all that? What possibly can you do with these kinds of powers? Any cancer is a combination of pains and disease/insects. Usually pains create minor damages to a particular area of the body. Even if pain leaves that body, the minor damage inside the body or inside any organ starts inviting cancer/infectious diseases/ insects. And once they start attacking/eating any part of the body, those insects do not give up until they completely destroy that part of the body or organ.

عندما يسيطر الشخص 100 % علي الحشرات، فالسرطان سينتهي.أما بالنسبة للآلام، كما قلت من قبل عدة مرات، ليس من الصعب علي العلوم الطبية أن تسيطر علي الألم و تبعده عن أي جزء من جسم أي إنسان. يجب علي العلوم الطبية أن تبدأ في البحث والتجارب لإكتشاف الطرق السليمة لنظام الإشعاعات للعمل ضد الآلام.لقد تعلمت من تجربتي أنه يمكن السيطرة علي الآلام بإستخدام نفس أنواع الإشعاعات. حتي الآلام يمكن أن نقسمها إلي فئات فرعية، لكن لا يزال نظام الإشعاعات المتمايلة، مؤثراً في كل أنواع الآلام. أقدر أقسم الآلام إلي فئات فرعية ثلاثة:

1. آلام ترسل إشارات ألم إلي مفاصلنا، عضلاتنا، أعضائنا، عمودنا الفقري، أو ألي أي مكان، أو إحداث ألم بها.

2 . آلام تحدث شعور بالحرق أو شعور مؤلم في أي جزء من جسمنا. يمكن أن تشعر بشعور الحرق في قدمك أحياناً، و في جمجمتك أحياناً أخري، وفي كل مكان. هذه الآلام تحدث شعور بالحرق و الألم معاً.

3. يحدث النوع من الألم عادةً الحكة.، فأحياناً يحدث طفح جلدي لنا بسبب بعض الحشرات أيضاً. لكن هذا النوع من الآلام به كهرومغناطيسية، و أنا متأكد أن العلوم الطبية ستسيطر عليها تماماً.

هناك عمل آخر للآلام ، وهو، إذا لم تستهدف الأعصاب، فهذه الآلام تقيم في جسمنا، ولكننا لا نشعر بأي شعور مؤلم. بالنسبة لي، هذا العمل من الآلام، هو قوة قاتلة و أكثر خطورة.

Even if there is powerful and effective tool or cure to control pain in the body, medical science still needs to discover the repelling rays system to repel pain from human body; if we just organize ourselves to hunt and kill cancer/infectious diseases/insects to hunt and kill them, we will be able to control and cure cancer problems 100 percent.

The nature and configuration of pain is similar to a demon's. Cancer/infection diseases/insects are mostly really kind of very big groups of insects, very tiny and invisible to the naked eye. Pains move electromagnetically; the average size of pain is almost equal to a small fly or a big mosquito, but pains are not insects. Their mechanism is similar to electromagnetism and rays. I am sure it is nothing personal, but the pains go inside our joints, muscles, organs, and other part of the body just to reside there.

Definitely this is an extremely mean and hurtful action, but they do that all the time everywhere; somehow either the pains are very good at it or it just happens that while attacking and hurting us they target mostly our nerves. Why do pains target nerves? Either they like to do it or maybe there is something attractive in our nerves for pains.

Only thing common between pains and our nerves is some electrically or some signals from different nerves in different part of the body to our brain all the time. And pains are very good in using our nerves by pinching or hurting them to send a pain signal to different parts of the body. According to my theory, main problem in cancer/infection disease/insects, they are too many, they are too many, and they are everywhere. One will behave total 100 percent control on insects, cancer will be a history.

عندما تكون هذه الآلام داخل أجسامنا، ولكن لا نعلم عنها شيئاً، و أمثلة قليلة لهذه الأنواع من آلام مثل الفشل الكلوي، ومرض السكري، وأمراض الغدة الدرقية، وما شابه ذلك. هناك عملية آخري أو عمل آخر للآلام نصف مؤذ أو أقل إيلاماً ، أو غير مريح تماما. خلال هذه العملية يملأ الألم أجزاء، وأنابيب، وأعضاء جسمنا، ويترك مساحة أقل لدوران الدم؛ في بعض الأحيان يسد الألم تماما الأنابيب، و قنوات السمع، أو أنابيب الكلى وغيرها، ليسبب الفشل العضوي أو إرتفاع ضغط الدم أو إنخفاضه، أو الاكتئاب، وغيره، ولذلك فعلاج كل هذه لآلام ليس بعيداً جداً. يجب علي العلوم الطبية إتخاذ خطوة في حرب الآلام الغير مرئية هذه، والامراض السرطانية الغير المرئية / الحشرات ضد جسم الإنسان.

إن الروح هي طاقة إيجابية دائمة في جسم الكائن الحي. إن الروح موجودة داخل الجسم حتى يكون الجسم على قيد الحياة. الروح تبقينا على قيد الحياة. الروح هي مزيج من آلاف الطاقات الإيجابي الأصغر أي أن مزيج من كل الطاقات الإيجابية هي روح داخل الجسم. تكون الآلاف الطاقات الإيجابية مسؤولة وحدها عن القيام بوظائف جسدية مختلفة في الجسم الحي . ضع في الإعتبار أن كل هذه الطاقات الايجابية هي الروح.

كل هذه الطاقات الإيجابية في الجسم الحي هي المسؤولة عن القيام بالمهام أو العمليات الفردية . اذا كان لدينا خمسمائة نوع من الهرمونات المختلفة في أجسادنا، هذا يعني أن الطاقة الإيجابية مسؤولة بشكل فردي، عن وظيفة وعمل هذا الهورمون. نفس الشيء ينطبق على كل عظمة، كل مفصل و كل عضلة، كل عضو، وحتى دمنا. جميع أجزاء جسمنا لديها طاقة إيجابية. أن الطاقة الإيجابية هي المسؤولة عن وظائف الجسم. إن الطاقة الإيجابية محجوزة داخل جسمنا، و لديها قدرات محدودة.

SEE & CONTROL DEMONS & PAIN

As for pains, as I said before several times, it will not be a very big deal for medical science to control and repel a pain from any part of any human body; medical science only needs to start research and experiments to discover the proper rays system for this operation against pains. I have learned from my experiences that all kinds of pains can be controlled with the use of the same kind of rays. Even pains can be subcategorized into three subcategories, but still, the same communication reeling rays system will be effective for all kinds of pains. According to my knowledge and experiments, I can subcategorize pains into three categories.

1. Pains that send or create hurtful feelings in our joints, muscles, organs, backbone, or anywhere.

2. Pains that create a burning and hurtful feeling anywhere in our body. That burning is sometimes in your feet, sometimes in your skull, or anywhere. These pains bring burning and hurting together.

3. The third kind of pain usually creates itching issues. Sometimes our body gets a rash due to minor insects also. But itching pain due to these kinds of pain is the same electromagnetic issue, and I am sure very soon medical science will have total control of it.

Another action of pains is, if they are not targeting nerves, then, even these pains are residing in our body but, we do not feel any hurt feeling. To me, that action of pains is more killing and dangerous force, when these pains are inside our bodies, but we are not aware about them; a few examples of these kinds of pains may be kidney failure, diabetes, thyroid issues, and the same kinds of other issues.

يمكننا زيادة صلاحيات الطاقة الإيجابية باستخدام أو من خلال إتباع قواعد صحية للمعيشة. يمكننا تناول الطعام الصحي، والحفاظ على الجسم قوي وصحي، وتجنب العادات السيئة وغير الصحية. و أيضاً الحفاظ على النهج الإيجابي وتجنب التفكير السلبي. هذا هو الشيء الوحيد الذي يمكننا السيطرة عليه لجعل طاقاتنا الإيجابية أقوى. كما قلت، إن الطاقة أو الطاقات الإيجابية للشخص العادي لديها صلاحيات محدودة،لأنها تعمل داخل جسمنا الحي فقط. وكما شرحت سابقا، كل طاقة إيجابية لديها مسؤولية منفصلة. على سبيل المثال، إذا كانت الطاقة الإيجابيةهي المسؤولة عن انتاج الانسولين في جسمك، فهذا هو عملها، وهذا هو كل ما يمكنها القيام به.

وهذه الطاقة لن تذهب إلى مفاصل الركبة لدينا ولن تساعدة في تشغيل الركبة. نفس الشيئ، الطاقة الايجابية تكون مسؤولة عن السيطرة علي وظيفة مفاصل الركبة وعملياتها، وستقوم الطاقة بذلك. وهذه الطاقة الإيجابية لن تذهب إلى البنكرياس وتسيطرة على انتاج الانسولين.إن الطاقات الايجابية ليست سوى طاقاتنا الداخلية. انها تبقينا على قيد الحياة، ولها قوة محدودة فقط للقيام بالعمل / المهام الموكلة لها.

بالمقارنة مع الطاقات الإيجابية، وكل الطاقات السلبية، كل الطاقات الخارجية. الطاقات الخارجية ليست جزءاً من الروح. الطاقات السلبية ليست مفيدة في تشغيل أي من وظائف أو عمليات جسمنا. هذه الطاقات السلبية تتكون أساسا من الأمراض،والعلل، والجن.

Another operation or action of pains is semihurtful or less painful or just uncomfortable. During this action they fill up parts, tubes, and organs of our body and leave less space for blood circulation; sometimes they totally block tubes, hear, or kidney tubes, etc., to either cause organ failure or high blood pressure or low blood pressure or depression, etc., so a cure for all these pains is not too far. Medical science only needs to step in in this war of invisible pains and invisible cancer diseases/insects against the human body.

The soul or spirit is the permanent positive energy of a living body. Souls/spirits reside inside the body until the body is alive. The soul/ spirit keeps us alive. The soul/spirit is a combination of thousands of smaller positive energies. The combination of all positive energies is a soul/spirit within the body. In a living body, thousands of positive energies are individually responsible for performing different bodily functions. Keep in mind that the combination of all these positive energies is the soul/spirit.

All these positive energies in the living body are responsible for doing individual functions or operations. If we have five hundred kinds of different hormones in our bodies, then a positive energy is individually responsible for the function and operation of that hormone. The same applies to each bone, each joint, each muscle, each organ, and even our blood. All parts of the body have a positive energy. That positive energy is responsible for bodily functions. Positive energy is confined inside our body and has limited powers.

إن الأدوية الإيجابية مثل الفيتامينات والأقراص، و أدوية الشراب ليست طاقات إيجابية. إن هذه الأدوية الإيجابية تساعد فقط على تعزيز طاقاتنا الإيجابية الداخلية حتى تقدر تعمل بشكل أفضل ومحاربة الطاقات السلبية الخارجية. نفس الشيئ، فتناول الغذاء الجيد،و القيام بالتدريبات، والعادات الصحية تزيد قوة الطاقات الإيجابية الداخلية.

أي طاقة سلبية خارجية (مثل المرض أو العلة أو الألم أو الجن) لا يمكن أن تضر أو تفسد أي عضو، لا يمكن أن تجعلنا مريضين، لا يمكنها السيطرة على عقلنا، لا يمكن أن تجعلنا غاضبون عضباً حاداً ، لا يمكن أن تلحق الضرر في مفاصل الركبة أو تؤلمنا، ولا تقدر توقف إنتاج هرمون الانسولين، لا يمكن أن تضر مفاصل الركبة أو أي مفصل آخر، لا يمكن أن تضر وظيفة الغدد الدرقية، لا يمكن أن تحدث مشاكل صحية، و لا يمكن أن تلحق الضرر بالكبد أو بالكلى ما لم الطاقة الخارجية السلبية أقوى من الطاقة الداخلية / طاقة إيجابية.

يمكننا زيادة صلاحيات الطاقة الإيجابية باستخدام أو من خلال إتباع قواعد صحية للمعيشة. يمكننا تناول الطعام الصحي، والحفاظ على الجسم قوي وصحي، وتجنب العادات السيئة وغير الصحية. و أيضاً الحفاظ على النهج الإيجابي وتجنب التفكير السلبي. هذا هو الشيء الوحيد الذي يمكننا السيطرة عليه لجعل طاقاتنا الإيجابية أقوى.

كما قلت، إن الطاقة أو الطاقات الإيجابية للشخص العادي لديها صلاحيات محدودة،لأنها تعمل داخل جسمنا الحي فقط. وكما شرحت سابقا، كل طاقة إيجابية لديها مسؤولية منفصلة.

SEE & CONTROL DEMONS & PAIN	رضوان قرشي

We can increase the powers of positive energy by using or by adopting healthy rules of living. We can eat healthy, keep our body strong and healthy, and avoid bad and unhealthy habits. Keep a positive approach and avoid negative thinking. This is the only thing we can control to make our positive energies stronger. As I said, the positive energy or energies of a normal person have limited powers, and they can function only within our living body. And as I explained earlier, each positive energy has a separate responsibility. For example, if a positive energy is responsible for producing insulin in your bodies, then this is its job, and that's all it can do.

This energy will not go to our knee joints and help operate the knee. In the same way, positive energy is responsible for controlling the function of knee joints and their operations, and the energy will do only that. That positive energy will not go to the pancreas and control the production of insulin. Positive energies are only our internal energies. They keep us alive, and they have limited strength just to do the work/functions assigned to them. As compared to positive energies, all negative energies all external energies. External energies are not part of the soul or spirit. Negative energies are not helpful in running any of our body's functions or operations.

These negative energies mainly consist of diseases, sicknesses, and demons. Positive medications like vitamins, pills, and syrups are not positive energies. These positive medications are only helps to strengthen our internal positive energies so that they can do a better job and fight against external negative energies.

على سبيل المثال، إذا كانت الطاقة الإيجابيةهي المسؤولة عن انتاج الانسولين في جسمك، فهذا هو عملها، وهذا هو كل ما يمكنها القيام به. وهذه الطاقة لن تذهب إلى مفاصل الركبة لدينا ولن تساعدة في تشغيل الركبة. نفس الشيئ، الطاقة الايجابية تكون مسؤولة عن السيطرة علي وظيفة مفاصل الركبة وعملياتها، وستقوم الطاقة بذلك. وهذه الطاقة الإيجابية لن تذهب إلى البنكرياس وتسيطرة على انتاج الانسولين.إن الطاقات الايجابية ليست سوى طاقاتنا الداخلية. انها تبقينا على قيد الحياة، ولها قوة محدودة فقط للقيام بالعمل / المهام الموكلة لها. بالمقارنة مع الطاقات الإيجابية، وكل الطاقات السلبية، كل الطاقات الخارجية. الطاقات الخارجية ليست جزءاً من الروح. الطاقات السلبية ليست مفيدة في تشغيل أي من وظائف أو عمليات جسمنا. هذه الطاقات السلبية تتكون أساسا من الأمراض،والعلل، والجن.

إن الأدوية الإيجابية مثل الفيتامينات والأقراص، و أدوية الشراب ليست طاقات إيجابية. إن هذه الأدوية الإيجابية تساعد فقط على تعزيزطاقاتنا الإيجابية الداخلية حتى تقدر تعمل بشكل أفضل ومحاربة الطاقات السلبية الخارجية. نفس الشيئ، فتناول الغذاء الجيد،و القيام بالتدريبات، والعادات الصحية تزيد قوة الطاقات الإيجابية الداخلية.

أي طاقة سلبية خارجية (مثل المرض أو العلة أو الألم أو الجن) لا يمكن أن تضر أو تفسد أي عضو، لا يمكن أن تجعلنا مريضي، لا يمكنها السيطرة على عقلنا، لا يمكن أن تجعلنا غاضبون عضباً حاداً ، لا يمكن أن تلحق الضرر في مفاصل الركبة أو تؤلمنا، ولا تقدر توقف إنتاج هرمون الانسولين، لا يمكن أن تضر مفاصل الركبة أو أي مفصل آخر، لا يمكن أن تضر وظيفة الغدد الدرقية، لا يمكن أن تحدث مشاكل صحية، و لا يمكن أن تلحق الضرربالكبد أو بالكلى ما لم الطاقة الخارجية السلبية أقوى من الطاقة الداخلية / طاقة إيجابية.

In the same way, good food, workouts, and healthy habits increase the strength of internal positive energies. Any negative external energy (like disease or sickness or pain or demons) cannot damage any organ, cannot make us sick, cannot control our mind, cannot make us extra angry, cannot damage knee joints or give us pain, cannot stop production of insulin hormone, cannot damage knee joints or any other joint, cannot damage function of thyroid glands, cannot create health problems, and cannot damage livers or kidneys unless the external negative energy is more powerful than the internal/positive energy.

Internal positive energies are strong enough to do the regular operations of organs, and they are powerful enough to save us from the attack of external energies. But internal positive energies have limited powers and are only responsible for performing particular functions.

However, negative external energies have unlimited powers. We only feel pain or experience sickness—including production of the insulin hormone or any other hormone, heartburn or stomach ulcers, mental sickness, arthritis or any joint pain, liver damage or kidney-function failure, infections, etc., as well as shortness of temper, insomnia, and extremism—when external negative energies beat our internal positive energies. The internal/positive energy never gives up as long as we are alive. Positive energy in scientific language is the body's immunity. If internal positive energy, i.e., immunity, is strong enough to protect our body from the attack or external disease/pain, we will stay healthy.

ونظرا لخبرتي ومعرفتي، أعتقد أن الآلام لا تحبذ أي جسم معين للعيش فيه أوالإضرار به و إتلافه. بالنسبة لهم، كل البشر والحشرات والزواحف سواء.. هم بالتأكيد لا يريدون الصراع كثيراً، لهذا فمعظمهم يفضلون الأجسام المتضررة بالفعل أو المرضى أو الأعضاء، بغض النظر عما إذا كانوا بشراً أو حيوانات أخرى.

في هذه الأيام، ونتعلم المزيد والمزيد عن الأمراض الجديدة والآلام، والعلل. والسبب في ذلك يرجع ذلك إلى أن عدد السكان في كل شيء يتزايد، ومعظم الناس يتحركون ويسافرون من مكان ما من عالم إلى مكان آخر، أما الصحة الحيوانية ليست بمثل هذه الأهمية في معظم مناطق العالم. من المكن أن يمرض الحيوان ويموت. بعد بضعة أيام، تخرج الأمراض منهم، وكذلك تخرج الآلام منهم، إنها لا تذهب بعيدا جدا؛ أينما وجدت أعضاء تالفة، تخترق ذلك الجسم وتبدأ في إتلافه أكثر، و إذا لم تعثر على جسم تالف أو مريض، تذهب الآلام فقط داخل الجسم السليم وتبدأ الإضرار بها.

لقد إعتدت علي قتل الحشرات والزواحف في كثير من الأحيان، ولكن منذ بدأت أشعر بهؤلاء الجن، أصبح لدي الكثير من المشاكل في قتلهم لأنني لا أريد الجن الذين يوجدون بهم، أن يزوروا جسدي. في حالتي، وأنا أجادلهم أو أصر على أن يعودوا إلى الجسد الأصلي، أو إذا كان هذا الجسم ميت، أنا أطلب منهم أن بحثوا عن شيئا من هذا القبيل ولكن ليس أنا. أنا قادر علي القيام بذلك، ولكن في حالات الناس العاديين، أفضل شيء هو الإبقاء على المنازل وأماكن العمل بدون حشرات والابتعاد عن الحيوانات، وبخاصة الحيوانات المريضة . أو إذا كنت لا تزال ترغب في ابقاء الحيوانات، يجب الحفاظ علي صحتهم. أنا لا أعرف إذا كان هذا سهلاً أو ممكناً للجميع.

SEE & CONTROL DEMONS & PAIN

If positive energy or immunity power decreases then all kinds of external negative energy, i.e., sickness/pain, will come to our body and will keep us sick and damaged. So when we take painkillers or other mediations, they increase the strength of our internal positive energies so that we can fight against external negative energies. But external negative energies have more strength and can work against our body for a long time and damage them completely. If the organs or parts of the body are completely damaged, then the only thing that will help the internal positive energy is replacing those damaged organs or parts. And we must keep taking the related medications to increase the powers of internal positive energies.

Every disease, sickness, and pain is fixable. But can anyone be sure about how long we can fix them? Internal positive energy has limited powers. If someone is using the right medication, then a person like me can help him or her by using powers to remove those external negative energies (demons) from his mind or body. I can only help to reduce the pressure of external negative energy, and I can easily remove that external negative energy; however, it is your responsibility to fix your organs and take proper medications to increase the strength of your positive internal energies so that they can function better. The animals around us are an especially big cause of the spread of diseases. Given my knowledge and experience, I believe that pains do not favor any particular body to live in or damage. For them, all humans, insects, and reptiles are the same. They definitely don't want to struggle too much. That's why most of them prefer already damaged or sick bodies or organs, regardless of whether they belong to humans or other animals.

رضوان قرشي

تذهب هذه الحشرات والزواحف والفئران، وغيرها من الحيوانات في كل مكان وتجلب جميع أنواع الأمراض القذرة والخطيرة إلى منازلنا وأجسامنا. هذه دورة، حياة و علي الشخص أن يفكر في كيفية حل هذا الأمر. ولكن يمكن أن تنشر الحيوانات المريضة المرض بسهولة في كل مكان.. تنمو الآلام أو الجن، كما أفتراض أنها بسرعة كبيرة، وبما أن نموهم يزيد، فإنهم تحتاجون إلى مزيد من الأجسام، وهذا يعني أن المزيد من الناس سوف يصابون بالمرض. أنا متأكد من أنك تدرك أن الجن والآلام كلها أشياء غير مرئية في العالم المادي وأنهم لا يموتون بسهولة.

تبلغ أعمارهم مئات السنين. إنهم في مهمة. بعد أن يقتلوا الشخص، يختاروا شخص آخر. وعندما يكونون في الجسم، يقومون تضر بإتلافه و كذلك إتلاف الأعضاء وخلال ذلك الوقت، وانهم يتكاثرون ويزيد عددهم.

تختلف الآلام و الجن عن بعضها البعض، كما يختلف البشر و تختلف الحيوانات البرية أو الزواحف السامة عن بعضها البعض. عندما يقتل الأسد غزالا، يأكل الأسد أولاً. عندما ينتهي الأسد من تناول الغزال، يأتي حيوان ثاني أقل قوة، و يبدأ في تناول بقايا لحم الغزال، و بعد ذلك يأتي ثالث أقوى حيوان يأكل بقايا اللحم. هكذا تأكل كل هذه الحيوانات. وأخيرا، تهاجم جميع الحيوانات الصغيرة أو الحشرات بقايا لحم الغزال الذي تم صيده. نفس الشيئ بمجرد أن يهاجمنا مرض ما، فإنه يأتي مع مجموعة ويظل يمهاجم أجسامنا حتى يلحق بها الأضرار تماما. في ما يخص أعضاء الجسم التالفة، يجب أن نتعامل مع سلسلة من الأمراض، والعلل، والآلام. لا أحد يستطيع أن يقتلهم. نكزن محظوظين فقط، إذا إستطعنا علاج الأعراض و الابتعاد عن مصدر المرض، سنكون قادرين على أن نصبح طبيعيين 100 %.

These days, we are finding and learning more and more about new diseases, pains, and sicknesses. The reason for this is because the population of everything is increasing; most people are moving and traveling from one part of the world to another, and animal health is not as important in most areas of the world. One animal may get sick and die. After a few days, diseases come out from them. Pains in their bodies come out from them, and they do not go too far; wherever they find damaged organs, they penetrate that body and start damaging them even more. If they do not find a damaged or sick body, they just go inside a healthy body and start damaging it. I used to kill insects and reptiles frequently, but since I started sensing these demons, I have developed a lot of problems killing them because I do not want their demons to visit my body. In my case, I argue with them or insist that they go back to the original body, or if that body is dead, I ask them to find something similar but not me. I am able to do it, but in normal people's cases, the best thing is to keep houses and workplaces insect free and stay away from animals, especially sick animals. Or if you still want to keep animals, then take care of their health. I don't know if this is easy or possible for everyone.

خلاف ذلك، بمجرد وجود هذه الأمراض و العلل في أجسامنا مرة أخرى،سيتمكنون من إصابتنا. هذه المشكلة موجودة مدى الحياة، مثل والقرحة الصداع النصفي، تلف الكبد،، الفشل الكلوي السكري، والتهابات البواسير والالتهابات الأخرى، وأنواع مختلفة من السرطانات. أجسادنا المريضة وأعضائنا التالفة هي طعام هذه الأمراض، حيث يأكلون أجسادنا وأعضائنا وتلحق الضرر به أكثر وأكثر من كل يوم. في العلم الحديث، لدينا أدوية معالجة جيدة جداً لعلاج الأضرار الناجمة عن هذه الأمراض. ولكنه من الصعب جدا، على تلك الأدوية المعالجة إبعاد هذه الأمراض بعيدا عن الأجزاء التالفة أو المجروحة من الجسم، إنهم لا يتركوه. نحن تناول المسكنات والمضادات الحيوية والأدوية العلاجية، ولكن تضرنا الآلام مرة أخرى. عند هذه النقطة، إذا كان الشخص يستخدم دواء معالج جيد جدا، سأستطيع أنا أو شخص مثلي أن ساعدهم على إزالة تلك الآلام من الجسم التالف أو المتضرر. بعد ذلك، يجب علي الشخص أن يستخدم النوع الصحيح من الأدوية المعالجة لإصلاح الأضرار. لقد خضت هذه التجربة المجنونة التي لا تصدق عدة مرات. لقد أصبحت الآلام وعدد لا يحصى من الامراض أصدقائي. لكن المشكلة هي أنها لا تشبه سوى النار، وحروقها.

يمكن للأمراض والآلام، البقاء خارج الجسم. وحتى ولو كانوا يتصرفون وكأنه أصدقاء. يمكن أن تقلل الآثار ولكن لا يزال تأثيرها هو الألم، فبمجرد أن تذهب الأمراض و الآلام إلى الجسم أوأي جزء منه، يشعر هذا جزء بالألم. هذا كله جنون، ولكن يمكنني التعامل مع هذا العالم طوال الوقت . وفقط أولئك الناس الذين جربوا قوتي مباشرة يؤمنون فعل، و أنني أستطيع علاجهم.

SEE & CONTROL DEMONS & PAIN

This is a cycle, and someone needs to think about how to fix it. But sick animals of all kinds can easily spread disease and sickness everywhere. Pains or demons; however, it is my assumption that they grow really fast, and as the growth increases, they need more bodies, which means more people will get sick. I am sure you understand that demons and pains are all invisible things in the physical world and that they do not die easily.

They are hundreds of years old. They are on a mission. After they kill one person, they choose someone else. And when they are in a body, they are damaging that body and its organs, and during that time, they are reproducing and increasing their numbers.

Different Pains and different demons are different from each other in the way human and wild animals or poisonous reptiles are different from each other. When a lion kills a deer, that lion eats first. Once that lion is finished eating the deer, the second strongest animal will come and start eating the leftover meat of the deer. After that, the third strongest animal will eat the leftover meat. In this way, all these animals will eat. And lastly, all the small animals or insects will attack the leftover meat of the hunted deer. In the same way, once a disease attacks us, it comes with a group and keeps attacking our bodies until it has damaged us completely. In regards to damaged organs, we have to deal with a line of diseases, sicknesses, and pains. No one can kill them. Only with luck and if we fix the symptoms and stay away from the source of the disease will we be able to become 100 percent normal.

رضوان قرشي

لم يكن صعباً بالنسبة لي إثبات أي شيء، كل يوم تقريبا، وأرى العديد من الناس يعانون من مشاكل مختلفة، وأساعدهم من خلال إبعاد آلامهم عنهم. إنهم بالتأكيد لا يعيشون في المياه، وذلك لأن تكوينهم الأساسي كهربائي. هذا هو السبب في أنهم لا يحبون المياه. نحن نتحدث فقط عن الجن في الوقت الحالي. هم في كل مكان، ولهم قوى غير عادية. أعلم أنهم يعيشون في الهواء لأني أشعر بها أحياناً يكونون قريبين جدا من الجدران والسقوف إذا لم تطيروا في الهواء، وأعلم أيضا أنهم يعيشون داخل أو فوق الأشجار و هم ينشطون أنفسهم من المجال الكهرومغناطيسي للجو الطبيعي ....

أعلم أنهم يستطيعون العيش داخل أي جسم حي، وبغض النظر عما إذا كان هذا الجسم لإنسان،أ وحيوان، أوحشرات،أوطيور، أوزواحف. كل هذه الأجسام سواء بالنسبة لهم. يمكنهم اختيار أي الجسم، كما يمكنهم التبديل بينها وقتما يريدون. ولكن تذكر أنه على الرغم من أنهم يعيشون في الهواء، الأشجار، والأجسام، وصفاتهم ما تزال على حالها. إذا كانت تحلق في الهواء، فإنها يمكن أن تذهب بسهولة في جسم أي حيوان، أو البدء في العيش داخله. هذا صحيح بالنسبة لهم جميعاً.

الجن فقط في حاجة الى لغة للتواصل معنا أو مع الحيوانات الأخري. وبالنسبة لهم جميعا، لديهم لغة واحدة فقط، وهي لغة التنويم المغناطيسي. على الجانب الآخر، نحن لسنا بحاجة لأي لغة خاصة التواصل معهم، إنهم يستمعون لنا طوال الوقت.إنهم فضوليون جدا. أنهم يتحتفظون بمعلومات عنا. إذا كان الجن جدد بالنسبة لنا، فإنهم يمكنهم أن يحفروا داخل ذاكرتنا ويعرفون عنا الكثير من المعلومات بسهولة، لذلك فهم يستمعون لنا، ويفهمون لغتنا، بغض النظر عن ما إذا كنا نتحدث باللغة الإنجليزية أو أي لغة أخري، هذا لا يعني أنهم سوف يطيعوننا عندما يسمعوننا.أنهم لا يطيعوننا معظم الوقت،. ولكن إذا ما أصبحوا صادقون معنا، وسوف بفعلون الكثير من أجللنا.

44

إذا ما قرر الجن أن يصبحوا ضدنا، سوف يحدثون الكثير من العقبات. لا يملك الجن الكثير من ا لمسئوليات مثلنا، انا أتحدث عن الوظائف، والمال، والمنازل، والتأمين، وغير ذلك.بالنسبة للمشاكل والمشاجرات، ويتصارع الجن مع بعضهم البعض.

إن لغة الجن هي التنويم المغناطيسي، وإذا فهمت التنويم المغناطيسي قليلا، ستعرف أنها خدعة. اذا يستخدمه شخص ما عليك، لا تعتقد بالضرورة أن هناك جني يتواصل معك أو يحاول يؤثر عليك. إذا كان الجن ينومك مغناطيسياً، وسوف نرى ما يريدونك أن تراه. ستفكر في كل ما يغذوتيه عقلك فقط.. وإذا كان الجن وينومنك، لن تستطيع التغلب عليهم. نفكر فقط ما يريدون منا أن نفكر فيه، نحن نرى ما يريدون لنا أن نرى.

إذا الجن في كل مكان حولنا، وهم أعداء لنا، ما الذي يمكن أن يفعلوه؟ يمكنهم أن يظلوا يضالوننا طوال الوقت عن طريق تنويمنا مغناطيسياً. يستطيع هؤلاء الجن أن يذهبوا أينما نذهب قبل وصولنا ويضللون غيرنا من الناس عن طريق تنويمهم مغناطيسياً. سوف تواجه مشاكل في كل مكان أينما ذهبت، مهما كنت تعمل. إذا كان الجن أصدقاء لشخص ما، فأنهم ينظفون المسارات الخاصة بهم. هؤلاء الناس لديهم حظا سعيدا في كل مكان. هذه المجموعات من الجن تصل أينما كانوا سيذهبون من قبلهم، وينومون الجميع مغناطيسيا ويحافظون على مسار الشخص خالياً من جميع المشاكل. كل الجن تقريبا لا يغيرون أماكنهم. إذا كانوا يعيشون في منزل، أو مكتب، أو متجر، فهم يعيشون هناك على مدى أجيال. إنهم لا يسمحون للجن أو أسر أخرى في الأماكن الخاصة بهم بسهولة. وهناك عدد قليل من الجن يعيشون في مكاتبنا، ومنازلنا، أو المحلات التجارية، بينما يسافرعدد قليل معنا.

Otherwise, once they make room in our bodies again, they can infect us. This is a lifetime problem, like ulcers, migraines, liver damage, diabetes, kidney failure, hemorrhoid infections, other infections, and different kinds of cancers. Our sick bodies and damaged organs are their food. They eat our bodies and organs and damage them more and more every day. In modern science, we have very good healing medications to heal the damages caused by these diseases. But it is very difficult for those healing medications to move these diseases away from the wounded or damaged parts of the body. They do not leave. We take painkillers, antibiotics, and healing medications; but the pains damage us again. At this point, if someone is using a very good healing medication, I can or a person like me can help them remove those pains from the damaged body. After that, someone needs to use the right kind of healing medications to fix the damages. I had this crazy and unbelievable experience several times. Pains and a myriad of sicknesses have become my friends. But problem is that they are just like fire, and fire burns. Diseases, pains, and sicknesses can stay out of the body. So even they are acting or behaving like a friend. They can reduce the effects but still their effect is pain; once they go to a body or a part of a body, that part will feel the pain. This is all crazy, but I deal with this world all the time. And only those people who experience my power firsthand actually believe me. It is not difficult for me to prove anything. Almost every day, I see several people with different problems and help them by taking their pains away from them. Surely, they do not live in water, because their basic configuration is *electric*.

That's why they do not like water. We are only talking about demons right now. They are everywhere, and they have extraordinary powers. Because I sense them and feel them, I know they live in the air. Sometimes they are very close to walls and ceilings if they are not flying in the air. I also know that they live inside or on trees& energize themselves from electromagnetic field of natural atmosphere . . .

I know that they can live inside any living body, regardless of whether it's a human's, animals, insects, bird's, or a reptile's. All these bodies are the same for them. They can choose any body and can switch whenever they want. But remember that although they live in the air, trees, and bodies, their qualities are still the same. If they are flying in air, they can easily go into any animal's body or start living inside it. This is true for all of them.

Only demons need a language to communicate with us or other animals. And for all of them, they just have one language, and that language is hypnotism. On other hand, we do not need any special language to communicate with them. They listen to us all the time. They are very nosy. They keep information about us. If they are new to us, they can dig inside our memory and easily find out a lot of information about us.

So they listen to us, and they understand our language, regardless of whether we speak English or another language; however, that does not mean they will obey us when they hear us. Most of the time, they do not obey us. But if they become sincere with us, they will do much for us.

إن الجن فضوليون جداً ويهتمون بشكل كامل بشؤوننا. أنا آسف أن أقول اننا تحت سيطرتهم تماما في معظم الوقت، وأننا عادة ما نفعل ما يريدون منا أن نفعله. بغض النظر عن صدق الجن، هم في الأساس غير مطيعون، و سلبيون. إنهم يستخدمون التنويم المغناطيسي، يمكنهم أن يظهروا لنا أي شيء أثناء يقظتنا. عندما يظهرون لنا أشياء ليبست موجودة في الواقع، نسمي ذلك"خدع بصرية".

يستطيع الجن أن يظهروا لنا أي شيء أثناء نومنا، ونحن نسمي تلك الأشياءالأحلام نحن نظن أننا نرى ما كنا نفكر فيه مؤخراً في أحلامنا. هذا خاطئ تماما. نحن نرى فقط ما يظهره الجن لنا في الأحلام. أحيانا يحدث أن نرى ما كنا نفكر فيه، ولكن هذا يحدث لأن الجن معنيون كثيرأبشؤوننا وحياتنا. وبناء على ذلك، ونحن نعتقد أن تلك الأحلام هي ناتجة من عقولنا، ولكنفي واقع الأمر، إن الجن مسؤولون تماما عن ذلك. عادة، حلم واحد لا يأتي من اثنين من الجن. جني واحد يظهر لنا حلماً واحداً. اذا كان هناك أكثر من جني حولنا، وعادة ما يتناوب الجن علينا، إعتمادا على الأقوى منهما.

يظهر لنا الجن عادة مشاكلنا العائلية، وشؤوننا، مشاكل أعمالنا، وغيرها في أحلامنا. إذا كانوا يشاهدون الأفلام معنا، فإنهم يمكن أن يظهروا لنا الفيلم كله مرة أخرى. إذا كنا في غابة أو إذا كان لدينا حيوانات برية أو زواحف سامة داخل أوحول بيوتنا، يخرج الجن منها، وتخترق أجسامنا، وسوف تكون أحلامنا مجرد كوابيس. هذا الجن ليس هو الجن العادي الذين يشاركون عادة في حياتنا أو شؤوننا. هذا ا الجن الجديد عادة ما يأتي من الحيوانات الأخرى، ليس لديه أكثر من الكوابيس أو جن مخيف.

46

And once they decide to go against us, then they will bring many obstacles. Demons do not have as many liabilities as we do. I am talking about money, jobs, houses, and insurance, among others. As far as problems and fights, demons have more fights and wars between themselves.

The demon's language is hypnotism; if you understand hypnotism a little bit, then you know it is a trick. If someone uses it on you do not necessarily think that a demon is communicating with you or trying to influence you. If a demon hypnotizes you, you will see whatever they want you to see. You will think only of whatever they feed your mind. And if demons are hypnotizing you, you will not be able to beat them. We think only whatever they want us to think. We see whatever they want us to see.

If demons are all around us and they are our enemies then what can they do? They can keep us misguided all the time by hypnotizing us. These demons can reach wherever we go before us and misguide other people by hypnotizing them. Wherever you go, whatever you do, you will face problems everywhere. If demons are friends of someone, then they clean up their paths. Those people have good luck everywhere. These groups of demons reach wherever they're going before them and hypnotize everyone and keep the person's path clear of all problems.

Almost all demons do not change their places. If they are living in a house, office, or shop, they live there for generations. They do not easily allow demons or other families in their particular places. A few live in our houses, offices, or shops, and a few travel with us.

تذكر دائما أنك إذا أردت أن تحكم حقا أي نوع من الجن موجودون حولك، أو من أين جاء الجن، أنت تحتاج إلى تحليل أحلامك. إذا كان لديك الكثير من الجن داخل أو حول لمنزلك، سوف تواجه أحلام مختلفة كل ليلة، وخاصة إذا كان لديك الكثير من الأشجار حول منزلك؛ قد يعني هذا وجود عدد كبير من سكان الجن. إذا كان يتحكم بك جني واحد بالكامل، سيكون لهذا الجن السيطرة الكاملة عليك، و سيظهرجني واحد فقط لك أحلامك.ولكن إذا كنت شخص قوي التفكير، لن يكون هناك جني واحد أو جني موجود بصفة دائمة حولك. وسوف تتعامل مع مختلف الشياطين طوال الوقت.

على أي حال، إذا كنت ترى أحلام مختلفة تماما عن أفكارك وكنت ترى السحالي أو القطط والكلاب في أحلامك، هذا يعني على الأرجح وجود جني داخل تلك الحيوانات لفترة طويلة، وبأن هو كل ما يعرفه. لهذا فهم يظهرون لك هذه الأحلام. إذا كان لديك صديق يتحدث إليك عبر الهاتف من بلد مختلف عن بلدك، فإن الجن الذي عنده قد يختار زيارتك لسبب ما. سوف يريك هذا الجن الجديد غالباً أحلام تتعلق بصديقك أو ببلده،أو بشؤونه. باختصار، الجن لا يظهرون لنا كل ما نريد ان نراه. أنهم يظهرون دائماً لنا ما يريدون أن يظهروه لنا. هذه هي هوايتهم. إنهم يفعلون ذلك من أجل أنفسهم، وليس من أجلنا.

يمكنني أن أسأل الشياطين من حولي لتريني بعض الأحلام، قد لا تكون أنت قادر على، ولكن . لدي جن لمختلفون يزورونني كل يوم أو أحيانا كل ساعة، وهذا هو السبب في أن أحلامي مختلفة طوال الوقت. في بعض الأحيان، أحلم ببعض الأحلام المعقدة، ولكنك ستفاجأ، لأن في بعض الأحيان لا أتعترف علي أي من الناس في تلك الأحلام. أنا أفترض مجرد افتراض هو أن هؤلاء الجن يجيئون حولي لأنني إزيلهم من أشخاص مختلفين في مناطق مختلفة من العالم، إنهم يجيئون حولي، ليظهروا لي أحلام عن حياة أو شؤون مضيفيهم السابقين.

SEE & CONTROL DEMONS & PAIN

Demons are very nosy and take full interest in our affairs. I am sorry to say that we are totally under their control most of the time and that we usually do what they want us to do. Regardless of the sincerity of demons, they are basically naughty and full of negativism. Demons use the power of hypnotism. They can show us anything while we are awake. When they show us something that isn't really there, we will think that a "trick of the eyes." And they can show us anything during our sleep, and we call those dreams.

We think we see whatever we recently had on our minds in our dreams. This is totally wrong. We see only whatever demons around us show us in dreams. Sometimes it happens, and we see whatever we had on our minds, but that's because demons are so much involved in our affairs and lives. Consequently, we think that those dreams are coming from our own minds, but in actuality, the demons around us are totally responsible for that. Usually, one dream does not come from two demons. One demon shows us one dream. If we have more than one demon around us, these demons usually take turns, depending on which is more powerful. Demons usually show us dreams about our family problems, affairs, and business problems, among others. If they are watching movies with us, they can show us the whole movie again. If we are around a jungle or wild animals or if we have poisonous reptiles inside or around our homes, demons come out from them and penetrate our bodies; our dreams will just be nightmares. These demons are not the regular demons that are usually involved in our lives or our affairs. These new demons usually come from other animals, and they do not have much material other than nightmares or scary demons.

رضوان قرشي

يمكن لأي شخص استخدام هذه الممارسات في ما يتعلق بالأحلام. إذا كنت تشهد وتري أحلاماً خطيرة ومخيفة حقا وتريدها أن تتوقف، يمكنني أن أرشدك في كيفية وقفها. هذه الكوابيس لا تأتي من الجن الخالصين، إنهم يأتون عادة من الجن الذين يأتون من الحيوانات البرية أو الزواحف. إنهم يظهرون لنا أحلام مخيفة و هذه هي هوايتهم، وانهم حقا يستمتعون بها عندما يخيفوننا و يرون رد فعلنا علي تلك الأحلام المخيفة.

عندما يكون لديك حلم مخيف، فقط تذكر بأن هؤلاء الجن يلعبون معك. لا تتصرف كأنك خائف على الإطلاق.، فبمجرد أن تستيقظ من كابوس، لا تصرخون أوتتصرف بخوف. فقط إنظر نحو كتفك اليسرى وتقول للجن، "أنت تهدروقتك.لست خائفا من هذا الحلم لذا يرجى تركني و تبحث عن شخص آخر. "ومع ذلك، لا يمكنك الكذب علي الجن لأنهم يقرأون في عمق عقولنا.

إذا كنت حقا لا تريد أن تبقي الكوابيس لديك، لابد أن تسيطر على مشاعرك وخوفك. تستطيع التأثيرات الخارجية أن تساعد على زيادة قوة طاقتنا الإيجابية الداخلية لحمايتنا من أعمال الطاقات السلبية الخارجية (أي الجن أو الأمراض) مثل الانفلونزا، البرد والسعال والحمى.الأشجار على قيد الحياة مثلنا. عندما تستخدم الطيور مناقيرها الحادة لعمل ثقوب في جذع شجرة أو عمل مجرفة في أي فرع من الشجرة، يمكن أن يقام عش في تلك الثقوب. عندما تصنع الطيور حفرة في أي جزء من الشجرة، والطيور لا يهمها ما إذا كانت تصرفاتهم سوف تضر بالشجرة. نحن مثل الأشجارتماماً، وتلك الآلام هي مثل الطيور. هذه الآلام تضر أجزاء من أجسادنا حتى يتمكنوا من الحصول على الطاقة. هذه الآلام لا يهمها كم نتحمل من الألم بسبب أفعالهم.

Always remember that if you want to really judge which kind of demon you have around you or from where a demon came, you need to analyze your dreams. If you have too many demons inside or around your house, then you will experience different dreams every night, especially if you have a lot of trees around your house; it could mean there is a significant population of demons. If you are completely possessed by a single demon, then that demon will have complete control, and it will be only one that shows you your dreams. But if you are a strong-minded person, then no single or permanent demon will be around you. You will be dealing with different demons all the time.

Anyway, if you are seeing dreams totally different from your thoughts and you are seeing dreams about lizards or cats or dogs, that means the demon was likely inside those animals for a long time and that's all it knows. That's why they are showing you these dreams. If your friend in a different country talks to you over the phone, that demon may choose to visit you for some reason. This new demon will mostly show you dreams related to your friend or your friend's country, and it will show you dreams about your friend's affairs.

In short, demons do not show us whatever we want to see. They always show us whatever they want to show us. This is their hobby. They do that for themselves, not for us. You may not be able to, but I can ask demons around me to show me some particular dreams. I have different demons that visit every day or sometimes every hour, and that's why my dreams are different all the time.

لا يهمها، بل هي تحدث مجرد جروح /إصابات من أجل تنشيط نفسها أومن أجل حياتهم. نفس الشيئ، إذا ذهبت إلى تلك الشجرة و قمت بتنظيف العش الموجود في الشجرة وتزيل الطيور من العش، ما سيحدث بعد ذلك؟ لن يكون هناك ثقب في جذع الشجرة أو في فرعها. لن يكون هناك طيور حول الثقب الموجود في الشجرة. ولكن إذا كان هناك ثقب في جذع أو فرع من شجرة، يأتي طائر آخر وسوف يجد الحفرة، وهذا الطائر الجديد سيحاول عمل عش في هذه الحفرة، و إذا كان الطائر الجديد أكبر في الحجم من الطائر القديم، قد يحاول الطائرالجديد عمل ثقب أكبر، سيحدث هذا مزيدا من الألم للشجرة. لكن الطيور لا تبالي بالشجرة. إذا لم تصلح الشجرة الثقب الموجود في الجذع أو في الفرع ستأتي طيورجديدة بإستمرار، وتظل تضر الشجرة. وبالمثل، فإن أجسامنا لن يتم علاجها ي عن طريق أخذ الدواء المناسب و إجراء جراحة. ستظل الآلام الجديدة و الأمراض تأتي وتهاجم أعضائنا الجريحة.

يمكنني إزالة الألم، والمرض، أو المرض من الشخص، ولكن إذا استمرت الأعراض و لا أحد يهتم بها،سوف يأتي مرض آخر بسرعة كبيرة. ولكن هناك شيء آخر، ونحن ندعوه الحظ السيئ. قد لا يكون لديك أعراض، ولكن ربما لسوء الحظ، سيكون عليك التعامل أو العيش مع شخص مريض، هذه الآلام ستنتقل لجسمك بكل سهولة.

ربما لن تشعر بأي ألم لبضعة أيام أو أسابيع أو أشهر، ولكن في نهاية المطاف، فإن هذه الآلام ستتلف جزء من جسمنا بالتغلب على طاقاتك الإيجابية. وبعد ذلك ستدحث دورة من المشاكل و يبدأ المرض.

Sometimes, I have some complicated dreams, but you would be surprised, because sometimes I do not recognize any of the people in those dreams. I just assume that because I remove demons from different people in different parts of the world; those demons come around me and show me dreams about the lives or affairs of their previous hosts. Anyone can use these practices in regards to dreams. If you are experiencing and seeing really dangerous and scary dreams and you want them to stop, I can guide you in how to stop them. These nightmares do not come from our sincere demons. They usually come from demons we get from wild animals or reptiles. Showing us scary dreams is there hobby, and they really enjoy it when they scare us and see our reactions to those scary dreams.

When you have a scary dream, just remember that these demons are playing with you. Do not act like you are scared at all. Once you wake up from the nightmare, do not yell or act scared. Just look toward your left shoulder and say to the demon, "You are wasting your time. I am not scared of that dream so please quit wasting your time with me and find someone else." However, you cannot lie to demons, because they can read deep inside our mind.If you really do not want to keep having nightmares, you need to control your feelings and fear. External influences can help increase the powers of our internal positive energy to protect us from the actions of external negative energies (i.e., demons or diseases) like flu, cold, fever, cough.

ليس ضرورياً أن نكون مرضى أوأن يكون لدينا جروح أو صابات، و هذا يدعو الآلام داخلنا أو من حولنا. إن الجن متواجدون حولنا باستمرار. الجن لا يسببون الألم مثل الآلام والمرض، ولكن بسبب سلبيتهم، يشعرالجميع بشيئ من المرض العقلي أو المزاج المنحرف.

من المهم ان يكون لكل جزء من جسمنا جسم يعمل بشكل كامل، ولكن إذا كنا نتحدث عنجس يعمل بكفاءة أقل من أقل 100 في المئة، ويمكن أن نقول أنه جسم يعمل بشكل غير كامل. هكذا هناك أمثلة عديدة للجسم الذي يعمل بشكل غير كامل. لكن لا يزال، وهناك لفئات للجسم الذي يعمل بشكل غير كامل.. اسمحوا لي أن أشرح. اذا فقد شخص ما يده أو ساقه أوأذنه أو عيهن أو أصبعه أو إهامه أو شيئا من هذا القبيل، يصبح الجسم غير كامل، ولكن تعمل أعضاء الجسم بشكل لأن دائرة الدم تعمل بشكل جيد. لكننا نستطيع أن نعيش حياة طبيعية بجسم غير كامل.. الشرط الثاني هو إذا كان لدي الجسم بعض المشاكل مع أي عضورئيسي، مثل القلب والكبد والكليتين والرئتين والمثانة وغيرها، يستطيع اللشخص يعيش حياة طبيعية. وأنا على استعداد لوصف إحدي تجاربي، عندما أصيب شخص أثناء وقوع حادث، كان هذا الشخص علي ما يرام تماما في كل مكان، لقد تضرر فقط في الجانب الأيسر من دماغه. لم يعتقد أحد حتى يعيش هذا الشخص بعد هذا النوع من التلف في الدماغ. وكان هذا المريض يحصول على علاج جيد في المستشفى، و كنت على استعداد للقيام ببعض التجارب لإختبار قواي.لقد كنت علي اتصال معه بشكل مستمر، لمدة عام كامل تقريبا، بالتخاطر و كنت أبقى كل أنواع طاقات السلبية الخارجية بعيدا عن جسده لانقاذه من الآلام، الالتهابات، وغيره من الأمراض. منذ البداية، وكنت على يقين من أن كل نضالي و جهودي ستجعل هذا الشخص شخص عادي تماما، ولهذا أنا لا تسمح لأي طاقة خارجية سلبية أن تخدعني.

Trees are alive like us. When birds use their sharp beaks to make holes in the stem of a tree or make a hole in any branch of the tree, they can set up a nest in those holes. When birds make a hole in any part of the tree, birds don't care how much their actions will hurt a tree. We are exactly like trees, and those pains are like birds. These pains damage parts of our bodies so that they can have energy.

They do not care how much pain we endure because of their actions. They don't care; they just make wounds/injuries in order to get energized them or live their lives. In the same way, if you go to that tree and clean the nest from the tree and remove the bird from the nest, what will happen after that? There will be no nest in that hole in the stem or branch of the tree. There will be no birds around that hole in the tree. But if the hole is there in the stem or branch of the tree, another bird will find the hole, and this new bird will try to make a nest in that hole. And if the new bird is bigger in size than the old bird was, then the new bird may try to make the hole even bigger, and that action will create more pain for the tree. But birds do not care about the tree. If the tree does not fix that hole in the stem or branch, new birds will keep coming and hurting the tree. Similarly, our body will not be fixed by taking proper medication and having surgery. New pains and diseases will keep coming and attacking our injured organs. I can remove a pain, sickness, or disease from a person, but if symptoms persist and nobody takes care of those symptoms, another disease will come pretty quickly. But there is another thing, and we call that thing bad luck. You may not have symptoms, but with bad luck—maybe you will have to deal with someone or live with someone who is sick—these pains will transfer to your body very easily.

أنا لا تترك هذا الجسم غير المراقب لفترة طويلة للحصول على أفضل نتيجة. الوقت ولكني تعلمت شيئا واحد بعد كل هذا النضال، و هو أنه يمكن أن يكون للشخص بعض الأجزاء المفقودة أو تكون بعض أجزاؤه مريضة جزء من الجسم، والتي ما تزال تعمل وتعمل بشكل عادي أوشبه عادي، ولكننا لا نستطيع الوصول إلي حل وسط فيما يتعلق بالمخ.

في حالة تلف بعض أجزاء من المخ أو فقدها، وهو ما يعني فقد بعض القدرات أو الحالة السوية الطبيعية، لذلك حتى لو كافحت كفاحاً شاقاً، وقضت الكثير من الوقت، لقد تعلمت أن هناك لابد من وجود مخ طبيعي متكامل، للحفاظ على كل جزء من أجزاء الجسم، و تعلمت أن المخ غير الكامل يستطيع أن تبقينا على قيد الحياة ولكن لا يستطيع أن يجعلنا نعيش حياة الطبيعية 100 في المئة. هذا الشخص لا يزال على قيد الحياة، ولكني لا أفعل أي شيء بعد الآن له. هذا الشخص لديه بعض المشاكل، وأنا واثق من أن بعض المشاكل تكون نتيجة لهجمات الطاقات السلبية الخارجية أيضا. أنا واثق من انه مع مرور الوقت سوف يتحسن أكثر من ذلك، لكنني لست متأكدا كم من الوقت يستغرقه ذلك. لكن أنا سعيد على الأقل أنه لا يزال على قيد الحياة حتى مع وجود بعض المشاكل البدنية الصغيرة ومشاكل في الكلام. أنا متأكد أن الله سوف يساعده و أنه سيكون طبيعي بنسبة 100% يوماً ما. كانت هذه تجربة واحدة إستطعت فيها المساعدة في علاج الإصابة، ولكن لم يتمكن كفاحي من المساعدة في تجديد أجزاء أو أنسجة المخ المفقودة / التالفة، لكني متأكد من أن العلوم الطبية سوف تكون قادرة على الوصول إلي تحقيق هذا الهدف أيضا. إن إرتعاش العين هو مثال شائع جدا من الجن أو شبه الجن أحيانا أي الآلام.

Maybe you will not feel any pain for a few days, weeks, or months; but eventually, those pains will damage a part of our body by defeating your positive energies. And then a cycle of problems and sickness will start.

We do not need to be sick people or have wounds or injuries to invite pains inside or around us. Demons are always around us. Demons do not hurt like pains and disease, but because of their negativism, everyone feels some mental sickness or extreme temperament.

Each and every part of our body is important to have a complete operational body, but if we talk about a less than 100 percent operational or perfect body, we can say it is a semi operated body. So there are several examples of an incomplete operational body. But still, there are some categories of an incomplete body or incomplete body operation. Let me explain. If someone loses a hand or leg or an ear or an eye or a finger or a thumb or something similar, it will make our body incomplete, but because blood circuit is still okay, organs function okay, so we can still lead normal life with the incomplete body. Second condition is if a body has some issues with any major organ, like the heart, liver, kidneys, lungs, bladder, etc., someone can still lead a normal life. I am ready to describe here one of my experiences when someone was hurt during an accident. That person was perfectly okay from everywhere; he only damaged the left side of his brain. Nobody even thought that that person will even survive after that kind of brain damage. That patient was getting good treatment at the hospital, and I was willing to do some experiments to test my powers.

يمكن أن يحدث هذا بسبب تدخل الجن أو شبه الجنفي أمور الفرد. انهم ببساطة يلعبون علي أعصاب وعضلات جسم شخص ما ليسبب ارتعاش والتهاب منطقة معينة.

ولكن إذا كان الإرتعاش على مستوى أعلى، هذا يعني أن عدد من الجن و أشباه الجن يتدخلون بالسيطرة على الأعصاب وتضغط علي أعصاب وعضلات مختلفة مما يسبب حركات غريبة وإرتعاش في مختلف أجزاء الجسم، مثل اليد،الأصابع، الرقبة، الرأس والساقين، إلخ... إذا كنت تريد أن تجري تجربة، يمكنك القيام بها بنفسك. فقط أنت تحتاج الى بعض الثقة. أنا لا أعرف كم يستغرق من لوقت ليستمعوا إليك. والسبب هو أنهم يستمعون لنا فقط عندما يعتقدون أنه يمكنك أن تجعلهم يستمعون إليك من خلال إستخدام بعض القوى. قم بذلك كلما عاني شخص ما من مشكلة إ. تبقي ارتعاش العين. ضع إصبعك في المنطقة المتضررة وتواصل مع الجن أو شبه الجن لإنهاء إحدث الإرتعاش . سيري معظمكم أن العين سوف تتوقفعن الإرتعاش.

لكن بالنسبة لمعظمكم سوف يبدأ الإرتعاش مرة أخرى بعد ثوان قليلة، و السبب في ذلك هو أن الجن أو شبه الجن الذين يسببون الآلام، لا يستمعون بسهولة حتى يعرفون أنك ستتمكن من وقفها. إنهم لا يهتمون، لأنهم يعرفون أن أكثرنا لسنا مدركين لها، وغير قادرين على رؤيتهم، والأهم من ذلك، أننا لا يمكننا القيام بأي شيء ضدهم لوقفهم. هنا، أنا مختلف عن الناس العاديين.، لأن الله وهوبني القدرات لإقناعهم أو الإصرار علي أن يتوقفوا عن الضغط علي المريض. أنا الآن أحاول نقل معرفتي ووعي للعلوم الطبية، في محاولة لإعطاء العلوم الطبية بعض النظريات والاتجاهات البشرية حتى تكون لدي البشر سيطرة أفضل على أجسادهم والمناطق المحيطة بهم. وأنا واثق هذا سيحدث أن يوماً ما . .

Continuously, for almost whole year, I was in contact with him telepathically and kept all kinds of external negative energies away from his body to save him from pains, infections, and other diseases. From the very start, I was sure that all my struggle and efforts will make that person a completely normal person. This is the reason; I never allow any external negative energy to dodge me. To get the best result, I never left that body unattended for long time. But after that entire struggle, I learned one thing. And that thing is someone can have some parts missing or someone can have some sick part of their body and still act and operate normally or semi normally, but we cannot compromise with the case of the brain.

If some portion or some area of the brain is damaged or missing, it means for sure some abilities or capabilities or some normality's will be missing. So even if I struggled hard and spent a lot of time, I learned that the complete physical brain is needed to keep each and every part of the body. I learned that an incomplete brain can keep us alive but cannot give us 100 percent normality. That person is still alive, but I am not doing anything anymore for him. He has some issues; I am sure right now some issues are due to the attacks of external negative energies also. I am sure with time he will improve more, but I am not sure after how long. But I am happy at least he is still alive even with some minor physical and speech issues. I am sure God will help him and one day he will be 100 percent normal. So that was one experience where I was able to help cure an injury, but my struggle and help cannot regenerate missing/damaged brains part or tissues. But I am sure medical science will be able to go that far to achieve this goal also.

رؤية الجن و الآلام السيطرة عليها

يظل الجن، والألم، والأمراض / الحشرات، باقون في حجمهم الأصلي، عندما تكون في الجو. الجن لديهم القدرة علي الإستحواذ علي الجسم، وهذا يعني أنهم موجودون في كل مكان داخل الجسم ولديهم سيطرة جسدية وعقلية جيدة جدا علي هذا الجسم بالذات. ستزداد سيطرة الجن يوما بعد يوم إذا بقي في هذا الجسم لفترة طويلة. يمكن أن يوسع الجن السيطرة علي جسم ما، فقط عندما يكونون داخل أي شخص، لكنهم لا يستطيعون نشر أنفسهم في الغلاف الجوي،فهم قادرون على السباحة والطيران في الهواء. بدون جسد، يمكن أن يبقي الجن فقط في حجمهم و شكلهم الأصلي في الجو المفتوح . الجن غير مؤذيين تماما عندما لا يكونون داخل الجسم. إنهم أشياء صغيرة فقط في الغلاف الجوي.

الجن غير مؤذيين تماما. ويمكنهم السفر أو التنقل عن طريق خطوط الهاتف والإشارات الكهرومغناطيسية، مثل الإنترنت أو التلفزيون، بسهولة جدا. خط الهاتف هو أفضل وأسهل طريقة للإنتقال من جسم إلي آخر. الجن لديهم قوى خارقة للطبيعة غير عادية التحرك / الإمتصاص من الغلاف الجوي للأجسام بكل الطرق الممكنة. ولا يوجد حدود لقدراتهم وقواهم، يمكنهم أن يمتصوا أو يستحوذوا عنكبوت صغير ويسيطروا عليه تماما جسدياً وعقلياً. يمكن لبعض الجن أن يذهبون داخل جسم الإنسان أو الفيل يفعلوا نفس الشيء، فهم يستحوذون علي الجسم ويسيطرون عليه جسديا وعقليا. إن قوى السفر لدي الجن، و قدراتهم الإستحواذية، وقدرات الإمتصاص، والسيطرة ليست قوى محدودة.

كان الله كريماً معهم حقا عندما منحهم القوى الخارقة. تعتبر الآلام أشباه للجن، وهم عبارة عن 50 % مثل الجن. لا تستطيع الآلام السيطرة علي الجسم، كما أنهم لا يستطيعون السيطرة علي الجسم جسدياً و عقلياً.

SEE & CONTROL DEMONS & PAIN	<div dir="rtl">رضوان قرشي</div>

Eye twitching is a very common example of sometimes demons or sometimes semi demons i.e., pains. This can happen due to an individual's involvement with a demon or semi demon. They simply play with the nerves and muscles of someone's body to cause twitching and inflammation in a particular area.

But if twitching is on a higher level, it means several demons and semi demons are involved in controlling and pinching different nerves and muscles to cause weird movements and twitching of different parts of the body, like the hand, fingers, neck, head, legs, etc. If you want to do an experiment, you can do one by yourself. Only you need some confidence. And I do not know for how long they will listen to you. The reason is they only listen to us when they believe you can make them listen to you by using some powers. Do this whenever someone has eye twitching problem. Keep your finger at the affected area and communicate with the demon or semi demon to quit doing it. Most of you will experience that the eye will stop twitching.

تستطيع الآلام نشر نفسها بمنتهي السهولة عندما تكون داخل الجسم. تعتبر الآلام أشياء طائرة، وحجمها الأصلي صغير جداً. تظل الآلام في حجمها الأصلي في الهواء المفتوح، ولا تستطيع توسيع نفسها في الجو المفتوح. تستطيع الآلام أيضا ضغط وتوسع نفسها وفقا لحجم العضو أو الأنبوب. لا توسيعالآلام لتغطي أو تستحوذ علي الجسم كله. توسيع الآلام نفسها فقط عندما يريدون سد قنوات الدم أو التنفس، أو صمامات القلب، أو قنوات الكليتين، إلخ...

يستطيع الألم ا لتحرك بسهولة داخل الجسم من خلال إشارات العصب لدينا . يمكن للآلام نشر الأذي عندنا من خلال عصب نظام التوزيع لدينا. آلام لديها خاصية الإيذاء أو السد عن طريق التوسيع. آلام لديها قدرات محدودة مقارنة بالجن. الآلام مخلوقات بلا قلب وقاسية، لهذا سميته "الآلام"، لكن هذا لا يعني أنهم لا يستطيعون أن يصبحوا أحد الأصدقاء. ثق بي، إنهم أصدقاء جيدون على حد سواء مثل الجن. أي ألم أو جني يمكن أن يصبح صديقك. ثق بي، وبمجرد أن يصبحوا أصدقاء، يطيعون ويستمعون أكثر من الأصدقاء من البشر أو الحيوان، الحيوانات الأليفة. لا مجال للمقارنة مع أي شخص. ولذلك فمن الواضح أن الآلام لا تستحوذ علي أي شخص ولا يمكنها أن تقوم بالتنويم المغناطيسي أو تسيطرعلي أي مخ. الآن الأمراض / الحشرات ضئيلة جدا وغير مرئية للعين المجردة. لا يمكنها أن تطير. إنها تستطيع أن تمشي وتقفز من مكان إلى آخر أو من جسم إلى آخر.إن المرض / الحشرات ليس لديه أي قوى خارقة للطبيعة. لا يمكن أن تتمدد أو تستحوذ علي أي شخص.إنها ليست سوى طفيليات جائعة، على استعداد أن تأكل وتدمر أجسادنا وأعضائنا.سأحاول أن أشرح الصلاة في هذا القسم. وسوف أقسم هذا القسم إلى نوعين من الصلوات. نوع واحد من الصلاة، وهو عندما نحاول أو عندما نرسل تمنياتنا ونطلب مباشرة من الله أن يسمعنا من خلال الإستجابة لمطالبنا ورغباتنا. أنا لا أتحدث عن هذه الصلاة.

Rizwan Qureshi	رؤية الجن و الآلام السيطرة عليها
But for most of you, it will start twitching again after few seconds. Reason is demons or semi demons that cause pains do not listen easily until they know you can stop them. They do not care, because they know most of us are unaware of them, unable to see them, and, most importantly, cannot do anything against them to stop them. Here, I am different from normal people. God gifted me abilities or capabilities to convince or insist them to stop. Now I am trying to transfer my knowledge and awareness to medical science, trying to give medical science some theories and directions so human being have better control of their bodies and surrounding. I am sure one day .	انا اتحدث عن الصلاة أو الدعاء، وعندما نقرأ الكتاب المقدس، الكتاب المقدس الصحيح،وكلام الله الصحيح من قبل الملائكة والأنبياء، في شكل دعاء مقدس أو صلاة مقدسة أو كتاب مقدس. الدعاء المقدس أو الصلاة المقدسة لها قوى سحرية. الدعاء المقدس أو الصلاة المقدسة أو الكتب المقدسة بلغاتها الأصلية لها قوة توليد الإشعاعات. كل كلمة وسطر في الكتاب المقدس لديها القوى لتوليد نوع معين من الأشعة أثناء الدعاء أو الصلاة أو أثناء قرأتنا الكلمات المقدسة / السطور مرارا وتكرارا. ليست كل صلاة أو دعاء ،الكلمة الواحدة. السطور في الكتاب المقدس الصحيح لديها نفس التأثيرات.
Demons, pain, and diseases/insects, some more basic difference are demons, pains, and diseases all of them stay in same and in their original size when, they are in atmosphere. Demons have the quality to possess a body, meaning they are everywhere inside the body and have very good physical and mental control of that particular body. The demons' control will increase day by day if the demons stay in that body for a long time. Demons possessing a body can expand themselves only when they are inside anybody. In the atmosphere they cannot expand themselves.	كل كلمة /سطروقسم له استخدامه وتأثيره الخاص. نحن (البشر) لانقرر، لسنا قادرون، و غير مصرح لنا تحديد أي دعاء مناسب أوصلاة مناسبة لأي غرض. إذا كنت تقرأ كتابك المقدس، إذا كنت تقرأ ملخص للكتاب المقدس، إذا كنت تذهب لبيت من بيوت الله، أو إلي مكان للعبادة، سوف يتمكن رجال الدين، من وصفك بمنتهي السهولة، أي دعاء من الكتاب المقدس مناسب لأي غرض؟. تذكر دائما أنه عند قراءة الصلاة المقدسة أو الدعاء المقدس، حدد دائما الأرقام الفردية. أنا أفضل أن يكون الحد الأدنى11 مرة، لتوليد ما يكفي من الإشعاع من صلواتكم لغرض خاص. كيف يمكنك استخدام وتطبيق تلك الصلوات و الإشعاعات لإنجاز مهمة معينة، سأذكر ذلك لاحقا في هذا الكتاب في مكان ما.على سبيل المثال، يمكن لرجال الدين أن يقولوا
They are capable of swimming and flying in the air. In an open atmosphere, without a body, they can stay only in their original size and shape. Demons are totally harmless when they are not inside a body. In the atmosphere, they are just small flying objects. They are totally harmless.	لك بسهولة جدا أي دعاء مناسب أو صلاة مناسبة للتخلص من الجن.، كما يمكنهم أن يقولون لك أي صلاة أو دعاء مخصص لنقل أو إرسال رسالتك أو طلبك إلى الله، حسب الأولوية.

SEE & CONTROL DEMONS & PAIN

Demons can very easily travel or transfer through telephone lines and electromagnetic signals, like the Internet or TV. The phone line is the best and easiest way to move from one body to a second body. Demons have extraordinary supernatural powers moving/ absorbing from atmosphere to bodies in all the possible ways. Their abilities and powers are not limited. They can absorb or possess a small spider and totally control the spider physical and mentally. Some demons can go inside the body of a human or elephant and do the same thing—posses the body and control them physically and mentally. Demons' traveling powers, possessing powers, absorbing powers, and controlling powers are not limited.

God was really generous when he awarded them supernatural powers. Pains are semi demons and are 50 percent like demons. Pains cannot possess bodies. Pains cannot control bodies physically or mentally.

But pains can expand themselves very easily when they are inside a body. Pains are also flying objects. Pains are also very small in their original shape. In open atmosphere, pains stay in their original shape .Pains cannot expand themselves in their original shape. Pains cannot expand themselves in open atmosphere. Pains can also compress and expand themselves according to the size of an organ or tube. Pains do not expand to cover or possess a whole body. Pains only expand themselves when they want to block blood or a breathing tube or valves of the heart or tubes of kidneys, etc...

رضوان قرشي

يمكنهم أيضاً أن يدلوك علي صلاة معينة أو دعاء معين، من الكتاب المقدس للتخلص من السحر الأسود من حولك. يمكن لرجال الدين أيضاً أن يقولوا لكم أي صلاة أو دعاء تحتاج إلى قراءتها في كثير من الأحيان عندما يكون لديك الرغبة في الحصول على ثروة أكبر وأكبر. نحن نعرف جميعا، أن العلم الحديث هو إختراعنا نحن البشر (الرجال و النساء الذين يعيشون في هذا العالم). لكن من الذي خلقنا؟ الله سبحانه وتعالى. لاتوجد آلة، ولا جهاز كمبيوتر، ولا علم حديث يقترب من مستوى ذكاء البشر. الكتاب المقدس يدلنا علي الكثير من الاشياء التي تعطينا المبادئ التوجيهية لنحيا حياة أفضل. لكن وجهة نظري هي أن آثار قراءة الكتاب المقدس في صلواتنا مختلفة، و بالتكرار، قراءة نفس الدعاء المقدس أو الصلاة المقدسة يولد بعض أشاعات خاصة. وإذا إستخدامنا هذه الأشعة للقيام بمهمة محددة، وسوف نكون ناجحين. الماء المقدس هو مثال واحد علي ذلك، تذكر، أن أدمغتنا خلق الكلمات السحرية في الكتاب المقدس كلاهما من صنع الله.

للكلمات المقدسة والصلاة أو الدعاء صلاحيات لا تصدق، مثل أمخاخنا، إن الاستخدام السليم لهذه الكلمات المقدسة والصلاةو الدعاء يولد أنواع مختلفة من الإشعاعات أو "الموجات". كما قلت سابقا، أن كل شيء، الأشعات أو الموجات، لها قوى مختلفة، قوى سحرية، معظمها، تستخدم غالباً لتحقيق مهمة خاصة أو غرض خاص.

و الآن أنا أعطي توجيهات واضحة للعلوم الطبية لإكتشاف هذه الأشعة علمياً .كما نعرف جميعا بالفعل، جميع أنواع الأشاعات أوالموجات هي من الذرات الصغيرة، وليس صعباً على العلم الحديث إكتشاف أي إشعاع أو موجة يتكون من أي نوع من الجزيئات، والجزيئات الكهرومغناطيسية...

Pain can very easily travel inside our body through our nerve signals. Pains can spread hurt through our nerve distribution system. Pains have the quality to hurt or block by expanding. Pains have limited powers as compared to demons. Pains are heartless and mean creatures. That's why I named them "pains," but it does not mean they cannot become a friend. Trust me, they are equally good friends like demons. Any pain or demon can become your friend. Trust me, once they become friends, they obey and listen way more than human friends or animal pets do. No comparison is possible with anyone. So it is clear that pains cannot possess anybody and pains cannot hypnotize or control any brain. Now diseases/insects are very tiny and are invisible to the naked eye. They cannot fly. They can walk and jump from one place to another place or one body to another. Disease/insects do not have any supernatural powers. They cannot expand or possess anybody. They are just hungry parasites, ready to eat and destroy our bodies and organs. I will try to explain prayer in this section. I will divide this section into two kinds of prayers. One kind of prayer is when we try to or when we send our wishes and requests directly to God and request God to listen to us by fulfilling our demands and wishes. I am not talking about this prayer. I am talking about prayer, when we read holy book, true holy book, & true words from God, by Angels and by prophets in shape of a holy prayer or holy book. Holy prayers have magical powers. Holy prayers or holy books in their original language have the power of generating rays. Each and every word and line in the holy book has powers to generate some specific kind of rays during prayer or during the time when we read the holy words/lines repeatedly. Not all prayer, word.

بمجرد أن يصبح العلم الحديث قادراً على إكتشاف نوع الجزيئات، الخطوة الثانية هي أن يحب أن تعرف العلوم الحديثة تركيبة تلك الأشعة أو الموجات. هذا كل شيء، بمجرد أن نعرف تلك الأشعاعات والموجات، سيكون لنا اليد العليا على الطاقة السلبية الخارجية. سيكون لدينا السيطرة الكاملة واليد العليا علي العالم الغير مرئي الموازي. إذا كان العالم الحديث ليس متبحراً في الدين كثيراً، ولا يعرف أي صلاة أو دعاء أو ما هي الكلمات المقدسة التي يحتاج اليها ليبدأ بها، يجب عليه أن يتصفح فقط الانترنت و يبحث في الكتب المقدسة المختلفة للديانات المختلفة. سوف تدلك شبكة الإنترنت، علي الصلاة التي يمكنك استخدامها لصد الجن أو الآلام أو الأمراض. العلم الحديث يجب أن يبدأ بتلك الكلمات المقدسة والصلاة أو الدعاء. وفي المستقبل، يجب عليها الاستمرار في إيجاد المزيد والمزيد من الأشاعات والموجات باستخدام نفس التقنية. قد يستغرق ذلك بعض الوقت، ولكني أفشي الأمر في الوقت الحالي. لا تفكر، ما معنى الكلمات المقدسة أو الصلوات المقدسة، و فقط قم بقراءتهم مرارا وتكرارا بأعداد فردية لتوليد أشعة أكثر و موجات أكثر؟ كل كلمة، كل سطر، كل دعاء أو صلاة في الكتاب المقدس لديها بعض التأثير السحري. أنا أقول لك الآن أن العلم الحديث سيدلك في المستقبل علي ان هذه الكتب المقدسة، في حد ذاتها، لديها الحلول والعلاجات لكل شيء. هذه الكتب المقدسة، والكلمات المقدسة، والأسطر، والأشاعات والموجات هي علم كامل. الآن مهما كانت هناك أشياء مفقودة، و شعور العلوم الحديثة بالعجز ضد الكثير من الآلام والأمراض، لابد للعلم الحديث أن يبدأ في البحث في الاتجاه، الذي سوف أقترحه عليكم و سترونه، لن يستغرق ذلك شهورا حتى والحديثة وعلي العلم الحديث أن يعالج ويجد الحل لكل ألم، ومرض.

SEE & CONTROL DEMONS & PAIN

I am talking about prayer, when we read holy book, true holy book, & true words from God, by Angels and by prophets in shape of a holy prayer or holy book. Holy prayers have magical powers. Holy prayers or holy books in their original language have the power of generating rays. Each and every word and line in the holy book has powers to generate some specific kind of rays during prayer or during the time when we read the holy words/lines repeatedly. Not all prayer, word. Lines in a true holy book have the same effects. Every word/ line and section has their own use and impact. We (humans) do not decide, are not capable, and are unauthorized to decide which prayer is suitable for which purpose. If you read your holy book, if you read summary of holy book, if you to the house of God, or place of worship, you religious leaders, will be able to describe you very easily, which prayer from holy book is suitable for which particular purpose? Always remember that when you read a holy prayer, always select odd numbers. I prefer a minimum of eleven times. Read continuously at least eleven times to generate enough rays from your prayers for some particular purpose. How you can use and apply those prayers and rays for some particular task, I will describe later in this book somewhere. For example, your religious leaders can tell you very easily which prayer is suitable to get rid of demons. They can tell you which prayer is specific for conveying or sending your message or request to God on a priority basis. Your religious leaders can tell you about some specific prayer from the holy book to get rid of black magic around you. Your religious leaders can tell you which prayer you need to read frequently when you have the desire to have more and more wealth.

رضوان قرشي

والآن اسمحوا لي أن ألخص مرة أخرى. يجب إبقاء كل من الآلام والأمراض / الحشرات بعيدا عن الجسم للبقاء في صحة جيدة، لنظل بصحة جيدة 100 %. هذا ممكن عمليا من خلال استخدام العلاج المناسب و الملابس المطاطية /البلاستيكية. لكن لصد الألم و إبعاده عن الجسم، يجب علي العلوم الطبية إكتشاف بعض نظم الأشاعات أوالموجات. لقد قدمت أدلة قليلة على كيفية القيام بذلك، و سوف أكتب المزيد من المعلومات حول هذا في وقت لاحق في هذا الكتاب.

إن الروح هي المسؤولة عن إبقائنا على قيد الحياة، و هي الطاقة الإيجابية، و ليس لديها إرادة حرة. إنها ليست سوى أمر من الله. بمجرد ترك الروح للجسم، تنتهي مدة صلاحيته أجسادنا أو تموت. بمجرد موت الجسد، تترك الروح هذا الجسد الميت فوراً، وقفاً لأمر الله، إما أن تنقل إلى جسم حديث الولادة أو تقف، وتنتظر لإعادة الحياة إلى جسم جديد. يمكن مقارنة العلاقة بين الروح والجسد البشري بالكهرباء والكمبيوتر. في هذا المثال، الروح هي الكهرباء وجسم الإنسان يشبه جهاز الكمبيوتر. نفس الشيىء، تستخدم الكهرباءلإعطاء الطاقة لمعدة مختلفة لجعلها تعمل، و جسم الإنسان يحتاج إلى روح لجعله على قيد الحياة و يعمل.. بطريقة مماثلة، أرواحنا هي الكهرباء التي تحافظ على إبقاء الجسم على قيد الحياة وبعمل. الطريقة الطبيعية لجهاز الكمبيوتر تأتي من عقل جهاز الكمبيوتر، معالج جهاز الكمبيوتر، أما جسم الإنسان لديه المخ، وبنفس الطريقة جهاز كمبيوتر يحتوي على لوحة المفاتيح و ماوس وطابعة، ماسحة ضوئية، وما إلى ذلك، الجسم البشري لديه الساقين واليدين والأذنين والأصابع، الشعر والعينين، الخ...

As all of us know, modern science is an invention of us humans (men and women living in this world). But who created or made us? The Almighty God. Still there is no machine, no computer, no modern science that even comes close to the IQ level of humans. The holy book says a lot of stuff that gives us guidelines to live and lead better lives. But my point is the effects of reading holy book on prayers are different. Repeatedly reading the same holy prayer generates some special rays. And if we use those rays for a specific task, we will be successful. Holy water is one example of this. Remember, our brains and the magical words in the holy book are both created by God.

Like our brains, holy words and prayers have incredible powers. Proper use of those holy words and prayers generates different kinds of rays or "waves." As I said before, everything, rays or waves, has different powers, magical powers, mostly, well, to use for a special task or for a special purpose.

Now I am giving clear directions to medical science to discover these rays scientifically. As all of us already know, all kinds of rays or waves are comprised of small particles; it is not difficult for modern science to discover which ray or wave is composed of which kind of particles, electromagnetic particles. Once modern science is able to discover the type or kind of particles, the second step is they need to find out the composition of those rays or waves. That's all. Once we have the knowledge of those rays and waves, we will have the upper hand on external negative energy.

نفس الطريقة التي يمكن للحاسوب أن يستمر في العمل بدون الطابعة، الماوس، لوحة المفاتيح، الماسحة الضوئية، و الشاشة ولكن الكمبيوتر لا يزال يعمل بدون تلك الأدوات، لكن لا يمكن تنفيذ جميع المهام بسبب الكهرباء،الكمبيوتر ليس معطلاً،إنه لا يزال يعمل لكن نظرا لعدم وجود الأدوات التنفيذية المطلوبة سوف يكون أداءالكمبيوتر غير كامل. نفس الشيئ، جسم الإنسان لديه روح تشبه الكهرباء. ويمكن للجسم البقاء على قيد الحياة، دون بعض الأعضاء، مثل العينين والساقين واليدين والشعر، والأصابع، وما إلى ذلك، لكن جسم الإنسان لن يكون مفيدا تماما أو يعمل علي أكمل وجه نظرا لغياب بعض الأدوات أو الأجزاء.

الآن يحتاج الكمبيوتر الدوائر المناسبة بشكل مستمر للتأكد من تدفق الكهرباء في كل جزء من جهاز الكمبيوتر. يوجد في جهاز الكمبيوتر، دوائر نحاسية وأسلاك موصولة بشكل صحيح مع مختلف أجزاء الكمبيوتر، مثل القرص الصلب، المعالج، محرك الأقراص، اللوحة الأم،المحول، والصمامات، وما إلي ذلك. إذا كان أي من هذه الأجزاء الأساسية أو الأسلاك حرقت أو قطعت، سيقضي ذلك على جهاز الكمبيوتر. نظرا لقطع الأسلاك، حتى مع وجود الكهرباء، فإن توفرها لا جدوي له لذلك الكمبيوتر. لن يعمل الكمبيوتر و سيكون معطلاً. في نفس الشيئ ، يمكن للجسم البشري البقاء على قيد الحياة بدون عدة أجزاء، ولكن إذا توقفت أي قناة دم رئيسية، أو عضو، مثل القلب أو الكبد أو المخ، عن العمل تماماً، سيتوقف جسم الإنسان عن العمل أو سيكون ميتا.

We will have total control and an upper hand on the parallel invisible world. If a modern scientist is not involved with religion too much and does not know which holy prayer or holy words he needs to start with, he should just go on the Internet and search different holy books of different religions. On the Internet, they will even tell you which prayer you can use to repel demons or pains or diseases. Modern science needs to start with those holy words and prayer. And in the future, they should keep finding more and more rays and waves by using the same technique. It may take some time, but I am exposing right now. Do nothing, what is the meaning of holy words or holy prayers, just read them repeatedly in odd numbers to generate more and more rays and waves? Every word, every line, every prayer in the holy book have some magical effect or impact. I am telling you right now that modern science will tell you in future that these holy books, in themselves, have solutions and cures for everything. These holy books, holy words, lines, rays, waves are complete science. Now whatever is missing and modern science feel helpless against a lot of pains and diseases, modern science in to start research in the direction, I am suggesting to them, and you will see, it will not take even months and modern science will have cure and solution for every pain, and disease. Now let me summarize again. To stay 100 percent healthy, we need to keep both pains and diseases/insects away from our body. This is practically possible by the use of proper medication and rubber/ plastic clothing. But to repel a pain and keep that pain away from a body, medical science needs to discover some system of rays or waves. I provided few clues on how to do it, and I will write some more about it later in this book.

يمكن استخدام الكهرباء لجهاز كمبيوتر آخر جديد أو لمبة أو فرن أو تلفزيون أو مروحة لجعلها تعمل أو تكون حيوية. بطريقة نفسه، يمكن أن تخرج الروح من الجثة وليس عليها أي قيود. روح ليس عليها أي قيود لذلك، ستذهب فقط إلي جسم إنسان آخر مولود حديثا، بإرادة الله و أمره، يمكن أن يرسل الملائكة بالروح لإعطاء حياة جديدة لأي شخص، أي حشرة أو حيوان أو طائر أو زواحف أو إلى أي جسم إنسان جديد. نفس الشيىء، الكهرباء ليس لديها أي حكمة، فالروح أيضا ليس لديها أي حكمة. نفس الشيىء الكهرباء توفر الطاقة لجهاز الكمبيوتر لجعله يعمل، والروح توفر الطاقة لجسم الإنسان لإبقائه على قيد الحياة. نفس الشيىء يعتبر المعالج هو عقل جهاز الكمبيوتر، وكذلك مخ الإنسان هو عقله يزداد ذكاء جهاز الكمبيوترو آدائه بإضافة برمجة أكثر وأكثر، و كذلك بإضافة وبرامج إلكترونية أكثر تقدما هذا ليس له أي علاقة بالطاقة الكهربائية. بغض النظر عن مدى صغر الكمبيوتر أو ذكائه، خلاصة القول ان لا يفرق ذلك مع الكهرباء. تبقي الكهرباء الكمبيوتر يعمل، بغض النظر عن ما إذا كان الكمبيوتر قديماً أو جديداً ، بطيئاً أو سريعاً . بمجرد أن يتعطل الكمبيوتر أو يتأووقف عن العمل، يتلف، سوف تذهب الكهرباء إلى جهاز كمبيوتر آخر أو جهاز كهربائي آخر.

ينمو جسم الإنسان والدماغ البشري مع مرور الوقت، بنفس الطريقة . يتعلم مخ الإنسان أشياء جديدة كل يوم، وجسم الإنسان يصبح أكثر وأكثر قوة أو يزداد ضعفا يوما بعد يوم، وإذا حصل مخ الإنسان على المزيد من التعليم والخبرة، فإنه يصبح أكثر ذكاءً. الروح ليس لها أي علاقة بهذا النمو أو الذبول التدريجي . الروح لا تصبح ذكية أو غبية أو كبيرة أو شابة مع مرور الوقت. سوف يظهر التغير فقط ، بالإيجاب أوالسلب، في المخ البشري. ستبقى الروح هي نفسها، مثل مفهوم الكهرباء.

Spirits are responsible for keeping us alive. Spirits are positive energy. Spirits do not have free will. Spirits are just an order of God. Once a spirit leaves our body, our bodies expire or die. Once a body dies, the spirit leaves that dead body immediately and, as per God's order, either transfers to a newborn body or stands by, waiting to bring life to a new body.

The relation between a spirit and a human body can be compared to electricity and a computer. In this example, the spirit is electricity and the human body is similar to a computer. In the same way electricity is used to give power to different equipment to make them operational, the human body needs the spirit to make it operational and alive. In a similar way, spirits are the electricity that keep our body alive and operational. They way all indigenous of a computer come from the mind of a computer, computer processer, human body has a brain. In the same way a computer has a keyboard, mouse, printer, monitor, scanner, etc., the human body has legs, hands, ears, fingers, hair, eyes, etc. The way a computer can still stay in operation or alive with the help of elector ally without a printer mouse, keyboard, scanner, monitor but without these tools, computer is still alive but cannot perform all functions due to electricity, computer is not dead, still alive or on but due to absence of required tools operational performance will be in complete. In the same way, the human body has a spirit, which is similar to electricity. A body can still stay alive without some tools, like the eyes, legs, hands, hair, fingers, etc., but the human body will not be completely useful or 100 percent operational due to the absence of some tools or parts.

إن وظيفة الروح هي مجرد تنشيط الجسم البشري أو غيره من الأجسام ليظلوا باقين على قيد الحياة، وحتى يستمروا في أداء وظائفهم. بمجرد أن تؤدي الأجسام وظائفها، تتحرك الأرواح لآداء مهامها الأخرى لتوفير الطاقة لأجسام أخرى بأمر الله.

و الآن، بعد أن شاهد الكل في بعض الافلام التي تدور حول تحول الأرواح إلى أشباح، بمجرد يموت الشخص في جو سيئ، يحدث شيء غير عادي حول الأشخاص خلال فترة وفاتهم. حسنا، إن فكرة الأشباح صحيحة. ولكن مرة أخرى تلك الأشباح ليست هي روح هذا الشخص الميت. الأرواح ليس لديها مخ لتقرر أي شيء من تلقاء نفسها. الارواح لها مخ يساعدهم على أداء وظائفهم لإبقائنا على قيد الحياة من خلال توفير طاقة الحياة لنا. هذا كل ما في الأمر الأرواح لا تنتظر ثانية واحدة حول الجثة. الجدول الزمني للأرواح ضيق للغاية و هو مكتوب بالفعل. ترك الروح جسد ما، و يجب عليها الذهاب علي الفور لتوفر لجسم آخر الطاقة أو الحياة، و بمجرد أن يختل الجسم أو يموت، تترك الروح أجسادنا فورا. وتذهب الى جسم آخرى جديد فورا لتوفر له الطاقة أو حياة. إذا، من هم هؤلاء الأشباح؟ . إنهم في الواقع الجن الذين عاشوا مع أن الإنسان أو الحيوان عندما كان على قيد الحياة. بغض النظر عن كيفية تصرف هذا الجن معنا أو مع الآخرين ولكن لا يزال هؤلاء الجن مخلصون جدا و مرتبطون بهذا لإنسان، الذي يستحوذون علي جسده أو يعيشون في نفس البيت مع هذا الإنسان أو البقاء حول هذا الإنسان. لذلك إذا حدث بالصدفة، أن شخص ما واجه بعض الأوضاع السيئة قبل موته أو أن شخص ما قتله أو حدث أي شيء غير مريح حقاً للإنسان قبل وفاته، قد لا يكون الناس الآخرين علي علم بكل ذلك، لكن الجن من حولهم عادة ما يكونون علي علم بجميع الحوادث أو عن كل شيئ سيئ أو مؤلم بنسبة 100 %.

SEE & CONTROL DEMONS & PAIN

Now the computer needs proper circuitry continuously to make sure electricity flows in each and every part of the computer. In a computer, copper circuits and wires are properly connected with different parts of the computer, like the hard drive, processor, motherboard, transformer, fuses, etc. If any of these basic parts or a wire burns or disconnects it will kill the computer. Due to the broken wires, even if electricity is available, that available electricity will be useless for that computer. The computer will not be functional or will be dead. In the same way, the human body can stay alive without several parts, but if any major blood tube or organ, like the heart or liver or brain totally stops working, the human body will be nonfunctional or dead.

Electricity can be used for another new computer or a bulb or oven or TV or fan to make them operational or alive. In a same manner, the spirit can come out of a dead body and does not have any restrictions. The spirit does not have any restriction that, for sure that spirit will go only in another newly born human body. From the order of God, and under the administration of God, angels can send that spirit to give a new life to anybody—any insect or any animal or any bird or any reptile or to any new human body. In the same way electricity does not have any wisdom; spirits also do not have any wisdom. In the same way electricity provides energy to a computer to make it function, spirits bring energy to the human body to keep it alive. In the same way the processor of a computer has the intelligence, the human brain also has the intelligence. They were performing, and intelligent of a computer can be increase by adding more and more programming and by adding more and more advance software's and it has nothing to do with electricity power ,

هناك حالات، في هذه الحالة إذا كان الجن أيضا متعلقين بالشخص الميت كثيراً، بالتأكيد، بعد وفاة هذا الشخص، فإن هذا الجن يثأرون له من الشخص المعني . تذكر، بمجرد أن يقرر الجني الإنتقام من شخص ما، ثق بي،لا يستطيع أي شخص طبيعي أو عادي، أن يتخيل هذا الموضوع. أسهل شيء يمكن أن يقوم الجني به فورا لمضايقة أو تخويف الشخص هو أن يجعلوهم يرون أحلام مخيفة جدا ومؤذية بواسطة التنويم المغناطيسي.الناس ترى أشياء مخيفة من حولهم.كذلك يسمعون ضوضاء مخيفة وغريبة. هذا لا يحدث في العالم المادي الحقيقي، يحدث الجن كل هذا في عقولنا من خلال استخدام التنويم المغناطيسي. كلما زاد تحكم الجن بنا، تحدث حوادث أكثر إخافة ووحشية من حولنا.

الآن، الحالة الثانية. عندما يرى الجيران وحتى الناس الذين يعيشون في منزل معين، في وقت بعض التحركات في هذا المنزل من حولهم، مع وجود حالة مخيفة وغريبة. عندما يري جسم ال أو صورة للشخص الذي مات بالفعل منذ فترة أو منذ زمن بعيد، تتحرك، يعتقدون، لسبب ما، أن الشخص الميت تحول إلى شبح وعاد إلى منزله للإنتقام من شخص ما أو لسبب آخر. وأحيانا يعتقد الناس أن الشخص الذي مات بالفعل منذ بعض الوقت أومنذ زمن بعيد، أن جسده ذهب ، لكن روحه لا تزال تعيش في ذلك المنزل لسبب ما. حسنا، لذلك علينا أن نفهم بشكل واضح جدا أنه لا توجد فكرة شبح لشخص ميت، فبمجرد موت الشخص، و بمجرد أن يتم دفن جثمانه، يتم إغلاق هذا الفصل. لن يعود ذلك الشخص الميت أو جثته أبدا إلى أي مكان مثل منزله أو أي مكان آخر. لا تقلق من أن شبح الشخص الميت أو من أن تعود الجثة في أي وقت مضى إلى أي مكان أو أي مكان آخر.

Regardless how much computer is small or intelligent or sum it make no difference to electricity. Electricity still keeps the computer energized regardless of whether the computer is old or new or slow or fast. Once computer is dysfunctional or non-operational or damaged, electricity will go to another computer or another electric appliance.

In the same way, the human body and human brain grows with time. The human brain learns new things every day, and the human body gets more and more powerful or gets weaker day by day; if a human brain gets more education and experience, it gets more intelligent. The spirit has nothing to do with all of this growth or decline. The spirit does not get smart or dumb or old or young with time. Only changes, positive and negative, will appear in the human brain or body. The spirit will stay the same, like the concept of electricity. The job of the spirit is just to energize the human body or other bodies to keep them alive until they are operational and functional. Once the bodies are functional, spirits move to other assignments to provide energy to other bodies under the order of God.

Now, as all of have seen in some movies about spirits turn into ghosts, once someone dies in a bad atmosphere, something unusual happens around them during the time of their death. Okay, the concept of ghosts is correct. But again those ghosts are not the spirit of that dead person. Spirits do not have a brain to decide anything by themselves. Spirits only have as much brain that can help them to perform their jobs to keep us alive by providing us the energy of life.

حتى لو هذا لم يكن مفهوم شبح الشخص الميت حقيقياً . ليس هناك وجود لشبح أي شخص ميت. كما شرحت بالفعل حول موضوع الارواح، ليست هناك أرواح هائمة هنا وهناك لأي شخص ميت. هذا كله خيال، أحدثه هؤلاء الجن الذين يريدون تخويفنا فقط للاستماع بالوضع أو أنهم إبتدعوا كل هذه الصور لتخويفنا، و مضايقتنا للإنتقام منا.

مرة أخرى، ليس من الصعب على الاطلاق، علي الجن أن يرينا جسم أو صورالشخص الميت بالفعل تحرك ، طوال الوقت أو بين الحين و الآخر في مكان معين أو في المنزل أو في أحلامنا.

الجن يتساوون في القدرة على أن يجعلونا نري أو نسمع أي شيء أثناء النوم في شكل حلم أو حتى أثناء يقظتنا و وعينا.الجواب البسيط هو قوة التنويم المغناطيسي. لذلك ينبغي أن يكون واضحا لنا أن بمجرد موت شخصاً ما، يكون قد مات و رحل.جسم الشخص وميت و شبحه أو روحه لا وجود له. لا شيء في أي مكان. إنهم لايعودون.

لا يوجد أي مفهوم للشبح في الحياة الحقيقية. ليس هناك روح معلقة وراء أي شخص. مهما ما نراه يحدث حولنا في بعض الأحيان،مثل شبح أو روح شخص ميت أثناء النوم أو عندما نكون مستيقظين، هو كله من الدراما التي يقوم بها الجن في ذلك المكان المحدد أو البيت. الآن الأمرفي يديك، يمكنك التحكم بها ورفض كل هذه المواقف البذيئة والمخيفة التي أحدثها الجن أو إستمرار خضوعك للمضايقة و الخوف طوال الوقت. لن يستسلم الجن، حتى تظهر لهم الثقة الحقيقية.وسوف يستمر الجن في مضايقتك وتخويفك حتى يكتشفوا أن لا شيء يجدي معك تذكر دائما أن الخطوة الأولى والأهم للخروج من هذه الحالة والمشكلة هي البدء في رفض وتجاهل أحلامنا بنسبة 100 %.

That's all. Spirits do not wait for one second around a dead body. Spirits' schedules are very tight and already written. Spirits leave one body, and immediately they have to go to another body to provide that body energy or life. Now when, spirits are only a source of providing us energy or life and they leave our bodies immediately once our bodies are dysfunctional or dead. And go to another new body immediately to provide them energy or life, so, who are these ghost are? These ghosts are actually those demons who lived with that human when that human or animal was alive. Regardless of how these demons behave with us or others but still these demons are very sincere and attached with that human, whose body they possessed or live in the same house with that human or stay around that human. So by chance, if that particular person faces some bad situation before his/ her death or someone kill them or anything really uncomfortable happen to that human before their death, other people may be not aware about all that, but demons around them usually 100 percentAware about all incidents or about all bad or painful. Situations, in this case if those demon were too much attached. With the death person, for sure, after the death of that person, those demons will take his revenge from the concern person. Remember, once a demon decides to take revenge on someone, trust me, a normal or common person, even cannot imagine about it. The easiest and immediate thing demons do to harass or scare a person are to show them very scary and nasty dreams by hypnotism. People see scary things around them. They hear scary and weird noises. This does not happen in the real physical world. Demons create all that in our minds by the use of hypnotism.

تلك الأحلام، بغض النظر عما إذا كانت أحلام جيدة أو سيئة، وليس لها أي علاقة بواقع الحياة. أنا حتى لا أناقش أحلامي مع أي شخص بغض النظر عن كون هذه الأحلام جيدة أم سيئة. إن الأحلام مثل الأفلام التي نشاهدها على شاشة التلفزيون تماماً. هذا الجن ليس لديه أي شيء آخر للقيام به. كلما ظللت قلقاً و خائفاً من أحلامك، كلما أكثر الجن من إظهار أحلاماً أكثر توتراً و سوءً و إخافةً. هذه الأحلام ليس لها تأثير حقيقي على الحياة الحقيقية. لذلك من اليوم أن تجعل عقلك يبدأ برفض وتجاهل أحلامك كل يوم في كل وقت. درب نفسك علي هذا كلما أظهرلك الجن من حولك أي حلم غريب أو مخيف، فقط إنظر نحو كتفك الأيسر في أي وقت لتحدث بصوت عال هكذا: "أيها الجني، أنا تعبت من حماقتك، إترك اللعب معي، لا تهدر وقتك معي، إذا كنت تريد أن تريني بعض الأحلام، إذن أرني حلم عن XYZ. "لذلك أنت بحاجة إلى إخبار هؤلاء الجن أنك لا تخاف ولا تهتم بتلك الأحلام.

وإذا كنت تخبرهم ما تريد أن ترى في أحلامك بثقة 100 % وستفاجأ بعد أيام قليلة، عندما تجدهم بدأوا يستمعون إليك. سرطان الدم هو هجوم مشترك من الألم ومرض السرطان /الحشرات. أن الألم المسؤول عن بدء أو إنشاء سرطان الدم، يتواجد فوق منطقة الصدر هذا الألم موجود في عظام الرقبة، والجمجمة، عظام اللثة والأنف .

بمجرد أن يبقى هذا الألم و المرض هناك لفترة من الوقت، فإنها تحدث بعض الأضرار الطفيفة داخل كل هذه العظام. ،و بمجرد أن تبدأ هذه الحشرات في أكل وتخريب داخل العظام، هو يبدأ سرطان الدم. فكلما شعر المرء بألم طفيف في العنق أوعظام اللثة أو الأنف أو الجمجمة، يجب أن يأخذ على محمل الجد وتناول كل دواء وعلاج ممكن من البداية لتجنب سرطان الدم.

The more control demons have on us, the more scarily and wild incidents will happen around us. Now, second situation. When neighbors and even people who live in that particular house, sometime see some movement in that house around them, with all other scary and weird situation. When people see a moving body or an image of that person who already died some time ago or a long time ago, they think, for some reason, that the dead person turned into a ghost and came back to his house to take revenge on someone or for some other reason. And sometimes people think that the person who already died some time ago or a long time ago, his body is gone but his spirit still living in that house for some reason. Okay, so we need to understand very clearly there is no concept of any ghost of a dead person. Once a person is dead, once his body is buried, that chapter is closed. That dead person or the body of the dead person will never come back to any place like his house or any other place. So quit worrying about this that the ghost of a dead person or maybe that dead body will ever come back to that place or any other place. Even this concept of a dead person's ghost is not real. There is no existence of any ghost of any dead person. As far as I already explain about spirits, there are no spirits wandering here and there of any dead person. These are all imagination, created by those demons who want to scare us just to enjoy the situation or they create all these images to scare us, harass us to take some revenge on us.

Again, this is not difficult at all, for demons to show us moving bodies or images of an already dead person, all the time or once in a while in a particular place or house or in our dreams.

لا يمكن للجنأن يبقوا في الجو المفتوح طوال الوقت، وخصوصا في موسم البرد. يحتاج الجن إلى بعض الأماكن للعيش، بغض النظر عن الجو، فهم موجودون حول الأشجار أو الحيوانات أو الطيور أو الزواحف أو في الناس أو منازلهم،أو أماكن العمل أو المحال التجارية، وما إلى ذلك إذا كان لديك المزيد من الأشجار في جميع أنحاء منزلك، ستجد أن معظم الجن يعيشون حول تلك الأشجار. لكن هذا لا يعني انك لن يكون لديك أي شيطان في منزلك. ولكن إذا لم يكن لديك أشجار خارج منزلك، فإن معظم الجن يعيشون داخل منزلك. هذا شيء جيد وسيء أيضاً. إذا لم يكن لديك شجر حول منزلك أو قريب منك، وسوف يعيش معظم الجن في منزلك، ولكن أنا واثق أن عددهم ليس كثيراً جداً . ولكن إذا كان لديك الكثير من الأشجار خارج منزلك، و سيتجد الكثير من الجن يعيشون على تلك الأشجار، لذلك أنا لا أعرف ماذا أفعل. ماذا يجب أن أفعل في رأيك ؟ هذا قد يبدو جنونياً ، ولكن أحيانا أشعر أن هذه الرغبات الحادة أن الجن يغذون عقولنا تشكل شيئ جذاب و جميل للغاية، في الحياة. أنا لا أتحدث عن الأنشطة الإرهابية. أنا لا أتحدث عن الإضرار شخص ما أو قتله. انا اتحدث عن عاطفة نحو الأشياء والأفكار، وغيرهم من الناس. عندما كنت شخص عادي، كنت ألهث وراء رغباتي مثل المجنون .

ولكن عندما لا يدفعني الجني كثيراً تجاه أي رغبة معينة أو أي شخص معين، أشعر تماما ي شخص ممل. مع عدم وجود الرغبة، لا يكون لدي أي طموح، وبالتالي، أستطيع التخلي عن أي شيء أو الإستسلام.

لا يتركنا الجن في سلام، إنهم يزعجوننا بإستمرار طوال الوقت، ليس لأنهم أعداؤنا، السبب هو أننا هوايتهم.

Demons are equally capable of showing us or making us hear anything during sleep in shape of a dream or even if we are up and conscious. Simple answer is the power of hypnotism. So it should be clear to us that once someone is dead, they are dead and they are gone. Their dead bodies or ghost of that dead person or the spirit of that dead person has no existence. Nothing, nowhere, they never come back.

There is no concept of ghost in real life. There is no spirit hanging behind anyone. And whatever we see happens around us sometimes, as ghost or spirit of a dead person during sleep or when we are up, is all drama of demons in that particular place or house. Now it is in your hands; you control it and reject all these naughty and scary situations created by demons or keep yourself harassed and scared all the time. Demons will never give up until you show true confidence. Demons will keep harassing and scaring you until they figure out nothing is working on you. Always remember the very first and most important step of coming out of these situation and problem is start rejecting and ignoring our dreams 100 percent.

Those dreams, regardless of whether they are good dreams or bad dreams, has nothing to do with real life. I even do not discuss my dreams to anyone regardless of how well they are or how bad they are. Dreams are just like the movies we watch on TV. These demons have nothing else to do. More you will be concerned, worried, scared about your dreams; these demons will show you more and fuller of tension and nasty and scary dreams

انهم يريدوننا أن نمتعهم إن الجن يثيرون بعقولنا بإستمرار الرغبات والأمنيات، بعد ذلك، يدفعوننا بإستمرار للجري وراء تلك الأمنيات و الرغبات. يجعلنا الجن نبقي تعساء و غاضبون عندما لا نحصل علي كل ما نرغب فيه. إنهم يشعرون بأفضل شعور عندما يسيطرون علينا. إن الأشجار الخضراء هي مجرد بيوت للجن، إنهم يعيشون على الأشجار لعدة سنوات. مئات فقط أو أكثر يعيشون على شجرة واحدة. إنهم لا يرغبون أن يعبث شخص ما بشجرتهم، تماما مثل أي شخص لا يريد تدمير منزله. إن قطع أو تقليم الشجرة مزعج جدا للجن.

كما قلت، إنهم لهم عقل مثلنا، ولكن لديهم أفضل السبل لإيذاءنا والإنتقام منا. لا يقتصر إنتقام الجن علي شخص واحد، لكنهم ينتقمون لأجيال. قد يبدو هذا جنونياً، لكن قد يكون مفيداً للحد من غضبهم، في حالة إحتياجك لتقليم أو قطع الشجرة. قبل قطع أي شجرة، إذهب قريباً من الشجرة و تحدث إليها: "من يعيش على هذه الشجرة، إنني بحاجة إلى إذن لقطع هذه الشجرة ". فقط إشرحوا لهم عذرك لقطع تلك الشجرة وقولوا لهم أن ينتقلوا إلى مكان آخر. إعطيهم ما لا يقل عن خمسة عشر يوما قبل قطع تلك الشجرة. عادة، هم لا يتضايقون جدا عندما نستأذنهم.

أعتقد أن معظم الناس في هذا العالم لا يؤمنون بفكرة الجن، معظم الناس لا يعتقدون أن هناك عالم موازي وأن عدد سكان هذا العالم الغير المرئي هو أعلى بكثير من عدد سكان العالم المرئي. معظم الناس ليس لديهم أدنى فكرة أن هذا العالم الغير المرئي يشاركنا حياتنا و يتدخل في شؤوننا. ربما بعد أن يقرأ الناس هذا الكتاب، وسوف يتعرف عدد قليل من الناس علي مفهوم هذا العالم الغير مرئي على الفور. ولكن بالنسبة لمعظم الناس سيظل العالم الغير مرئي، لغزا لم يحل. ولكن على الجانب الآخر، أنا أشعر أنه بالرغم من كون كل الجن والأمراض لغزاً بالنسبة للإنسان، إلا أنني لغز محير للجن والأمراض.

Rizwan Qureshi	رؤية الجن و الآلام السيطرة عليها
These dreams have no real impact on real life. So from today, make your mind start rejecting and ignoring your dreams every day all the time. Train your mind for this. Every time demons around you show you any scary weird dream, just look toward your left shoulder anytime and talk loudly like this, "Mr. Demon, I am tired of your crap, quit playing with me, quit wasting your time on me, if you want to show me some dreams, then show me dream about XYZ." So you need to tell those demons you are not scared and interested in those dreams.	أنا أقوم بمفاجأتهم بإعلامهم عندما يكونون بالقرب مني.وعندما أشير بإصبعي إليهم وهم يطيرون في الهواء. وعندما وأبقي عيناي ناظرةً إليهم مباشرة .
And if you tell them what you want to see in your dreams with 100 percent confidence, you will be surprised after a few days when those demons start listening to you.	إنه مفهوم غريب جداً ، أن يكون من الممكن أن تطلب من أي جني، يستحوذ علي جسم أي إنسان في أي جزء من العالم، المغادرة. يمكنني إقناعهم بمغادرة ذلك الجسم، ولكن في بعض الأحيان لابد أن أصر علي ذلك. الإصرار هو إجراء يستغرق بعض الوقت. ولكن خلال عملية إخراج جني من شخص ما، يأتي إلى معظمهم في البداية بمجرد أن يقرروا ترك هذا الشخص. إنهم عادة ما يكون في منتهي التعاسة والغضب مني في لقائنا الأول،لكن بعد أربعة و عشرون ساعة أو أقل، يسامحونني ويصبحون أصدقائي. أنا عادة أطلب من الجميع مغادرة منزلي في اليوم الثاني أو الثالث، وهم يستجيبون لي معظم الوقت.
Blood cancer is a combined attack of a pain and cancer disease/ insects. That pain responsible for starting or creating blood cancer resides above the chest area. This pain resides in the neck bone, skull, bones of gums and nose. Once this in stay there for a while, it creates some minor damages inside all these bones. Once damages are there, it opens door for cancer disease/insects to go inside the bones. Once these insects start eating and damaging inside the bones, it is the start of blood cancer. So whenever someone feels minor pain in neck of gum or nose or skull bones, all take it very seriously and do every possible medication and cure from very beginning to avoid blood cancer.	إذا اخترت بيتاً معيناً أو منطقةً معينةً، بدلا من الشخص، فإنني أستطيع نقل كل الجن إلي ذلك المنزل أو هذه المنطقة. أطلب منهم أن يذهبوا إلى مكان آخر، و لكن معظمها يأتي إلي. إن عدم معرفة كم عدد الجن في هذه الألم بالذنطقة أو أي نوع من القوى يتميزون بها، قد يكون مشكلة بالنسبة لي، و يكون التعامل مع العديد من الجن أمراً صعباً حقا. أنهم عادة ما يفاجئون، وأنا أفاجأ أيضاً . وانا بحاجة الى ما لا يقل عن أربع وعشرين ساعة حتى يتسنى لهم فهمي و معرفتي قبل أن يغادروا. لقد أجريت هذه التجربة عدة مرت، والشيء الوحيد الذي تعلمته أن الإنشغال بأكثرمن جني أو العبث معه في وقت واحد، ليست فكرة جيدة. إن الجن هم الوحيدون الذين لديهم القدرة علي أن يظهروا لنا الأحلام .

67

SEE & CONTROL DEMONS & PAIN

Demons cannot stay in open atmosphere all the time, especially in cold season. Demons need some places to live, regardless of whether they are trees or animals or birds or reptiles or human or their houses or their workplaces or shops, etc. If you have more trees around your house, most of the demons will live on around those trees. But it doesn't mean you will have no demon in your house. But if you do not have trees outside your house then most of the demons will be living inside your house. This thing is good and this thing is bad too. If you do not have tree around your house or close by, most demons will be living in your house, but I am sure not too many. But if you have a lot of trees outside around your house means, a lot of, too many demons will be living on those trees a lot of population of demons live on trees so I do not know what to do. What do you think I should do? This may sound crazy, but sometimes I feel that these extreme desires that demons feed our minds make up the very attraction and beauty of life. I am not talking about terrorist activities. I am not talking about damaging or killing someone. I am talking about a passion for things, ideas, and other people. When I was a normal person, I was running after my desires like crazy. But when no demon pushes me too much for any particular desire or person, I feel just like a dull person. With no desire, I have no ambition, and consequently, I can give up on anything. Demons cannot leave us in peace. Demons keep us disturbed all the time but not because they are our enemies. The reason is that we are their hobby. They want us to entertain them. Demons continuously create desires and wishes in our minds. After that, demons continuously push us to run after those wishes and desires.

رضوان قرشي

فالأحلام لا تأتي من عقولنا. يستطيع الجن قراءة عقولنا بسهولة وإنهم حتى يستطيعون العثور على معلومات عميقة داخل أدمغتنا. الجن هم الذين يظهرون لنا الأحلام بتنويمنا مغناطيسياً. الناس العاديون عادة ما يكونون تحت تأثير جني واحد على الأقل. ويظهر هذا الجن لهم أحلام أحيانا لتخويفهم، وأحيانا لمضايقتهم، وأحيانا أخري لتكشف لهم عن الشئون التي تحدث من حولهم. هذه هي هواية الجن، وعقولنا ليست سوى لعب بالنسبة لهم.

إذا كنت لا تري حلماً، فلا يوجد جن من حولك، إذن هم لا يلعبون في عقلك عندما تكون نائما. وأنا أتعامل مع جن جدد هذه الأيام، إنهم يعاملونني كشخص عادي و طبيعي في البداية بدلامن إستخراج معلومات من عقلي. أنهم يحاولون أن يظهروا لي أحلام حول الشخص، أوالأسرة أو منطقة، الذين إنسحبت منهم، ونتيجة لذلك، أرى ناس غرباء والمنازل غريبة، ومشاكل غريبة في أحلامي. هذا جنون، لكن هذا يحدث كل يوم. في الوقت الذي يعرفني الجن، فأنهم لا يهتمون بإضاعة وقتهم معي ليظهروا لي الأحلام. ومع ذلك بحلول ذلك الوقت، سوف يوجد جن شخص آخر يتسكع حولي.

إنها حقيقة تجريبية، وهو إعتقاد يعتقده جميع الناس المتدينون، أن أي نوع من الجن، أو أي نوع من المرض، يكون وراءه دائما اللحوم الحمراء. تكون اللحوم الحمراء لبقرة أو ثور عادة. بصراحة، ليس لدي أي مشكلة مع أي نوع من أنواع اللحوم أو أي نوع من الطعام، ولكني شخص غير طبيعي، فليس لدي أي مشكلة مع الجن، فهم يستمعون لي، وعادة لا يؤذوني. لكن الشخص العادي يتجنب دعوة الجن أو مرض، يعيش الجن والمرض داخل اللحوم الحمراء ويتتبعونها، لذا كن حذرا.

68

Demons keep us very unhappy and angry when we cannot get whatever we desire. They feel better when they have control over us. Green trees are just a house for demons. They live on trees for years. Hundreds or more just live on one tree. Just like we don't want anyone to destroy our houses, they do not like it if someone messes with their tree. Cutting or trimming a tree is very annoying to demons. As I said, they are like us mentally, but they have better ways to hurt us and take revenge on us. A demon's revenge is not limited to one person. Demons take revenge for generations. This may sound crazy to you, but it may be helpful to reduce their anger just in case you need to cut or trim a tree. Before you cut any tree, just go close and talk to tree: "Whoever lives on this tree, I need their permission to cut this tree." Just tell them your excuse for cutting that tree and tell them to move to another place. Give them at least fifteen days before you cut that tree down. Usually, they do not get too upset when we ask permission from them.

I believe most people in this world do not believe in the concept of demons. Most people do not believe that there is a parallel world and that the population of that invisible world is much higher than the population of the visible world. Most people have no clue that this invisible world is involved in our lives and our affairs. Maybe after they have read this book, a few people will gain a concept of this invisible world right away. But for most of the people, this invisible world will remain an unsolved mystery. But on other hand, I strongly feel that though all demons and diseases are a mystery to human beings, I am a mystery to demons and diseases.

اعتدت أن أكون مختلفاً . إنني بحاجة لعرض العديد من السلوكيات المتطرفة. لكن لأن الجن لا يستطيعون البقاء حولي لفترة طويلة، أشعر أنني محايد معظم الوقت. في هذه الأيام، يمكنني سحب نفسي بسهولة من أشياء كثيرة، حيث أنني لا أشعر بكره شديد أو حب شديد لأي شيء أو أي شخص. عموما، أنا أكثر مسؤولية، ولكن سلوكياتي المتطرفة تقل. هؤلاء يبقينا الجن مستمرين في حياتنا، عندما يصرون على أن تكون لدينا هوايات، وأشياء نحبها، و أشياء نكرها، والمسابقات، وأن يكون لدينا رغبات طوال الوقت. إن سلبية سيئة للغاية بالنسبة لنا من ناحية، ولكنهم بطريقة أو بأخرى، يمكنوننا من الحفاظ على أ نشطتنا ونظل نسعي وراء رغباتنا، وأنا أعتقد أن ذلك هو الشيئ الجذاب في الحياة.

ثق بي، إن التنويم المغناطيسي أداة قوية للغاية، ويمتلكها الجن، إنهم يضيفون أنواع مختلفة من الأفكار السلبية والإيجابية تجاه الناس. يقنعنا الجن بإستمرار بمشاعرنا تجاه الناس من خلال التنويم المغناطيسي.

أحيانا يستغرق ذلك وقتاً طويلاً، ولكن في نهاية المطاف، سوف يكون على اقتناع الشخص العادي سهلاً. يمكن أن يجعلنا الجن نكره شخص ما أو شخص ما نحب شخص ما بسهولة جدا عن طريق استخدام التنويم المغناطيسي.

هذا صحيح. لا يمكن السيطرة علي الروح أو يملي عليها أمر ما من خارجها، بواسطة التخاطر أو التنويم المغناطيسي. إنها لا تشارك في عمليات التخاطر والتنويم المغناطيسي، فهي لديها مصادر خارجية. نحن نرسل تعليمات إلى الجن عن طريق التخاطر، وهم يتغلبون علي الطاقات الإيجابية و يسيطرون على عقولنا للتفكير في بعض الامور.

I surprise them by informing them when they are close to me. I surprise them when I point my finger at them as they are flying in the air. And I surprise them when I keep my eyes pointed straight at them.

This is a very strange concept, but it is possible to ask any demon possessing any human body in any part of the world to leave. I can convince them to leave that body, but sometimes I need to insist. Insisting is a procedure, and it takes some time. But during the process of taking out a demon from a person, most of them come to me first once they decide to leave that person. They are usually very unhappy and angry with me during our first meeting. After twenty-four hours or less, they forgive me and become my friend. I usually ask everyone to leave my house on the second or third day, and they listen most of the time.

Instead of a person, if I chose a particular house or a particular area, I was able to move all the demons in that house or area. I ask them to go to some other place, and most of them come to me. Not knowing how many demons are in that particular area or what kind of powers they have can be a problem for me, and handling numerous demons is really difficult. They are usually surprised, and I am surprised too. And I need at least twenty-four hours so that they understand and learn about me before they leave. I performed this experiment several times, and the only thing I learned was that it is not a good idea to get involved or mess with so many demons at one time.

وهذا ليس صعباً على الجن. هذه هي اللغة التي يستخدمونها للتواصل مع أي عقل. إذا كنت خبيراً في التنويم المغناطيسي وتحاول تنويم شخص ما مغناطيسيا، وأنت لا تقوم بالتنويم المغناطيسي حقاً، الجن الخاصين بك هم الذين يقومون بالتنويم المغناطيسي حقاً !

لدينا الملايين من الجن حولنا. صغر حجمها يسمح للملايين منهم بالتجمع في غرفة صغيرة جداً. عادة، ضعاف العقل من الناس يعطون السيطرة الكاملة للجن على عقولهم. الجن هم أصدقائهم الحقيقيون، وأنهم أصدقاء للشياطين. عندما تزداد سيطرة الجن على عقل شخص ما، فإنهم عادةلا يريدون ترك الشخص بسبب الصداقة التي تربطهم بهم، هذا يحدث للأطفال، فضلا عن الناس من جميع الأعمار. عادة، يقوم الجن بتنويم هؤلاء الناس مغناطيسياً، و من خلاله، يظهرون للناس ما يريدون. هذا هو جهد فردي من أحد الأصدقاء من الجن نحو الإنسان الذي يسيطر عليه الجن. لا يجلب الحجم والشكل الفعلي للجن أي فائدة لأي انسان، لذلك باستخدام التنويم المغناطيسي، يقوم الجن بتشكيل صديق وهمي من الجن في شكل إما شبح أو صورة إنسان لهذا الإنسان على نحو خاص.. بهذه الطريقة، يتحدث بعض البشر مع هؤلاء البشر أو الجن على شكل شبح الذين شكلهم أصدقائهم من الجن لهم،يتحدثون إليهم في خيالهم، والتي أنشأتها أصدقاء شيطان عنهم. يظن هؤلاء البشر أنهم يرون ويتحدثون إلى جن حقيقيون حقاً ، ولكن في الواقع هذا هو حلم اليقظة الخاص بهم. سترى حفنة من الناس يتحدثون إلى أنفسهم. إنهم في الواقع يتحدثون إلى الجن الخاص بهم.

إذا كنت تقود السيارة، لا يمكن للجن أن يحركوا أو يحولوا توجيهك،ولا يستطيعون دفع الفرامل. يمكنهم، مع ذلك، أن يدغدغونك أو يصيبونك بجروح بالغة في الجسم في ثواني، كما يمكنهم أن يجعلوك تنام بسهولة في ثوان.

.

Demons are the only ones that can show us dreams. Dreams do not come from our minds. Demons can easily read our minds and even find information deep inside our brains. Demons are the ones that show us dreams by hypnotizing us. Normal people are usually under the influence of at least one demon. And that demon shows them dreams sometimes to scare them, sometimes to harass them, and sometimes to reveal affairs around them. This is the hobby of demons, and our minds are just like toys for them.

If you are not seeing a dream, no demon is around you, or they are not playing with your mind when you are sleeping. These days, I have to deal with new demons. New demons treat me as a regular and normal person at first instead of digging up information from my mind. They try to regular and normal person at first instead of digging up information from my mind. They try to show me dreams about the person, family, or area I pulled them out of. As a result, I see strange people, strange houses, and strange problems in my dreams. This is crazy, but it happens every day. By the time that demon learns about me, they do not bother to waste time with me by showing me more dreams. By then, however, I will have someone else's demon hanging around me.It is an experimental truth, a belief held by all spiritual people, that any kind of demon, or any kind if disease, always goes behind red meat. Usually, red meat belongs to the cow or bull. Honestly, I do not have any problem with any kind of meat or any kind of food, but I am an abnormal person. I do not have any problem with demons. They listen to me, and they usually do not hurt me. But a normal person needs to avoid inviting demons or disease, and demons and disease live inside red meat and follow red meat, so be careful.

الجن أقوياء للغاية، لكنهم لا يستطيعون قيادة السيارات من تلقاء انفسهم، إنهم بحاجة إلي أجسام للقيام بهذه الأفعال. يمكن للجن أيضا أن يجعلونا ننام أثناء قيادتنا للسيارات. يمكنهم تنويمنا مغناطيسياً، و يدفعوننا للإنتحار عن طريق أن نصطدم بشجرة أو قطب بسياراتنا، ولكنها يحتاج الجن دائماً إلي أجسام للوفاء برغباتهم. لو قمنا بزيادة ضبط النفس، ويمكننا أن نقلل من وجود الجن في حياتنا وعقولنا.

إن التخاطر والتنويم المغناطيسي وكلاهما مختلفين، لكنهما يسيرا جنباً إلى جنب. من المستحيل عملياً العثور علي إنسان له القدرة على أن ينوم مغناطيسياً شخص ما. بالنسبة لي، يبدو هذا مستحيلاً إلى حد ما. تقريبا كل خبراء التنويم المغناطيسي يستخدمون الجن الخاص به لمساعدتهم الناس بحاجة إلى مهارة تواصل مثل التخاطرليستطيعوا التواصل مع الجن الخاص بهم. على سبيل المثال،اذا كان هناك من يرسل جن إلى غيره الذين يبعدون عنه بمائة ميل، هذا يعني أنه لديه أو أنها لديها بعض الجن تحت سيطرته أو سيطرتها. إذا كان لديك جن تحت سيطرتك، وقمت بإرسالهم مع تعليمات إلي شخص ما، سيذهبون إلي ذلك الشخص للبدء بتنفيذ التعليمات. التخاطر يسمح للشخص بقراءة عقول الآخرين. عندما يستخدم الشخص التواصل بالتخاطر مع شخص آخر، فإن هذا الشخص يرسل إثنين من الجن على الاقل.

هناك جزء واحد مهم في التنويم المغناطيسي، و هو التخاطر والجن فقط يمكنهم القيام به.هناك طريقتان متاحتان يمكن للمرء أن يستخدمهما للتخاطر لقراءة عقول الناس:

SEE & CONTROL DEMONS & PAIN

I used to be different. I need to exhibit many extreme behaviors. But because demons cannot stay around me for a long time, I feel neutral most of the time. Nowadays, I can easily withdraw from many things. I do not feel too much hate or love for anything or anyone. Overall, I am more responsible, but my extreme behaviors are reducing. These demons keep us going when they insist that we have hobbies, likes, dislikes, competitions, and desires all the time. On the one hand, a demon's negativism is extremely bad for us, but somehow, they keep us active and keep us running behind our wishes and desires, and I think that is the attraction of life.

Trust me, hypnosis is a very strong tool, and demons have this tool. They add different kinds of negative and positive thoughts toward people. Demons continuously convince us about feelings for people through hypnosis.

Sometimes it takes a long time, but eventually, a normal person will be convinced easily. By using hypnotism, demons can make us hate someone or love someone very easily.

This is true. The soul/spirit cannot be controlled or dictated externally by telepathy or hypnotism. They are not involved in the processes of telepathy and hypnotism. Those have external sources. We send instructions to demons by means of telepathy, and demons defeatpositive energies and control our minds to think certain things. And this is not difficult for demons. This is the language they use to communicate with any mind.

رضوان قرشي

1- قم بإرسال إثنين من الجن إلى الشخص الذي تريد قراءة عقله. كلا الجنيين سوف يتلقيان تعليماتك بالتواصل معهم من خلال استخدام التخاطر. وسيقوم كلاهما بقراءة أفكار هذا الشخص باستخدام التنويم المغناطيسي. بمجرد أن يحصل جني واحد لإمداد عقلك بكل المعلومات الجديدة بالتنويم المغناطيسي. بهذه الطريقة، يقوم جني واحد بقراءة عقل هذا الشخص بإستمرار، و الجني الأخر ينقل جميع المعلومات إلى عقلك.

2. عند إرسال إثنين من الجن لشخص واحد، لابد أن تتأكد من ألا يوجدد تعارض بين هذين الجنيين، و أنهما يمكنهما التواصل بسهولة فيما بينهما، وأن في وسعهما.التواصل مع بعضهما البعض باستخدام المجالات والنظم المغناطيسية و الكهرومغناطيسية التي تستخدم أيضا المجالات. هذا مشابه تقريبا للتخاطر، ولكن لأن هذا التواصل يحدث بين إثنين من الجن، فإن الوسط مختلف، إلا أن القواعد هي نفسها كما في التخاطر. في هذا الإجراء، يقوم جني واحد بقراءة العقل، ويقوم بنقل جميع المعلومات إلى الجني الثاني بالقرب منك، و سوف يقوم الجني الثاني بفك كافة المعلومات في عقلك عن طريق استخدام التنويم المغناطيسي. الآن أنت تفهم أنه لا يمكن للجن أن يقوموا بتنويمنا مغناطيسياً بمساعدكبيرة لست مهتماً بقراءة عقول الآخرين، لأنني لست شخصاً فضولياً جدا. لكني لا أزال، لدي الكثير من المشاعر طوال الوقت.

أعتقد أن الجن يستمتعون بحياتهم بأ ن يكونوا داخلنا أو حولنا. نحن نخضع لهم معظم الوقت، دون أدنى دليل. نحن مجرد لعب أو وسائل للجن. إنهم يعيشون بداخلنا ويستمتعون بحياتهم. لابد لنا أن نقر ونختار مزاجهم.

If you are a hypnotism expert and you are trying to hypnotize someone, you are not really performing hypnosis. Your demons are really performing hypnosis for you!

We have millions of demons around us. Their small size allows millions of them to gather in a very small room. Usually, weak minded people give total control of their minds to their demons. Demons are their true friend, and they are friends to demons. When demons get that much control over someone's mind, they usually do not want to leave the person because of the friendship they have developed. This happens to kids as well as people of all ages. Usually, demons hypnotize those people, and through hypnotism, they show the people whatever they want. This is an individual effort of a friend demon toward a demon-controlled human. Actual size and shape of a demon will not bring any interest to any human. So by using hypnotism, demons create an imaginary demon friend in a shape of either a ghost or a human for that particular human. This way, some humans talk to those humans or ghost-shaped demons in their imagination, created by their demon friends for them. Those humans think they are really seeing and talking to a real demon, but actually it is all their open eyes dream world. You will see a bunch of people talking to themselves. Actually they talk to their demon. If you are driving, demons cannot move or turn your steering, and they cannot push the breaks.

They can, however, tickle you or badly hurt your body in seconds. They can easily make you asleep in seconds as well.

كذلك لابد أن نتبع تعليماتهم. لابد أن ندخن السجائر بغضب للغاية لإرضائهم. يجب أن تبقى في حالة حزن وإكتئاب لارضائهم. لابد أن نصبح متطرفين، كي يشعروا بالسعادة.. يجب أن نتصرف بطريقة سلبية لأنهم يريدون منا ذلك كي يشعرون بالسعادة. إنهم فقط ينوموننا مغناطيسيا، ونحن نفعل ما يريدون، لكنهم أكثر سيطرة، يمكننا أن نبدأ في مقاومة نفوذها.إنه شيئ صعب، ولكننا نستطيع التحكم في عقولنا. يمكننا أن نفعل أي شيء.هل التنويم المغناطيسي والتخاطر ممكن من أي مكان وفي أي مكان؟. يتوقف ذلك حقاً على مدى مهارتك ومدى قوة عقلك. هذا كله لعبة عقول. إذا كان عقلك قوي بما فيه الكفاية، يمكن أن يكون الجميع عبيدك، يتبعونك، ويستمعون إليك. إذا عقلك ضعيفاً، سوف يرسلك الجن إلى مستشفى للأمراض العقلية.

التخاطر يسمح للشخص بالسيطرة على عقل شخص آخر. حسنا، في الواقع، إن الشخص لا يسيطر على العقل ولكنه يغذيه بالتعليمات وهذه التعليمات تأتي دائما من الجن. بمجرد تلقي الجن التعليمات، فإنهم يبدأون إجراءاتهم فوراً. ويمكن لخبراء التخاطر الوصول بسهولة إلى أي عقل في أي مكان في هذا العالم. كل هذا يعتمد على مدى قوة عقلك. أي عقل قوي بهذه المهارات يستطيع السيطرة على أي عقل في أي جزء من العالم.. لا يمكن القيام بالتنويم المغناطيسي من مسافة بعيدة. ويمكن أن يقوم به الجن، وليس الإنسان. وهذا الجن يجب أن يكون قريباً منك كي يقوم بتنويمك مغناطيسياً. هل نحن بحاجة إلى إعداد، أم يمكننا أن نبدأ فقط بالقيام بالتنويم المغناطيسي أو بإستخدام التخاطر؟ربما هناك فرق بيني وبين بعض خبراء التخاطر و التنويم المغناطيسي.

Demons are extremely powerful, but they cannot operate or steer cars by themselves. They all need bodies to fulfill these actions. Demons can also make us sleep when we are driving. They can hypnotize us and push us to commit suicide by running a car into a tree or pole, but demons always need bodies to fulfill their desires. If everyone increases their self-control, we should be able to reduce the presence of demons in our lives and minds.

Telepathy and hypnotism are both different, but they go together. It is practically impossible to find a human with the ability to hypnotize someone. To me, it seems rather impossible. Almost all hypnotism experts use their demons to help them. People need a communication skill like telepathy to communicate with their demons. For example, if someone sends a demon to someone else who is one hundred miles away from him, this means he or she must have some demons under his or her control. If you have demons under your control and you send those demons to someone with instructions, those demons will go to that person and start doing there. Telepathy can allow one to read the minds of other people. By using this technique, you can easily read the thoughts of other people. When someone makes a telepathy connection with another person, they usually send at least two demons to that person. One important part of telepathy is hypnotism, and only demons can perform hypnosis.

There are two possible ways one can use telepathy to read people's minds:

الآخرين، وعادة، هؤلاء الناس لابد أن يمارسوا هذه المهارات على أشخاص معينين لفترة من الوقت قبل أن يتمكنوا من إرسال التعليمات، و عادة، هذه الممارسة لابد من إرسال الجن الخاص بهم فيها. هؤلاء الممارسين لتلك المهارات يمنحون الجن الخاص بهم بعض الوقت لإقامة وإجراء التنويم المغناطيسي لعقول الآخرين. عادة، كل شخص لديه بالفعل مجموعة من الجن من حوله. أحيانا يكون هؤلاء الجن مع هؤلاء الناس منذ طفولتهم.

في حالتي، الفرق الوحيد هو أنني لم يكن لدي أي سيطرة على أي جني معين. يمكن لعقلي التحليق في أي مكان في العالم بسهولة.

ويمكنني إقناع أي جني بتلقي التعليمات مني، ولكن هذا ليس محل إهتمامي. كم من الوقت يستمر آثار التنويم المغناطيسي؟ إن عقولنا قوية جدا، ونحن الذين نتحكم في عقولنا. يمكن أن تقع عقولنا تحت تأثير الجن، ويمكنهم أن يبقونا تحت تأثير التنويم المغناطيسي. وبمجرد أن نتحرر من التنويم المغناطيسي، نعود إلى وضعنا الطبيعي، ولكن معظمنا لايدرك الجن وتنويمهم المغناطيسي لنا. هذا هو السبب في أننا نشعر وكأننا لنا أفكارنا الخاصة، كلما ألقت الجن شيئاً في عقولنا. وعندما يكون تطرأ فكرة ما في عقولنا، يصبح من الصعب تجاهل تلك الفكرة. عادة، يلقي الجن بأشياء في عقولنا لعدة ساعات و بعد ذلك يتركوننا وشأننا لمعرفة ردود الفعل لدينا تجاه ضغطهم علينا لفترة طويلة. أو إذا ظل الجن حولي، يساعدونني عادة، ويبقون على مسافة معينة مني.

عادة، كل شخص لديه جني واحد أو أكثر حوله أو داخله، لكن ليس لدي أي جني داخل جسدي معظم الوقت. لا يمكن لأي أحد منع الجن من التوجه إلي داخل أجسامنا. إنهم يذهبون داخل جسدي ولكن لا يبقون هناك لفترة طويلة.

74

1. Send two demons to the person who's mind you want to read. Both demons will receive your instruction when you communicate with them by using telepathy. Both of them will read the thoughts of that person's mind by using hypnotism. Once they get the information, one demon will keep reading the mind of the person, but the second will come back to you and feed all the new information to your mind through hypnotism. This way, one demon will continuously read the mind of that person, and the other demon will transfer all the information to your mind.

2. When you send two demons to one person, you need to make sure that those two demons have no conflicts with each other and that they can easily communicate with each other. Demons can communicate with each other by using magnetic fields and systems that also utilize electromagnetic fields. This is almost similar to telepathy, but because this communication is happening between two demons, the traveling medium is different. Otherwise, the rules are the same as they are for telepathy. In this procedure, one demon will read the mind of the person and transmit all the information to a second demon near you. The second demon will decode all the information in your mind by using hypnosis. Now you understand that demons cannot hypnotize us from a significant assistance. I have no interest in reading other people's mind, because I am not a very nosy person. Still, I get a lot of feelings all the time.

I think demons enjoy their lives by using or residing inside or around us. Most of the time, we obey them without the slightest clue. We are just toys or mediums for demons. They live and enjoy their lives inside us. We have to adopt their temperaments.

رؤية الجن و الآلام السيطرة عليها

يمكنني إزالة الجن من الأجسام كل يوم، لكنهم يستحوذون علي جسم آخر بسرعة. الجن يتواجدون داخل وخارج أجسادنا طوال الوقت، ولكن في حالة الناس العاديين، لديهم القليل من الجن الدائمين. لذلك ما أقوم به، هو أنني أستخدام أي جني حول أي شخص في أي جزء من العالم، بدلاً من الإبقاء علي بعض الجن الدائمين حولي لهذا الغرض. هذا التخاطر المجنون يجعل كل شيء. سهل جدا بالنسبة لي، إنني فقط أصل إليهم، و أقدم نفسي، وأوجه لهم تهديدات للإبتعاد عن هذا الشخص اذا لم يستجيبوا لي. معظم الوقت، غالباً ما يكفي هذا بالنسبة لهم، وهم يستمعون إلي. أنهم يزورونني قبل أن يبدأوا في طاعتي، ربما لمجرد أن يتحققوا من هذا الشخص المجنون. يستطيع الجن الإستحواذ علي أي جسم وإستخدامه ضد أي شخص. الجن أجسام لمادية، ولكنهم هل ليسوا في صلابتنا. إن أجسادهم المادية مثل الهواء، لكنهم ليسوا هواءً خالصاً، و قوتهم غير عادية. بعض الناس يعتقدون أن الجن نوع خاص من الغاز الذي يمكن إستخدامه كمصدر للطاقة. إنهم مخطئون تماماً في ذلك. الجن الطائر غير مؤذي مطلقاً، فهم لا يستطيعون أن يؤذوا أحداً، ولا يمكن أن يقوموا بتنويمه مغناطيسياً. تبدأ قوتهم في العمل فقط عندما يخترقون الجسم. بمجرد أن يدخلون الجسم، يستطيعون نشر أنفسهم. إذا كانوا يغطيون الجزء السفلي من الجسم، لا يمكن أن يقوموا بتنويم العقل مغناطيسياً والسيطرة عليه من هناك. ألف شيطان يجب أن يكون الجني حول الرأس، عنداالأذن اليسرى بالتحديد، ليقوم بتنويمنا مغناطيسيا والسيطرة على العقل. خلال عملية التنويم المغناطيسي الذي يقوم بها الجن، و عادة ما يجري داخل العقل جدال كبير، و كلما زادت قوة الشخص، إزدادت مقاومته لتأثير الجن. يجب أن يكون الجن قريبين جدا بالنسبة لنا، خصوصا قرب أذننا اليسرى لدينا، لتنويمنا مغناطيسياً إنهم لا يستطيعون تنويمنا مغناطيسياً من منطقة نائية بإستخدام التخاطر.

We have to follow their instructions. We have to smoke cigarettes for extremely angry to please them. We have to stay sad and depressed to please them. We have to become extremists so that they feel good. We have to act in negative ways so that they feel because demons want us to. They just hypnotize us, and we do whatever they want; however, more control to these demons, we can start resisting their influence. It is difficult, but we are the bosses of our own minds. We can do anything. Is hypnotism and telepathy possible from anywhere? It really depends on how skilled you are and how powerful your mind is. This is all a game of minds. If your mind is powerful enough, everyone could be your slave, follow you, and listen to you. If your mind is weak, these demons will send you to a mental hospital

Telepathy allows one to control someone else's mind. Well, actually, one does not control the mind but feeds it instructions, and those instructions always come from demons. Once demons receive the instructions, they start their procedures immediately. Telepathy experts can easily access any mind anywhere in this world. This all depends on how powerful your mind is. A powerful mind with these skills can control any mind in any part of the world. Hypnotism cannot be done from a remote distance. And hypnotism can be done by only demons, not by a human. And that demon needs to be close by you to hypnotize you.

Do we need a setup, or can we just start hypnotizing or using telepathy? Maybe there is a difference between me and some other experts of telepathy and hypnotism.

بمجرد أن تخترع العلوم الطبية آلة تؤثر علي الجن والأمراض، سيستطيع الأطباء إزالة أوسحب هذه الطاقات السلبية من اجسادنا. عندما لا يتواجد الجن حولنا، سيكون لديهم القليل من السيطرة على أنشطتنا وسلوكياتنا. عندما لا يتواجد الجن حولنا، سيكون لديهم القليل من السيطرة على أنشطتنا وسلوكياتنا. إن مستقبل صحتنا مشرق جدا. أرجو أن تدرس العلوم الطبية نظريات التي أجريتها للبحث، وبعد ذلك، لن تستغرق وقتاً طويلاً لإختراع الآلات المناسبة للعلاج. لدينا بالفعل دواء حديث لعلاج الأضرار.

إن الحيوانات أو حتى الجن، مثل الأرواح ليس لديها أي لغة للتواصل معنا أو مع أي جسم أخر أو أي جني أو ألم أو مرض. إن أرواح لا يمكن السيطرة عليها، و لايمكنها التواصل مع غيرها من الأرواح.الأرواح لا شيء، إنها مجرد أمر من الله. مرة أخري، إن الروح مثل الطاقة التي تمد جسم معين كما قدر الله. جميع الجثث تتماثل. إن جثة الإنسان أو الحيوان أو الحشرة أو أي طائر، تتماثل جميعها بعدالموت. الطريقة التي يموت بها الكثير من الحيوانات / الطيور / الحشرات، كل يوم في ظروف سيئة أو في حالة سيئة للغاية، لكننا لا نرى أي أشباح تتسكع حول منازلنا أو في طريق أي حيوان أو طير أو حشرة. يستطيع الجن المتواجدون حولنا بعد وفاة شخص معين أن يظهروا لنا أشباح هؤلاء الأشخاص الذين ماتوا، من خلال التنويم المغناطيسي. والآن نستطيع أن نتحكم في مدة بقائنا تحت سيطرة هؤلاء الجن والسماح لهم بمضايقتنا، و إشعارنا بالخوف، طوال الوقت.

الروح ليست مسؤولة عن أفعالنا الجيدة أو السيئة. أيا كانت أفعالنا جيدة أو سيئة نقوم بها، فإن جسدنا المادي وعقولنا هي المسؤولية تماماً عن ذلك. الأرواح فقط هي المسؤولة عن تنشيط أجسامنا المادية لإبقائنا على قيد الحياة. مهما فعلنا من أفعال جيدة أو سيئة، فالروح ليست مسؤولة عن ذلك.

Rizwan Qureshi	رؤية الجن و الآلام السيطرة عليها

Rizwan Qureshi

Usually, those people have to practice on particular people for a while before they can send instructions. Usually, that practice involves them sending out their demons. They give their demons some time to set up and feed hypnotism into the minds of others. Usually, everyone already has a group of demons around them. Sometimes these demons are from their childhood. In my case, the only difference is that I do not have any control over any particular demon.

My mind can fly anywhere in the world quite easily. I can convince any demon to take instructions from me, but this is not my field of interest.

How long does the effects of hypnotism last? Our minds are very powerful, and we are the bosses of our minds. Our minds can come under the influence of demons, and they can keep us hypnotized. Once we are free of hypnotism, we return to normal, but most are not aware of demons and their hypnotism. That's why we feel like we are thinking our own thoughts whenever demons feed something into our minds. And when something keeps coming to our minds, it can become difficult to ignore that idea. Usually, demons feed stuff into our minds for few hours and then leave us alone to see our reactions to their pressure for a long time. Or if they still stay around me, they usually help me, and they maintain a certain distance from me.

تظل قدرة أوقوة أوشدة،أوطاقة الروح دائما هي نفسها، فهي لا تنقص ولا تزداد بمرور الوقت. فقط جسمنا المادي/ عقلنا هو الذي تتغيرأوضاعه بالصغر أو الكبر، ولكن الروح لا تغير قوتها أو طاقتها.الأرواح لا تكبر أو تصغر في العمر. الأرواح تبقي علي نفس الحالة ووفقاً لترتيب إلهي معين، والأرواح تمد الأجسام المختلفة بالطاقة فقط أو تبقيها علي قيد الحياة، وفقاً لجدولهم. تنتقل الروح إلي جسم آخر لإمداده بالطاقة أو يبقيه علي قيد الحياة الجسم الذي كان ميتاً.

كما ناقشت سابقاً أن جسدنا المادي أو العقل هو المسؤول عن أعمالنا الجيدة أو السيئة، و الأرواح لا علاقة لها بذلك. منح الله الإرادة الحرة والتعليمات الواضحة الخاصة بالخير و الشر لعقلنا في شكل الكتب المقدسة، الأنبياء المقدسون، أو ديننا. إذا كان هناك يوم القيامة لتقرير نتيجة أفعالنا الجيدة أو السيئة في هذا العالم أثناء وجودنا فيه، ليتم تقرير ما إذا كنا سنذهب إلالجنة أم أننا نستحق الجحيم، وسوف يتم إعادة تنشيط جثثنا وسيتم بث الروح الجديدة لجثثنا لإحيائنا، بالنسبة لي العود للحياة هو لمواجهة يوم القيامة، و ما يعقبه من نتيجة في شكل الجنة أو الجحيم.هذا ليس ضروريا، سوف نحصل على نفس الروح لتنشيط جسمنا أو لتجعلنا على قيد الحياة مرة أخرى.أثناء حياتنا بعد الموت. إما في الجنة أو في الجحيم.

اذا كان هناك من يفكركيف سوف نعود على قيد الحياة مرة أخرى لابعد موتنا. لا تقلق. هذا الأمر يرجع إلي الله. وسوف يقوم الله بإعادة تنشيط أجسادنا، كما فعل الله ذلك في المرة الأولى، أو ببساطة سوف نولد من جديد كما ولدنا أول مرة في هذا العالم،. ولكن في الحياة الثانية، سوف تكون في أجسامنا أرواح جديدة، لنولد من جديد ليوم القيامة، وأنا ليس لدي أية معلومات حتى الآن في أي مرحلة من العمر، سوف نكون. عندما نولد من جديد، أنا لا أعرف، سوف نكون أطفالاً أم صغاراً أم كبارا .

SEE & CONTROL DEMONS & PAIN

Usually, everyone has a demon or demons around or inside them, but I do not have any inside my body most of the time. Nobody can stop demons from going inside our bodies. They go inside my body but do not stay there for long. I can remove demons from bodies every day, but they quickly possess another. Demons are in and out of our bodies all the time, but in case of normal people, they have few permanent demons. So what I do, I just use any demon around any person in any part of the world, instead of keeping few permanent demons around me for this purpose. This crazy telepathy makes everything very easy for me. I just reach them, introduce myself, and make threats to them to move away from that person if they will not listen to me. Most of the time, it is enough for them and they listen. Sometimes they visit me before they start obeying me, maybe just to check who that crazy person is. Demons can possess a body completely and can use that body physically against anyone. Demons are physical bodies, but they are not solid like us. Their physical bodies are like air, but they are not plain air. Their powers are extraordinary. Some people think demons are a special kind of gas that can be used as an energy source. They are completely wrong about that. Flying demons are totally harmless. They cannot hurt anyone. They cannot even hypnotize anyone. Their powers start working only when they penetrate a body. Once they come inside a body, they are able to expand themselves. If they are covering the bottom part of a body, they cannot hypnotize and control a mind from there. A demon needs to be around the head, specifically our left ear, to hypnotize and control the mind.

رضوان قرشي

إن الشخص أو نحن سنولد من جديد في العمر الذي كنا فيه في حياتنا الأولى في العالم. لا نعرف حتى الآن.

الآن بإختصار، لا توجد أشباح لجثث الأشخاص الذين ماتو أو الأرواح. إنهم الجن فقط الذين يختصون بأجسام هؤلاء الناس، أو الجن الذين من حولنا، هم الذين يحدثون كل الدراما الشبح هذه، لتخويفنا ومضايقتنا. في الحياة الثانية والدائمة الحياة التي تكون بعد الموت، بعد هذه الحياة المؤقتة والعالم، وسيتم إعادة تنشيط أجسامنا إما بنفس الروح، أو ربما بروح جديدة لتعطينا الحياة مرة أخرى. والله سيهب لنا روحاً جديدةً أو ربما نفس الروح الدائمة لإبقائنا على قيد الحياة إلى الأبد، ولكن لا نعرف عن الحياة دائمة بعد يوم القيامة، هل سيكون في الجنة أم في الجحيم؟

الروح ليست سوى مجموعة من التعليمات، و ليس لديها أي أحاسيس أو مشاعر حب أو كره. و لا ليس لديها أي ذاكرة لتذكر من الذين كانوا قد خدموهم بالفعل، أو من الذين يخدمونهم الآن، و من الذين كانوا سيخدمونهم في المستقبل. هذا شائع جداً، خصوصا بين الأطفال في الليالي المظلمة، عندما نرى حركات غير عادية في الغابات أو الأشجار. هذه هي قوة الجن.

الجن يستطيعون أن يظهروا لنا أجسام تتحرك مثل الأشباح الموجودة في الأشجار وفي أفنيتنا الخلفية المظلمة أو في المناطق الفارغة و مظلمة في منزلنا. إن الجن يلقون في عقلنا الأفكار المخيفة، لجعلنا نخاف أ. الشياطين إطعام كثر و أكثر. الجن دائماً ما يلقون الأفكار المخيفة في عقولنا مثل شخص يتحدث خلفلنا في الظلام. أحيانا يظهر لنا الجن في الظلام أجسام قبيحة المنظهر مثل أشباح تتحرك في غرفنا المظلمة أو خارجها قرب النوافذ لتخويفنا.

78

During the process of hypnotism by demons, we usually have a big argument inside the mind; the stronger the person, the stronger the resistance to the demon's influence. Demons need to be very close to us, especially near our left ear, to hypnotize us. Demons cannot hypnotize us from a remote area by using telepathy. Once medical science invents a machine that can affect demons and diseases, doctors will be able to remove or pull these negative energies out of our bodies. When no demons are around us, they will have little control over our activities and behaviors.

The future of our health is very bright. Medical science needs to consider my theories for research. After that, it will not take long to invent the proper machines for treatments. We already have modern medication to heal the damages.

Like animals or even demons, spirits do not have any language to communicate with us or any other body or any demon or pain or disease. Spirits cannot be controlled or can communicate with spirits. Spirits are nothing, just an order of God. If anything possibly can interact with spirits if with the order of God are only angels. Nobody else can interact or communicate with spirits. Again spirits are only like a power supply to a particular body for a certain specified true as scheduled by the God. All the dead bodies are same. A dead body of a human or an animal or insect or any bird, they are all same after death. The way a lot of animals/birds/insects die every day in bad or extremely bad condition, but we never see any ghosts hanging around our houses. Or on street of any animal or bird or insect. Only demons around us after the death of a particular person show us through hypnotism the ghosts of those peoples.

الجن يغذون عقولنا بعض الأفكار بأن الأشباح سوف تظهر أمامنا فجأة ، و تقوم بدفعنا أوالإمساك بنا، أو إلحاق الضرر بنا أو فعل أي شيء مخيف بنا بدنياً لهذا لابد أن تكون واثقاً من أن الجن لا يمكنهم تغيير أنفسهم إلى الجسد المادي، و كذلك لا يستطيعون تغيير أنفسهم إلى شبح غاضب أوإلي ساحرة. يستطيع الجن أن يظهروا لك أشباح قبيحة مختلفة ومخيفة فقط بواسطة تنويمك مغناطيسياً ولكن ثق بي لن يكون هناك أي شيء فعلي،أوأي جسد مادي للشبح. الجن حقيقة واقعة، ولكن لا يمكنهم التحول أن إلى شبح مادي أو ساحرة مادية. حتى لو كنت ترى شبح قبيح ما أمامك، لا تشعر بالخوف من ذلك الشبح. هذا كله دراما من التنويم المغناطيسي يقوم بها الجن.وتذكر أن الجن غير قادرين على السيطرة على الجو لعمل ظلال من الأشباح أو الساحرات في الهواء أو في الأشجار أو في الجو. يستطيع الجن إظهار صورهذه الأشباح أو الساحرات فقط من خلال التحكم في عقولنا، فقط عن طريق إستخدام التنويم المغناطيسي.

أيا كان ما نراه من شبح مخيف في الظلام في كل مكان ليس موجوداً بالخارج؛ يأتي ذلك كله من الجن، وهم يستخدمون عقولنا لإظهار تلك الصورلنا لتخويفنا. كن واثقاً أن تلك الصور هي نتيجة إستخدام الجن لقوي التنويم المغناطيسي فقط ليضايقوننا. لا توجد قوة بدنية في صور تلك الأشباح، وهي غير قادرة علي إيذاءك أو قتلك. كلما زاد شعورك بالخوف، كلما زادت رؤيتك لصور تلك الأشباح.

لابد أن ترفض كل تلك الأفكار وصور الأشباح وتصرف بثقة أكثر وأكثر وحاول السيطرة أكثر وأكثر علي عقلك لهزيمة هذا سهلاً، لكنه ليس مستحيلاً. الشيء الوحيد الذي يمكن ان يفعله الجن ربما هو الإستحواذ علي جسمك وعقلك وجعلك تفعل ما يريدون منك القيام به.

Now it is in our hand, for how long we want to keep us in the hand of these demons and let them keep play with us to keep us scared, harassed at the time. Spirits are not responsible for our good or bad deeds. Whatever good or bad deeds we do, our physical body and brain are totally responsible for that. Spirits are only responsible for energizing our physical bodies to keep us alive. Whatever we do well or bad, things or deeds, spirits are not responsible for that.

The capacity, strength, intensity, or power or energy of spirits always stays same. The energy or strength of spirits do not decrease or increase with time. Only our physical body/brain changes their conditions to young or old, but spirits do not change their strength or energy. Spirits do not go older or younger. Spirits stay in same condition and as per assigned schedule from God, spirits just energies or keep alive different bodies according to their schedule. Spirits switch or move to next assigned body to energies or bring to life once last or ex-body or dead.

As I discussed that our physical body or brains is responsible for our good or bad deeds spirits have nothing to do with that. Our mind is granted a free will from God with clear instructions of Good and bad in shape of holy books, holy prophets, or our religion. If there will be a judgment day to decide the result of our good or bad deeds in this world during our stay in this world, to decide whether we will go to heaven or we deserve hell, our dead bodies will go be re energized our dead bodies, new spirits, will be assigned to us to me come alive again to face the judgment day and the consequences after judgment day in or result shape of heaven or hell.

بنفس الطريقة،يستطيع الجن أن يستحوذوا علي جسم أي إنسان آخر أو حيوان ويجعلوه يفعل ما يريدون منهم أن يفعلوه.

يستطيع الجن أن يضروك أو يؤلموك جسديا، عندما يستحوذون علي جسمك. عندما يوجد الجن داخل جسمك ، يستطيع قتل أي شخص أو يتسبب في إحداث أي نوع من الألم فقط عندما يكون داخل هذا. لكن لابد أن نكون واثقاً. إذا أظهرلك الجن بعض صور الأشباح أو الساحرات في الظلام، فإن هذه الأشياء تكون وهمية. لا توجد أي قوة بدنية. تلك الأشباح والساحرات تخوفك فقط، ولكنها لا يمكن أن تؤذيك جسدياً. تذكر أن صور الأشباح تلك أو الساحرات لا يأتون من عقل شخص آخر، إنما يأتون من عقلك فقط. يجب أن تظهر المزيد من الثقة ورفض سيطرة هذا الجن، ولن يكون هناك أي شبح قبيح أوساحرات بعد الآن، أنا أعلم، هذا لا شيء بالنسبة لي. لا يستطيع أي جني السيطرة علي، لكن في حالتك، أنت فقط تستطيع أن تساعد نفسك. سوف أعطي تعليمات واضحة بشأن كيفية التخلص من الجني الموجود في جسمك أو في محيطك، في كتابي في وقت لاحق. إتبع تعليماتي وقم بها كل يوم، و سوف تكون حياتك سهلة وطبيعية جداً .

ليس هناك طريقة لإبعاد الجن عنا طوال الوقت، بغض النظر عن مدي قوتنا. ولكن اسمحوا لي أن اقول لكم، فقط فكري في هذا، الآن يمكننا أن نقاتل أو نقاوم الجن أو نترك قتالهم، واسمحوا لي ان اقول لكم ما هو العيب في ذلك. كلما إستحوذ الجن علي الجسم والعقل، الأمر يحتاج إلى بعض الوقت ليكون للسيطرة على هذا الشخص أكثر وأكثر. حتى إذا كنت قررت عدم محاربة هؤلاء الجن كل يوم باستمرار، ستزيد سيطرة جني واحد أو أكثر عليك وعلى عقلك. هذه السيطرة على الزيادة الجن تزداد يوماً بعد يوم، لذلك بدلا من إعطاء عقلك لسيطرة هذا الجن، وتفقد الكثير و الكثير كل يوم، من الأفضل مواصلة القتال معهم، والتخلص منهم كل يوم و كل ساعة .

This is not necessary, we will get the same spirit to get energize our body or make us alive again. During our life after death. Either in heaven or hell. If someone is thinking, how, we will get alive again once we will be dead. Don't worry about it. This is the responsibility of God. And God will reenergize our bodies the way God energizes our bodies the first time or simply we will be born again the way we born first time in this world. But in second life when our bodies will be reassigned new spirits, to reborn us for the judgment day, I do not have any feed yet, in which age cycle, we will be. When we will be reborn, I do not know, we will be a kid or young or old. A person or we will reborn in the age whatever we have in our first life in the world. Do not know yet.

Now shortcut, there is no ghost or dead human bodies or spirits. Only demons from those people of bodies or demons around us create all this ghost drama to scare and harass us. In second and permanent life of death from this temporary life and world, our bodies will be reenergized with either same spirits or maybe new spirits to give us life again. God will assign a new or maybe same spirit permanently to us to keep us alive forever, but no idea order that permanent life after judgment day will be in heaven or hell?

Spirits are only a set of instructions. Spirits do not have any emotions or like or dislike feelings. Spirits do not carry any memory to remember to whom they already served, to whom they are serving right now, and to whom they will serve in the future. This is very common especially among kids when in dark nights we see unusual movements in the woods or trees. This is the power of demons.

رؤية الجن و الآلام السيطرة عليها

أنا أعلم، بمجرد أن يذهب الجن القديم، و سيحاول الجن الجدد زيادة السيطرة عليك، لذلك يجب التخلص منهم.. بنفس الطريقة يجب الإستمرار في قتال هذا الجن كل يوم. وبهذه الطريقة يأتي الجن ويذهبوا، ولكنهم لن تكون قادرة على السيطرة عليك بقدر كبير، نظرا لقلة الوقت المتاح لتواجدهم حولك، فإذالم يكن الإنسان شريراً أو شيطاناً، فهذا هو المصدر الخارجي الوحيد لجعل شخص ما شريراً أو شيطاناً. يجب أن تسيطر علي نفسك، و تبقي الجن بعيداً عنك، وهكذا لن يكون هناك شر أو شيطان في أي مكان، إن هذا ممكناً، لكنه صعب إلي حد ما، لكن إستمر في المحاولة. لذلك بإختصار، يمكن لجني واحد ولكنه دائم، أن يحول حياتك إلي جحيم أكثر صعوبةً وأشد جنوناً، لهذا يجب أن تجنبهم عيداً عن عقلك/رأسك طوال الوقت.

الأمراض صيادية وطفيلية. فإذا حدث في عائلة واحدة أن شخص واحد تألم ومات بسبب نوبة قلبية أو سرطان أو غيره أو أي مرض خطير. تلك الآلام والمرض لا تذهب بعيداً جداً بعد أن تقتل هذا الشخص.إن الآلام هي الخطوة الأولى التي تتلف الجسم. فبمجرد يموت شخص في العائلة، تخرج الآلام فوراً من هذه الجثة،لأن الجن و الآلام لا تعيش و تبقي في الجثة الهامدة.لذلك فبمجرد أن يموت شخص في عائلة ما، يتحرك الألم إلى أقرب شخص متاح. عادة ما يكون هذا الشخص التالي ليس جاراً و ليس الشخص الأقرب. ربما كنت تريد معرفة السبب؟ السبب في ذلك هو التعاون المتبادل بين الآلام والأمراض، فهي لا تترك الجثة تماماً قد يستغرق ذلك بعض الوقت، لكن عادة ما تعود تلك الأمراض إلى نفس البيت أو نفس العائلة، بعد أن تنتهي من جثة الميت تماما يعود المرض لجسم جديد، و يشترك مع الآلام في إيذاء و أكل الجسم الجديد وفي خلال تلك الفترة تستهدف الآلام والأمراض نفس العائلة الواحد تلو الآخر عادةً.

Demons show us moving bodies like ghosts in trees and our dark backyards or in vacant and dark areas of our house. Other than these demons create or feed scary thought also in our mind to make us more and more scared. Demons always feed scary thoughts to our minds like someone is talking behind us in the dark. Sometimes demons show us dark ugly-looking bodies like ghosts moving in our dark rooms or outside by the windows to scare us. Demons feed thoughts in our minds that suddenly some ghost will appear in front of us and push us or catch us or hurt us or do something scary physically. So be confident about it; for sure demons cannot change themselves to a physical body. Demons cannot change themselves to an angry ghost or witch. Demons can show you different scary and ugly ghosts only by hypnotizing you. But trust me there will not be anything in real, on any physical body like a ghost. Demons are reality, but demons cannot convert themselves into a physical ghost or witch. Even if you are seeing some ugly ghost in front of you, do not get scared of that ghost. This is all hypnotism drama from demons. And remember, demons are not capable of controlling the atmosphere to create shades of ghosts or witches in the air or in the trees or in the atmosphere. Demons are only capable of creating these images of ghosts or witches by controlling our minds, only by the use of hypnotism. Whatever scary ghost we see in dark everywhere is not out there; it is all coming from demons, and demons are using our minds to create those images and show us to scare us. Be confident; those are only images in a result of use of hypnotism powers from demons to harass us. There is no physical strength in those images of ghosts. Those images of ghosts are not capable of hurting or killing you. More you will get scared, more you will see those ghost images.

لذا كن حذراً؛ ولا تسمح لهم بأن يصيبوكم الواحدا تلو الآخر. قم بإستخدام إجراءات العلاج الخاصة بي،و قم بإيذاء هذه الأمراض قبل أن تضرك.

لا يمكن للشخص العادي معرفة ما إذا كان الجن موجوداً أم لا في وقت معين. أنا أكد لكم أن كل بيت مليئ بالجن. لكن في بعض الأحيان لا يكون الجن قريبين منا للغاية، عندما نريد التواصل معهم. ليس لدي هذه المشكلة، ولكني أتحدث عنك. السبب في ذلك هو أنك عندما ترغب في التعامل أو التواصل مع الجن، يجب أن تكون وثقاً جداً من أن هناك جني واحد أو أكثر موجودون حولك ويستمعوا لك في هذا الوقت بالذات.

للتأكد من وجود الجن حولك في هذا الوقت بالذات، فإنك تحتاج إلى قتل بعض الحشرات من حولك. لأني أنا متأكد بنسبة 100 % أنه سيكون هناك جن من حولك إذا قتلت عنكبوت أو أكثر أوالصراصير، أو سحالي. وإذا كنت لا تريد قتل الحشرات، قم بتخويف قطة من حولك فقط ؛ بعد عدة مرات كل الجن الوجودون بالقطط سوف تخرج وتقفز عليك. لذلك هذه وسيلة لجمع بعض الجن حولك.

سألني شخص ما إذا كان من الممكن السيطرة على جني أو أكثر،و بدلا من السيطرة، هل من الممكن هناك جعل الجن أصدقاء بطريقة أو بأخرى، بعد ذلك، إذا طلب الشخص من الجن القيام ببعض الاشياء، في المقايل، هل سيطلب هذا الجن من الشخص فعل شيئ ما؟ أول شيء، مجرد أن يصبح الجن أصدقاء لك، سوف يستمعون لك، وسوف يحاولون فعل أي شيء من أجلك، كل ما هو ممكن في حدود سلطاتهم. إلي إي مدي يستطيع الجن فعل أشياء من أجلنا، و ما هي الإحتمالات الجيدة و السيئة ؟، وسأذكرذلك في مكان ما في هذا الكتاب في وقت لاحق.

Rizwan Qureshi	رؤية الجن و الآلام السيطرة عليها

Rejects all those thoughts and images of ghost and act more and more confident and try to have more and more control of your mind to defeat these demons. It is not easy, but it is not impossible.

The only thing demons could possibly do is possess your body and mind and make you do whatever they want you to do. Same way, demons cans possess anybody of any other human or animal and make them do whatever they want them to do.

Demons can damage or hurt you physically when they possess your body. When a demon is inside your body demons can kill anybody or give any kind of pain or gangers only when inside that body. But be confident. If demons are showing you some images of ghosts or witches in the dark, those ghosts and witches are imaginary. Without any physical strength. Those ghosts and witches only scare you, but they cannot hurt you physically. Remember, those images of ghosts or witches are not coming from someone else's mind; those images of ghost come from your mind only. You show more confidence and reject the control of those demons; there will be no ugly ghost or witches anymore, I know; it is nothing for me. No demon can control me. But in your case, only you can help yourself. In my book later on I will give clear instructions on how to get rid of a demon from your body and from your surroundings; follow my instructions every day and do it every day. Your life will be very easy and very normal. There is no way we can keep demons away from us all the time, regardless of whatever powers we got. But let me tell of you just think that, now we can fight or resist demons and quit fighting against them, let me tell you what is disadvantage of that.

شيئ ما يتعلق بهذا السؤال، وهو هل سيطلب منا الجن فعل شيء أم لا؟ الجواب بسيط، وهو أن الجن منقلون تماماً بقوى خارقة للطبيعة، فهم يمتلكون قوة التنويم المغناطيسي. الجن لا يعتمدون علينا بأي حال من الأحوال، . ليس هناك شيء لا يستطيعون لحصول عليه بأنفسهم. ذلك لذلك فالجواب هوأنه بسبب قدراتهم الخارقة والتنويم المغناطيسي ، يمكنهم الحصول على أي شيء منا، و يمكن جعلنا نفعل أي شيء لهم دون أن يطلبوا منا ذلك، فقط عن طريق إستخدام قواهم.

لذلك لا تقلق بشأن ذلك، فالجن لا يطلبون منك أي شيء، الجن لا يطلبون، إنما يأخذون فقط ما يريدون. إنهم يقومون بما يريدونه منا أو من أي شخص آخر. ويمكنهم إجبار أي شخص القيام بأي شيء يريدونه بسهولة جداً.يعيش الجن في مجموعة في مكان معين. إنهم لا يسافرون معنا. عادة يبقى جني واحد، من مجموعة الجن، حولنا أو يسافر معنا. لدينا جن مختلفين في منزلنا. لدينا جن مختلفون في الكراسي الخلفية لسياراتنا و في مكاتبنا.

عادة لا يسمح الجن للآخرين من الجن بالمجيء إلى أراضيها، ما لم يكن لديها تفاهم جيد جداً بينهم. تعامل الشخص العادي مع جن مختلفين في أماكن مختلفة. لا شك أن كلما زادنت قوة الجن، كلما زادت سيطرتهم وهم يستحوذون على جسمنا معظم الوقت . يستحوذ بقية الجن على أجسامنا بينما يكون البعض الآخر مشغولاً في مكان ما أو يستريحون في مجموعتهم. هذا صحيح بالنسبة للجن الباقين حولنا. يعيش القليل من الجن داخل أجسامنا. إنهم يسافرون معنا معظم الوقت أينما ذهبنا.

SEE & CONTROL DEMONS & PAIN

Whenever demons possess a body and mind, it takes some time to have more and more control of that person. So if you decide not to fight against those demons every day constantly, one or few demons will have more and more control on you and your mind. This control of demons increase more and more day by day. So instead of giving permanent controls of your mind to these demons and lose more and more every day, it is better to keep fighting with them and get rid of them every day every hour.

I know once old demons leave, new demons will try to increase control of you; you should get rid of them. Same way keeps fighting with these demons every day. This way demons will come and go, but they will not be able to have too much control on you due to less available time around you if human is not an evil or devil then this is the only external source of making someone evil or devil. Control yourself and keep them away from yourself. There will be no evil or devil anywhere. Practically possible but a little bit difficult, keep trying. So shortcut, once single but permanent demon can make your life more hell more difficult and crazier. So avoid it and keep them moving out of your mind/head all the time.

Diseases are hunters and parasites. In one family if one person suffered and died due to heart attack or any cancer or any other serious disease. Those pains and disease after killing that person do not go too far. Pains are the first step to damage a body. Once a person dies in a family, pains immediately come out of that dead body because demons and pains do not live and stay on a dead body. So once a person in a family dies, pain moves to the nearest available person.

علي حد علمي المحدودة فإنني أعلم أن الجن أو الألم مشابهان للتركيبة الكهرومغناطيسية. وهو عالم غير مرئي، عملياً لا يستطيع جسم أي إنسان أو حيوان، أو حشرات المرور خلال خط هاتفي. فعندما يكون شخص ما علي خط الهاتف الآخر، بغض النظر عن مدي بعد المسافة، ميلاً واحداً بعيداً عنا أو عدة آلاف من الأميال، بستطيع الجن و الآلام التنقل ذهاباً وإياباً إلي خط الهاتف الآخر، و يقوما إما بإختراق جسم الشخص الموجود علي الخط الآخر للهاتف، أو ينتقلا في الجو المحيط به، أو إذا لم يكن ذلك الشخص واضعاً سماعة الهاتق في أذنه.، لذلك أي شخص ينتمي إلي هذا العالم المرئي لا يمكنه التنقل ذهاباً وإياباً من خلال الهاتف، لكن الجن و الآلام يمكنهم ذلك. بنفس الطريقة، يمدد الجن الصغير جداً نفسه، عندما يكونون في الجو المفتوح، و ذلك لإختراق جسم الإنسان، أو أي جسم آخر للإستحواذ عليه. مهما كان صغر ا حجم هذا الجن، فهم ينشرون أو يمددون أنفسهم لتغطية الجسم كله أوالإستحواذ عليه لتحقيق السيطرة عليه. ماذا ستقول العلوم الطبية والحديثة في هذا الموضوع، إذا لم يعتقد شخص ما، في هذه النقطة ، بأن الجن يمكنهم التنقل من خلال خط الهاتف، أو إعتقد حتي أن الجن لا يمكنهم نشر أو تمديد أنفسهم أثناء عملية الإستحواذ علي الإنسان أو علي أي جسم آخر؟. لا تضيع الوقت، قم بعمل تجربة كي تقنع نفسك وبقية العالم، حتى نتمكن من الإنتقال إلى الخطوة التالية.

فإذا كانت الجن و الآلام مصنوعين من أحد أنواع التركيبة الكهرومغناطيسية، هذا يعني أنني قادر على رؤية تلك التركيبات الكهرومغناطيسية، أي الجن والآلام. ليس علي الصراع من أجل رؤية الجن والآلام و هما يطيران في كل مكان. ليس لدي الجن أي سيطرة على هذا، إنني أراها طوال الوقت. لكن ليس لدي أي سيطرة علي نفسي أو علي محيطي لرؤية الملائكة.

84

Usually that next person is not a neighbor of or not a nearest person. You may want to know why? Reason is mutual cooperation between pains and diseases do not leave even dead body completely. It may take some time. But usually those diseases come back to same house or same family after they are done completely with the dead body. During the time when the disease comes back to new body and joins the pains and starts hurting and eating new body. Usually these pains and diseases target the same family one by one. So be careful; do not allow them to hurt you one by one. Use my cure procedures and hurt these diseases before they hurt you.

A normal person cannot figure out whether a demon is present or not at a particular time. I am giving you assurance that every house is full of demons. But sometimes demons are not available very close to us, when we want to communicate with them. I do not have this problem, but I am talking about you. Reason is when you want to deal or communicate with a demon; you need to be very confident that one or more demons are present around you and listening to you at that particular time.

So to make sure some demons are around you at that particular time, you need to kill some insects around you. For I am 100 percent sure you will have a demon around you if you kill a spider or more spiders, cockroaches, or lizards. If you do not want to kill insects then just scare a cat around you; several times all demons from cats will come out and jump on you. So this is a way to gather some demons around you.

لا أستطيع رؤية الملائكة كلما أردت أن أراهم، ولا أستطيع التواصل معهم. ليس لدي أي طريقة للوصول إلى الملائكة. لكني أستطيع ريتهم وقتما أرادوا لي أن أراهم. ولكني ما زلت لا أستطيع التواصل معهم. ولا أستطيع السيطرة عليهم مطلقاً. في السنوات العشر الماضية رأيت الملائكة فقط خمس أو ست مرات فقط لبضع ثوان من حولي، هذا كل شيء. لكني أستطيع أن أتحكم في رؤية الجن والألم، وأنا قادر تماماً وكلياً علي أن أراهم، و أشعر بهم، والتواصل معهم، بغض النظر عما إذا كانت أمامي أو في جزء من العالم. لذلك كم من الوقت سيستغرق العلوم الحديثة لإكتشاف كل ما لديهم من نظريات علمية؟

يعلم الله كم هو صعب بالنسبة لي الإفصاح عن كل هذه المعلومات و الكتابة عنها، ولكن نأمل أيضا أن كل هذا النضال فتح أبواب جديدة للعلوم الحديثة حتى يتمكنوا من مساعدة البشرية أكثر وأكثر. بالنسبة للملائكة، وإما أنني ليس لدي إمكانية لرؤيتهم، أو ربما هم ليسوا حولي، ولكن بالتأكيد، ليس لدي أي فكرة، ولا رؤية، ولا إحساس لرؤية أو التواصل مع الملائكة. الملائكة، كما رأيتهم، حجمهم مساو لجني عادي صغير. لكن الملائكة مشابه للضوء الذهبي للنجوم البراقة بشكل واضح جداً. و تواجدوا حولي لبضع ثوان فقط ، هذا كل شيء. سيكون من الصعب للغاية الكشف عن حالتي أو حالة، عندما كنت قادرا على رؤية هؤلاء الملائكة. هذا كل ما أعرفه عن الملائكة. وأنا متأكد أن الكثير منا قد يكون بالفعل رأوا الملائكة أو ربما سوف يروها الملائكة، من الجائز أن يروها يوماً ما. ليس لدي أي شيء آخر عن الملائكة، وهذا هو كل ما يمكنني أن أقول لكم عنهم وكيف يبدو شكلهم. هذا مجرد جزء من تجربة حاولت القيام بها عدة مرات. أنا لم أقم بإجراء أي تجارب على شخص حالته جيدةأو شخص طبيعي . أحيانا أختارأن أعرفهم فقط ، إنني أقوم بإجراء بعض التجارب أيضاً أثناء معرفتي بهم..

SEE & CONTROL DEMONS & PAIN

Someone asked me if someone gets a control of a demon or more than one demon or instead of control, if someone make a demon friend somehow, after this, if that person asks his demon or demons to do some stuff, in reply, do demons demand something from that person? First thing, once demons become your friend, they will listen to you and will try to do anything for you, whatever is possible under their powers. How much they can do for us and what is good and bad possibilities are there, I will describe somewhere in this book later on.

As far as this question, if in response, demons demand something from us or no? Simple answer is demons are fully loaded with supernatural powers. Demons have the power of hypnotism. Demons, in any way, are not dependent on us. There is nothing they cannot get by themselves. So answer is due to their supernatural powers and hypnotism demons can get anything from us, and demons can make us do anything for them without asking us just by using their powers.

So do not worry about it that demons will demand anything from you. Demons do not ask; they just take it; they just do it whatever they want from us or from anybody else. Demons can compel anyone do anything they want very easily. Demons live in a group in a particular place. Demons do not travel with us. Usually from whole group, only one demon stays around us or travels with us. We have different demons in our house. We have different demons in backseats of our cars we have different demons in our offices.

رضوان قرشی

قبل بضعة أشهر إخترت واحد من شخصيات إحدى القنوات التلفزيونية لأعرف معلومات عنه. في الخطوة الأولى، أرسلت عدد من الجن إلى الرجل، كي يزيدوا حدة سلوكه، أنا آسف؛ لقد نسيت أن أقول لكم أن هذا الرجل كان يتصرف بالفعل بشكل عدواني ومجنون. أثناء برنامجه الحواري. من هذه التجربة، تعلمت من هذه التجربة أنه إذا كان شخص ما يتصرف بشكل مجنون وعدواني، من السهل جداً جعله يكون أكثرعدوانية وجنوناً. بالمقارنة بهذه الأنواع من الناس، إذا إخترنا شخص ما أقل تطرفا أو غير متطرف، إما أن يكون من الصعب جعلهم يتصرفون بعدوانية وجنون بشدة، أو أن الأمر سيستغرق بعض الوقت لجعلهم يتصرفون بعدوانية وجنون بشدة.

أنا لا أقول أنه هذا ليس من ممكناً، في الواقع كل شيء ممكن، ولكن لماذا يتم إيذاء شخص ما عندما يكون طيباً؟. على أي حال، أنا أصف هذه التجربة، وكيف أكبر أو أزيد السلوك العدواني لشخص يتصرف بجنون. بالفعل في الخطوة الأولى، أرسل سبعة من الجن الواحدا تلو الآخرإلى مضيف في برنامج حواري أو الشخصية التلفزيونة لتضخيم و تكبير تطرفه، و جنونه، و سلوكه العدواني، لقد كانت تجربة جيدة. لقد إستطاع الجن تزويد حدة تطرفه، ولكنهم لم يقضوا الوقت الكافي حول هذا الشخص. و السبب وراء ذلك هو أن الجن الخاص بي كان يجب أن يقاتلوا الجن الذين كانوا بالفعل حول هذا الشخص. انتظرت النتائج لمدة سبعة أيام، وبعد سبعة أيام، أدركت أنه شيئ صعب و يستغرق وقتاً طويلاً. وبهذه الطريقة، بلا سبب، كان يجب علي مجموعتين من الجن أن يحاربوا مع بعضهم البعض ويقتلون بعضهم بعضا. لقد إنتظرت بضعة أيام، وأخيرا، حتى لو لم أكن راغباً ومستعداً للقيام بذلك ولكنني قمت بذلك، لممارسة وإستكمال تجربتي.

Usually demons do not allow other demons to come to their territory, until unless all of these demons have very good understanding with each other. A normal person deal with different demons at different places. No doubt, more powerful demons are more dominant and they possess our body most of the time. Rests of the demons possess our body when others are busy somewhere or resting in their group. This is true about demons stay around us. Few demons live inside our body. They travel with us most of the time wherever we go.

As much I learn from my limited knowledge is a demon or a pain something similar to electromagnetic structure. Invisible word, practically no human body, animal, or insects can travel through telephone line. Someone (anything, human) is at the second end of the phone line, regardless, one mile away from us or several thousand miles away from us, demons and pains travel back and forth on back ends of the phone line either penetrate in their bodies or if end users are not keeping phone on their ear, then these demons and pains move into the surrounding atmosphere. So anybody who belongs from this visible world cannot travel back and forth through a phone line, but demons and pain can. Same ways, very small demons, when they are in open atmosphere, expand themselves once they penetrate in a human or any other body to possess that body. Very small in size that demon, how come, spread or expands them to cover or possesses to have control of whole body. So what medical and modern science will say, of question, if at this point someone even think that demons cannot travel through phone line. Or think even that demons cannot spread or expend themselves during the process of possess in a human or other body. Do not waste time; do experiment to convince yourself and rest of the world. So we can move on to next step.

لقد قمت بإجراء إتصال توارد خواطر، مباشرة مع الجن المرتبطين بذلك الشخص. أولاً، أقنعت هؤلاء الجن بألا يشعروا بعدم الأمان بسبب إتصالي بهم عن بعد ثانياً أقنعتهم بأنه لا داعي للهرب من هذا الشخص. لقد طلبت منهم عدة مرات ألا يأتوا إلي و أن يبقوا مع هذا الشخص. لقد أمهلتهم بضعة ساعات.لكن على أي حال بعد ساعات قليلة، وأجريت إتصال توارد خواطر مع هؤلاء الجن من جديد وأعطيتهم تعليمات قليلة. لمزيد من الإطمئنان، إتصلت بهم ثلاث مرات في الأيام الثلاثة التالية، وأعطيتهم نفس التعليمات. و بعد أيام قليلة تعلمت أن الذهاب مباشرة إلى الجن المتواجون حول شخص ما وإعطائهم بعض التعليمات. بدلا من إرسال جن جدد إلى شخص ما، أسهل ومباشر أكثر. يكون الجن الموجودون بالفعل حول شخص ما يتصلون و يسيطرون بشكل كامل علي هذا الشخص بالذات، فبدلاً من إرسال فريق جديد من الجن لشخص ما، الأفضل والأسهل هو استخدام الجن الذين يختصوا به لإنجاز مهمة خاصة. فإذا كنت لا تريد لأي شخص أن يزيد حدة مزاجك الخاص وتصرفاتك المتطرفة، يجدر بك التحكم بشكل أفضل في أعصابك. تذكر دائماً،أن حتى الأشخاص العصيون ،و الهادئ، والأكثر تحملاً وصبراً، يكون الجن أقل تأثيراً عليهم. إن الجن لا يستطيعون التحكم بسهولة بهذه الأنواع من الناس. كلما تصرفت بعدوانية و جنون و عصبية، كلما زادت سيطرة الجن عليك.

لن تعلم إذا كان هناك شخص ما يقوم ببعض التجارب عليك.، لذلك يجب عليك السيطرة على عقلك، ورفض المزاج السلبي والسيئ دائماً .قم بفعل أفضل ما لديك، لا تؤذي مشاعر الآخرين فقط بإستخدام لسانك لنطق ألفاظ بذيئة. كن حذرا قبل إغضاب شخص ما، فأنت لا تعلم من هو الذي تغضبه وماذا يمكن أن يفعل.تكون تجارب الجن هذه عادة مؤقتة. ولكن لا تقم بتحدي أي جني.يستطيع هؤلاء الجن إفساد حياة أي شخص في وقت قصير جداً على المدى الطويل. لذا كن حذرا عندما تتحداهم..لا أستطيع أن أقوم بأي تجارب على شخص مجهول أو غير موجود.

So if demons and pains are made of some kind of electromagnetic structure, this means I am capable of seeing those electromagnetic structures, i.e., demons and pains. I do not have to struggle to see demons and pains flying everywhere. Demons do not have any control on this. I see them all the time. But I do not have any control on myself or surrounding to see angels.

I cannot see angels whenever I want to see them. I cannot communicate with angels. I do not have any access to angels. But I can see angels whenever they want me to see them. But still no communication with them. And no control on them at all. In the last ten years I have seen angels only five or six times just for few seconds around me, that's all. But demons and pain, I am fully and totally in good command to see them, sense them, and communicate with them, regardless of whether they are in front of me or in part of the world. So how long will it take for modern science to discover all their theories scientifically?

I hope God knows how difficult it is for me to expose and write all this information, but hopefully, all these struggles will open new doors for modern science so they can help mankind more and more. In the case of angels, either I do not have vision to see them, or maybe they are not around me, but for sure, I have no clue, no vision, and no sense to see or sense or communicate with angels.

يجب أن أتعامل مع شخص يمكن الوصول إليه، لمعرفة نتيجة التجربة فعلاً . وعادة ما يكون العاملين في اوسائل الإعلام والسياسيين هم الأكثر شعبية والأسهل في الوصول إليهم.. يمكنك أن ترى نتيجة تجاربك على الفور. وأنا لا أقتصر على بلد واحد، لذا يرجى ألا تفترض فقط وأني وراء أي شيء يحدث لك. ربما هناك شخص آخر، ليس أنا.

سوف أصف بالتفصيل الكامل في وقت لاحق في هذا الكتاب، كيف يمكن للشخص جذب الجن ، والتفاعل معهم، وجعل الجني أحد الأصدقاء، والتواصل معه، واستخدامه في أشياء مختلفة. سأذكر في التفاصيل، ما يزيد أو ينقص علي ذلك أيضا. سأصف لك كثيراً كيفية إنقاذ نفسك من الجن، و الألم والمرض، ولكني الآن، وأصف الفائدة السلبية أو ربما بعض الفائدة الممكنة للجن. فقط لأقوم ببعض التوعية للقراء بالجن. إذا قمت بعمل أي تجربة على شخص ما، أنا متأكد 100 % من عدم ترك أي آثار جانبية لهما في المستقبل، حيث أني دائما أمسح المناطق المحيطة بهم، من تجربة الجن أو آلام. لقد أجريت نوع من التجارب علي شخص آخر، ذات مرة، و خلال إحدى المقابلات معه، قررت أن أطلب من الجن الذهاب إليه وتجميد عقله. بطريقة ما كان ذلك يحدث ولكن ليس بشكل جيد بما فيه الكفاية، لقد واجهت نقس المشكلة في وقت لاحق ، أن هناك صراع بين الجن المتواجدين حول هذا الشخص والجن الذين أرسلهم إليه، حيث يقوم الجن من كلا الطرفين بإضاعة الوقت في الجدل والقتال مع بعضهم البعض، بدلا من القيام بهذه المهمة للمرة الأولى قمت بنفس الممارسة للإتصال التخاطري مع الجن المتواجدين حول هذا الشخص. في اليوم الأول أعطيتهم تعليمات قليلة لتجميد عقل هذا الشخص مؤقتاً خلال المقابلات والحديث فقط لبضع دقائق.

Angels, as I saw them, they were of equal size to an average small demon. But angels were very clearly similar to light-gold sparkling stars. And they were around me just for few seconds; that's all. It will be very difficult to reveal my condition or situation, when I was able to see those angels. That's all I know about angels. I am sure a lot of us may already have seen angels or maybe will see angels, once they will then sometime. Do not have anything else about angels; that's all I can tell you about angels, how they look like.

This was just part of an experiment I tried few times. I never did any experiments ever on a normal or a good person. Sometimes I just choose to learn about them, and during this learning, I do a few experiments also. Few months ago I choose one anchor from a one TV channel to learn something about him. At first step, I send several demons to that guy to amplify his conditions. I am sorry; I forgot to tell you this guy was already acting too wild and crazy during his talk show. From this experiment, I learn that if someone is already acting crazy and wild, it is very easy to make them wilder and crazier. As compared to those kinds of people, if we choose someone less extremist or a zero extremist, either it will be difficult to make them too wild and crazy or it will take some time to make them extremist, wild, and crazy.

لكن شيئاً لم يحدث ذلك اليوم، إما أن هذا الشخص قوي العقل جداً، أو يرفض لسيطرة ذلك الجن بسهولة جدا، أو الشيء الثاني الممكن ربما لم يستمع الجن الخاص به إلى تعليماتي. في اليوم التالي، إتصلت مرة أخرى هؤلاء الجن بالتخاطر. هذه المرة، ووجهت لهم تهديد واضح بأنهم إذا لم يتبعوا تعليماتي اليوم فقط لبضع دقائق، سأقوم في اليوم التالي بتحرك كل هؤلاء الجن بعيداً عن هذا الشخص لهذا الشخص لتحقيق سيطرتي وتعليماتي. وهذه هي المرة الأولى التي إستمع فيها الجن لي، وأعتقد أن هؤلاء الجن فعلوا ذلك لأنهم لم يكونوا على إستعداد لترك ذلك الشخص.

مرة أخرى، أجريت تجربة واحدة علي شخص آخر عن طريق إستخدام الجن المتواجدين حوله. هذه المرة، وطلبت منهم أن يجعلوه يقول بعض الاشياء، أشياء لم يكن ليقولها في حالته العقلية الطبيعية، و هكذا يمكننا إستخدام هؤلاء الجن بمئات الطرق لإجراء نشاط سلبي، فالجن يحبون السلبية، وهم دائما على إستعداد لفعل أي شيء سلبي. تذكر دائما أنهم لا يحتاجون تعليماتي أو تعليماتك للقيام بأعمال سلبية، حتى و لو لم يطلب أحد منهم ذلك، و مع ذلك لا يزال 7 إلي24 من الجن مشغولون بإحداث السلبية و نشرها. تذكر دائما، ليس هناك جني خاص، أو منفرد أو شرير. عندما يتصرف كل هؤلاء الجن و الآلام بشكل سلبي فردي أو جماعي، فهم يعتبرون من الشياطين والشرور. تذكر دائما، لا يستطيع ذلك الجن فعل أي شيء، لن تكون سياسات الشياطين و الشر ناجحة إلا إذا كان لديهم سيطرة علينا، لذلك إفعل ذلك أفضل لديكم لرفضها من خلال رفض كل أنواع التطرف والسلبية، وما إلى ذلك إذا لم تتمكن من السيطرة على نفسك، فلا تشكو لأحد.

SEE & CONTROL DEMONS & PAIN

I am not saying it is not possible; actually everything is possible, but why hurt someone when they are good people. Anyway, I am describing this experiment, how to amplify or boost wild behavior of an already-crazy person. In the first step, I send one by one seven demons to that talk show host or TV anchor to amplify his extremism, craziness, and wild behavior; it was a good experiment. Those demons were able to amplify his extremism, but those demons were not getting enough time around that person.Reason behind was my demons had to fight with those demons first, who were already around that person. I waited for the results for seven days. After seven days, I figured out it is a difficult and long way to go. And this way, for no reason, two groups of demons have to fight with each other and kill each other. I wait for few days and finally, even I was not willing and ready to do it but, I did to practice and complete my experiment. I established a telepathic contact, directly to the demons of that person. First, I convinced those demons not to feel insecure due to my remote contact with them. Second I convinced them not to run away from that person. I asked them several times not to come to me and stay with that person. I give them a few hours. But even I said do not come to me; still they send one demon to me to check who was the contact person. Anyway after few hours, I established my telepathic contact with those demons again and give them a few instructions. Just to stay on safe side, I contact them three times in next three days and gave them same instructions. After few days, I learn that it is more direct and easier to go directly to demons around someone and give them some instructions. Instead of sending brand-new demons to someone.

رضوان قرشي

من الصعب جداً الحفاظ على الجسم خالياً من الجن وآلام في طوال الوقت. إن هذا ممكناً، لكن هذا يستغرق وقتاً طويلاً جدا و محاربو الجن و الآلام بإستمرار. من ناحية أخرى، يعد إستخدام الجن والآلام سلبياً، أمراً سهلاً جداً. كما وصفت سابقاً إن التجميد المؤقت للعقل / الذاكرة، يزيد من درجة من السلوكيات المجنونة، الخ. والآن أصف، كيف يمكن للشخص إستخدام الجن والآلام لجعل شخص ما يشعر بالمرض. لدينا هنا خيارين مرة أخرى. إما إرسال جني لشخص ما بالتعليمات. وسوف يذهب هذا الجني إلي الشخص وأثناء إقامته معه ، سيستمر الجني في دعوة جميع أنواع الآلام والمرض من كل مكان إلى جسم هذا الشخص بشكل مستمر.

هناك عدد قليل من الخيارات ، يمكنك أن تعطي الجني مجموعة واضحة من التعليمات بعدم دعوة جميع أنواع الآلام أو المرض، ولكن يدعو أنواع معينة من الآلام والمرض. يمكنك أن تعطي التعليمات للجني بإرسال كل أنواع الآلام والمرض لكلى شخص ما بإستمرار بدلاً من الجسم كله. وعادة يتبع هؤلاء الجن تعليماتك. الكل يعاني عادة من نوع ما من الآلام، تكون قوية جداً في بعض الأحيان، و ضعيفة في أحيان أخري. يمكنك الإتصال بتلك الآلام مباشرة في عضو معين من أعضاء شخص معين، وتعطيهم تعليمات لزيادة هجومهم أو الإضرار بجسده بسرعة. إذا كانت هذه الآلام قوية، يستمعون لك عادة و يقومون بزيادة مهاجمة الجسم لإحداث المزيد من الأضرار. في هذه الحالة لا فائدة من الجني. الاحتمال الآخر هو إذا قمت بإرسال مجرد مجموعة طاقة من الآلام لشخص معين مباشرة. حتى لو وجد بعض الجن بالفعل حول هذا الشخص، ولكن لسوء الحظ لا يقو هذا الجن بالجدال، أو بمحاربة، أويقطع هجوم الألم علي نفس الجسد .

Demons already present around someone usually have fully contact and control of that particular person. So instead of sending a new team of demons to someone, it is better and easier to use their own demons for some particular task. So if you do not want anyone to amplify your temperament and extremism, you better control your temperament. Always remember, even temperamental people, easygoing people, people with more tolerance and patience have less impact of demons on them. Demons cannot control easily those kinds of people; you will act wild crazy and short temperament person, and demons will have more and more control on you.

And you never know if someone is doing some experiments on you. So control your mind, and always reject negative and bad temperament. Try your best; do not hurt someone's feelings just by using your blunt tongue and wordings. Always be careful before you upset someone; you never know who is who and what they can do. These demon experiments are usually temporary. But do not ever challenge any demon. These demons can screw up anyone in a very short time for long term. So be careful when you challenge them.

I cannot do any experiments on an unknown or unavailable person To really know the result of an experiment I really need someone who is more accessible. And usually media people and politicians are more popular and more accessible. You can immediately see the result of your experiments. I am not limited to one country. So please do not just assume I am behind anything happening to you. Maybe someone else. Not me.

رؤية الجن و الآلام السيطرة عليها

يدع الجن تلك الآلام تدخل داخل هذا الجسم، و مجرد دخول الآلام داخل جسم معين، فإنها تبدأ تقيم به و على الفور تحدث ضرر في أي مكان تجده داخل الجسم.

هناك هواية أخري سهلة جدا ومفضلة للجن، هي جعل الشخص الطبيعي مريض نفسي وعقلي عن طريق التحكم في المخ من ذلك الشخص من خلال التنويم المغناطيسي. الجن لا يحتاجون إلى أي تعليمات من أي شخص للقيام بذلك. إنهم بالفعل مشغولون بإيذاء كل شخص آخر عقلياً و معنوياً بدون توقف لذلك الاختصار، هناك الملايين من الاستخدامات السلبية للجن، كأن يستخدمون في إيذاء الإنسان عقلياً وجسدياً، ومعنوياً. بغض النظر عن ما إذا كنا نطلب من الجن القيام بهذه الأشياء أم لا، إنهم يفعلون كل هذه الأنشطة السلبية، وسوف يستمرون في فعل ذلك إلى الأبد. لذلك هذا هو الوقت المناسب عندما يستيقظ الناس و العلوم الطبية الحديثة ليقوموا بتحسين الوعي لمحاربة الأفعال الشيطانية للجن، والآلام، والأمراض.

عادة، يستخدم بعض أطباء الجن، الجن الخاص بهم على شخص ما لتنويمه مغناطيسياً ويظهرون لهم أي صورة أو فيلم، و كل ما يريدون أن يظهروه لهم. عادة، ما يذهب الناس إلى هذا النوع من الناس لمعرفة ما اذا كان هناك شخص ما يريد أن يقتلهم أو يقضي علي أعمالهم. هؤلاء العرافين، وعادة ما يستخدمون الجن، ليظهروا لنا عدد قليل من الصور أو الأفلام من أذهاننا. يحدث هذا عندما نكون مستيقظين. هذه ليست مفاجأة، لأن الجن عندما يقومون بتنويمنا مغناطيسياً أثناء النوم ليظهروا لنا أحلامنا، إذاً ليس صعباً علي الجن إظهار بعض الصور أو ملئ مرآة بواسطة تنويمنا مغناطيسياً. نحن دائما نريد أن نعرف إذا كان هناك شخص ما وراء حظنا السيئ أو المواضيع الأخي في حياتنا، على الأقل الناس يريدون معرفة من هو عدوهم.

Later in this book, I will describe in full detail how someone can attract, interact, make a demon friend, communicate with a demon, and use a demon for different things. I will describe in details, plus and minus of this also. A lot of time, I am and I will describe how to save yourself from demon, pains and disease, but right now, I am describing negative or maybe some possible use of demons just to provide some awareness about demons to readers. If I ever did any experiment on someone, 100 percent I make sure not to leave any side effects for them in the future. I always clear their surroundings from experiment demons or pains. One time, I did some kind of experiment to another person. During one of his interviews, I decided to ask demons to go and freeze his mind. Somehow it was happening but not well enough.

Later on I find out the same problem, that conflict between the demons around that person and the demons I send to him. Instead of doing the job, most of the time demons of both parties wasting time in argument and fighting with each other. First time I did same practice of telepathic contact with the demons around that person. First day I gave them few instructions to freeze that person's mind temporarily during interviews and speech just for few minutes.

يستفيد أطباء الجن من هذا الوضع، و يستخدمون الجين الخاص بهم، و هؤلاء الجن يقومون بقراءة عقل هؤلاء الناس عن طريق التنويم المغناطيسي. يقوم طبيب الجن بوضع مرآة أمام هذا الشخص. عند هذه النقطة يقوم الجن بتنويم هذا الشخص مغناطيسيا مرة أخرى ويظرون له صورة عدد قليل من الأعداء المشتبه بهم من قبل ذلك الشخص فهذا إجراء يتحكم فيه طبيب الجن جيداً .

الجن ليسوا طاقة إيجابية. فهم ليسوا مسؤولين عن إبقائنا على قيد الحياة وأداء وظائف الجسم وعملياته. أما الروح ، فهي الطاقة الإيجابية التي تقتصر وتنحصر في داخل أجسامنا بقوة ثابتة. 'إن الجن والمرض مدعوون في منزلنا (أي الجسم والبيئة)، لكنهم يمثلون حكلاً ثقيلاً عندما يكونون داخل منزلنا أو جسمنا.يعتبر الجن والمرض طاقات سلبية خارجية يمكن أن تدخل داخل أجسامنا بسهولة. و مجرد أن يذهبوا داخل الجسم، تقوم روحنا أو الطاقة الإيجابية يحمايتنا من أفعال الجن السلبية. لكن الطاقة الإيجابية محدودة، إنها تعمل بشكل فردي و محدود، و تعمل علي أجزاء الجسم المنفصلة الطاقة السلبية خارجية، و يمكنها أن تزيد من قوتها عن طريق إستخدامها أو عن طريق دعوة المزيد من الجن أو مرض للدخول داخل أجسامنا.ليس لقوة الجن حدود على صلاحياتهم. إنهنم يستطيعون زيادة قوتهم لهزيمة الطاقة الإيجابية الداخلية، و بمجرد أن تتغلب الطاقة السلبية على الطاقة الإيجابية الداخلية (أي نظام المناعة لدينا)، ونمرض ونعاني من الآلام مثل الإلتهابات، والنوبات القلبية، والشلل، و النزيف، و حتي فشل الآعضاء .

But nothing happened that day. Either that person was very strong mentally or rejecting the control of those demons very easily, or second possible thing was maybe his demons were not listening to my instructions. Next day, I contacted the demons again telepathically. This time, I clearly threat demons around that person that, if they will not follow my instructions today just for few minutes, next day, I will move all those demons away from that person to that person to fulfill my controls and instruction. And the first time those demons listened to me I think was because those demons were not ready to leave that person.

Another time, I did one experiment to another person by using demons around him. This time, I ask his demons to make him say some stuff, whatever, he will never say in right condition of his mind. So we can use these demons in hundreds of ways for a negative activity. Demons love negativity. Demons are always ready to do anything negative. Always remember, demons do not need my or your instructions to do negative work, even if no one asks them, still 24-7 demons are busy doing and spreading negativism. Always remember, there is no special or single devil or evil. All these demons and pains once they are acting negative individually or collectively are the devils and evils. Always remember, these demons cannot do anything there's devil or evil policies or agent a will never be successful unless, they will have control on us. So do your best to reject them by rejecting all kinds of extremism, negativism, etc. If you cannot control yourself, then do not complain to anybody. It is very difficult to keep a body free of demons and pains all the time.

إذا كنت لا أعمل على شخص ما لبضعة أيام، فإني أشعر بالإسترخاء والراحة، و لكن لا يكون ذلك ممكناً بالنسبة لي في كل وقت، لأني مشغول دائما بمساعدة شخص ما، بغض النظر عما إذا كانوا يدركون مساعدني لهم أم لا. "حالة فراغ" هي عندما يكون الشخص مثل البيت الشاغر لسنا مهيئين ليكون لدينا جن أو مرض في جسمنا. نحن أفضل بدونهم، ولكن الجن مهيئون لإيجاد وسط يمكنهم إختراقه، و التمدد فيه، و يبدأون في العيش به. إن الجن مزعجون، و لكنهم أجسام مادية، ومع ذلك، هم مثل الهواء تماماً، ولتأمين وسط ما، يختارون أي جسم، بغض النظر عما إذا كان جسم إنسان أو حيوان . إنهم لا يهتمون كيف كثيرا بمدي إيذاء / إتلاف الوسط أو الجسم. بعد أن أفرغ من العمل على شخص ما وتخليص جسمهو جسمها من هذا الجن و هذا المرض، وبعدذلك ، يصير في جسمه أو جسمها مساحة فارغة، مما يعني إمكانية إختراق الجن و الأمراضالجسم النظيف بسهولة. لذا كن حذرا وإبق بعيداً عن الأجسام المريضة.

ويتحكم الجن بالمرضي بأي لوح من أنواع المرض العقلي. وهب الله الجن بالكثير من القوى للسيطرة على العقول من خلال التنويم المغناطيسي. أنهم يتصرفون بشكل مختلف. في حالات نادرة، . خلاف ذلك، ليس لديهم تعاطف مع البشر. وسوف يولدون كل أنواع الصفات السلبية داخلنا، مثل الغيرة، والجشع، والغضب، والتعصب، نفاد الصبر والشك وعدم الثقة، والمرض. لدي القليل من السيطرة عليهم بعون الله. إنني أستخدام إجراءات مختلفة لتعطيل سيطرتهم.. لا أعتقد أن هذا من ممكن للشخص العادي. ويمكن لشخص مثلي تخفيف الضغط من الجني. والباقي في يديك، بالتحديد كيف يمكنك التكيف و التحرك بسهولة وسرعة نحو نهج إيجابي وطريقة تفكير إيجابية، فإذا دربت نفسك على التصرف والتفكير بشكل إيجابي، وسوف تجعل من الصعب على الجن أن يجعلك مريض عقلياً.

It is possible but very time-consuming and continuous fight of me with demons and pains. On the other hand, the negative use of demons and pains is very easy. As I described above, temporary, mind/memory freeze increases the degree of crazy behaviors, etc. Now I am describing, how someone can use demons and pains to make sick. Here we have two choices again. Either sends a demon to someone with instruction. That demon will go to that person and during that stay amount that person, that demons will keep inviting all kinds of pains and disease to that body continuously from everywhere.

There are few more options you can give that demon clear set of instructions not to invite all kinds of pains or disease, guest invites some particular kinds of pains and disease. You can give instruction to a demon to send continuously all kinds of pains and disease to someone's kidneys instead of the whole body. And usually those demons follow your instructions. Everybody usually has some kind of pains, sometimes very powerful, sometime weak. You can contact directly those pains in a particular organ of a particular person and give them instructions to increase their attack or damage that body quickly. If those pains are powerful, usually, they listen to you and increase attack on that body to create more damages. In this case no use of a demon. Another possibility is if you just send a directly a power group of pains to a particular person. Even some demons already around that person, but by bad luck demons do not argue, fight, or interrupt pain attack to same body. Demons let those pains go inside that body. Once pains go inside a particular body, they start residing and immediately damage body wherever they find room inside a body.

لدينا دائماً الأفكار الإيجابية والسلبية.اذا كنت لا تزال تختار التمييز بين الجيد والسيئ، الإيجابية والسلبية، الحق والباطل، الصواب والخطأ، سيكون لديك متسع من الوقت لهزيمة الجن.

إذا كنت شخص عادي، ستأتي كل الأفكار الإيجابية والجيدة من عقلك، وكل الأفكار السلبية والسيئة تأتي من جني حولك. إذا رغبت في التغلب على جني ما وتستعيد سيطرتك، عليك أن تبدأ الآن. إبدأ برفض كل الأفكار السيئة والسلبية، وتوقف عن التشكك الشديد.قم بالحد من الغيرة. حاولة الحد من التنافس السلبي. كن دائماً على يقين من القرار الإيجابي. هذه وسيلة ممكنة لتدريب الجن من حولك أن يكون أقل سلبية. أنا واثق من أن الجن لن يحبذ هذا السلوك،ولكن هذا قرارك سواء كنت تريد أن تجعل الجني يتحكم بك، و يجعلك تتصرف بجنون أو الحفاظ علي السيطرة علي نفسك و تجبر الجن على مساعدتك في مسارك الإيجابي. وسوف تحتاج إلى الكثير من الممارسة. ببساطة،رفض الأفكار السيئة يعني ان لدينا المزيد من السيطرة على عقولنا.وقبول الأفكار السيئة يعني مزيد من سيطرة الجن على أذهاننا.

إذا كان هناك أي شخص يقول شيئا عن الجن، أنهم سحرة ويمكنهم تحقيق ثلاث رغبات أو يمكنهم أن يجعلونا أغنياء، أصدقائي، إنهم يروون لكم قصصاً. إن الجن الحقيقيين أقوياء جداً ولكنهم في الغالب يستخدمون قوتهم بشكل سلبي. إذا وجدت من أي وقت جني له صفات الجن السحرية الموجودة في القصص، وسوف أشارك خبرتي ومعرفتي مع الجميع. وأتمنى لو وجد مثلهذا الجن كي أستطيع أن أقول: "نعم، في حاولة جعل الجن أصدقائك ". أفضل شيء هو الإبتعاد عنهم، هذا ليس سهلاً لكنه ليس مستحيلاً . القتال مع الجن مثل القتال مع الهواء.

Rizwan Qureshi	رؤية الجن و الآلام السيطرة عليها
Another very easy and favorite hobby of demons is to make a normal person psycho and mentally sick by controlling the brain of that person through hypnotism. Demons do not need any instruction from anyone to do this. They are already busy nonstop hurting every other person mentally and morally. So shortcut, there are millions of negative uses of demons to hurt mentally, physically, and morally a human. Regardless of whether we ask demons to do these things or not, they are doing all these negative activities, and they will keep doing it forever. So this is the time when common people and modern medical science needs to wake up and improve awareness to fight against the devil activation of demons, pains, and disease.	هل يستطيع الجن أن يسمعنا؟ نعم، يمكن لجميع الجن أن يسمعونا، وهم يهتمون جداً بحياتنا، ويتناقشون في أمورنا مع الجن الآخرين. إنهم يعرفون تاريخ عائلتنا بسبب عمرهم. الجن لا يتحركون بسهولة. بعض من هؤلاء الجن يعيشون في بيوتنا أو في أماكن العمل أوفي الأشجار، و بعضهم يعيشون بشكل دائم داخل أجسامنا. أنهم يعيشون بشكل مريح أكثر في تلك المناطق مثل المنزل أومكان العمل، والمناطق التي لا تستخدم كثيراً أو أماكن مظلمة في الغالب. إنني أراهم أحيانا يطيرون في غرفة واحدة في بيتي، كما أراها ملاصقة للسقوف أو الجدران. نادراً ما أستخدم تلك الغرفة. أنا أذهب إلى هناك مرتين في اليوم فقط لألبس أحذيتي في. لقد رأيت الكثير منهم في الحمام الكبير أيضاً، أنا لا أذهب هناك عادة.
Usually, some demon doctor uses their demons to hypnotize someone and show them any photo or movie, whatever they want to show us. Usually, people go to these kinds of people to find out if someone wants to kill them or kill their business. Those fortune-tellers usually use their demons to show us a few photos or films from our mind. This happens when we are awake. This is not a surprise, because when demons hypnotize us during sleep in order to show us our dreams, then this is not difficult for demons to show a few photos or a fill in a mirror by hypnotizing us. We always want to know if there is someone behind our bad luck or issues. Or at least they want to know who their enemy is. That demon doctor takes advantage of the situation. They use their demons. Their demons read the mind of those people by hypnotism. And then that demon doctor keeps a mirror in front of that person.	أنا لا أرى أي جن في الحمام الذي أستخدامه أو في أي حمام آخر في المنزل. نه شيئ غريب، لكني رأيت عدة مرات، حفنة منهم تحلق حولي، لكنهم كانوا يحافظون على أن يكونوا علي مسافة مني. أنا ممتن دائماً لرعايتهم وإخلاصهم. في بعض الأحيان أنها تبين لي ذلك من خلال القيام بأشياء من هذا القبيل.على أي حال، والجن لا يتركون المنزل الذي يعيشون فيه،بغض النظر عن الذي يعيش في هذا المنزل. أنهم لا dسمحون لجن آخرين بالمجيئ إلى مكانهم. إذا كان الجن يعيشون داخل جسد شخص ما، وأنا لا أتحدث عن المرض ولكن عن الجن، فإنهم يتحركون ويذهبون مع هذا الجسم في كل مكان. يعد هؤلاء الجن أجزاء من شخصياتنا. في الأساس إن الجن، بغض النظر عن عدد هم، هم علي الأقل مخلصون لنا، لكنهم في الأساس، فهي الطاقة السلبية، و.يحبون الاشياء السلبية. عندما تفعل شيئا سيئا وكنت وتصاع نفسك، فإن عقلك أو طاقتك الإيجابية ستحاول إيقافك،لكن هذه الجن يصرون على أن نفعل شيئاً سلبياً طوال الوقت.

At that point those demons hypnotize that person again and show him the picture of few suspected enemies of that person in the mirror. So this is a very controlled hypnotism procedure by a demon doctor.

Demons are not positive energy. Demons are not responsible for keeping us alive and performing bodily functions and operations. The soul/spirit is a positive energy that is limited and confined inside our bodies with a fixed strength. Demons and disease are uninvited guests in our house (i.e., our body and environment). They are not a problem when they are outside of our house or our body, but they are a burden when they are inside our house or inside our body. Demons and disease are external negative energies that can go inside our bodies easily. And once they go inside our body, our soul/spirit or positive energy protects us from a demon's negative actions. But positive energy is limited, and it works individually for separate parts of the body. Negative energy is external, and they can increase their power by using it or by inviting more demons or disease into our bodies. Demons have no limits on their powers. They can increase their strength to defeat internal positive energy. Once negative energy beats the positive internal energy (i.e., our immunity system), we get sick and suffer pains like infections, heart attacks, paralysis, hemorrhages, and even organ failure.

If I am not working on someone for a few days, I experience a relaxed and comfortable condition. But that is not possible for me all the time, because I am always busy helping someone, regardless of whether they are aware of that help or not.

عادة، ما يحدث في الواقع يعتمد على من لديه المزيد من السيطرة، إذا كان للجن مزيد من السيطرة علينا، سنستمع لهم ونتبعهم. لكن إذا كنا نسيطر على عقولنا، فلن نفعل أشياء سيئة أو خاطئة بسهولة. الجن لا يستفيدون بشيء من هذا، إنها مجرد هواية لهم. عادة، يبقى الجن داخل أجسامنا إلى الأبد ما لم يقم شخص ما مثلي بإزالتها من جسم شخص آخر، وفي هذه الحالة، يصبح جسد الشخص طبيعياً لفترة من الوقت. ثم يأتي جني آخر و يبدأ العيش في ذلك الجسم. قد يبدأ الجني بمساعدة الشخص أحياناً، ولكن في معظم الوقت سوف يحدث مشاكل. أستطيع ان أحدثكم عن نفسي. كانت لي عادات قليلة، و كنت فقط أريد بعض الأشياء. وسوف أترك كل شيء وأنا لن أنهي هذا العمل. ولكن لأن لدي سيطرة أكثر علي نفسي، فأنا شخص مختلف. أنا لست نشط للغاية. أنا بطيئ جداً، وأفكر كثيراً قبل أن أفعل شيئاً. أنا لا أتلهف للقيام بأشياء مجنونة. أنا أكثر نضجاً وأكثر حساسيةً في الوقت الحاضر. لدي مجموعة من الناس (الأهل والأصدقاء). أنني أقوم بتنظيف أجسادهم كل يوم، ومزاجهم يتغير كذلك. لا أحد منهم يتصرف بتطرف بعد الآن. لكن الناس العاديون يكونون تحت تأثير نفس الطاقات السلبية والجن منذ طفولتهم، لذلك فإن عاداتهم وأمزجتهم هي نفسها.

بإختصار، الجن يحبون أن يعيشوا في مكان واحد أو جسم واحد. إنهم لا يتحركون بسهولة. إذا كان الجن سلبيون للغاية، و الإنسان ضعيف عقلياً، سترى الكثير من الأمثل لبشر يكلمون أنفسهم طوال الوقت، ونحن نعتبر هذا النوع من الناس مجنون أو مريض عقلياً.

رؤية الجن و الآلام السيطرة عليها

يمكننا وصف المرض في فئتين:

1. المرض المؤلم: الحشرات غير المرئية التي تأكل أجزاء الجسم و تلف أعضاؤه و أجهزته بشكل مستمر. هذا عمل مشترك من الآلام والحشرات. بغض النظر عن كمية المسكنات والأدوية التي نتناولها، تستطيع هذه الحشرات الغير مرئية أن تقتل . يمكن نقلها بسهولة من الجسم، لكنها لا تموت. إلا أنها سوف تجد جسماً آخروتبدأ في إتلافه.

2. الأمراض الغير الغير مؤلمة: وهذه الآلام الغير مرئية تحدث الكثير من المرض في جسمنا أيضاً، لكنها لا تأكل أجسامنا أو أعضائنا. أنها تشاركنا طعامنا كمصدر للطاقة بالنسبة لها. لكنها تسد أو توقف عمل الأنابيب المختلفة في الكلى والقلب، أو المخ، بل يمكن أن تتسبب في الفشل الكلوي والسكتة القلبية، أو تمدد الأوعية الدموية.

ما هو التخاطر والتنويم المغناطيسي؟ التخاطر والتنويم المغناطيسي ليسا نفس الشيء. التخاطر هو شكل من أشكال الإتصال يسمح لك بالتحدث على إنفراد مع شخص ليس أمامك. يمكنك التواصل عقلياً مع أي شخص في أي جزء من العالم.إن روحنا هي الطاقة الإيجابية التي تحافظ على حياتنا وتجعل وظائف الجسد تعمل. لا يمكن لأحد يستخدم الإتصال بالتخاطر للوصول إلى الروح. نحن نتواصل دائما مع الجني أو الجن الموجودون حول الشخص، بإستخدام تقنيات التخاطر، حيث يمكننا أن نعطي الجن الخاص به تعليمات، والتي يمكن تجعل مضيفيهم يفكرون في شيء معين. الجن لا يستخدمون التخاطرمع البشر أو الحيوانات، لكنهم يستخدمون التخاطر ليتواصل مع بعضهم البعض، أما البشر فيستخدمون التخاطر للتواصل مع غيرهم من البشر.

Rizwan Qureshi

"Vacuum condition" that the person is like a vacant house. We are not designed to have a demon or disease in our body. We are better without them, but demons are designed to find a medium where they can penetrate, expand, and start living. Demons are mean, and they are physical bodies; however, they are just like air, and to secure a medium, they choose anybody, regardless of whether they are human or animal. They don't care how much they hurt/damage the medium or that body. After I work on someone and clean his or her body of these demons and disease, after that, his or her body has an empty space, which means demons and disease can easily penetrate that clean body. So be careful and stay away from sick bodies.

People with any kind of mental sickness are being controlled by demons. God has gifted demons with lots of powers to control minds through hypnotism. In rare cases, they act differently. Otherwise, they have no sympathy for human beings. They will generate all kinds of negative qualities in us, such as jealousy, greed, anger, intolerance, impatience, suspicion, mistrust, and sickness. I have a little control over them with help from God. I use different procedures to disrupt their control. I don't think this is possible for a normal person. Someone like me can reduce the pressure from a demon. The rest is in your hands, namely how easily and quickly you adapt and move toward a positive approach and way of thinking. If you train yourself to behave and think positively, you will make it difficult for a demon to make you mentally sick person. We always have positive and negative thoughts. If you still have a choice to differentiate between good and bad, positive and negative, true and false, right and wrong, then you still have time to defeat a demon.

SEE & CONTROL DEMONS & PAIN

If you are a normal person, all positive and good thoughts are coming from your mind. All negative and bad thoughts are coming from a demon around you. So if you still want to beat a demon and regain your control, you need to start practicing right now. Start rejecting all bad and negative thinking. Stop getting too suspicious. Reduce jealousy. Try to reduce negative competition. Always be sure about positive decision. This is a possible way to train a demon around you to be less negative. I am sure demons will not like this behavior, but this is your decision—whether you want to give your control to a demon and act crazy or keep your control and compel that demon to help you in your positive path. You will need a lot or practice. Simply, rejecting bad thoughts means we have more control over our mind. And accepting bad thoughts means demons have more control of our mind.

If anyone says anything about demons—that they are magical and can fulfill three wishes or can make us rich—my friends, they are just telling you stories. Real demons are very powerful but mostly use their negative powers. If I ever find a demon with qualities of the magical demons in stories, I will share my knowledge and experience with everyone. I wish they existed so that I could say, "Yes, try to make demons your friend." The best thing is to stay away from them. It is not easy but not impossible. Fighting with demons means fighting with air.

Can demons hear us? Yes, all demons can hear us, and they take full interest in our lives and discuss us with other demons. They know our family histories because of their age.

رضوان قرشي

ولكننا لا نتواصل مع عقول البشر مباشرة. نحن نتصل بجن البشر الآخرين ونعطيهم تعليمات. بعد ذلك، يستخدام الجن التنويم المغناطيسي للسيطرة على الطاقة الإيجابية لدينا و علي عقولنا.التنويم المغناطيسي هو اللغة التي يستخدمها الجن للتواصل مع لبشر والحيوانات والحشرات. يستطيع الجن أن يظهروا لنا ما يريدون في أحلامنا، عن طريق إستخدام التنويم المغناطيسي. يجيد الجن إستخدام التنويم المغناطيسي الذي يستطيع الجن من خلاله أن يظهروا لنا أي شيء يريدونه في عالمنا الحقيقي أيضاً. هذه النوعية من السيطرة على شخص ما في وتغذيتة أو تغذيتها بأفكار مختلفة، أو أحلام، أو عواطف، هذا هو التنويم المغناطيسي.

كيف يعمل التخاطر والتنويم المغناطيسي؟ ما هي الأجزاء السهلة و الصعبة؟ التنويم المغناطيسي هو إجراء من شأنه أن يمكن الجن من إلقاء أفكار في عقول المخلوقات الحية. فكر في الأمر بهذه الطريقة، يمكننا أن نلعب دي في دي، ثم نغير الأقراص ونشاهد فيلم آخر. التنويم المغناطيسي يعمل بطريقة مشابهة، يمكن إعتبار جهاز الدي في دي هو أحلامنا، ويستطيع الجن أن يظهروا لنا أي شيء يريدونه. وكلما كنا واقعين تحت سيطرتهم، كلما لاحظنا كل ما يريدون.

الآن يمكن للإنسان القيام التنويم المغناطيسي. عادة يكون لدي خبراء التنويم المغناطيسي جن أقوياء جداً معهم، وهم فقط يطلبون من هؤلاء الجن لتنفيذ تلك العمليات. التخاطر هو الوضع العادي للإتصال بالجن. ولكن عندما يكونون حولنا، لا نكون في حاجة إلى إستخدام قوي التخاطر للتواصل معهم. نستطيع أن نتكلم كلام عادي، و يمكن للجن أن يسمعونا بسهولة. ولكن عندما نكون في حاجة إلى التواصل مع شخص ليس أمامنا، نكون بحاجة لمهارة التواصل هذه.

98

Rizwan Qureshi

Demons do not move easily. Some of them just live in our houses or business places or trees. Some of them permanently live inside our bodies. They live more comfortably in those areas like the house or workplace, areas that are not in use or mostly dark. I sometimes see them flying in one room in my house. I see them stuck on ceilings or walls. I rarely use that room. I go there twice a day only to put my shoes on. I saw a lot of them in the big restroom too. Usually, I don't go there.

I don't see any demons in the restroom I use or any of the other rooms in the house. It is funny, but several times, I saw a bunch flying around me, and when I walked, they moved as well. But they maintain a certain distance from me. I am always thankful for their care and sincerity. Sometimes they show me by doing stuff like that. Anyway, demons do not move from the house they are living in, regardless of who lives in that house. They don't allow other demons to come to their place. If demons are living inside the body of a person—I am not talking about disease but about demons— then they move and go everywhere with that body. Those demons are parts of our personalities. Basically, demons, regardless of how many there are, are at least sincere with us. Basically, they are negative energy. They like negative stuff. When you are doing something bad and you are conflicted, your mind or your positive energy will try to stop you, but these demons insist that we do something negative all the time. Usually, what actually happens depends on who has more control. If the demons have more control over us, we listen to them and follow them. But if we are in control of our mind, we do not do bad or wrong stuff easily.

رؤية الجن و الآلام السيطرة عليها

لقد تعلمت أن التخاطر طريقة فعالة للتواصل مع الجن، والمرض، والآلام. لقد كنت قادراً على إستخدام هذه المهارات في أي جزء من العالم بدون أي صداقة السابقة مع هؤلاء الجن، ولكن الناس العاديون يحتاجون إلى الإتصال بهؤلاء الجن.

هل يمكننا التواصل مع الجن بدون التخاطر؟ نعم، يمكننا التواصل مع الجن، والمرض، والآلام بطريقة عادية، لكنهم عادة لا يهتمون بالمحادثة الطبيعية. يحتاج المرء لممارسة التخاطر للإتصال عن بعد، و. عادة لا يكشف الناس عن كيفية ممارسة التخاطر حقاً.

لست متأكداً من عدد الأشخاص القادرين فعلاً على إجراء هذا الشكل من أشكال الإتصال. الناس العاديون يعتقدون دائماً أنهم يمارسون التواصل مع عقل إنسان آخر، ولكن في واقع الأمر، هم يتواصلون مع جن ذلك الشخص. معظم خبراء التخاطر يرسلون جنهم عادة ليكونوا حول أولئك الناس الذين يكونون بحاجة إلى التواصل معهم، ويبدأ الجن بتنويم الناس وفقاً لتعليمات التي مستضيفهم عند قراءة هذا الكتاب، قد يبدو كل شيء في غاية السهولة، ولكن كن حذرا. الجن ليسوا مزحة. فهم أقوياء جداً، وهم لا يوقعون أنفسهم تحت سيطرة أي أحد أن بسهولة.

عند ممارسة معظم الناس التخاطر أو التنويم المغناطيسي، وهو ما يعني أنهم يفتحون عقولهم لهؤلاء الجن. كل هذا يعتمد على مدى قوة عقلك. معظم الوقت، بدلاً من أن يستمع الجن لتعليماتنا، يحدث العكس. هؤلاء الناس عادة إما يموتون بسبب حادثة ما، أو أن يصبحوا مختلين عقلياً بشدة. وتذكر أننا هواية الجن المفضلة. أنا أتعامل مع الآلاف الجن طوال الوقت، ولكن بالنسبة للشخص العادي، جني واحد يكفي لجعل هذا الشخص مختل عقلياً أو مجنون. عندما تقرر ممارسة أي مهارة خطرة مثل التخاطر أو التنويم المغناطيسي، تأكد من أنك تعرف الآثار الجانبية.

99

Demons get nothing from this. This is just their hobby. Usually, demons inside our bodies will stay forever unless someone like me removes them from someone else's body, and in that case, the person's body will be neutral for a while. Then another demon will come and start living in that body. They may start helping the person sometimes, but most of the time they will create problems. I can tell you about myself. I had few habits; I just wanted some things. I'll leave everything. I won't finish that work. But because I have control over myself, I am a different person. I'm not too active. I'm very slow, and I think a lot before I do something. I'm not dying to do crazy stuff. I'm a little bit more mature and more sensible nowadays. I have a group of people (friends and family). I clean their bodies every day, and their temperaments change as well. None of them act extremist anymore. But normal people are under the influence of the same negative energies and demons from their childhood, so their habits and temperaments are the same.

Shortcut, demons like to live in the same place or same body. They donot move easily. If they are too much negative and human is Mentally weak then you can see a lot of examples of those people talk to themselves all the time, and we consider those kinds of people crazy or mentally sick. We can describe disease in two categories:
1. Painful disease: Invisible insects that eat body parts and organs damage the body parts and organs continuously. This is a combine action of pains and insects. Regardless of how many painkillers and medications we take, these invisible insects can kill. They can easily be moved from one body, but they do not die. They will find another body and start damaging that body.

هل هناك أي آثار جانبية لممارسة التنويم المغناطيسي والتخاطر؟ إن كلا الجن وآلام أوالمرض أجسام مادية ، ولكن غير مرئية لمعظمنا. كلا الجن والمرض مشابهان للهواء. لا يمكننا وؤية الهواء، لكننا يمكن أن نشعر به. إننا لا نستطيع أن نرى الجن والمرض، و معظمنا لا يشعر بها ، إلا أنها هي أجسام مادية مثل الهواء. ولكن يستطيع كل منا الشعورالآثارة، في شكل مرض أو مشاعر مريضة أو آلام. لأجسام المادية فقط يمكنها إحداث تأثيرمثل هذا.

كيف يمكنك أن تعرف ما إذا كنت تحت تأثير جني ما؟ كيف يمكنك معرفة ما إذا كان لديك أي جن من حولك؟ شيئ بسيط جداً، إذا كنت لا تحلم أثناء النوم، فلا وجود للجن حولك، ولكن إذا كنت تحلم أثناء النوم، فإن لديك جن حولك.

إذا كنت تعاني من أنواع مختلفة من أحلام كل ليلة، إذاً أنت تحت تأثير أكثر من جني. إنني أشعر بقوة أن كل من هو تحت تأثير أكثر من جني سيصبح مريض عقلياً عاجلاً أو آجلا.الجن ليسوا مثل الآلام أوالمرض. إنهم أكثر إهتماماً بالسيطرة على عقولنا. بعض الناس لديهم شخصيات قوية للغاية.

في حالة هؤلاء الناس، بدلا من يقعوا تحت سيطرة الجن، هؤلاء الجن يتبعونهم. الجن أذكياء جداً. بالنسبة لمعظمهم يكون مستوى ذكائهم مساوي لذكاء طفل في الثانيةعشرة من عمره.ومع ذلك، هم أكثر براءة منا. المشكلة الوحيدة هي أن الجن أصدقاء أفضل من البشر و يسهل التعامل معهم. ولكن قليل من البشر أذكياء جداً و لهم عقول قوية، و نواياهم وأهدافهم قوية. في حالة هؤلاء الناس، أشعر بقوة بأن الجن مجرد أتباع لهم. عندما يحدث هذا، يساعد الجن هؤلاء الناس في مساعيهم. ولكنني واثق أنه بإمكانك إحصاء تلك الأمثلة القليلة على أصابعك.

2. Painless diseases: These invisible pains also create a lot of sickness in our body, but they do not eat our body or our organs. They share our food as energy. But they block or stop different tubes in the kidneys, heart, or brain; they can cause kidney failure, heart attack, or aneurysms.

What is telepathy and hypnotism? Telepathy and hypnotism are not the same. Telepathy is a form of communication that allows you to privately talk with someone who is not in front of you. You can mentally communicate with anyone in any part of the world. Our soul/ spirit is a positive energy that keeps us alive and operates our bodily functions. No one can communicate by using telepathy to access souls. We always communicate with the demon or demons around that person. By using telepathy techniques, we can give instructions to their demons, which can then cause their hosts to think something in particular. Demons do not use telepathy on humans or animals, but demons use telepathy to communicate with each other. Humans use telepathy to communicate with other humans. But we are not communicating with their minds directly.

We are communicating with their demons and giving them instructions. After that, demons use hypnotism to control our positive energy and our minds. Hypnotism is a language that demons use to communicate with humans, animals, and insects. By using hypnotism, demons can show us whatever they want in our dreams. Demons are so good at using hypnotism that they can show us anything they want in the real word too. This quality of controlling someone in and feeding him or her different thoughts, dreams, or emotions is hypnotism.

يذكرنا الجن الصادقون إذا نسينا الأشياء. إنهم يلقون في أذهاننا مشاعر مختلفة ليجعلونا نشتبه بالآخرين.إننا ننسى الأشياء مرات عديدة، و ثم فجأة، مهما كان الشي الذي نسيناه، نتذكره في عقولنا، ولكن من الذي يذكرنا بكل هذه الامور التي ننساها؟يستطيع الجن الذين يلقون بأشياء مشبوهة في أذهاننا تجعلنا نشك في الآخرين.

هل هناك أي طريقة للشخص العادي أن يخرج الجن من جسم الرجل أو المرأة؟ لا، هذا مستحيل عملياً، ولكن إذا إتصلت برجال الدين عندك قد يكونون قادرين على توجيهك بشأن كيفية تقليل ضغط الجن. يمكنهم أن يوجهوك بسهولة في وسائل منع مشاكلالجن. في هذا النظام الذي خلقه الله، كل شيء ممكن.

ليس من الصعب بالنسبة لي إبقاء الجن بعيداً عن أي شخص. الجن يسمعوك في كل وقت، ولكن جعلها يستمعون إليك و يستجيبون لك ليس سهلاً. يستطيع الجن والمرض من حولنا الإستماع إلينا في كل وقت، لكننا لا نستطيع أن نسمعهم. لكي ينقلوا رغباتهم لنا، فإنهم ينومون عقولنا مغناطيسياً.إنهم يعرفون مشاكلنا، و يعرفون أنهم هم المسؤولون عن آلامنا وأمراضنا، ولكنهم لا يهتمون. من الصعب جداً وقف أنشطتهم السلبية.

لكنك قادر على إرغامهم بالتوقف عن فرض سيطرتهم و عن القيام بمخالفات. عدا ذلك، فإنه من الصعب حقاً السيطرة علي أنشطتهم. هل يمكنك محاولة الحد من سيطرة هؤلاء؟ إذا كنت تريد الحد من سيطرتهم علي عقلك، الشيء الوحيد الذي يمكنك القيام به هو جعل نفسك أقل إثارة للإهتمام بالنسبة لهم. وكيف يمكنك أن تفعل ذلك؟ يمكنك تقليل السلبية، والعنف، والتطرف في شخصيتك.

SEE & CONTROL DEMONS & PAIN	رضوان قرشي
How do telepathy and hypnotism work? What are the easy and difficult parts? Hypnotism is a procedure that demons pursue to feed something into the minds of living creatures. Think of the way we can play a DVD and then change discs and watch another movie. Hypnotism works in a similar way. The DVD could be considered our dreams, and demons can show us anything they want. The more we are under their control, the more we will observe whatever they want.

Now man can perform hypnosis. Usually, hypnotism experts have very strong demons with them, and they just ask those demons to perform those operations. Telepathy is a normal mode of communication with demons. But when demons are around us, we do not need to use the powers of telepathy to communicate with them. We can just talk normally, and they can hear us easily.

But when we need to communicate with someone who is not in front of us, we will need this communication skill. I have learned that telepathy is an effective way of communicating with demons, disease, and pains. I am able to use this skill in any part of the world without any previous friendship with those demons, but normal people need to have more connection with those demons. | تجنب العصبية و كن صبوراً. لا تغضب بكل بسهولة، كذلك تجنب المنافسة. إذا قمت بالسيطرة علي صفاتك السلبية، سيهتمون بك بشكل أقل بالتأكيد و سيبحثون عن شخص آخر. كل الجن مختلفون.

بعضهم لديه قوي قليلة، والبعض الآخر لديه قوى مختلف، إلا أن هناك بعض الأشياء المشتركة عند كل الجن، وهي قدرتهم علي إختراق الأجسام، وكلهم قادرون علي تمديد أنفسهم بقدر يريدون. كذلك كل الجن قادرون على التنويم المغناطيسي.

عندما يسيطر الجن علي العقول، يحدثون كل أنواع الأمراض العقلية والسلوكيات العنيفة. الأمراض تحدث كل أنواع الإعياء. هناك شيء آخر. هذا الشيء الثالث هو الشعور الداخلي، لكني لا أستطيع أن أجد كلمة واحدة لتفسير ذلك. يمكننا النظر في إضطرابات النوم، عندما تكون متعباً ولكنك غير قادر على النوم. هذا ليس مرضاً، ولكنها بعض المشاكل العميقة الي يحدثها الجن. التعصب ليس مرضاً، ولكن الجن يبقونا في حالة من عدم الصبر وعدم التسامح طوال الوقت، هذا يبقينا بعيداً عن دراساتنا، كما أنهم يبقونا في حالة كسل. هذا كله ليس مرضاً، ولكننا نعاني من كل ذلك بسبب سيطرة الجن علينا.
الحياة أفضل بكثير عندما لا يوجد الجن حولنا. سيكون لدينا رغبات أقل توحشاً وجنوناً عندما لا يوجد الجن حولنا، و لن يستطيع أحد أن ينومنا مغناطيسياً عندما لا يكونوا موجودين. بالاضافة الى ذلك، لن يوجد توترة أو مرض لو لم يتواجد الجن. حولنا. إنني أشعر بقوة بأن هذه الحياة ستكون سلمية جداً بدون الجن.
لقد تمت برمجة جسمي على الشعور بمزيد من الألم مقارنة بالشخص الطبيعي. بالنسبة لي، فإنه لا فرق عندي إذا كان شخص ما يعاني من مجرد صداع، حمى، سرطان، أو فيروس نقص المناعة البشرية، فكل هذه الأمراض تتساوي بالنسبة لي... |

Can we communicate with demons without telepathy? Yes, we can communicate with demons, disease, and pains in a normal way, but they usually do not pay attention to normal conversation. For remote communication, one needs to practice telepathy. Usually, people never reveal how to really practice telepathy.

I am not sure how many people are really capable of this form of communication. Normal people always think they are practicing communicating the mind of another human, but in actuality, they communicate with the demons of that person. Most telepathy experts usually send their demons around those people with whom they need to communicate, and those demons start hypnotizing the people according to their host's instructions.

When you are reading this book, everything may sound very easy, but be careful. Demons are not a joke. They are very powerful, and they do not give their control to anyone that easily. When most people practice telepathy or hypnotism, it usually means that they open their minds to those demons. This all depends on how strong your mind is. Most of the time, instead of a demon listening to our instructions, the opposite happens. These people usually either die because of some accident or they become extremely mentally ill. And remember that we are a favorite hobby for demons. I deal with thousands of demons all the time, but to a normal person, a single demon is enough to make that person mentally ill or crazy. When you decide to practice any dangerous skill like telepathy or hypnotism, make sure you know about the side effects.

رؤية الجن و الآلام السيطرة عليها

بمجرد أن أبدأ العمل على شخص ما، لا توجد أية قيود أو حدود، فلا أستطيع أن أقتصر على علاج صداع شخص ما، سأسبب إزعاجاً لجميع الأمراض والعلل داخل الجسم. وسوف أكون قادراً على إخراجهم من هذا الشخص، ولكن بعد ذلك، إذا كان هذا الشخص لا يريد مرض جديد، هو أو هي بحاجة إلى إصلاح الأضرار من خلال تناول العلاج المناسب أو إجراء عمليات جراحية سليمة. وأستطيع أن أساعد في إبعاد الطاقات السلبية للجن والأمراض بعيداً عن هذا الشخص، ولكن لابد أن تعالج الأعراض في أقرب وقت ممكن لتجنب الدعوات المتواصلة للأمراض والإلتهابات، و الإعياء إن مرض السكروالعديد من الأمراض الداخلية الأخرى خالية من الألم. عادة، لا يشعر الناس بأي ألم من تلك الأمراض إلا بعد أن تتسبب تلك الأمراض للأعضاء في أضرا بالغة لها. لكن في حالتي، جسمي حساس للغاية لجميع هذه الأمراض. كلما تواجد مرض، أوإعياء، أو جن حولي، إنهم يبقونني متألماً الألم ولا أشعر بالراحة بشكل كبير، حتى يغادروا هم أو أجبرهم على مغادرة جسدي. بالمقارنة مع الناس العاديين، وهؤلاء الأفراد لا يشعرون بأي شيء، لذلك لا يشعرون بأي مشاكل. ولكن نظرا لحساسيتي الزائدة، أبقى غير مرتاح جداً حتى يترك الجن والأمراض جسدي.

يكون الأشخاص الهادئون، أو البطيئون وحتى العصبيون، أقل عرضة للوقوع تحتسيطرة الجن. إن السلبية، والعنف، والحالات التطرف هي الصفات الرئيسية للجن. في الأساس، ونحن نتحكم في عقولنا. لا يستطيع الجن تغييرنا بسهولة. لهذا فإن الناس الذين يتصرفون بعنف وعصبية وخيانة للأمانة و سلبية، وتطرفاً بالفعل، هم الأكثر شيوعاً بين الجن. يستطيع الجن بسهولة استخدام الناس للقيام بأنشطة سلبية. معظم الجن لا يحبون حتى الناس الذين يتسمون بالهدوء، و البطئ، والناس الهدوء.

SEE & CONTROL DEMONS & PAIN

Are there any side effects to practicing hypnotism and telepathy? Both demons and pains or disease are physical bodies but invisible to most of us. Both demons and disease are similar to air. We cannot see air, but we can feel air. We cannot see demons and disease, and most of us cannot feel them either; however, they are physical bodies like air. But almost all of us can feel effects in the shape of sickness or sick feelings or pains. Only physical bodies can create an impact like this.

How do you know if you are under the influence of a demon? How can you know if you have any demons around you? It is very simple. If you are not dreaming during sleep, no demons are around you, but if you are dreaming during sleep, you have demons around you.

If you are experiencing different kinds of dreams every night, then you are under the influence of more than one demon. I strongly feel that anyone who is under the influence of more than one demon will become mentally sick sooner or later.

Demons are not like pains or disease. They are more interested in controlling our minds. Some people have extremely strong personalities. In their cases, instead of controlling, those demons follow them.

Demons are very smart and intelligent. For most of them, their level of intelligence is equal to a twelve-year-old kid. However, they are more innocent than we are. The only problem is that demons are better friends than human and they are very easygoing. But a few humans are extremely intelligent with very strong minds. Their intentions and goals are strong.

رضوان قرشي

لكن ذلك لا يعني أن هؤلاء الناس ليسوا تحت تأثير الجن، ولكن هؤلاء الجن قد يكونوا أقل خطورة. إن الحفاظ على الهدوء ممارسة جيدة للغاية، عدواني لتجعل نفسك أقل إثارة للإهتمام الجن .

ربما لا يتبع الجن والآلام أو المرض تماماً جميع قواعد المجال الكهرومغناطيسي، ولكن لديهم شيء مشابه جداً للمجال الكهرومغناطيسي. وإنني أشعر بقوة بأن هذا المجال الكهرومغناطيسي هو المسؤول عن تنقلهم خلال خطوط الهاتف و إنتقالهم من مكان إلى آخر في ثوان، بغض النظر عن المسافة. في البداية، واجهت الكثير من الألم والمرض لأنني كلما إتصلت مع أي ألم أو مرض آخر داخل شخص، كان كل جني أو مرض يخرج من هؤلاء الأشخاص، تتخزن داخل جسدي. لقد أجريت تجارب قليلة. وبعد تلك التجارب، تعلمت أن أثناء عملية إخراج الجن أو الآلام أو الأمراض من شخص ما، إذا كنت أمسك أي معدن أو إذا كنت أبقي قدمي عاريتين على أرضية خرسانية أو إذا كنت ألمس جدار من الطوب، لا يتخزن الجن والأمراض في جسدي. كان هذا مشابهاً لعبورهم من جسدي إلي تلك المعادن، والجدران، والأسمنت، أو أرضيات السيراميك. بعد ذلك، علمت أن هذا الجن،لدي الآلام والأمراض شيء مشابه جداً للجاذبية. إذا كان الجن بنتقلون من جسم إلي آخرمن خلال خطوط الهاتف أو المجالات الكهرومغناطيسية وإذا إة من ونتقلوا من جسم واحد إلي جسمي، يتم تخزينها داخل جسدٍي. ولكن خلال تلك العملية برمتها، إذا كنت مستلقياً على الارض بشكل صحيح، سوف يمرا لجن والمرض من جسدي. ومعظمهم سيذهب إلى الأرض نتيجة لمبدأ الجاذبية. بعد ذلك، بدأت أشير علي الناس أن يبقوا أ قدامهم وأيديهم على أي جدران من الطوب والأسمنت والسيراميك أوالأرض أو علي مختلف المعادن.

104

In the case of these people, I strongly feel that demons just follow them. When this happens, demons help those people in their endeavors. But I am sure you can count those few examples on your fingers.

Sincere demons remind us if we forget things. They feed different feelings into our mind to make us suspicious about other people. Many times, we forget things. Then suddenly, whatever we forgot comes to our minds, but who reminds us of all this forgotten stuff? The demons that feed suspicious things in our mind can make us suspect other people.

Is there any way for a normal person to take a demon out of his or her body? No, it is practically impossible, but if you contact your religious leaders, they should be able to guide you on how to reduce the pressure of demons. They can easily guide you in ways to prevent problems from demons. In this system created by God, everything is possible. It is not difficult for me to keep demons away from anyone. Demons hear you all the time, but making them listen to you is not easy. Demons and disease around us are able to hear us all the time. We cannot hear them. To convey their wishes, they hypnotize our minds. They know our problems. They know they are responsible for our pains and sicknesses, but they do not care; it is very difficult to stop their negative activities.

But you are capable of compelling them to cease their influence and stop their wrongdoing. Other than that, it is really difficult to control their activities. Can you try to reduce their control?

بهذه الطريقة، سينتقل أي جني أومرض إلى الأرض. حاول القيام بذلك عدة مرات في اليوم، وستجد أن ذلك سيساعدك، فإذا كنت تعاني من صداع أو ألم آخر، مثل إلتهاب المفاصل، وأنا لا أتحدث عن الأمراض، لا تتحدث إلى أي شخص سليم صحياً، ولكن فقط إستخدام الهاتف على الأذن في الجانب المصاب قليلاً لثواني أو لدقائق كحد أقصى. وإذا كان من قبيل المصادفة أنهم لا يستخدمون مكبر الصوت في هواتفهم، و يبقون سماعة الهاتف على آذانهم، فإن فرصة إنتقال الألم من خلال المحادثة القصيرة تصل إلى نسبة 90 في المئة. بعد ذلك أنت تحتاج فقط إلى إصلاح لأضرار التي سببها الألم، من خلال تناول الدواء. إذا كنت تتحدث لعدة اشخاص لفترة قصيرة جداً، فهناك فرصة 100 في المئة أن الألم الذي تعاني منه سيختار شخص ما من هؤلاء لأشخاص في الطرف الآخر من خط الهاتف .

لذلك عليك أن تعرف، إنه إذا كنت في حالة مؤلمة، وكنت تتناول بعض الأدوية منذ ساعات قليلة مضت، ولكنها لم تنجح في التخلص من هذا الألم، تذكر، بمجرد البدء في تناول حبوب مسكنات الآلام، سوف يبدأ الألم في البحث عن ضحية أضعف، وستكون على إستعداد لترك جسدك. خلال هذه العملية إذا بدأت تتكلم على الهاتف لفترة قصيرة جداً من الوقت مع العديد من الناس، وهم لا يستخدمون مكبر الصوت في الهاتف، ويضعون سماعات الهواتف على آذانهم خلال المحادثة الهاتفية معكم، وهناك إحتمالات 99 في المئة ، أن يختار الألم شخص ما من بين هؤلاء الناس وينتقل لأي شخص منهم خلال محادثة هاتفية قصيرة جداً. هكذا تعرف، أتك بهذه الطريقة يمكنك أن ترسل الألم إلى شخص آخر.

If you want to reduce the control they have over your mind, the only thing you can do is make yourself less interesting to them. And how can you do it? You can reduce the negativism, violence, and extremism in your personality. Avoid short temperaments and do not become impatient. Do not get angry too easily. Avoid competition as well. If you control your negative qualities, they will definitely be less interested in you. They will look for someone else. All demons are different. Some have a few powers, and others have different powers; however, a few things are common between all demons. All of them are capable of penetrating bodies.

All of them able to expand themselves as much they want. All demons are capable of hypnotism.

When demons are controlling minds, they create all kind of mental illnesses and violent behaviors. Diseases create all kind of sicknesses, pains, and illnesses. There is another thing. This third thing is an inner feeling. I cannot find a single word to explain it. Consider a sleep disorder when you are tired but unable to fall asleep. This is not a disease but some deep problem created by a demon. Intolerance is not a disease, but demons keep us impatient and intolerant all the time. They keep us away from our studies, and they keep us lazy. All these are not disease, but we suffer all of these because of the control demons have over us. Life is much better when demons are not around. We will have less wild and crazy desires in our minds when demons are not around us. No one can hypnotize us when they are gone. Plus, there is no sickness or tension if demons are not around. I strongly feel that life would be very peaceful without demons.

لذلك لا تتحدث علي الهاتف مع أي شخص، بمجرد أنك كنت تعاني من الألم، و عليك تناول مسكنات الألم أيضا، و هكذا تنقذ هؤلاء الناس من هجوم الألم.الخاص بك عليهم. بالتأكيد، في مكان ما في هذا الكتاب، وسوف أصف كيفية البدء في التواصل والصداقة مع الجن من حولنا، و ما يزيد أو ينقص عليها.و الآن أنا أصف كيفية إستخدام الناس و كيف يمكنهم إستخدام، و كيف ينبغي إستخدام ،و عدم إستخدام الجن لهذا الغرض. وهناك الكثير من الناس يذهبون إلي أطباء الجن لإحداث الكثير من الجاذبية أو المحبة عند صديق ذكرا أو أنثي.عن طريق إستخدام الجن. يمكنك العثور على الكثير من أطباء الجن في مناطق مختلفة من العالم في كل مكان. سوف تكون قادراً حتى على القيام بذلك بنفسك في المستقبل. لذلك بدلا من إستخدام عبارة "أطباء الجن"، أفترض فقط أنه يمكنك القيام بذلك بنفسك. سأفترض فقط أنك ذكر و ستستخدم الجن الخاص بك لإجتذاب أي سيدة أو العديد من النساء إليك أو السيطرة عليهن.القاعدة بسيطة، تحتاج إلى أن تطلب صراحة ما تريده من الجن الخاص بك. تأكد من أن تقول للجن الخاص بك بألا يحدثوا بعض المرض و غيره من المشاكل لهم. آمل أن يستمعوا إليك، و يستجيبوا لك، ولكنني أشك في ذلك.إذا أرسلت جني لينوم إمرأة ما مغناطيسياً، بحيث يولد الجني بعض الحب والجاذبية لك في مخيلتها، و سوف تبدأ في التفكير فيك فوراً. تذكر دائما، أن البشر هم المتحكمون في عقولهم، حيث يمكنهم رفض أية أفكار بسهولة أحياناً، وأحياناً أخري من الصعب الخروج من فخ جني قوي. الآن الخطوة الأولى، هي أن يجد الجني الخاص بك لنفسه مكاناً بين الجن الموجودون حول تلك المرأة.

My body is programmed to feel more pain compared to the normal person. To me, it makes no difference if someone has just a headache, fever, cancer, or HIV. All these diseases or sicknesses are the same for me. Once I start working on someone, there are no restrictions or limits. I cannot limit myself to someone's headache. I will disturb all sicknesses and diseases inside the body. I will be able to move them out of that person, but after that, if that person does not want to contract new disease, he or she needs to fix the damages by taking the proper medication or undergoing the correct surgeries. I can help keep the negative energies of demons and diseases away from that person, but the symptoms still need to be fixed as soon as possible to avoid continuous invitations to diseases, infections, and sicknesses. Diabetes and several other internal diseases are pain free. Usually, people do not feel any pain from those diseases until they damage the organs badly. But in my case, my body is extremely sensitive to all these diseases. Whenever disease, sicknesses, or demons come around me, they keep me in pain and very uncomfortable until they leave or I compel them to leave my body. As compared to normal people; these individuals do not feel anything. That is why they feel no problems. But because of my extra sensitivity, I stay very uncomfortable until demons and diseases leave my body. Slow, calm, even-tempered people are less likely to be under the influence of demons. Negativism, violence, and extremism are the main qualities of demons. Basically, we are the bosses of our minds. Demons cannot change us easily. That's why people who already exhibit violence, short tempers, dishonesty, negativism, and extreme behavior are more popular among demons.

إما أن يصل الجني الخاص بك إلي عقلها بسهولة ، أو أن يضطر إلي القتال مع الجن التواجدون حول تلك المرأة بالذات، لذلك قد يكون هذا هو السبب في أن الجني سيأخذ وقتاً طويلاً لينوم هذه المرأة مغناطيسياً . الآن هناك ظرفان واحد أن نفترض فقط أن الجني الخاص بك سيصل إلى عقل تلك المرأة بطريقة ما ولن يكون صعباً علي الجن تنويم تلك المرأة مغناطيسياً، وأن حبك وإنشاء علاقة بك أصبح وشيكاً و فورياً، يمكنك ان تطلب من الجني الخاص للضغط علي تلك المرأة عن طريق التنويم المغناطيسي. لن يستغرق ذلك وقتاً طويلاً، وسوف تري تلك المرأة حولك على الفور.

لكن تذكر أنك أنت و الجني الخاص بك بهذه الطريقة، لا تعطيان ما يكفي من الوقت المناسب لتلك المرأة لتعلم الكثير عنك وتفكر فيك قليلاً وتحسم أمرها. هذا قد يفعل أمرين، قد تأتي لك تلك المرأة على الفور ولكن ربما أنها لم تحبك، و ستنصرف عنك بسرعة. و الشيئ الثاني، ربما تبدأ تحبك على الفور، و يروق الأمر لك. إنني أعتقد دائما أن كل ما تحتاجه هو أن تتصرف ببطيء وثبات وتدريب الجن الخاص بك بنفس السرعة.

والآن إذا عدنا إلى الخطوة الأولى، عندما قررت أن ترسل الجن الخاص بك لإمرأة ما، إذا كانت محاطة فعلاً بجن خاص بها، أو جن آخرين حولها، أرسلهم رجال آخرون، و في هذه الحالة، لن يجد الجني الخاص بك فرصة للوصول بسهولة إلى عقل تلك المرأة . تذكر دائما، أن الجن يتقاتلون فيما بينهم طوال الوقت، كما يمكنهم بسهولة قتل بعضهم البعض. إذا كان الأمر كذلك فإذا كان الجن الخاص بك ليس قوياً بما فيه الكفاية، قد يموت بسبب علاقة الحب الخاصة بك، فإن لم تسمع رداً مرة أخرى قريباً من الجن الخاص بك، فهذا يعني أنه ضحى بحياته من أجل علاقة الحب الخاصة بك.

Demons can easily use these people for negative activities. Most demons do not like eventempered, slow, and calm people. But that still does not mean that these people are not under the influence of demons, but those demons may be less dangerous. It is a very good practice to keep calm and quiet. Stay cool and patient and nonviolent and non aggressive to make yourself less interesting for demons.

Maybe demons and pains or disease do not follow exactly all the rules of electromagnetic field, but they have something very similar to electromagnetic field. And I strongly feel that this electromagnetic field is responsible for their traveling through the phone lines and transferring from one place to another in seconds, regardless of the distance. In the beginning, I faced a lot of pain and sickness because whenever I communicated with any pain or sickness inside another person, every demon or disease coming out of those people was stored inside my body. Instead of storing all these demons and diseases inside my body, I did a few experiments. And after those experiments, I learned that during the process of taking out demons or pains or diseases from someone, if I was holding any metal or if I was keeping my bare feet on a concrete floor or if I was touching a brick wall, those demons and diseases were not stored in my body. They were like a current passing from my body and going inside those metals, walls, cements, or ceramic floors. After that, I learned that these demons, pains and diseases had something very similar to gravity. If they are traveling from one body to another body through telephone lines or through electromagnetic fields and if they come from one body and enter mine, then they will be stored inside my body.

لتجنب هذه المأساة يجب أن تتصرف بذكاء ومنذ البداية، يجب عليك أن تطلب من الجن الخاص بك العمل بذكاء وبحذر. يجب علي الجن الخاص بك أن يصل إلي تلك المرأة عندما يكون الموجودون حولها، مشغولون في مكان ما، أ ويستريحون، أو يمكن أولا أن يختلط الجن الخاص بك مع هؤلاء الجن ببطيء وثبات، و بمجرد أن يصبح الجن الخاص بك أصدقاء للجن الموجودون حول تلك المرأة، سيكون من السهل جداً علي الجن الخاص بك إقناع هؤلاء الجن والمرأة ليكونوا في صالحك.

كل تعليماتي ليست لك فقط ، فهي أيضاً لجميع الجن. هناك طريقة أخرى يمكنك إختيارها لإستخدام الجن في تحقيق الحب الذي تريده، ذلك إذا لم تكن في عجلة من أمرك، مجرد إعطاء أوامر أو تعليمات إلى الجن الخاص بك ليتصرف بطريقة سهلة. إطلب منهم زيارة تلك المرأة يوماً بعد يوم، و يلقي في عقلها بعض الأفكار عنك في بضع دقائق ثم يتركها وحدها، و بهذه الطريقة سوف لدي الجن الخاص بك طريقاً سهلاً للوصول إلى الجن المتواجدون حول المرأة، و الوصول إليها بالتأكيد أيضاً جميع. وآمل أن لا تستخدم هذه الحيلة الواحدة مع عدة نساء مرة واحدة.

هناك ظرف آخر أو طريقة أخري يمكن أخذها في الإعتبار. إذا لم يجد الجن الخاص بك طريقة بطريقة ما للوصول إلي الجن التواجدون حول تلك المرأة أو أنهم لم يستطيعوا الصول إليها، إسمح لي أن أقدم لك بعض الإقتراحات، حسنا، إنتقل الآن إلى الخطوة التالية. ربما يحاول آخرون مثلك الوصول إلى تلك المرأة تحديداً. هذه مشكلة أخرى. أو ربما أن تلك المرأة مرتبطة بالفعل برجل آخر، في هذه الحالة، يكون الجن المختصون بذلك الرجل ضد الجن المختصون بك أيضاً في هذه الحالة، يصبح الوضع أكثر وأكثر تعقيداً.

But during that whole process, if I am grounded properly, demons and disease will pass from my body. Most of them will go into the ground as a result of the principle of gravity. After that, I started suggesting that people keep their feet or hands on any brick walls, the cement or ceramic floor, or various metals. This way, any demon or disease will go toground. Try it several times a day, and you'll find that it helps. If you are suffering from any pain, like headache or another pain, like arthritis, I am not talking about diseases, do not talk to any healthy person, but using your phone on ear at affected side just for few seconds or maximum a minute. And by chance if they are not using speaker phone and keeping phone on their ears 90 percent chance are your pain will transfer to them during short conversation. After that only you need to fix damages caused by that pain by taking some medication. And if you are talking to several people for very short conversation, there is a 100 percent chance your pain will choose someone from several people at the other end of the phone line.

So you know, if you are in painful condition and you are taking some pills since last few hours but unsuccessful in getting rid of that pain, but remember, once you start taking painkiller pills, usually pain will start looking for a weaker victim and ready to leave your body. During this process if you start talking on the phone for very short period of time with several people and those people not using speaker phone, they are keeping phone on their ears during phone conversation with you, 99 percent chances are your pain will choose someone among those people and transfer to anyone of them during very short phone conversation. So you know, this way you can send your pain to someone else.

لهذا أياً كان الذي يملك المزيد من القوي والجاذبية للمرأة سيفوز في السباق. إستمري في العمل. وسوف تحصل علي ما تريد. الآن يمكنني أن أقترح عليك طريقة أخرى سهلة و ستكون هذه الطريقة سهلة جداً بالنسبة لك، وللجني الخاص بك، إذا كنت ترغب في ذلك، وهي طريقة كافية بالنسبة لك. تذكر دائما، أنك ليس لديك جن قليلون من حولك، إنهم أحيانا يكونوا بالمئات و أحياناً أكثر من ذلك. لذلك عليك إعطاء تعليماتك و أوامرك كثيراً، حتي يتبع معظم الجن أوامرك معظم الوقت .

لابد أن تدرب الجن الخاص بك علي أحلامك. تذكر، بمجرد أن يكون لديك أكثر من جني حولك، كل ليلة أثناء نومك ، سيقوم جن مختلفون أو مجموعات منهم بالإتصال بعقلك من خلال التنويم المغناطيسي ليظهروا لك الأحلام، لذلك لابد أن تدرب الجن الخاص بك و تعطيهم الأوامر و التعليمات المناسبة لإظهار أو لجلب المرأة المفضلة لديك في أحلامك طوال الوقت. من فضلك قم بمراجعة القوانين المحلية الخاصة بك، إذا كان يعتبر هذا غير قانوني في منطقتك! وأنا أعلم أنه منذ عدة سنوت سألني شخص ما ذات مرة أن أساعده في الوصول إلى امرأة ، وأعتقد أن اسمها جيني. حافولت ي البداية القيام ببعض الإجراءات وأرسلت بعض الجن لاقناعها بصديقي. بعد أيام قليلة، إقتنعت به، لكن كان لديها موافقاًما منه لأنه كان يشكو منها.

لذلك فإن الخطوة التالية، بدلا من إضاعة المزيد من الوقت في إقناع إمرأة، أنشأت إتصال مع عقلها للوصول إلي الجن الموجودون في عقلها أو حولها. أتذكر عدة مرات أنني أقنعت هؤلاء الجن لعدة أيام وأعطائهم تعليمات و أوامر واضحة مرارا وتكرارا.

So do not call anyone, once you are suffering from any pain and take up painkillers also, so you can safe those people from the attack of your pain. For sure, somewhere in this book, I will describe how to start communication and friendship with demons around us, with plus and minuses. Right now I am describing how people use and can use, should use and should not use demons for this purpose. A lot of people reach demon doctors to create a lot of attraction or love in a male or female friend for them by the use of demons. You can find a lot of demon doctors everywhere in different parts of the world. Even you will be able to do this by yourself in the future. So instead of using the words "demon doctors," I just assume you are practicing this by yourself. I just assume you are a male and you will use your demons to attracts or control any women or many women toward you.

The rule is simple; you need to tell your demon openly what you want. Make sure to tell your demons not to make those people sick or create some other problems for them. I hope they will listen to you, but I doubt it. So if you send a demon to a woman so a demon can hypnotize that woman and generate some love and attraction for you in her mind. Demons are very powerful in hypnotizing anyone. As soon as demon will feed some thoughts in her mind, she will start thinking about you immediately. Always remember, humans are the bosses of their minds. Humans can reject any thoughts sometimes easily; sometimes it is difficult to come out from the trap of a powerful demon. Now in the first step, your demon has to make room around that woman, among demons around here.

أعتقد أني عملت في هذه المهمة، لمدة يومين ثم تركتها، وأعتقد بقدر ما أتذكر، أن المهمة كانت ناجحة. تذكر دائما، انها إن إرسال جني موجهة إلى شخص ما طوال الوقت ليست فكرة جيدة، و السبب في ذلك هو أن الجن طاقات سلبية ؛ وآثارها، ونتائجها سلبية. إذا سيطر الجن سيطرة كاملة على دماغ أو عقل أي شخص، فإنهم يمكنهم أن يجعلوه مريضاً جسدياً أو عقليا، لذلك يجب أن يكون لديك قوي كافية للسيطرة على الجن قبل إستخدامهم .

تأكد، أنك عند إرسالك الجن لشخص ما، لإنجاز مهمة ما، أنك قمت بإرشادهم و توجيههم للهدف. الشياطين.الجن ليسوا قططاً أو كلابا، إنهم مخلوقات خارقة و قوية في هذا العالم، إذا كنت تفهم المواد المشعة، وهذه الأنواع من المواد المشعة تنبعث منها بإستمرار إشعاعات مشعة. كما تعلم، لقد إكتشف العلم الحديث هذه المادة المشعة منذ زمن طويل، نظرا لنوعية ما ينبعث منها بإستمرار من إشعاعات قاتلة للأجسام الحية والبشرية وغيرها. إكتشف العلم الحديث تلك الأشعة المشعة القاتلة لإستخدامها. و بمجرد أن إكتشف العلم الحديث أن هذه المواد المشعة قاتلة للبشر و الكائنات الحية الأخرى، بدلاً من أن يثبط العلم الحديث إستخدام هذه الأشعة، فإنه شجع إستخدامها، و إستخدمها أخيراً لعمل قنبلة نووية. إذاً من الذي أوجد المواد المشعة؟ من الذي أوجد هذه المواد المشعة القاتلة التي تخرج منها هذه الإشعاعات القاتلة؟ بالتأكيد المخ البشري. والسؤال المطروح الآن هو الذي خلق العقل البشري؟ العلم الحديث أم الله ؟ المشكلة في العلوم الطبية والحديثة هو أنها تؤمن فقط وتعتقد في كل ما تراه، أو تسمعه، وتشعر به، هذا كل ما في الأمر. . إذا كان الأمر كذلك، إذا كانت العلوم الطبية والحديثة لا يمكنها رؤية الألم في الجسم، وذلك لا يعني عدم وجود الألم. ويمكنني أن يثبت لأي طبيب أوباحث أنني أستطيع إبعاد الآلام في بضع ثوان عن الجسم بواسطة الإتصال فقط.

Either your demon will get access to her mind easily or may your demon has to fight with the demons around that particular woman. So this may be the reason why your demon will take a long time to hypnotize that woman. Now there are two conditions—one, we just assume that your demon will get access to the mind of that woman immediately somehow. It will not be difficult for that demon to hypnotize her about your love and involvement of you is looking for short-term and immediate relationship, you can ask your demon to push that woman hard by hypnotism. It will not take a long time, and you will see that woman immediately around you.

But remember, this way you and your demon are not giving enough time to that woman to learn and think about you a little bit and settle down. So it may do two things. She may come to you immediately but maybe she never liked you and back off quickly. Second thing maybe she starts liking you immediately and it works for you. I always think you need to act slow and steady and train your demons also for same pace.

Now if we go back to the very first step, when you decided to send your demon to a woman. If that woman is already surrounded with some of her demons and some other demons are also around her come or send by few other men. In this situation, your demon will not get easy access to the mind of that woman. Demons already around that woman will not give away access to your demon to reach her mind or brain. Always remember, demons fight with each other all the time and are very easily capable of killing each other. So if your demon is not strong enough, your demon may die due to your love affair.

حسنا، وجهة نظري هي، ما لذي نحتاج إليه أكثرالآن؟ هل نحتاج الأشعة المشعة للقنبلة النووية لقتل الأجسام الحية والبشرية وغيرها، أم "أشعة" تصد الجن أو الآلام عن أجسامنا ؟ فكيف إعتقد العلم الحديث أن الله خلق المواد المشعة التي يوجد بها إشعاعات مشعة قاتلة ولكن الله لم يترك أو يخلق نظام "أشعة" لصد أو السيطرة على الآلام واالجن و ذلك لحماية الأجسام الحية والبشرية وغيرها من الجن والآلام. هكذا سأفصح لك عن أصل الإشعاعات والموجات لصد الجن والآلام. لماذا علي أن أقول هذا، لأن إما أن العلوم الطبية لم تهتم بمصدر الإشعاعات لصد الجن والآلام، أو أنها لا دراية لها بتلك الإشعاعات.

إن كل الكتب المقدسة، كل الكلمات المقدسة باللغة الأصلية، والكلمات الأصلية فقط، وليس ملخص ، أو ترجمة، هي مصدر للأشعة التي تصد الجن والآلام. جميع المواد الموجودة على هذه الأرض لا تنبعث منها إشعاعا ت لصد الجن و الآلام هناك قليل من الكلمات المقدسة،بغض النظر عن معانيها هي كلمات وسطور مشعة في الكتب المقدسة، هي كلمات فعالة في صد ودحر الجن والآلام لحماية البشر والأجسام الحية الأخرى. تلك الصياغات و السطور المقدسة باللغة الأصلية، لديها قوة حارقة للجن و الآلام بدون قراءتها مراراً وتكراراً. هذه الإشعاعات الحارقة التي تخرج أثناء الصلاة، نحن بحاجة إلي الإكثار من الصلوات المقدسة لمحاربة أو الجن والآلام. مرة أخرى، للكلمات المقدسة في الكتاب المقدس والصلاة المختلفة، إستخدام مختلف. لكنني أتكلم هنا عن الصلاة المشعة أو كلمات الكتب المقدسة لصد وهزيمة الجن والآلام بدون قراءة مراراً وتكراراً ، تلك الكلمات المقدسة تجلب قوة لصد الجن والآلام. هذا فقط لإكتشاف أشعة بالحدة المناسبة، لمحاربة الجن والآلام.

So if you do not hear back from your demon soon, it means your demon sacrificed his life for your love affair. To avoid this tragedy of your demon, you should act smart and from the beginning you need to ask your demons to act smart and careful. Your demons need to reach that woman when other demons around her are busy somewhere else, resting, or first, your demons need to mix up with those demons slow and steady. Once your demons will become the friend of other demons around that woman, it will be very easy for your demon to convince those demons and that woman in your favor.

All of my instructions are not only for you; they are for all demons also. Another way you can choose to use your demons to achieve your love if you are not in hurry. Just give commands or instructions to your demons to play easy. Tell them to visit that woman every other day and feed something about you in her brain for few minutes and then leave her alone. This way your demon will have easy access to both demons around her and definitely her too. I hope you will not use this trick to several women in one time.

Now consider another condition. If somehow your demon cannot get access around those demons around that woman or herself to that woman. Then let me give you few more suggestion. Okay, now move to next step. Maybe like you, some other people trying to reach that particular woman. This is another problem. Or maybe that woman is already involved with another man; in that case, the demons form that man will come against your demon also. In this case, the situation is getting more and more complicated.

العلوم الطبية فقط هي التي يجب أن تثري أو تضخم هذه الإشعاعات وإستخدامها لضرب الأهداف إلكترونياً. الطريقة الثانية، أنه حتى تصل العلوم الطبية إلى نقطة تحول، فإن قراءة هذه الكلمات المقدسة في الصلوات المقدسة مراراً و تكراراً، يولد موجات وأشعاعات طاردة لمحاربة الجن والآلام. لذلك لا تعتقد أن الله لم يقدم لنا أي شيء لسلامتنا و إنقاذنا من الآثار السلبية الناجمة عن الجن والآلام. يقين، الله لديه علاج لنا ضد الجن والآلام، ولكن العلوم الطبية لا تزال غير مدركة له. و لكني أنا واثق أنه في يوم ما، قريباً جدا ستكتشف العلوم الطبية هذه الموجات والإشعاعات في المستقبل .

في الخطوة الثانية، يجب علي العلوم الطبية لديها زيادة قيمة أو تضخيم هذه الإشعاعات الحارقة وإستخدامها إلكترونيا في مجال مكافحة الآلام والجن الخفية. إن الكتب المقدسة علم كامل.كل صلاة، كل سطر من الكتب المقدسة يولد أو ينبعث منه إشعاعات.و الآن مسؤولية العلوم الطبية و الحديثة إكتشاف كل هذه الموجات والإشعاعات وإثراءها وتضخيمها ومن ثم إستخدامها إلكترونيا لعلاج كل مشكلة على هذه الأرض. آمل ألا يستغرق العلوم الطبية والحديثة وقتاً أكثر من اللازم،للإعتقاد ولفهم توقعاتي، ونظرياتي. هذا مثل واحد بسيط علي سبيل المثال، لكيفية إستخدام هذه النظريات، إذا كان أي شخص لديه أي ألم في أي جزء من جسمه، و قرأت مراراً الصلاة المقدسة، ما لا يقل عن 11 مرة كحد الأدنى باللغة الأصلية، وتضخمها إلكترونياً، وتطبقها على مكان الألم، و في غضون ثوان قليلة، لن تتحتمل للآلام والجن آثار تلك الصلوات المقدسة، وستترك ذلك المكان أو الجسم على الفور.

So whoever will have more powers and attraction for that woman will win the race. Keep working. You will get it. Now another and easy way I can suggest to you. This will be very easy for you and the demon if you like it and it's good enough for you. Always remember, you do not have only a few demons around you; sometimes they are in the hundreds and sometime more. So you need to give your instruction and commands frequently so most of them follow your commands most of the time.

You need to train your demons about your dreams. Remember, once you have more than one demon around you, every night during sleep, different demons or groups of demons will contact your mind through hypnotism to show you dreams. So you need to train your demons and give them proper instructions and command to show you or bring your favorite woman in your dreams all the time. Please check your local laws; this is not illegal in your area! I know one time someone asked me to help him to get access to a woman few years ago. I think her name was Jeanie. I tried some procedure first and sent a few demons to convince her for my friend. After a few days, she was convinced for him but still she had some attitude with him as he was complaining about her.

So the next step, instead of wasting more time and convince her, I established telepathic contact with her mind to reach demons in or around her mind. I remember I convinced those demons several times for several days and give them clear instructions and commands again and again. I worked on that assignment; I think for two days and then let it go. I think as much, I remember, that mission was successful.

الأحلام هي أول إتصال صالح للجن بنا. يستخدام الجن عقولنا أو دماغنا ومهاراتهم في التنويم المغناطيسي لإعداد الأحلام لنا. لقد كانت فكرتي عن الأحلام مثلك ومثل اللآخرين منذ بضعة سنوات مضت . الأحلام هي جزء مهم جداً من حياتنا. لقد كنت أبحث دائما عن رسالة وراء أحلامي. ولكن منذ بدأت رؤية، وإستشعار عن بعد، والتواصل مع الجن، علمت الكثير من الأشياء الغريبة والمثيرة للدهشة. سأصف الآن آلية الأحلام ومهارة التنويم لدي الجن بالتفصيل. لكن قبل ذلك سأسدي لك نصيحة واحدة بسيطة عن الأحلام، والأمر يرجع إليك، فإما أن تستمع لي وتجعل حياتك سهلة أو لا تستمع لي، و تظل خائفاً ومضايقاً نفسك من هذه الأحلام الغريبة المخيفة بقية حياتك. الأحلام ليس لديها حكم علي حياتنا الحقيقية، إنها تماماً مثل الأفلام المختلفة أوالدراما التي نشاهدها على شاشات التلفزيون كل يوم، وهي لا يكون لها أي تأثيرفي حياتنا الحقيقية. أحلام لا تتوقع أي شيء عن ماضينا أوحاضرنا أو مستقبلنا أو ماضي أو حاضر أو مستقبل أي شخص آخر . أفضل طريقة للتعامل مع الأحلام هي أن نراها أو نشاهدها كفيلم دون أخذها على محمل الجد، فبمجرد إستيقاظك في الصباح، لا تضيع حتى دقيقة واحدة في القلق حول الأحلام، و حاول أن تواجه أحلامك و تسيطر عليها.

سأشرح الطريقة التي تستطيع بها السيطرة علي الجن المتواجدون حولك والتواصل معهم و كيفية مواجهة أحلامك وفقاً لرغباتك وإرادتك في مكان ما من الكتاب . على أي حال، لقد وصفت الأحلام قليلاً في كتاب الأول، والآن سأعطي المزيد من التفاصيل. يستخدم الجن مهارتهم في التنويم المغناطيسي مثل فيلم دي في دي، دماغنا يكون مثل مشغل الدي في دي، وعيوننا ترى، بغض النظر عما إذا كنا مستيقظين أم نائمين.

SEE & CONTROL DEMONS & PAIN

Always remember, it is not a good idea to keep sending a guided demon to someone all the time. Reason is demons are negative energies; their effects and results are negative. If demons establish total control of a brain or mind, they can make that person mentally or physically sick. So you should have enough powers to control demons before you use them.

Make sure, if you are sending your demons to someone, to achieve some task once the job is done, you guided and targeted demons. Demons are not cat or dogs. Demons are powerful supernatural creature in this world. If you understand radioactive materials or substances, these kinds of substances continuously emit radioactive rays. As you know modern science discovered a long time ago these radioactive substance due to the quality of those substance of emitting continuously those human and other living bodies, killing rays. Modern science discovered that those killing radioactive rays from these radioactive substances to use the quality of chain reaction of these radioactive substances and rays. Once modern science finds out those radioactive materials are killer for humans and other living bodies, instead of discouraging it, modern science encourage it and finally use it to build a nuclear bomb. So who created those radioactive substances? Who created those killing radioactive rays coming out of those radioactive killing rays? Definitely the human brain. So now the question is who invented the human brain? Modern science or the God? Problem with medical and modern science is they just have faith and believe whatever they can see, hear, and sense, that's all.

رضوان قرشي

الجن قادرون على إظهار أي شيء لنا مثل فيلم أو مسرحية لشخصيات واقعية حولنا في أحلامنا. نحن أو عقولنا لينا قادرون علي صنع أو إحداث الأحلام بدون وجود جني. لدينا الكثير من الروابط، و الإتصالات، وتأثير الأحلام من حولنا، في حياتنا، لكننا لا ندرك تماماً تأثير الجن في حياتنا. يصعب جداً علي الشخص العادي تصور وفهم ذلك، لكن الأحلام هي أسهل طريقة لشرح فكرة الجن لشخص ما. بنفس الطريقة، أحلامنا هي أسهل طريقة لتحليل الجن من حولنا. لدينا دائما مجموعة من الجن حولنا في منزلنا أو في مكان آخر. عادة يسافر معنا جني واحد فقط إذا كان يستحوذ علي جسمنا في ذلك الوقت. و خلاف ذلك، الجن لا يسافرون معنا.

يعيش الجن في منزلنا ولا يذهبوا إلى مكتبنا معنا. والسبب في ذلك هو أن كل مكان، بغض النظر عما إذا كان مكتبنا / ورشة عمل،مرحاض، مرآب، محل، فندق، و متجر، يستحوذ عليها مجموعة معينة من الجن. هؤلاء الجن يعيشون هناك، و هم لا يسمحون للجن الآخرين بالدخول إلي منازلهم بسهولة. إذا حدث بالصدفة أن شخص ما لديه جني واحد فقط حوله / حولها، فإن الجني نفسه يسيطر على عقله أثناء نومه عن طريق التنويم المغناطيسي، للإتصال بعقله أو دماغه لنقل مجموعة كاملة من الشخصيات من حوله مع نوع من الدراما أو الحدث. الجن لا يتركون أجسام البشر أو الحيوانات بسهولة ما لم يمت الجسد. يرتبط الجن مع هذه الأجسام بشدة، حيث يقيمون فيها طوال حياتهم، بغض النظر عن ما إذا كان هذا الجسم هو جسم إنسان أو عنكبوت أو سحلية أو قطة أو أي شيء آخر. عادة، نضيف جني جديد حولنا بمجرد أن نقتل أي حشرة أو الزواحف حولنا. ردود الفعل الأولى والمباشرة من الجن تظهر أخياناً في شكل نوع من الألم أو المرض، والثانية على الفور وسوف يكون رد الفعل الثاني المباشر، هو الأحلام المخيفة و السيئة.

114

Rizwan Qureshi

So if medical and modern science cannot see pain in a body, it does not mean there is no pain. I can prove to any medical doctor or scientist in a few seconds by moving pains away from their bodiesby just communication.

Okay, my point is what do we need more right now? Radioactive rays of nuclear bomb to kill human and other living bodies or "rays" to repel demons or pains from our bodies? How come modern science thinks that God has created radioactive material with radioactive rays to kill bodies but God did not leave or make any system of "rays" to repel or control pains and demons to protect human and other living bodies from demons and pains. So I am going to tell you the origin of rays and waves to repel demons and pains. Why I have to tell because either medical science never pay attention to the source ofrays to control and repel the demons and pains, or really modern and medical science is not aware about it. All holy books, all holy words in original language, original words only, not summary, or a translation, are the source of rays to repel the demons and pains. The way all available substances on this earth do not emit rays to repel demons or pains.

There are few holy wording, regardless of their meanings are, radioactive wordings and lines in the holy books, are effective to repel and defeat demons and pains to protect humans and other living bodies. Those holy wordings, line, or prayers in original language has the burning powers for demons and pain without reading them repeatedly. Those burning rays come out from holy prayers needed to be amplified or enriched to fight against demons and pains.

رؤية الجن و الآلام السيطرة عليها

إذا كنت ترى نفس الأحلام طوال الوقت أنت وأفراد عائلتك، هذا يعني أنك لم تقم بإضافة أي جني جديد من حولك.

عادة ما يرتبط الجن جداً بالأجسام التي يقيمون فيها. على سبيل المثال، يقيم الجن في جسم الإنسان و عادة تعيش داخل أو خارج الجسم، حول نفس الشخص أو الأسرة. تبدل الجن الأجسام عندما تنتهي أو تموت الأجسام القديمة . إذا لم تكن شخصاً إجتماعياً، لن يكون لديك تنوع في أحلامك. لأنه بمجرد أن تجتمع مع ناس أقل ، ستمتص أو تجذب عدداً أقل من الجن، إلي مجموعة الجن الموجودون حولك. إذا كنت لا تقتل الحشرات، هذا يعني أنك لم تضف جن جديد من حولك. إذا كنت موجوداً مع بعض الناس، بل يعني عدم وجود أي جن إضافين جدد ولكن إذا كنت شخصاً إجتماعياً جداً وتجتمع مع مختلف الناس طوال الوقت. كنت كثير السفر والذهاب هنا وهناك طوال الوقت. إذا كنت تتحدث إلي ناس جدد ومختلفون على الهاتف طوال الوقت، وتقتل الحشرات الصغيرة في كثير من الأحيان، مثل العناكب والصراصير، أو السحالي، وغير ذلك، يكون هذا مؤشراً واضحاً بأنك كل مرة تقوم فيها بإضافة المزيد من الجن الجدد حولك، من أشخاص جدد، ومكان جديد، و من الحشرات الميتة، لذلك إذا كانت شخصيتك من هذا النوع، ستكون أحلامك مختلفة جداً طوال الوقت. ولأنك قد إستوعبت الكثير من الجن من أنواع مختلفة من الناس و من مناطق وحشرات، سيكون من الصعب جداً على جني واحد فقط الحفاظ على سيطرتك. بنفس الطريقة، سيكون إنتاج أحلامك، مثل إنتاج الفيلم، سوف تكون أكثر تعقيدا وتضم الكثير من الشخصيات والكثير من الشخصيات الجديدة والغريبة في أحلامك بالتأكيد.

115

Again, in holy book, different prayers, different holy wordings have different use. But because here I am talking about radioactive prayers or wording of holy books to repel and defeat demons and pains.Without even reading repeatedly, those holy wording is bringing strength to repel demons and pains. This is just to discover the rays or waves of suitable intensity to fight against demons and pains. Only medical science has to enrich or amplify those rays and use them to hit the targets of pains and demons electronically. Second way, until medical science will reach to a turning point, reading of those holy prayers repeatedly generate repelling waves and rays to fight against demons and pains. So do not think God never made anything for our safety to save ourselves from the negative effects of demons and pain. For sure, God had a cure for us against demons and pains, but still medical science is not aware about it. But I am sure one day, very soon in future, medical science will discover these waves and rays.

And in the second step, medical science has to enrich or amplify these burning rays and use them electronically in the fight against the invisible pains and demons. Holy books are complete science. Every prayer, every line of holy books generates or emit rays. Now this is the responsibility of modern and medical science to discover all those waves and rays, enrich and amplify them and then use them electronically to cure each and every problem on this earth. I hope it will not take too much lone time for medical and modern science to believe and understand my prediction, and theories one simple example, how to use it, if anyone has any pain in any part of body.

سيظهر لك الجن الذي يخرج من سحلية ، حلماً به سحالي، لأن هذا هو كل ما يعرفه الجني. بنفس الطريقة سيظهر لك الجن الذين إمتصصتهم أو جذبتهم من مختلف الناس، أحلام عن هؤلاء الناس وعائلاتهم حيث كان الجن يعيشون. سوف تكون محظوظاً إذا أظهر لك جني واحد فقط، حلماً فيني حين ينتظر الباقي لدورهم. لكن هذا ليس صحيحا. سيقرأ هؤلاء الجن بعض الاشياء عنك من عقلك بواسطة التنويم المغناطيسي، ثم تقوم مجموعة الجن بأكملها بإضافة الأشخاص الذين سبق لهم الإقامة بداخلهم، إلى حلمك الذي ينتجونه، كما أنهم سيظهرون لك أحلام معقدة وطويلة للغاية.في الصباح عندما تستيقظ، سوف تفاجأ بأحلامك والشخصيات الغريبة في أحلامك. ليس خطئك أنك تري كل هؤلاء الناس الغرباء غير المعروفين في أحلامك أو إذا كنت ترى أحلام مخيفة أو سيئة للغاية.

ولكن هذا ليس خطأ الجن أيضاً، والسبب، هو أنهم يظهرون لك كل ما يعرفونه. في هذه المرحلة أنت تحتاج إلى النظر أساساً نحو كتفك الأيسر وتتواصل مع الجن الموجودون حولك في كل مرة تذهب فيه إلى السرير، وتقول لهم بوضوح أنك لا تحب الحلم الذي أنتجوه. قل لهم بوضوح ما تريد أن تراه في أحلامك، وأطلعهم علي صور الناس الذين تريد أن تراهم في أحلامك. ستكون هذه عملية مستمرة، لأنك لا تعرف من هو الجن الموكل إليه إنتاج الحلم لك في تلك الليلة تهمة القيام الإنتاج حلم بالنسبة لك في تلك الليلة. هكذا تحدث لهم بوضوح ماذا تريد، والشيء الثاني، إذا كانوا سيخيفونك أو ينتجون لك الأحلام المزعجة، لا تشعر بالخوف على الإطلاق. لا تبقى هادئاً، قل لهم بوضوح أنك لم تحب و لم تقدر الأحلام التي يظهرونها لك. إذا كنت واثقاً بما فيه الكفاية وشعرالجن أنك كنت واثقاً أيضاً، ثق بي، سوف تتغييرالأحلام التي تعيشها،.

Read repeatedly the holy prayer, at least minimum eleven times in original language, amplify it electronically and apply it to the place of the pain within few seconds. Dreams are the first valid and confirmed contact of demons with us.Demons uses our mind or brain and their skill of hypnotism to create dreams for us. Until a few years ago, I was same about dreams like you and others. Dreams are a very important part of our lives. I was always looking for a message behind my dreams. But since I started seeing, sensing, and communicating with demons, l learned a lot of weird and surprising stuff. I am going to describe the mechanism of dreams and skill of hypnotizing a demon in detail right now. But before this, I am giving you one simple advice about dreams, and it depends on you; either you listen to me and make your life easy or do not listen to me and keep getting scared and keep harassing yourself from these scary, weird dreams for the rest of your life. Dreams have no convicts with our real life. Dreams are just like different movies or dramas we watch on TV every day. Dreams do not have any impact on our real life. Dreams do not predict anything about ours or anyone else's past, present, or future. The best way to deal with dreams is just to see them or watch them as a movie without taking them seriously. Once you wake up in the morning, do not even spend one minute worrying about dreams. Try to manage and control your dreams.

The way I explain somewhere in the book control and communicate with demons around you and manage your dreams according to your wishes and will. Anyway, I described a little bit about dreams in book 1; now I am going to give more details.

وسوف تشاهد في أحلامك كل ما تريد مشاهدته.ستكون هذه خطوتك الأولى لبدء التواصل مع الجن. بمجرد أن تعرف طريقة التواصل معهم، فإنهم يستمعون إليك , يستجيبون لك ، و يمكنك أن تطلب منهم أكثر وأكثر.سأصف لك في مكان ما في هذا الكتاب مايمكنك توقعه من الجن أن يفعلوه لك.

أشعر في المستقبل، في وقت قادم، أنه عندما يذهب الناس إلى الفراش للنوم في عجلة من أمرهم، وعلى وجه الخصوص. قبل أن يذهبوا إلى النوم، سوف يخبرون غيرهم من أفراد الأسرة والأصدقاء مقدماً ما سيرونة في أحلامهم، و كيف يحدث الحلم. إن الأحلام التي يظهرها جني واحد، تكون أقل تعقيداً و به شخصيات محدودة.

هؤلاء الجن لديهم مؤامرة والتوتر أقل. وعادة، نحن نعلم بالفعل جميع الشخصيات في حلمنا إذا كانت هي نفسها و أن الجن الموجود من حولنا لفترة طويلة ويشارك في ذلك. ولكن إذا قمنا بإضافة المزيد و المزيد من الجن حولنا، من أشخاص مختلفين طوال الوقت، فهم في نهاية لن يجلسوا وينتظروا دورهم. سوف يعمل المزيد والمزيد من الجن معاً ببطئ و ثبات، بدلاً من القتال مع بعضهم البعض للوصول إلى عقلك،و ينتجون لك الحلم معاً.

بعد تلك اللحظة سوف يكون في حلمك الكثير من الشخصيات الجديدة والغريبة، حتى ولو كنت لم ترهم في أي وقت مضى في حياتك، ولكن لهم علاقة بالجن الجدد الخاص بك في الماضي. عندما ترى مثل هذا التنسيق الجيد بين هؤلاء الجن من حولك لإنتاج مثل هذا المستوى الجيد العالي من الأحلام، يمكنك البدء في مطالبة وتوجيه الجن بنوع القصص التي تريد أن تراها في أحلامك. يمكنك أن تقول للجن الخاصة بك عن تسلسل القصص والشخصيات الموجودة في أحلامك، وربما يمكنهم الإختيار قبل أن ينتجوا لك حلما.

SEE & CONTROL DEMONS & PAIN

Demons use their skill of hypnotism as a DVD movie, our brain as a DVD player, and our eyes to see, regardless of whether we are up or sleeping. Demons are capable of showing us anything like a movie or drama of real characters around us in our dreams. We or our brains are not capable of making or creating or seeing dreams without a demon. We have a lot of connections, contacts, influence of dreams around us, in our life. But we are totally unaware about the influence of demons in our life. It is very hard to imagine and understand for a normal person. But dreams are the easiest way to explain a demon to someone. Same way our dreams are the easiest way of analyzing the demons around us. We always have a group of demons around us in our house or another place. Usually only one demon travels with us if that demon possesses our body at that time. Otherwise, demons do not travel with us. Demons live in our house and do not go to our office with us. The reason is everyplace, regardless of whether it is our office/workshop, restroom, garage, shop, hotel, store, is possessed by a particular group of demons. Those demons live there. Demons do not allow other demons to enter their houses easily. If by chance someone has only one demon around him/her, the same demon will control your mind during your sleep by the hypnotism contact with your mind or brain to transfer a full set of characters around us with some kind drama or incident. Demons do not leave the bodies of humans or animals easily unless the body dies. Demons are much attached with those bodies where they reside all their lives, regardless of whether that body is a human or a spider or a lizard or a cat or anything else. Usually, we add new demons around us once we kill any insect or reptile around us.

يمكنك أن تقول التوفيق وترشد الجن الخاص بك إذا كنت تريد أن تكون شخصية ذات طابع خاص في حلم من نوع خاص. الأمر كله بيدك، كيف توجه، وتستخدم، أو تسيئ إستخدام الجن الخاص بك، بمجرد أن يبدأوا في الإستماع لك وإتباعك. قد ترغب في معرفة كيف ينتج الجن أحلامنا. كما تعلم فإن أدماغتنا أو عقولنا لا تحتاج إلي عيون لرؤية أو تصور أي شيء، أليس كذلك؟ يمكننا أن نتصور أي شيء يمكن لأي شخص القيام به في خيالنا. ولكن لا يمكننا تحويل خيالنا إلى فيلم. ولكن الجن يمكنهم ذلك، إذا أغمضت عينيك وبدأت في إنتاج أي شيء تريده في عقلك، إبدأ بتذكير نفسك بأي فيلم أو شريط فيديو لأغنية أو أي شيء يحدث في حياتك أو أي شيء تريد أن تراه يحدث في حياتك، يستطيع عقلك أن يتخيل بسهولة و يظهر لك كل ذلك. لكن الألوان ليست كما هي في الواقع، وكذلك ليس هناك تسلسل في الخيال مثل ما يوجد في فيلم ما.وبالتالي فإن آلية الدماغ قادرة على تشغيل، ورؤية الأشياء مثلما هي في الحياة الحقيقية، إن مخنا قادرعلى أن يكون مثل جهاز الدي في دي أو جهاز عرض مع الموسيقى التصويرية. إغمض عينيك الآن، وتخيل شيئا، ستلاحظ إذا كان لديك مشهد تشاهده في خيالك، فإن عقلك مستعد لتشغيل أي خيال أو أفكار تريدها في أي وقت علي هذه الشاشة في خيالك، لكن الألوان ليست كما هي في الحقيقة، و أنت لا تستطيع أن تشعر وكأنك تشاهد فيلماً حقاً، أو أن هذا ما يحدث حقاً في حياتك الحقيقية. لذلك ينبغي أن يكون الأمر واضحاً لك، أن مخنا مجهز بالفعل تماماً، بآلية لتشغيل ومشاهدة أي خيال بغض النظر عن ما إذا كنا مستيقظين أم نائمين، وبغض النظر عن ما إذا كانت أعيننا مفتوحة أم مغلقة. الآن نحن نحتاج إلى الجزء المفقود. نحن لا نريد ان نضيع وقتنا في إنتاج الخيا، و الإستمرار في مشاهدة خيالات عديمة اللون والصراع مع الخيالات، و بخاصة عندما لا تبدو حقيقية. هكذا هنا نحن بحاجة إلى الجن لإنتاج قصص أو أفلام وتشغيل نظام الدي في دي في مخنا.

118

The very first and immediate reactions of the demons come out sometimes, some kind of pain or sickness, and second immediate reaction will be scary and nasty dreams. If you are seeing the same dreams all the time about you and your family members, this means you did not add any new demon around you.

Demons usually are very attached with the bodies in which they reside. For example, demons reside a in a human body and usually live inside or outside around same person or family. Demons switch bodies when old bodies expire or die. If you are not social person, you will not have variety in yourdreams. Because once you meet with less people, you will absorb or attract fewer demons around you in your group of demons. If you arekilling no insects, it means you are not adding new demons around you. If you around some people, it means no new addition of any demons. But if you are very social and meet with different people all the time. You travel a lot and go here and there all the time. If you talk to new and different people on the phone all the time, you kill small insects frequently, like spiders, cockroaches, or lizards, etc..

This is a clear indication that all the time you add more and more new demons around you, from new people, new place, and from the dead bodies of insects, so when you are this kind of personality, your dreams will be very different all the time. And because you have absorbed a lot of demons from different types of people and areas and insects, it will be very difficult for only one demon to keep your control.

الآن هناك فرق كبير بيننا و بين الجن الذين ينتجون الخيال ويحولوه إلى جسم آخر. يمكننا أن نتصور أي شيء لفترة طويلة، ولكن لا يمكننا ان نشغل أو نقل خيالنا إلى مخ شخص آخر. ولكن أداة التنويم المغناطيسي قادرة على نقل الخيال والفكر إلى الاللدي في دي ونظام الشاشة في مخنا. الآن خلال أحلامنا، نحن لا نشاهد خيالنا ولكن الخيال والأفكار التي تأتي من الجن، وهذا هو السبب في أننا لا نملك أي سيطرة على تلك الأحلام.. لا يمكننا تغيير أي شيء أو أي موقف في أحلامنا. لهنا نحن بحاجة لتوجيه الجن لدينا، لما نريد. نحن بحاجة ألي تثقيف الجن الموجودون حولنا، بما نحب و ما نريد رؤيته و مدة الرؤية.

بنفس الطريقة، نحن بحاجة لتوجيه هؤلاء الجن، بما لا نحب ولا نريد أن نشاهده في الأحلام. مرة أخرى، الأحلام هي مجرد أفكار فقط والخيال من جني واحد أو عدد من الجن، وهي ما ينقله الجن إلى شاشة مخنا، ليبينوا لنا أفكارهم في شكل فيلم من واقع الحياة أو حلم، لهذا ليس للأحلام أي علاقة بحياتنا الحقيقية. أحلام لا تملك أي تأثير على حياتنا الحقيقية. هكذا يرجى التمتع بكلا الأمرين، حياتك و أحلامك، فلا تسيئ إستخدامهما أو تفسدهما.

ليس من الصعب على الجن إنتاج قصة أو حلم، بنفس الطريقة التي نسرد بها القصص أو الكذب أو الحقائق، أو نروي قصصاً مختلفة لأطفالنا أوغيرهم، و هي صحيحة في بعض الأحيان ووهمية أحياناً أخري. نفس الشيئ، الجن يحكون لنا قصة في شكل حلم، و يتواصل الجن مع المخ عن طريق أداة أو لغة التنويم المغناطيسي.

SEE & CONTROL DEMONS & PAIN

Same way, your dream production, like a movie production, will be more complicated and comprised of a lot of characters and, for sure, a lot of new and strange characters in your dreams. Demons that come out from a lizard will show you dreams about lizards, because that's all the demon knows. Same way demons you absorbed or attract for different people will show you dreams about those people and families where that demon used to live. You will be lucky if only one demon will show you a dream and the rest waits for their turn. But this is not true. These demons will read some stuff about you from your mind by hypnotism, and then the whole group of demons will add their ex-residents as the characters of your dream product and will show you very complicated and long dreams. In the morning when you will wake up you will be surprised about your dreams and strange people in your dreams. This is not your fault when you are seeing all these strangers' unknown people in your dreams or if you are seeing extremely scary or nasty dreams.

But this is not fault of demons either, reason, they are showing you all this because that's all they know. At this point you need to look toward mainly you're left shoulders and communicate with demons around you every time you go to bed, clearly tell them if you do not like their dream production. Tell your demons clearly what you want to see in your dreams, show them the pictures of people you want to see in your dreams. This is a continuous process, because you never know who is in charge demon that night to do dream production for you that night. So talk to them clearly what do you want, and second thing, if they should scare or bad dreams, do not get scared at all. Do not stay quiet.

رضوان قرشي

هذه القدرة، والإمكانية للجن،بأن يخبرونا بأفكارهم وخيالهم، هذا كله حلم . الجن فقط هم الذين يملكون إدراج أوتشغيل أفكارهم أو خيالهم في نظام الدماغ، ثم يستطيع المخ أن يشاهد ويسمع الأحلام. نحن نشارك الجن في عملية الأحلام بنسبة 50 % ، لذلك تستطيع أن تخبرهم بما تريد أن ترى، وليس هذا صعباً على الجن. لابد للجن وحدهم أن يبدأ وا في التفكير من عقلك أيضاً خلال عملية إنتاج الأحلام لك.

قد تسألني ما الذي يحصل عليه الجن من عملية الأحلام برمتها .إنهم يسيطرون على عقولنا وأفكارنا، ويتمتعون بتخويفنا، و تهديدنا، وتضليلنا، لكن يجب أن يتغير هذا الآن. سيعرف كل الجن ببطيء وثبات الآن، أنك على علم بهم وبأنشطتهم. إذا كان الأمر كذلك و هم يريدون حقاً أن يصبحوا أصدقائك، فهم بحاجة للإستماع إليك ومتابعتك. حظاً سعيداً في أحلامك!

تعريفي للشئ الغير طبيعي، هو كل شيء أو كل شيء أقل من الطبيعي أو أعلي من الطبيعي، بالنسبة للظروف والناس. في أي مجال، في الألعاب، في العمل الإبداعي، والكتاب ومخرجي الأفلام والسياسيين والزعماء الدينيين والمعلمين،المدربين، وما إلى ذلك، بغض النظر عن المعرفة والخبرة مجال معين الذي يقتصر علي 40-50 عاما. الحيوانات والطيور،الزواحف والحشرات ليس لديها الكثير من الخيارات أيضاً، بغض النظر عما إذاكانوا يريدون البقاء أو العيش في مكان معين أو حول شخص معين إذا كانوا لا يريدون . مثلاً إذا أراد الحصان البقاء معنا في غرفة نومنا أو في المطبخ، فهذا غيرممكن في معظم الوقت. أوإذا أرادت مجموعة كبيرة من العناكب السامة الكبيرة البقاء في غرفة نومنا أو في المطبخ، وتريد أن تتحرك بحرية هنا وهناك، لا يكون هذا ممكناً معظم ذلك الوقت، لم يكن ممكنا. بالمقارنة مع الحيوانات والطيور والزواحف،الخ، ونحن البشر لدينا المزيد من الحرية لتقرير إلى أين نذهب وما نريد القيام به.

120

Tell them clearly that you did not like and appreciate the dreams that they are showing you. If you are confident enough and demons also feel you are confident, trust me, your dream life will change, and you will be watching in your dreams whatever you want to watch. This will be the first stop of yours, to start communicating with demons. Once your figure out, they listen, you can start asking them more and more. Somewhere, in this book, I will describe what you can expect from your demons to do for you.

I feel in the future, time is coming, when people will go to bed to sleep in hurry and specially. And before they will go to the bed, they will tell other family members and friends in advance what are to how and how they will be seeing in their dreams. Dreams created by one single demon are less complicated with limited characters.

Those demons have less conspiracy and tension. And usually, we already know all the characters in our dream if same and a demon around us for a long time is involved in it. But if we are adding more and more demons around us from different people all the time, then eventually they are not just going to sit and wait for their turn. Slow and steady more and more demons will start working together and instead of fighting with each other to get access over to your mind, they will create dream together.

After that moment your dream will have a lot of new and strange characters, even you have never seen them ever in your life, but they are related to your new demons in the past.

بالتأكيد، لدينا بعض القيود الإجتماعية والقيود.لا نزال نحن أكثر حرية في إختيار الجو المناسب والبيئة الصالحة والناس الأصلح للبقاء في الأنحاء.وعادة ما نحن نختار نفس النوع من الأصدقاء والبيئة التي نحبها، طبقاً لمستوى ذكائنا وهواياتنا.

إذا أحببنا ركوب الخيل وسباق الخيل، سوف نبقي بالقرب من نفس النوع من الناس لأننا سوف نحب صحبتهم. بنفس الطريقة، إذا أحببنا لعب الغولف، سنكون موجودين حول الناس الذين يلعبون أو يحبون لعبة الغولف. بنفس الطريقة، إذا كان شخص ما مدمن كحوليات أو مدمن مخدرات بشكل سيء، سيتسكع مع نفس النوع من الناس، كذلك الرسامين والكتاب و منتجي الأفلام والمخرجين، الجميع يحبون البقاء مع معظم من يشبهونهم من الناس إلي حد كبير. نحن نعيش قرابة مائة عام كحد أقصى. مقارنة بنا،عادة ما يعيش الجن لاف السنين في الحياة الواحدة.

نظرا إلى الإطار الزمني، الجن هم أكثر دراية منا. ليس لدي الجن حدود كبيرة، أين و مع من يعيشون؟ و من الذين لا يستطيعون العيش معهم؟. يتبع الجن رغباتهم و إختياراتهم بنفس الطريقة بالضبط التي نحب و نميل إلي جو معين، أوبيئة معينة، أو صحبة معينة من الناس نظل حولهم. فالجن كانوا يرغبون في العيش داخل جسم العنكبوت، إنهم يعيشون داخله، وبمجرد موت العنكبوت، يتركونه. وإذا كان الجني يريد البقاء حول الإنسان، بغض النظر عن عدد الأجسام التي يقوم الجن بتبديلها في كل مرة واحدة يموت فيها أحد البشر وذلكسوف يجد الجن ويختار جسم إنسان آخر. والآن كما وصفت عدة مرات، يتفاعل الجن بشكل كامل مع أحوالنا، و هوايا تنا وشؤوننا، غيرها من الأنشطة طوال الوقت. الجن لا يتعلمون منا بالقدر الكافي، إنهم يعلموننا عن طريق تغذية مخنا بالآراء والأفكار طوال الوقت.

SEE & CONTROL DEMONS & PAIN

When you see such a good coordination among these demons around you to produce such a good high level of dreams, you can start to demand and guide your demons which kind of stories you want to see in your dreams. You can tell your demons the sequence stories and the characters of your dreams, possibly they can choose before they create a dream for you. You can tell and guide your demons if you want to be a special character in a special kind of dream. This is all in your hand, how you want to guide, use, or misuse your demons once they start listening and following you. You may want to know how demons create our dreams. As you know our brain or minds do not need eyes to see or imagine something, right? We can imagine anything any person doing anything in our imagination. But we cannot convert our imagination into a movie. But demons can. If you close your eyes and start creating anything in your mind you like, start reminding yourself about any move or video of a song or anything happening in your life or anything you want to see happening in your life your mind can easily imagine and able to show you. But colors are not right, and there is no sequence in imagination like a movie. So the brain mechanism is capable of playing and seeing things like real life, like our brain is able to act like a DVD or a projector with soundtrack, close your eyes right now and imagine something. You will notice if you have a scene to watch your imagination, your mind is ready to play any imagination or thoughts on that screen whenever, whatever you want to see in your imagination. But colors are not right and you cannot feel like you are really watching a movie or this is really happening in your life in actual.

كما قلت، والجن يحبون البقاء حول الناس الذين يحبونهم، فعلي سبيل المثال، إذا كان الجن يحبون الشاعر وشعره، سوف يبقون معه طوال حياته، وبعد وفاة هذا الشاعر، لن يبدأ الجني في العيش في جسم قطة، لكنه سيبحث عن شاعر آخر، بغض النظر عن ما إذا كان رجلاً أو إمرأة.، بهذه الطريقة لمجرد الإستمتاع بنفس الهواية من الشعر،فالجني ، قد يصل عمره إلي آلف أو ألفي عام، ويعيش داخل شعراء مختلفين و حولهم. يعيشون داخل وحول الشعراء. حسناً، هذه مدة طويلة. إفتراض فقط وجود شاعر، صغير جداً، شاعر شاب فقط ربما في الثلاثين من عمره، وقرر هذا الجني الإنضمام لصحبة هذا الشاعر الشا ب.

وهكذا فإن عمر الشاعر الشاب 30 عاماً فقط، بينما عمر الجن الموجودين حول هذا الشاعر 2000 عاماً مع خبرة ومعرفة بالشعر لفترة طويلة. سيتلقى الشاعر الشاب بإستمرار أفكار ورؤي من الجن في شكل أحلام أو أفكار طوال الوقت و هذا يساعده على إبداع مستوى عال من الشعر. الشيء نفسه صحيح في المجالات الأخرى، عندما يكتب الناس روايات وقصص ناجحة للغاية، وينتجونو يخرجون أفلام جيدة، ذكية جداً، وما إلى ذلك، يحدث ذلك معظم الوقت بسبب مساعدة وخبرة الجن اللطيف.

إن العمل الإبداعي والتطرف هما نفس الشيء. وحيثما كانت الأجواء، والبيئة، والجهود الغير طبيعية متوفرة، سيوصل الشخص إلى مستوى رفيع في مهنته أو في مجاله أو هوايته. أي شيء به مستوى عا لي من التطرف، وإيجاباً أو سلباً، يكون للجن دائماً علاقة به. فيعليه. ولا شك، كل شخص يقوم بإبداع تحفة ما، يكون لديه دائماً عاطفة زائدة تجاه عمله. وهذه العاطفة الزائدة والمستوى العالي جداً لمحبة عملهم بجعله استثنائي في مجال عمله., وهكذا كل ما لا نستطيع أن نفعله بنجاح بأنفسنا بمستوى عال جداً، يساعدنا الجن الموجودون حولنا،

Rizwan Qureshi	رؤية الجن و الآلام السيطرة عليها
So it should be clear to you that our mind is totally already equipped with the mechanism of playing and watching any imagination regardless of whether we are up or sleep, regardless of whether our eyes are open or close. Now he needs the missing part. We do not want to waste our time to create an imagination keep watching colorless and struggling imaginations and especially when they do not seem real or true. So here we need the demons to bring stories or movies and play in the DVD system of our brain.	في تحقيق إنجاز عالي المستوى في مجال معين عن طريق وضع خبرات معرفتنا في أدمغتنا بإستخدام التنويم المغناطيسي .

So it should be clear to you that our mind is totally already equipped with the mechanism of playing and watching any imagination regardless of whether we are up or sleep, regardless of whether our eyes are open or close. Now he needs the missing part. We do not want to waste our time to create an imagination keep watching colorless and struggling imaginations and especially when they do not seem real or true. So here we need the demons to bring stories or movies and play in the DVD system of our brain.

Now there is a little difference between our and demons creating imagination and transfer them to anotherbody. We can imagine anything for long time, but we cannot play or transfer our imagination to someone else's brain. But the tool of hypnotism is capable of transferring imagination and thought to the DVD and screen system of our brain. Now during our dreams, we are not watching our imaginations but the imagination and thoughts of demons. Because all those imaginations and thoughts come from demons, that's why we do not have any control over those dreams.

We cannot change anything or any situation in our dreams. So here we need to guide our demons, what we want. We need to educate demons around us, what we like and want to see and for how long. In the same manner, we need to guide those demons, what we do not like and do not to want to watch during dreams. Again, dreams are just thoughts and imagination of a demon or several demons, what they transfer to the screen of our brain to show us their thoughts as a real-life movie or a dream. So dreams do not have anything to do with our real life.

أنا متأكد من أنني فعلت أشياء غبية كثيرة في حياتي، ربما عن طريق الخطأ، ولكني فعلت الشيء التالي، لأن شخص ما ظل يدفعني للقيام به،وأخيراً، قررت أن أفعل ذلك كتجربة أخرى. لا شك في أن هذه التجربة كانت ناجحة جداً، حتى أنني كنت واثق من أنني لن أفعل ذلك مرة أخرى أبداً. سألني صديق شخص ما إذا كان هناك أي وسيلة ليؤدي حصانه أداءً إستثنائياً في سباق الخيل. شرحت له وسيلة ممكنة،لا وهي إضافة بعض الجن الأقوياء لحصانه وترك هؤلاء الجن يعملون على هذا الحصان على الأقل لمدة إسبوع. عند هذه النقطة، لو لم نتحدث عن فعل أي شيء حقاً، فقد ظننت أنه يريد فقط أن يعرف ، و لهذا قمت بتوجيهه فقط. ولكن هذا الرجل كان جاداً جدا، وبطريقة أو بأخرى، كان واثقاً بأنني كنت على حق. لم أقل نعم فوراً. لقد إستغرق مني هذا بعض الوقت لأقول نعم. على أي حال، لم يكن هذا سهلاً. أنا فقط لا يمكن أن أطلب من قليل من الجن من حولي أو في أي مكان الذهاب والبدء في تعزيزوتضخيم دماغ ذلك الحصان. يجب أن أجد بعض الجن المتوحشون و الغريبي الأطوار حقاً، الذين يحبون البقاء في جسم حصان.

ينبغي أن يكون لدي بعض الجن الذين يشعرون حقاً بالراحة مع حصان وقادرون على القفز في عقل هذا الحصان. كان من السهل فقط أن أسأل قليل من الجن عشوائياً الذهاب لتعزيز هذا الحصان، ولكن كان من الصعب العثور على جن مناسبين لهذا الغرض. على أي حال، وطلبت من ذلك الشخص إحضار بعض الصور ومقاطع الفيديو لثلاثة أو أربعة خيول مثالية حقاً وممتازة في السوق لغرض هذا السباق....

SEE & CONTROL DEMONS & PAIN

Dreams do not have any impact on our real life. So please enjoy both, your life and your dream life, and do not misuse them and mess them up together. It is not difficult for demons to create a story or a dream. The way we tell stories or lies or truths, or we make and tell different stories to our kids or others, sometimes true and sometimes imaginary. Same way demons just tell us a story in the shape of a dream. Demons communicate with our brain with the tool or language of hypnotism; this capability and ability of a demon, telling us their thoughts and imagination, is collectively a dream. Only demons have to insert or play their thoughts or imagination in our brain system. Rest, our brain system is capable to watch and hear the dreams. We are 50 percent partner with these demons in the process of dreams. So you can tell them what you want to see, and it is not difficult for demons. Only demons have to start thinking from your mind also during the process of creating dreams for you. You may ask me what demons get from the whole process of dreams. Definitely control of us, control of our brain and thoughts, enjoyment by scaring us, enjoyment by threatening us, enjoyment by misguiding us. But this should change now. Now slow and steady all demons will know that you are aware about them and their activities. So if the really want to become your friend, they need to listen to you and follow you. Good luck with your dreams!

My definition of abnormal is everything below normal or everything above normal in conditions and people. In any field, games, creative work, writers, movie directors, politicians, religious leaders, teachers, coaches, etc., regardless of our field of knowledge and experience about a particular field is limited to forty to fifty years.

رضوان قرشي

ينبغي أن يكون لدي بعض الجن الذين يشعرون حقاً بالراحة مع حصان وقادرون على القفز في عقل هذا الحصان. كان من السهل فقط أن أسأل قليل من الجن عشوائياً الذهاب لتعزيز هذا الحصان، ولكن كان من الصعب العثور على جن مناسبين لهذا الغرض. على أي حال، وطلبت من ذلك الشخص إحضار بعض الصور ومقاطع الفيديو لثلاثة أو أربعة خيول مثالية حقاً وممتازة في السوق لغرض هذا السباق.. ثم طلبت منه أن يجلب حصانه في مكان محدد، حيث يمكن أن أذهب بسهولة، على مقربة من أي منزل مثلاً. والآن الجزء الصعب، ويكاد يكون من المستحيل بالنسبة لي دائماً في ذلك الوقت. لقد أنشأت إتصال توارد خواطر مع الجن الموجودون حول هؤلاء الخيول. وكان عندي صور ومقاطع فيديو.، و طلبت من االجن الموجودون حول ذلك الحصان، , حاولت إقناعهم، وإدراجهم طوال يوم كامل أن يذهبوا إلى ذلك الحصان الذي أمامي. أعتقد أنن كررت هذه التجربة سبع مرات في ذلك اليوم. وكانت هذه تجربتي الأولي والأخيرة للتعامل مع الحيوان، ولكن كانت تجربة ناجحة. الإستخدام الإيجابي للجن في السباق. من الصعب جداً إستخدام أي جني في عمل نشاط إيجابي. على أي حال. أنا لا استخدم إسم بلد ما، ولكن أشعر أن هذا البلد الأسيوي به سكان من الجن الأكثر سلبية علي الأرض. السبب في ذلك هو كثرة عدد السكان والمنازل القديمة والقذرة والمناطق، بالاضافة إلى أن الكثير من الناس مرتبطون بأعمال السحر الاسود. الأولمرة كنت تعلم عنه قبل عدة سنوات خلال مباراة كريكيت بين بلدين. عندما تلقيت بعض المشاعر لمكافحتها، لكن في البداية لم أكن على إستعداد للإعتقاد بأن الناس يستطيعون فعل مثل هذا الشيء السيئ فقط للفوز في لمباراة ما.

Rizwan Qureshi	رؤية الجن و الآلام السيطرة عليها

Animals, birds, reptiles, insects do not have too many choices, regardless of whether they want to stay or live at a particular place or around particular person if they do not want to. Like if a horse wants to stay with us in our bedroom or in our kitchen, it is not possible most of the time. Or if a big group of poisonous big spiders want to stay in our bedroom or in our kitchen and want to move freely here and there. Most of the time, it is not possible. As compared to animals, birds, reptiles, etc., we humans are freer to decide where to go and what to do. Definitely, we have some social restrictions and limitations. Still we have more freedom to choose the right atmosphere and environment and people to stay around. Due to our intelligence level and hobbies, usually we choose same kind of friends and environment whatever we like

If we like horse riding and horse racing, we will stay around same kind of people because we will like their company. Same way, if we like to play golf, we will be more around people who play or like golf. Same way, if someone is alcoholic or badly addicted to drugs, he will hang around the same kind of people. Painters, writers, movie producers, directors, everybody likes to stay around people most match for them. We live around a hundred years maximum. As compared to us, usually demons live thousands of years in a single life.

Due to time frame, demons are more knowledgeable than us. Demons do not have too many limits, where and with whom they can live with and who they cannot live with?. The way we like a particular atmosphere, environment, and company of suitable people to hang around, exactly same way, demons follow their wishes and choices also.

خلال هذه المباراة بشكل خاص، وكان كل ضارب كرة محاطاً بعدد لا يحصى من الجن لجعله كثير الحركة و شديد العصبية. لم أكن أفهم ذلك في لك الوقت، ولكن أنا أفهم الآن كيف يمكن لمجموعة من الجن الموجهين والذين لهم هدف، يجعلون ضارب الكرة كثير الحركة والعصبية. يستطيع الجن، عن طريق التنويم المغناطيسي، الإصرار على إستمرار ضارب الكرة في الوقوع في الخطأ، والسيطرة على لعبة الكريكيت، وخسارة المباراة. لقد فوجئت، ولكني أعتقد أن الناس يعتقدون حقاً أن. كل شيء مباح في الحرب. هكذا، فأي لاعب كريكيت يقرأ هذه الحادثة، وتذكر في المرة القادمة، خلال اللعبة، إذا شعرت في أي وقتبضغوط، شديدة، أو حركة زائدة أو عصبية، أو أنك غير مرتاحاً، قم برش رذاذ الماء المقدس كل 30 دقيقة مباشرة على وجهك وأذنك ورأسك وعنقك. بنفس الطريقة، قم بشرب الماء المقدس كل ساعة خلال المباراة وسوف تشعر بأنك تستطيع السيطرة على نفسك. ثق بي، لا يمكن للجني التغب علي الماء المقدس، ولكن تأثير المياه المقدسة يكون مؤقتاً، لذلك تحتاج إلى إستخدامه كثيراً في أغلب الأحيان عليك وعلى محيطك.

أنا لا أعرف ما الذي يحصل عليه هؤلاء الجن من هذه المبادلات. لكن هذه هي هوايتهم. إنهم ينوموننا مغناطيسياً ويدفعوننا إلى العمل بطرق سلبية. أنا لا أعرف ما الذي يحصلون عليه من كل ذلك، ولكن تأثيرها تحدث و تنتشر السلبية بشكل أكبر، ومع ذلك، يمكنك عكس هذا الوضع بالإنضباط والممارسة. كلما شعرنا بإندفاع قوي نحو رجل أو إمرأة، عندمانشعر بالحب أكثر من اللازم أو الكراهية أكثر من اللازم نحو شخص ما، عندما نريد فقط أن نأكل شيئاً ما على الفور، أو عندما يكون لدينا مجرد رغبة لممارسة الجنس في أسرع وقت ممكن، وتذكر أن الجن مسؤولون بنسبة 99 في المئة عن كل هذه الدوافع!

SEE & CONTROL DEMONS & PAIN

They want to and like to live inside a body of spider, they live inside a spider, and once one the spider die, they leave it. And if a demon wants to stay around a human, regardless of how many bodies that demon has to switch every time one human dies, that demon will find and choose another human body. Now as I described several times, demons take full interact in our affairs, hobbies and other activities all the time. Demons do not learn from us as much; they teach us by feeding ideas and thoughts in our minds all the time.

As I said, demons want to stay around people whom they like. For example, if a demon likes a poet and his poetry, that demon will stay around that person his whole life. After the death of that poet, that demon will not start living in a body of a cat, that demon will look for another poet, regardless of whether it's a man or woman. This way just to enjoy same hobby of poetry, a demon, whose age maybe one thousand years or two thousand years was living inside and around different poets, for that long okay just assume there is a poet, very young poet only age maybe thirty years, and if that demon who likes poetry decided to join the company of that young poet.

So even that young poet is just thirty years old but the demon around that poet is two thousand years old with experience and knowledge of poetry for that long. The young poet will continuously receive ideas and vision from his demons in shape of dreams or thoughts in mind all the time that will help him to create high level of poetry.

رضوان قرشي

ما هي بعض العلاجات للمشاكل الناجمة عن الجن؟ بمجرد أن ينتبه العلماء إلى نظرياتي، أنا متأكد من أنهم سوف يكونون قادرين علي إختراع الآلات التي تقلل من تأثير الجن، والمرض، والآلام في أجسامنا، ولكن حتى ذلك الحين، أقترح علي الجميع إستخدام بعض الحيل للحد من المشاكل التي يسببها الجن. ومع ذلك، يمكن إستخدام هذه الحيل فقط لمحاربة الجن، ولا تعمل على مرض أو الآلام. هذه الحيل ما يلي:

١. الجن يحبون اللحوم الحمراء فقط. م أفهمه هو أن الجن يحبون لحوم البقر. إذا كان لديك المزيد من لحم البقر، وتتناول المزيد من لحم البقر، هذا يعني أنك تدعو الجن أكثر وأكثر في منزلك وفي جسمك.

٢. قم بفرك ما لا يقل عن خمسة ليمونات صغيرة أو الليمون الحامض في أجزاء مختلفة من جسمك، وخصوصاً حول رأسك وأذنيك وعينيك، وصدرك لمدة دقيقتين. ثم حرك يدك حول جسمك سبع مرات. تأكد من الخضوع لهذه العملية عند قيادتك للسيارة. تجنب المناطق السكنية، وقم بإختيار الطرق الرئيسية، وبعد تحريك يدك في جميع أنحاء جسمك سبع مرات، لا تضيع الوقت بعد الآن. إستمر في القيادة، وإفتح النافذة وقم بإلقاء جميع الليمون أو الليمون الحامض نحو أي شجرة. هناك فرصة 60 % أن يتركك الجن الموجودون حول جسمك لتتبع تلك الليمونات أو الليمون الحامض. إذا كنت تشعر بالضغط، كرار هذه العملية كل يوم أو كل يوم و آخر أو على الأقل مرة في الأسبوع.يمكنك أيضا قطع الليمون أو الحامض إلي نصفين، و قم بفرك تلك القطع علي ذراعك اليسرى و علي كتفك، ثم ألقها من سيارتك بإتجاه شجرة خضراء. لا توقف السيارة أثناء هذه العملية.

126

Same thing is correct of other fields, when people write extremely successful novels, stories, produce and direct good movies, extra intelligent, etc., most of the time this happens due to the help and experience of nice demons.Creative work and extremism is same thing. And wherever abnormal atmosphere, environment, efforts will involve, it will take that person to extreme level of his profession or field or hobby. Anything with too extreme level, positive or negative, always demons are involved in it. No doubt, every person who creates a masterpiece always has extra passion about his work. And this extra passion and extremely high level of love with his work make them extraordinary in their fields. So whatever we cannot do successfully by ourselves on a very high level, demons around us to help us to achieve the highest level achievement in a particular field by putting their knowledge experiences in our brains by using hypnotism.

I am sure I did several stupid things in my life, maybe by mistake, but the following thing, I did because someone kept pushing me to do it, and finally, I decided to do it as another experiment. No doubt the experiment was very successful; till I am sure I will not do it again ever. Spend whole daft for this experiment. One friend of someone I know asked me if there is any way if his race horse shows extraordinary performance in horse race. I explained to him the possible way of adding some powerful demons to his horse and let those demons to work on that horse at least a week. At this point, without talking about really doing anything. I thought he just wanted to know that's why I just guided him. But that guy was very serious, and somehow, he was confident that I was right. I did not say yes immediately.

3. الجن لا يتركون أجسام البشر بسهولة، خصوصا إذا كانوا يعيشون حول هذه الأجسام لفترة طويلة. و لكي تطردهم، خاذ ما لا يقل عن 15 عصا مليئة بأوراق النعناع الأخضر، ثم ضعهم في وعاء معدني مليئ بالماء، قم بغلي المياء مع أوراق النعناع لمدة لا تقل عن ثلاثين دقيقة، و قم بشرب ماء النعناع كل ثلاثة أيام. هذا سوف يقلل من ماء النعناع من سلبية هؤلاء الجن من حولك، و لن يحدثوا مشاكل في عائلتك أو في شؤون أعمالهم، وقد يصبحوا أقل ايجابية و داعمون بسبب ماءالنعناع.

4. كما وصفت من قبل، يمكنك إستخدام الماء العادي في زجاجة رش، و يمكنك رش كل ركن من منزلك غالباً. حاول تغطية كل مكان من السقف إلى الأرض.، يمكنك القيام بذلك في كثير من الأحيان. الماء لا يقتل الجن، ولكنهم لا يحبون المياء. المياه يبقيهم غير مرتاحين. إذاقمت بذلك في كثير من الأحيان، فإن الجن لن يبقوا حولك أو في منزلك لفترة طويلة. قم بتفعل الشيء نفسه في سيارتك. سوف تحتاج إلى رش الماء بشكل روتيني لأنه بمجرد أن تترك مجموعة من الجن منزلك سوف يكون فارغاً لفترة أخرى، وستأتي مجموعة أخري من الجن لاحتلال المكان، و إذا واصلت رش الماء، سوف يستمرون في مغادرة منزلك .

5. يمكنك أيضاً إستخدام ما المبيدات الحشرية كثيراً، ولكن تأكد من رشها في الهواء نحو السقف. لا تترك أي ركن غير مراقب. رش في كل مكان في أغلب الأحيان، وستدهش بالنتائج.

لا يوجد الجن داخل الجسم معظم الوقت، إنهم يحيطون بالجسم بطريقة أو بأخري، و بهذه الطريقة، فهي داخل الجسم، ولكن بعض أجزاء منه تكون أيضاً فوق الجلد. كلما تنقل الجن عن طريق خطوط الهاتف، عادة ما تلصق بآذاننا، رؤسنا، ورقابنا، وخصوصا آذاننا اليسري..

It took me some time to say yes. Anyway, it was not easy. I just cannot request few demons around me or anywhere to go and start boosting and amplify the brain of that horse. I should find some really strange and wild demons who like to stay in a body of a horse.

I should have few demons who really feel comfortable with horse and able to jump start with the mind of that horse. It was easy if I just ask randomly few demons to go and amplify that horse, but it was difficult to find suitable demons for that purpose. Anyway, I asked that person to bring some pictures and videos of three or four really ideal and perfect horses in market for this race purpose. Then I asked him to bring his horse at a specific place, where I can go easily, i.e., close to any house. Now the hard part and almost impossible for me always at that time and still. I established telepathic contact with the demons of those horses. I had pictures and videos. I request, convince, and insert whole day long to all the demons around those horses and invite them to that particular horse in front of me. That particular day, I think I repeated that experiment seven times. That was my first and last experiment dealing with an animal but it was successful. Positive use of demons in race. It is very difficult to use any demon for positive activity. Anyway, I am not using the name of country, but that Asian country I feel has the population of most negative demons on Earth. The reason is that there is too much population, dirty and old houses and areas, plus too many people involved in the business of black magic. First time I learn about negative demons, several years ago during a cricket match between two countries.

في تلك اللحظة، لم يكن الجن قد إخترقوا أجسامنا تماماً . في ذلك الوقت، يجلسون فوقنا ، ويحفرون داخل عقولنا بإستخدام أذننا اليسرى معظم الوقت، لمعرفة المزيد عنا أو باستخدام قوي التنويم المغناطيسي لديهم.. إذا لاحظ عالم الطب شخصاً عادياً يتكلم على الهاتف مع شخص مريض أو حاد المزاج جداً، أو شخص متطرف في أي مجال، أنا واثق من أن الجن سوف ينتقلون عبر خطوط الهاتف ويستحوذون علي الشخص الآخر. وتستطيع العلوم الطبية إستخدام الآلات الحديثة للكشف عن الأشاعاتوالإشارات، وبمجرد أن تستطيع العلوم الطبية الكشف عن الجن أو المرض، أنا واثق من أنها ستستطيع العثور بسهولة على أن علاجات يستطيع الشخص العادي إستخدامها ضدهم.

تذكر دائماً أن الجن والمرض / الآلام ليسوا نفس الشيئ، فالجن مختلفون. فهم لا يضرو ننا، و لكنهم يستخدموننا مثل الألعاب بالنسبة لهم. إنهم يسيطرون علي عقولنا، ومعظم الوقت، نحن نفعل مايريدون منا ان نفعل. معظم الوقت، ونحن نعتقد ما يريدونه منا. إننا نفكر فيما يريدون منا التفكير فيه معظم الوقت. قد تسألني، ماذا يجني الجن من هذا؟ الجواب البسيط هو أن هذه هي هوايتهم، و نحن ننخرط في أمورنا و عائلاتنا، وهم يتخذ ون قرارات بشأن ما نحتاج إلى القيام به. أنهم يبقوننا غاضبين ويجعلوننا نتصرف كل أنواع التصرفات السلبية. عملياً، ليس من الممكن تعطيل سيطرة الجن. إذا قام شخص مثلي بأخذ الجن الموجودن حولك أو داخلك،سيستحوذ عليك جن آخرون في غضون بضعة أيام أو ربما ساعات قليلة. يمكن للجن رؤية أنك متاح للإستحواذ عليك، وعلى الفور يأتي إليك جني جديد، وسوف تفسح مكاناً حولك وداخلك في غضون ثوان قليلة.

When I receive some feelings to fight against it. But at first I was not ready to believe that people can do such a bad thing just to win a game. During that particular match, every batsman was surrounded by uncountable evil demons to make them hyper and nervous. I did not understand it at that time, but I do understand now how a group of targeted and guided demons can make a batsman extra hyper and nervous. Demons, by doing hypnotism, continuously can insist a batman to keep making mistakes, control the cricket, and lose the game. I was surprised, but I think people really believe that everything is fair in war. So if any cricket players reading this incident remember next time, during the game, if you ever feel pressured, hyper, nervous, or uncomfortable, spray holy water every thirty minutes directly on your face, ear, neck, and head. Same way drink holy water every hour during the game you will feel in control of yourself. Trust me, no demon can beat holy water, but the effect of holy water is temporary, so you need to use it frequently on you and your surroundings.

I don't know what these demons get out of these trade-offs. But this is their hobby. They hypnotize us and push us to act in negative ways.I do know what they get from all that, but their influence does create and spread more negativism. However, you can reverse this situation with discipline and practice. Whenever we feel strongly pushed toward a man or woman, when we feel too much love or too much hate toward someone, when we just want to eat something immediately, when we just have a desire to have sex as soon as possible, remember that demons are 99 percent responsible for all of these impulses!

رؤية الجن و الآلام السيطرة عليها

ولكنك لن تعرف هذه التغييرات لأن كل الجن يتصرفون إلى حد كبير بنفس الطريقة. قد تكون أحلامك مختلفة، ولكن قد يكون ذلك تغييراً كبيراً.من ناحية أخرى، المرض أو الآلام لا ينوموننا لسيطرون على عقولنا، إنهم لا يتورطون في عائلتنا أو شؤوننا التجارية. إن المرض والآلام مجرد طفيليات ، فهم يأكلون وينشطون أنفسهم من أجسادنا وأجهزتها، إلا أنهم لايهتمون إذا كانوا يؤذوننا أو يقتلوننا.

من المحتمل يستطيع العلم الحديث أن يكشف الجن والمرض والآلام،أو الامراض التي تصيبنا. يستطيع علماء العلوم الطبية إستخدام أي شخص، ولكن إذا طلبت مني المساعدة. إن تقنياتي في غاية البساطة. أستطيع التحدث لأي شخص لديه أي نوع من الألم، بحيث يمكن لعلماء العلوم الطبية، إستخدام المعدات الخاصة بهم لمراقبة إجراءاتي. يمكنني إستخدام قوتي لسحب الألم ليخرج من هذا الشخص المريض، وسوف ينتقل الألم إلي من خلال أية وسيلة نستخدمها للتواصل. أستطيع أن أفعل هذاعدة مرات حسب الحاجة. إذا تلقيت أي جني أو ألم من خلال الهاتف، يمكنني أن أخرجه بسهولة من جسدي حتى أكون مستعداً مرة أخرى لهذه التجارب. بهذه الطريقة البسيطة جداً يستطيع علماء العلوم الطبية مراقبة ما يخرج من الشخص المريض وينتقل إلي عن طريق خطوط الهاتف و يدخل في جسدي. وفقاً لنظريتي، بمجرد أن تكتشف العلوم الطبية تلك الأشعة، سوف يستطيعون إيجاد علاجات لجميع أنواع العلل والمرض فقط بإزالة الأجسام الغير مرئية من شخص ما.

إنني لم أر أبداً أي شيء مثل حورية، أو شبح، أو ساحرة، أو أي شيطان في شكل إنسان. إنني أراهم دائماً في أشكالهم الأصلية الخاصة، هم أجسام طائرة صغيرة بأشكال مختلفة، فبعضهم علي شكل دائري، و آخرون علي شكل خيوط. يتأثر القلب عادة بحجب و توسيع الطاقة السلبية.

What are some of the cures for the problems caused by demons? Once scientists pay attention to my theories, I am sure they will be able to invent machines that reduce the influence of demons, disease, and pains in our bodies, but until then, I suggest everyone use a few tricks to reduce the problems caused by demons. However, these can only be used to fight against demons. These will not work on disease or pains. These tricks include the following:

1. Demons like red meat only. My understanding is that demons like beef. If you have more beef and eat more beef that could mean you are inviting more and more demons into your house and into your body.

2. Rub at least five small lemons or limes on different parts of your body, especially around your head, ears, eyes, and chest for two minutes. Then move your hand around your body seven times. Make sure you undergo this process when you are driving. Avoid residential areas. Choose major roads. After you move your hand around your body seven times, do not waste time anymore. Keep driving. Open a window and throw all the lemons or limes toward any tree. There is a 60 percent chance the demon around your body will leave to follow those lemons or limes. If you feel pressure, repeat this process every day or every other day or at least once a week. You can also cut a lemon or lime in half, rub those pieces on your left arm and shoulder, and then throw them out of your car toward a green tree. Do not stop your car during the process.

3. Demons do not leave human bodies easily, especially if they have been living around those bodies for a long time. To exorcise them, take at least fifteen sticks that are full of green mint leaves…

وبسبب خاصية التوسع هذه، يمكن لهذه الأمراض سد الأوعية الدموية و إعاقة الدورة الدموية.

تتأثر الكلى عادة بنوعين من الطاقات السلبية أوالأمراض. واحد منها يسد بالتوسع. المرض الأول يسد فقط الأنابيب الرئيسية في الكلى لعرقلة مهامهم. النوع الثاني من أمراض الكلى هو نتيجة حشرات غير مرئية تأكل تتلف الكلى بشكل مباشر. وبناء على ذلك، يحدث للناس إلتهابات في الكلى وحصى في الكلى أحياناً.إإن الجن أقوياء و أذكياء جداً بالمقارنة بالمرض و الآلام. الجن ليسوا طفيليات، وليسوا طاقات إيجابية، لأنه يمكن إستخدام الجن في أي من الإتجاهين. الجن يحبون أن يفعلوا أشياء و تصرفات سلبية. يمكننا إستخدام الجن في الأشياء الجيدة ولكن ليس لفترة طويلة.

الجن يفعلون أفعال وأشياء إيجابية لبضع ساعات أو أيام. الطاقات الايجابية هي نفوسنا أو أرواحنا والملائكة،التي تتبع فقط أوامر الله. يستطيع الجن إقامة علاقات صداقة مع أي إنسان أو حيوان، وبمجرد أن يصبح الجن أصدقاء مخلصين لشخص ما، سوف يتبع أوامر هذا الشخص بدون مناقشة.

كما أوضحت، كل الجن يبقون في مجموعات كبيرة أو في قبائل تقريباً، يكون هناك عادة،أصحاب عمل ضمن تلك القبائل أو الجماعات، و يتبع جميع الجن في المجموعة أو القبيلة أوامر رئيس الجن.بمجرد أن يصبح رئيس الجن من أصدقاء أي إنسان، يستطيع هذا الإنسان إستخدام هذه القبيلة من الجن بأكاملها لفعل كل يريده هو أو هي فقط بتمرير الأوامر إلى رئيس الجن. وسوف يقوم رئيس الجن بتمرير نفس الأمر إلي بقية المجموعة، أو القبيلة من الجن.بمجرد أن يقترب الإنسان من الموت، يستطيع هو أو هي نقل تلك الصداقة مع الجن إلى إنسان آخر،

130

3. Demons do not leave human bodies easily, especially if they have been living around those bodies for a long time. To exorcise them, take at least fifteen sticks that are full of green mint leaves. Put them in a metal bowl with water. Boil the water and mint leaves for at least thirty minutes. Drink that mint water every three days. This mint water will reduce the negativity of those demons around you that they will not create problems for your family or business affairs. They may even become a little positive and supportive because of the mint water.

4. As I have described before, you can use plain water in a spray bottle. You can spray each and every corner of your house frequently. Try to cover everywhere from the ceiling to the floor. Do this frequently. Water does not kill demons, but they do not like water. Water keeps them uncomfortable. If you do this frequently, demons will not stay around you or in your house for a long time. Do the same thing in your car as well. You will nccd to spray watcr routinely because once one group of demons leaves, your house will be vacant for another group of demons to occupy. If you keep spraying water, they will keep leaving your house.

5. You can also frequently use insect killers, but make sure you spray it in the air toward the ceiling. Do not leave any corner unattended. Spray everywhere frequently, and you will be surprised with the results.

Most of the time, demons are not completely inside the body. Somehow they surround the body. In this way, they are inside the body, but some parts are also above the skin. Whenever demons travel through the telephone lines, they are usually stuck in our ears, heads, and necks, especially our left ears.

و ستبدأ نفس المجموعة من الجن في إتباع أوامر الإنسان الجديد. لا يمكن لأي إنسان إجبار أو دفع الجن أن ينفذوا لهم أوامرهم. هذا هو كل شيء فيما يتعلق بالصداقة والإخلاص.

البشر يستخدام البشر المختلفون مجموعات من الجن لأغراض مختلفة. لقد وصفت عدد قليل بالفعل، ولكن إسمحوا لي أن أصف عدد قليل آخر. يستخدم أطباء الجن الجن لأغراض علاجية. إن الجن أكثرقوة من الأمراض والآلام. عندما يمرر الإنسان المعالج أوامر للجن الموجودون حوله أو حولها بتطهير جسم الشخص من كل الأمراض والآلام، فإن الجن يقومون بتطهير الجسم في ثوان. لكن تذكر، أن الجن لا يفعلون أشياء إيجابية لفترة طويلة. الآن سأشرح كيفية القيام بهذه العملية، والإيجابيات والسلبيات لإستخدام الجن لإزالة العلل، والأمراض، والآلام.بالطريقة التي يعالج بها المعالج هذه العلل و الأمراض.

ولكني أقول أن هذا إجراءاتي هي الأفضل الأشاعات والمجالات الكهرومغناطيسية. وسأستمر في مطالبة وتصرالعلوم الطبية و الحديثة آلات بإختراع آلات لتنظيف جسم الإنسان من كل الأمراض والحشرات الغير مرئية 'والآلام بإستخدام الأشاعات والمجالات الكهرومغناطيسية.ويمكن للمعالج تمرير الأوامر إلى الجن لتطهير الأجسام، وسوف يستمع الجني إلى الإنسان، ولكن يجب أن نتذكر أن المعالج يستطيع عكس الإجراء وجعل هؤلاء الجن يصيبون الجسم بمجموعة من الأمراض أو الآلام المختلفة .

وهذا هو الأسهل للجن القيام به. بالاضافة إلى ذلك، أنهم يحبون كل أنواع الأنشطة السلبية. لا يمكمن الإعتماد علي المعالجين، فقد لا يوفرون حلاً دائماً، لهذا يجب علي العلوم الطبية أن تتدخل وتجد حلاً دائماً لهذه الأمراض والآلام. لدينا بالفعل جميع أنواع الأدوية العلاجية والعمليات الجراحية.

SEE & CONTROL DEMONS & PAIN	رضوان قرشي

At that moment, demons have not completely penetrated our bodies. At that time, they sit on top of us and dig inside our minds by using the   left ear most of the time to learn more about us or use their hypnotizing powers. If a medical scientist observes a normal person who is on phone with a sick person who has a very short temper or someone who is an extremist in any field, I am sure that demons will travel via the phone lines and possess the other person. Medical science can use modern machines to detect the rays and signals. Once medical science is able to detect demons or disease, I am sure they will be able to easily find the cures that a normal person can use against them.

Always remember that demons and disease/pains are not the same things. Demons are different. They do not hurt us, but they use us as toys. They control our minds, and most of the time, we do what they want us to do. Most of the time, we think whatever they want us to think. You may ask me, what do demons get from this? The simple answer is that this is their hobby, and we get involved in our affairs and families, so they make decisions about what we need to do. They keep us angry and make us perform all kinds of negative acts. Practically, it is not possible to disrupt the demon's control. If someone like me takes the demon around you or inside you out, another will possess you within a few days or maybe a few hours. Demons can see that you are available for possession, immediately new one will come to you, and will make room around and inside you within a few seconds. And you will never know about these changes because all demons pretty much are the same way. Your dreams may be different, but that may be the extent of the change.

لا توجد أدوية مثالية يمكنها جعل الشخص الغير طبيعي أو الشخص المريض عقلياً يعود إلى حالته العقلية الطبيعية. الأطباء يعطون أو يحقنون المرضى العقليين بالمهدئات إلى، و بمجرد أن ينام المريض عقلياً، عادة ما يتم تقليل ضغط الجن عليهم لبضعة أيام. هذا هو السبب الذي يجعل الأطباء يشيرون بإنتظام علاج المرضى العقليين بهذه الأدوية، تجعل الناس المصابين بأمراض عقلية في حالة إرتخاء وهبوط معظم الوقت، وفي هذه الحالة، لا يستطيع الجن إستغلال هذا الشخص، فالشخص الطيئ أوالذي يشعر بالنعاس هو ببساطة أقل فائدة للجن. هذا هو السبب الذي يجعل الجن ينومون مغناطيسياً هذا الشخص بإستمرار، ويصرون على أن المرضى العقليين لا يتناولون أي دواء له أي تأثير على الجن، فهم يقاومون الأدوية تماماً. الأدوية غير فعالة تماماً ضد الجن.

الجني لا يتخلى عن قيادة لإنسان لجني آخربسهولة. لا يحدث ذلك دون قتال. نحن لا ندرك ذلك، ولكن الجن يتصرفون مثل وكأننا من ممتلكاتهم. الشياطين إنهم يعاملوننا كما لو كنا ألعابهم.يستخدم منا الجن كيفما أرادوا من خلال تنويمنا مغناطيسياً. ولكن لايدع جني ما الحيوان الذي يسيطرون عليه لجني آخر ما لم يكن الجني الجديد أكثر قوة. يقع بعض الناس تحت سيطرة أكثر من جني. الشخص الذي يقع تحت تأثير أكثر من جني قوي يصبح شخصاً مريضاً للغاية و لديه مشاكل السلوك المتطرف. الجن لا يحبون الأشخاص الباردين، و المعقولين، إنهم يفضلون عادة الإستحواذ علي الأشخاص سريعي   الغضب،   و   العنيدين، والمتطرفين.بصراحة، ليس من الصعب على الجنجعل أي شخص مجنون، ولكن الأشخاص السريعي الغضب بشكل غير طبيعي عرضة للسلوك المتطرف، و هم مهمة سهلة بالنسبة للجن.

On the other hand, disease or pains do not hypnotize us in order to control our minds. They do not get involved with our family or business affairs. Disease and pains are pure parasites; they eat and energize themselves from our bodies and organs. They do not care if they hurt or kill us.

Modern science could potentially detect the demons, disease, pains, or sicknesses that plague us. Medical scientists can use anyone, but if I have to help, I will. My techniques are very simple. I can talk to any person who has any kind of pain so that medical scientists can use their equipment to observe my procedure. I can use my power to pull the pain out of that sick person, and that pain will travel to me through whatever medium we use to communicate. I can do this as many times as needed. If I receive any demon or pain through the telephone, I can easily take them out of my body so that I am ready again for the experiments. In this very simple way, medical scientists can observe what is coming out from the sick person and traveling through phone lines and going into my body. According to my theory, once medical science is able to detect those rays, they will be able to find cures for all kind of sicknesses and disease by just removing the invisible bodies from someone.

I have never seen anything like a fairy, a ghost, a witch, or any demon in the shape of a human being. I always see them in their original shapes, small flying objects in different shapes. Some are round. Some are like threads. The heart usually is affected by the blocking and expanding of negative energy. And because of this expanding quality, these diseases can block the blood vessels and interrupt blood circulation.

عادة ما يكون للجن السيطرة الكاملة علي هذا الشخص. إذا أراد جني آخر السيطرة علي هذا الشخص، يجب علي هؤلاء الجن أن يحارب بعضهم البعض لتغيير أمر السيطرة. يكون الجن خارج أجسامنا أجسام طائرة و صغيرة حقاً. إنهم أشبه بالحشرات المرئية! إنهم ليسوا مثل ما نراهم في أفلام الرعب أو الصور المخيفة. إنهم غير مؤذيين تماماً عندما يطيرون في الهواء من حولنا. أحيانا أري عدة مئات من الجن يطيرون من حولي في غرفة صغيرة جداً. حتى الآن، لم أر أي من جني يمدد جسده عندما يطير في الهواء، ولكن يستطيع الجن تمديد و ضغط أجسامهم بسهولة وفقا للجسم الذي يخترقونه أو يستحوذون عليه. ما إنهم يستطيعون إتلاف أي عصب أوعضو من أعضاء الجسم بكل سهولة ،يمكنم حتي الذهاب بسهولة إلى أي عرق، أو شريان أو أنبوب، واستخدام خاصية إمكانية الضغط/ التمدد لسد هذه . عن الأماكن، إن الأذن اليسرى هي الطريق نحو أدمغتنا و عقولنا بالنسبة للجن. إنهم يصلوا إلي عقولنا لتنويمنا مغناطيسياً عن طريق استخدام الأذن اليسري، معظم الوقت. أي شخص لديه مشاكل في أذنه أو أذنها اليسري قد يكون أو تكون تحت تأثير جني .

الجن هم الذين يثنوننا عن زيارة الأطباء أو رجال الدين. الجن هم السبب الرئيسي للمرض العقلي في البشر. إن الجن والأمراض يسببون الكثير من الإضطرابات البدنية والعقلية في أدمغتنا وأجسامنا. إن الشخص المريض عقلياً يقع تحت سيطرةجني واحد أو أكثر إلى حد كبير. يمكننا أن نميز الشخص الذي يتصرف بجنون من حولنا. يستطيع الأطباء والناس العاديين الآخرين الحكم بسهولة علي شخص معين إذا كانت هناك دلائل على وجود مرض عقلي به، ولكن هذا الشخص المريض عقلياً لا يدرك أبداً أنه يتكلم ويتصرف أو أنها تتكلم و تتصرف يشكل مجنون.

SEE & CONTROL DEMONS & PAIN

Kidneys are usually affected by two kinds of negative energies or diseases. One blocks, by expanding. The first disease just blocks the major tubes in the kidneys to disrupt their functions. The second kind of kidney disease is the result of invisible insects that eat and directly damage the kidneys. Consequently, people get kidney infections and sometimes kidney stones. Demons are way powerful and intelligent as compared to disease and pains. Demons are not parasites. Demons are not positive energies, because demons can be used either way. Demons really like to do negative things and actions. We can use demons for good stuff but not for a long time.

Demons do positive actions and things for few hours or days. Positive energies are our souls or spirits and angels, which only follow God's commands. Demons can befriend any human or animal, and once demons become sincere friends with someone, they will follow that person's commands without asking any questions.

As I have explained, almost all demons stay in big groups or tribes, and usually, there are bosses within those tribes or groups. All demons in a group or tribe follow the command of a boss demon. Once that head demon becomes a friend to any human, that human can use that whole tribe of demons to do whatever he or she wants just by passing commands to the head demon. And the head demon will pass the same command to the rest of its group or tribe of demons. Once that human is near to death, he or she can transfer that friendship with demons to another human, and the same group of demons will start following the commands of the new human. No human can compel or push demons to do his or her bidding. This is all about friendship and sincerity.

هذا لأن ذلك الشخص المجنون خاضع لسيطرة التنويم المغناطيسي لجني ما. الجن يقنعون هذا الشخص المجنون والمختل عقلياً بإستمرار أنه ليس مريضاً أو أنها ليست مريضة، و أنه او أنها على ما يرام تماما. قد يعتقد هذا الشخص المريض عقلياً أن الجميع من حوله أو من حولها خاطئ ، أو مجنون، أو مريض عقلياً. إذا كان لديك تجربة الوجود مع شخص مريض عقلياً ، وي تعرف أنه لا يريد تناول أي أدوية، وأنهم لا يحبون الأطباء، و لا يحبون صحبة رجال الدين، السبب في ذلك هو الجن.

لا يستطيع الناس العاديون أن يشعروا بالجن.بمجرد أن تصبح قادراً على الشعور/ الإحساس بهم، فلن تكون قادراً على تحملهم. هل ستكون غير مرتاحاً ومنزعجاً حتى يغادرون جسمك. لذلك يجب شكر الله علي أن الناس الطبيعيون ليس لديهم أدنى فكرة أو مشاعر عندما يبدأ الجن الإقامة داخل أجسادهم. ثق بي، ليس من السهل التخلص من أي من جني موجود في جسمك. لقد واجهت الكثير من المشاكل. خلاف ذلك، أنا قادر علي الإصرار على أن يستمعوا إلي. عادة، ما يحدثون لي بعض المشاكل، ولكن بمجرد أن أتعرف عليهم، يثقون بي، ويصبحون أصدقاء لي أفضل من البشر، و يتصرفون بشكل أفضل من البشر.أقل نهم أقل ضرراً من البشروالحيوانات. هذا صحيح في حالتي.و ليس صحيحاً بالنسبة للجميع. لذلك تذكر لايستطيع المرء أن يوقف قدوم الجن إلى بيوتنا أو أجسادنا،ولكن من خلال التحكم في سلوكنا وعقولنا، فإننا نستطيع أن نقلل من تأثيرهم علي أجسامنا وحياتنا.

القاعدة البسيطة هي التالي: نحن بحاجة إلى جعل أنفسنا أقل إثارة للإهتمام بالنسبة لهم

Different humans use groups of demons for different purposes. I already described a few, but let me describe a few more. A few demon doctors use demons for healing purposes. Demons are way more powerful than diseases and pains. When a human healer passes a command to his or her demons to cleanse someone's body of all diseases and pains, the demons will cleanse the body in seconds. But remember, demons cannot do positive things for a long time. Now I will explain how this process works and the pluses and minuses of using demons to remove sickness, diseases, and pains the way a healer treats them, but I will say that my procedure is better— electromagnetic rays and fields. And I will keep requesting and insisting that medical and modern science may invent machines to clean a human's body from all invisible insects' disease and pains by using rays and electromagnetic fields.

A healer can pass commands to demons to cleanse bodies, and the demon will listen to that human; however, you should remember that the healer can reverse the procedure and make those demons infect a body with a bunch of different diseases or pains.

And this is easier for demons to do. Plus, they like all kinds of negative activity. Healers may not be reliable, and they may not offer a permanent solution, so medical science needs to step in and find a permanent solution for these diseases and pains. We already have all kinds of healing medications and surgeries.

There are no perfect medications that can bring an abnormal or mentally sick person back to a normal mental condition. Doctors feed or inject sedatives into mentally sick people.

إنهم يحبون التطرف، والغضب، والاكتئاب،السلبية، والعادات السيئة مثل الشرب والأدوية. إترك الأشياء و العادات السيئة ، و تقلباتك المزاجية السيئة، و هكذا سيصبح الجن أقل إهتماماً بك، و سيبحثون عن شخص أكثر إثارة للإهتمام بالنسبة لهم.لقد كنت أقتل الحشرات والزواحف في كثير من الأحيان، ولكني منذ بدأت أن أشعر بهؤلاء الجن، أواجه الكثير من المشاكل في قتلهم، وذلك لأنني لا أريد للجن أو الأمراض الخاصة بهم زيارة جسدي. في حالتي، أقوم بمجادلتهم أو الإصرار على أن يعودوا إلى الجسد الأصلي، أو إذا ذلك الجسد ميتاً، أطلب منهم أن يجدوا شيئاً من هذا القبيل ولكن ليس أنا.

نحن الذين نتحكم في عقولنا. والمشكلة الوحيدة هي أنه إذا لم يكن لدينا عقول قوية، سيستطيع الجن تنويمنا مغناطيسياً وإستخدامنا بسهولة، كما يحلو لهم، لكننا لا زلنا متحكمين في عقولنا، ولكن الجن يضخمون و يزودون كل شيئ بطريقة سلبي. إذا كنا قليلوا الغضب، سوف جعلوننا أكثر غضباً، و إذا كنا قليلوا الحزن، سوف يدفعوننا إلى مزيد من الإكتئاب ونحن نصر على الإنتحار، و علي قتل شخص ما، أو جرح شخص ما. إذا كنا لا نحب شخص ما، سيقوم الجن بزيادة الكراهية له. وبسبب طبيعتهم السلبية، يضطر الجن أن يأخذونا إلي المسار السلبي.على الرغم من أننا أرباب العمل من عقولنا، و بالرغم من أننا نتحكم في عقولنا فنحن ما زالنا نتبع تعليماتهم و نحن غير مدركين ذلك.

بمجرد أن ندرك أن كل الظروف القاسية أو المتطرفة ليست قادمة من عقولنا ولكن نتيجة لعب الجن بنا، سنكون بحاجة للبدء في ممارسة السيطرة على سلوكياتنا المتطرفة. ليس من السهل على أي شخص التخلص من لأمزجة الحادة. يمكنك على الأقل محاولة مكافحة هذه التأثيرات السلبية.

SEE & CONTROL DEMONS & PAIN	رضوان قرشي

Once the mentally ill person goes to sleep, the pressure from demons is usually reduced for a few days. This is the reason why doctors regularly suggest those medications for the treatment of mentally ill people. Those medications keep mentally ill people at ease and down most of the time. In that condition, demons cannot use that person. A slow or sleepy person is simply less useful to demons. That's why demons continuously hypnotize that person and insist that the mentally ill person not take any medication that has any effects on demons. Demons are completely resistant to medications. Medications are totally ineffective against demons.

A demon does not give up command of a human to another demon easily. It never happens without a fight. We are not aware of this, but demons act like we are their property. Demons treat us as their toys. Demons use us however they want by hypnotizing us. But one demon will never let another demon take over the animal they possess unless the new demon is more powerful. Some people are under the influence of more than one demon. The person who is under the influence of more than one powerful demon will become an extremely ill person with extreme behavior problems.

Demons do not like cool, sensible, and normal people. Demons usually prefer possessing the bodies of short-tempered, stubborn, and extreme people. It is easy for demons to exploit these kinds of people. Honestly, it is not difficult for demons to make anyone crazy, but abnormally short-tempered individuals and people prone to extreme behavior are an easy task for them.

إذا حاولت ذلك و لكن ما زالت لا تستطيع السيطرة على عقلك وسلوكك، عندها تكون في حاجة لشخص مثلي يمكنه تحريك الجني بعيداً عنك. عادة، ما يكون الجن حولك أو داخلك منذ طفولتك، وهؤلاء هم أشد ويقاومون كثيراً قبل خروجهم من شخص ما، لأنهم يعتقدون أنك من ممتلكاتهم، أو لعبتهم أو مكان لإقامتهم. مرة شخص ما يأخذ هذا الشيطان بعيدا عنك، وسوف يكون لديك مكان فارغ متاح للجن جديد. لكن يكون لأحد السيطرة القوية عليك إذا حافظت ممارسة السيطرة والحد من السلوكيات السلبية، وقللت من الغضب، وحافظت على مزاج بارد.أستطيع أنا أو شخص مثلي إزالة هؤلاء الجن منك أنت لإعطائك وقتاً كافياً للحفاظ على السيطرة والحفاظ على عقلك. بمجرد أن تترك الإستماع وإتباع الجن، لن يضيعوا وقتهم معك. سيجدون شخصاً آخر أكثر إثارة للإهتمام بالنسبة لهم. أخيرا، ستصبح المتحكم في عقلك مرة أخرى!

يغذي الجن عقولنا بالدروس/ الرغبات المتوحشة والمجنونة طول الوقت.و ليس لديهم ما يفعلونه إذا لم يقاتل بعضهم البعض. إذا كانوا حولنا طوال الوقت، سيغذون عقولنا برغبات متوحشة وسيئة بواسطة تنويمنا مغناطيسياً. وسوف يظلون يصرون على إنتحار شخص ما، أو أنهم سوف يحدثون رغبات جنسية أو غيرة أو كراهية أو أنوع آخر من الرغبات السلبية والسيئة. هذا كله يأتي دائماً من الجن الموجودون حولنا. أحياناً يصرون أن تصفع شخص ما أو تلكمه بدون سبب. يمكنهم بسهولة تضخيم أو زيادة غضبنا.

إنهم يستطيعون أن يجعلونا أكثر حزناً بسهولة، أو يجعلوننا نشعر بالكآبة بدون سبب. إذا كنت تشعر بالصفات الأكثر سلبية في نفسك، لابد أن تبدأ في رفض كل هذه الأفكار و الرغبات السلبية للحد من سيطرة الجن على عقلك. إذا إتبعتهم، سوف يتمتعون أكثر وسوف نظل في ورطة طوال الوقت. إن الجن مسئولون عن تغذيتنا بكل الأفكار المجنونة والرغبات الموجودة في أذهاننا.

Rizwan Qureshi	رؤية الجن و الآلام السيطرة عليها
Demons usually have total control and command of that person. If another demon wants to take command of that person, those demons have to fight with each other to change the command. Outside our bodies, demons are really small flying objects. They are similar to visible insects! They are not like what we see in horror movies or scary pictures. They are totally harmless when they are flying in the air around us. Sometimes I have seen several hundred demons flying around me in a very small room. Until now, I have never seen any of demons expanding their bodies when they are flying in the air, but demons can easily compress and expand their sizes according to the body they penetrate or possess. They can very easily damage any nerve or organ of a body. They can easily go into any vein, artery, or tube and use their compressing/expanding qualities to block it. For demons, the left ear is the path toward our brains. Demons reach into our brains to hypnotize us by using our left ear, most of the time. Anybody who has problems with his or her left ear could be under the influence of a demon.

Demons are the ones that discourage us from visiting doctors or religious people. Demons are the main cause of mental sickness within humans. Demons and diseases cause a lot of physical and mental disorders in our brains and our bodies. The mentally sick person is pretty much under the control of one or more demons. We can see if someone is acting crazy around us. Doctors and other normal people can easily judge when a particular person is exhibiting signs of a mental illness, but that mentally sick person never realizes that he or she is talking and acting crazy. | إذا كان أي شخص يقول شيئا عن الجن، أنهم سحرة ويستطيعون تحقيق ثلاث رغبات أو يمكن أن تجعلونا أغنياء، أصدقائي هم يحكون لكم قصصاً. الجن الحقيقيون أقوياء جداً، لكنهم يستخدمون سلطاتهم السلبية غالباً. إذا وجدت في أي وقت جني به صفات الجن السحري الموجود في القصص، سأشارك خبرتي ومعرفتي مع الجميع. أتمنى لو وجد مثل هذا الجن كي أستطيع أن أقول: "نعم، حاول جعل الجن أصدقاءك "إن أفضل شيء هو الإبتعاد عنهم. ليس هذا سهلاً، لكنه ليس مستحيلاً. القتال مع الجن يعني القتال مع الهواء.

لقد تحدثت إلى العديد من الأشخاص الذي إدعوا أن الجن زاروهم وتواصلوا معهم في شكل البشر. لقد سألتهم فقط إذا كان هذا صحيحاً حقا، وإذا كان الجن يستطيعون عكس العملية وتغيير أنفسهم من شكل الإنسان إلى شكل الجن مرة أخرى. ولكن لم يحدث شيئ من هذا القبيل. حتى اليوم، عندما أصبحت قادراً على الشعور، والإحساس، ورؤية الجن. لم أر أي جني يأتي إلي في شكل إنسان أو تواصل معي مثل البشر. أنا أتعامل مع العديد من الجن كل يوم،بعضهم لطيف للغاية، والبعض الآخر في غاية الخطورة، لكنهم دائماً ما يكونون في شكلهم الحقيقي، وهو، أجسام طائرة صغيرة مماثلة للحشرات الطائرة. أنا أتواصل مع الجن أربع وعشرين ساعة، سبعة أيام في الأسبوع. طلبت أن يظهر أي من هؤلاء الجن لي ما إذا كانوا يستطيعون تغيير نفسها في أي شكل مثل الإنسان أو الحيوان، لكن هذا لم يحدث أبداً. ونتيجة لذلك، أشعر بقوة أن كل هذه القصص عن الجن الذين يتجول في شكل البشر ليست سوى قصص. إذا كان هناك أي تغيير في معرفتي أو خبرتي، وسوف أخبر الجميع بطريقة أو بأخرى. |

That is because that crazy person is under the control of a demon's hypnotism. Demons continuously convince that crazy and mentally ill person that he or she is not sick, that he or she is perfectly okay. This mentally ill person may believe that everybody else around him or her is wrong, crazy, or mentally sick. If you have experience being around a mentally sick person, you know that they do not want to take any medications, that they do not like doctors, and that they do not like the company of religious people. The reason is demons.

Normal people cannot sense demons. Once you are able to sense/feel them, you will not be able to tolerate them. You will be uncomfortable and disturbed until they leave your body. So thank God that normal people have no clue or feelings when demons start residing inside their bodies. Trust me; it is not easy to get rid of any demon from your body. I went through so many problems. Otherwise, I am able to insist that they listen to me. Usually, they create some problems for me; however, once we have been introduced, they trust me, and they become better friends than humans. They behave better than humans.

They are less harmful than humans and animals. This is true in my case. This is not true for everyone. So remember that no one can stop demons from coming into our homes or our bodies, but by controlling our behaviors and minds, we can reduce their influence in our bodies and lives.

لدينا الملايين من مختلف أنواع الجن من حولنا، داخل منزلنا، حول منزلنا أو في مكان العمل،وفي كل مكان. إن الجن يظهرون إلى حد كبير نفس النوع من الصفات والعادات والأمزجة كما يفعل البشر، على سبيل المثال، الجيد،و السيئ، و السيئ جداً،أو الغير مطيع، والشرير، و المتطرف، والغير مؤذي، و الغيور والغاضب، و المطيع، والعاصي، الخ.

كما وصفت عدة مرات، فالجن، أو جماعة أو قبيلة الجن، يعملون معاً و يستخدمون لغتهم غير العادية للتنويم المغناطيسي،أو أنهم يملكون جسم ما ويدعون مختلف أنواع الحشرات الغير مرئية لإحداث أنواع مختلفة من الآلام أو تضر أعضاء الجسم المختلفة.

لا يهم اذا كان شخص ما هو صحي جداً أو جميل، أو صاحب عمل ناجح، أو غني جداً، فإن هذا الجني، أو جماعة أو قبيلة الجن يستطيعون أن يختاروا أي شخص بسهولة جداً.

يستطيع هؤلاء الجن أن يجعلوا الشخص الذي يتمتع بصحة جيدة للغاية، شخصاً مريضاً بسرعة كبيرة، إنهم يستطيعون إتلاف جمال شخص ما في بضعة أيام، و كذلك تستطيع هذه المجموعات من الجن أن يجعلوا الشخص الغنيا جداً فقير للغاية عن طريق إحداث كل أنواع المشاكل في مجال أعمال شخص ما. هذه الشياطين، وكذلك يستطيع هؤلاء الجن جلب الكراهية بين الزوج والزوجة أو بين المحبين بإستخدام التنويم المغناطيسي.

لماذا يفعل الجن مثل هذه الامور؟ الجواب هو: حسب طبيعة الجن، هم يحبون الأنشطة السلبية، أو في بعض الأحيان نجعله تعساء بسبب أفعالنا. وأنا متأكد بنسبة 100 في المئة أن معظمهم يتصرفون ضدنا ويحاولون تدمير حياتنا أو صحتنا أو أسرتنا أو أعمالنا.

138

Rizwan Qureshi	رؤية الجن و الآلام السيطرة عليها
The simple rule is the following: we need to make ourselves less interesting for them. They like extremism, anger, depression, negativism and bad habits like drinking and drugs. Quit the bad stuff and curb your bad temperament and they will be less interested in you and look for someone more interesting for them.	نحن لدينا رغبتين أو حجتين أو خيارين طوال الوقت. القلب يمكنه تأييد مسار واحد، ولكن العقل يمكنه أن يد لك علي مسار آخر، و هكذا يوجد إثنين من التعليمات، واحد يأتي من عقلك، والثاني يأتي من الجن الموجودون حولك أو داخلنا. جسدي لا يستطيع أن يتحمل الجن حولي أو بالقرب مني، لذلك ليس لدي إختيار لإقناعهم بمغادرة المكان الخاص بي عدة مرات في اليوم. أنا آسف، ولكن ليس لدي أي خيار.
I used to kill insects and reptiles frequently, but since I started sensing these demons, I have developed a lot of problems killing them, because I do not want their demons or diseases to visit my body. In my case, I argue with them or insist that they go back to the original body, or if that body is dead, I ask them to find something similar but not me. We are the bosses of our minds. The only problem is that if we don't have strong minds, demons can easily hypnotize and use us however they like. Still, we are the bosses of our minds, but demons amplify everything negative. If we are a little bit angry, they will make us angrier. If we are a little bit sad, they will make us more depressed and insist that we commit suicide, kill someone, or hurt someone. If we do not like someone, demons will increase that hate. Because of their nature of negativism, demons are compelled to take us on a negative path. Even though we are the bosses of our minds, we still follow their instructions unconsciously.	تذكر دائماً، فإنه ليس من الصعب على أي جني تنويم الإنسان أو الحيوان مغناطيسياً، وجعل أي شخص يقوم بأي نشاط بدني، مثل لكم شخص ما، أو قتل شخص ما، أو حتي فتح الصنبور. نحن نقم بهذه الأفعال إما أثناء النوم أو عندما نكون يقظين، ولكن قد نكون غير مدركين لهم تماماً هذا كله يتوقف على مدى ضعف عقولنا. أحياناً تقوم الحيوانات أو الزواحف أو الطيور من حولنا بعمل أنشطة للجن.

ألا تعتقد أن هذا العالم الخفي يضرنا ويقتلنا بالفعل؟، ألا ينبغي أن نتوقف عن إيذاء وقتل بعضنا البعض على الأقل؟. يستطيع الجن، والآلام، والأمراض أن يتنقلوا بمنتهي السهولة من خلال خط الهاتف، وخاصة من جسم مكتظ. لهذا السبب أكره إجراء المكالمات الهاتفية والرد عليها. لا يستطيع السحر الأسود أو الجن هزيمة الكتب المقدسة أو الإجراءات المقدسة. عندما نستخدم مكبر الصوت في الهاتف، تنتقل هذه الآلام و هذا الجن القادمين عن طريق خط الهاتف إما إلى الجو المفتوح من حولنا أو يعودون إلى المصدر في الطرف الآخر من خط الهاتف. |
| Once we are aware that all extreme conditions are not coming from our minds but a demon playing with us, we need to start practicing controlling our extreme behaviors. It is not easy for anyone to get rid of temperaments. | من السهل جداً إستقبال أو إستيعاب الجن من أي مكان، ولكن من الصعب جداً التخلص منهم، وخاصة هؤلاء الجن الذين يهاجمون العقل مباشرة ليثوموا بتنويم الناس مغناطيسياً، ويحثونهم على القيام بشيء معين ، لأن الجن يتبعون أوامر طبيب الجن. هؤلاء الجن هم الأكثر خطورة وضررا بالمقارنة مع الجن العاديون. |

SEE & CONTROL DEMONS & PAIN

You can at least attempt to fight these negative influences. If you try but still cannot control your mind and behavior, this is the time when you need someone like me who can move that demon away from you. Usually, demons have been around or inside you since your childhood, and these are tougher and they resist a lot before they leave someone, because they think you are their property, toy, or residence. Once someone takes that demon away from you, you will have an empty place or a vacancy available for a new demon. But no one will have strong control of you if you keep practicing to control and reduce negative behaviors, lessen anger, and keep a cool temperament. I or someone like me can remove those demons from you to give you enough time to maintain control of your mind. Once you quit listening and quit following demons, they will not waste their time with you. They will find someone else more interesting for them. Finally, you can become the boss of your mind again! Demons feed wild and crazy lessons/wishes to our minds all the time. Demons are free creatures with a lot of time in their hands. They have nothing to do if they are not fighting with each other. If they are around us all the time, they will feed wild and bad wishes into our minds by hypnotizing us. They will keep insisting that someone commit suicide, or they will create sexual desires or jealousy or hatred or other kinds of negative and bad wishes. These always come from demons around us. Sometimes they insist you slap someone or punch someone for no reason. They can easily amplify or boost our anger. They can easily make us sadder. They can keep us depressed for no reason.

لا يوجد أحد لا يعاني من سيطرة الجن، إلا إذا كان الشخص يرش أي نوع من الماء المقدس مباشرة علي الوجه، والأذن والرأس والعنق والصدر على الأقل مرتين يومياً. ليس هدف من المناقشة من الذي يقع تحت تأثيرالذي لا يقع تحت تأثيرهم. هناك درجة أو مستوى من سيطرة الجن على الجسم. عادة ما يحدث الجن الطبيعيون حالة من السلبية والتطرف. قد لهذه تؤدي بنا هذه الظروف إلى أي حالة غير طبيعية أو مستوى غير طبيعي لأي موقف، مثل الحب الشديد أو الكراهية الشديدة والغيرة الشديدة أو المنافسة الشديدة، ونفاد الصبر، أو فرط الحركة، أوالغضب، أو العصبية، أوالاكتئاب، أونوبات القلق، أو محاولات الانتحار، أو اليأس، أو المبالغة في ردود الفعل، أوالرغبات الجنسية، و تناول الطعام بكثرة، أوالسياسة، أوالحديث، أوالهدوء، الخ.

خلال سيطرة الجن، إذا كانت السيطرة بمستوى عادي، سيعانى الناس عادة من الحالات المذكورة أعلاه. لكن أحياناً، إما بدون سبب، أو سأقول ربما ينزعج الجن لسبب ما منا في بعض الأحيان . في تلك الحالة يكون هجوم الجن على الدماغ أو العقل أكبر بكثير بالمقارنة بسيطرة الجني الطبيعي. هذا ليس ضرورياً. يستهدف الجني الشخص الذي يشعر بالضيق أو الغضب منه، وأحيانا يستهدف أي فرد آخر من العائلة أيضاً.

سأقول إن الأشخاص الأضعف عقلياً، في الأسرة. في بعض الأحيان، يكون هؤلاء الناس أهداف سهلة للغاية، الأشخاص الذين لا يسافرون أولا يتحركون كثيراً ولكنهم يبقون فقط في مكان معين أو يبقون في المنزل أكثر من اللازم أو يبقون في غرفة معينة أكثر من اللازم أو يبقون تحت شجرة في الليالي المظلمة أو يقتلون بعض الحشرات أو الزواحف أو أخيراً، أقول حظ سيئ.

140

If you feel more negative qualities in yourself, then you need to start rejecting all those negative thoughts and wishes to reduce their control of your mind. If we follow them, they will enjoy more and will keep us in trouble all the time. Demons. are responsible for feeding us all the crazy thoughts and wishes within our mind. If anyone says anything about demons—that they are magical and can fulfill three wishes or can make us rich—my friends, they are just telling you stories. Real demons are very powerful but mostly use their negative powers. If I ever find a demon with qualities of the magical demons in stories, I will share my knowledge and experience with everyone. I wish they existed so that I could say, "Yes, try to make demons your friends." The best thing is to stay away from them. It is not easy but not impossible. Fighting with demons means fighting with air.

I talked to several people who claimed that demons visit them and communicate with them in the shape of humans. I just asked them if this was really true and if the demons could reverse the process and change themselves from a human to a demon again. But nothing happened like that. Until today, when I am able to sense, feel, and see demons, I never see any demon come to me in the shape of a human or communicate like a human.

I deal with so many demons every day, some extremely nice, others extremely dangerous, but they are always in their real shape, that is, small flying objects similar to flying insects. I communicate with demons twenty-four hours all seven days a week.

رؤية الجن و الآلام السيطرة عليها

ولكن تذكر، إشعور أي شيءإذا بدأت تشعر أن هناك شيئ غير طبيعي حدث عقلياً حولك، لا تضيع وقتك، تبدأ في تناول أي دواء تستطيع الحصول عليه من الأطباء لتحسين قوتك البدنية. لا تستخدم الدواء الذي يجعلك تشعر بالدوار أو في حالة سكر، لأنني أؤمن بقوة أن تلك الأنواع من الأدوية التي تبقي عليكم الشعور بالنعاس، فإن هذه الأدوية تبهج الجن و تزيد من سيطرتهم علي عقل شخص ما. ـ أنت بحاجة إلى البقاء في حالة تأهب مثل الشخص العادي. تدرب وإقنع عقلك برفض الرقابة الخارجية للجن علي عقلك. إرفض كل السلوكيات الشاذة، و السلبية و البطيئة والمفرطة، و المتطرفة. تناول الأدوية لتقوية نفسك. بمجرد أن تصل إلى هذا المستوى، بحث عن الماء المقدس، وبغض النظر عن مقدار إنزعاج شخص ما، رش الماء المقدس بإستمرار كثيراً و مباشرةً على وجهه و رأسه وأذنينه ورقبته، وصدره. ثق بي، لا يوجد أي جني يمكنه أن يقف أمام الماء المقدس. لكن تذكر، أن تأثير المياه المقدسة (بسبب موجات والإشعاعات) مؤقتة جداً. لهذا السبب، يعود الجن على نحو غير عادي مرة أخرى بعد بضعة ساعات، لذلك تحتاج إلى أن رش الماء المقدس كثيراً جداً.

أفضل طريقة هي عند رش الماء المقدس على نفسك، قم برشه في الهواء في كل مكان في منزلك أيضاً،وهذا سيساعدك على التخلص من الجن الشرير، وستخفض/تقتل سلبية الجن من حولك. نظراً لكثرة رش الماء المقدس في منزلك، سوف ينتقل الجن إلى تلك المناطق أو الزوايا حيث لا يمكن أن يصل الماء المقدس إليهم، أو أنهم سوف يغادرون منزلك، لهذا من الأفضل الإستمرار في عمل هذه الإجراءات بشكل منتظم.

إن سيطرة الجن المتوحش والشرير يتيح لنا استخدام قدرتنا وقوتنا المادية الكاملة، كل ما نستخدمه عادةً في الظروف العادية.

SEE & CONTROL DEMONS & PAIN

I demand that anyone show me if these demons can change themselves into the shape of any human or animal, but it never happens. As a result, I strongly feel that all those stories about demons wandering in the shape of humans are just stories. If there is any change in my knowledge or experience, I will notify everyone somehow.Around us, inside our house, around our house or workplace, and everywhere, we have millions of different kind of demons. Demons exhibit pretty much the same kind of qualities, habits, and temperaments as humans do—for example, good, bad, very bad, naughty, evil, extremist, harmless, harmful, jealous, angry, obedient, disobedient, etc.

As I described several times, demons—or group or tribes of demons operate together and use their extraordinary language of hypnotism or they possess a body and invite different kinds of invisible insects to create different kinds of pains or to damage different body organs.

It doesn't matter if someone is very healthy or beautiful, is a successful business owner, or is very wealthy; this demon—or group or tribe of demons—can choose any person very easily.

Very quickly, those demons can make that healthy person extremely sick;

رضوان قرشي

إن سيطرة الجن لا تجلب أي قوة إضافية لجسمنا ولكن سيطرة الجني علي عقلنا، يعطينا حرية إستخدام قوتنا البدنية بكامل طاقتها دون رعاية من أحد.

عادة يبدو صوتنا مختلفاً وثقيلاً قليلاً. وبالتأكيد، ليس لدينا أي سيطرة علي أنفسنا، وهذا هو السبب الذي يجعلنا نتصرف بشكل غريب حقاً، ومجنون،وخطير. حتى الآن، ليس لدي العلوم الطبية أي دواء أو موجات/ أشاعات مباشرة للإصرار على مغادرة سيطرة أي جني علي الجسم. لذلك إستخدام المياه المقدسة وإستمر في رشها كل ساعة، عندما تكون حالة المريض سيئة جداً، يجب رش ذلك الماء حسب الحاجة. سأكتب تفاصيل كاملة عن كيفية تحويل الماء العادي إلى ماء مقدس في وقت لاحق في الكتاب. تذكر دائما، أن خلال عملية رش الماء المقدس، يجب إبقاء قدميك على أرضية سيراميك أو أسمنت أو علي أي معدن. وهذا يوفر للجن والآلام مساراً سهلاً ليتركوا الجسم.إن وضع قدميك في كثير من الأحيان علي السيراميك البارد أو أرضية أسمنت شيئ صحي جداً للجميع..سيساعد ذلك كثيراً الناس الذين يعانون من آلام في أقدامهم، أو ألم حارق في أقدامهم أو في أي جزء من الجسم . وعندما تظل حافي القدمين على السيراميك البارد أو علي أرض أسمنتية، فإن الآلام والجن وهم أجسام مادية، و كهرومغناطيسية ستنسحب من جسمنا نتيجة لتأثير قوي الجاذبية، إذا وضعت أقدامك علي الأرض أو علي أي معدن أو أسمنت.

لا يقوم الجن بأفعال مؤذية كثيراً أو يحدثوا ظروفاً حادة، فهم. في بعض الأحيان يبقون حولنا ولا يضايقونا كثيراً.إذا كنا لا نغضبهم أو نزعجهم بلا سبب.أحيانا يحب الجن عدد قليل من الناس. و الآن مشكلة حب شخص ما هذه، لها جانب إيجابي و جانب سلبي.

All the time, we have two desires or arguments or choices. The heart may be endorsing one path, but the mind may be telling you to embrace another. Out of these two, one instruction is coming from your mind, and the second is coming from demons around and inside us.

My body cannot tolerate demons around or close to me, so I have no choice but to convince them to leave my place several times a day. I am sorry, but I do not have a choice.

Always remember, it is not difficult for demons to hypnotize any human or animal and make one do any physical activity, such as punching someone, killing someone, or even turning on the faucet. We do these actions either during sleep or when we are awake, but we may be totally unaware of them. That all depends on how weak our minds are. Sometimes animals or reptiles or birds around us do activities for demons.

Don't you think this invisible world is already hurting and killing us? And shouldn't we stop hurting and killing each other at least? Demons, pains, and diseases can be transferred very easily through the phone line, especially from an overcrowded body. That's why I hate making and answering phone calls.

No black magic or demon can defeat holy books or holy procedures. When we use a phone with the speaker on, these pains and demons coming through the phone line either move to the open atmosphere around us or go back to the source on other end of phone line.

الجانب الإيجابي للجن بهذه الطريقة، عندما يحب الجني شخص ما، يقوم بمساعدته كثيراً. الشياطين دائماً يجدون الوسائل ويواصلون البحث عن سبل مساعدة هذاالشخص بكل وسيلة ممكنة. الجن يفتحون أبواب النجاح لهذا الشخص طوال الوقت، أما الجانب السلبي للجن أنهم حتى لو كانوا يحبون شخص ما، فهم يحاولون بإستمرار فرض سيطرتهم على ذلك الشخص. إما في الأحلام أو في واقع الحياة ، افهم يحاولون إقناع هذا الشخص بإستمرار بأنهم ما زالوا حوله. ربما لا توجد للجن أي نوايا سيئة تجاه هذا الشخص، ولكن عندما يرى الناس الطبيعيون شخصاً يتحدث إلى الهواء أو يتفاعل مع صديق وهمي، عادة يعتبر الناس العاديين هؤلاء الأنواع من الناس مرضى عقليين. يبدأ الجن في إظهار هؤلاء الأشخاص الوهميون لهؤلاء الناس إما في شكل إنسان أو في شكل شبح حوله أو حولها، وفي هذه الحالة يصبح هؤلاء الأشخاص غير طبيعيين و يظلوا يبحثون ويركضون وراء ذلك الصديق الوهمي ليتواصلوا معه أكثر وأكثر.

توجيه لهؤلاء الناس، يرجى محاولة فهم أن كل ما تراه أمامك و بعيداً عنك قليلاً، ليس حقيقية، و أن هؤلاء الجن ليسوا أصدقائك. أصدقائك من الجن الموجودون داخل رأسك يظهرون لك بعض الصور الوهمية في شكل إنسان آخر أوالحيوانات أو في شكل أشباح. المشكلة في هذاا النوع من السيطرة من الجن علي العقل البشري أو المخ، أنه يؤدي في نهاية الأمر إلي بعض المرض العقلي لهذا الشخص عاجلاً أو آجلاً. إذاً جعل الجن صديقك ليس فكرة سيئة، ولكن لا تدعهم يلعبون بعقلك. تذكر دائما أن الجن في النهاية ، أقوى المخلوقات على الأرض، فبمجرد أن يكون لديهم المزيد من السيطرة عليك، سوف تتصرف مثل الجن بشكل أكبر وأقل من البشر.

It is very easy to receive or absorb demons from anywhere, but it is very difficult to get rid of them, especially those demons that attack the mind directly to hypnotize people and urge them to do something in particular because the demons are following the commands of the demon doctor. Those demons are way more dangerous and harmful compared to regular demons.

There is nobody who is not suffering from the possession of a demon, unless someone is spraying any kind of holy water directly to their face, ear, head, neck, chest at least twice a day every day. Who is under the possession of a demon and who is not is not the point of the discussion. There is a degree or level of possession on a body by a demon. Normal demons usually create the situation of mainly negativism and extremism. These conditions can take us to any abnormal condition or abnormal level of any situation, like too much love or hate, too much jealousy or competition, impatience, being hyper, anger, short temperance, depression, anxiety attacks, suicide attempts, hopelessness, overreactions, sexual desires, too much eating, politics, talking, quiet, etc.

During the possession of a demon, if that possession is of a normal level, usually people suffered from above-mentioned conditions. But sometimes, either for no reason, or I will say, sometimes, maybe demons get upset for some reason from us. In that condition demons attack on our brain or mind is way up as compared to normal possession of a demon. This is not necessary, the demon only targets that person, with whom they are upset or angry; sometimes they target any other member of the family also.

هناك شيءآخر نحن بحاجة دائماً لتذكره، و هو عدم وجود فرق بين قوي الجن و قوي الشر. إذا كثرت سيطرة الجن أكثر علي مخك، سيأخذونك إلي الإجاه الخاطئ، حيث لا يمكنك التمييز بين الصواب والخطأ. لذا كن حذراً قبل أن تخسر 100 في المئة من السيطرة علي عقلك.

في مكان ما، وصفت بالفعل عدد قليل من الطرق التي قد تستطيع بها الآلام أن تضر بنا. الألم يحدث مشاعر إيذاء. قد يحدث الألم شعور حارق و مؤلم في نفس الوقت، ويمكن أن تحدث الآلام حكة أيضاً. أغلب الناس تقريباً خاضوا بعض التجارب فيما يتعلق بالطفح جلدي أو الحكة من حين إلي آخر. يصاب بعض الناس بلحكة، أو التورم أو الطفح جلدي بسبب لدغات الحشرات. أنا لا أتحدث عنهم. هذا الطفح الجلدي يؤدي إلي الحكة وعادة ما يقضي عليها سريعاً جداً ، بمجرد أن يستخدم الشخص أي كريم أو مرهم للحكة.

إنني أحاول أن أشرح هنا الجسم الكهرومغناطيسي المادي، مثل الجن أو الآلام. الله يعلم أنني لم أكن على إستعداد للكتابة عن هذا، و لكني كنت في حاجة إلى ذلك، حتي تتركني الآلام الحكة هذه. على أي حال،هذا النوع من آلام الذي يحدث الحكة وإحمرار الجلد أو الوجه أو أشياء من هذا القبيل، لا يحدث ذلك في الجلد بسبب لدغ أي حشرات. قول أن هذا يأتي فقط لشخص ما، ربما الحظ السيئ فقط. لذلك فالحكة التي أعاني منها لا يجدي معها أي كريم مضاد للحكة أو رش لمضاد حيوي. إذا لم يجدي كريم الحكة ورذاذ المضادات الحيوية، هذا يعني أن هذا النوع من ألم الحكة لم يحدث بواسطة حشرة.

144

I will say that the people who are most mentally weak in the family, Sometimes, those people are very easy targets, those who do not travel or move too much but just stay at particular place or stay at home too much or stay in a particular room too much or stay under a tree in dark nights or kill some insects or reptiles or finally, I will say bad luck. But remember, whenever you start feeling anything happening mentally abnormal around you, do not waste time start taking any possible medication you get from doctors to improve your physical strength. Don't use medication that makes you dizzy or intoxicated, because I strongly believe that those kinds of medications which keep you sleepy are more cheerful of demons to have more and more control of someone's mind. You need to stay alert like a normal person. Train and convince your mind to reject the external control of a demon on your mind. Reject all abnormal negative slow and hyper, extreme behaviors. Take medications to strengthen yourself. Once you come to this level, find any holy water, and regardless of how much someone gets upset, keep spraying that holy water frequently, directly to his face, head, ears, neck, and chest. Trust me, there is no demon that can stand in front of the holy water. But remember, the effect of holy water (due to the waves and rays) is very temporary. For that reason, demons unusually come back after a few hours, so you need to spray that holy water very frequently.

The best way is when you spray holy water on yourself spray holy water in the air everywhere in your house also this will help you to get rid of evil demons; it will reduce/kill the negativity of demons around you.

هذا النوع من الحكة / الألم به بعض الخواص الكهرومغناطيسية، مثل الجن أو الالام الأخرى. مثل إحمرار الوجه وحكة، هذه أجسام مادية ولكنها غير مرئية. ما هو العلاج بالنسبة لهم؟ بصراحة، أنا لا أعرف حالياً. الشيء الوحيد، الذي تعلمته في الأيام القليلة الماضية، أنهم لم يستمعوا لي عندما كنت أحاول التواصل معهم. الطريقة الوحيدة التي يتركوني بها، هي كلما كنت أغطي كل أجزاء جسمي بملابسي. لقد كان هجومهم عادة على تلك الأجزاء العارية من الجسم، أو الغير مغطاةبملابسي.بالتأكيد أنا بحاجة لمعرفة المزيد، ولكن حتى الآن، أنهم يغادرون جسدي بمجرد أن أغطي جسدي بملابسي.

ربما يسأل شخص ما، ما هي النسبة المئوية للجن، والنسبة المئوية للألم، والنسبة المئوية للمرض في الغلاف الجوي؟ أنا أقول أن الهواء مليئ بها. إن الجن والآلام الجسدية كائنات مادية و لكنها كهرومغناطيسية . الأمراض أو الحشرات كائنات مادية ولكن ليست كهرومغناطيسية. عندما يقوم شخص ما غير طبيعي بإستقبال جني أو ألم في جسمهم، وتذكر دائماً أنهم قد يكونوا محليين أو قد يتصلون بك من مسافة بعيدة، سواء من الهاتف أو البث الحي للتليفزيون، أو الإنترنت..كما وصفت عدة مرات، فإن الخطوة الأولى أو الهجوم الأول للآلام لإحداث أضرار طفيفة بالجسم. ربما تترك الآلام هذا الجسم، لكنها تفتح باب دعوة مستمرة للسرطان/ مرض/ الحشرات في هذا الجسم. الآلام، و الجن، يكاد يكون من المستحيل قتلهم الآن.لكن السبب الرئيسي للسرطان هو هذه الأمراض/الحشرات المتوفرة محليا .

لكن ليس من الصعب قتل هذه الحشرات / الأمراض. الآن يجب أن تعرف، وإلا فإقرأ هذا الكتاب مرة أخرى.

Due to the frequent spray of holy water in your House, demons will move to those areas or corners where holy water cannot reach them or they will permanently leave your house. But for sure, after some time some new ones will come to your house, so it is better keep doing these procedures on a regular basis.

The possession of a wild and evil demon lets us use our full physical capacity and strength, whatever usually we do not use in normal circumstances. Possession of a demon do not bring any extra strength to our body but demon's control of our brain, give us freedom to use our physical strength with full capacity without care of anybody.

Usually, our voice sounds a little different and heavy. And definitely, we do not have any control on us that is why we act really strange, crazy, and dangerous. Until now, medical science does not have any direct medication or waves/rays to insist any demon to leave the possession of a body. So use holy water and keep spraying every hour, when conditions of a patient is very bad, then with time spray as needed. I will write complete details how you can convert regular water to holy water later in the book. Always remember, during the process of spraying holy water, keep your feet grounded with ceramic or cement floor or any metal. This provides demons and pains an easy path to leave a body. Grounding your feet frequently with cold ceramic or cement floor is very healthy for everyone. People with pains in their feet, or burning pain in their feet or any part of the body will help them a lot. When they will stay barefooted on cold ceramic or cement floor.

هكذا هناك نسبة ما بلا شك من الأمراض / الحشرات في كل مكان في السرير، أو علي الكراسي، أوعلي السجاد، أو علي الأشجار، هكذا فهي علي كل الأجسام سواء كانت حية أو ميتة. هكذا هم موجودون في كل مكان بكثرة، ولكن بفضل الله، ليس من الصعب صيدهم وقتلهم. الجن والآلام يغطون الكثير من المناطق في هواء الغلاف الجوي. لكني عادة ما أراهم في كل مكان في الهواء الطلق. الجن والآلام مثلنا.لذلك حتى لو أنهم ليسوا في كل مكان في الهواء ولكن لا يزال هناك الكثير منهم، لا يحصى عددهم. بصراحة، أنا لن أقلق بشأن الجن والآلام، حيث أننا بطريقة ما، قد نكون قادرين على التخلص من جميع حشرات مرض / سرطان هذه بسرعة. إذا إستطعنا بطريقة ما تعقب وقتل جميع هذه الحشرات، كل الإصابات الكبيرة، و الأمراض، وأمراض السرطان ستكون 100 في المئة تحت السيطرة. في الكتاب المقبل، وسأحاول تقديم بعض الخيارات الممكنة لكيفية إمكان خفض مستوى الطاقة للجن والآلام الموجودون حولنا. الجن والآلام لديهم رغبة حرة مثلنا. الإرادة الحرة تعني أنني يمكنني إختيار أي متجر لشراء بقالتي أو بنزيني، أليس كذلك؟ لا يمكنك إلقاء اللوم على الله لشرائك مشترواتك، أو بقالتك، أو بنزينك من محل واحد أو متجر وليس من محل آخر. بنفس الطريقة، وأنا وأنت لدينا إرادة حرة إما في التصويت لصالح الحزب الجمهوري أو الحزب الديمقراطي في الإنتخابات، أليس كذلك؟ هذه إرادة حرة أو مشروع حر، أليس كذلك؟ لذلك أنت وأنا لايمكننا أن نلقي باللوم على الله لهذه المناقشة، أليس كذلك؟ لذلك أقول لك أنني متأكد بنسبة 100 في المئة من أنك الجن والآلام لديهم 100 في المئة إرادة حرة.، أما الملائكة والأرواح ليس لديهم أي إرادة حرة على الإطلاق. لذلك بما أن الجن والآلام، بما في ذلك المرض / الحشرات، لديهم إرادة حرة مثلنا بنسبة 100 في المئة، فعلي من يتم إلقاء اللوم على أفعالهم؟

Pains and demons are physical, electromagnetic bodies. Ground to any metal or cement floor, this will pull them out of our body due to the powerful effect of gravity. Not all the times, demons acts like too much hurtful or create extreme conditions. Sometimes they just stay around us and don't bother us too much, if we are not making them angry or upset for no reason. Sometimes demons like a few people.

Now this problem of liking someone has a positive approach and has a negative approach. The Positive approach of a demon is this way, when a demon likes someone; he helps that person a lot. Demons always find and keep looking for the ways to help that person in every possible way. Demons open doors of success to that person all the time. The negative approach of demons even if they like someone is that they continuously try to establish control over that person. Either in dreams or in real life, demons convince that person continuously that they are still around that person. Maybe demons do not have any bad intentions for that person, but when a normal people see a person talking to air or interacting with an imaginary friend, they usually consider those kinds of people mentally sick.Demons start showing that imaginary people either in human shape or in a shape of ghost around him or her. In this situation they become a little abnormal and keep looking and running behind that imaginary friend to communicate with them more and more.

A guideline, of those people, please try to understand that whatever you see in front of you and a little far from you are not real, those are not your demon friends.

إذا قتل رجل في الشارع رجلاً آخر بإطلاق النار عليه بالصدفة، من الذي يمكن توجيه اللوم إليه لقتل ذلك الرجل، وهو لديه إرادة حرة لإتخاذ القرار؟ نحن لا نلقي باللوم على الله طوال الوقت، نحن نلوم هذا الرجل لقتله الرجل الآخر، أليس كذلك؟ أنا أقول لك أن الجن،و الآلام والأمراض لها أيضاً إرادة حرة. يمكنهم إختيار أي شخص لإيذائه والإضرار به، نتيجة لإرادتهم الحرة. وأعتقد أن هذا يكفي للنقاش في هذا الموضوع، يمكنك أن تقررمن الذي يتحمل مسؤولية الإرادة الحرة لأعمال الجن والآلام؟

إن حجم وشكل الجن والآلام يتراوح بين النمل الصغير والصراصير. إن أشكالها إما أن تكون مثل بعض الحشرات أو العنكبوت أو فقاعة ماء أو خيوط طائرة أيضاً. حتى الآن كان أكبر جني رأيته، كان في حجم الصرصار وكان مدوراً. وكان ذلك الجني الوحيد و أكبر جني رأيته. لم أر أكبر منه حتي الآن. في الشكل الدائري يكونون بنفس حجم الذبابة أو أصغر. من فضلك، من أجل الله، إترك التفكير في الجن أنهم يكونون علي شكل إنسان أوحيوان، أو أشباح أو ساحرات أو مارد، أو وحوش، لن يستغرق وقتاً طويلاً، عندما يستطيع العلم الحديث أن يكون قادراً على رؤيهم إلكترونياً أيضاً أنا واثق من أنه سيكون نفس الشيء بالطريقة التي أصف بها هذه الأشكال. بالنسبة إلي تحويل الجن أنفسهم بشكل سحري، علي شكل جسم إنسان أو حيوان، فليس هذا ممكناً أيضاً، فهم لايمكنهم تحويل أنفسهم إلى شكل إنسان أو حيوان. الشيء الوحيد الممكن لهم هو التنويم المغناطيسي. إنهم يقومون بالتنويم المغناطيسي، وإظهار صور من البشر أو الحيوانات أو الأشباح أو الوحوش وغيرها، ويستخدمون هذه الصور في أحلامنا، وحتى في. يقظتنا. أنا متأكد من أن الجن يستمتعون بتلك الحالات التي نصبح فيها نحن البشر خائفين جداً أثناء الكوابيس وغيرها من الأشياء المتعلقة برؤية الأشباح / السحرة / الوحوش.ربما يفعلون ذلك لمضايقتنا، من فضلك سيطر على نفسك، , وكن واثقاً، وإجعلهم أصدقائك بدلاً من أن تظل خائفاً منهم طوال الوقت.

SEE & CONTROL DEMONS & PAIN

Your demon friends inside your head show you some imaginary i mag in the shape of another human or animals or in the shape of a ghost. The problem with this kind of control of a demon on human mind or brains, eventually bring some mental sickness to that person sooner or later. So it is not a bad idea to make a demon your friend, but do not let them play with your brain. Always remember ultimately that they are demons, the most powerful creatures on the earth, so once they will have more and more control of you then you will be acting more like demons and less like humans. Another thing we always need to remember is that there is no separation between devil powers or evil powers, most of the demons are really either evil or devil. So if there is more control of a demon on your brain, he can take you to the wrong direction, where you cannot distinguish between right and wrong. So be careful before you lose 100 percent control of your brain. Somewhere, I already described a few ways the pains can possibly hurt us. Pain creates hurt feelings. Pain can create burning and hurting feeling at the same time; pains can create itching also. Almost everybody should have some experience of rash or itching issues once in a while. Sometimes people get itching, swelling or rash due to bites of any insects. I am not talking about them. Those rashes and itching issues usually go away pretty quick once someone uses any ointment or itching cream. Here, I am trying to describe and explain an electromagnetic physical body, like demons or pains. God knows I was not willing to write this. But I need to so these itching pains leave me alone. Anyway, this kind of pains which create itching and skin issues or face redness or similar issues, do not come to skin due to any insect bites. I will say they will just come to someone, maybe just bad luck. So what I am experiencing is no itching cream or antibiotic spray is working on them. If itching cream and antibiotic spray is not working on them, it means this kind of itching pain is not caused by an insect.

رضوان قرشي

إذا كنت في منزلك وسمعت أصواتاً غريبة تخرج من الغرفة الأخرى مثل التصفيق، فإنني أشعر بقوة أنه من التنويم المغناطيسي.السبب هو أن السبيل الوحيد لسماع الجن بدون التنويم المغناطيسي مماثل لصوت تنفس ثقيل علي مسافة قريبة جداً من صدري أو بعض الأصوات المماثلة، و الأصوات التي نشعر بخروجها من معدتنا.

أنا أعلم أن عندما يأتي جني بالقرب مني طوال الوقت، فإنه يصدر أصواتاً مثل الشخص الذي يمضغ العلكة. أعتقد أنهم يصدرون أصواتاً ليثيروا إهتمامنا أو ربما لإعلامنا بوجودهم. فلا تخافوا من هؤلاء الجن، إنهم ليسوا بهذا السوء. إنهم بحاجة إلى القليل من التدريب والقليل من السيطرة. كما قلت عدة مرات، وأرى أن الوقت سيحين قريباً جداً. وأنا واثق أن كل واحد منا يجب أن يمر بتجربة كهذه، بغض النظر عن ما إذا كنت أوليت ذلك إ هتماماً أم لا.أحيانا بدون سبب، تشم شيء رائحتة أقول أنها سيئة، أغلب الوقت.

تلك الروائح الكريهة هي جن أيضاً. أنا لا أعرف حقاً السبب الحقيقي، ولكن إذا كثرت الكثافة السكانية للبشر في مدينة أو بلد معين يتسبب في مزيد من سكان الجن، والآلام، والأمراض في تلك المناطق المعينة. هناك أسباب أخري لزيادة سكان الجن، مثل الأماكن المظلمة والقذرة، و كذلك إستخدام الكثير من اللحوم الحمراء، الخ.هذه هي نصيحتي لهؤلاء الناس الذين لا يحترمون الآخرين ويؤذون مشاعرهم طوال الوقت "نتذكر دائما، أن الجميع سواء كان إنسان أو اي جسم حي آخر، لديه جني واحد فقط داخل جسمه، لكن يحيط به دائماً مجموعة كبيرة من الجن من حوله، و بخاصة الإنسان، وأنا أقسمه إلي إمرأة و رجل.

بغض النظر،عما يفعله الجن معنا أو كيف يعاملوننا، لا يزال هؤلاء الجن لديهم إرتباطات وإخلاص مع الشخص بالذات الذين يكونون حوله أو حولها. لذلك من الأفضل أن تكون حذرا قبل أن تسبب مشاكل كثيرة جداً لنفسك بلا أي سبب أو من أجل أشياء صغيرة كن حذراً.

148

Rizwan Qureshi	رؤية الجن و الآلام السيطرة عليها

هناك أمثلة لا تحصى من الناس، وعندما يكونون في منتهى الأنانية أو الشر أوالقسوة مع الناس. هناك بعض المعلمين، وربما ليس في الولايات المتحدة الأمريكية، حقيقي يؤلمون، ويضربون، كذلك يوجد بعض الآباء/الأشقاء، و بعض الأزواج حقاً يسيئون التصرف مع زوجاتهم، وبعض الآباء / الأشقاء يجعلون حياة الأخت / الإبنة جحيم حقاً وهناك الكثير من الأمثلة المختلفة. وفجأة يصاب هؤلاء الأنواع من الناس ببعض الأنواع الخطيرة من الأمراض مثل فيروس نقص المناعة البشرية أو السرطان أو يواجهونالحوادث، وما إلى ذلك . هذا العالم الخفي من الجن هو ذاتي التشغيل. إنهم يتخذون قراراتهم بأنفسهم ويبدأون في جعل حياة شخص ما جحيماً. هناك عالم خارج الولايات المتحدة الأمريكية، حيث لا تعد حقوق الإنسان شيئاً بالنسبة للناس. قد يكون هذا سبب آخر لخلق الله للجن والآلام، كي يظل الإنسان تحت السيطرة من خلال خلق الخوف من حوادث المرض والموت. هذا السؤال مثير للإهتمام للغاية. كيف سنتصرف إذ الم يكن لدينا مخاوف من الجن والمرض والآلام، والحوادث، والموت؟.

إنني أفكردائماً ماذا سيحدث معي إذا بقيت على قيد الحياة لسنوات قليلة زائدة؟ إسمحوا لي أن أشرح.، كل يوم أكون علي إتصال بالعديد من الجن الجدد طوال الوقت، و كل جني يمثل جماعة أو قبيلة من الجن، وبمجرد أن أتعرف علي جني واحد أو مجموعة واحدة من الجن، فإنهم لا تأتون بالقرب مني بالقدر الكافي، إنهم بحاجة إلى التوصل مع جسم إنسان للإستحواذ عليه.

إنهم ليسوا بحاجة إلى أن يأتوا بالقرب مني، فأنا عادة أتعرف علي إشاراتهم المختلفة بمجرد أنهم يريدون أن يخطروني بوجودهم حولي. ما أقصده هو أن الجن الجدد فقط يأتون بالقرب مني للغاية، و يستحوذون علي جسدي لبضع دقائق، هذا كل ما يمكنهم القيام به. لا يبقى جني في جسدي لفترة طويلة، فقط لبضع دقائق .

This kind of itching/pain has some electromagnetic quality like demons or other pains, like face redness and itching, these are physical but invisible bodies. What should be the treatment for them? Honestly, I do not know right now, the only thing, I learned in the last few days, that they do not listen to me when I was trying to communicate with them. The only way they were leaving me alone was whenever I was covering all the parts of my body with my clothes. Usually their attack was on those parts of the body that were naked or not covered with my clothes. Definitely I need to learn more, but until now, they are leaving my body once I cover my body with my clothes.

Someone may ask what is the percentage of demons, percentage of pain, and percentage of disease in the atmosphere? I will say air is full of them. Demons and pains are physical but electromagnetic objects. Diseases or insects are physical but not electromagnetic bodies. When someone abnormal receives a demon or a pain in their body, always remember they may be local or they may connect to you from far distance either from phone or live TV or live Internet conversation. So demons and pains around or inside you can get from anywhere. But disease or insects are always local. They do not come through the phone line or live TV or live Internet. As I described several times, initial or first step or attack is done by pains to create minor damages to body. Then maybe pains leave that body, but they open a continuous invitation door for cancers/disease/insects in that body. Pains, demons, it is almost impossible to kill them right now. But main reason or cause of cancer is these locally available diseases/ insects.

But it is not difficult to kill these insects/diseases. By now you should know; otherwise, read this book again. So there is a percentage, no doubt of diseases/insects are everywhere in or beds, chairs, carpets, trees, so in all bodies whether dead or alive. So everywhere, a lot, but thanks to God, it is not difficult to hunt and kill them. Demons and pains cover a lot of area of air atmosphere. But usually I see them everywhere in open air. Demons and pains are like us, so even if they are not everywhere in air but still a lot, uncountable. Honestly, I will never worry about, demons and pains as much, if somehow, we will be able to get rid of all these disease/cancer insects quickly. If somehow we hunt and kill all these insects, all major infections, diseases, or cancer diseases will be 100 percent under control. In next book, I will try to bring some possible options how possibly we can reduce energy level of demons and pains around us.

Demons and pains have free will also like us. So free will means I can choose any shop to buy my grocery or gas, right? You cannot blame God for my buying my shopping, my groceries, and gas from one store or shop but not from other one. Same way, I and you have free will to either vote for Republican Party or Democratic Party in elections, right?

لكنهم مازالوا يستغرقون أربع وعشرين ساعة بالنسبة لهم ليتعلموا تماماً، ويصبحوا أصدقائي. لذلك أنا أفكر ماذا سيحدث لي إذا ظللت إتعرف علي عالم الجن لبضعة سنوات، وماذا سيكون مستقبلي؟

نأمل أن أبقى طبيعية عقليا وجسديا. أي فكرة. سنري من الذي سيكون في السيطرة للجن أم لي؟ سألني شخصما سؤال حول ماذا سيحدث إذا إستطاع الشخص العادي بطريقة أو بأخرى، الآن أو في المستقبل، أن يجعل الجن أحد أصدقائه؟، عادة يريد الناس بنسبة 100 في المئة السيطرة على الجن لإستخدامهم في أغراض خاصة قليلة أو كثيرة. بنفس الطريقة، التي أطلب بها من أصدقائي من الجن أن يفعلوا الكثير من الاشياء لي وللآخرين الذين يخصوني. والسؤال هو، إذا ظللنا نطلب بإستمرار من الجن القيام بعمل لنا، وعادة ما يتبعون ويطيعون الأوامر والتعليمات.السؤال هو، هل سيطلب الجن منا القيام بشيء لهم مقابل خدماتهم لنا؟

الإجابة عن هذا السؤال: لا تقلق بشأن الجن. الشياطين، فلديهم قوى كثيرة، قوى خارقة للطبيعة، حتى أنهم لا يحتاجون أن يطلبوا منا أي شيء.. إنهم فقط يأخذون ما يريدون. و يفعلون فقط ما يريدون فعله. إنهم لا يعتمدون علينا.أنا واثق من أن الجن سيكونون سعداء بالقدلر الكافي إذا أصبح البشر بطريقة أو بأخرى أصدقائهم ويظلون على إتصال بهم. وأعتقد أن هذا سيكون كافياً للجن. أشعر بنفس الطريقة مع الجن الموجودون حولي، فهم يستمعون لي، و يطيعوني، و يتبعون أوامري وتعليماتي معظم الوقت، طوال الوقت، إنهم لا يزالون حولي وسعداء بي. , و هكذا إذا حاول شخص ما مضايقتك بالجن، لا تقلق بشأنهم، بطريقة ما أنا واثق من أن الجن لا يتوقع أي شيء منا، يكفيهم أن نعاملهم كأصدقاء لنا و نظل علي إتصال بهم.

Rizwan Qureshi

This is free will or free enterprise, right? So you or me cannot blame God for this discussion, right? So I am 100 percent sure telling you that demons and pains have 100 percent free will. Angels and spirits do not have any free will at all. So demons and pains, including disease/insects, once they have 100 percent free will like us, who will be blamed for their actions? If a man on the street kills another man by gunfire, by chance, who will be blamed for the action of that killing once that man has a free will to make his decision? We do not blame the God all the time; we blame that man for killing another man, right? So I am telling you demons, pains, and diseases also have free will, they can choose anyone to hurt and damage due to their free will. I think this is enough discussion about this topic, the rest you can decide. Who to blame for the free will actions of demons and pains?

Size and shape of demons and pains are between small ants and cockroaches. Their shapes are also either like some insects or like a spider or like a water bubble or like flying threads. Until now, the biggest demon I have seen was the size of a cockroach and it was round. That was the only one and the biggest I have even seen that big; otherwise, in round shape they are around same size like a fly or smaller. Please, for God's sake, quit thinking about demons in the shape of humans, animals, or ghosts or witches or Jennies or monsters, etc. Time is not far when modern science will be able to see them electronically too. I am sure it will be the same thing the way I am describing these shapes. As far as demons converting magically themselves into a human body or any animal, etc., this is not possible also.

رؤية الجن و الآلام السيطرة عليها

بغض النظر عما إذا كنا في البداية أو بعد فترة، سيحبني الجني أو لا يحبني، لكنه سيتعلم شيئاً واحداً عني، إما لي أو عن أي شخص ما حولي قريب مني، أن لن يستطيع الجني أن يسيطر علي جسمي أو علي جسم أي شخص آخر لمدة طويلة. هذا كله ضد طبيعة الجن تماما، فهم يحبون دائما أن يسيطروا على الجسم المادي.

الآن في حالتي، أنا لا أسمح لهم بالإستحواذ علي جسدي. إذا قام الجن بذلك، سأقاومهم حتى يتركوني وشأني. أحب القيام بنفس الشيئ مع الأشخاص القريبين مني أو حولي. الجن لا يحبون الإستحواذ علي الجسم بشكل مؤقت. الجن لا يحبون تترك الجسم ويستمرون في الذهاب و الإياب علي لإدارة وضعي، , و بمجرد أن يعرف الجن أنني مصدر متاعب لهم، بغض النظر عما إذا كانوا يحبوني أم لا، سيحاولون الإبقاءعلى ضحاياهم من البشر بعيداً عني قدر المستطاع. السبب في ذلك هو بما أنني أقاتل هؤلاء الجن، يوجد بالكاد بشر من حولي. أنا لا أعرف ماذا يغذي الجن به العقول، و كيف يفعلون ذلك.مع ضحيتهم من البشرعن طريق التنويم المغناطيسي، في هذه الأيام وأنا لا أرى أي شخص حولي لفترة طويلة. حسنا، دعنا نري من على إستعداد للمغادرة.

ما هو مفهوم الشيطان أو الشر؟ بالنسبة لي، في الأساس، الشيطان أو الشر ليسا مخلوقان آخران، الشيطان أوالشر ليسا مخلوقان. في الواقع الشيطان أو الشر هما حالة. يستطيع الشيطان / الشر التواجد في شكل إنسان فقط. بالنسبة لي أفضل شيطان/ شر يكون مزيجا من شر الإنسان وشيطان الجن. الشيطان والشر ليسا مخلوقان مستقلان في هذا العالم. الجن الأكثر سلبية والبشر الأكثر سلبية هم أفضل تمثيل للشيطان أو الشر.

151

Demons cannot convert themselves either into any human or animal. The only possible thing is hypnotism. They hypnotize and create images of humans or animals or ghosts or monsters etc. and use those images during our dreams and even when we are up. I am sure demons enjoy the situations we humans get so scared during nightmares and other stuff related to seeing ghosts/witches/monsters.Maybe they do this to harass us, please control yourself, be confident, and make them your friends instead of getting scared of them all the time.

If you are in your house and you hear some weird noises coming out from the other room like clapping, I strongly feel it is hypnotism. The reason is that the only way I hear demons without hypnotism was similar to heavy breathing very close to my chest or some similar noises, and the voices, sometimes we feel coming out from our stomach.

I know one demon came close to me all the time, and that demon makes noises like if someone is chewing gum. I think they make noises to get our attention or maybe to notify us about their presence. So do not get scared of these demons they are not that bad. They need a little training and a little control. As I said several times, I see that time is coming very soon. I am sure everyone of us should experience similar thing like this and regardless of whether you paid attention to that or not. Sometimes for no reason, you just smell something most of the time I will say badly.

لذلك إذا كنت بحاجة إلى إيجاد شيطان /شر، لا تبحث هنا وهناك، فيقيناً، يوجد إما شيطان أو شر بيننا، إما في شكل إنسان أو شيطان سلبي للغاية، أو مزيج من الإثنين معاً. الشيطان والشر ليسا صورة أو جسم، بل هو إتجاه الذي يوصلنا إلى أن مستوى عالي من الشر والشيطان. كل منا، بغض النظر عنما إذا كنا بشر أو جن لديها إرادة حرة لتقرير أي إتجاه يكون أفضل بالنسبة لنا. الشر هو إتجاه الذي يتبعه الشيطان ليصبح عضوا من أتباع الشيطان و نقوم نحن البشر و الجن على حد سواء، بالكفاح ضده، ونستطيع إختيار الإتجاه الصحيح والمستقيم نحو مشيئة الله. حتى بالنسبة للبشر، كل واحد منا والشياطين، نحن البشر و الجن أحرار في تقرير ما نريد أن نصبح عليه، و كلانا لا نريد أن نصبح شراً أو شيطاناً.

لديك مسار حر، إرادة حرة وخيارات حرة، وفكر وحلل حياتك وإتجاهاتك و قم بإختيار الإتجاه نحو إرادة الله. كل ما أقترحه أو أعطي تفاصيل عن أي علاج أو إجراءات علاجية أو وصف للعالم الغير مرئي وغيره من الأشياء المختلفة في هذا الكتاب،والكتاب الأول، و في الكتاب القادم. فقد تعلمت على مدى فترة من عدة سنوات، كما مررت بالكثير من الظروف المؤلمة، و في النهاية إلى وصلت إلي حل. لم أكن على إستعداد للإستماع أو التعلم،و لكن علمتني الطبيعة الأم بطريقتها الخاصة. وإذا كنت لا أوافق و تجنبت / بعض التغذية أوتعليمات، وضعت الطبيعة الأم لي في وعاء الطبخ، وبدأت تطبخني حتى أتعلم أوأكون على إستعداد للتعلم أو الفهم الصحيح.

الآن، حتى ولو كنت لا تمارس أي شيء لإقامة علاقة أو صداقة بينك وبين الجن من حولك، بمجرد أن تشعرأنك واثق من أن لديك بعض الجن حولك وأنهم أصدقائك في تلك النقطة، فإن الوضع سيكون مختلفاً. ولكن الآن، عندما لا تكون على علم، و حتى لو لم يكن لديك أي ثقة أنبوجود أي جن من حولك، والذين يستمعون إليك طوال الوقت...

Those bad smells are demons also. I do not know really the true reason, but more population of humans in a particular city or country cause more population of demons, pains, and disease in those particular areas. Other than the reason of population of humans, some other reasons are suitable for more population of demons is dark and dirty places, too much use of red meat, etc. This is my advice for those people who disrespect other people and hurt their feelings all the time", always remember, everyone whether he is human or another living body, has only one demon inside his body, but in surrounding atmosphere there is always a big group of demons around them, especially human, and I can subdivide it to a man and a woman.

Regardless, what demons do with us or how they treat us, still all those demons have attachments and sincerity with that particular person whom they are around. So you better be careful before you just for no reason or for very small things create a lot of troubles and problems for yourself. Be careful. There are uncountable examples of people, when they were very selfish or mean or cruel with people. Some teachers, maybe not in USA, really hurt, beat, some father/brother, some husbands really misbehave with their wives, some father/brother really make the life of their sister/daughter hell.

There are lots of different examples. And suddenly those kinds of mean people catch some kind of dangerous disease like HIV or cancer or face accidents, etc. This invisible world of demons is self-operational. They make their own decisions and start up running someone to make their life hell.

إفعل شيئاً واحداً، وبهذه الطريقة يمكنك البدء في التواصل معهم.

إذا كنت تقود السيارة و أوقفك ضابط شرطة، أو كنت في العمل و كان رئيسك في العمل يسيئ معاملتك، أو إذا كان لديك بعض المشاكل مع صديقتك أو صديقك أو زوجتك أو زوجك، إنظر بشكل رئيسي نحو كتفك اليسرى، ولكن هذا ليس ضرورياً،و تأكد أنك وحدك في هذا الحديث، لا يجب أن يوجد إنسان آخر ما، و قل ثلاث مرات بصوت عال (ليس كثيراً)، "أصدقائي الجن الموجودين حولي أو في بيتي،أرجوكم أن تأتوا بالقرب مني، إني بحاجة لأتحدث إليكم ". وبعد ثوان قليلة، قل الشيء نفسه مرة أخرى، ثم مرة أخرى، قل الشيء نفسه بعد ثواني قليلة أخري. قم بإختيار غرفة أو مكان في المنزل أقل إستخداماً و يظل مظلماًمعظم الوقت، لأن معظم الجن يبقون في الظلام و في المكان الأقل إستخداماً. و بعد أن تناديهم ، مرر طلبك لهم مثل،"صديقتي، غير راضية عني. أرجو إقناعها لتصبح طبيعية معي "أو" لقن رئيسي درساً "أو" إقنع ضابط الشرطة بأن يهدأ وألا يعطيني تذكرة مخالفة. ". إطلب أي شيء؛ وكن واثقاً من أنهم يصغون إليك، ولكن مدى السرعة التي سيعملون، يعتمد ذلك علي مدي إستعدادهم لذلك، لكن لن يستغرق ذلك وقتاً طويلاً.

إستمر في ممارسة، وقريباً جداً سوف تشعربهم حولك. يمكنك أن تطلب منهم ما تريد أن تراه في أحلامك، وسوف يستمعون إليك. الشيء الأكثر أهمية، هو قراءة كتابي أمامهم لذلك سيكون من السهل جداً على الشياطين من حولك فهم ما تقوم به، ولماذا تفعل ذلك. حظاً سعيداً.

There is a world outside USA, where human rights are nothing for people. This may be another reason God created demons and pains to keep the human race under control by creating the fear of disease accidents and death. This is a very interesting question. How will we behave if we will have no fears of disease, demons, pains, accidents, and death?

I always think what will happen with me if I stay alive for few more years? Let me explain. Every day, I come in contact with several new demons all the time. Every demon represents a group or tribe of demons. Once I get introduced to one demon or one group of demons, they do not come close to me as much; they need to come to a human body to possess it.

They do not need to come close to me; I usually recognize their different signals once they want to notify me about their presence around me. The point is that only new demons come very close to me and possess my body for few minutes, that's all they can do. No demon stays in my body for a long time, just for a few minutes. Still, it takes twenty-four hours for them to completely learn and become friends with me. So I am thinking if I will get introduced in the demon's world for few more years, what will be my future? Hopefully, I will stay normal mentally and physically. I have no idea, We will see who will be in the control—demons or me? Someone asked me a question that if somehow, right now or in the future, a normal person will be able to make a demon a friend, what will happen after that? Usually 100 percent people want to control a demon to use them for few or more particular purposes.

لا يستطيع الجن أن يحققوا لك الفوز في أرقام اليانصيب، ولا أداء أي نوع من السحر لك، كذلك لا يستطيعون الوفاء بثلاثة أمنيات سحرية أو حتى أمنية واحدة سحرية لك، لذلك لا تضيع وقتك في هذه الأشياء. لقد قمت بذلك بالفعل بشكل صحيح جداً، وقضيت الكثير من الوقت في ذلك. الجن قادرون على فعل معظم الأشياء المتعلقة بالتنويم المغناطيسي أو الحصول على المعلومات أو نقلها من هنا إلى هناك، وبعض الأنشطة السلبية والمتطرفة الأخرى. لا يستطيع الجن تحريك شيئاً مادياً لك أو حتى لأنفسهم. إنهم لا يستطيعون سرقة أي أموال أو مجوهرات أو أي نشاط آخر. يستطيع الجن تنويم جسد مادي آخر مغناطيسياً، مثل البشر أو الحيوانات، للقيام بأي نشاط بدني. لكن الجن لا يستطيعون أداء أي نوع من النشاط البدني. الجن لا يستطيعون أن يمسكوا يدنا أو كتفنا، مثل أي إنسان آخر؛ ولا يستطيعون عضنا أو دفعنا،مثل البشر أو الحيوانات الآخرين . إنهم يستطيعون إختراق جسمنا ومن السهل جداً أن يؤذوننا الجسم بأي شكل من الأشكال. حتى أنهم يستطيعون التسبب في أزمة قلبية للشخص بالهجوم في ثوان و سد صمامات القلب. يستطيع الجن أن يتسببوا لنا في أي نوع من الألم الجسدي أو إحداث أضرار جسيمة في أي عضو من أعضاء الجسم. هذا ليس هذا شيئاً صعباً بالنسبة لهم. ولكن إذا كان لديك فلساً واحداً، ضع العملة على طاولة أمامك؛ الشياطين لن يستطيع الجن تحريك العملة على الإطلاق. و لا يستطيعون القيام بأي نشاط جنسي مع أي واحد منا، بغض النظر عما إذا كنت رجلاً أو امرأة. ولكن خلال النشاط الجنسي بين جسدين ماديين، بغض النظر عما إذا كانوا من البشر أو الحيوانات، يستمتع الجن بتلك الأنشطة الجنسية أكثر من تلك الآجسام المادية، لذلك آمل أن تفهم أنهم يجعلونا نقوم بالكثير من المرح، حتى يتمكنوا من الإستمتاع أيضاً. مثل الشرب، والمخدرات، والجنس، بالإضافة إلى السلوك المندفع والأنشطة السلبية.

Rizwan Qureshi	رؤية الجن و الآلام السيطرة عليها
Same way, I ask my demon friends to do a lot of stuff for me and for others on my behalf. The question is, if we continuously ask a demon to do work for us and they usually follow and obey the commands and instructions, the question is, will demons ask us in return to do something for them for their services to us?	في الأساس هذا هو مفهوم السيطرة علي الجسد المادي بغض النظر عن ما إذا كان جسد إنسان أو حيوان، انهم يستحوذون علي الأجسام المادية للتمتع بجميع الأنشطة البدنية التي يقومون بها بما في ذلك الأكل والشرب. وهذا هو السبب في أننا نكون أكثر نشاطاً عند القيام بالكثير من الأشياء بسبب ضغطهم.
Answer for this question: do not worry about demons. Demons have so many powers, supernatural powers; even they do not need to ask us anything. Demons just take whatever they want. Demons just do whatever they like to do. Demons are not dependent on us. I am sure demons will be happy enough if somehow humans become their friends and stay in contact with them. I think that will be enough for demons. I feel the same way with demons around me. They listen to me, they obey me, they follow my commands and instructions most of the time, all the time; still, they are around and happy with me. So if someone tries to harass you with demons, do not worry about them. Somehow I am sure demons do not expect anything from us; it is enough for them if we treat them as friends and stay in their contact.	كل شيء كثير، أكل كثير، وحشية أكثر، أدوية أكثر، شرب أكثر، مزيد من الجنس وغيره، حتى يتمكنوا من الإستمتاع أكثر ولكننا نحصل علي بعض المتعة من ذلك أيضاً. بإختصار، الجن يضخمون ويعززون كل حالة تتعلق بالمتعة، والتطرف، والسلبية. فكن حذراً.
	لا يمكنك التعامل مع الجن كما تتعامل مع الحيوانات إذا كنت لا تريد صراعاً بينك وبينهم. لا يهم لا يهم ماذا تريد؛ سيأخذ الجن أماكنهم أو سيحتلون بعض المساحة كيفما يريدون على أي حال. لكن أنا أتحدث عن تنمية صداقة بينك وبين الجن. الشياطين. تذكر دائماً أن الجن يحبون أن يعيشوا في نفس الجو، وما نحبه لأنفسنا، بمعنى ألا يكون الجو حاراً جداً ولا بارداً جداً. بالنسبة للأماكن النظيفة والقذرة، من الأفضل أن تكون حذراً، لأن الأماكن النظيفة والجميلة تجلب جن لطفاء، و أكثر حساسيةً، وبالتأكيد لهم خلفية جيدة. إذا ظل مكانك قذر وسيئ، بهذه الطريقة ستدعو الجن الشرير، والمقرف، و القذر إلى مكانك. كما يعلم الجميع، عادة، يكون المرآب و السندرات أماكن أقل إستخداماً، ولكن نظراً لظروف الطقس، يعيش الجن هناك ولكن ليس بشكل دائم. بسبب البرد الشديدا أو الحر الشديد، سيتحركون ذهاباً وإياباً طوال الوقت.
Regardless whether in beginning or after sometime, a demon likes me or dislikes me, but he learns one thing about me, either I or someone close around me, that a demon will not be able to have possession on my body or anyone's body for long time. This is totally against the nature of demons. Demons always like to have a possession of a physical body.	

Now in my case, I do not allow them to possess my body. If demons do, I will resist them until they leave me alone. I like to do the same thing with people close to me or around me. Demons do not like a temporary possession of a body. Demons do not like to leave my body and keep coming back and forth to manage the situation with me, so once they figure out, I am a trouble for them, regardless of whether they like me or not, demons will try to keep their human victims away from me as much possible. The reason is that since I am fighting with these demons, I hardly have any humans around me. I do not know how and what demon feed the minds of that human victim by hypnotism these days I do not see anyone around me for long time. Well, let's see who else is ready to leave.

What is the concept of a devil or evil? To me, basically, devil or evil are not creatures. Devil or evil is not a creature. Actually devil or evil is a condition. Devil/evil can exist in shape of a human only. A devil/evil maybe we can see in shape of a demon only. To me, the best devil or evil should be a combination of an evil human and a devil demon. Devil or evil is not a separate creature in this world. More negative demons and more negative humans are the best representation of devil or evil. So, if you need to find a devil/evil, d'not look here and there, for sure, either devil or evil is just among us, either in the shape of a human or a very negative demon or the combination of both. Devil or evil is not a picture or a body; it is a direction that promotes us to that high level of evil and devil. Both of us, regardless human or demons, we have a free will to decide which direction will be best or most suitable for us.

الآن لديك خياران: إما ترك البيت كله لهم ليعيشوا في أي مكان يريدون. لكن في هذه الحالة سوف يقومون بمقاطعتك، و إزعاجك، وسوف يحدثون مشاكل لك، إذا لم يعجبهم شيء. الخيار الثاني هو تترك غرفة صغيرة لهم فقط، و إجعل تلك الغرفة مظلمة معظم الوقت. حافظ على تلك الغرفة جميلة ونظيفة وإستخدمها فقط لأشياء بسيطة. لا تجلس في تلك الغرفة وقتاً طويلاً، و لا تأكل ولا تنام هناك، مجرد إستخدامها فقط في بعض الأغراض السريعة .

بمجرد أن تقرر أنك سوف تترك غرفة واحدة لهم، وإستخدم هذه الغرفة في أضيق الحدود وإبقها مظلمة معظم الوقت. الخطوة الثانية قم برش الماء المقدس و مبيد الحشرات كل يوم في كل مكان في المنزل. قل لهم بصوت عال أنك خصصت تلك الغرفة لهم كي يعيش الجن كلهم هناك. لن ينتقلوا إلى تلك الغرفة المعينة فورا، ولكن في أيام قليلة. هذا لا يعني أن الجن سيقتصروا على تلك الغرفة المعينة.

لكنهم سيستمرون في الطيران في كل مكان في المنزل. سوف يشاهدون التلفزيون معك، و يستمعون إلى مكالماتك الهاتفية، و كذلك سيتقاسمون بعض أنشطتك البدنية، ولكنهم سعيشون في تلك الغرفة بالذات في المجموعة أو العائلة. ستكون هذه هي الخطوة الأولى لتفادي الصراع مع الجن.سوف يكون الجن سعداء جداً بك بهذه اخطوة. بهذه الطريقة ستكون على علم أيضاًعندما تكون في حاجة إلى التواصل مع الجن، فهذه الغرفة الخاصة سيكون مكان أفضل وأسرع للوصول إليهم. تذكر دائما أن تتصرف بشكل جيد معهم، و إترك لهم بعض الأماكن على وجه الخصوص، وحتى إذا كانوا أكثر وأكثر ودية، لا تتخلى أبداً عن الإحتياطات لحمايتك و حماية عائلتك،

156

Evil is a direction which the devil follows to become a member of devil followers or we both, human and demons, can fight against it and can choose the direction of right and straight toward God's will. So for both of us, humans & demons, it is in our hand we are free to decide what we want to become, we or demons do not want to become evil or devil.

You have free path, free will, free choices, think and analyze your life & directions and choose the direction towards the will of the God. Whatever I propose or give details of any cure or cure procedures ordescription of the invisible world and different other stuff in this book, book 1 and in next book. I learned over a period of several years. I went through a lot of painful conditions to finally come to a solution. I was not ready to listen or learn, Mother Nature taught me in its own way. Still, if I do not get agree and avoid/some feedings or instructions, Mother Nature puts me in a pot and start cooking me until I learn or ready to learn or understand properly.

Right now, even if you do not practice anything to establish relationship or friendship between you and demons around you, once you feel confident that you have some demons around you and they are your friends at that point, the situation will be different. But right now, when you are not aware, even you do not have any confidence that there are any demons around you, who are listening to you all the time, do one thing, this way you can start communicating with them.

قم برش الماء المقدس دائما على وجهك ورقبتك و رأسك، و أذنك، وفي كل مكان في المنزل لتجنب سيطرة الجن "الدائمة على عقلك / جسمك أو منزلك. وهذا الماء المقدس سيحدهم وسيجعلهم تحت السيطرة إلي حد ما.

إسمح لي أن أشرح لك، ربما بعد ذلك ستفهم بشكل أفضل و تكف عن القلق حول هذا الموضوع. حسنا، فكر في طبيب الجن. وهؤلاء الناس يقضون حياتهم كلها ليكون قليل من الجن حولهم أو يخضعوهم لسيطرتهم. ولا شك، أنه في نهاية المطاف سيكون لديهم قليل أو كثير من الجن حولهم، وبدون شك هؤلاء الجن سيطيعونهم و يتبعونهم. ولكن راقب أطباء الجن هؤلاء، فهم ليس لديهم إكتفاء من الناحية المالية. ستري أطباء الجن هؤلاء يبحثون عن الأغنياء أو الأشخاص الآخرين ليستمروا في الذهاب إليهم للحصول علي بعض المساعدة في أمور أسرهم و أعمالهم من خلال الجن المدربين بقوة. تذكر دائماً أنه ربما لأول مرة يستخدم أطباء الجن، الجن الخاص بهم لحل مشاكلك أو قضاياك الحقيقية. و الآن المشكلة هي هذه، أنك سوف تذهب إلى طبيب الجن مرة. واحدة وتحل مشاكلك، وسوف تدفع له أجره، وينتهي عملك معه، أليس كذلك؟ لكن المشكلة مع أطباء الجن هي أنهم بحاجة إلى المال طوال الوقت. حتى أن بعد مروربعض الوقت، قد يحدث طبيب الجن مشكلة وهمية أو مؤقتة لك عن طريق إستخدام الجن الخاص به. لماذا؟ السبب من الأسباب، حتى على إتصال به طوال الوقت لحل القضايا الخاصة بك، وبهذه الطريقة يستطيع طبيب الجن كسب المال منك طوال الوقت. لهذا السبب قررت أن أكتب في هذا الكتاب كل خدعة وعلاج للتعامل مع الجن بنفسك، وبمجرد أن تتدرب على هذه الخدع و العلاج و لإجراءات، لن تحتاج أبدا إلي الذهاب إلى أي طبيب جن.

If you are driving and a police officer stops you, if you are at work and your boss is mean with you, or if you have some problem with your girlfriend or your boyfriend or your wife or husband, mainly look towards your left shoulder, but this is not necessary; make sure you are alone in this conversation, no other human at least say three times loudly (not too much), "My demon friends around me or in my house, please come close to me, I need to talk to you." After few seconds, say the same thing again, and then again say the same thing after few seconds. Choose a room or place in the house least in use and mostly stay dark most of the time, because most of the demons stay in a dark and the places which are least used. After calling them, pass your request to them like, "My girlfriend, she is unhappy with me. Please convince her to become normal with me" or "Teach my boss a lesson" or "Convince the police officer to calm down and not give me a ticket." Ask for anything; be confident that they are listening to you, but how fast they will act, it depends if they are ready for that, but it will not take long time.

Keep practicing, and very soon you will be experiencing them around you. You can ask them what you want to see in your dreams; they will listen to you. The most important thing, read my book in front of them so it will be very easy for demons around you to understand what you are doing and why you are doing it. Good luck. Demons cannot bring winning lottery numbers. Demons cannot perform any kind of magic for you. Demons cannot fulfill three or even one magical wish for you, so do not waste your time on these things. I already checked very properly and spent already a lot of time on it.

ربما سيأتي أطباء الجن في المستقبل، لإقتراض الجن الخاص بك منك. من فضلك لا تعطي الجن الخاص بك لأحد.

لا تفهم ذلك؟ سأشرح لاحقاً.كما وصفت عدة مرات، فإن أجسادنا المادية تكون دائماً تحت إستحواذ جني واحد على الأقل طوال الوقت. هؤلاء الجن يقيمون في جسمنا و يسافرون معنا. أنا أتحدث عن الناس العاديين الذين لا يستخدمون أي إجراءات أو علاج للتخلص من الجن. إن عقولنا و أجسامنا بمثابة لعبة لأولئك الجن. الآن عندما نبدأ صداقة (أنا أتحدث عن صداقة الرجل / المرأة)، مستحيل أن يسمح لنا هؤلاء الجن عقلياً بالبدء في علاقة أو صداقة ما لم يكن الجن المسيطرون على عقولنا و أجسامنا نحن و الطرف الآخر على حد سواء لديهم فهم جيد للغاية وصداقة بينهم. إذا كنت شخص قوي جداً و ترفض أن يتحكم بك ذلك الجني الخاص بصديقك، عن طريق التنويم المغناطيسي، ضد إرادة هؤلاء الجن الموجودين حولك، سيحدث هؤلاء الجن مشاكل بينك وبين صديقك عن طريق التنويم المغناطيسي ، إن عاجلا أو آجلا، وفي نهاية المطاف سوف تفكك علاقتك مع صديقك. أنا آسف ولكن هذا هو الواقع. لذلك أي علاقة أو صداقة تبدأ ببطئ ستجلب للجميع فهماً جيداً للبشر والجن على حد سواء. عادة هذا النوع من الصداقات والعلاقات تظل في حالة جيدة لفترة طويلة أو إلى الأبد لأن لا أحد يعمل ضدها، لا البشر ولا الجن. الشيء نفسه بالضبط، ينطبق علي حالة الكراهية أيضاً. إذا كنت تريد أن تكره شخص ما، تأكد من أن الجن الخاص بك وبه يكرهون بعضهم البعض، و أيضاً كي تجعل هذه علاقة الكراهية ناجحة وكاملة، كيف؟ تحدث معهم.

بمجرد أن تعلم كيفية التواصل مع الجن وتبدأ في إعطاء هذه الأوامر والتعليمات، عند هذه النقطة تحتاج إلى فهم أمرين أو مشكلتين.

Rizwan Qureshi

Demons are mostly capable of doing stuff related to hypnotism or transferring or obtaining information from here to there and some other negative and extreme activation. Demons cannot move anything physically for you or even for themselves. Demons cannot steal any money or jewelry or any other activity. Demons can hypnotize another physical body like humans or animals, to perform any physical activity. But demons cannot perform any kind of physical activity. Demons cannot hold our hand or shoulder, like any other human; demons cannot bite or push us, like other humans or animals. Demons can penetrate our body and very easily hurt our body in any way. Even they can give any one heart attack in seconds by blocking heart valves. Demons can give us any kind of physical pain or severe damage to any organ of our body. This is not a big deal for them. But if you have a penny, set the coin on the table in front of you; demons cannot move that coin at all. Demons cannot and do not do any sexual activity with any of us, regardless of whether you are a man or woman. But during the sex activity between two physical bodies, regardless of whether they are humans or animals, demons enjoy sexual activities more than those physical bodies, so hopefully you understand they make us do a lot of fun things, so they can enjoy also. Like drinking, drugs, sex, plus extreme behavior and negative activities. So basically this is the concept of a possession of a physical body regardless of whether it is a human or animal, they possess physical bodies to enjoy all physical activities including eating and drinking. That's why during the possession of a demon, we are more active to do a lot of stuff due to their pressure.

رؤية الجن والآلام السيطرة عليها

الأول هو أنك كلما طلبت من الجن فعل أي شيئ لك، ضع في إعتبارك دائماً أن هؤلاء الجن ليسوا الوحيدين في العالم. النقطة هي أن الجن الخاص بك قد يواجه بعض العقبات أو المشاكل في الوفاء بأوامرك بسبب بعض الجن الآخرون من الطرف الآخر. على سبيل المثال، تطلب من الجن الخاص بك للذهاب وتنويم امرأة مغناطيسياً، لتنجذب إليك. ليس من الصعب عليهم القيام بذلك، كما أنه من الصعب للغاية علي المرأة أيضاً مقاومتهم.

لكن إذا كان هناك بعض الجن حول هؤلاء النساء يحمونهن من الجن الآخرين. قد يكون هؤلاء الجن أكثر قوةً وعدداً بالمقارنة مع الجن الخاص بك، وهذه هي المشاكل المحتملة القليلة التي يواجهها أصدقائك من الجن الخاص بك، أثناء عملية تنفيذ أوامرك. لذلك لا تعتقد أنهم لا يحاولون لكنهم يستغرقون بعض الوقت. المشكلة الثانية المحتملة التي يواجهها الجن، هي أنهم لابد أن يتابعوك ويحلون مشاكلهم الخاصة أيضا. ولذلك فإن أفضل طريقة للحصول علي أفضل نتيجة، هي أن تذكرهم بالمهمة بين الحين والآخر، حتى لو كانوا على إستعداد للتخلي، فبمجرد أن تطلب منهم مرة أخرى، لن يتخلوا عن الإستمرار في المحاولة. وإذا كانوا يتحركون ببطئ لإنجاز مهمتك، بسبب أي شخص آخر، سوف يفعلون الأفضل. تذكر دائماً، لا يوجد جني واحد فقط. سيكون لديك دائما الكثير من الجن حولك. هكذا فبدلاً من أن تطلب واحداً فقط، يجب عليك أن نطلب منهم كلهم الذهاب ومساعدتك في شؤونك الخاصة.

هذا هو القانون الخامس لنيوتن- عادة ما يتبعك الجن بسهولة أكثر، بمجرد أن يروا أن لديك المزيد من القوة، لذلك حسن قوتك، و تعلم المزيد والمزيد.

159

Everything is more, more eating, wilder, more drugs, more drinking, more sex, etc., so they can enjoy more but we are getting some fun out of it also. Shortcut, demons amplify and boost every condition related to fun, extremes, and negativism. Be careful.

You cannot treat demons as you treat animals if you do not want a conflict between you and demons. It does not matter what you want; demons will take it or occupy some space the way they want anyway. But I am talking about developing a friendly atmosphere between you and demons. Always remember demons like to live in the same kind of atmosphere, whatever we like for ourselves, i.e., not too much hot or cold. As far as clean and dirty places, you better be careful. Clean and nice places will bring neat and nice demons, more sensible and definitely with a good background. If you keep your place dirty and nasty, this way you are inviting evil, nasty, and dirty demons to your place. As everyone knows, usually, garage and attics are least used places, but due to weather conditions, demons will live there but not permanently. Due to too much cold or hot weather, they will be moving back and forth all the time. Now you have two choices— either leave the whole house available for them and they can live anywhere they want, but in this case they will be interrupting you, bothering you, and will create problems for you, if they do not like something. Second choice is just leave a small room for them. Keep that room dark most of the time. Keep that room neat and clean and just use for minor things. Do not sit in that room for long time; do not eat there. Don't sleep in that room. Just use it for some quick purpose.

أشعر دائماً أن هذا أكثر إستقامة، وأقل إستهلاكاً للوقت، وأقل توريطاً مع الجن المتطفلين، فقط قم بإجراء إتصال توارد خواطر مع الشخص المعني، و قم بالتهديد، وإترك تعليمات واضحة لعدد قليل من المرات، ولا تقلق بشأن هذا الموضوع بعد الآن، لأن هذا يحقق نتائج حقاً. على أي حال، إستمر بتذكيرهم بما تريد منهم أن يفعلوه، وثق بي أنهم سوف يفعلون لك ما تريد. كل شيء يستغرق وقت. الصداقة الجديدة مع الجن تستغرق وقتاً أطول قليلاً بالنسبة لهم ليتبعوك على الفور، ولكن مع مرور الوقت سيكونون أكثر وأكثر طاعةً وصادقةً معك وسيتبعون أوامرك. كل الجن في الأساس نفس الشيئ، ولكن الفرق الوحيد بينهم هو حجمهم وقوتهم وذكائهم. لا يوجد نموذج خاص، عرق، أو حجم الجن مخصص للإنسان أو الحيوانات أو الحشرات مثل العناكب. يستطيع نفس الجن ضغط أو تمديد نفسه بسهولة جداً. تعمل لغتهم أو أداتهم، و تنويمهم المغناطيسي بنفس الطريقة مع كل شخص، كل شيء، بغض النظر عما إذا كانوا إنسان أوحيوان، أو حشرة، أو زواحف. كما وصفت عدة مرات،الجن أجسام مادية ، و كهرومغناطيسية، ولايموتون مع الأجسام التي يقيمون فيها.

بمجرد موت الجسد المادي، يخرج الجن فوراً منه. و يبحثون عن جسم آخر حر مباشرةً، أو إذا لم يتم العثور على جسم متاح أو حر، سيصارعوا مع بعضهم البعض للسيطرة على أي جسم معين ليعيشوا فيه. كما وصفت عدة مرات، يعيش الجن لآلاف السنين في حياة واحدة، وخلال تلك الحياة الواحدة التي تستغرق ألف سنة، يحاول الجن العيش في العديد من الفصائل المختلفة.

قد سبب للبقاء في جسم من نفس النوع من الحشرات، هو الفهم الأفضل لمجتمع العنكبوت.

Once you decide you will leave one room for them and will use that room the least and keep it dark most of the time, then the second step spray holy water every day in whole house but not too much in that room. After spraying holy water and insect killer in house everywhere, loudly tell them that you make that room for them so all of them can live there. Not immediately but in few days, they will move to that particular room; it does not mean demons will limit themselves to that particular room.

Still they will be flying everywhere in the house. They will be watching TV with you. Listening to your phone calls. Sharing some of others your physical activities, but in group or family they will be living in that particular room. This will be the very first step to avoid a conflict with demons. This step, demons will be very happy with you. This way you will be aware also when you need to communicate with demons; that particular room will be the best and quickest place to reach them. Always remember behaving nicely with them, leaving some place for them in particular, and even they are more and more friendly; still never give up precaution for you and your family's protection. Always spray holy water on your face, neck, head, ear, and everywhere in house to avoid demons' permanent control over your mind/body or your house. This holy water will keep them within limits and a little bit under control.

Let me explain to you; maybe then you understand better and quit worrying about it. Okay, think about a demon doctor. These are those people who spend their whole lives to have few demons around them or under their control.

ربما إرتباط فوري أكثر مع عائلة من العنكبوت، والأطفال, و أولادهم، وذلك لأن خلال عملية التكاثر هذه، والجو العائلي في سنوات عديدة، يقوم الجن بتطوير علاقة إرتباط، وإنجذاب، ومشاركة مع هذا النوع من السلالات. ربما كان مجتمع العنكبوت أكثر ملاءمة بالنسبة لهم بعد قضاء سنوات عديدة حولهم. بنفس الطريقة يعيش بعض الجن في الزواحف والحيوانات، و في بعض أجسام البشر لآلاف السنين في حياة واحدة.

الآن وجهة النظر التي أريد تفسيرها هنا هي أن هناك إختلاف في مستوى العقل، فرق في مستوى الذكاء، والحكمة بين جميع هذه الأجسام المادية، مثل السحلية، العنكبوت، والحيوانات،والبشر. بنفس الطريقة هناك فرق كبير بين الأنشطة والهوايات أيضاً. الآن يمكنك أن تفترض بسهولة الفرق بين الجن فيما بينهم. فالأنشطة، والهوايات، وكل شيء سيكون مختلفاً بشكل كبيربين الجن الذين يقضون آلاف السنين في أجسام العناكب، و الذين يعيشون بإستمرار في جسم الإنسان. حسنا، وهكذا، هذا هو الفارق الأول بين الجن عندما يشاركون مع إثنين من السلالات أو الأعراق المختلفة، لهذا السبب سيختلف جداً مستوى الحكمة وأشياء أخرى. الآن أتكلم عن الجن الذين يعيشون في أجسام البشر، ولكن يختلف مستوى العقلين البشريين و تختلف سلوكياتهما. إذا كان الأمر كذلك، إذا قضي جني واحد آلاف السنين في جسم شخص من عائلة فقيرة جداً، وغير متعلم، وعائلة بسيطة، و يتعاطي المخدرات و الكحوليات، و الجني الثاني قضي آلاف السنوات في جسم شخص من الطبقة الراقية جداً، غني ومتعلم ومتدين جداً، و أجسام نظيفة من الأسرة البشرية. سيختلف الجنيين بسبب إختلاف الجو بين نفس العرق. واحد سيئ للغاية / مدمن كحوليات / مدمن مخدرات،، متوحش، سيئ، بينما الجن الآخر، متدين، ونظيف، ومتعلم، أو مثقف، وما إلى ذلك، لذلك عندما نرى ناس من حولنا، وإذا كان هؤلاء الناس جيدون، هذا يعني بهم الجن الخاص بهم أيضاً جيدون وراضون بهم.

SEE & CONTROL DEMONS & PAIN

No doubt, finally they have few or more demons around them and no doubt these demons obey them and follow them. But watch. None of those demon doctors will be financially self-sufficient. You will always see those demon doctors looking for rich people or other people to keep going to them to get some help through demon doctor's powerful trained demons about their family issues or business issues. Always remember may be for the first time your problems or issue maybe real and that demon doctors use his demons to resolve your issues. Now the problem is this—you will go to that demon doctor one time and will resolve your issues; you will pay him his fee and you should be done with him, right? But the problem with demon doctors is that they need money all the time. So after some time, even that demon doctor can create some fake or temporary problem for you by the use of his demons. Why? The Reason is, so you can stay in his contact all the time to resolve your issues; this way that demon doctor can make money from you all the time. That's why I decided to write each and every trick and cure to handle demons by you in this book. Once you practice these tricks cures and procedures, you will not need ever to go to any demon doctor.

Maybe in future, demon doctors come to you to borrow your demons from you. Please do not give your demons to anyone. You do not understand this? I will explain later on. As I described several times, our physical bodies are always under the possession of at least one demon all the time. Those demons reside in our body and travel with us. I am talking about normal people who do not use any procedures or cure to get rid of demons. Our minds and bodies are like a toy for those demons.

هنا وجهة نظري هي أن أجسادنا دائماً على إستعداد لإستيعاب الجن من الآجسام المكتظة. بعض الناس الطيبين قد يكون لديهم حشد كبير من الجن الجيدون جداً من حولهم، وبنفس الطريقة قد يكون الناس السيئة جداً حشد كبير من الجين السيئين داخل أو حول أجسادنا.ذلك لا يحدث فقط عندما تمر بشخص ما،إنه عادة ما يحدث إما أثناء الإتصال الهاتفي أو أثناء المحادثات. وجهاً لوجه أنا آسف إذا كنت ما زلت غير قادر على شرح وجهة نظري. لكن بإختصار كنا قادرون على ترك الأجسام اليشرية المرئية، أو هيئات حقوق الإنسان، ولكن الجن الغير مرئيين بمجرد أن يعلقوا بأجسام البشر، هذا يعني أنهم قد يبقون حول جنسنا، أو سلالة عائلتنا المقبلة لعدة آلاف من السنين. لذا كن حذرا، حاول دائماً أن تبقى حول الرجال المتدينين والمثقفين، و لو لبضع ثوان أو دقائق، لتحصل على بعض الجن الجيدون حقاً منهم. بالضبط نفس الشيء صحيح فبمجرد البقاء مع أهل الخير سوف تتحول إلي إنسان جيد أو طيب. السبب هو أن هؤلاء الجن، لا يغيرون أنفسهم إلى جيد أو سيئ، ولكن من المؤكد أنهم قادرون على تغير نا إلي جيد أو سيئ بسبب سلطاتهم الخارقة. بعض الجن أكثر ذكاءً و بعضهم أقل ذكاءً، لذلك لا نتوقع نفس المستوى من الذكاء لكل جني.

قد يكون الجن من حولك، من خلفية مختلفة ولهم تجربة مختلفة. ربما يخرج أحد هؤلاء الجن من سحلية أو قطط أو كلاب، أ والأشجار القديمة،أو من شخص مدمن، أو من كنيسة أو غيرها من الأماكن الدينية، أو يخرج من شخص مدمن كحوليات.

أنا واثق، أنه ربما سيكون من الصعب عليك جداً معرفة ذلك لفترة طويلة ، حتى أنه يمكنك أن تشعر بالجن من حولك وأنهم أصدقائك، لكنهم لا يزالون لا ينفذون ما تطلبه منهم،ا بالطريقة التي تريدها.

Now once we start a friendship (I am talking about man/woman friendship), there is no way those demons will allow us mentally to start a relationship or friendship unless the demons controlling either minds or bodies have a very good understanding and friendship. If you are a very powerful person and you reject the control of that demon, hypnotizing you against the will of those demons around you, sooner or later, by hypnotism, these demons will create problems between you and your friend, and eventually you will have a breakup with your friend. I am sorry but this is a fact. So any friendship or relationship start with low speed or pace bring everyone in good understanding, humans and demons both. Usually those kinds of friendship and relationships stay in good shape for a long time or forever because no one is working against it—no human or demon. Exactly, same thing is true in case of hate also. If you want to hate someone, make sure your and their demons hate each other also to make this hate relationship successful and perfect, how? Talk to them.

Once you learn how to communicate with demons and you will start giving those commands and instructions, at that point you need to understand two things or two problems. One is, whenever you ask demons to do something for you, always keep in mind that they are not the only demons in the world. The point is that your demon may face some obstacles or problems due to some other demons from the other party to fulfill your command. For example you ask your demons to go and hypnotize a woman to get attracted toward you. It is not difficult for them to do it. It is also very difficult for the woman also to resist them.

على سبيل المثال إذا كنت تريد تغييررأي سياسي في قضية معينة أو إذا كنت تريد إمرأة تأتي إليك لتغازلك. الآن أنت تطلب من الجن ما تريده كل يوم، ولكن لا شيء يحدث أو يحدث بشكل بطيئ جداً. السبب وراء ذلك سبق أن قلت لك عنه في البداية. كل جني لديه مجال إختصاص محدد. وإنهم يعرفون كيفية التنويم المغناطيسي، ولكن إذا كان الجن الموجودون حولك لا يعرفون أي شيء عن السياسة أو لا يجيدون التعامل مع المرأة أو على الأقل لا يفهمون كيفية إقناع إمرأة بالتنويم المغناطيسي، حتى تبدأ في الإنجذاب إليك بدون الشك فيك.

لذلك لتحقيق أغراض محددة أو معينة، ستحتاج إلى أن يكون لديك جن متخصصون في مجال معين. فكيف تقوم بذلك؟

ليس لدي أي فكرة كيف ستكون قادر على العثور على جن مناسبين لآداء عمل معين، ولكني أقول لك كيف تستطيع أن تفعل ذلك. يمكنك الممارسة أيضاً، ربما في يوم من الأيام سوف تكون قادراً على القيام بذلك. لا أستطيع أن أعلم أي شخص هذا، لأنني إكتسبت هذه القوة بشكل طبيعي. بدون القيام بأي ممارسة. على أي حال، عادة لتحقيق الإتقان في العمل و لكي تفعل شيئا في وقت أقل، أقوم عادة بسحب بعض الجن من هنا و هناك، يتصلون بنفس المجال، و أحتفظ بهم حولي لبضعة أيام قليلة. ثم أطلب منهم ما يجب القيام به. فقط على سبيل المثال، إذا كان يجب علي التعامل مع بعض السياسيين، سأقوم بسحب الجن من ذلك السياسي نحوي، ثم أعطيهم الأوامر والتعليمات للقيام بشيء ما. أفضل جزء في هذه النظرية هو أن نفس الجن سيعودون إلى السياسي و يقومون بتغيير رأيه بطيء وثبات حول موضوع معين.

But if there are some demons around those women and they are protecting them from other demons. May be those demons are more powerful and more in numbers as compared to your demon; these are few possible problems your demon friends may face during the fulfillment process of your command. So do not think they are not trying but it takes some time. The second possible problem with demons is that they have to follow you and have to resolve their own problems also. So the best way to have better result is that you need to remind them of the task every now and then, so if they were ready to give up, once you ask again, they will not give up and keep trying. And if due to some else, they were moving slow for your task, they will do better. Always remember, they are never only one. You will always have a lot of demons around you. So instead of asking only one, you should ask all of them to go and help you with your issues.

This is Newton's law number five—demons usually follow you more easily once they see more power in you. So improve your power. Learn more and more. I always feel it is straighter, less time consuming and less involvement of outsider's demons. Just establish a telepathic contact with the concerned person and leave threat and clear instruction few times and quit worrying about it anymore, because this really works.

Anyway, simply keep reminding them what you want them to do; trust me they will do it for you. Everything takes time. New friendship with demons may take a little longer for them to follow right away or immediately, but with time they will be more and more obedient and sincere with you and with your commands.

يخرج من نفس الرجل السياسي أصلاً؛ بهذه الطريقة سيكون كل منهما سعيداً وأنا سوف أصل إلي هدفي. أحياناً يستغرق تحقيق مثل هذا النوع من الأهداف شهوراً. وإذا كنت بحاجة إلي شيء بسرعة، فإن أفضل طريقة هي التخاطر. مجرد إتصال توارد خواطر مع الجن الموجودين حو ل أي شخص معين عدة مرات و يجب أن تترك أوامر وتعليمات واضحة، و سوف تحصل على النتيجة التي تريدها بعد مرور بعض الوقت.

الجن أجسام مادية ولكنهم نوع من الأجسام الكهرومغناطيسية. يتحرك الجن أو يحلقون في المجال أو النظام الكهرومغناطيسي، خلقهم خاصةً بسبب هذه النوعية من سرعة السفر أو الإنتقال للجن التي تشبه سرعة الصوت أو الضوء أو في مكان ما من حوله، حيث يستطيع الجن في ثانية واحدة، الإنتقال من زاوية واحدة من الأرض إلى زاوية ثانية من الأرض. أنامتأكد من أن العلم الحديث سيعطينا بيانات أكثر دقة في المستقبل، حتى ذلك الحين،إفترض فقط أنني أقترب من الصواب. أحاول هنا أن أشرح لكم طريقة الإتصال بين الجن. إنهم يرسلون إشارات علي شكل أشعة لبعضهم البعض في المجال الكهرومغناطيسي، في جميع أنحاء العالم رسالة إشارات.

لكن الجن لا يعتمدون على أي نوع من الأسلاك أو المعدات لإرسال الإشارات الخاصة بهم في أي مكان في العالم. شيء آخر مهم للغاية وغير عادي و هو أن إرسال إشارات إلى أي جزء من العالم لأي جني معين، لا يقتصر على جني واحد فقط. يمكن لجني واحد إرسال إشارات الرسالة بإستخدام تردد معين يأخذ إشارة رسالته إلى كل من أصدقائه من الجن أو الأسرة من الجن، والتي ينبغي ضبطها لتصل إلى المستوى نفسه من التردد.

All demons are basically the same, but the only difference between them is size, power, and intelligence. There is no special design model, race, or size of demons made especially for human or especially for animals or especially for insects like spiders. The same demon can compress or expand very easily. Their language or tool, hypnotism, works the same way for everybody, everything, regardless of whether they are human, animal, insect, or reptile. As I described several times, demons are physical, electromagnetic bodies, and demons do not die with the physical bodies in which they reside.

Once physical body is dead, demons come out of the body immediately and find another free body immediately or if they cannot find a vacant or free available body, they will fight with each other to get the possession of any particular body to reside there. As I described several times, demons live for thousands of years in a single life. During the single life of thousand years, demons try to live in several different species.

The reason of staying in the body of same kind of insect may be better understanding with spider community. Maybe more attachment with immediate family of spider, kids their kids, because during whole that process of reproduction and family atmosphere in so many years, demons develop attachment, attraction, and involvement in that kind of race. Maybe that spider community more suitable for them after spending so many years around them. Same way some demons live in reptiles, some in animals, and some in human bodies for thousands of years in one single life.

بهذه الطريقة، سيكون لدي الجن مستويات مختلفة من الإشارات المحددة لبعض ترددات معينة. تنشر المستويات المختلفة من الترددات إشارات الرسائل الخاصة بها إلى كل مكان وقتما يريدون ارسال رسائلهم، فمن السهل جداً علي الجن للسفرو الإنتقال عبر خطوط الهاتف أو التلفزيون أو الإنترنت، و الإشارات في كل مكان في أي ركن من أركان العالم.

الجن يستخدمون تقنية جيدة للغاية للسفر، و الإتصال. آمل في يوم من الأيام أن تتعلم العلوم الحديثة وتصل إلى هذا المستوى حيث أننا سنكون قادرين على التواصل والسيطرة على العالم الغير مرئي من الجن. الآن لماذا شرحت لك كل المعلومات الواردة أعلاه؟ كنت أحاول أن أبين لك إذا كنت تفهم الجن جيداً حقاً يستطيع هؤلاء الجن نشر رسائلك في جميع أنحاء العالم في غضون ثوان قليلة. يفهم الجن اللغات المحلية فيما بيننا فقط، و لكن عندما يتحدثون مع بعضهم البعض، يكون شكل من أشكال التخاطر، ولنه ليس مرتبطاً بجني واحد أو منطقة معينةا. يستطيع الجن إستخدام إشارات مختلفة بترددات مختلفة لنقل رسالتهم من أي مكان إلي أي مكان، للتواصل مع الأجسام الحية، بغض النظر عما إذا كانت للبشر، أوالأشجار،أ والحشرات أوالحيوانات، يستخدم الجن لغة التنويم المغناطيسي. إذاكنت تسيطر علي الجن الخاص بك، فهو يستطيع نشر رسالتك للجن اللاخرين في جميع أنحاء العالم في بضع ثوان. أحيانا أشعر أنني ربما أستطيع الوصول إلى شبكة من الإتصالات الكهرومغناطيسية للجن في جميع أنحاء العالم، عالمهم، العالم الغير مرئي، أشعر بقوة أنني لست بحاجة إلي ذلك، أن. أستمر في البقاء قريب من الشخص العادي، وأود أن أتجنب و أحافظ على نفسي ضمن الحد المسموح به. ولكني غير متأكد من كيفية، الحد من نفسي. سوف نرى.

Now my point to explain here is there is a difference of mind level, difference of IQ level, difference of wisdom level between all these physical bodies, i.e., spider, lizard, animals, and human. Same way there is a big difference between activities and hobbies also. Now you can easily assume the difference between the demons. The activites, hobbies, and everything will be way different between a demon who spends thousands of year in bodies of spiders a who is continuously living in a body of a human. Okay, this was first difference between demons when they were engaged with two different breeds or races. So for that reason the level of wisdom and other things will be different too. Now I am taking about demons residing in human bodies, but the level of two human minds and behaviors are different. So if one demon spends thousands of years in the body of very poor, uneducated and backward family, drugs and alcoholic and second demons spend thousand years in the body of a human of very high class, rich, educated, very religious, and clean bodies of human family. So due to even same race but different atmosphere, both demons will be different. A very bad/alcoholic/ drug-addicted, wild, nasty, dirty, and the other demon should be very religious, clean, educated, or informative, etc., so when we see people around us, and if these people are doing good, it means their demons are also good and satisfied with them.

Here my point is our bodies are always ready to absorb demons from overcrowded bodies. Some good people may have too much crowd of very good demons around them, same way very bad people may have too much crowd of nasty and bad demons inside or around our bodies it just do not happen, when you just pass someone,

نحن البشر ننقسم إلى بلدان ومدن وبلدات، ومنازل للحصول على مزيد من الحرية بشكل آمن , و بإحتكار مطلق. نحن لا نسمح لأي شخص للدخول و إقحام أي غريب في بلادنا، مدينتنا، بلدتنا، أو منزلنا، بنفس الطريقة بالضبط، ينقسم الجن أيضاً إلى فئات سكنية، حيث يعيش الجن في مكان معين، منزل، أو شجرة في مجموعة. في منزل خاص حيث يعيش مجموعة معينة من الجن، هم لا يسمحون لأي جني جديد أو أقوى. يحارب الجن علناً وبشكل أكبر من البشر لتأمين مكان معيشتهم.

هذا امر جيد بالنسبة لنا، هذا يعني أننا عندما نكون في المنازل أو في متاجرنا أو مكاتبنا، لسنا في حاجة للتعامل مع الغرباء والجن الجدد طوال الوقت. بمجرد أن نكون في منزلنا، يكون الجن الذين يعيشون في منزلنا هم المسؤولون عنا. مرة واحدة ونحن في سيارتنا. الشياطين يعيشون ا. لذلك على الأقل سنكون في مأمن من هجمات و إستحواذ الجن الجدد. نحن البشر حتى لا نتصور ما يحدث طوال الوقت من حولنا، أو بين الجن. ربما يكون الأمر مختلفاً بالنسبة لنا من حيث مفهوم وجود منزل و شجرة في فنائنا. ولكن بالنسبة للجن كلا المكانين هما نفسهما، لا فرق بينهما. القليل من الجن يجعلون من منزلنا مكان لمعيشتهم أو منزلهم، والآن تخيل فقط لو أتي شخص وحاول طردنا من بيوتنا التي نعيش فيها منذ عشرين أو ثلاثين أو خمسين سنة ؟ كيف ستشعر؟ وإلى أي مدي ستغضب؟ تخيل الآن كم عمر الجن، وتخيل، منذ متى، يقيم أو يعيش هؤلاء الجن في تلك الأشجار أو في هذه المنازل أكثر منا، لذا كن حذرا لا تختار معركة مع الجن وحاول تدريبهم على إختيار بعض زوايا المنزل الأقل إستخداماً، بدلا من العمل ضدك، فهؤلاء الجن يجب أن يساعدوك ويدعموك بكل الطرق الممكنة التي في وسعهم. ينقسم هذا العالم إلى قسمين، واحد مرئي والثاني عالم غير مرئي.

it usually happens either telephone conversation or during face-to-face talks. I am sorry if still I am unable to explain my point. But shortcut we are capable of leaving visible human bodies, but invisible demons once stuck with them it means they may stay around our breed, race or next family for several of thousand years. So be careful, even for few seconds or minutes, always try to stay around good religious and educated people, so you may get some really good demons from them. Exactly the same thing is true for once to stay around company of good people you will turn good. The reason is that these demons do not change themselves to good or bad, but for sure they are capable of changing us to good or bad due to their supernatural powers. So some demons are more intelligent and some less, so do not expect the same level of intelegence from each and every demon.Demons around you, maybe from different background and with different experience. Maybe one of these demons comes out from lizard or cats or dogs, or old trees, out of some drug-addicted person, or out of a church or another religious place, or came out from an alcoholic person, etc. I am sure, for a long time, maybe it will be very difficult for you to figure that out, you can even feel that demons are around you and they are your friends, but still, whenever you ask them to do something, it is not happening the way you want it. For example if you want to change the mind of a politician on a particular issue or if you want a woman come to you and start flirting with you. Now you are asking your demons every day, but still nothing is happening or is happening very slow. The reason behind that I already told you about in beginning. Every demon as their specific field of expertise.

نحن أصحاب المنزل في العالم المرئي، ولكن، هؤلاء الجن الذين يعيشون في هذا المنزل، في العالم الغير مرئي يطالبون بذلك البيت.أعلم أن هذا شيئ صعب ومعقد بالنسبة لك، ولكن المور تسير على النحو في العالم الغير مرئي، سنكون ضد الجن كثيراً، وسوف يكونون ضدك. لا اعتقد ان هذه فكرة جيدة.

لا يعيش الجن على جثث الموتى، بغض النظر عما إذا كانوا بشراً أوحيوانات، أو حشرات. في كل مكان في هذا العالم، ونحن. دعوني اقول لكم شيئاً واحدا حول هذا الموضوع. ليسلدي أي تجربة لإستشعار أو رؤية جني يخرج من النمل الصغير، لأنني لا أقتل أي نملة.

في الغالب لقد أحسست ورأيت الجن يخرج من السحلية، و العنكبوت، و الصرصور، والإنسان. بسبب أن طرق الوصول إلي الأجسام الحية الأخرى محدودة، لا أستطيع مناقشة أمرهم بثقة بنسبة 100 في المئة. حسنا، نعود إلى المناقشة الأصلية، في كل مكان تعيش أجسام حية، سواء كان إنسان أ و حيوان أو طيور أو حشرات وغيرها، لذلك ربما تعيش كل تلك الأجسام تحت سيطرة الجن الموجودين من حولهم معظم الوقت. عادة يعيش الجن أو يقضون حياتهم حول نفس النوع من السلالات أو يمكنك أن تقول نفس النوع من النسل طوال حياتهم. ولكن هناك إحتمال في حالة عدم توافر جسم حي من نفس السلالة / العرق، سوف يبحث الجن عن أجسام حية أعلى أو أفضل للجن الذين يخرجون من جثث الحيوانات أو الحشرات، أو أشجار، أو الزواحف. الآن هناك مكان من حولنا، ربما نجد كل أنواع الأجسام الحية ولكن ليست أجسام البشر، أي المقابر، أو المدافن.

They know how to hypnotize, but if demons around you do not know anything about politics or your demons are not good to handle a woman or at least they do not understand how to convince a woman hypnotically so she startsto be attracted to you without suspecting you. So for all specific or special purposes, you need to have particular demons that have specialties in a particular field. So how to do this?

I have no idea how you will be able to find suitable demons for a particular job, but I am telling you how I can do it. You can practice also, maybe one day you will be able to do it. I cannot teach anyone this because this is power I achieved naturally, without doing any practice. Anyway, usually to bring perfection in work and do something in less time, usually I pull some demons from here and there, related to the same field. I keep them around me for a few days. Then I ask them what needs to be done. Just for example, if I have to deal with some politicians, I will pull several demons out from that politician toward me, and then I will give them commands and instructions to do something. The best part behind this theory is that the same demons will go back to the politician and will change his mind slow and steady about some particular subject. Originally these demons come out from the same politician; that way both of them will be happy and I will get my target. Sometimes it takes months to achieve such kind of goals. And if I need something fast, the best way is telepathy. Just establish a telepathic connection with the demons around any particular person several times and leave clear commands and instructions to their demons; after some time you will get the result you want to have.

غالباً ما نجد الكثير أجسام البشر لكنهم موتى، و الأجسام الحية الوحيدة التي تعيش في المقابر أو المدافن، و المتاحة للجن هي الأشجار، والحشرات والطيور القليلة، أو عدد قليل من الحيوانات.كما وصفت عدة مرات يحب الجن الأماكن المظلمة والأقل إستخداماً.بمرور الوقت يعتاد الجن علي تلك الأماكن. الجن يحبون لأماكن الهادئة، لا يوجد بها تدخل، مظلمة، و لا يستخدم كثيراً. بمرور الوقت، يزيد إحتكار الجن ولن يتحملوا دخول و خروج أي شخص يأتي إلى تلك الأماكن. يعمل الجن علي تعزيز وتضخيم مستوى الخوف عند الإنسان خلال زيارته للمقبرة أو المدفن. السبب، ربما لأن الجن يتمتعون بذلك. لكن السبب الآخر المحتمل لزيادة مستوى الخوف عند البشر، هو أنه ينبغي لهم تجنب الذهاب إلى تلك الأمكان بقدر المستطاع .

الجن لا يخططون لشيء يخيفنا أولكيفية زيادة مستوي الخوف لدينا. يقوم الجن فقط بقراءة عقولنا. فبمجرد أن يعرفوا أننا تبحث هنا وهناك، إذا كان بإمكاننا أن نرى أي شبحم، أو جسم مخيف هيئة يمشي وراءنا أو أي شبح يراقبنا من الأشجار، وما إلى ذلك، يعرف الجن أننا ممتعون للغاية بالنسبة لهم، إنهم يأتون وراء نا أثناء طريقنا إلى منزلنا وبطريقة ما يجعل لإقامتهم مكاناً حولنا. ستعلم خلال هذا النوع من التجارب، أنك ستلاحظ أنك ترى سلسلة من الكوابيس بدون توقف. ستجعلك الصفات البسيطة جداً، تشعر بالخوف والمضايقات، و سيهتم الجن بمضايقتك أكثروأكثر من ذلك.

إن قمت برفضهم، سوف يقلعوا عن مضايقتك وتخويفك و ربما تركوك وحدك قريباً جداً. يوجد الجن حولنا أو حول أجسام البشر أمامنا، لن تعرف كيف يريدون معاملتنا.

Demons are physical but some kind of electromagnetic bodies. Demons move or fly in electromagnetic field or system, created especially for them due to this quality the traveling speed of demons, which is like the speed of sound or light or somewhere around it. In one second, a demon can move from one corner of the earth to second corner of the earth.

I am sure modern science can give us more precise data in the future; until then, just assume I am plus or negative close to right. Here, I am trying to explain to you the way of communication between demons. Demons send signals in the form of rays to each other in the electromagnetic field, all around the world, message signals.

But demons are not dependent on any kind of wiring or equipment to send their signals anywhere in the world. Another extremely important and extraordinary thing which is that sending signals to any part of the world to any particular demon is not limited to only one demon. One demon can send message signals by using a specific frequency that will take his message signal to all of his friends or family demons, which should be tuned up to the same level of frequency. This way, demons have different levels of signals set for some particular frequencies. Different level of frequencies spread their message signals to everywhere whenever they want to send their messages. It is very easy for demons to travel through phone lines or TV or Internet, signals everywhere in any corner of the world. Demons are using extremely good technology for traveling, for communication.

لكن حتى يصبح الجني صديقك، ويقرر أن يتصرف بشكل لطيف معك، كل الشياطين تكون نفس الشيئ الجن يعتبروننا مثل اللعبة. لا يهتم الجن كم يخيفنا أو يجعلونا مريض عقلياً أو جسدياً

أنهم مشغولون فقط بالتمتع عندما نكون متضايقون، أو خاوئفون أو مرضي.الآن هل تعتقد أن تدريب هؤلاء الجن فكرة جيدة ، أكثر و أكثر من ذلك، و إعطائهم أفكار أكثر وأكثر، و ربما كيف يستطيع الجن أن يخيفونا أكثر وأكثر؟ منذ ستون عاماً، لم يكن لدينا العديد من القنوات التلفزيونية أو أفلام الرعب، والشر، و الأفلام السيئة. لكن هناك الآن توجد أفلام رعب وشر، و قتل لا تعد ولا تحصى، نحن خائفون من تلك الأفلام الشريرة المقرفة لكنك لا تعرف أبداً، ربما أنك تشاهد تلك الأفلام الشريرة، و المرعبة و المقرفة تحت ضغط من الجن الموجودين حولك. الآن لديك خياران لتجنب هذا الوضع. الأول هو رفض هذه الأفلام المرعبة والشريرة، فبمجرد ألا أحد يشاهد أحد هذه الأفلام، لن ينتج أو ينفذ أحد هذه الأفلام. الخيار الثاني هو تدريب نفسك، و ستفهم100 في المئة تصرفات الجن ليظهروا لنا كوابيس أفكار تخيفنا، عادة ما يغذي الجن بها أذهاننا للتمتع بأوضاعنا. ما زلت اعتقد أن مشاهدة أفلام الرعب والشر ليست فكرة جيدة.

هذه الأفلام تقوم بتدريب الجن من حولنا لجعل الحياة جحيماً بالنسبة لأصحاب القلوب الضعيفة والجبناء من الناس، بإ ظهار الكوابيس. لهم. أنا لست شجاعاً أيضاً، ولكن مفهوم والوعي بالجن و أفعالهم واضح جداً. لهذا السبب أنا لا زلت خائفاً من الكلب أو أي حيوانات لبرية أخرى، ولكني لست خائفاً من الجن بالمرة. قد تسألني لماذا؟.

Hopefully one day modern science will learn and reach that level where we will be able to communicate and control the invisible world of demons.Now why did I explain to you all of the above information? I was trying to tell you if you have really good understanding of demons, those demons can spread your messages all over the world within a few seconds. With us, demons understand local languages only. But when they talk to each other, it is a form of telepathy but not limited to one demon or one particular area.

Demons can use different signals of different frequencies to transmit their message anywhere everywhere to communicate with living bodies, regardless of whether they are human, trees, insects, animals, and demons use language of hypnotism. If you have control on your demon, your demon can spread your message all over the world in a few seconds to other demons. Sometimes I feel I may have access to the electromagnetic network of communication of demons all over the world, their world, invisible world, I strongly feel I do not need that. To still stay close to a normal person, I should avoid and keep myself within limit. But not sure how, I will be able to limit myself. We will see.

We humans are divided into countries, cities, town, homes to have more freedom securely and monopoly. We do not allow anybody to enter & insert any outsider in our country, city, town, or home. Exactly same way, demons are also subdivided into residential categories. Demons live in a particular place, house, or tree in a group. In a particular house where a particular group of demons live, they do not allow any new or stronger demon. Demons fight openly and way more than human to secure their living place.

لأنني أعرف الجني لن أو لا يمكن أن يعضني، ولكن الكلب يمكنه ذلك. بالنسبة لقدرة الجن علي أن تضر بنا من خلال جعلنا مرضى جسدياً أو عقلياً. لتجنب هذا، يجب علينا أن نجعل كل هؤلاء الجن الموجودون حولنا أصدقائنا. بمجرد أن يصبح الجن أصدقائنا، فإنهم لا يجرحون أصدقائهم. حالتي عكس ذلك تماماً، أي حيوانات برية أو زواحف تجعلني خائفاً بسهولة جداً، ولكن الجن، وحتى لو حاولوا، لأن يجعلوني خائف، لا يستطيعون، لأنهم يدعون أنهم أشباح كبيرة و سيئة وقبيحة ، لكنهم ليسوا كذلك.

لذلك يجب أن تفهم هذا، وتكف عن الخوف منهم. إذا فهمت علم وظائف الأعضاء لدي وإرشاداتي، و لن تخاف من الجن بعد ذلك في وقت قريب جداً. هل سمعت من أحدهم قول أن هذا المكان يحالفني الحظ فيه أو هذا المكان لا يحالفني الحظ فيه؟ بنفس الطريقة، بمجرد أن يتزوج شخص ما أو يخطب إمرأة، إما أن يتحسن أو حظهم أو حياتهم أو يسوء حظهم أو حياتهم أحياناً.

ثم يقولان عادة لبعضهما أنهما لم يكونا محظوظين مع بعضهما. هذه هي أمثلة بسيطة جداً للنزاعات الناشئة عن الجن. المثال الأول عن المنزل / المكتب / الأعمال التجارية، إسمحوا لي أن أفسر. لا شك، عندما لا يعيش أحد في بعض الأماكن الشاغرة لفترات و فترات طويلة، مع عدم وجود أماكن مضاءة، وتظل الأماكن مظلمة معظم الوقت.

بنفس الطريقة إذا كان هناك منزل كبير و يعيش به فقط عدد قليل من الناس، وعادة ما يكون معظم المنزل غير مستخدم، ومعظم الغرف تظل مظلمة معظم الوقت، تكون هذه الأنواع من الأماكن مثل الجنة بالنسبة للجن.

170

This is good for us, in this sense, that when we are at homes or shops or offices, we do not need to deal with strangers and new demons all the time. Once we are in our house demons living in our house are in charge of us. Once we are in our car. The demons live in our car are the owner or in charge of us. So at least in a few places, we are safe from the attacks and possessions of new demons. We humans even cannot image what happens all the time around us, among demons. Maybe it is different for us the concept of a house and a tree in our yard. But for demons both places are same. Few demons make our house as their living place or home, now just imagine if someone just comes and tries to kick us out from our homes where we are living there since the last twenty or thirty or fifty years? How will you feel? How angry will you get? Now imagine the age of demons and imagine, since how long, those demons are staying or living on those trees or in these houses way more than us. So be careful do not pick a fight with dcmons & try to train thcm to choose some least in use corners of the house, instead of working against you, these demons need to be helping and supporting you in every possible way they can. This world is divided into two parts; one is visible and second is invisible world. We are owners of the house in the visible world but in the invisible world, those demons live in that house and claim that house. I know it is difficult and complicated for you, but this is the way it is in invisible world. You will go against them too much, demons will go against you. I don't think it is a good idea.

Demons do not live on dead bodies, regardless of whether they are humans, animals, or insects. Everywhere in this world, we have humans, animals, insects and other living bodies everywhere. Let me tell you one thing about this topic.

بمجرد أن يكون للجن السيطرة الكاملة علي مثل هذا المكان، ثق بي سيكون من الصعب للغاية تعديل وضع هؤلاء الجن، فإذا قرر شخص ما أو أي أسرة قررت إستخدام هذا المنزل و بدأوا يعيشون هناك، مقارنة مع بيت عادي، مستخدم بطريقة عادية منتظمة، يتأقلم الجن عادة وفقاً للأفراد والمساحات الموجودة في ذلك المنزل. ليس هذا فقط. هؤلاء الجن عادة ما يتعلق الجن جداً بأفراد الأسرة في تلك المنازل. لكن المنازل الشاغرة لفترة طويلة أو الأماكن أو الغرف في منازل الغير مستخدمة لفترة طويلة أوالأقل إستخداماً أو التي تظل مظلمةً طوال الوقت، عادة ما يشغل الجن هذا النوع من المنازل والأماكن فوراً وبشكل كامل. مستحيل أن يغير الجن أوضاعهم فوراً بمجرد أن تنتقل إلي ذلك البيت، إذا كنت تعتقد ذلك، حتى و لو كان طبيب الجن سيقدم لك المساعدة، لا أزال أعتقد بقوة أن الإنتقال إلي هذا المنزل الشاغر بإستعجال أو على الفور ليست فكرة جيدة. أفضل فكرة وسياسة جيدة للإنتقال إلى مثل هذا المنزل، أن تنتقل فيه خطوة خطوة، و أن يستغرق ذلك بعض الوقت للتحرك في بدلا من التحرك في في يوم واحد. أشعر إذا لم يكن الجن في ذلك المنزل سيئون حقاً وشريرون، وربما سيتأقلمون مع مرور الوقت، إذا قمت بالإنتقال إلي ذلك المنزل في خطوات والتحدث إليهم أيضاً.

السبب وراء محاولتي توجيهك إلي الإتجاه الصحيح، هو أنك قد تعرف عن نفسك، ولكنك لن تعرف أبداً إذا بدأ أطفالك في مواجه بعض المشاكل أو أي شخص آخر في الأسرة. لا شك، والجن هم العقل المدبر، حينما يريدون إيذاء شخص ما أو على إستعداد للعب مع شخص ما. لذا أعتقد أن عليك نقل متعلقاتك أولاً إلي ذلك المنزل. الا تأخذ أي أطفال أو نساء معك. أولاً قم بإضاءة الأنوار داخل و خارج البيت. إذهب إلى كل غرفة و شجرة، وركن من أركان المنزل.

I do nothave any experience of sensing or seeing a demon coming out for small ants, because, I never kill any ant. Mostly I have sensed or seen demons coming out from a spider, lizard, cockroach, human. Due to my limited access to other living bodies, I cannot discuss about them with 100 percent confidence. Okay, come back to the original discussion, everywhere we have living bodies, whether human, animals, birds, insects, etc., so possibly all these living bodies are under the possession of demons around them most of the time. Usually, demons live or spend their lives around The same kind of race or you can say the same kind of breed all their lives. But there is a possibility in case of unavailability of a living body of same breed/race, that demon will look for superior or better living bodies for those demons whom come out from the dead bodies of animals insects trees or reptiles. Now there is a place around us where possibly we can find all kinds of living bodies but no human bodies, i.e., cemeteries or graveyards.

In a cemetery or a graveyard, mostly we have a lot of human bodies but dead; the only available living bodies available for demons in graveyards or cemeteries are trees, insects, few birds, or few animals. As I described several times demons like dark and least-in-use places. In time, demons get habitual of it. Demons like quiet, no interference, dark, and not-in-use place. With time, their monopoly will increase and they will not tolerate anybody to go or to come to those places, demons make sure to boost and amplify the fear level of a human during the visit to a graveyard or cemetery. The reason is maybe that demons enjoy it. But another possible reason of increasing the level of fear in humans is that humans should avoid going to these place as much possible.

كن واثقاً.و تذكر دائماً أن كل الجن ويراقبوك ويستمعون إليك، فابدأ في التحدث مع الجن في كل غرفة و.قل لهم بوضوح أنك قمت بإستئجار أو شراء هذا المنزل، وأنك لا تريد قتال أي جني، وأنك ليس لديك أي مكان آخر لتعيش فيه، ستكون على ما يرام إذا كان هؤلاء الجن سوف يعيشون في مناطق مختلفة من منزلك.

قل للجن أين تريدهم أن يظلوا معظم الوقت. شيء من هذا القبيل، سيسمع جميع الجن كل ما تقوله. الآن اليوم الثالث، خذ بعض الماء المقدس، ومكافح الآفات، ومبيد الحشرات معك. قبل البدء قل لكل الجن أنك ستقوم برش مكافح الآفات ، وقاتل الحشرات، والماء المقدس لتنظيف المنزل. و قل لهم أن يذهبوا خارج البيت، خلال عملية الرش، إذا أرادوا ذلك. قم برش كل شيء ، قم برش رذاذ الماء المقدس داخل المنزل فقط ، بشكل صحيح في كل ركن من المنزل. لا تقم برش أي ماء مقدس خارج المنزل. و أقترح أن تترك الأنوار مضاءة. إذهب إلى هناك لبضع ساعات لمدة عشرة أيام قادمة علي الأقل. وتحدث مع الجن كل يوم، وأخبرهم أنك ستنتقل إلي هذا البيت. وأنه لن يكون لديك أي مشكلة إذا أراد الجن أن يعيشوا في زوايا قليلة من المنزل.

قبل البدء في رش الماء المقدس، قل للجن أنك سترش الماء المقدس. قم برش رذاذ الماء المقدس في الأيام العشرة المقبلة كل يوم، و خلال كل هذا، وبسبب الماء المقدس، سيختفي الشر والجن من منزلك. حافظ على رش قاتل الحشرات كل يوم، بمجرد أن تزول الحشرات، سيزول الجن الموجودون معها أيضاً. إشعر بالراحة، فسوف يكون هناك نوع عادي من الجن من حولك. سيعاني أطفالك أفراد العائلة قليلاً من الكوابيس في الأيام القليلة الأولى، ولكنك ستحتاج إلى الحفاظ على رش الماء المقدس مرتين في اليوم في كل مكان في المنزل. قم برش رذاذ الماء المقدس على وجهه و رأس وعنق و أذني جميع أفراد الأسرة. وسيستسلم الجن في غضون أيام قليلة،و بهذه الطريقة، لن يكون لديك مشكلة مع الجن طوال حياتك. وسوف يتأقلمون مع عائلتك قريباً.

Demons do not plan anything to scare us or how to increase our level of fear. Demons just read our minds. Once demons figure out that we are looking here and there, if possibly we see any ghost a scary dead body walking behind us or any ghost watching us from trees, etc., demons figure out we are a very enjoyable for them, they come behind us all the way to our house and somehow make room for their stay around us. You will learn, during these kinds of experiences, you will observe or see nonstop series of nightmares. So simple formulas will make you more scared and harassed, demons will care and harass you more and more.

If you reject them, they will quit harassing and scaring and may be they will leave you alone pretty soon. Demons are around us or around human bodies before us, you never know, how, they want to treat us. But until a demon becomes your friend and decides to behave nicely and gently with you, all demons are the same. Demons consider us as a toy. Demons do not care how much they scare us or make us sick mentally or physically.

They are just busy enjoying when we get scared, harassed, or sick. Now do you think it is a good idea to train these demons, more and more, and give them more and more ideas, how possibly, demons can scare us more and more? Sixty years ago, we did not have many TV channels or horror, evil, and nasty movies. But now there are countless horror, evil, and killer movies. We are scared of those nasty evil moves but you never know, may be you are just watching and those nasty horror and evil movies under the pressure of demons around you.

لا تحاول أبداً إفتعال إشتباك أو محاولة إيذاء الجن. أما فيما يتعلق برش الماء المقدس، ذلك لمجرد الحفاظ على سلامتك، ولذا فإنني لا يمكنني المساعدة في ذلك. يجب علي الجن أن يتحملوا. لا يمكننا قتل الجن. إنهم أجسام كهرومغناطيسية. هيكلها مجرد إشارات إلكترونية. الماء المقدس هو بمثابة حل لهم. هذا هو السلاح الوحيد لدينا لصد الجن عن جسمنا وعن منزلنا. لا يمكنن قتا ل الجن، فعددهم الكثيف و قواهم أكبر من إمكانية تعاملنا معها بمجرد أن يقر الجن أن يكونوا ضد شخص ما، فإنهم يحدثون له سلسلة من المشاكل والصراعات لنا بدون توقف في كل مكان لذلك بدلاً من السعي وراء هذه الطريقة، سوف نحاول أن نجعلهم أصدقاء. سأكتب عدة إجراءات حول كيفية جعل الجن أصدقائك في وقت لاحق في هذا الكتاب. لذلك عندما يقول الناس بعض الأماكن يحالفهم الحظ فيها، بينما لا يحالفهم الحظ في أماكن قليلة، هؤلاء الجن هم السبب الرئيسي لذلك. إذا كانت هذه الجن يعملون لصالح شخص ما، فإنهم يقومون بمساعدته طوال الوقت، و فتح أبواب جديدة للنجاح له، و يزيلون العوائق من طريقه عن طريق تنويم أصدقائه و أعدائه مغناطيسياً. بمجرد أن يعمل الجن الخاص في صالحك، يفعلون كل ما يمكنهم لجعلك شخصاً ناجحاً. مهما فعلت، و أينما ذهبت، الجميع وكل شيء جيد سيكون في صالحك. الآن بنفس الطريقة إذا لم يكن الجن سعداء بك، ثق بي، أينما ذهبت و مهما فعلت، سيجلب لك هؤلاء الجن كل عقبة ممكنة في طريقك. سأقول لماذا تقاتلهم. لماذا لا تجعلهم فقط أصدقائك، عندما يكون ذلك من السهل جداً وليس مستحيلاً. سيحاول الجن أن يظهروا لك أشباح في جميع أنحاء المنزل، وحول الأشجار، و أكثر الخدع شيوعاً، هي أنك سترى شبح أو صورة فقط في مكان ما حولك .

SEE & CONTROL DEMONS & PAIN	رضوان قرشي

Now you have two choices to avoid this situation. One is to reject these horror and evil movies. Once nobody watches these movies, nobody will make or produce these movies. Second way is to train yourself and 100 percent understand the actions of demons of showing us nightmares and scare us and reject all those nightmares, seeing dreams and scary thoughts usually demons feed in our mind to enjoy from our situations.

I still believe it is not a good idea to watch horror and evil movies. These movies train demons around us to make the life hell for people with weak hearts and cowards by showing them nightmares. I am not a brave person either, but concept and awareness of demons and their actions is very clear. That's why I am still scared of a dog or any other wild animals, but not scared of demons anymore. You may ask me why? Because I know a demon will not or cannot bite me but a dog can. As far as demons can hurt us by making us physically sick or mentally sick, to avoid this, we should need to make all these demons around us our friends. Once demons become friends, they do not hurt their friends. My case is totally opposite; any wild animal or reptile can make me scared very easily, but demons, even if they try, cannot make me scared, because they pretend, they are bad and ugly looking big ghosts, but they are not.

So you need to understand this and quit getting scared of them. If, you will understand my physiology and guide lines, very soon you will not be scared of demons any more.

يتظاهر الشبح بالإختباء في مكان بمجرد أن يراك. حتى لو ذهبت وراء تلك الصورة أو الشبح، فإنك لن تجد أي شيء في أي مكان. حتى لو كنت جريئاً حقاً وتطلب من تلك الصور أو الشبح أن يأتوا أمامك، فإنهم لن يفعلوا ذلك. أو حتى في بعض الأحيان، تراهم من مسافة ينتقلون من هنا إلى هناك، لكنهم لن يأتوا أمامك وجهاً لوجه. الآن يجب أن تعرف كل ما يحدث بينك وبين الجني الذي يسيطر علي عقلك. الجن يرسلون باستمرار إشارات إلكترونية إلي عقلك ليونوموك مغناطيسياً. الآن هناك إحتمالان. إذا كان الجني قوي جداً جداً، وإذا عقلك ليس قوي جداً في الحقيقة، في كلتا الحالتين سوف تكون قادراً على رؤية تلك الصور أو الأشباح بسهولة جداً.

الآن الأمر في يدك، إفهم الجن و تنويمهم المغناطيسي، و قم برش الماء المقدس على نفسك وحولك وعلاج هذه المشكلة من حولك أو تظل خائفاً أنت وعائلتك وتجعل حياتك جحيماً هذا هو مجرد تفكير منطقي سليم. إذا كان هناك أي شبح حقاً، لماذا لا يهاجمك ذلك الشبح فقط و يقتلك؟ إذا كنت تعرف مسبقاً، أن الجن يريد ون تخويفك بحيث يجعلوك تترك ذلك المنزل.

هذا كل ما يمكنهم القيام به. يظهرون لك الكوابيس أثناء النوم، كما يظهرون لك ويضايقونك بإظهار لك صور لأشباح تمشي و تختبئ، وتجعلك مريضا جسدياً ولكن إذا كنت ترش رذاذ الماء المقدس على نفسك، هذا الماء المقدس سيعمل كحل أو يزيل المجال الكهرومغناطيسي حول الجن. هذه المياه المقدسة ستؤثر علي الجن، بشكل مشابه لما يفعله الماء بمجرد رشه على دائرة إلكترونية نشطة.

مرة أخرى تلك الأشباح هي مجرد خيال وهمي التي أحدثه الجن من حولنا فقط لمضايتنا معظم الوقت. انهم لا يستطيعون القيام بأكثر من هذا. لذا يرجى الإسترخاء والهدوء.

Have you ever heard from someone that that place was lucky for me or that place was unlucky for me? Same way, once someone gets married or gets engaged with each other, their luck or life either improves or sometimes gets worse. Then they usually say that they were not lucky for each other. These are very simple examples of the conflicts created by demons. First example about house/office/business let me try to explain. No doubt when no one lives at some vacant places for long, long times, places with no lights, places stay dark most of the time, the same way if in a big house and just a few people live there, and most of the house is usually not in use, and most of the rooms stay dark most of the time, these kinds of places are heaven for the demons.

Once demons have complete possession of a place like this, trust me it will be very difficult for demons to get adjusted; if someone or any family decides to use that house and start living there. As compared to a normal house, which is already in use in a regularway, demons in those houses usually adjust themselves according to the people and space in that house. Not only this. Those demons are usually very attached with the family members in those houses. But longtime vacant houses or places or rooms in a houses, not in use for long time or least in use or stay dark all the time, usually demons occupy those kind of houses and places immediately and completely. There is no way, if you think, those demons in that house will adjust immediately once you decide to move in that house. Even if a demon doctor offers you help, still I strongly think it is not a good idea just move in that vacant house in rush or immediately.

كل شخص لديه مجموعة من الجن من حوله، بمجرد أن يخطب الرجل المرأة أو يتزوجها، عادة عندما ينتقل الناس من مكان ما إلى بيت آخر ، يرتبط الجن الموجودون حول هؤلاء الناس بهم حقاً ويحاولون الإنتقال معهم أيضاً في المنزل الجديد. الآن هذا الزواج الجديد أو الخطبة تجمع بين اثنين من الجن مختلفين من مختلف القبائل والجماعات معا. فإذا تأقلم كلا الفريقين من الجن مع بعضها البعض، ستكون الحياة جيدة. سوف يقوم الجن من كلا الجانبين بمساعدة ودعم ال و الرجل و المرأة المتزوجين حديثاً، في جعل حياتهما ناجحة. وسيكون حظهم جيد، حتى الرجل و المرأة سيكونان بخير مع بعضها البعض، ولكن إذا كان الجن من كلا الجانبين يتقاتلان مع بعضها البعض، هذا يعني أن الجن من كلا الجانبين سوف يبذلان كل جهد ممكن لإحداث صراعات و مشاكل لا توقف بين الرجل والمرأة بواسطة لتنويمهما مغناطيسياً أو تضليلهما ضد بعضهما. وسوف يفعل الجن كل شيء لتدمير العلاقة بين ذلك الرجل والمرأة. لماذا يحدث هذا؟ لأن هؤلاء الجن يسيطرون عليك، و سوف يقررون من الذي يمكن أن تعيش معه، و من الذي لا يستطيع. أن يعيش معك. إذا كنت لا تريدهم أن يسيطروا على حياتك، لا تبقي الجن في جسمك أو منزلك. بمجرد أن يذهب هؤلاء الجن، قد يأتي إليك جني جديد قريباً، على الأقل ، وسوف تستطيع الحفاظ على زواجك.

أنا متأكد أنك سيكون لديك بعض القضايا الجديدة مع الجن الجدد أيضاً. يمكنك أن تقرر بشأنهم أيضاً. إذا كان هؤلاء الجن الجدد يريدون البقاء حولك، يجب عليهم أن يكونوا داعمين لك ويساعدوك، وإلا أنا لا أقول أن الجن دائماً مخطئون. ويمكن للجن رؤية ما لانستطيع أن سماعه او رؤيته. إذا كان لديك جني من حولك منذ طفولتك، أنا متأكد من أنه ينبغي أن يكون مخلصاً جداً ومتعلقاً بك.

رضوان قرشي

The best idea and good policy is to move into houses like this, step by step and take some time to move instead of moving in in one day. I feel if demons in that house are not really, really bad and evil, may be they will adjust with time, if you move in that house in steps and talk to them also. The reason why I am trying to guide you to the right direction is that you may know about yourself but you never know if your kids start facing few problems or someone else in the family.

الآن بطريقة ما إذا إكتشف الجني الخاص بك أي شيء خاطئ خاص بزوجك، مثل الخيانة أو عدم الإخلاص أو أي شيء مماثل، سوف يبدأ الجني الخاص بك في العمل ضد زوجك أيضاً. حظاً سعيداً، ومرحباً بك في عالم الجن. إذا كنت لا تزال ترغب في تغيير أي شيء في حياتك الخاصة، فقط إستخدم إجراءاتي وقم بإرسال الجني الخاص بك لشخص آخر.

بمجرد أن يصبح الجن أصدقائك، عادة ما تكون على إستعداد أن يتبعوك ويطيعوك طوال الوقت. حتى أن الجن الخاص سيطيعون شخص ما إذا طلبت منه القيام بذلك. إنهم يكونون لطفاء و مطيعون للغاية بمجرد أن يصبحوا أصدقائك، إن صداقة الجن صداقة نقية 100 في المئة. تذكر أن الجن الخاص بك متعلق بك كثيراً، إنهم لن يريدوا أن يتركوك أبداً، ولكن إذا كنت أصررت، و قمت بدفعهم إلي الذهاب والعيش مع شخص آخر وإطاعته، سوف يقومون بذلك.نصيحتي لك ألا تعطي أصدقائك من الجن المخلصين لك لأي شخص آخر.

No doubt, demons are master mind, once they want to hurt someone or ready to play with someone. So I think you need to move your stuff in that house first. Start going there just for few hours. Do not take any kids or women with you. First switch on all the lights inside and outside the house. Go to each and every room, tree, and corner of the house. Be confident. Always remember all demons are watching you and listening to you. Start talking to demons in each and every room.

أنا لا أحبذ تدريب الجن علي القيام بأعمال سيئة أو غير قانونية أو منافية للأخلاق. الجن هم 100 في المئة مخلوقات سلبية خارقة للطبيعة. إذا واصلت مطالبة الجن ببذل المزيد والمزيد من الأعمال القذرة، والشريرة، والسيئة، هذا يعني أنك مسؤول عن تحويلهم إلى شيطان و جني شرير. ماذا عن أنك بدلاً من أن تطلب منهم أن يفعلوا أشياء سيئة وشريرة، تدريبهم على القيام بأشياء جيدة؟. إن الجني الواحد الذي حولك هو دائماً جزء من مجموعة كبيرة أو قبيلة من الجن. فإذا كنت تدرب جني واحد فقط، و تحوله هذا إلي جني جيد، فإن تدريبك سيذهب إلي كامل مجموعة الجن. هكذا يمكنك إستخدام الجن الطيب الخاص بك للمساعدة وإصلاح الكثير من الأشياء السيئة والشريرة من حولك. على سبيل المثال، إذا كان هناك شخص ما مدمناً للكحول أو المخدرات،

Tell them clearly that you rent or bought this house, and that you do not want to fight with any demon; you do not have any other place to live, you will be okay if these demons will live in different areas of your house. Tell demons where you want them to stay most of the time. Things like this, whatever you say; all demons will be listening to you. Now the third day, take some holy water, pest control, and insect killer with you. Before you start tell all the demons that you are spraying pest control, insect killer, and holy water to clean the house. Tell demons if they want, during that spray they can go outside from the house. Spray everything and last spray holy water only inside the house, very properly in each and every corner of the house. Do not spray any holy water outside the house. I will suggest leave lights on. At least go there for a few hours the next ten days. Every day, talk to demons and inform them that you are moving in this house. And you do not have any problem if demons want to live in few corners of the house. Before you start spraying holy water, tell demons that you are going to spray holy water. Spray holy water for the next ten days every day. During all this, due to holy water, evil and devil kind of demons will be gone from your house. Keep spraying insect killers every day; once insects will be gone, their demons will go with them too. Rest, you will have normal kind of demons around you. First few days your kids and family members will suffer a little bit with the nightmares. But you need to keep spraying holy water twice a day everywhere in the house. Spray holy water on all family members' face, head, neck, ears. Those demons will give up in a few days. This way, you will not have a lifetime problem with demons. They will adjust with your family soon.

يستطع الجني الخاص بك إصلاح الشخص و الجن الموجودون حوله على حد سواء هؤلاء الجن الذين كانوا مسؤولون عن جعل ذلك الشخص مدمناً للكحول. الجن هم بالفعل أشرار والشياطين.

لذلك قم فقط بتدريبهم علي أن يصبحوا طيبين، و هكذا يمكنك إستخدام الجن الطيب الخاص بك لتحويل الكثير جداً من الجن إلى أن يصبحوا طيبين أيضاً. أنا أعلم، أنه يجب أن تعرف أنه من السهل جداً أن تكون سيئ و شرير. من الصعب أن تصبح طيباً، وخاصة بالنسبة للجن. أعرف مسبقاً أنه يمكنك أن تحول الشر الجني الشرير إلي جني طيب. لماذا؟ إلى أي مدى وإلى متى يمكن أن تذهب لشخص ما سيئة والشر؟ إلي أي مد، و كم ستغرق من الوقت أن يصل الشخص إلي ذروة السوء و الشر؟.سيأتي الوقت الي يصل فيه إلي ذروة الشر و السوء. السوء و الشر لا حدود لهما أنت لا تعرف أبداً، ربما كان الجني الخاص بك مستعد ليصبح جني طيب أيضاً. و ربما تعب بالفعل من جعل الناس مرضى، وجعل الناس يخافون، إلخ... لقد رأينا عدد لا يحصى من الناس لهم عادات سيئة للغاية مثل تعاطي المخدرات والكحول والسرقة والقتل وغير ذلك، وفجأة تغيرت حياتهم. فجأة و في غضون بضعة أيام تغيروا بنسبة 100 في المئة، وأصبحوا حقاً طيبون و متدينون.

لقد حدث شيئان من حولهم. الأول أنهم لا يزال لديهم إرادة لأن يصبحوا طيبين، والثاني أنهم بطريقة ما خرجوا من سيطرة الجني الشيطان، الذي كان مسؤولا عن كون الناس أشخاص سيئون بنسبة 99 في المئة. هؤلاء الجن الشريرون والشياطين هم المسؤولون أساساً عن نشر أو تغذية كل العادات السيئة والشريرة مثل تعاطي المخدرات، ونشر المخدرات والكحول والقتل والغش والتطرف والسلبية.

Do not ever try to pick a fight or try to hurt demons. As far as spraying holy water, it is just for your safety, so I cannot help with that. Demons need to tolerate that. We cannot kill demons. Their structure is just electronic signals. Holy water is just like a solution for them. This is the only weapon we have to repel demons from our body and from our house. We cannot fight with demons. Their population and powers are too much for us to handle. Once demons decide to go against someone, they can keep creating a series of nonstop problems and conflicts for us everywhere. So instead of going that way, we will try to make them friends. I will write several procedures on how to make demons your friends later on in this book. So when people say some places are lucky for them and few places are unlucky for them, these demons are the main cause for that. If these demons are in favor of someone, demons help those people all the time. Open new doors of success for them. Remove obstacles from their ways by hypnotizing their friends and enemies. Once your demons are in your favor, they do every possible thing to make you a successful person.Whatever you do, wherever you go, everybody and everything is good and in your favor. Now the same way if demons are not happy with you, trust me wherever you go whatever you do, these demons will bring every possible obstacle in your way. I will say why fight with them. Why not just make them your friends, when it is very easy and not impossible. Demons will try to show you walking ghosts all over the house, around the trees; the most common trick is that you will see a ghost or just an image somewhere around you. That ghost will pretend to hide somewhere once he sees you. Even if you will go behind that image or ghost, you will not find anything anywhere.

الجن لديهم إرادة حرة أيضاً مثلنا، فهم أحرار في إختيار الجيد أو السيئ، كل ما يعتقدون أنه يعمل من أجلهم. لدينا ميزة واحدة، و هي أن الجن ليسوا موحدين. الشياطين. بمجرد أن يحد الجن ويتخذون قراراً بإنهاء البشر / الحيوانات / الطيور / الزواحف / الحشرات / الأشجار من هذه الأرض، فلن يستغرق ذلك سوى يوم واحد. لم يخلق الجن من دم ولحم مثلنا أو مثل المخلوقات الحية الأخرى على هذه الأرض. الجن لديهم مقاومة ضد الإشعاع. و لكن ليس لدينا مقاومة ضد الإشعاع. الشياطين ليس لديهم مقاومة ضد الإشعاع الخارج من الصلاة المقدسة والكلمات المقدسة. ولكن هذه الإشعاعات من الكلمات المقدسة والصلوات المقدسة هي فقط للمساعدة والتوجيه للكشف أو إكتشاف المواد التي لديها القدرة على صد الجن.

في الأرض.، المياه المقدسة هي أداة أساسية تستخدم ضدهم بالتأكيد، ولكن هذا لا يكفي. إنهم يحتاجون إلى المزيد من القوة. منذ اليوم الأول، كان العلم الحديث يعمل جاهداً للعثور على اليورانيوم والبلوتونيوم، وهما المسؤولان عن نشر الإشعاع في كل أنحاء العالم في أي لحظة ضد البشرية والسلالات الحية الأخرى ولكن ليس الجن.

يستطيع الجن البقاء على قيد الحياة بسهولة جداً في جو مليئ بالإشعاع. في الحقيقة، يستطيع الجن تنشيط أنفسهم بسهولة في هذا النوع من الإشعاع. إذاً، ما الذي نقوم به ضد أنفسنا؟ بقدر ما تعلمت من واقع تجربتي الشخصية، أن الجن يحبون أن يصبحوا أصدقائنا، ون أن يتبعوننا و يطيعوننا. والآن هناك طريقة بأي حال من الأحوال، إذا قرر كل واحد منا تحمل المسؤولية في تغيير جني واحد من كونه شرير إلي جني طيب ولطيف؟. أنا أعرف ، و سأقول لك كيفية القيام بذلك.

Even if you act really bold and ask those images or ghost to come in front of you, they will not. Or even sometimes, you see them from a distance moving from here to there, but they will not come in front of you face-to-face. Now you should know everything which is happening between you and the demon controlling your brain. Demons are continuously sending electronic signals to your brain to hypnotize you. Now there are two possibilities. If the demon is very, very powerful or if your brain is not really too strong, in both cases you will be able to see those images or ghosts very easily.

Now this is in your hand. Understand the demons and their hypnotism and spray holy water on yourself and around you and fix the problem around you or keep scaring yourself and your family and make your life hell. This is just common sense. If there was really any ghost in reality, why not that ghost just attacks you and kills you? If you already know, demons want to scare you so you leave that house.

That's all they can do. Show you nightmares during sleep, and harass you when you are up by showing you walking and hiding images of ghosts, and make you sick physically. But if you just spray holy water on yourself, that holy water will work as a solution or removal of the electromagnetic field around demons. This holy water will affect a demon, the same way water affects an energized electronic circuit once you spray water on top of it. So again those ghosts are just imaginary imagination created by the demons around us just to harass us most of the time. They cannot do more than this. So please relax and calm down.

في وقت لاحق في هذا الكتاب، سوف أكتب عن القليل من الإجراءات التي أنت في حاجة لإستخدامها لجعل الجن أصدقائك. بمجرد أن تبدأ في الحصول على مؤشرات واضحة وإشارات منها رداً من الجن على إتصالاتك بهم؛ من فضلك لا تطلب منهم أو تدفعهم للقيام بأفعال شريرة أو سيئة. سوف يحب الجن أن يفعلوا أشياء سيئة و شريرة لك،لكن بطريقة ما إذا كنت تتصرف بكثير من المسؤولية وبشكل مختلف، و كانت بداية تدريب الجن الخاص بك جيدة بنسبة تقارب100%. لا تتورط بدينك أو دينهم. أنت تحتاج فقط البدء في التواصل معهم، إبدأ في شرح العادات السيئة والأشياء السيئة الواحد تلو الآخر. تم تدريب الجن علي أن يكونوا شياطين أو أشرار أو أبالسة، لكن الجن ليسوا مثل الملائكة. الجن مثلنا، إن لديهم إرادة حرة، و يمكنهم الإختيار أي الإتجاهين، الجيد أو السيئ. لابد أن تشرح لهم العادات الجيدة الواحدة تلو الأخري. لابد أن تشرح لهم كيف أنهم يسيئون إستخدام قواهم لإيذاء وترويع الناس طوال الوقت.

فبدلا من إظهارالكوابيس، يستطيع الجن أن يظهروا لكل شخص أحلام لطيفة و مبهجة حقاً، هذا ليس من الصعب بالنسبة لهم. لن تمر فترة طويلة،و سوف تكون قادراً على تحويل الجن الشرير إلى جن طيب. أنت لا تعرف أبداً، قد تحول مجموعة كاملة من الجن من حولك.

إن فكرة ممارسة الجن الجنس معنا، فكرة مجنونة. الله يعلم من الذي إكتشف أو إخترع هذه الفكرة؟ إن ممارسة الجنس مع جني هو تماما مثل ممارسة الجنس مع عنكبوت صغير أو ذبابة. الجن أنفسهم ليس لديهم أي حياة جنسية. يختلف الجهاز التناسلي لديهم عن الكائنات الحية العادية. الهيكل، والملمس، والنظرات، والحجم، مادة الجسم، الجنس،الوزن والغذاء، ليس هناك شيء مشترك بين الإنسان والجني، فقط إستخدام العقل، والأفكار، والتفكير، والعواطف، والإستراتيجية، و الذكاء، والغضب، والمشاعر، والمتعة والحزن وغيرها، مماثلة بالضبط.

179

Every person has a group of demons around them. Once a man and woman get married or get engaged, usually when people move from one place to another house, their demons are really attached to them and try to move with them also in the new house. Now this new marriage or engagement brings two different demons from two different tribes or groups together. So if the demons of both groups adjust with each other, life will be good. Demons of both sides will help and support the newly married man and woman to make their life successful. This will be their good luck, even the man and the woman are okay with each other, but if demons of the both sides start fighting with each other, it means demons from both sides will do each and every effort to create nonstop conflicts and problems between man and woman by hypnotizing them or misguiding them against each other. Demons will do everything to destroy the relationship between that man and the woman. Why is this happening? Because these demons have your possession. Now these demons will decide with whom you can live or with whom you cannot. So if you do not want them to control your life, do not keep these demons in your body or house. Once these demons will go away, you may get new one soon, at least, you will be able to maintain your marriage.

I am sure you will have some new issues with new demons too. You can decide about them too. So if those new demons want to stay around you, they need to be supportive and helpful; otherwise,I am not saying, demons are always wrong. Demons can see whatever we cannot hear and see. So if you really have a demon around you since your childhood, I am sure that demon should be very sincere and attached to you.

بالنسبة للشكل، يختلف شكل الجن كثيراً عن الإنسان بقدر إختلاف شكل العنكبوت بالمقارنة بشكل الإنسان. ولكن استخدام العقل يكون مثل الإنسان، والعادات كذلك، حتى ولو كانوا يعيشون في جماعة، لا يزال نظام الإنجاب يختلف عن البشر. ليس لدي الجن أي شريك جنسي أو حياة جنسية، فهم لا ينقسمون إلى جنسين.لا يوجد أي تفضيل أو خيار خاص أي جني سوف يذهب إلى امرأة لامتلاك جسدها وعقلها،و أي جني سيذهب الى رجل ليمتلك جسده. نظرا لقدرة العقل المماثلة، ومستوى الذكاء، والعواطف، يعيش الجن ويستمتعون بحياتهم المادية في أجسامنا بما في ذلك أجسام الحيوانات والطيور وغير ذلك وهذا ليس قرارهم، إنهم مخلوقون لنفس الغرض. إذا لم يكن هناك حن من حولنا. أقول أننا سنتتصرف مثل الملائكة بنسبة 50 في المئة . إنه موضوع سيئ، لكن إسمح لي أن أشرح. الجن ليس لديهم أي شريك جنسي أو جهازأو جسم لهذا الغرض، ولكن عقولهم، و رغباتهم، و أمانيهم، وعاداتهم مثلنا تماماً أو أقول أكثر تحمساً منا. يستحوذ الجن علي أجساد البشر أثناء النشاط الجنسي، كما يستحوذ عليه أثناء شرب الكحول أو تعاطي المخدرات. هذه هي لعنة الجن. إنهم يعتمدون على أجسامنا للتمتع برغباتهم وأمانيهم. إنهم لا يستطيعون شرب الكحول، و لا يستطيعون القيام بأي نشاط جنسي و لا يستطيعون عمل الكثير من الأشياء الأخرى مثل الكراهية أو الحب مع بعضهم البعض. لكنهم مهيئون ليكون لديهم كل هذه الأمنيات والرغبات. لذلك كان يجب علي الجن إستخدام أجسامنا من أجل الإستمتاع بحياتهم و تحقيق رغباتهم، لأنهم شركائنا في جميع الأنشطة الممتعة، و هذا هو السبب في أنهم يدفعونا بإستمرار إلى الإنخراط أكثر وأكثر في هذه الأنشطة، حتى لو كان الكثير من العادات سيئة. بالنسبة للنشاط الجنسي، لا يقوم الجن بأي نشاط جنسي معنا أو مع أي حيوان آخر.....

Rizwan Qureshi

Now somehow if your demons find out anything wrong about your husband, like cheating or insincere or anything similar, your demon will start working against your husband too. Good luck. Welcome to the demons' world. If you still do not want to change anything in your life, just use my procedures and send your demon to someone else.

Once demons become your friends, usually they are ready to follow and obey you all the time. Even your demons will obey someone else if you ask them to do that. They are extremely nice and obedient once they become your friend. Demon's friendship is 100 percent pure. Remember, you are sincere and demons are too much attached to you, they do not want to leave you ever, but if you will insist and push them to go and live and obey someone else, they will. My advice to you, do not give your sincere demons friends to anyone else.

I will prcfcr not to train dcmons to do bad or illegal or below ethics things. Demons are 100 percent negative supernatural creatures. They love to do bad and evil things. If you will keep asking those demons to do more and more dirty, evil, and bad things, it means you are responsible for turning them to a devil and evil demon. What about instead of asking them to do bad and evil things, train them to do good stuff? One single demon around you is always a part of a very big group or tribe of the demons. If you just train one demon and convert that demon to a good demon, your training will go to whole group of that demon. Then you can use your good demon to help and fix a lot of bad and evil things around you.

رؤية الجن و الآلام السيطرة عليها

إنهم فقط يستحوون علي كلا الشريكين، بغض النظر عن هويتهما. بمجرد أن يستحوذ الجن علي أجسامنا، سيصبحون جزء من جسمنا. أيا كان، ما نستمتع به، سوف يحصل الجن على نفس النوع من مشاعر المتعة خلال أي نشاط بدني. هذا عكس إشارات الحلم. تماماً، فالجن يرسلون إشارات أو رسائل إلى عقولنا ليظهروا لنا الأحلام. إذا كنت عكست ذلك، و إستوعبت أو إستقبلت الإشارات أو الرسائل من عقولنا، سنستمتع، ونشعر بإحساس الأنشطة الجسدية والعقلية التي نقوم بها، تحت تأثير التنويم المغناطيسي الذي يقومون به. أقصى ما يمكن أن يفعله الجني بالنسبة للنشاط الجنسي مع الإنسان من خلال جلب شريك جنسي واقعي في حلم ذلك الإنسان بالذات.

خلال الأحلام، لا يمكن لأحد معرفة ما إذا كان ذلك حقيقية أم حلم، إذاً هذا هو أقصى ما يمكن للجن القيام به لتحقيق رغباتهم و أمانيهم. لذا الرجاء التوقف عن مضايقة نفسك، فليس هناك شيطا أي جني يمكن أن يأتي إليك في أي شكل، و يؤذيك لمجرد إرضاء نفسه. انا لا أقول أن الجن لا يريدون ذلك. أنا أقول أنهم غير قادرون على القيام بذلك. لا تبالي بالأمر و إستمر في رش الماء المقدس في كل مكان للإبقائهم بعيداً عنك عندما تكون مستيقظاً. أنا آسف أنه لا توجد وسيلة، تنقذك منهم بمجرد أن تنام. الآن أعود إلي موضوع سابق عندما كنت أناقش كيف يمكن لشخص سيء للغاية أن يتحول إلى شخص جيد جداً ومتدين. الشخص السيئ يشارك في عادات سيئة وغير صحية بسبب تأثير و سيطرة الجن الأشرار للغاية والشياطين. هؤلاء الجن لا يتهمون إذا كان تأثيرهم السيئ يدفع شخص ما نحو تدهور حقيقي في الصحة، وأخيرا إلى الموت. مجموعة الجن الطيبون والصالحون من يبقون دائما حول الإنسان الطيب و الصالح للغاية . الآن إذا حدث بالصدفة، أن شخصا سيئاً حصل على فرصة للبقاء حول شخص طيب و صالح لبعض الوقت، لو بالصدفة قرر جني طيب واحد التغلب على جميع الجن الشياطين ويستحوذ...

For example, if someone is alcoholic or drug addicted, your demon can fix both human and their demons responsible for making him alcoholic. Demons are already evil and devils. So just train them to turn to be good. Then you can use your good demons to convert so many demons to be good too. I know and you should know that it is very easy to be bad and evil. To become good, it is difficult especially for demons. I already know that you can convert an evil demon to a good demon. Why? How far and for how long someone can go for bad and evil? Time will come when a person or a demon will reach at the peak of evil and bad. Bad and evil has a limit. So you never know; maybe your demon is ready to become a good demon too. Maybe your demon is already tired of making people sick, making people scared, etc. We all have seen uncountable people with extremely bad habits like using drugs, alcohol, stealing, killing, etc., and suddenly their life is changed. Suddenly within a few days they are changed 100 percent and became really good and religious. Two things happened around them. One they still have the will of becoming good, second somehow they come out from the possession of that devil demon, who was 99 percent responsible for them being bad people. These evil and devil demons are mainly responsible for spreading or feeding all bad and evil habits like use of drugs, spreading drugs, alcohol, killing, cheating, extremism, and negativism. Like us, demons have free will too. Demons are free to choose good or bad, whatever they think works for them. We only have one advantage that demons are not united. Once demons get united and decide to finish humans /animals /birds / reptiles/insects/trees from this earth, it will take only one day.

على جسد شخص سيئ، وهكذا سيكون جني واحد قادراً على تغيير العادات السيئة لذلك الشخص في غضون يوم واحد عن طريق إستخدام التنويم المغناطيسي. العادات الحسنة والعمل الصالح معدية أيضاً. إذا كان الأمر كذلك بطريقة ما قمت بتحويل جني واحد فقط إلى جني طيب، فإنك لا تعرف إلي أي مدى ستذهب رسالتك. سيكون جني واحد قمت بتدريبه قادراً على التوجيه في الإتجاه الصحيح، لا يمكن أن تعرف كم من البشر وكم من الشياطين سيقوم بتوجيهم.

كل جني لديه معرفة مختلفة. لذلك لا أستطيع أن أعتمد على جن قليلون فقط أو جن من بلد معين. لهذا السبب، سحبت أو دعوت جن من مناطق مختلفة من العالم. وهذه الزيارات من الجن من هنا وهناك لا تتوقف أبداً طالما بقيت على قيد الحياة.

هؤلاء الجن، بغض النظر عما إذا كانوا أشرار أو طيبين، يجلبون جميع أنواع من المعلومات فذهني متزامن مع عقولهم طوال الوقت. إنهم يساعدوني طول الوقت للحصول على المزيد والمزيد من المعلومات منهم. إذا لم أكن مقتنعا بشيء ما، فإنهم يشرحونه لي حتى أفهم وجهة نظرهم. أنا لا أعرف قدر المعلومات التي سوف أحصل عليها منهم في المستقبل، لكنني لا أعرف ما إذا كنت سوف أستطيع كتابة كتاباً آخر بسهولة، بعد الكتاب القادم. هذا هو السبب في أنني سوف أحاول أن أضع تفاصيل أكثر وأكثر في هذا الكتاب وفي الكتاب القادم. في الواقع، هذه الرسالة هي للجن الموجودين حولك، حتى يتمكنوا من الإتصال بي أيض.

بمجرد تمرير الأمر إلى أصدقائك من الجن، قد تضطر إلى تذكيرهم من وقت لآخر إذا كان هناك شيء مهم جداً بالنسبة لك. عادة، تحتاج لتذكيرهم من وقت لآخر قبل أن يتباطأوا بعد ثلاثة أيام.، الأشياء الحقيقية المهمة، تحتاج إلى تذكيرهم في كثير من الأحيان.

Demons are not made of blood and meat like us or other living creatures on this earth. Demons have resistance against radiation. We do not have resistance against radiation. Demons do not have resistance against the radiation coming out from holy prayers and holy words. But those radiations of holy words and holy prayers are just to help and guideline to detect or discover substances on this earth that have the capability of repelling demons. Definitely, holy water is a basic tool to use against them, but it is not enough. It needs more strength. Since the very first day, modern science has been working hard to find uranium and plutonium, which is responsible for spreading radiation all over the world any second against human and other living breeds but not demons.

Demons can very easily survive in the atmosphere full of radiation. In actual, demons can energize themselves easily in that kind of radiation. So what are we doing against ourselves? As much as I learn from my personal experiences, demons love to become our friends. Demons love to follow and obey us. Now is there any way, if every one of us decides to take responsibility of changing one demon from evil to be a good and nice demon?. I know and I will tell you how to do it. Later in this book, I will write a few procedures; you need to use them to make demons your friends. Once you start getting clear indications and signals from them in response to your communications with demons; please do not ask or push them to do evil or bad stuff. Demons will love to do bad and evil stuff for you, but if somehow you act a little more responsible and different, and from very beginning of training your demon approximately 100 percent good., do not get involved with your or their religion..

رؤية الجن و الآلام السيطرة عليها

يمكنك كتابة بعض التفاصيل على قطعة من الورق و تعلقها في الغرفة التي تعتقد أنهم عدداً فيها أو يسكنون بها أكثر.

لا تقلق أبداً من ذلك، في المقابل سيكون لديك أي شيء تفعله للجن بمجرد أن تطلب منهم فعل أشياء لك طوال الوقت. ثق بي، أنت لست بحاجة للقيام بأي شيء من أجلهم. سيكون هذا كافياً لهم بمجرد أن تصبح صديقهم. شيء آخر هو أن كل ما يريدونه هو عادة ما يرغبون في الإستحواذ علي جسم إنسان أثناء ممارسة مختلف الأنشطة البدنية أو وقتما يريدون. و هكذا فهم يحصلون بالفعل علي أكثر من كفايتهم.

إذا كان يجب إستخدام الجن في فعل شيئاً سيئاً حقاً، سأقول لك لا تستخدم الجن الخاص بك لأنك ستعرضه للخطر. إذا كنت حقاً بحاجة إلى فعل شيء شرير ضد شخص ما، ث أقترح عليك أن تذهب إلى مقبرة أو مدفن. إبحث عن شجرة وسط المقبرة أو المدفن، و قم بتعليق تعليماتك المكتوبة بخط اليد في مكان ما على الشجرة، و قم بإستدعاء الجن الموجودين في جميع أنحاء المقبرة ما لا يقل عن ست مرات، قل لهم كل ما تريد. أنت بحاجة للذهاب إلى هناك ما لا يقل عن ست مرات في نفس الوقت كل يوم، بمجرد أن تكون على إستعداد لترك تلك الشجرة في المقبرة، إترك رطل واحد علي الأرض على الأقل من لحوم البقر لهم.

قل لهم بوضوح: " لقد أتيت بهذا اللحم لكم حتى تستمتعوا بها." أنا متأكد أنك بمجرد أن تغادر المقبرة أو المدفن، بعض الجن سيأتي خلفك، لذلك بمجرد أن تعود إلى سيارتك، قم يرش رذاذ الماء المقدس في كل مكان في السيارة،و علي وجهك، و رقبتك و رأسك و أذنك، و صدرك.

SEE & CONTROL DEMONS & PAIN

You just need to start communication with them, start explaining about bad habits and bad stuff one by one. Demons are trained to be devils or evil or Satan, but demons are not like angels. Demons are like us. Demons have free will. They can choose either way, good or bad. You need to explain to them good habits one by one. You need to explain to them how all the time they misuse their powers to hurt and scare people. Instead of showing nightmares, demons can show every one really nice and pleasing dream. This is not difficult for them. It will not be a long time, when you will be able to turn an evil demon to a good demon, you never know, you may convert the whole group of demons around you.

This is such a crazy idea or thought that demons do sex with us. God knows who discovered or invented this idea? Doing sex with a demon is just like doing sex with a small spider or a fly. Demons themselves do not have any sex life. Their reproductive system is different from regular living creatures. Structure, texture, looks, size, body material, gender, weight, food, there is nothing common between a human and a demon, only use of brain, thoughts, thinking, emotions, strategy, intelligence, anger, feelings, enjoyments, sadness, etc., are exactly similar. In looks, a demon is as much different from a human as much a spider is different in looks as compared to a human. But the use of brain is the same, habits are the same as human. Even they live in a group; still their reproductive system is different from a human's. Demons do not have any sex life or sex partner. Demons are not divided into two genders. There is no preference or special choice of any demon that which one will go to a woman to possess her body and brain or which one will go to a man to posses his body.

يجب أن تطلب من الجن أن يعودوا للمقبرة، ويستمتعوا بلحم البقر، و يقوموا بالعمل، مهما كان ما تطلب منهم القيام به. قم برش رذاذ الماء المقدس مرات عدة للتأكد من أن هؤلاء الجن عادوا إلى المقبرة. أنت لا تحتاج إلى أن تأتي بهم إلى منزلك.

كل مجموعة من الجن، وحتى مجموعة الجن الموجودين في منزلك،دائماً ما يكون لديها جني يتزعم جماعة أو قبيلة الجن، و عادة ما يكون ذلك الجني هو الأكبر و الأقوى بين جميع الجن في مجموعة معينة. الجن الأقوى عادة ما يبقي حول البشر. عادة ما يبقي بقية الجن أو يعيشون داخل أو حول الأشجار والحيوانات والطيور والزواحف والحشرات، وما إلى ذلك. عادة كل الجن في مجموعة معينة يسمعون و يطيعون زعيم أو قائد الجن.وعادة ما يبقي زعيم الجن حول البشر. الآن عندما تجعل جني صديقك، ينبغي أن يكون الجني الزعيم. إذا بدأ الجني الزعيم الإستماع لك و طاعتك، هذا يعني أن بقية الجن سيستمعون إليك أيضاً. الآن إذا كنت قلدراً على تحويل جني ليكون طيباً وداعما، هذا يعني أن رسالتك بالإتصاف بالطيبة سوف تذهب تلقائياً إلى جميع الجن في تلك المجموعة.

تبحث الآلام دائماً عن بعض المسافة بين عضلاتنا. هذه الآلام تنجح في إيجاد بعض المساحة بجرد إستخدام عضلاتنا بطريقة غير عادية، مثل إذا بدأنا فجأة القيام ببعض التمرينات، أو الركض، أو حمل الأوزان الثقيلة. و بهذه الطريقة تستطيع الآلام العثور علي مساحة قليلة لإختراق داخل عضلاتنا، فإذا فرد شخص ما عضلاته قليلاً أكثر من المعتاد.

Due to same brain capacity, IQ level, and emotions, demons live and enjoy their physical lives in our bodies including the bodies of animals, birds, etc. This is not their decision. They were created for the same purpose. If there is no demons around us. I will say 50 percent of us should be acting like angles. It is a bad topic but still let me explain. Demons do not have any sex partner or system or body for this purpose, but their brain, desires, wishes, and habits are exactly like us or I will say way more excited than us. During the sex activity demons possess the bodies of humans or animals. They also possess their bodies during drinking alcohol or using drugs. This is the curse of demons. They are dependent on our bodies to enjoy their desires and wishes. They cannot drink alcohol; they cannot do any sex and a lot of other stuff like hate or love with each other. But their brain is designed to have all these wishes and desires. So to enjoy their lives and to fulfill their wishes demons have to use our bodies, because they are our partners in all enjoyable activities that's why they continuously push us to get involved more and more in these activities, even if a lot of habits are bad. Now sex activity, demons do not do sex with us or any other animal. They just posses both partners, regardless who they are. Once demons possess our body and then they are part of our body. Whatever, we enjoy a demon will get the same kind of enjoyment feelings during any physical activity. This is just reverse of dream signals. Demons send signals or messages to our brains to show us dreams. If you reverse it, absorb or receive signals or messages from our brains, you'll enjoy, and feel the sensation of physical mental and emotional activities we do, under their hypnotism.

خلال التدريبات هذا يتيح قليل من المساحة للآلام لإختراق ذلك المكان وتبدأ الإقامة هناك، و هذا سيحدث الكثير من الألم وحالة مؤلمة لأي شخص. الآن إذا إستمر الشخص في القيام بالتمرينات أو فرد العضلات، هذه الحركات المستمرة للعضلات تزعج آلام عادةً، و تجعله يترك الجسم في غضون أيام قليلة إذا لم يتم تلف العضلات، أما في حالة تلف العضلات، تبقي الآلام عادة هناك حتى تشفي.

آلالام تريد البقاء في الجسم طوال الوقت، لأن الجو المفتوح لا يجذبها. الآلام مختلفة عن الجن في هذا الصدد، فالجن يبقون في الجو المحيط كثيراً أو قول معظم الوقت من حولنا. بمجرد أن تكون الآلام داخل عضلاتنا، إنهم عادة ما يبحثون عن العصب أو العظم أو المفصل لتتعلق بمصدر للحصول على بعض العصير أو الطعام للحفاظ على نفسها نشيطة.

الأمراض / الحشرات تحتاج إلى التنفس مثلنا، وهذا هو السبب في أن الأمراض / الحشرات تحرك كثيراً داخل وخارج الجسم المصاب. آلام ليست مثل الأمراض / الحشرات.، فهي لا تتنفس مثلنا، إنها تبقى داخل جسمنا أو داخل عضلاتنا أو أعضائنا لمدة غير محددة من الوقت لتتمكن من الإستمرار الحصول على الغذاء أو مصدر للطاقة لتنشيطها. بمجرد أن تخترق الآلام داخل العضلات، فإنها تحاول عادة الذهاب أعمق وأعمق في المفاصل أو الأعضاء، و أثناء ذلك تلحق الآلام الضرر بأعضائنا ومفاصلنا، وأجزاء أخرى من الجسم حقاً. الآلام لا تضرنا لأنها تريد ذلك، لا، فخلال وجودها داخل جسمنا، تتحرك هنا وهناك للحصول على مصدرمن المواد الغذائية أو الطاقة، وخلال هذا البحث تلحق عدد من الأضرار في جسمنا.

185

SEE & CONTROL DEMONS & PAIN

The maximum a demon can do about a sexual activity with a human is by bringing a virtual sex partner in the dream of that particular human. During dreams, nobody can figure out if it is real or a dream, so this is the maximum a demon can do to fulfill their desires and wishes. So please quit harassing yourself; there is no demon can come to you in any shape and hurt you just to please himself. I am not saying that demons do not want to. I am saying they are not capable of doing it. So just take it easy and keep spraying holy water everywhere to keep them away from you when you are up. I am sorry but there is no way, if there is nothing can save you from them once you sleep. Now I am going back to a previous topic when I was discussing how a very bad person turns to a very good and religious person. A bad person was involved in bad and unhealthy habits due to the influence and the possession of extremely evil and devil demons. Those demons do not care if their bad influence is pushing someone toward real bad health and finally to death. Good and righteous group of demons always stay around extremely good and righteous human. Now if by chance that bad person gets a chance to stay around that good and righteous person for some time, if by chance even one single good demon decides to beat all the devil demons and possess the body of a bad person, that one single good demon will be able to change the habits of that bad person within one day by the use of hypnotism. Good habits and good deeds are contagious also. So if somehow you just convert one demon into a good demon, you never know how far your message will go. And one single demon trained by you will be able to guide in right direction you never know how many human and how many demons he will direct. Every demon has a different knowledge.

رضوان قرشي

بمجرد أن يحدث تلف بسيط بسبب هذه الآلام، سيفتح ذلك الأبواب للأمراض / الحشرات أن تأتي داخل جسمنا، وتبدأ في أكل عضائنا وأجزاء من الجسم، و هذا يحدث في نهاية المطاف إلتهابات وسرطان داخل الأجسام. آلام،عادة ما تكون الآلام واحد أو اثنين فقط، 'إنها لا تحتاج إلى الكثير من الطاقة. لكن الآلام هي المسؤولة كلياً عن إحداث أضرار طفيفة جداً داخل الجسم. هذا الضررهو بداية إصابة كبيرة في المستقبل، وسرطان خطير. لا يمكننا قتل الآلام في الوقت الحالي. ولكن في المستقبل القريب،ستستطيع العلوم الطبية أن تتصدها عن أجسامنا بسهولة، بإستخدام بعض نظام الإشعاعات إلكترونياً. إن السبب الرئيسي للإلتهابات الكبيرة والسرطانات هو هذه الأمراض / الحشرات. يمكنك قتل هذه الأمراض والحشرات بسهولة جداً عن طريق إستخدام إجراءات العلاج بمساعدة طبيبك. هذه الآلام تحدث كل أنواع إلتهاب المفاصل،مشاكل المفاصل، وآلام الصداع النصفي فقط عندما يريدون البقاء داخل الجسم وتمتص المواد الغذائية أو الطاقة من أعصابنا، و مفاصلنا، أو أنسجتنا. كلما زادت الطاقة التي يحتاجون إليها، زاد الضرر و نلاحظ مشاعر أكثر إيلاماً.

كانت هذه فكرة سيئة ومخيفة بالنسبة لي وهي سحب بعض الجن من منطقة تحت تهديد الإشعاع.. إنني أقوم بهذا النوع من التجارب المجنونة على نفسي طوال الوقت، لهذا السبب أعتقد في يوم من الأيام سأموت في ثانية خلال هذه التجارب المحفوفة بالمخاطر. على أي حال، كان لابد من التأكد إذا كان البشر لا يمكنهم الذهاب إلي منطقة معينة، بسبب تسرب من مفاعل نووي، لا يمكن للإنسان أن يذهب بدون حماية خاصة، إذا بقي الجن هناك أو يتعرضون للإشعاعات النووية التي تقتلهم ايضاً؟. هذا لن يحدث على الفور فقط . لقد إستغرق الأمر مني بعض الوقت.

186

So I cannot depend on just a few demons or demons from a particular country. For this reason, I was pulling or inviting demons from different areas of the world. These visits of demons from here and there will never stop as long as I live. These demons, regardless of whether they are evil or good, bring all kind of information for me. My brain is 100 percent synchronized with their brains all the time. They help me all the time to get more and more information from them. If I am not convinced about something, they explain it to me until I understand their point of view. I do not know how much more information I will get from them in future, but I do not know if I will write another book easily, after the next book. That's why I will try to put more and more details in this book and next book. Actually, this message is for the demons around you, so they can contact me also.

Once you pass a command to your demon friends, you may have to remind them every now and then. If something is really important for you. Usually, you need to remind them every now and then before they slow down after three days. Real, important stuff, you need to remind them frequently. You can write some details on a piece of paper and hang in the room where you believe they are most in numbers or more populated. Do not ever worry about that; in return you will have to do anything for demons once you ask them to do stuff for you all the time. Trust me; you do not need to do anything for them. This will be enough for them once you become their friend. Another thing is whatever they want is usually they like to possess human body during different physical activities or whenever they want. So they are already getting more than enough.

عندما أنشأت علاقة توارد خواطر مع تلك المناطق لمجرد ثواني. كان عدد وقوة الحن مرتفع جداً في تلك المناطق التي يوجد بها تسرب إشعاعي، لدرجة أنه عمل علاقة توارد خواطر حتى لمجرد بضع ثوان، جلبت حفنة من الحن لي من تلك المناطق. لقد كان الإستشعار، و المظهر والسلوك كذلك، والإستماع، والإتباع، كان كل شيء مماثل لكل شيئ عند الجن من أي منطقة أخرى أو بلد آخر. ولكن أقول أن المعرفة لديهم كانت ذات تقنية عالية جداً. كنت تقرأ الآن، سوف تقرأ المزيد من الأشياء في وقت لاحق في هذا الكتاب، آمل أن نفتح أعيننا ونحن نفعل شيئاً لتأمين العنصر البشري على هذه الأرض. المواد إن المواد النووية والإشعاعية من المصادرالنووية، هي الطاقة الأكثر قوة، التي يستخدمها الجن ليزودا أنفسهم بالطاقة. على الجانب الآخر الإشعاع النووي طاقة غيرمناسبة للجنس البشري. يصبح الجن العادي قوي للغاية ومدمر للعقل و الجسم البشري بمجرد أن ينشط الشيطان نفسه من إشعاع نووي نشط.

أحيانا يكون الجن من حولنا أبرياء جداً لدرجة أنهم لا يستطيعون معرفة ما إذا كنا نرغب/ نتمنى شيء أو أننا سعداء فقط بالوضع ولكن لا نرغب في شيء. في بعض الأحيان تكون درجة إخلاصهم ومساعدتهم كبيرة للغاية حتى أنهم ليس لديهم أدنى فكرة عن أنهم يساعدوننا أو أنهم يحدثون مشاكل لنا. مثال بسيط، إذا كنت في صحة جيدة وليس بك مرض بالصدفة منذ عدة أشهر. بحيث أنك تشعر شعورجيد بسبب ذلك، وإذا قررت أن تخبر أحداً عن ذلك مثل، "لم يحدث لي مرض أو لم أصب بالبرد منذ ستة أشهر". هنا أنت شاكر لأنك ليست مريضاً، لكن لديك الجن الخاص بك سوف يعتقدون أنك نادم و لديك رغبة في أن يحدث لك المرض أو البرد. ليست من الصعب علي الجن فتح الأبواب في جسمنا لهذه الأمراض. لذلك أنت بحاجة لتدريبهم بشكل صحيح حتى يفهموا ما تريده، وما هو جيد بالنسبة لك.

SEE & CONTROL DEMONS & PAIN

If you have to use demons to do something really bad, I will say do not use your demons because you may put them in danger. If you really need to do something evil against someone then I will suggest you to go to a graveyard or cemetery, find a tree in the middle of the graveyard or cemetery. Hang your handwritten instructions somewhere on the tree. At least six times call the demons around in the graveyard and tell them whatever you want. You need to go there at least six times at the same time every day. Once you're ready to leave from that tree in the graveyard, leave at least one pound ground beef for them.

Tell them clearly, "I bring this beef for you so you can enjoy it." I am sure once you leave from graveyard or cemetery some of the demons will come behind you. So once you come back to your car, spray holy water everywhere in your car, your face, neck, head, ear, and chest. You need to tell those graveyard demons to go back, enjoy the beef, and do the work, whatever you ask them to do. Spray holy water several times to make sure those demons go back to the graveyard. You do not need to bring them to your house.Every group of demons, even the group of demons in your house, always has a group leader or a tribe leader demon. Usually that demon is the biggest among all demons and the most powerful demon in a particular group.

Most powerful demons usually stay around humans. The rest of the demons usually stay or live inside or around trees, animals, birds, reptiles, insects, etc. Usually all the demons in a particular group listen and obey the command of a leader demon. Usually leader demons stay around humans. Now when you make a demon your friend, it should be the leader demon.

يمكنك تدريبهم، إذا كنت واثقاً بما فيه الكفاية، ولا تشعر بالخوف منهم، إبداً على الفور. تذكر، أنهم بحاجة إلى التدريب والتوجيه طوال الوقت. إن عقل الجن و عقل الألم مختلفان، و لكن.الشكل يتشابه لكليهما. لإلكهرومغناطيسية على حد سواء. لكن برمجة عقولهما مختلفة.

تمت برمجة عقل الجن على نفس مستوى عقل الإنسان، بالنسبة لمستوى الذكاء،و الأمنيات، والرغبات والتفاهم، أما الآلام، تمت برمجة عقولها على مستوى قتل وأكل الحشرات فقط. آلام ، ليس لديهم أي شعور أو إرتفاع لمستوى الذكاء، وهم يتطلعون فقط لمصدر طاقة، أومكان للعيش داخل الجسم.

لا تعتقد أن كل الجن سعداء بي. ولا شك، أن دائرة أصدقائي من الجن تكبر أكثر و أكثر كل يوم، لكنني أشعر بقوة أن هناك الكثير من الجن والآلام لا يزالون غير راضين عني،.و السبب هو أنني أقوم بسحبهم أو نقلهم من مكان إلى آخر طوال الوقت. أنا واثق من حفنة منهم قد تكون غير سعيدة لأنه كان ربما كانوا غير مستعدين لترك ضحاياهم أو الأجسام الموجودون بها، لكنني أصر على أنهم يقومون بذلك. أنا لا أعرف ماذا يمكنني أن أفعل. إنهم يقومون بفعل أشياء سيئة جداً في المقام الأول عن طريق إيذاء الناس، بالصداع النصفي، إلتهاب المفاصل، وآلام المفاصل وغيرها، حتى لو كنت يمكنني أن أساعدشخص ما، نني إلأشعر لم لا؟ لم يكن لي الكثير من الأصدقاء على أي حال، ولكن بما أنني أعبث مع الجن والآلام، وأطلب منهم مغادرة بعض الأجسام، أشعر أن هؤلاء الجن يبقون ضحاياهم بعيداً عني بقدر الإمكان، عن طريق تنويمهم.

If the leader demon starts listening and starts obeying you, it means the rest of the demons will listen to you also. Now if you will be able to convert a demon to a good and supporting demon, it means your message of being good will automatically go to all demons of that group.

Pains always look for some space between our muscles. These pains get successful to find some room once we use our muscles in an unusual way, like if we suddenly start working out, jogging, or pulling heavy weights. This way pains can find a little bit room to penetrate inside our muscles during the period when we use our muscles a little more than usual. During the stretching exercises, if someone stretches their muscles a little bit more, this will create a little bit of room for the pains to penetrate there and start residing there. This will create a lot of pain and sore condition for anyone. Now if someone continues to work out or stretch muscles, these continuous movements of the muscles usually bother the pains, and they leave that body within a few days if muscles are not damaged. In case of damaged muscles, usually pains stay there until muscles heal.

Pains want to stay in our body all the time because somehow open atmosphere does not have any attraction for the pains. Pains are different from demons in this regard. Demons stay in the surrounding and open atmosphere a lot or I will say most of the time but around us. Once pains are inside our muscles, usually they look for a nerve or bone or joint to get attached with a source to get some juice or food to keep themselves energized.

إنني أبذل قصاري جهدي، إذا عرف الناس المزيد عن الجن و خرجوا كلياً من فخ الخوف والرعب، أشعر بأن الجن سيكونون السبب الأخير لجعل حياتنا جحيماً. أنا لا أقول أنني كنت مختلفاً في البداية، لقد كنت خائفا أيضاً. ولكن عندما كنت خائفاً، لم يكن هناك شخصاً واحداً يستطيع أن يقول لي شيئاً غير مخيف عن الجن. كلما تحدثت أكثر إلى الناس، و سمعت قصصاً أكثرإخافة من أشخاص مختلفين، كلما زاد خوفي ومضايقتي.و الآن أنا قادر على رؤية الجن، و الإحساس بهم، و التواصل معهم، وشرح كل شيء عنهم و عن أعمالهم.

إذاً كم من الوقت سيستغرق الناس كي يتعلموا ويفهموا الجني الحقيقي؟من المهم جداً الخروج من الخوف والمضايقات من الجن إذا كنت ترغب في التواصل معهم لتصبح صديقهم. لا يمكنكما التأقلم معاً. أذكر أن شخص ما قال لي ذات مرة أن هناك شبح كان يعيش على شجرة في وسط الشارع، ونحن عشنا هناك ما يقرب من ست سنوات. في كل تلك السنوات الست، لم أمر بتلك الشجرة في الليل وحدي ابداً. عندما كنت طفلا، قال لي أحد جيراني عن الشارع المتجه نحو المقبرة أو المدفن، أن كل من سار في ذلك الشارع التي مرت بعد حلول الظلام، يسيرشبح أنثي ذات أنف طويل جداً،وراءه، وربما تقتله. أتذكر أننا عشنا في هذا الحي لعدة سنوات، وأنا لم أستخدم هذا الشارع للذهاب إلى أي مكان. هناك شخص ما كان يقول لي طوال الوقت أنه رأي شخص ما أمامه يجري و يختيئ في مكان ما. يقول شخص ما أنه يسمع مجموعة من الأصوات من الطابق العلوي الشاغر.أحيانا يرى بعض الناس أشباح يراقبونهم من الأشجار؛أحيانا نرى أشباح تقف و تراقب من نوافذ مظلمة.أنا لا أقول أن هؤلاء الناس مخطئون، لقد مررت بظروف و حوادث مماثلة لهذه الحوادث، و أكثر منها سوءاً .

189

SEE & CONTROL DEMONS & PAIN	رضوان قرشي
Diseases/insects need to breathe like us; that's why diseases/insects move frequently in and out of an infected body. Pains are not like diseases/insects. Pains do not breathe like us, so they stay inside our body or inside our muscles or organs for an indefinite amount of time, and they keep getting food or a source of energy to energize themselves. Once pains penetrate inside a muscle, they usually try to go deeper and deeper into joints or organs. In this course, pains really damage our organs, joints, and other parts of the body. Pains do not damage us because they want to. No, during their stay inside our body, pains move here and there to get connected with the source of food or energy; during this search they create several damages to our body. Once the body gets damaged just a little bit due to these pains, it will open doors for the diseases/insects to come inside our body and start eating different organs and parts of the body that eventually creates infections and cancer inside the bodies. Pains, usually one or two only, even they do not need too much energy. But pains are totally responsible for creating very minor damage inside the body. That damage is the beginning of a future big infection and a serious cancer. We cannot kill pains right now. But in the near future, medical science will be able to repel them easily from our body with the use of some system of rays electronically. Main cause of major infections and cancers are these diseases/insects. You can kill these diseases and insects very easily by using my cure procedures with the help of your doctor. These pains create all kinds of arthritis, joint issues, and migraine pains just when they want to stay inside the body and suck their food or energy from our nerves, joints, or tissues.	ولكن الآن بمجرد أنني فهمت الجن وأعمالهم التي تضايقنا وتخوفنا، أصبحت لا أشعر بالخوف من الجن بعد الآن، ولكنني لا زالت خائفاً من مختلف الزواحف والحيوانات البرية. السبب في ذلك هو أنني أعرف أن هؤلاء الحيوانات قد يؤذونني، فالجن يستطيعون أن يجعلوك مريضاً، ولكن لا يمكن ان يؤذوك مثل الحيوانات البرية التي تستطيع أن تضرك. مرة أخرى، بالنسبة لرؤية أشباح تجري هنا وهناك، فهذه هي قوى التنويم المغناطيسي من الجن. إن الطريقة التي يظهرون لك بها بالأحلام، تبدو تماماً مثل الحياة الحقيقية أثناء النوم، إنها نفس الشيء، ولكن الفكرة , والإستخدام والغرض مختلفين تماماً . عندما كنت طفلاً، كنت معتاداً في الليل على إبقاء وجهي وجسمي مغطى تماماً ببطانية بسبب خوف غير مرئي. إذا إضطررت لقيادة سيارتي إلى مكان ما ليلاً، حتي الضباب، يخيفني ثناء القيادة. وأستطيع أن أعطي لك مليون مثال لإثبات مدى شعوري بالرعب، و الخوف ، والجبن طوال حياتي. لم يتغير شيء بعد، ولكني أصبحت فقط لا أخاف من الجن، أوالأشباح، أوالليالي المظلمة، أوالغرف المظلمة أوالشوارع المظلمة، أو الأشجار الكبيرة القديمة بعد الآن. أنا لا أقول أن الجن لا يضرون، .إنهم يمكنهم ذلك، ولكن بمجرد أن يدخلوا داخل جسمك، إنهم يمكنهم أن يسببوا لك الصداع أو بعض العلل و الأمراض الأخرى الصغيرة أوالكبيرةا، وهذا هو كل ما يمكنهم القيام به. لا يوجد شبح طويل القامة طوله 30 قدم، يخرج من الظلام و يأكلنا. شيء مثل هذا. هل سمعت عن الكثير من قصص الأشباح الصحيحة أبداً، هل سمعت أبداأي شخص أبداً يقول أنه شاهد شبحاً يخرج من شجرة ويسحب أو يرفع شخص ما بأيديهم ويذهب بعيدا، أبداً، فلايستطيع الجن تفعل أي شيء مادي بأنفسهم، إنهم يعتمدون علي جسمنا و أجسام غيرنا بنسبة 100 % ، لتنفيذ شيء مادي ضد أي شخص. إذا كان لدينا سيطرة جيدة جداً علي عقولنا، لن يستطيع الجن إستخدام جسم أي شخص عن طريق إستخدام التنويم المغناطيسي لأداء أي نشاط بدني لأنفسهم، ولكنه ليس

190

The more energy they need, the more damage they create and the more hurtful feelings we observe. That was such a bad and scary idea for me to pull some demons from an area under threat of radiation. I do all the time these kinds of crazy experiments on myself. That's why I believe someday I will be dead in seconds during these risky experiments. Anyway, I had to check if humans cannot go in a particular area, due to the leakage of a nuclear reactor, no human can go without special protections if demons are still there or are exposed to nuclear radiation killing them too? It will not just happen immediately. It took me some time.

When I established telepathic connection with those areas just for seconds, the population and the strength of the demons was so high in those radioactive radiation leakage areas that even a telepathic connection just for few seconds brought bunch of demons to me from those areas. In sensing, in looks, behavior wise, listening, following, everything was same like demons from any other area or country. But I will say their knowledge was very high tech. You are reading right now and you will read more stuff later in this book, hopefully open our eyes and we are doing something to secure human race on this earth. Nuclear substances and the radiation from nuclear sources, are the most powerful energy, demons use to energize themselves. On other hand nuclear radiation is most unsuitable energy for human race. A very regular demon becomes extremely powerful and damaging for human brain and body once that demon energize himself from nuclear radio active radiation.

من السهل الفوز على التنويم المغناطيسي للجن إنهم أقوى منا بمراحل، كلما زاد تعاملي مع الجن كل يوم، كلما زادت معرفتي بهم أكثر. الآن، أنا لست خائفاً من الجن بالمرة عند هذه المرحلة. أنا واثق أن هناك الكثير من الجن لديهم قوى أكثر.. أنا متأكد من أنهم يمكن أن يؤذوني جسدياً أو يجعلوني مريضاً أو يسببوا لي بعض الآلام في أي وقت يريدونه، لكنهم لا يستطيعون أن يخيفوني بإظهار أشباح أو سحرة لي أو عن طريق إستخدام حيل التنويم المغناطيسي الخاصة بهم . في أول محاولة لهجوم مخيف، يغذي الجن ويحدثوا خوفاً و أفكار وأحلام مخيفة في أذهاننا بواسطة التنويم المغناطيسي، و بمجرد أن يدركوا أننا خائفين، في الخطوة القادمة يبدأون بإظهار أشباح مخيفة، وسحرة، وحوش قبيحة، ولكن وهمية لتخويفنا.

ما الذي يجنوه من هذا؟ في الحقيقة أنا لا أعرف، ولكن بمجرد أن يصبح الجن صديقك، أنا لا أرى أي سبب لإستمرارهم في إستخدام هذه الحيل الوهمية لتخويف الناس المختلفين. هل يحبنا الجن؟ نعم، في الواقع لا يستطيع الجن عمل الكثير في حياتهم الخاصة.

معظم الجن يعيشون حياتهم في حياتنا. ففي النهار هم مشغولون بجعلنا غاضبين، متطرفين، مدمنين للكحول، أو أن نصبح أشخاص سلبيين، أما في الليل فهم مشغولون بإظهار الأحلام. لنا. إذاً متى يحصلون على وقت لأنفسهم؟ إن الجن مشغولون بنا طوال الوقت. فالآن هم من حولنا طوال الوقت على أي حال، لذلك نحن بحاجة لتدريبهم بشكل صحيح لإستخدامهم في أنشطة إيجابية. أحيانا يتصرف الجن بغرابة قليلاً، فهم يخرجون من الزواحف أو الحيوانات عادة، و يتجهوا نحو الهدف. لا شك في أن جميعلهم يتصرفون بوحشية وجنون حقاً في البداية. أستطيع أن أعطي لكم مثالين على ذلك.

Sometimes demons around us are so innocent that even they cannot figure out that either we are wishing /desiring for something or we are just happy with the situation but not wishing for something. Sometimes the degree of their sincerity and help is so high even they have no clue that they are helping us or they are creating problems for us. Simple example if you are healthy and have no sickness by chance since last several months, So you feel good about it and if you decide to tell someone about it like, "I did not get sick or get a cold since last six months." So here you are thankful for not being sick, but your demons will think you are regretting and desiring to get sickness or cold. This is not difficult for demons to open doors in our body for these diseases. So you need to train them properly so they really understand what you really want and what is good for you.

You can train them, if you are confident enough and do not feel you are scared of them then start immediately. Remember, they need training and guidelines all the time. Brain of a demon and brain of a pain is different. Structure is same for both—electromagnetic. But programming of both brains is different.

The brain of a demon is programmed at the same level as the human brain, for IQ level, for wishes, and desires and understanding. Pains, their brain are programmed at the level of killing and eating insects only. Pains do not have any sense or high IQ level. They just look for energy source and place to live inside a body.

Do not think all the demons are happy with me. No doubt, the circle of my demon friends is getting bigger and bigger every day, but I strongly feel there are a lot of ..

واحد من الجن يأتي من طائر، وكان هذا الطائر الكبير وحده علي الطريق و كان إسمهbrassards براساردز، على ما أعتقد. كنت أرى تلك الطيور دائماً تأكل جثث ألحيوانات النافقة أو الميتة، في الطرق وغيرها من المناطق. لقد مررت بهم عدة مرات من قبل، و لكنني لم ألتقط أي جني من تلك الطيورمن قبل.

هذه المرة مرت فقط بهذا الطائر، لقد كان الطائر وحيداً. لم يكن هناك جثة على جانب الطريق. لقد بدا لي أن الطائر مريض في ذلك الوقت. أعتقد أن هذا كان السبب وراء قفز الجني إلي من ذلك الطائر. في الواقع لم يقفز الجني علي، ولكن علي سيارتي، وبمجرد أن أصبح الجن في سيارتي، بدأت في الشعور به. لقد كنت أبعد أميالاً من منزلي، و قررت أن أقدم نفسي إلي ذلك الجني. لم يأت الجني بالقرب مني في ذلك الوقت. ولكن عندما بدأت الحديث معه، قفز ذلك الجني فورا علي، وخلال ثوان، إستحوذ علي جسدي. لقد شرحت للجني عن أفعاله ومشاعري تجاهه، و خرج مني قبل وصولي إلى بيتي.

أنا أتركهم وحدهم عادة في اليوم الأول، وبخاصة عندما يخرجون من حيوان أو زواحف. من السهل التعامل معهم بعد أربع وعشرين ساعة، ولكن هذا الجني فهمني حتى قبل أن أدخل إلي بيتي. لقد تصرف هذا الجني بطريقة لطيفة معي حقاً. من اليوم الأول، أنا لم أتحدث معه بمجرد أن دخلت المنزل. كان هناك جني جديد من حولي، ولكنني لم يحاول دفعه بعيداً عني، السبب هو أن هذه كانت هذه المرة الأولى التي يكون لدي جن من هذا النوع من الطيور. أنا لم أحاول أن أرسله بعيداً عني مطلقاً. وكنت أتوقع كالعادة، أن يستكشف ذلك الجني العالم خلال إقامته في جسم ذلك الطائر المقرف. ولكنه كان يحاول أن يكون لطيفاً حتى من اليوم الأول.

demons and pains may be still unhappy with me. Reason because I pull or move them from one place to another place all the time. I am sure a bunch of them may be unhappy because may be they were not ready to leave their victims or bodies but I insisted them to do so. I do not know what else I can do. They are doing a bad thing in the first place by hurting people from migraine, arthritis, joint pains, etc., so if I can help someone, I feel why not? I never had too many friends anyway, but since I am messing with demons and pains and asking them to leave certain bodies, I feel these demons are keeping their victims away from me as much they can by hypnotizing them.

I am trying my best if people learn more about demons and totally come out from their trap of fear and scare; I feel demons should be the last reason to make our life hell. I am not saying I was different in the beginning. I was scared too. But when I was scared, there was no single person who can tell me anything about demons that was not scary. The more, I talk to people, the more I hear scary stories from different people; these things were scaring and harassing me. Now when I am able to see demons, I am able to sense demons, I am able to communicate with demons. I am explaining each and everything about demons and their actions. So how long people will take to learn and understand the real demon? It is very important to come out from the fear and harassment of the demons if you want to communicate with them to become their friends. You cannot do together. Still, I remember once someone told me that a ghost lived on the tree in the middle of the street. We lived there almost six years. In all the six years, I never passed from that tree in nighttime by myself ever.

هذا الجني لم يحاول أن يظهر لي أي شيء غريب أو مخيف للغاية. لقد جمعت لديه القليل من المعلومات من عقلي و من هنا وهناك، أنا واثق من نفسي. لقد كان الجن يظهرون لي أحلام طوال الليل، عني و عن إنسان آخر. أظل أناضل من أجل فهم ما كان يحاول إظهاره لي.طوال النهار. ولكن وجهة نظري هنا هي أنه حتى لو كان هذا الجن خرج من طير بري جداً، فإنه لا يزال يحاول بذل قصارى جهده ليكون لطيفاً معي، لمجرد أنني تواصلت معه فقط لبضع دقائق. ماذا أفعل؟ قلت له فقط بثقة بأني أعرف أنه حولي، وقلت له بوضوح أني أعرف أنه خرج من ذلك الطير المريض أو ربما بعض الأمور القليلة. وكان هذا كافياً ليفهمني ذلك الجني. سيتعلم أكثر من ذلك في غضون بضعة أيام. بمجرد أن يكون حولي لبضعة أيام، انا متأكد من أنه سينقل الكثير من علمه إلى ذهني عن الجن وعالمهم، و بعد بضعة أيام، عندما يسألني إذا كنت أريد له أن يفعل أي شيء لي، وسوف أعطي له شيئاً يفعله.

وهكذا، أرأيت كم هو سهل وبسيط جعل الجن صديقك؟ يمكنك أن تفعل ذلك أيضاً. كل ما تحتاجه هو شيئين. أولاً، لا تخف منهم بعد ذلك. الثاني، أن تكون علي ثقة بأنهم حولك ويستمعون لك بنسبة 100 %.

لقد حدث حادث آخر في عملي في مكتبي. أنا أحتفظ عادة بفخ غراء للجرذان في مكتبي للتخلص من الحشرات. لقد سبق و طلبت من كل الجن إبلاغ الجميع عن ذلك، كي يكونوا حذرين. على أي حال، في اليوم الثاني في العمل، عندما فتحت باب المكتب، قفز علي جني واحد و قلت له أنا متأكد فقط أنك شخص جديد هنا، و لهذا السبب قفزت علي.

SEE & CONTROL DEMONS & PAIN

When I was a kid, someone in my neighborhood told me about the street going towards the cemetery or graveyard that whoever walked or passed that street after dark, a very long-nosed female ghost usually comes behind him and maybe kills him. I remember we lived in that neighborhood for several years; I never used that street to go anywhere. All the time, someone tells me that they see somebody running in front of them and hiding somewhere. Someone says they hear a bunch of noises from a vacant upper floor. Sometimes people see some ghosts watching them from the trees; sometimes we see ghosts standing and watching from dark windows. I am not saying these people are wrong. I went through way worse conditions and incidents, similar to these incidents. But now once I understand the demons and their actions of harassing and scaring us, I do not feel scared of demons anymore, but I am still scared of different reptiles and wild animals, the reason is because I know those animals can hurt me.

Demons can make you sick but cannot hurt you like a wild animal can hurt you. Again, as far as seeing ghosts running here and there, these are the hypnotizing powers of demons. The way they show you dreams, exactly look like real life during sleep, same thing, just a different idea, different use and purpose. When I was a kid, in night time, I used to keep my face and body totally covered with a blanket due to some unseen fear. If ever I had to drive my car off somewhere in the nighttime, even scary fogs used to scare me during driving. I can give you one million examples to prove how much I was terrified, scared, and a coward all my life.

رضوان قرشي

ثم نظرت حولي و عثرت على سحلية عالقة في فخ الغراء، وقام رجل أعمال الصيانة بإلقاء فخ الغراء هذا في القمامة في الدقائق القليلة القادمة. لكن كان ذلك الجني حولي طوال اليوم، لم يكن بالقرب مني ولكنه كان في الغرفة مع الآخرين، حتى أنه جاء معي إلى بيتي. إنه لم يقترب مني و لهذا لم أتواصل معه. بمجرد أن أنام، يبذل الجني قصارى جهده لإظهار أكثر الأحلام شراً لي، وربما كل ما يقدر على أن يظهر لي إياه. أنا لا أتذكر كل شيء ولكن في جزء من الحلم أظهر لي نوع من الغراء الكثيف يخرج من أنفي. و كلما أخرجت ذلك الغراء من أنفي، كلما خرج أكثر من أنفي. أنا لا أعرف كم من الوقت كنت أحلم، و أخيراً إستيقظت، فتحت عيني وقلت له أشياء قليلة فقط وعدت الى النوم. قلت له: "الآن أنت بخير. الآن لا تضيع وقتي بعد الآن. إذا كان يمكنك أن تظهر لي أحلام جيدة، فلا بأس. وإلا إتركني وحدي. أو أعطي فرصة للجن الآخرين الذين يستطيعون أن إظهار أفضل الأحلام. " قلت ذلك فقط وعدت إلى النوم. و مر بقية الليل بخير. الآن وجهة نظري هنا هي أنك بمجرد أن تقتل هذه الأجسام التي يستحوذ عليها الجن، من الواضح أن ذلك سوف يزعجهم و سيتضايقون منك، لأنهم عادة ما يتعلقون جداً بتلك الأجسام.. حتى لو كنا نريد ذلك، فإننا ر نستطيع قتل الجن، لذلك عادة ما نقتل الأجسام التي تحت إستحواذهم. الآن هذا مثال حدث من هذا القبيل. أنا الذي قتلت السحلية، وهذا الجني خرج من ذلك الجسم، وكان مستاءً مني، وربما كان يحاول أن يعطيني بعض المرض مثل الصداع أو آلام الظهر. المقبل، وبمجرد أن نمت، بدأ يظهر لي أحلام سيئة. هذا كل ما يمكن للجن القيام به بمجرد أن يغضبوا من شخص ما. وإذا كنت شخص ضعيف العقل، سيبدأون يظهرون لك أشباح وهمية، و سحرة، وهذا هو كل ما في وسعهم القيام به. لذلك فالأمر متروك لك، إما أن تظل خائفاً طوال الوقت أو تبدأ في التحدث معهم. قل للجن الموجودين حولك ،

194

Still nothing changed, but only I am not scared of demons, ghosts, dark nights, dark rooms, dark streets, or old big trees anymore. I am not saying demons cannot hurt. They can, but once demons will go inside your body, they can just give you a headache or some other minor or major sickness; that's all they can do. There is no thirty-feet-tall ghost to come out of the dark and eat us.

Nothing like this. Have you ever heard all lot of true ghost stories, have you ever heard anybody saying that they have seen a ghost coming out from the tree and pulling or lifting someone in their hands and went away, never. Demons cannot do anything physical by thenselves Demons are 100 percent dependent on our and other bodies to perform something physical against anyone. If we have very good control of our minds, then demons cannot use the bodies of anyone by the use of hypnotism to perform any physical activity for themselves. But it is not that easy to beat the hypnotism of demons.

They are way, way powerful than us. The more I deal with demons every day, the more I learn about them. Now at this point, I am not at all scared of demons. I am sure there are a lot of demons with a lot of powers. I am sure they can hurt me physically or make me sick or give me some pains anytime they want, but they cannot scare me by showing me ghosts or witches or by using their tricks of hypnotism. In first attempt of a scary attack, demons feed and create fearful and scary thoughts and dreams in our minds by hypnotism.

"حسناً، أنا آسف إذا كنت قد فعلت شيئاً خاطئاً. ولكني أعيش هنا، ولا أستطيع الإ بقاء علي جميع أنواع الحشرات في بيتي. لذا أرجو منكم الرحيل، و لا تضيعوا وقتي وقتكم. إذا كنتم تريدون الخروج من المنزل والبحث عن سحلية أخرى، ولكن لا تأتوا بها إلي منزلي ". كن حذراً في المستقبل، وتكلم فقط بنفس الإسلوب وبثقة. إن الجن بحاجة إلى أن يدركوا أنك على دراية تامة بهم. لا يهم إذا كنت في وقت ما تغضب إذا كان لا يعجبك ما يقومون به. الآن بعد ذلك قم برش رذاذ الماء المقدس عليك و في منزلك، حتى يغادروا منزلك. أرجو أن تعلم شيئاً.

لا يريد العديد من الناس التحدث عن الجن، لأنهم خائفون منهم. الجن ليسوا بهذا السوء. أترى كم إنني أناقش الجن في الكتاب الأول والثاني. هل تشعر أنني خائفاً من الجن؟، وأود لك أقول كيفية السيطرة على الجن. أنت بحاجة لتدريب نفسك أولاً، ثم ستكون قادراً على تدريب الجن من حولك. إذا كنت تستطيع تدريب كلب أو قطة وتصبح صديق لهما في عشر سنوات، ثق بي، سوف يستغرق منك يوماً واحداً فقط لتصبح صديقاً معه للجن. إن المادة الفيزيائية / والنسيج والقوى تختلف عنا، بخلاف ذلك المستوى العقلي ومعدل ذكائهم مثل الإنسان. لكن الجن يستخدمون / يضيعون معظم مواهبهم، وذكائهم ومستوى ذكائهم فقط لتخويفنا ويضيعون كل وقتهم في للعثور على مزيد من السبل لإحداث نوع مختلف من المخاوف و تغذيتها في أفكارنا وأحلامنا طوال الوقت. الآن هذا هو الوقت المناسب عندما يحتاجون إلى بعض التدريب الإيجابي منك، وذلك بدلاً من إضاعة وقتهم، سيقوم الجن بعمل شيء جيد ومفيد لهم و لنا. هذا ممكن فقط بمجرد أن تبدأ في تجاهل الكوابيس، و ترفض دائماً كل الأفكار والمشاعر المخيفة. إذا حاول تخويفك، إرفض ذلك تماماً، وإبدأ في السخرية من تلك الأفكار والأحلام المخيفة.

Then once they figure out we are already scared, in next step they start showing us scary but imaginary ghosts, witches, and ugly monsters to scare us. What do they get from this? I really do not know, but once demons become your friend, I do not see any reason why they will keep doing these imaginary tricks to scare different people. Do demons like us? Yes, actually demons do not have too much to do in their own lives.

Most of the demons live their lives in our lives. In daytime they are busy making us angry, extremist, alcoholic, or a negative people. In nighttime they are busy showing us dreams. So when do they get time for themselves? All the time, demons are busy with us. So now they are around us all the time anyway, so we need to train them properly and need to use them for positive activities. Sometimes demons act a little bit weird. Demons come out from reptiles or animals usually right on target. No doubt all of them are really wild and act really crazy in the beginning. I can give you two examples. One demon came out of a bird. That big bird was by the road by itself named brassards, I think. I always see those birds eating dead animals' bodies by the roads and other areas. I passed by them several times before, but I never picked any demon from those birds before.

يمكننا تعقب وقتل الأمراض / والسرطانات / والحشرات بسهولة جداً، و لكننا لا يمكننا قتل الجن أو الآلام. إن الجن والآلام أجسام مادية، ولكن نسيجهم / أو تكوينهم كهرومغناطيسي. لم يخلق الجن و الآلام من دم ولحم مثلنا، فهم لا يستخدمون الأكسجين أو ثاني أكسيد الكربون لأغراض التنفس.

إن عدد سكان الجن مرتفع للغاية، وهم يقتالون بعضهم البعض طوال الوقت. السبب الأول بشكل أساسي هو الزيادة السكانية، و السبب الثاني في ذلك هو الإستحواذ الزائد علي الجسم الحي، بغض النظر عما إذا كانوا من البشر أو حيوانات، أو حشرات، أو زواحف. عادة يعيش ثلاثة أو أربعة أشخاص، في منزل صغير، ولكن يمكن أن نتوقع بسهولة أن الحد الأدنى من الجن الذين يعيشون في المنزل الصغير نفسه، يصل إلي 500-1000 جني. إذا كان لديك أشجار حول منزلك فأننت تبحث عن آلاف الجن حول المنزل أيضاً، ولكن معظم الجن يظلون مشغولون بالجسم الموجود تحت حوزتهم. على الفور, قد يكون هذا الجسم من الأشجار، أوالبشر أوالحيوانات أوالزواحف أوالحشرات. لا يمكن لجني واحد جيد تغيير كل سلالة الجن. نحن بحاجة إلى إقناع كل جني من حولنا للبدء في التفكير الإيجابي إن عدد سكان الجن أكثر من اللازم. كل جني يبحث عن أجسام البشر أو الحيوانات أو طيور أو زواحف أو حشرات ليعيشوا فيها ويستمتعوا بالحياة المادية والرغبات. إن نسبة الأجسام الحية المتاحة تصل إلي 1:1000 + من الجن. هذا هو سبب صراع الجن طوال الوقت للإستحواذ علي جسمٍ حي.يستطيع الجن قتل بعضهم البعض بسهولة جداً. لا يستطيع الجن تنويم كل منهم الآخر مغناطيسياً .

196

This time, I just passed this bird. The bird was by itself. There was no dead body by the road. That bird seemed sick to me at that time. I think that was the reason the demon from that bird jumped on me. Actually not on me but in my car. Once the demon was in my car, I started sensing that demon. I was a few miles away from my house. I decided to give my introduction to that demon. The demon was not coming close to me at that time. But when I started talking to him, that demon immediately jumped on me and, within seconds, possessed my body. I explained to that demon about his actions and my feelings about him. He came out of me before I reached my house.

Usually, I leave them alone the very first day, especially when they come out from an animal or reptile. After twenty-four hours, it is easy to handle them. But this demon understood me even before I went inside my house. This demon I feel behaved real nice with me from the very first day; I did not talk to him once I was at home. A new demon was around me, but I did not try to push him away from me, The reason was that was the first time when I have a demon from this kind of bird. I did not try to send him away from me at all. I was, as usual, expecting that demon will explore his world during his stay in the body of that nasty bird. But he was trying to act nice even from the very first day.

That demon did not try to show me anything weird or scary the very first night. He collected a little bit information from my mind and from here and there, I am sure about me. All night long, that demon was showing me dreams about me and some other human.

رؤية الجن و الآلام السيطرة عليها

الجن يتواصلون مع بعضهم البعض من خلال إستخدام مبدأ التخاطر، أي إرسال الإشارات الإلكترونية لبعضهم البعض داخل الجو في المجال الكهرومغناطيسي. لا يمكننا قتل أي جني أو ألم، ولكن لدينا الكثير من الطرق لصد الجن عن جسم ما أو عن مكان معين.

يعيش الجن في منزلنا أو من حولنا، بغض النظر عن ما يفعلون بنا، من خلال وضع أفكار مخيفة في أذهاننا، أو إظهار الكوابيس، أوأشباح وهمية، أو سحرة، لا يزال هؤلاء الجن هم الأكثر إخلاصاً، والآكثر تعلقاً، وأكثر وديةً معنا. السبب وراء ذلك هو أن الجن وعائلاتهم يعيشون معنا أو حولنا نحن وعائلاتنا، وأنت لا تعرف منذ متى. كان ذلك. أحيانا منذ آلاف السنين. إن الجن الموجودون حولنا هم الأكثر تعلقاً بنا، بالمقارنة بالجن الآخرون الذين يعيشون على الأشجار أو في المنازل في الحي. هؤلاء الجن لا زالوا لا يتبعوننا، عن كونهم مخلصون لنا، و لهذا عليك التواصل معهم و تدريبهم على المشاركة في الإتجاه الصالح بدلا من الإتجاه الشرير.

أنت بحاجة لتقول لهم ما تريد وما لا تريد. سيستغرق ذلك بعض الوقت ، لكن في نهاية الأمر سوف يستمعوا إليك. أنا لن أقترح عليك أن تطلب من الجني الخاص للذهاب إلى مكان آخر أن يفعل لك شيئاً.السبب أنه بمجرد أن يخرج الجن من المنزل، سيكون منزلك مفتوحاً لجن جدد. أنت لا تعرف أي نوع من الجن الجدد سيكونون أو حتى، أن شخص ما يمكن أن يرسلهم لك خصيصاً ليصيبوك أنت و عائلتك، أنت لا تعرف. الآن بمجرد أن يصبح الجن أصدقائك، كن حذراً بالنسبة عدد قليل من الأشياء. أنت لا تعرف إمكانيات وقدرات أصدقائك من الجن،.

SEE & CONTROL DEMONS & PAIN	رضوان قرشي

And all day long, I was struggling to understand what he was trying to show me. But here my point is, even if that demon came out from a very wild bird, still he was trying his best to be nice with me just because I communicated with him just for a few minutes. What did I do? I just told him with confidence that I know he is around. I told him clearly that I know he came out from that sick bird or may be a few more things. This was enough for that demon to understand me. In a few days, he will learn more, once he will be around for few days, I am sure he will transfer a lot of his knowledge to my brain about demons and demons' world. After a few days, when he will ask me if I want him to do anything, I will give him something to do.

So, you see how easy and simple it is to make a demon your friend? You can do it also. You just need two things. First, do not get scared any more of them. Second, 100 percent confidence and believe that they are around you and listening to you.

Another incident happened at my work in my office. Usually, I keep rat glue trap in my office to get rid of insects. I already told all demons to inform everyone about it, so they should be careful. Anyway, the next day at work, when I unlocked the office door, one demon jumped on me. As usual, I just told him that I am sure you are someone new around here that's why you jumped on me. Then I looked around. I found a lizard was stuck in the glue trap. Maintenance man trashed that glue trap in the next few minutes. But that demon was around me all day long. He was not close to me but in the room with others. He even came with me to my house.

ولكن ينبغي لك أن تعلم أن الجن يستطيعون قتل بعضهم البعض بسهولة جداً. كي تحصل على المزيد من الحماية، يعيش الجن في جماعة في مكان معين أو منزل، ولكي يحصلوا على مزيد من القوي ضد مجموعات أخرى من الجن، فهم يعيشون معاً في مجموعة لدعم بعضهم البعض، وتأمين مكان إقامتهم من مجموعات الجن الأخري. هذا هو السبب في أن معظم الجن لا يسافرون معنا. الآن بمجرد أن يصبح الجن أصدقائك و طلبت منهم القيام ببعض الأشياء المختلفة لك، سوف يفعلون ذلك. ولكنهم قد يتقاتلون مع الجن الآخرين أثناء تلبية أوامرك. قد تفقدهم، بمجرد أن يقتلهم جن أو مجموعة من الجن أكثر قوة . ثاني شيئ، أنك سوف تفقد الجن المخلصين. الآن سوف تفتح باب بيتك لجن غرباء جدد. قد يكون الجن الجديد جيد و قد يكون سيئ، أنت لا تعرف أبداً. يتواصل الجن مع بعضهم البعض عن طريق إرسال إشارات إلكترونية إلى بعضهم البعض، ولهذا يستطيع الجن دائماً توصيل رسالتك إلى الجن الآخرينفي أي جزء من العالم.. هذه هي أسهل طريقة وأكثر أمناً لإرسال رسالتك من خلال الجن الخاص بك لجن شخص آخر لإقناعهم بشيء، و بهذه الطريقة لن يخرج الجن الخاص بك من بيتك إلى منزل غريب ويتعاملون أو يصارعون مع بعض الجن الآخرين لتنفيذ أوامرك. على سبيل المثال، إذا كنت سياسيا و تريد إقناع الناخبين بالتصويت لصالحك، يجب أن تعطي الجن الخاص بعض التفاصيل، وتطلب منهم البدء في الإتصال بجن الناخبين المختلفين عن طريق إرسال إشارات لإقناعهم بالتصويت لك. بمجرد أن يستطيع الجن الخاص بك إقناع الجن الخاص بالناخبين، ليس من الصعب علي الجن حول الناخبين إقناعهم بالتصويت لك، لذلك انت بحاجة لتعليم هذه الأفكار للجن الخاص بك، حتى يتمكنوا من مساعدتك أكثر. أنا واثق أنه من الصعب عليك فهم أهمية جني واحد صادق و مخلص حقاً واعتقد، إسمحوا لي أن أقدم لكم مثالاً واحداً.

He did not come close that's why I never communicated with him. Once I went to sleep, that demon did his best to show me the nastiest dreams, whatever possibly he was able to show. I do not remember everything but in part of the dream he showed me some kind of thick glue coming out of my nose. The more I took that glue out of my nose, the more it came out of my nose. I don't know for how long I was dreaming. Finally, I woke up. I just opened my eyes and told him just few things and went back to sleep. I told him, "Now you're okay. Now do not waste my time anymore. If you can show me good dreams, its fine, otherwise, leave me alone. Or give chance to other demons that can show better dreams." I just said that and went back to sleep. Rest of the night was okay. Now here my point is once you kill the bodies these demons possess, obviously they will get upset with you because usually they are very attached with those bodies. Even if we want to, you cannot kill demons, so usually we kill the bodies under their possession. Now this is an example of an event like that. I killed that lizard. That demon came out from that body. The demon was upset with me, maybe trying to give me some sickness like headache or back pain. Next, once I slept, it started showing me nasty dreams. That's all demons can do once they get angry with someone. And if you are a weak-minded person, they will start showing you imaginary ghosts and witches; that's all they can do. So it's up to you if you keep getting scared all the time or start talking to them. Tell demons around you, "Okay, I am sorry if I did something wrong. But I live here. I cannot keep all kinds of insects in my house. So please move on. Do not waste my time and your time.

لا توجد وسيلة، أحصي بها عدد أصدقائي من الجن. كم منهم لا يزالون حولي، وكم منهم قمت بإرسالهم إلي مكان ما ليفعلوا شيئاً، وكم منهم ظلوا على إتصال بي لتلقي أي أمر مني،إذا كان لدي شيء لهم يفعلونه من أجلي. إن إحصائهم مستحيل. ولكني ما زلت أتنكر عندما جعلت الجني الأول صديق لي. الجني الأول و المرة الأولى، وكان ذلك الجني حولي لعدة أشهر. أنا متأكد من أنني أرسلته إلي مكان ما خاطئ، لختفقد إختفي فقط إلى الأبد، ولم أسمع منه مرة أخرى. كان ذلك الجني كثير التعلق بي ، حتي أنني كل صباح أطلب منه أن يوقظني مهما كان الموعد، و يقوم هو بايقاظي دائماً بالضبط في الوقت نفسه. إذا حدث في يوم من الأيام، ولم أطلب منه أن استيقظ في أي وقت معين، إنه ينتظر دائما حتى الساعة 8:00 صباحا وبعد ذلك يبدأ فقط بدغدغتي في كل مكان حتى أستيقظ وأخبره بالميعاد الذي أريد أن أستيقظ فيه. معظم الوقت، أقول له أنني أريد أن أنام لمدة ساعة أخرى. عادةً ما أراوغه دائما حول الوقت الذي أريد أن النوم فيه، 30 دقيقة اخرى، بدلاّمن أن أحدد له وقتاً معيناً.، ولكنه يعود لي بعد ثلاثين دقيقة بالضبط، ليوقظني مرة أخرى.كل صباح. أحاولت أن اراوغ معه عدة مرات، لكنه ظل يعود مراراً وتكراراً ليوقظني حتى، أستيقظ أخيراً. في وقت ما إذا تأخرت ساعة متأخرة في العمل، فإنه بعد فترة زمنية معينة، يأتي للعمل دائماً، ويسألني لماذا تأخرت جداً. . لقد كان فضولياً لذلك، ففي كل صباح خلال التدريب الذي أقوم به، قال أنه يريد أن يعرف خططي لهذا اليوم. كان يريد أن يعرف دائماً إذا كنت سأذهب إلى مكان آخر غير العمل.

If you want go outside and find another lizard, do not bring that lizard in my house." Be careful in future. Just talk like this on and on with confidence. Demons need to realize that you are totally aware of their presence. It does not matter if you get angry sometimes when you do not like whatever they do. Now after this, spray holy water on you and in your house so they leave your house. I hope you learn something.

Several people even do not want to talk about demons, because they are so much scared of them. Demons are not that bad. See how much I am discussing demons in the first and second books. Do you feel I was scared of demons? I should be telling you how to control the demons. You need to train yourself first then you will be able to train demons around you. If you can train and become friendly with a dog or a cat in ten years, trust me, then it will take you one day only to become friends with a demon. The physical material/texture and powers are different from us, otherwise mentally and IQ level of demons is same like human. But demons are using/wasting most of their talent, smartness, and IQ level just to scare us and spend all their time to find more ways to create different kind of fears and feed them in our thoughts and dreams all the time. Now this is the time when they need some positive training from you, so instead of wasting their time, demons do something good and beneficial for them and for us. This is possible only once you start ignoring nightmares; always reject all scary thoughts and fearful feelings. If demons try to scare you, totally reject it and start making fun of those scary thoughts and dreams.

و إذا كنت سأقود سيارتي في إتجاه مختلف غير المعتاد، إنه دائما يعرف أين أنا ذاهب، و بمجرد أن أقول له التفصيل، فإنه يعود دائماً، للمنزل ويقيم فيه. لقد كنت مندهشاً حقاً وسعيداً عندما زارني في عملي لأول مرة. كنت أتحدث إلى بائع في ذلك الوقت، و في الوقت نفسه بالضبط ظهر لي في التو وبدأ يعطيني إشارات ليقول لي أنه موجود حول لزيارتي. لقد تجاهلته لبضع دقائق، و لكنه ظل يرسل لي إشارات ليقول لي مرحباً.

أخيراً، وفي دقائق قليلة، عندما فرغت من التعامل مع البائع، وجدت زاوية هادئة كنت قادراً على التحدث مع ذلك الجني. أخيراً، وسألته: "ماذا تفعل هنا؟" وبعد ذلك اليوم، إعتاد على زيارتي هنا وهناك طوال الوقت, لقد كنت ذات مرة متأخراً عن العمل أو لسبب آخر. لقد كان هذا الجني طيب و صديق لطيف للغاية. لكن أنا لا أعرف ماذا حدث له؛ و فجأة، إختفى تماماً. أنا واثق من أن جني أكبر أو أكثر قوة منه قام بقتله. السبب لا يزال مجهولاً بالنسبة لي.

أنا لا أتذكر إذا بكيت من أجل أي صديق من البشر أبداً،ولكني لا زالت تدمع عيني،من أجل ذلك الجني بمجرد أن أفكر فيه ؛و كل يوم دارت الحياة؛و يأتي حولي عدد لا يحصى من الجن، بعضهم يظلون حولي، و بعضهم، أرسلته لمكان ما ليفعل شيئاً. و بعد ذلك، أحعل من كل حني صديق لي، ولكني لن أتعلق بأي أحد مثلما تعلقت بذلك الجني الأول.

يعيش الحن الأصدقاء المخلصون حولك وفي بيتك لحمايتك من أنشطة غيرها من الجن الشرير والشياطين. نحن بحاجة لتقدير إخلاصهم . لكنك لا تزال تحتاج إلى رش الماء المقدس داخل بيتك وعلى نفسك كل يوم لطرد الشر والشياطين من بيتك.

Rizwan Qureshi

We can hunt & kill diseases/cancers/insects very easily. But we cannot kill demons or pains. Demons and pains are physical bodies, but their texture/configuration is electromagnetic. Demons or pains are not made of blood and meat like us. Demons do not use oxygen or carbon dioxide for breathing purposes.

Population of the demons is extremely high. Demons fight with each other all the time. One reason is mainly overpopulation and the second reason is over possession of a living body, regardless of whether they are human, animal, insect, or reptile. Usually in a small house three or four people live, but in the same small house, you can easily expect a minimum of five hundred to one thousand demons. If you have trees around your house then you are looking for thousands of demons around your house too. But most of the demons stay engaged or busy with the immediate body under their possession. That body may be trees, human, animals, reptiles, insects, etc. One single good demon cannot change the whole race of the demons. We need to convince each and every demon around us to start thinking about positivity. The population of demons is too much. Each and every demon looks for a living human or animal or bird or reptile or insects bodies to live and enjoy their physical life and desires. The available living bodies are 1:1000+ ratio of the demons. That's why to have a possession of a living body, demons fight with each other all the time. Demons can kill each other very easily. Demons cannot hypnotize each other. Demons communicate with each other by using the principle of telepathy, i.e., sending electronic signals to each other within the atmosphere's electromagnetic field. We cannot kill any demon or pain, but we have a lot of ways to repel demons from a body or from a particular place.

رؤية الجن و الآلام السيطرة عليها

قبل رش بيتك، يمكنك أن تطلب من أصدقائك من جن الخاص بك الإنتقال إلى منطقة معينة حيث لا ترش بها المياه المقدسة. لابد أن تفعل ذلك، بغض النظر عن ما إذا كان الجن طيب أم سيئ، قلمياه المقدسة مشكلة لكل جني. لا يهتم الشياطين و الجن الأشرار بالبقاء في المنزل حيث يقوم شخص برش المياه المقدسة في كثير من الأحيان.

لا شك أن الجنس البشري، أي إنسان يستطيع صنع أو دعم أي نوع من أنواع الأسلحة المشعة، بغض النظر عن ما إذا كان متعمد أو غير متعمد،كل ذلك يعمل من أجل الشياطين و الجن الشرير. هؤلاء الناس يعملون علي تدمير الجنس البشري، وترك كل شيء على هذه الأرض لشياطين والجن الشرير. عادة ما نكون تحت سيطرة جني واحد فقط في وقت واحد. لكن هناك عدد قليل من الحالات مع أنواع قليلة من الناس، لديهم مزيد من القدرة على إستيعاب مزيد من الجن الشرير و الشياطين من الغلاف الجوي. عادة، الناس العصبيون والمتطرفون للغاية، وأثناء حالة الغضب الشديد، و المرضى، وجميع الزعماء الدينيين و الدعاة وجميع السياسيين القذرين والأشرار، و النساء المهووسات، المرضي العقليين، والسكاري / و مدمني الكحول / مدمني المخدرات، المتطرفين، و السلبيين. هذه هي الأمثلة.

هذه الأنواع من الناس عادة ما يكونون تحت سيطرة جني واحد فقط، ولكنهم محاطون بعدد لا يحصى من الجن طوال الوقت.إن وجود هذا العدد الكبير من الجن من حولهم، يبقيهم في هذه الحالات المتطرفة. بمجرد أن يتحدث أحدهم معهم على الهاتف أو يجتمع معهم بشكل شخصي، وأحيانا حتى الأشخاص العاديون في مزاجهم، و النظيفين، والأصحاء، و كذلك الناس المعتدلين، يستوعبون الجن الأشرار من هؤلاء الأشخاص الذين يتكلمون معهم علي الهاتف أو يقابلونهم، لذا كن حذراً، إذا

SEE & CONTROL DEMONS & PAIN

The demons live in our house or around us, regardless of what they do with us, by creating fearful thoughts in our minds by showing us nightmares, imaginary ghosts, witches, still these demons are most sincere, most attached, and most friendly with us, the reason behind it is because these demons and their families are living with or around us and our families, you never know since how long. Sometimes since thousands of years. Demons around are more attached with us as compared to other demons that live on trees or in neighborhood houses. Regardless, these demons are sincere with us, still they really do not follow us. That's why you need to communicate with them and train them to get them more involved in the righteous direction instead of the evil one.

You need to tell them what you like and what you do not like. It will take some time, but finally they will listen to you. I will never suggest you to ask your demon to go somewhere else to do something for you. The reason is that once they will leave the house, your house will be open for new demons, and you never know which kind of new demons they will be or even someone can send them especially to hurt you and your family, you never know. Now once demons become your friends then be careful about a few things. You really do not know about the powers and capabilities of your demon friends, but you should know that demons can kill each other very easily. To have more protection, demons live in a group in a particular place or house. To have more powers against other groups of demons, they live together in a group to support each other and to secure their residence from another group of demons.

رضوان قرشي

كنت شخصاً متماسكاً و معتدلاً، إبق بعيداً عن هؤلاء الناس المتطرفين، و إلا سوف تكون في نفس الحالة. الحظ السيئ هو عندما تشاهدها مباشرة على شاشات التلفزيون أو الإنترنت، سوف تكون قادراً على إستيعاب بعض من الجن الأشرار. لذلك يجب أن تبقي نفسك بعيداً عن الجن الشرير، لابد أن تظل بعيداً عن كل هؤلاء الناس المتطرفين. إذا شعرت بأنك قمت بإمتصاص بعض الجن الأشرار بالصدفة من هؤلاء الناس المتطرفين، فالأفضل لك أن تشرب و ترش الماء المقدس على نفسك كثيراً للتخلص من هؤلاء الجن الأشرار. عليك أن تكون ذو شخصية قوية جداً، ويكون عقلك قوي جداً لأخذ الجن الأشرار في إتجاهك. ولكن إذا لم تكن بتلك القوة، سوف يقوم هؤلاء الجن الأشرار بتغييرك أنت و حياتك وأنت في أي وقت من الأوقات. هؤلاء الجن هم معجزات إلكترونية من الله.

لا تجدي مسكنات للآلام، ولا كريم الحكة، و لا المراهم، و لا الأقراص، و لاالمضادات الحيوية، و لا مضادات الجراثيم و لا مضاد العدوى و لا الأدوية، لا شيء يعمل ضد الجن. لا يمكنك صد أ وتدمير، أو قتل أي جني بأي من الأدوية المذكورة أعلاه.. أنت تحتاج لفهم بنية الجن، كي تفهم بشكل أفضل . الجن يتحركون ويسافرون من هنا إلى هناك طوال الوقت. نناقش الآن خط الهاتف أولاً، لديك نوعين من الهواتف، الخطوط الأرضية والهواتف المحمولة الاسلكية أو الهواتف المحمولة، الهواتف. كيف تعمل؟ بغض النظر، هناك من هو الذي على الهاتف معنا، فقط في الغرفة المجاورة أو شخص ما يكلمنامن كراتشي أو طوكيو،سنسمع كل الإشارات الصوتية لكلا الصوتين في نفس الوقت تقريباً . ويمكن هذا أن يدلكم علي سرعة إنتقال تلك الإشارات الصوتية عبر خطوط الهاتف أوالأقمار الصناعية. الآن عندما يستخدم هؤلاء الجن أو الآلام، خطوط الهاتف للتنقل، وبغض النظر عن الخطوط الأرضية أو خطوط لاسلكية، فهم ينتقلون بالضبط بنفس الطريقة وبنفس السرعة كإشارة الصوت الإلكترونية.

Rizwan Qureshi	رؤية الجن و الآلام السيطرة عليها

That's why most demons do not travel with us. Now once demons are your friends and you ask them to do different stuff for you, they will do it. But during this they may have to fight with other demons to fulfill your commands. You may lose them once a more powerful demon or a group of demons may kill them. Second, you will lose your sincere demons. Now you and your house will be open for new strange demons. New one may be good may be bad, you never know. Demons communicate with each other by sending electronic signals to each other. So demons can always communicate your message to any part of the world to other demons around someone else. This is an easier, safer way to send your message through your demons to someone else's demons to persuade them with something. This way your demons do not go out of your house to some strange house and deal or fight with some other demons to fulfill your commands. E.g., if you are a politician and you want to convince your voters to vote for you, you should give some details to your demons and tell them to start communication by sending signals to demons of different voters to convince them to vote for you. Once your demons will be able to convince the demons of the voters, it is not difficult for the demons around the voters to convince them to vote for you. So you need to teach these ideas to your demons so they can help you more. I am sure it is difficult for you to understand the importance of even one but really true and sincere demon. I guess, let me give you one example. There is no way, if I can count all together, how many demons become my friends. How many still around, how many I send somewhere to do something and how many stay in contact to take any command, if possibly, I have something for them to do for me.

وهذا يمكن أن يعطيك فكرة بسيطة عن تكوين وهيكل ومادة الجني أو الألم .

يجب علي العلم الحديث أن يبدأ البحث في الإتجاه نفسه، أياً كان، ما إقترحه في الوقت الحالي. هو كيف يمكن لبعض الأشاعات إحداث بعض التشويش بين الإشارات الإلكترونية . إذ إستطاع العلم الحديث على نحو ما الكشف عن الجن إلكترونياً، وسوف لا يستغرق إكتشاف نظام أشعة طاردة للجن وآلام من الجسم الحي أي وقت، بدون الإضرار بالأجسام الحية للبشر/ الحيوانات و تدميرها. الآن فكر إذا لم يكن لديك غطاء عازل فوق الأسلاك النحاسية و أسلاك خطوط الهاتف. عندما يتحدث شخصين مع بعضهما البعض على نفس خط الهاتف، فهذا يعني أن إشارة إلكترونية أنتقلت من خلال تلك الأسلاك النحاسية من خط الهاتف، و كذلك ينتقل الجن و الآلام داخل هذه الأسلاك النحاسية أيضاً. هل هناك أي طريقة أو أي دواء، أو مرهم، أو مضادات حيوية، أوشراب معالج يمكن إستخدامها علي تلك الأسلاك النحاسية العارية لقتل إشارات هذا الصوت الإلكتروني التي تنتقل في هذه الأسلاك؟ لا، الشيء نفسه يحدث مع الجن . بل هي أيضاًأجسام كهرومغناطيسية وقادرة على السفر مثل أي إشارة إلكترونية. إذاً يمكن لأي نظام أشعة يحدث تشويه أو قتل أو صد للإشارات الإلكترونية في الأسلاك النحاسية، سواء زائدة أو ناقصة ستعمل علي الجن أيضاً. يستطيع الجن البقاء على قيد الحياة و ينتقلون بسهولة جداً في الأسلاك الكهربائية ويعيشون فيها، وكذلك ينتقلون في المناطق المصابة نتيجة للإشعاع. يستطيع الجن التنقل بسهولة جداً عن طريق إستخدام الهواتف أو خطوط الكهرباء أو أسلاك. و بطريقة مماثلة إشارات الإنترنت، وإشارات الإتصالات اللاسلكية، وإشارات التلفزيون، و إشارات الأقمار الصناعية، كل ذلك أيضاً مسار سهل جداً لتنقل الجن و الآلام.. يستخدم الجن هذه المسارات للإنتقال من شخص إلى آخر عادةً .

SEE & CONTROL DEMONS & PAIN

It is impossible to count. But I still remember when I made the very first demon my friend. Very first time and very first demon. That demon was around me for several months. Then I am sure I sent him to some wrong place; he just disappeared forever, never heard from him again. That demon was so much attached to me that every morning whatever time, I asked him to wake me up, he always wakes me up exactly at the same time. If some day, I never asked for any particular time to wake me up, he always waits until 8:00 a.m. After that he just starts tickling me everywhere until I wake up and tell him a particular time when I want to wake up. Most of the time, I just tell him that I want to sleep for one more hour. He comes back exactly one hour after to wake me up. I always dodge him about time that I want to sleep thirty more minutes, instead of telling him some particular time. But he comes back exactly thirty minutes to wake me up again. Every morning, I try to dodge him several times, but he never gives up and keeps coming back again and again to wake me up until, finally, I wake up and get up. If sometimes I was staying late at work, after certain time limit, he always comes to work and asks me why I am so late. He was so nosy; every morning during my workout, he wants to know my plans for the day. He always wanted to know, if I am going to some other place other than work. If I ever drive my car in a different direction other than the usual, he always comes to know where I am going. Once I tell him in detail, he always comes back home and stays at home. I was really surprised and happy when he visited me at my work the very first time. I was talking to some vendor at that time, exactly at the same time he just showed up and started giving me signals to tell me that he is around and visiting me.

رضوان قرشي

خلاف ذلك، المجال الكهرومغناطيسي الطبيعي موجود في الجو المفتوح وهو المسار الرئيسي لإنتقالات، وإتصالات الجن في كل مكان. أعتقد أنه لم يكن هناك في البداية هاتف أو خطوط كهرباء، وهذا هو السبب في حاجة الجن إلي مجال كهرومغناطيسي في الغلاف الجوي لغرض إنتقالاتهم وإتصالاتهم. ولكن الآن في العالم الحديث، فإنهم يستطيعون الذهاب من خلال خط الهاتف إلي أي جزء من العالم في ثوان دون شراء أي تذاكر طيران. هل يمكنك أن تتخيل الجن، كم هم مخلوقات مدهشة؟ أتدري من خلق الجن؟ أنا واثق من أنه ليس بشراً.

دعوني أقول لكم المزيد عن قوي الجن، يمكنك تقسيم الجن يشكل أوسع إلي فئتين، واحدة بالقوي الطبيعية، والثانية جن بقوي قوية للغاية. إنني أستطيع التفريق بين هذين النوعين من الجن عن طريق إعطائك مثال بسيط من أسلاك النحاس العارية لخط الهاتف و أسلاك نحاسية عارية من خط الكهرباء. عندما يتم توصيل هذه الأسلاك بمقبس الطاقة أو بالهاتف، ثم تنشط تماماً، الآن إذا لمس شخص ما هذه الأسلاك العارية من خط الهاتف والكهرباء الحية، هناك فرق هائل في الطاقة أو الصدمة بين هذين النوعين من الأسلاك. الشيء نفسه صحيح يالنسبة لهذين النوعين من الجن. الجميع يقع تحت سيطرة الجن العادي طوال الوقت تقريباً. لكن قواهم و آثارهم ليست ضارة ومؤذية للغاية. هذا هو السبب في أننا لا نشعر بوجودهم بسهولة داخل أجسادنا. لكن النوع الثاني من الجن قوي و مؤذ للغاية ، فمجرد أن يسيطر هؤلاء الجن علي جسم الإنسان وعقله، فإنهم لا يستغرقون وقتاً طويلاً في إفساد ذلك الشخص.

ويستطيع الجميع رؤية أو معرفة أن شخصا ما تحت سيطرة الجن بكل سهولة.

I ignored him for few minutes, but he kept sending me signals to tell me hello. Finally, in few minutes, when I was done with that vendor, I found a quiet corner where I should be able to talk to that demon. Finally, I asked him, "What are you doing here?" After that day, he used to visit me here and there all the time. Once, I was late at work or for some other reason. He was such a good demon and such a nice friend. But I do not know what happened to him; suddenly, he just disappeared. I am sure some bigger or more powerful demon killed him. The reason is still unknown to me. I do not remember if I ever cried for any human friend, ever.

But for that demon, still I get tears once I think about him. Then life moves on; every day uncountable demons come around me, some stay around, some I send to somewhere to do something, and after that, I will make every demon my friend, but I will not get attached with anyone as much as I was attached with that very first demon. Sincere and friend demons live around you and your house and protect you from the activities of other evil and devil demons.

We need to appreciate their sincerity. Still you need to spray holy water inside your house and on yourself every day to kick out evil and devil demons from your house. Before you spray, you can tell your demon friends to move to some particular area where you will not spray holy water. You need to do it because, regardless of whether demons are good or bad, holy water is a problem for every demon. Bad and devil demons do not bother to stay in a house where someone sprays holy water frequently.

رؤية الجن و الآلام السيطرة عليها

إن الجن العاديون يتصلون بي، و يستحوذون علي جسدي، داخله وخارجه طوال الوقت . أنا فقط أقول لهم أنهم في جسدي و يجب أن يتركوه. عادة ما يكفي هذا هو ما، و لا يستغرقون وقتاً في ترك جسدي. هذا لا يزعجني بالقدر الكافي. ولكن عندما يقفز علي جني من النوع الثاني و يستحوذ علي جسدي، أنا لا ألقول لهم أن يتركوني وأنتظر، لكتي لابد أن أصر على أن يغادروا جسدي فوراً، لأنني أتألم كثيراً الإستحواذ.

ليس لدينا أي نظام لصد وتدمير، أو قتل أي جني في الوقت الحالي. ولكن يمكن للجن أن يقتلوا بعضهم بعضاً بمنتهي السهولة . هناك الكثير من القصص المتعلقة بأطباء الجن المختلفين يحصرون الجن في زجاجة من المياه ويتخلصون منهم في النهر أو المحيط. و يظل هؤلاء الجن محصورون في تلك زجاجات الماء إلى الأبد في قاع المحيط حتى أن يقوم شخص ما بفتحها لإطلاق سراح هؤلاء الجن. نحن لا نعرف منذ متى وجدت من حولنا هذه القصص لأسر الجن في زجاجة ماء.

لكن أعتقد أن هذا هو الوقت المناسب الذي يحتاج الجميع فيه إلى معرفة الحقيقة حول هذه القصص الخيالية. وأنا واثق أن حتى أطباء الجن هؤلاءلا يدركون كيفية تعامل الجن الأقوياء مع الجن الآخرين. في الواقع، معظم أطباء الجن عادة ما يكون لديهم مجموعة قوية جداً من الجن.

كلما إتصل شخص ما بأطباء الجن لمساعدتهم ضد الجن الذين من حولهم سواء في منازلهم أو على الأشجار، يرسل أطباء الجن، الجن الأقوياء جداً الذين يخصونهم، لتنظيف ذلك البيت أو المنطقة المعينة من الجن العاديين الذين يعيشون عادةً هنا وهناك في مجموعات صغيرة.

SEE & CONTROL DEMONS & PAIN	رضوان قرشي

No doubt in human race, regardless of whether it is intentional or unintentional, any human make or support any kind of radioactive weapons is working for the evil and the devil demons. Those people are working to destroy human race and leave everything on this earth for the evil and devil demons on this earth. Usually in one time, we are under the possession of only one demon. But there are few conditions with few kinds of people, have more capacity to absorb more evil and devil demons from atmosphere. Usually, very short tempered, very extreme behavior people, during the condition when someone is extremely angry, sick people, all religious leaders and preachers, all dirty and mean politicians, bipolar women, mentally sick people, drunk/alcoholic/drug-addicted people, extremists, and negative people are the examples.

These kinds of people usually are possessed by only one demon but surrounded by uncountable demons all the time. The presence of so many demons around them keeps them in these extreme conditions. Once someone talks to them on the phone or meets with them in person, sometimes even normal-tempered, clean, healthy, and moderate people absorb few evil demons from them. So be careful if you are a very controlled and moderate person; stay away from these extreme condition people, otherwise, you will be in the same condition. Bad luck is even if you watch them live on TV or Internet, you will be able to absorb some of their evil demons. So to keep yourself away from evil demons, you need to stay away from all these extreme condition people. If by chance you feel you absorb some evil demons from these extreme people, you better drink and spray...

إن قصة حبس الجن في زجاجة مياه هي مجرد قصة. في الحقيقية، هؤلاء الجن من أطباء الجن يطوقون منزل معين أو شجرة أو منطقة، ويقتلون الجن العاديون والأقل قوة الذين يعيشون عادة في بيوتنا أو في الأشجار، أو حول بيوتنا. إن مجموعة الجن الأقوياء المرسلين من طبيب الجن مدربون عادة لقتل الجن الطبيعي من خلال مهاجمتهم في لحظة مفاجئة دون منحهم فرصة للجري أو إنقاذ أنفسهم. كيف يقتل الجن بعضهم البعض؟، إسمحوا لي أن أشرح لكم، ولكن قبل ذلك، تذكر دائماً أنه بمجرد أن يطلب أي شخص من طبيب الجن إرسال الجن الخا ص بهم لقتل الجن العاديين الموجودون حول منازلهم، يكون الجن التابعون لأطباء الجن أكثر تنظيماً، بالإضافة إلى أنهم أتوا لقتل جن آخرين، وذلك سهل بالنسبة لهم. ولكن بمجرد أن تدعو الجن التابعين لطبيب الجن، فهذا يعني أنك تقوم بإستبدال الجن الطبيعيين من حولك مع بالجن الإرهابيين التابعين لطبيب الجن . بمجرد أن يقتل الجن الإرهابيين، الجن الذين كانوا حولك في بيتك، لن يتركوا منزلك. تذكر أنك من الآن و صاعداً سيكون عليك التعامل مع هؤلاء الجن التابعين لطبيب الجن.سيترك أطباء الجن دائمًا بعض من الجن التابعين له حولك للحفاظ على السيطرة عليك. لن يتركك الجن التابعين لأطباء الجن وحدك. انهم يريدون دائماً أن يستمر إعتماد الناس عليهم. فإذا لم تكن خائفاً، يطلب أطباء الجن من الجن الخاص به أن يخوفوك لتركض وراء طبيب الجن لمساعدتك في التخلص من الجن الموجودين في بيتك أو عملك. بإختصار، أفضل شيء هو أن تبتعد عن أطباء الجن هؤلاء، حتى لا تعتمد عليهم إلى الأبد. ل ثانياً، بمجرد ألا تستخدمهم، فهذا يعني أنك لن تضطر للتعامل مع الجن المدربين بقية حياتك. أفضل شيء هو أن تحل مسألة الجن الوجودين حولك بنفسك. عليك القيام بثلاثة أشياء بسيطة. إجعل الجن أصدقائك. كيف؟، سأقول لك لاحقاً في هذا الكتاب.

holy water on yourself frequently to get rid of those evil demons. You need to be very, very strong personality with a very strong mind to take these evil demons in your directions. But if you are not that strong, these evil demons will change your life and you in no time. These demons are the electronic miracles of the God. Pain medication, itching cream, ointments, tablets, antibiotic, or antibacterial or anti-infection medicines, nothing works against the demons. You cannot repel, destroy, or kill any demon with any of the above-mentioned medications. To understand better, you need to understand the structure of demons. Demons move and travel from here to there all the time. Now discuss phone line first. You have two kinds of phones, i.e., landlines and wireless cell phones or mobile phones. How do they work? Regardless, someone is on phone with us just in the next room or someone calling us from Karachi or Tokyo, we will hear both voice signals almost at the same time. This can tell you the speed of traveling of those voice signals through phone lines or satellite. Now when these demon or pains, use phone lines to travel, regardless landlines or wireless lines, they exactly travel the same way and with same speed as a electronic voice signal. This can give you a little bit idea about the configuration and physical structure of a demon or a pain

Modern science needs to start research in the same direction, whatever, I am suggesting right now. How some rays can create some distortion between electronics signal. If somehow modern science will detect the demons electronically, it will take no time to discover the repelling rays system for the demons and pains from a living body without hurting or damaging human/animal living bodies.

الثانية، و إستمر في رش مكافح و قاتل الآفات والحشرات داخل منزلك طوال الوقت، هذا يعني أن كلما قلت أجسام الحشرات كلما قل من الجن. لشيئ الثالث، إستمر في رش الماء المقدس على نفسك وفي منزلك. سيكون حولك عدد قليل من الجن من حولك، وبالتأكيد سوف يكونون طيبين وداعمين لك. بطريقة ما، أنا واثق أن حتى أطباء الجن لا يدركون أن الجن المدربين يقتلون الجن الآخرين لمجرد إتباع أوامرهم،بغض النظر عن عدد الجن الطيبين و السيئين في مجموعة الجن الموجودين حولنا. أعتقد بقوة أن هذه فكرة سيئة جداً.

الجن، بغض النظر عن ما إذا كان لديهم قوي عادية، أو جن لديهم قوة قوية و كبيرة وغير عادية، ليس لأي منهم أي شكل مادي أو جسم مثل البشر. في الواقع إن حجم الجن ليس كبير وثقيل مثلنا. كل الجن حقاً إن الجن كائنات طائرة و صغيرة، وغير مرئية، و كهرومغناطيسية. أحجامهم تتراوح بين النملة إلى الصرصور الصغير. فما رأيك؟ كيف يقاتلون مع بعضهم البعض؟ حسنا، دعني اقول لك، الجن يرمون الشياطين أو يرشون نوع من الرذاذ على بعضهم البعض. أن ذلك الرذاذ يخرج منهم وكأنه رذاذ من أشعة الجن الآخرين. طبيعة الرذاذ يشبه السائل، ولكنه ينتقل أو يهاجم مثل الأشاعات القوية. نوع من السائل الغير ممغنط وغير كهرومغناطيسي. إذا كان هناك جني أكثر مكهرباً أكثر ، ونشيط أكثر، وأكثر قوة، هذا يعني أن رذاذ الأشعة المهاجمة / القاتلة، سوف يكون أكثر قوة وفتكاً. يحتاج الجن الأقل نشاطاً كمية أقل من رذاذ الأشعة القاتل، أ و من السائل بالمقارنة مع الجن الغير عاديين النشيطين والأقوياء. هذا هو الإسلوب والسلاح الذي يستخدمه الجن لقتل بعضهم البعض. يقتل الجن التابعون لطبيب الجن القليل من الجن فقط.

Now think if you do not have insulation coating over copper wires of the wires of phone lines, when two people talking to each other on same phone line, it means an electronic signal is traveling through that copper wire of the phone line and within those copper wires demons and pains travel also. Is there any way or any medication, ointment, antibiotic, medicated syrup you can use on those naked copper wires to kill that traveling electronic voice signal in those wires? No. Same thing with demons. They are also electromagnetic bodies and able to travel like any electronic signal. So whatever system of rays can create distortion or kill or repel the electronic signals in the copper wires, plus minus will work for the demons too. Demons can survive and able to travel very easily in live electrical wires and infected areas due to radiation. Demons can travel very easily by using phones or electricity lines or wires. Similar way, Internet signals, radio communication signals, TV signals, satellite signals, are also a very easy path of traveling for demons and the pains. Usually, demons use these traveling paths to move from one person to another. Otherwise, electromagnetic field naturally exists in the open atmosphere is the main traveling, communication path for all the demons everywhere. I guess in beginning there was no phone or electric lines that's why demons need a natural electromagnetic field in the atmosphere for the purpose of their traveling and communications. But now in the modern world, they can go through phone line to any part of the world in seconds without buying any airline tickets. Can you imagine about demons? What amazing creatures. Do you know who create demons? I am sure not any human.

لكن في الحياة الحقيقية، يقتل الجن بعضهم البعض طوال الوقت فقط للمحاربة خلال إمتلاك جسم أو مكان ما. إن الجن والآلام الأكثر إضراراً وإيذاءً، هم أولئك الذين يحصلون على فرصة لتنشيط أنفسهم بأشعة الراديو النووية النشطة. عادة عندما يستحوذ الجن أو الآلام من تلك الفئة، حتى لو إستحوذوا علي مجرد جسم الإنسان أو الحيوان أو الدماغ فقط أوالقلب فقط لبضع ثوان، سيفشل قلب الإنسان أو دماغه علي الفور في ثوان قليلة. ليس من الضروري أن يمتلك ذلك الجني الجسم البشري لقتل أو الإضرار بجسم الإنسان، لكن الإنسان أوالأعضاء البشرية لا تتحمل بأي شكل الجن النشيطين بالإشعاعات النووية. حتي الجن العادي يتنقل في ثوان معدودة من طرف واحد من الأرض إلى الطرف الآخر، كما يمكنهم التنقل عن طريق خطوط الهاتف أو غيرها من الوسائل الالكترونية.

ولا توجد وسيلة يمكننا بها إيقاف الجن عن إمتلاك أجسامنا. لذلك، ماذا سنفعل، إذا إنتقل القليل أو الكثير من الجن من هذا الركن من أركان الأرض إلى زاوية أخرى من الأرض، وقرررروا أن يستحوذوا علي بعض الأجسام الواحد تلو الآخر، بمجرد أن ينشطوا أنفسهم بالطاقة النووية النشطة أو الإشعاع؟ لقد كانت لي تجربة لأشعر بأثر رش رذاذ السوائل المهاجمة أو الأشعة مرة واحدة فقط . في منتصف الليل تحت الشجرة، عندما كنت أعبث مع الجن الموجودين على تلك الشجرة. لقد كنت أتحلي بالثقة المفرطة بالنفس كثيراً و أهتم قليلاً عند التعامل مع الجن في الماضي.. على أي حال، كان هذا خطأي، فالجن الذين على الشجرة هاجموا الجن من حولي للإستحواذ علي جسدي وعقلي. قام الجن على الجانبين بمهاجمة كل منهما على الآخر.
بالنسبة لي الجن من كلا الجانبين لديهما نفس النوع من القوى، ولكن الجن الموجودين علي الأشجار أكثر عدداً. أعتقد أن جميع الجن الموجودين من حولي قتلهم الجن الموجودون علي الأشجار، و لكني لم أسمح لهم بالبقاء من حولي لوقت طويل أيضا.

Let me tell you more about the powers of the demons. In a broader way, you can divide demons in two categories. One with the normal powers, second extremely powerful demons. I can describe or differentiate between these two types of demons by giving you a simple example of naked copper wires of a phone line and a naked copper wire of electricity line. When these wires are connected with the power outlet or phone jack and fully energized, now by chance, if someone touches these naked phone line wires and the live electric wire, there is a huge difference of power or shock between these two wires. Same thing is true with these two kinds of demons. Everybody is under the possession of a normal demon, almost all the time. But their powers and effects are not too much damaging and hurtful. That's why we never feel so much easily about their presence inside our bodies. But second kind of demons is extremely powerful and damaging. Once those demons take the possession of a human body and brain, they screw up that person and his mind in no time. And everyone can see or tell very easily that someone is under the possession of a demon.\

Normal demons contact me and possess my body all the time, in and out. I just tell them that they are in my body and they need to leave. Usually this is enough and within no time, they leave my body. It does not bother me as much. But when the second kind of demon jump on me and possess my body, I just cannot say to leave and wait. I have to insist them to leave immediately, because it hurts me a lot during the period of possession.

على أي حال، إن السائل أو الرذاذ الذي قام الجن بإستخدامه لقتل بعضهم البعض يعطي شعور مثل الماء ولكنه لم يكن هناك ماء. أتمنى أن أستطيع أن أشرح، لقد شعرت خلال قتالهم، أن شخصاً ما رمى آلاف الغالونات من الماء علي، ولكني ظللت أبحث حولي. لم يكن هناك ماء. أتمنى أن تفهم. ثم أنني لدي عدد قليل من أكثر التجارب مشابهة لهذه. و أخيراً، تعلمت أن المياه المقدسة تعتبر أداة أو سلاح يستخدم ضد الجن لصدهم. عندما تقرأ هذا الكتاب في منزلك، سيقرأ الجن الموجودون حولك في المنزل، هذا الكتاب أيضا، الواحد تلو الآخر، و لهذا إقرأ قراءة بطيئة وثابتة، وبهذه الطريقة يحصل الجن على فرصة لقراءة هذا الكتاب معك. وبمجرد أن تنتهي من قراءة هذا الكتاب، لا تعطيه لأحد. كل يوم، قم بفتح صفحة واحدة من هذا الكتاب، و إتركها مفتوحة في الغرفة أو المنطقة التي تعتقد أنك سوف تسمح الجن الخاص بك بالبقاء. لا يمكن أن تعرف كم عدد الجن الذين يعيشون حول المنزل. هكذا إترك هذا الكتاب مفتوحاً علي صفحات مختلفة كل يوم . بهذه الطريقة سوف يتمكن كل الجن تقريباً جميع الشياطين من قراءة تلك الصفحات الواحد تلو الآخر. من فضلك لا تسألني إذا كان الجن يمكنهم القراءة. لا يمكن ان تعرف منذ كم الاف من السنوات الماضية،و الجن موجودون في الأنحاء يستمعون و يقرؤن اللغات المحلية بمجرد أن تترك صفحات قليلة مفتوحة كل يوم، سيتمكن الجن من القراءة. وهذا سيفعل خيرات. أولا،سيعلم الجن أنك تعرفهم. بقدر ما يقرأ الجن، ما يقرب من 50 في المئة من التدريب ليصبحوا أصدقائك، وسوف يحصل عليه الجن من هذا الكتاب.

لن تعرف أبداً متى سيكون لديك جن غير مدعو من حولك في بيتك، بمجرد أن يكون هذا الكتاب هناك و يستطيع الجن قراءته، فإنهم سيغييرون سياستهم أو إستراتيجيهم تجاهك فوراً. بمجرد أن يبقوا حولك سيتعلمون المزيد عنك و عن سلوكك الخاص والودود تجاه الجن، لن تستغرق وقتاً طويلاً في تغيير موقفهم منك.

We do not have any system of repelling, destroying, or killing any demon right now. But demons can kill each other very easily. There are a lot of stories related to different demon doctors that they can confine demons in a bottle of water and throw them away in a river or ocean. And those captured demons stay confined in those bottles of water forever in the bottom of the ocean until someone opens that bottle to release those demons. Since how long these stories of capturing demons in the bottle of water are around us, we don't know.

But I think this is the time when everyone needs to know the truth about these fiction stories. I am sure even those demon doctors are not aware of how powerful demons treat other demons. In actual, most demon doctors usually have a group of very powerful demons.

Whenever someone contacts those demon doctors to help them against the demons around them either in their houses or on trees, demon doctors send their very powerful demons to clean that particular house or area from normal demons who usually live here and there in small groups. The story of confining demons in a bottle of water is just a story. In actual, those demons from demon doctors surround a particular house or tree or area and kill normal and less powerful demons that usually live in our houses or trees around our houses. The group of powerful demons from a demon doctor usually trains to kill normal demons by attacking them in a sudden moment without giving them chance to run or save themselves.

ثم في الخطوة الثانية، و عن طريق جعل من هذا الكتاب قاعدة، يمكنك البدء في التحدث إليه. أنت تحتاج فقط إلى أمرين، يجب أن تكون على ثقة بنسبة 100 في المئة من أن الجن حولك و يستمعون إليك. لا تشعر بالخوف على الإطلاق. خلال هذه العملية، إذا كنت تشعر ببعض الألم في مكان ما، قل لهم بوضوح أنك لا تحب أنهم يلحقون بك الضرر. إستمر فقط في الممارسة نفسها. في غضون بضعة أيام، سوف يبدأ الجن بإعطائك إشارات مختلفة لجذب إنتباهك، أو يصروا أن تتحدث إليهم.. مهما قلت للجن، سوف يبدأون في مناقشتك و مناقشة إتصالك بهم مع بعضهم البعض. لن يستغرق الأمر وقتا طويلاً عند كل منهم سوف ليبدأوا في إعطائك إشارة بسيطة مثل دغدغتك أو قرصك بلطيف أحياناً أو بقسوة أحياناً أخري، إذا كنت لا تستجيب لهم، سوف أعطيك إجراءات أكثر تفصيلا عن كيفية جعل الجن أصدقائك، في وقت لاحق في هذا الكتاب، و عن كيفية رشوتهم للإتصال بك، وكيف أنهم في البداية ربما سيحاولون الإتصال بك.

بعض الجن أقوياء جداً، وبعضهم لديهم قوى طبيعية. نفس الشيئ في البشر، فعقول أو أدمغة القليل من البشر قوية جداً، وعدد قليل آخر من الناس ضعفاء العقول. إن الجن إنتهازيون جداً. فبمجرد أن يقرروا فعل شيئ ما، إما لأنفسنا أو لشخص آخر، سيظل هؤلاء الجن ينوموننا مغناطيسياً، وسيظلوا يرسلون إشارات إلكترونية، و يظلوا يغذوننا بالأفكار و الأوامر ليصروا على أن نفعل أشياء معينة. يدفعنا الجن أحياناً بواسطة تغذية الافكار والأوامر لشيء جيد بالنسبة لنا، وأحيانا يفعلون هذا بنا ليستخدموننا لمساعدة شخص آخر. إذا كنت تفكر في ذلك، سوف تجد الكثير من الأمثلة في حياتك عندما فعلت الكثير من الاشياء نتيجة لتأثير الجن الموجودين حولك. على سبيل المثال، عندما كنت جالساً بشكل عادي، وإنتابتك فجأة رغبة في تناول الطعام، شيئاً مختلفاً..

How demons kill each other?, let me explain, but before that, always remember once someone asks any demon doctor to send their demons to kill regular and normal demons around their houses, the demons from demon doctors are more organized, plus they come to kill other demons, so it is easy for them. But once you invite the demons from a demon doctor, it means you are replacing normal demons around you with the terrorist demons from a demon doctor. Once those terrorist demons will kill demons around you in your house, they will not leave from your house. Remember, from then on you will have to deal with those demons from the demon doctor. Demon doctors will always leave some of his demons around you to maintain a control on you.

Demon doctors will not leave you alone. They always want to keep people dependent on them. If you are not scared, demon doctors will ask his demons to scare you so you will keep running back to those demon doctors to help you to get rid of the demons from your house or work. So in brief, best thing is you need to stay away from these demon doctors, so you will not be dependent on them forever. Second, once you do not use them, it means you will not have to deal with their trained demons for the rest of your life. The best thing is manage this demon issue around you by yourself. Three simple things. Make demons your friends. How? I will tell you later in this book.

Second, keep spraying pest control and insect killers inside your house all the time. So less insects' bodies means less demons. Third, keep spraying holy water on yourself and in your house. You will have only a few demons around you.

وأحياناً على الفور رغبة في شرب شيء ما، رغبة فورية في التدخين أو شرب الكحول،أ و رغبة فورية لممارسة الجنس، أو رغبة فورية لمقابلة شخص ما أو التحدث الى شخص ما، أو رغبة فورية لمشاهدة أي فيلم خاص، أو رغبة فورية في النوم..

سوف تفكر أكثر، وسوف تفاجأ أكثر بكثرة الاشياء التي يمكن أن نفعلها، بسبب تأثير التنويم المغناطيسي للجن من حولنا. سوف تفاجأ كم نحن نتبع هؤلاء الجن. الآن يرفض الناس ذوي العقول القوية تأثير الجن. إنهم يفعلون كل ما يبدر إلي ذهنهم في شكل مشاعر و أوامرمن الجن الموجودين حولهم. و الآن لا يقبل الناس الأكثر سيطرة على عقولهم التنويم المغناطيسي و أوامر الجن بسهولة. نتيجة لذلك، هذه الأنواع من الناس يديرون نقاشاً داخل عقولهم طوال الوقت. الجن يولدون مختلف الرغبات في العقول، وقد يرفض العقل البشري هذه التغذية للعقل عدة مرات، ولكن الجن لا يستسلمون حتى يقنعونا أو يصروا أن تتبع عقولنا الشهوات، أوالأفعال ، أو رغبات، أيا كان ما يولده الجن داخل أدمغتنا. إن الجن يصرون جداً علي توليد رغبات و أمنيات مختلفة، ليبقونا مشغولين بفعل شيئاً ما طوال الوقت، ولكن الجن من حولنا، أنا أتحدث عن الجن العاديون، ليس لديهم أي شيء آخر للقيام به.

نحن المهمة و الهدف الذي يشتغل به الجن أربعة و عشرون ساعة، سبعة أيام في الإسبوع، نحن لعبة الجن. نحن نوفر وسائل الترفيه والتمتع للجن بقبول أوامرهم و تغذيتهم لعقولنا. ليس للجن أي حياة مادية في حد ذاتها. ولكن دماغ الجن مليئ بنفس النوع من الرغبات والشهوات بنفس الطريقة بالضبط. يتمتع الجن بتحقيق كل رغباتهم و أمانيهم بإستخدام جسمنا .

أنا أشعر بشعور مختلف في هذه الأيام. لقد إعتدت أن أكون مختلف. لقد إعتدت علي الركض وراء رغباتي و أمنياتي مثل المجنون طوال الوقت. إذا كنت غير قادر على تحقيق أمنياتي أو رغباتي، كان ذلك يجعلني مستاءً وغير سعيد للغاية. لكني في هذه الأيام، عندما أكون تحت تأثير أقل للجن، أموت حقاً من أجل الحصول علي أي شيء. إذا إستطعت الحصول على شيء بسهولة، أكون سعيداً. إذا لم أتمكن من الحصول على شيء ما، أشعر أنني بخير بدون ذلك الشيئ. أشعر دائماً أنني شخص بطيئ و هادئ، سواء كنت تحت تأثير الجن أم لا. لا شيئ يجذبني كثيراً، حتى لو كنت أحب شيء ما كثيراً، ما زلت أشعر أنني بخير بدون ذلك. وأنا لا أشعر أو أري أي ضغط أورغبة شديدة لآركض وراء أي شيء.

Second, keep spraying pest control and insect killers inside your house all the time. So less insects' bodies means less demons. Third, keep spraying holy water on yourself and in your house. You will have only a few demons around you. And for sure they will be good and supportive to you. Somehow, I am sure even demon doctors are not aware that their trained demons kill other demons just to follow commands, regardless of how many demons are good and how many demons are bad in a group of demons around us. I strongly think this is a very bad idea.

لا أستطيع أن أبقي غاضباً من شخص ما لفترة طويلة. لا أستطيع الحفاظ على غضبي من أجل أي شيء أو أي شخص لفترة طويلة. أنا أستسلم بمنتهي السهولة. لكني ما زلت ، أشعر بالغضب أحياناً ولكن لبضع ثوان فقط. من الصعب جداً الحفاظ على غضبي حقا. هذه الأشياء غيرعادية جداً بالنسبة لي، إنني لا أعتقد حتى أن هذا يحدث لي. لدي الكثير من التوفيق طوال الوقت في كثير من الأشياء. أنا لا أشعر بطاقة مفرطة على الإطلاق. ن إدقات قلبي طبيعية 100 في المئة. لا يمكنني أن أتأقلم مع أي خطة، ولا أشعر بالحب أو الكراهية لأحد. الأمر يزداد صعوبة حقاً أن تكره شخص ما لفترة طويلة. إن مزاجي هدئاً جداً.

Demons, regardless of whether they have normal powers and strength or are big and extraordinary powerful demons, none of them have any physical structure or a body like a human. In actual size, demons are not big and heavy like us. All demons are really small flying, invisible, electromagnetic objects. Their sizes are between an ant to a small cockroach. So what do you think? How do they fight with each other? Okay, let me tell you. Demons throw or spray some kind of spray on each other. That spray comes out from them like a spray of rays on other demons. The nature of spray is like a liquid, but it travels or attacks like powerful rays. Some kind of demagnetized and de-electronize liquid. If a demon is more electrified, more energized, more powerful, this means the attacking/killing rays spray will be more powerful and killing. Less energized demons have less amount of killing spray of rays or fluid as compared to extraordinary energized and powerful demons. This is the style and weapon demons use to kill each other. Demons of the demon doctor just kill a few demons only. But in real life, demons kill each other all the time just to fight over possessing a body or place.

اسياً.ومسائل أخرى في الحياة. نفس الشيئ بالنسبة للدين، وبعد كل ما تعرضت له عيناي وحواسي، لا أستطيع التفكير في أي شيء آخرسوي الله. لقد إعتدت أن أكون شخص ذو سلوك متطرف، ولكني الآن لست شخصاً معتدلاً.

Most damaging and hurtful demons and pains are those who get chance to energize themselves from a nuclear radio active radiation. Usually demons or pains of that category even just possess a human or animal body or just brain or just heart for few seconds only, human heart or brain will fail immediately in few seconds. This is not necessary that demon possess that human body to kill or damage that human but human body or human organs do not have any kind of tolerance for demons energized of Nuclear radiations. Even normal demons travel in few seconds from one end of the earth to the other end of the earth. They can travel through phone lines or other electronic means.

And, there is no way, we can stop demons to possess our bodies. So, what we will do, if few or more demons just travel from this corner of the earth to the other corner of the earth and decide to possess few bodies one after one, once they are energized from nuclear radio active energy or radiation? Only one time I had experience to feel the effect of that attacking fluid spray or rays spray. In the middle of the night under the tree, when I was messing with the demons on that tree. I used to be so much overconfident and care less when dealing with the demons in the past. Anyway, that was my fault.

Demons on the tree attack the demons around me to take the command of my body and mind. Demons on both sides attack on each other. To me demons on both sides have the same kind of powers, but demons from the trees were more in numbers. I think all demons around me were killed by the demons from the trees. But I did not let them stay around me for a long time either.

أنا بطيء وهادئ بالمقارنة بشخص معتدل. أنا لا أريد أن أقود سيارتي بسرعة، وهذا هو تغيير كبير، فقد كنت أقود بسرعة طوال الوقت. وكنت دائماً في عجلة من أمري، كنت دائماً أقود سيارتي بسرعة. والآن أريد فقط أن أقود سيارتي بسرعة طبيعية جداً. أنا لا أشعر بأني في عجلة من أمري في أي شيء. لقد أصبحت لا أهتم كثيراً جدا بالكثير من الأشياء. لذلك أنا لا أعرف إذا كان الجميع سيحب مثل هذا النمط من الحياة. على أي حال لا تقلق بشأن ذلك لأنني مختلف، فلدي الكثير من التحكم والسيطرة على ذهني، ولدي القدرة على خوض الصراع، ومقاومة، وجدال الجن طوال الوقت، حتى أصدقائي من الجن يرسلون لي إشارات إتصال من خلال الحفاظ على بعض المسافة معظم الوقت. جسدي لديه الكثير من المقاومة ضد الجن. الجن الجديد فقط يحاول جديدة الإستحواذ علي جسدي ولكنه إستسلم في بضع ثوان. حتى لو إقترب مني أي إنسان، يترك الجن الموجودون حولهم، ليكونوا حولي. وعادةً لا يريد الجن أن يتركوا جسم الإنسان، وهذا هو السبب في أن الجن القوي يبذل قصارى جهده للحفاظ على أجسامهم البشر الذين يستحوذون عليهم بعيدا عني بتنويمهم مغناطيسياً. أنا قادر كثيراً على الحفاظ على ذهني وجسمي بعيداً عن إستحواذ الجن، و أعتقد أن هذا هو السبب في أنني أواجه وتيرة مختلفة وبطيئة في الحياة. لكن بالنسبة لك لكشخص عادي، مهما فعلت لا يمكنك رفض سيطرة الجن على عقلك طوال الوقت. لي انه من المستحيل بالنسبة للشخص العادي للحفاظ على أنفسهم بعيدا بنسبة 100 في المئة من الجن.

الحد الأقصى، الذي يمكن أن يفعله البعض، هو إستخدام كل ما لديهم و إجراءاتي ضد الجن؟ والحد الأقصى الذي يمكنك القيام به هو صد الجن الشرير عنك، لتجنب هذا السلوك المتطرف وتصبح شخص معتدل بتأثير الجن الطيب،

Anyway, that attacking fluid or spray demons use to kill each other with has the feeling like water but there was no water. I hope I can explain. During their fight, I felt someone throw thousands of gallons of water on me, but I kept looking around me. There was no water. I hope you understand. Then I have few more experiences similar to this. Finally, I learned about holy water as a tool or weapon to use against demons to repel them. When you are reading this book in your house, for sure maybe one by one demon around you in your house will read this book too, with you. So read slow and steady; this way demons will get chance to read this book with you. Once you finish rearing this book, do not give to anybody. Every day, open one page of this book and leave it open in the room or area where you think you will allow your demons to stay. You never know how many demons live around your house. So every day leave this book open, with different pages. This way almost all demons around you will be able to read those pages one by one. Please do not ask me if demons can read. You never know since last how many thousands of years, same demons are around and listening and reading the local languages. Once you will leave few pages open every day, so they can read. This will do good things. First, all of the demons will know about your knowledge about demons. When they read more, almost 50 percent of the training to become your friend, demons will get from this book.

You never know when you will have uninvited demons around you in your house, once this book will be there and they will be able to read it, they will change their immediate policy or strategy toward you.

اللطيف،الهادئ والودود، ولكن سيكون لديك جني طيب حولك، لذلك لا داعي للقلق بشأن بطء وتيرة الحياة. لأنه حتى لو أبقاك الجن الطيب والودود في حالة معتدلة، فإنه لا يزال سيطلب منك أن تحقق حفنة من الرغبات/ الأماني و أنشطة بدنية ممتعة لتقوم بها. لكن عند هذه النقطة، الشيء الإيجابي هو أنك من خلال معرفتك بكل هذه الأشياء عن الجن وأعمالهم، ستفهم بشكل أفضل قراراتك، و عقلك، وغضبك و تطرفك، و سيكون لديك فكرة جيدة للغاية في قبول ورفض سيطرة الجن على عقلك. وثمة مشكلة أخرى هي أن عقل الجن و عقل الإنسان متشابهان كثيراً جداً عندما نتحدث عن الرغبات والأمنيات. ففي 90 في المئة من الوقت لدينا تقريباً نفس الرغبات والأمنيات، أيا كان ما يغذية الجن في عقولنا للحصول على متع أكثر وأكثر و سعادة مادية. ولكن بوصفنا بشراً، نحن على إستعداد للتخلي بسهولة جداً عن أي رغبة أو أمنية، ولكن سيطرة الجن لا تدعنا نتخلي عن أي رغبة أو أمنية بسهولة، على سبيل المثال، من الذي يريد أن يرفض عندما يولد الجن رغبة فورية لممارسة الجنس أو لشرب الخمر أو للتدخين،أوالنوم قليلاً لفترة أطول، أو لا تقوم بعمل تمرينات، أو ألا تذهب إلى العمل، أو ألا تذهب إلى المدرسة، الخ. أليس كذلك؟ هذه هي وجهة نظري. رغبتك في الكثير من الأمور بشكل مستمر. تحب بعضها وربما لا تحب بعضها ، ولكن نظراً لسيطرة الجن، أنت لا تستطيع التفرقة بين الصواب والخطأ بسهولة. مشكلتي في هذه الأيام أنه لا يولد الجن لدي أي رغبات / أمنيات في نظامي معظم الوقت، فإنني أفكر وأتمنى الكثير من الأمور ولكني لست مستعدا للإقتناع بهم ومستعد للتخلي عن أي شيء بمنتهي السهولة . كما لاحظت كثيراً في هذا النوع من الحالات، أشعر أن هناك جاذبية أقل و متعة أقل في الحياة.

Then once they will stay around you they will learn more about you and your friendly behavior towards demons, you will not take long time to change them towards you. Then in the second step, making this book a base, you can start talking to them. Only you need two things, 100 percent confident that demons are around you and listening to you. Do not feel scared at all. During this process, if you feel some pain somewhere, tell them clearly you do not like if they are hurting you. Just keep doing same practice. Within a few days, demons will start giving you different signals to get your attention or to insist that you to talk to them. Whatever you will say to demons, they will start discussing you and about your contact with them with each other. It will not take time when all of them will start giving you simple signal like tickle you or sometimes pinch you nicely or sometimes hard, if you will not respond to them. Later in this book, I will give you more detailed procedures on how to make them friends, how to bribe them to contact you, and how possibly in beginning they will try to contact you.

Some demons are very powerful and some demons are with normal powers. Same way among humans, the minds or brains of a few human are very powerful and strong, and few people their minds or brains are weak. Demons are very pushy. Once they decide to do something, either for ourselves or for someone else, these demons will keep hypnotizing us, keep sending electronic signals, keep feeding thoughts and commands to insist us to do certain stuff. Sometimes demons push us by feeding thoughts and commands for something good for us; sometimes demons do this to us to use us to help someone else.

لذلك أنا حقًا أعرف ما يمكنني القيام به، لأنه لا يمكنني السماح لأي جني بالسيطرة على ذهني أو جسمي مرة أخرى. جسدي لا يمكنه ان تحمل وجودهم حتى ولو على مقربة مني. حتى الجن لديهم بعض مشاكل الحرق بمجرد أن يقتربوا مني، لهذا فهم لا يستطيعون البقاء بالقرب مني وقتاً طويلاً أيضاً. لذلك أعتقد انني سوف أعيش هذه الحياة البطيئة الوتيرة لبقية سنوات حياتي.

ولكن لا تقلق علي نفسك. لن تصل إلى هذه المرحلة. السبب في ذلك هو أنك لن يكون لديك أي فكرة عن الجن حولك بنسبة 90 في المئة من الوقت. حتى وإن كنت تحت تأثير الجن، أو عندما يقوم الجن بتنويمك مغناطيسياً والسيطرة عليك. والكثير من الأوقات التي لن يكون لها ما يكفي من الشجاعة لرفض بعض الرغبات / رغبات، بل سيكون لديك فكرة واضحة أن الجن يدفعوكم لذلك. لذلك أنت على ما يرام. وسوف تكون على ما يرام إذا أبقينت الجن الشرير بعيداً عنك، وتبقي الجن الطيب و المعتدل فقط حولك، فمن السهل جداً أن تصبح صديقاً للجن المعتدل بالمقارنة مع الشيطان و الجن الشرير. إذا كنت لا تحب أن تكون شخصاً ذو مزاج معتدل، إبق علي الجن الخاص بك ذو الطبيعة الشريرة و الشيطانية من حولك، ولا تقم برش أي ماء مقدس على نفسك وعليهم، وإلا فإن كل شيء سوف يتغير إلى المستوى المعتدل.

يستطيع الجن تدمير صورة وشخصية أي إنسان بمنتهى السهولة، كما يمكنهم جعل الشخص يقول أشياء خاطئة طوال الوقت، ومن ناحية أخرى، فإن هذا الشخص لن يعرف أبداً الفرق بين الصواب والخطأ بسبب قدرة الجن على تجميد العقل و ذاكرة. هذا هو تنويم مغناطيسي ثنائي الإتجاه من جنيين مختلفين. إذا سألتني، كيف سأفعل ذلك، إسمحوا لي أن أشرح لك.

If you will think about it, you will find so many examples in your life when you did so much stuff due to the influence of demons around you. For example, you were sitting in a normal way; suddenly you had a desire to eat something different, sometimes immediate desire to drink something, immediate desire to smoke or drink alcohol, immediate desire to have sex, immediate desire to meet someone or to talk to someone, immediate desire to watch any particular movie, immediate desire to go to sleep.

You will think more, you will be surprised more that how much stuff we do due to the influence of the hypnotism from demons around us. You will be surprised how much we follow these demons. Now people with strong brains are more capable of rejecting the influence of demons. But people with weak minds do not even think about rejecting the influence of demons. They just do every second whatever comes to their mind in the shape of feedings and commands from demons around them. Now people with a little bit more control over their minds do not accept hypnotism feedings and commands of demons easily. In the result of that, these kinds of people go through an argument within their minds all the time. Demons generate different desires in the minds, human mind may reject that feeding several times, but demons do not give up until they convince or insist our minds to follow the desires, actions, or wishes, whatever demons generate inside our brains. Demons are very consistent in generating different desires and wishes to keep us busy doing something all the time. We have a lot of stuff to do all the time, but demons around us, I am talking about normal demons, has nothing else to do.

أولاً سأرسل التعليمات والأوامر إلى الجن الموجودين بالفعل حول شخص ما، وسوف أطلب منهم إقناع شخص ما بواسطة التنويم المغناطيسي أن يقول شيئاً خطأً مراراً وتكراراً. من السهل أن إستخدام الجن الموجودين بالفعل بالقرب من شخص ما، و السبب أن هؤلاء الجن يستطيع بالفعل الوصول إلى عقل الشخص المستهدف، و في غضون بضعة أيام، سيكون هؤلاء الجن سيطرة كاملة علي ذلك الشخص، وسوف يجعلونه يقول أشياء خاطئة وكريهة طوال الوقت كلما فتح هذا الشخص فمه للحديث، وخلال هذا، من المهم أن إرسال عدد قليل من الجن من هنا وهناك لدعم الجن الموجودين بالفعل قرب ذلك الشخص.المستهدف. و الآن علي الجن الجدد الذهاب والبدء في تنويم نفس الشخص مغناطيسياً، لتجميد قدرته على معرفة الفرق بين الخطأ والحق. وعادة يجيد الجن منع العقل البشري على الفور من أن يستطيع رؤية أي شيء وراء كل ما يريده الجن. إن إشارات الجن ببساطة تجعل الشخص يفكر أنه على حق والجميع على خطأ. يكون هذا التحكم من إتجاهين من مجموعتين مختلفتين من الجن فعال حقاً وسهل العمل، أحيانا لمدة ثلاثة أو أربعة أيام، فقط عن طريق إرسال الأوامر مرة واحدة أو مرتين.

إذا كان الشخص المستهدف شخص ضعيف العقل، ستطول سيطرة الجن عليه لفترة أطول، ولكن إذا كان الشخص المستهدف شخص قوي في التفكير، سيدرك أخطائه في غضون ثلاثة أربعة أيام، وسيبدأ تصحيح نفسه بعد ثلاثة إلى أربعة أيام. الآن إذا كنت ترغب في إستهداف شخص بإستمرار، أقترح عليك إقامة إتصالات توارد خواطر مع الجن الموجودين حول الشخص المستهدف كل ثلاثة أيام .

We are the 24-7 hour assignment and target of the demons. We are the toys of the demons. We provide entertainment and enjoyment to the demons by accepting and following their commands and the feedings. Demons do not have any physical life by itself.But the brain of a demon is full of the same kind of wishes and desires exactly same way. Demons enjoy all their desires and wishes by using our bodies. I feel different these days. I used to be different. I used to run behind my desires and wishes like crazy all the time. If I was unable to fulfill my wishes or desires, it was making me very upset and unhappy. But nowadays, when I am less under influence of demons, I am really dying for anything. If I can get something easily, I am happy. If I cannot get something, I feel I am okay without it. Without or with less influence of demons on me, I always feel like a slow pace and calm person. Nothing attracts me too much, even if I like something a lot, still I feel I am okay without it. I do not feel or see any push or extra desire to run behind anything.

I cannot stay mad with someone for a long time. I cannot maintain my anger for anything or anyone for a long time. I give up very easily. Still, sometimes I get angry but just for seconds. It is very difficult to really maintain my anger. These things are so unusual for me, even I don't believe this is happening to me. I have a lot of OKs all the times about a lot of things. I do not feel hyper at all. My heartbeats are 100 percent normal. I cannot keep up with any plan, and do not feel love or hate for anyone. It is getting really difficult to hate someone for a long time. Temperament is very even.

Sometimes even it is difficult to pretend to be angry. I am suffering from a very slow pace in my life.

لن أفعل مع أي شخص أكثر من مرة واحدة؛ و السبب في ذلك هو أن ذلك قد يثير بعض المشاكل الخطيرة لكلا الشخصين على حد سواء بغض النظر عما إذا كانوا أشخاص أقوياء أو شخص ضعيف العقل. الأمر يعتمد أيضاً على قوي الجن بالإضافة إلي نفوذك علي الجن. إذا تبعك الجن وأطاعوا أوامرك بدون قيد أو شرط وبشكل صحيح، فإن الشخص المستهدف سيتكون في ورطة إلي أن تتغير أوامرك مع كل مجموعات من الجن، وأقترح عليك إستهداف الناس السيئون والمجانين أو المرضي العقليين؛ سوف تفاجأ بالنتائج. يستغرق الأمر بضعة أيام ليكون لتتحكم بشكل جيد في الناس ذوي الأمزجة أو السلوك المعتدل حقاً. عادة يكون السبب في ذلك هو أن الجن الموجودين حولهم ليسوا من فئة الجن الشربر. وأفضل شيء هو أن ترسل أوامرك لفترة معينة فقط.

بهذه الطريقة سوف تستسلم مجموعة خارجية ثانية من الجن على الأقل في فترة معينة. تذكر، نحن بشر، ولسنا من الجن. لذا الرجاء عدم إستهداف الناس الطيبين. إذا كنت في حاجة لإستهداف الناس المتطرفين، و السلبيين، والمجانين، والسيئين فقط. هذا ليس ضروريا، إذا كنا نفعل هذه الدراما لشخص ما، فالجن يقومون بذلك طوال الوقت مع الناس لتدمير وتشويه سمعتهم وكفاءتهم. أنا لا أفعل مثل هذه الامور مع أحد. ولكن إذا وجدت شخص ما بالصدفة، فأنا أحياناً أقوم بمجرد ممارسة بسيطة، ولكن ليس لوقت طويل. أنا دائماً ما يكون لدي مهلة زمنية للجن للإستسلام. هذه خدعة شائعة جداً، من الجن عندما يريدون إثبات أن بعض البشر مجانين و يعانون من حالة نفسية. آمل أنني كنت قادراً على توضيح ذلك. بإختصار، يضع الجن أشباح أو خيالات وجدران أمام أعيننا. نحن لا نستطيع أن نرى الفرق بين الصواب والخطأ و. أحيانا يجعلنا الجن عمياناً أكثر، حتى أننا لا نستطيع التفريق بين الخير والشر.

I used to be very biased politically and other matters in the life. Religion wise, after all the exposures to my eyes and senses, I cannot think about anything else other than God. I used to be an extreme behavior person, but right now I am not even a moderate person. I am way slow and easygoing even as compared to a moderate person. I do not want to drive my car fast. This is a big change. I used to drive so fast all the time. Always in a hurry, always drive fast. And now I just want to drive my car in the last and with a very normal speed. I do not feel hurry for anything. I am very careless about a lot of things. So I don't know if everyone will like a lifestyle like this. Anyway do not worry about it because I am different. I have a lot of control and command over my mind. I am so much able to fight, resist, and argue with demons all the time, even my demon friends send me contact signals by maintaining some distance most of the time. My body has a lot of resistance against demons. Only new demons try to possess my body but give up in a few seconds. Even if any human comes close to me, their demons have to leave their bodies until they are around me. Usually demons do not want to leave the human body that's why strong demons try their best to keep their human bodies away from me by hypnotizing them. I am a lot able to keep my mind and body away from the possession of a demon. I think that's why I am experiencing different and a slow pace of life. But for you as a normal person, even whatever you do you cannot reject a control of a demon on your mind all the time. To me it is impossible for a normal person to keep themselves away from demons 100 percent. The maximum, what some can do, even use all their and my procedures against demons?

الآن فإنكم كلكم ستسيطرون بشكل جيد جداً على الجن الموجودين حولك، لذلك يمكنك أن تقرر كيف ستستخدمهم. ستحتاج إلى أن تستخدمهم هنا وهناك، وإلا لن يكون لديك ما يكفي من الممارسة إذا احتجت إلى استخدامهم.

أفضل وسيلة هي نشر الخير فقط في كل مكان. الآن قد تسألني لماذا أكتب كل الأشياء في الأسطر أعلاه. السبب الرئيسي هو جلب بعض الوعي بين الناس أنهم لا يجب أن يقللوا من شأن أي شخص من حولهم، وهذا لا يعني أن الشخص الفقير والضعيف المظهر يكون دائماً ضعيفاً وغير قادر على القيام بأي شيء. أنت لا تعرف أبداً، ربما هذا يستطيع ذلك الشخص أن يضعك في ورطة كبيرة كلما أراد ذلك. هذا الشخص قد يبدو ضعيفاً، لكنك لا تعلم أبداً، قد يكون لديه جن أشرارو متوحشون للغاية من حوله، ليس من الضروري أن يفعل هوالكثير، فقط يمكنه تمرير أوامره إلى الجن الموجودين حوله، وسيكون ذلك أكثر شيئ كاف لهؤلاء الجن ليتصرفوا. لذلك كن حذراً. لا تجعل لك أعداءً. احترم الجميع دائماً، لأنك لا تعرف من الذي يغضب منك ويجعل حياتك جحيماً. سياستي هي تدريب كل شخص، بحيث إذا كان عاجزاً جسدياً، فإنه سيشعر بقوة و ثقة بسبب الجن الموجودين حوله. بنفس الطريقة، إذا كان هناك شخص ما قوي حقاً، يجب أن يكون حذراً قبل إزدراء أو جرح شخص ما. هل تعتقد أنني أؤمن بمفهوم توازن القوى؟ إذا لم أكن كذلك، لماذا أقوم بتدريبكم كلكم؟. لقد اعتدت في الماضي، أن أغضب كثيراً. كان ذلك سهلاً جداً. لقد كان لدي دائما الكثير من الطاقة والقوة لأغضب وأصبح في أي وقت ولأي شخص.لقد اعتدت أن أغضب حتى لأشياء بسيطة جداً بسهولة. لم أجد أبداً لدي أي مشكلة بفعل ذلك. لكن في هذه الأيام عندما لا يقع جسدي/عقلي تحت سيطرة الجن معظم الوقت، لا أشعر بما يكفي من النشاط لأغضب.

The maximum you can do is to repel an evil demon from you to avoid extreme behavior and become a moderate person with the influence of a good, nice, easygoing and friendly demon, The maximum, what some can do, even use all their and my procedures against demons? The maximum you can do is to repel an evil demon from you to avoid extreme behavior and become a moderate person with the influence of a good, nice, easygoing and friendly demon. Still you will have a good demon around you, so you do not need to worry about slow pace of the life, because even if a good and friendly demon keeps you in a moderate condition still will ask you to go for bunch of desires/wishes and enjoyable physical activities to do. But at this point, the positive thing is that by knowing all these things about demons and their actions, you will have better understanding of your decisions, your mind, your anger, your extremism, and you will have a very good idea of accepting and rejecting the demon control on your mind. Another problem is that the brain of a demon and the brain of a human are very much similar when we talk about desires and wishes. So 90 percent of the time we almost have same desires and wishes, whatever, our demons feed in our minds to get more and more physical enjoyment and happiness. But as a human, we are ready to give up very easily any desire or wish, but demon control do not let us to give up about any desire or wish easily. For example, who wants to reject when a demon generates an immediate desire to have sex or to get drunk or to smoke, sleep a little longer, or don't do workout, don't go to work, don't go to school, etc?. Right, Here is my point. You desire for a lot of things continuously.

ما زلت لا أحب الكثير من الأشياء، ولكن لا شيء يبقيني غاضباً لفترة طويلة. أشعر دائماً أنني ليس لدي الكثير من الطاقة لأغضب أوأثور على شخص ما. معظم الوقت، أشعر أني في منتهي الصبر و الراحة هذه الأيام. إنني دائماً أفاجأ لماذا لم يكن لدي ما يكفي من الطاقة للغضب. أشعر بأني كسول وبطيئ، وبمجرد أن يحين وقت الغضب. حتى عندما تكون هناك حاجة للتصرف بغضب حقاً، بسبب شيء ما يحدث من حولي، ولكن هذه الحالة تزول بمنتهي السرعة، وأعود إلى حالة الهدوء والإسترخاء الوضع في وقت قصير جداً. الآن بهذه المناقشة، يمكنك تصور مدى سهولة أن يبقينا الجن على إستعداد للثورة والغضب. إن إستحواذ الجن علينا يجلب لنا الكثير من الطاقة التي نستخدمها في الأنشطة السلبية، مثل الغضب الشديد، و عدم الصبر،سرعة الغضب، الخ.

بالتأكيد كل هذه الطاقات تأتي من أذهاننا، ولكن يجعلنا الجن نولد ونستخدم هذه الطاقات في السلوك المتطرف والسلبي. أشعر بقوة إذا الجن غير موجودون حول شخص ما، فهذا الشخص لا يمكنه أن يولد الكثير من الطاقة من قبل نفسه لإستخدامها في السلوك السلبي والمتطرف.فإذا كان إستطعنا بطريقة ما إبقاءأنفسنا بعيداً عن سيطرة الجن، سوف نكون أكثر إسترخاءً، وأكثر هدوءاً، وأكثر صبراً. سيكون لدينا المزيد من التسامح. لن نغضب بسهولة، و لن يكون من السهل على أي شخص إغضابنا بسهولة . أنا لا أعرف ماذا أقول من شأنه أن يساعدك أكثر. الآن سأحاول وصف حالة إستحواذ الجن علي شخص ضعيف حيث يتغير صوته وحركات جسمه يتغير صوت هذا الشخص تماماً ،و يصبح مختلفاً ومخيفاً عند سماعه.,و تزداد القوة و الوحشية في أجزاء الجسم عادة خلال حركات اليدين والساقين، من المؤكد أن تحدث هذه الحالة، عندما يخرج الجني من بعض الأجسام الغير آدمية، مثل سحلية كبيرة في العمر حقا، حقا القديمة أو نوع آخر مشابه من الأجسام الأخري، الكبيرة في العمر.

Some you like, some maybe you don't like, but due to control of demons, you just cannot figure out between right and wrong easily. My problem these days is that no demons are generating any desires/wishes in my system most of the time. My desires/wishes operated and controlled by the demons is off most of the time. I still think and wish for a lot of things but I am not ready to be persuaded by them and very easily ready to give up about anything. As much I observed in this kind of conditions, I feel, there are less attraction and less enjoyment in life. So I really don't know what I can do, because I cannot allow any demon to have control of my mind or body again. My body cannot tolerate their presence even close to me. Even demons have some burning problems once they come close to me, so they cannot stay close to me for a long time either. So I guess I will live this slow-paced life for the rest of the years of my life.

But don't worry about yourself. You will never come to this condition. The reason is that 90 percent of the time even you will not have any clue about the demons around you, even you are under influence of a demon, when a demon will be hypnotizing and controlling you. And a lot of times you will not have enough courage to reject some desires/wishes, even you will have clear idea that a demon is pushing you for that. So you are okay. And you will be okay until you will keep an evil demon away from you and keep only good, friendly, and moderate demons around you. It is very easy to become a friend of a moderate demon as compared to a devil and evil demon. If you do not like to be an even-tempered and moderate person, keep your evil and devil nature demons around you.

جدا هؤلاء الجن، متوحشون وأشرار مستوى بشكل متطرف. عادة ما تكون هذه هي المرة الأولى لهم في داخل جسم الإنسان. هؤلاء الجن ينزعجون ويغضبون للغاية ، إذا إضطروا لترك هذه الأجسام الغير إنسانية بسبب وفاتهم. هذا هو إحتمال إذا قتل ذلك الإنسان الضحية هذا الأجسام الغير إنسانية. مثل سحلية و نتيجة لذلك يخرج جني من تلك الأجسام الغير آدمية ليستحوذوا علي جسم الإنسان. هذا النوع من الجن ليس لديه أي جاذبية لأي جسم من الأجسام البشرية أو الغير آدمية، ولكنهم لا يزالون يستحوذون علي تلك الأجسام لمجرد الانتقام. و أفضل وجه للإنتقام هو تدمير عقل و جسم هذا الشخص، إذاً لا تفكر في جعل هؤلاء الجن أصدقائك من الخطوة الأولى. يجب عليك أولاً طرد هؤلاء الجن من ذلك الجسم. بمجرد أن يهدأ هؤلاء الجن، سيتواصلون معك، ولكنك لست بحاجة إلى أن تكون لطيفاً معهملي أن يهدأوا، الآن يمكنك أن تأخذ الشخص الضحية إلى المستشفى، ومنحهم الدواء و العلاج. قم بفعل كل ما ترضي به من وجهة نظر العلوم الطبية. ولكن لا تعطي المريض أدوية لإسترخاء المخ، مثل حبوب النعاس أو الدواء، إذاً إفعل كل ما يطلبه منك الطبيب هذا مهم، .ولكن حتى كل هذه الأدوية والعلاجات مهمة، ولكن لن يخرج الجني من هذا الجسم بسبب تلك الأدوية.

أعلم أنه أمر مزعج جداً عندما يرش شخص ما الماء على الوجه / الرأس / العنق / الأذن / الصدر / الظهر، ولكن بغض النظر عن كل ما يحدث فإن الضحية البشرية في حاجة إلى أن تلمس أرضية معدنية أو أسمنتية أو سيراميك من أي جزء من الجسم للوقوف عليها.

ثم في بداية كل ثلاثين دقيقة كل ساعة ثم بعد ذلك كل قم برش الماء المقدس في البداية كل ثلاثين دقيقة، ثم كل ساعة، ثم كل ساعتين ثم كل خمس...

Do not spray any holy water on yourself and on them; otherwise, everything will change to a moderate level. Demons can easily destroy the image and personality of any human very easily. Demons can make a person say some wrong stuff all the time. On other hand, that person will never figure out between right and wrong due to ability of demons to freeze his mind and memory. This is two-directional hypnotism by two different demons. If you ask me, how I will do it, let me explain to you. First I will send instructions and commands to the demons already around someone. I will ask them to convince someone by hypnotism to say something wrong again and again. It is easy to use demons already around someone, the reason is that those demons already have access to the mind of that targeted person. In a few days, usually those demons will have total command of that person. They will make him say wrong and crappy stuff all the time whenever this person will open his mouth to talk. During this, it is important to send a few more demons from here and there to support the demons already around that targeted person. Now new demons need to go and start hypnotizing the same person to freeze his ability to figure out the difference between wrong and right. And usually demons are so good in blocking the human mind immediately so humans cannot see anything beyond whatever demons want. Demons' signals simply make him think that, he is right and everyone else is wrong. This two-way control from two different groups of demons is really effective and easy work, sometimes for three or four days, just by sending commands one or two times. If target person is a weak-minded person then this control of the demons will work on him for a longer time, but if the targeted person is a strong-minded person,

ساعات، إستمر في رش الماء المقدس على الإنسان الضحية والمناطق المحيطة به بشكل مستمر. يحتاج ذلك الإنسان إلى شرب الماء المقدس بإستمرار. بغض النظر عن مدي قوة ذلك الجني أو مدي جنونه، هذا الماء المقدس سوف يركل ذلك الجني خارج ذلك الجسم، فالماء المقدس يحدث الكثير من تشويه في الجسم الكهرومغناطيسي للجن. لا يستطيع أي إنسان مساعدة ذلك الشخص بقدر ما يستطيع الماء المقدس مساعدته في ذلك الإنسان الضحية ضد سيطرة الجن الشرير. الجن مثلنا إلى حد كبير، أو أقول أنهم أكثر سلبية وتطرفاً منا، حيث أن لديهم جميع أنواع العواطف و الأمزجة السلبية. هل الجن يغارون وينتقمون؟ نعم، غيورين و إنتقاميون بشدة. فبمجرد أن يتعلق الجن بشخص ما، فهم يشعرون أن ذلك الشخص أو الإنسان أو الجسم من ممتلكاتهم. يعمل الجن بشكل غيور جداً بالنسبة لذلك الجسم أو الشخص، فهم لا يتحملون مجرد أن يحاول شخص ما الإقتراب من ذلك الإنسان. الآن للحفاظ على سيطرتهم علي ذلك الجسم أو الإنسان، سيستمر الجن في زيادة تأثيرهم و سيطرتهم علي ذلك الجسم بالقدر الذي يجعله يفقد السيطرة علي أجزائه، و هكذا سوف يقول ذلك الشخص كلاماً غريباً وبأصوات غريبة .

سيتحرك الجسم البشري هنا و هناك بشكل غير منتظم و غير طبيعي. فقد السيطرة على الدماغ وأجزاء الجسم. لا يهتم الجني الشرير بذلك الإنسان. يهتم ذلك الجني بالسيطرة علي ذلك الجسم بنسبة 100 في المئة بغض النظر عن ما إذا مات ذلك الجسم أثناء تلك السيطرة. قتل الشياطين. لا يوجد طبيب أو شيطان لا يستطيع أي جني آخر المساعدة أكثر أو أفضل من الماء المقدس في تقليل مغناطيسية الجسم الإلكتروني في ذلك الجني.

then he may realize his mistakes in three four days and will start correcting himself after three to four days. Now if you want to target someone continuously then I will suggest you need to establish telepathic contact with the demons around the targeted person every three days. I will not do this with anyone more than one time; the reason is that it may create some serious problem for both regardless of whether they are strong or a weak-minded person.

It also depends on the powers of the demons plus your influence on demons. If demons follow you and your commands unconditionally and properly, then that targeted person will be in trouble until you will change your commands with both groups of the demons. I will suggest you to target only bad and already-crazy/psycho people; you will be surprised with the outcome. It takes a few days to have really good control of even-tempered or moderate-behavior people. Usually the reason is that the demons around them are not from the evil category of the demons. The best thing is to send your commands only for a particular period. This way at least a second group of outsider demons will give up after certain period. Remember, we are human, not demons. So please do not target good people. If you need to just target extremists, negative, crazy, and bad people only. This is not necessary, if only we do this drama to someone, demons do this all the time with people to destroy and ruin their reputation and competence. I don't do things like this to anyone. But by chance, if I find someone, sometimes I do just a little bit practice, but not for long time. I always have a time limit for demons to give up. This is a very common trick of demons when they want to prove some human is crazy and psycho.

الأحلام شيئ كبير للغاية بالنسبة لنا حتى الآن ولكن سوف تكون مثل الأفلام في المستقبل. نحن نفكر دائماً في الأحلام ونحاول معرفة التوقعات والآثار المحتملة للأحلام في واقع حياتنا . كل شخص لديه توقعات وإفتراضات مختلفة حول أحلام معينة.

ثق بي، إذا كنا نخلط أحلامنا مع حياتنا الحقيقية والعملية، فإننا نضيع وقتنا و طاقتنا. إن الأحلام مثل الأفلام التي نشاهدها في حياتنا اليومية.تماماً. يقوم ممثلون مختارون فقط بالتمثيل في السينما، بينما. لكن الجن يختارون الموجودون حولنا يختارون الممثلين.. لأفلام الحقيقية لديها عملية كاملة من السيناريو، والحوارات، والممثلين، و المنتج، و المخرج، و المصور، والمحررين، وما إلى ذلك، و بعد عملية طويلة نحصل على فيلم واحد لمشاهدته. ثم نحتاج إلى تلفزيون ومشغل أفلام. بالرغم من أن أحلامنا تشبه الأفلام بنسبة 100 في المئة ، فهي لا تكلف أي شخص مالاً كثيراً، وكذلك لا يستغرق إنتاج حلماً وقتاً طويلاً. تستطيع عقولنا وعيوننا وآذاننا إستقبال أشعة الصور و الأصوات و ترجمتها في عقولنا وعيوننا وآذاننا. نتيجة لتلك الآلية المتوفرة بالفعل في عقولنا، نكون قادرين على رؤية الأفلام التي شاهدناها على جهاز الفيديو أو جهاز الدي في دي. هناك نظام آخر أو آلية أخرى في في عقولنا تمكننا من رؤية الأشياء والأفكار أو الصور في خيالنا. بدون إستخدام العينين. الجن مسؤولون تماماً، وليس عليهم أن تخوض عملية طويلة من ممثلين، و مخرج و عملية تحرير إلخ.. يستطيع الجن إنتاج حلماً من خيالهم. في الخطوة التالية،يقوم الجن بنقل حلم الخيال كإشارة إلكترونية إلي عقلنا،ثم يقوم عقلنا بترجمة هذه الإشارات في شكل حلم.

Rizwan Qureshi

I hope I was able to explain. Shortcut, demons put shades in front of our eyes; demons put walls in front our eyes. We cannot see the difference of right and the wrong. Sometimes demons make us so much blind even we cannot differentiate between good and the bad. Now all of you will have very good control of the demons around you, so you can decide how to use them. You need to use them here and there; otherwise, you will not have enough practice once you will need to use them.

The best way is just spread good everywhere. Now you may ask me then why I write all the stuff in the above lines. The main reason is to bring some awareness among people that they do not need to underestimate anyone around them. It does not mean a poor and a weak-looking person is always weak and incapable of doing anything. You never know; maybe this person can put you in a big trouble whenever he wants it. That person may look weak but you never know, he may have extremely wild and evil demons around him. He does not have to do too much. Only he has to pass his commands to his demons, and it will be more than enough for his demons to act. So always be careful. Do not make enemies. Always respect everyone. Because you never know who gets angry with you and make your life hell. My policy is to train everyone, so if he is helpless physically, will still feel strong and confident due to demons around him. Same way, if someone is really powerful and strong, he needs to be careful before he disrespects or hurt someone. Do you think I believe in the concept of the balance of power? If I did not why should I be training all of you? In the past, I used to get angry frequently. It was very easy.

رؤية الجن و الآلام السيطرة عليها

يجب أن يفكر الجن فقط في أي قصة وشخصيات في أفكارهم ومخيلاتهم. لإنشاء حلم، في الخطوة الثانية ينقل الجن تلك الأحلام والكوابيس، والقصص والأفكار المخيفة من نظام خيالهم لنظام خيالنا ليظهروا لنا الأحلام. . يمكننا القول بلغة الكمبيوتر أن الجن ينسخون أفكارهم وخيالهم ويلصقونها في موقع نظام خيالنا في عقلنا. خلال عملية نقل الجن قصصهم الوهمية إلى عقولنا، تقوم عقولنا بمعالجة وترجمة هذه القصص الخيالية من الجن لتجعل الأحلام تبدو لنا وكأنها 100% مماثلة إلى واقع أحداث الحياة. يفكر الجن وينقلون خيالهم في شكل إشارات إلكترونية. خلال عملية قيام الجن بتنويمنا مغناطيسياً ليظهروا لنا حلماً، لا تكون لدي أي سيطرة من عقلنا على الإطلاق.، كما أننا لا تكون لدينا أي سيطرة على الأحلام.

الأحلام هي محض أفكار شقية أو خطيرة أو قصص من عقل الجني. لا يمكننا تعديل أو تغيير أحلامنا. ولكن يمكننا أن نطلب من الجن أن يظهروا لنا الأحلام نفسها التي نحبها أو نريد أن نراها في أحلامنا، هذا سهل جداً. فقط يجب أن تطلب منهم ذلك بكل ثقة بنسبة 100 في المئة. أرى عادة الأحلام التي أريد أن أراها. في اليوم الأول، كل جني جديد يفعل ما يحلو له إظهاره، ولكن في اليوم التالي، يحتاجون إلى النظر وضع رغبتي في الإعتبار أيضاً، إذا كانوا لا يريدون أن يروني غاضباً و غير سعداء بهم. لي مفاجأة وغير سعيدة معهم. لذلك يمكنك ان تفعل الشيء نفسه أيضاً. قبل أن تنام، إنظر نحو كتفيك وأخبرهم بكل ثقة ما تريد أن تراه في أحلامك.

على أي حال، ليس لدينا أي سيطرة علي عقولنا خلال عملية الأحلام، بنفس الطريقة التي يكون لدينا بها السيطرة على عقولنا أثناء يقظتنا. علينا أن مشاهدة كل ما في أحلامنا. لا يمكننا تخطي أي جزء من أحلامنا لمجرد إما لأننا لا نحبه أو لا نرغب في مشاهدته. خلال الأحلام، ونكون تحت تصرف الجن تماماً، فكل ما يريدون إظهاره لنا، علينا فقط مشاهدته. لا نستطيع نحن و لا عقولنا أن نرفض سيطرة الجن وعملية الأحلام علي الإطلاق، ما لم يوقظنا شيء، وبمجرد أن نستيقظ، ستتوقف عقولنا عن تلقي إشارة إلكترونية من عقل الجني.

I always have a lot of energy and power to get angry and yell anytime at anyone. I used to get irritated and upset even for very minor things very easily. I never had any problem doing it. But these days when most of the time my body/mind is not under the possession of demons, I do not feel energetic enough to get angry. I still do not like a lot of things, but nothing keeps me upset for long time. I always feel I don't have as much energy to get angry or irritated at somebody. Most of the time, I feel very patient and very relaxed these days. It always surprised me why I don't have enough energy to get angry. I feel so lazy and slow, once the time comes to get angry. Even when I need to act really irritated due to something happening around me, but this condition goes away so quick and fast, and I come back to my calm and relaxed mode in no time. Now from this discussion, you can imagine how easily demons keep us ready to get irritated and angry. The possession of the demons bring in us a lot of energy to use for negative activities like to get extremely angry, act impatient, short-tempered, etc.

Definitely all these energies are coming from our mind, but demons make us generate and use these energies for extreme and negative behavior. I strongly feel if demons are not around someone, that person cannot generate so much energy by himself to use for negative and extreme behavior. So if somehow we can keep ourselves away from the possession of demons, we will be more relaxed, calmer, and more patient.

وسوف يخل ذلك تماماً بعملية إنتاج الحلم. ليس لدي الجن أي حلم بشكل مسبق بالنسبة لنا. الأحلام هي إنتقال حي للإشارات الإلكترونية من عقل الجني إلى العقل البشري. معظم الوقت، وبمجرد ان نعود الى النوم، تكون الأحلام مختلفة عن سابقاتها، لكن هذا ليس ضرورياً. إذا الجني هو نفسه، قد يستمر الحلم حول نفس الموضوع. وبمجرد أن نستيقظ، يستطيع معظمنا إستعادة سيطرتنا علي عقلنا بنسبة 100 % على الفور. إن الأشخاص ذوي العقول الضعيفة أو الواقعين كليا تحت سيطرة الجن يعانون من رؤية أشياء وهمية مثل الأشباح، والساحرات، أو المخلوقات الخيالية الأخرى، حتي أثناء يقظتهم. حتي عندما تصل. الجن يستخدمون آلية الخيال الموجودة في عقولنا لنقل أحلامهم، و أفكارهم، و قصصهم إلينا، من خلال إستخدام قوتهم في التنويم المغناطيسي. و تقوم عقولنا بترجمة تلك الإشارات الإلكترونية للتنويم المغناطيسي من الأحلام بسهولة، ويظهر الجن لنا القصص والحوادث، والصور.لأحلام، كأنها في الحياة الحقيقية. هناك القليل من الإختلاف بين رؤية الأحلام أثناء النوم، ورؤية بعض الصور في اليقظة. أولا، عملية رؤية الأحلام أثناء النوم لا تتدخل فيهاعيوننا، فعملية من حلم لا تحتاج إلي العينين، وهكذا فالأعمي يري الأحلام أيضاً. إن عملية رؤية الصور، مثل الأشباح أو الساحرات حول الأشجار أو في الأماكن المظلمة هو خلل من الجن عن طريق خلط إشاراتها الإلكترونية للأشباح الوهمية / الساحرات مع الأشاعات التي تدخل و تخرج من عيوننا. في كلمات بسيطة، يمكننا القول إن الجن يستطيعون أن ينومونا مغناطيسياً لنا حتى و لو كنا مستيقظين ويمكنهم أن يظهروا لنا ما يريدونه. نحن نحتاج إلي عيوننا لعملية رؤية صور الأشباح / الساحرات، و. الأمر معقد، أليس كذلك؟ أنا واثق من العلوم الحديثة سوف تتوصل إلي هذا قريباً، وسوف تجلب لنا المزيد من التفاصيل.

We will have more tolerance. We will not get angry easily. It will not be easy for someone to upset us easily. I don't know what else to say that will help you more. Now I will try to describe a condition of a possession of a demon on a very weak person when the voice and body movements of that person are totally changed, the voice of that person is different and scary when you hear him. During movements of his hands and legs, the power and the wildness of body parts are usually increased than normal. For sure this condition happens when a demon comes out from some inhuman body like a really, really old lizard or similar kind of another body but really old.

These demons are just wild and evil of very extreme level. Usually, they are first time inside a human body. These evil demons are extremely upset and angry once they have to leave those inhuman bodies due to their death. It is a possibility if that victim human killed those inhuman bodies like lizard, and as a result a demon comes out from that inhuman body and possesses the body of that human. These kinds of demons do not have any attraction for any human body or inhuman, but still they possessed those bodies just to take revenge. And their best revenge is to destroy the mind and body of that person. Don't even think about making these demons your friends in the first step. First step should be to kick them out from that body. Once they will calm down, they communicate with you. But until they calm down you don't need to be nice with them. Now you can take victim person to hospital, give them medication. Do everything that will satisfy you from the point of view of the medical science. But do not give patient brain-relaxing medications, i. e., drowsy pills or medication.

الآن الجزء التالي هو نوعية الأحلام، فالقليل من الجن يعمل بجد لإظهار أحلام عالية الجودة لنا، بغض النظر عن ما إذا كان ذلك لتخويفنا أو لجعلنا سعداء، حيث يستطيع جني واحد قراءة عقولنا، و بمنتهى السهولة يقومون بسحب بعض الشخصيات والقضايا من واقع الحياة من حولنا في حياتنا الحقيقية. لكن هؤلاء الجن لا يخوضون في التفاصيل أكثر من اللازم، فبمجرد أن يحصل الجن على بعض المعرفة الأساسية، والصور، و المعلومات من عقلنا، يقومون بإختلاق بعض القصص، ومزجها مع الناس أو الصور بشكل عشوائي في ذاكرتهم. هذا ما نحتاجه فقط من الجن الجدد والغرباء من حولنا. أما الجن الموجودون بالفعل بالقرب منا لسوا في حاجة إلى قراءة عقولنا للحصول على بعض المعلومات لأنهم عادة ما يكونوا على علم بهذا الموضوع. بمجرد أن يكون لديك بالفعل بعض الجن من حولك، إما أنت أو أحد أفراد الأسرة سيستوعبون القليل من الجن من هنا وهناك إما من خلال محادثة هاتفية أو أثناء السفر، و تأتي بكل هؤلاء الجن إلى منزلك. هذه هي عملية منتظمة للحصول على الجن من هنا وهناك. أحيانا هؤلاء الجن يبقون حولنا و في أحيان أخري يرجعون إلي أصحابهم الأصليين. إذا تأقلم الجن من حولنا أو حول منزلنا ضبط بسهولة مع جن جدد من مختلف العائلات أو الحيوانات أو المناطق، سنري أحلام معقدة جداً وفريدة من نوعها طوال الوقت. إذا كان الجن كسالى، ستكون أحلامهم بلا معنى بالنسبة لنا، أو ستكون أحلام قصيرة جداً. لكن إذا كان الجن يستمعون إلى كل ما تريد أن تراه، فهم أذكياء ولديهم كفاءة، و سوف تحب النوم أربعة و عشرين ساعة في الإسبوع حتى تتمكن من مشاهدة أحلامك. إذا كان شخص ما تحت سيطرة جني واحد تماماً، فسوف يكون هو الزعيم أو المسؤول عن الأحلام. هذا الجني سوف ينتجون الأحلام لنا، إما ما يحبه الجني أو ما نطلبه منه أن يظهرونه لنا في أحلامنا.

SEE & CONTROL DEMONS & PAIN

رضوان قرشي

So do everything whatever a doctor asks you to do. It is important. But even all those medication and treatments are important, but still that demon will not come out from that body due to those medications. I know it is very annoying once someone sprays water on you face/ head/ neck/ ear/ chest/ back, but regardless of whatever happens that human victim needs to touch some metal or cement, ceramic floor from any part of the body for the grounding purpose.

Spray holy water in beginning every thirty minutes then every hour then every two hours then every five hours, keep spraying holy water on the victim human and their surroundings continuously. That human needs to drink holy water continuously. Regardless of how much the powerful is a demon or how much that demon is mad, this holy water will kick that demon out of that body. Holy water creates a lot of distortion in the electromagnetic demon's body. No human can help that person as much as the holy water can help that human victim against the possession of an evil demon. Demons are pretty much like us, or I will say way more negative and extremist than us. Demons are full of all kinds of emotions and negative temperament. Do demons get jealous and revengeful? Yes, extremely jealous and revengeful. Once demons get too attached with someone, demons feel that person or human or body is their property. Demons act very possessive in case of that body or person. Demons do not tolerate once someone else tries to come close to that that human. Now to maintain their possession of that body or human, demons will keep increasing their influence and ..

لكن اذا حصل شخص ما علي جن من هنا وهناك، بالإضافة إلى الكثير من الجن الذين يعيشون مع الحشرات أوالزواحف، أ والفئران، أوالحيوانات من حولك أو حول المنزل، قد ينضم أيضاً هؤلاء الجن إلى عملية إنتاج الأحلام أحياناً . إذا أصبح هؤلاء الجن أصدقائك و كانوا على إستعداد ليظهروا لك كل ما تريد مشاهدته في أحلامك، فإن ذلك سيكون نجاحاً كبيراً في حياتك الترفيهية. وسوف يجلب الجن الجدد والغرباء دائماً، ؛ كل شيئ مخيف، و قذر، أو على الأقل ما لا ترغب في مشاهدته في أحلامك. عندما يقوم مجموعة من الجن بالسيطرة على عقلنا، وإنتاج حلم لنا، وسوف تكون تلك الأحلام أكثر تعقيداً وغرابة. إذا خرج الجن من سحلية، يعرف أو يهتم معظمهم بالسحالي فقط، و كذلك الجن الذين يخرجون من القطة / الكلب / فأر يعرفون عادة المزيد عن تلك الحيوانات. سيهتم هؤلاء الجن بنفس النوع من السلالة التي عادة ما يحبون أن يعيشوا فيها أو يبقوا حولها. إذا كان لدينا بعض الجن من مختلف المناطق أو الأسر من حولنا، أوسلالة مختلفة /عرق مختلف من حولك، فإذا جعلتهم أصدقائك، تخيل مدي سهولة إنتاج هذا الجن أحلام ذات درجة عالية لك. ليس من الصعب إقناع الجن أن يظهروا لك أحلام وفق رغباتك. أولاً،تتصرف دائماً بثقة بنسبة 100 في المئة عندما تتحدث اليهم. يجب أن تكون على ثقة تامة بأنهم حولك و يستمعون لك. أخبرهم كل ليلة بما تريد أن تراه في أحلامك قبل أن تنام. إذا كانوا لا يزالون انهم يسببون لك إزعاجاً، فبغض النظر عن ما يظهرونه لك في الأحلام، لا تهتم بها، و إستمر في أن تطلب منهم أن يستمعوا إليك، و إلا سيضيعون وقتهم. دعني أروي لك حادثة و احدة. إنها سيئة قليلاً ، ولكنها سوف تساعدك على فهم طبيعة الجن قليلاً.

سألني أحد الموظفين كيف يستطيع أن يتحدث مع الجن الخاص به ليجلوه يري الأحلام التي يريد أن يراها، و كالعادة، شرحت له كيف يقوم بذلك،

226

Rizwan Qureshi	رؤية الجن و الآلام السيطرة عليها

control of that body as much, when that human will lose control of their brain and body parts. In that condition, that person will say weird stuff in weird voices. The human body will move here and there totally in disorder and abnormal way. That evil demon does not have any care for that human. That demon is just concerned to keep hold of that body 100 percent regardless of whether that body dies during that killing possession of demons. No demon doctor or no other demon can help more than or better than holy water to demagnetize the electronic body of that demon.

Dreams are a very big deal for us until now but will be like movies in the future. We always think about dreams and try to find out possible predictions and impacts of dreams in our real life. Everyone has different predictions and assumptions about particular dreams.

Trust mc, if wc arc mixing our dreams with our real and practical life, for sure we are making a big mistake and wasting our time and energy. Dreams are just like movies we watch in our everyday life. In movies, only some selected actors do the acting. But in dreams, demons around us choose the actors. Real movies have a whole process of script, dialogs, actors, producer, director, cameraman, editors, etc., then after a long process we get one movie to watch. Then we need a TV set and a movie player. Even though our dreams are 100 percent like movies, but our dreams do not cost anyone that much money. Production of a dream is not that much time-consuming either.

و بعد إسبوع واحد واتتني فرصة للتحدث معه، وبدأ يحكي لي عن بعض أحلامه. إنه سيئ قليلاً، لكن قد يساعدك على فهم الجن. وقال، "قبل أن أذهب إلى الفراش للنوم، سألت الجن من حولي لمدة عشر دقائق على الأقل أن يذهبوا بي في هذه الليلة في كل الأماكن التي ذهبت فيها في كل يوم أو كل اسبوع أو كل شهر أو كل سنة.

و تأكد من أن جميع النساء الجميلات يجب أن يرتدوا ملابس خفيفة أينما ذهبت". حسنا، أيها القراء، انا آسف، لا أستطيع أن أكتب كلامه بالضبط. على أي حال لذلك قال أنه لا يرى نفس الحلم بالضبط طوال الليل. لم يسبق له ان استيقظت في أي وقت واحد خلال الليل. ولكن فقط والمشكلة في الحلم هو أن جميع النساء، أينما ذهب، كن يرتدين الثياب المناسبة والجميلة، لكنه كان يرتدي ملابس داخلية واحدة خلال زيارته إلى جميع الأماكن طوال الليل. ثم قال أنه تحدث إلى كل إمرأة و، ولكن خلال الحلم كله، وقال أنه كان يشعر بالحرج، والإهانة، والخزي، أينما ذهب طوال الليل في حلمه. حسنا، أنا لا أعرف ماذا أقول. قلت له فقط. ثم سألني مرة أخرى لماذا حدث هذا. وأجبته فقط، ربما يريد الجني الخاص بك أن يعطيك رسالة ما. قلت له أيضاً أن على الأقل أنك الآن تعلم أن الجني الخاص بك يصغي إليك، أو على الأقل هو علي هو إتصال بك الآن. في الحقيقة أنا لا أعرف ما إذا كان يفهمني أم لا، لكنه قال أنه سيقوم بممارسة أكثر وتركني. آمل أنه ربما تتعلم شيء من هذا الحادث أيضاً.

الماء نفسه لديه بعض صفات إزالة المغناطيسية. ولكن بالتأكيد، الماء المقدس هو أداة سلاح ممتاز، وأداة جيدة جداً لإزالة المغناطيسية. إن الجن هم أجسام مادية كهرومغناطيسية. إنهم يتنقلون في المجال الكهرومغناطيسي المتوفر طبيعياً في الجو المفتوح.

SEE & CONTROL DEMONS & PAIN

Our brain, eyes, ears are able to receive and decode rays of pictures and sounds in our brain, eyes, and ears. Due to that already-available mechanism in our brain, we are able to see movies we played on a VCR or a DVD player. There is another system or mechanism in our brain, and that mechanism enables us to see things and thoughts or images in our imaginations without the use of eyes. Demons are totally responsible for producing the dreams. Demons do not have to go any long process of actors, director, editing process etc. Demons are capable of producing a dream by their imagination. In the next step, demons transfer the dream imagination as an electronic signal to our brain. Then our brain decodes those signals in the shape of a dream. In easy and nontechnical language we can say demons hypnotize us to convey and convert their thought and imagination into our minds to show us dreams. To create a dream, demons have to just think about any story and characters in their thoughts and imaginations. In second step demons transfer those dreams, nightmares, their scary stories and ideas from their imagination system to our imagination system to show us dreams. In computer language you can say that demons copy their thoughts and imagination and paste in our imagination system of our brain. During the process when demons transfer their imaginary stories to our brains, our brains process and decode those imaginary stories of demons to show us dreams, to look like 100 percent similar to real-life events. Demons think , transfer their imaginations in shape of electronic signals. During the process, when a demon is hypnotizing us to show us a dream, we do not have any control of our mind at all. We do not have any control on dreams.

إن رش الماء المقدس في الهواء أو في الإتجاه المحتمل فيه وجود الجن يطيرون أو نحو وجهنا / رقبتنا / أذننا / رأسنا / صدرنا، سيحدث ذلك بعض التشويش في المجال الكهرومغناطيسي والجن الكهرومغناطيسيين. إن الماء المقدس ليس حلاً كاملاً أو دائماً ضد سلالة الجن. إن الماء المقدس مشكلة بالنسبة للجن ومسار إنتقالهم بالتأكيد. إذا قمت برش بعض الماء على دارة إلكترونية حية، قد يحدث إنقطاع للتيار الكهربائي. نفس الشيء بالضبط أو نفس العلاقة بين الماء المقدس والجن.

إن عقولنا آلات ممتازة. ينتهي العقل أو يموت مع عملية الموت. ولكن لن يحدث جنان أو حالة نفسية للمخ من تلقاء نفسه، يحدث خلل أو اضطراب أو مشكلة داخل المخ بمجرد أن تسبب الآلام الضرر المادي للمخ، و ذلك للحصول على إحتياجاتهم الغذائية أو الطاقة لتنشيط أنفسهم.

هذه الأضرار الطفيفة والأولية التي أحدثتها الآلام تفتح الأبواب لدعوة مختلف الأمراض / الحشرات داخل المخ. المشكلة الثانية التي تأتي إلى المخ هي عندما يسيطر هؤلاء الجن تماماً علي عقل الشخص أو هيئة الجسم الحي، ويجعله مجنون، و مريض نفسي ومتطرف بشكل سلبي، وسريع الغضب، و قليل الصبر، وغير متسامح، وما إلى ذلك، هذا يؤدي بالشخص نحو المرض العقلي. وعادة ما يحدث هذا عندما يبدأ الجن في إرسال إشارات إلكترونية من الأوامر والتعليمات لإحداث أفكار جديدة، والرغبات، أمنيات، وأحلام، أو بكلمات بسيطة، نستطيع أن نقول عندما يبدأ الجن في تنويم البشر مغناطيسياً للسيطرة عليهم. فإذا كان لدينا سيطرة على هذه الآلام، وسوف لا يحدث ضرر لعقلنا, ولن يحدث المرض الجسدي في نهاية المطاف. بنفس الطريقة، إذا كان لدينا سيطرة على الجن، لن تعاني عقولنا من أي مرض نفسي أو مشاكل بسهولة.

Rizwan Qureshi

Dreams are pure naughty or serious thoughts or stories from the brain of a demon. We cannot edit or change our dreams. But we can ask our demons to show us same dreams whatever we like or want to see in our dreams. It is very easy. Only you need to ask them with 100 percent confidence. I see usually whatever dreams I want to see. In the very first day, every new demon does whatever he wants to show, but in the next day, they need to consider my will too, if they do not want to see me upset and unhappy with them. So you can do the same thing too. Before you go to sleep, look toward your shoulders and tell them with full confidence what you want to see in your dreams. Anyway, during the process of dreams, we do not have any control of our minds the way we have control of our mind when we are up.

We have to watch each and everything in our dreams. We cannot just skip any portion of our dreams because either we do not like or we just do not want to watch. During dreams, we are totally at the disposal of the demons; whatever they want to show, we just have to watch. We or our brains cannot reject the control and the process of dreams at all, unless something wakes us up. Once we wake up, our brains will discontinue receiving the electronic signal from the brain of a demon. It will completely disturb the all process of dream production.

Demons do not have any prerecorded dream for us. Dreams are live transmission from an electronic demon brain to a human brain. Most of the time, once we will go back to sleep, dreams are different from previous ones, but it is not necessary.

رؤية الجن و الآلام السيطرة عليها

لن ترى أي غير طبيعية، والنفسية، لن تري أي شخص غير طبيعي أو مجنون من حولك إذا ترك الجن اللعب في عقولنا. سوف يتمتع الجميع بعقل هادئ و مسترخي،و سهل التعامل معه بالنسبة للشخص المصاب ببعض الأضرار العرضية في المخ، هذا قد يجعله مجرد معاق وغير قادر على إستخدام كافة وظائف المخ. إن تأثير أكثر إيذاءً و ضرراً للشخص الذي لديه بعض الأضرار العرضية في مخة بالمقارنة مع الشخص الذي يتمتع بمخ سليم وصحي إن ألأمخاخ السليمة و الصحية، لديها مقاومة أكثر للجن والآلام بالمقارنة بالمخ المتضرر بالصدفةأ.

ليس صحيحاً أن كل الجن يرغبون في العيش أو البقاء حول الأماكن القذرة. الجن يحبون أن يعيشوا في الأماكن المظلمة والأقل إستخداماً. الجن لا يحبون الطقس البارد، إنهم لا يحبون الهواء البارد، والأرض الباردة، و الماء البارد على الإطلاق؛ فكل هذه الأشياء لها آثار ضارة علي أجسامهم الكهرومغناطيسية، نظراً لطبيعتها الإلكترونية. الجن يحبون الغلاف الجوي الجاف والساخن. لا شك أن بعض الجن يعيشون حوال الأماكن القذرة، ولكن معظم الجن يحبون العيش في طقس معتدل/حار وأماكن نظيفة جداً. أعتقد أن هذا مجرد إختلاف في الرأي حول ما هو القذر بالنسبة لهم و بالنسبة لنا. نفس الشيئ ما هو النظيف بالنسبة لنا و لهم. مثل أن حفنة من الجن يحبون أن يعيشوا في جسم سحلية أو جرذ أسود قذر. وأنا واثق من أن تلك الأجسام مريحة جداً وأجوائها جيدة بالنسبة للجن هذا هو سبب وجودهم هناك. أنا متأكد من أنك أنت وأنا لا نستطيع التفكير بهذه الطريقة.

هذا مجرد إختلاف في الرأي. من حيث مفهوم ما هو قذر أو ما هو نظيف بالنسبة لهم أو بالنسبة لنا؟ ربما يكون لدي عدد قليل من الجن وقليل منا أرضية مشتركة بشأن هذه المسألة.

If the demon is the same, it may continue dream on the same subject. Once we wake up, most of us get 100 percent control of our brain back to us immediately. People with weak brains or totally under control of demons can see imaginary things like ghosts, witches, or other imaginary creatures, even when they are up. Demons use our mechanism of imagination of our brain to transfer their dreams, thoughts, and stories to us by the use of their power of hypnotism. Our brains easily decode those electronic hypnotism signals of dreams and show us as real life stories, incidents, and images. There is a little bit of difference between seeing dreams during sleep and seeing some images when we are up. First, the process of seeing dreams during sleep does not involve our eyes. Process of dream does not need eyes. So a person without eyes can also see dreams.

The process of seeing images, like ghosts or witches around trees or in dark places is a malfunctioning of demons by mixing their electronic signals of imaginary ghosts/witches with the rays in and out of our eyes. In simple words, we can say that demons can hypnotize us even when are alert and up, and demons can show us whatever they want to show us. For this process of seeing images of ghosts/witches, we need eyes. It's complicated, right? I am sure modern science will jump in this soon and will bring more details for us.

Now next part is quality of the dreams. Few demons really work hard to bring high quality dreams to us, regardless of whether to scare us or make us happy. One single demon is able to read our brain's memory and very easily can pull some real-life characters and issues around us from our real life.

دعوني أروي لكم حادثة واحدة مع جني خرج من جسم سحلية. لم أكن على إستعداد للمخاطرة لأنني كنت أعرف مسبقاً أن الجني خرج من سحلية. كنت على ثقة من أنه لم يكن منزعجاً مني إطلاقاً لأنني قمت بالفعل بالإتصال معه عدة مرات قبل أن أخلد للنوم.

حتى ذلك الحين، كان بخير. الآن من واقع تجربتي في الماضي بمجرد أن عرفت مدي قوة ذلك الجني، أدركت بالفعل أنه سوف يكون الجني الذي رسيظهر أحلام هذه الليلة.وكان ذلك الوقت الذي كنت طلبت فيه من الجن ألا يظهروا لي أحلاماً سيئة. "إذا كنت تريد أن تظهر لي حلماً، إظهر لي فقط الأحلام الجيدة، وإلا لا داعي للقلق بشأني". في ذلك اليوم، طلبت من الجني الذي خرج من جسم السحلية نفس الشيء، قلت: " إظهر لي الأحلام الجيدة والجميلة فقط ". و قد دعيت لحضور حفلة.طوال الليل، في حلمي، و كان بها كل أنواع الزينة والطعام للضيوف.

كان مكان الحفلة كبير حقاً، وجميل جداً. لكن المشكلة الوحيدة في هذا الحلم هو أنني كنت الإنسان الوحيد الذي دعي إلى هذه الحفلة. وكان بقية الضيوف كلهم الآلاف السحالي. وكانت الحفلة لطيفة جداً ومنظمة تنظيما جيداً. لم يحاول أحد إخافتي أو مضايقتي . وكان الجو لطيف جداً إذا كنت ترى الحفلة من وجهة نظري فقط . لكن الله وحده يعلم كم أخاف دائماً من السحالي وأكرههم. لذلك هذا لا يكفي فقط بالنسبة لك أن تخبر به الجن ليفعلوا لك الخير، لأنك لا تعرف ما هو الخير في عيونهم، ولهذا قم بتحديد ا ما تريد وماذا كنت تعتقد أنه جيد بوضوح دائماً حتي يكون لدي أصدقائك من الجن فكرة عن إختياراتك ما تحب وما تكره. بعد ذلك اليوم، أخبرهم بوضوح دائما ما أريد أن أرى في أحلامي، إذا سألوني. كما وصفت، لقد قسمت العالم الغير المرئي إلى ثلاثة أجزاء رئيسية. أنا واثق من أننا نستطيع تقسيمهم الى الآلاف من الفئات

But those demons really do not go into too many details. Once they get some basic knowledge, images, and information from our brain, they just make some stories, mix them randomly with people or images in their memories. This is needed by only new and strange demons around us. Demons already around us do not need to read our minds to get some information because usually they are already aware about it. Once you already have a few demons around you, either you or other family members absorb few demons from here and there either during phone talk or during traveling and bring all those demons all the way to your house. This is a regular process of getting demons from here and there. Sometimes those demons stay around us and sometimes go back to their original people. If somehow demons already around us or around our house easily adjust with the new demons from different families or different animals or different areas then all the time we will see very complicated and unique dreams. If demons are lazy, their dreams will make no sense to us, or they will be very short. But if demons are listening to you whatever you want to see and they are smart and efficient then you will love to sleep 24-7 so you can watch your dreams. If someone is totally under control of one single demon, then that demon is the boss or in charge of the dreams. That demon will create and produce dreams for us either whatever that demon likes or whatever we ask our demon to show us in our dreams.

But if someone is getting demons from here and there, plus a lot of demons who live with insects, reptiles, rats, animals around you or around your house, those demons with those living things, may join the dream production process also sometimes...

الفرعية، لكن سأترك هذا للعلوم الطبية. نبدأ الآن بالأمراض /الحشرات. فهي طفيليات تماماً. وأود، لو أستطيع أن أقول إن هذه الأمراض / الحشرات تشاركنا طعامنا، ولكن هذا ليس صحيحاً. هؤلاء الأمراض / الحشرات، في الحقيقة، تأكلنا، وتأكل أجزاء أجسادنا، وأعضاء أجسامنا. لأن الشيئ الثاني هو أن الآلام، على نحو ما، لا تستطيع البقاء في جو مفتوح لفترة طويلة.

تحتاج الآلام دائماً إلى جسم لتعيش أو تقيم فيه، وتشارك الأجسام الحية الغذاء بالتأكيد عندم اتعيش معها، و داخلها، بغض النظر عما إذا كانت تلك الأجسام لبشر أو حيوان، أوطيور، أو حشرات، أو زواحف، وما إلى ذلك كما وصفت عدة مرات، الآلام هي أجسام كهرومغناطيسية. إذاً أي نوع من الطعام تشاركه معنا؟كما قلت من قبل، الآلام دائماً بحاجة إلى جسم لتعيش فيه الآن أي نوع من الطعام تحتاجه هذه الآلام و من أين يمكنها الحصول عليه؟ تحتاج الآلام الكهرومغناطيسية إلى الغذاء في شكل طاقة من أجسادنا، تشبه الطاقة الكهربائية. تضرّ الآلام عادةً أعصابنا أو أنسجتنا لتشحن نفسها من تلك الأنواع من الطاقات. تستهدف الآلام دائماً أجزاء مختلفة جسمنا حيث يمكنها أن تشحن أو تنشط نفسها للبقاء على قيد الحياة.

عند هذه النقطة، أود أن أقول أن هذه الآلام لا تهتم عندما تقيم في مخ شخص ما، وتتلف بعض الأعصاب به، وبالتالي تستطيع أن تمتص بعض الطاقة من تلك الأعصاب للحفاظ على تنشيط نفسها و تستمر على قيد الحياة. لا تهتم الآلام على الاطلاق إذا تسببت أفعالهم بضرر دائم في شكل ألم في الرأس، وهو الصداع النصفي الذي يحدث كثير من الناس. نفس الشيئ بالضبط، تختار الآلام الأجزاء المختلفة من الجسم التي أعصاب و أنسجة أكثر، مثل عظام الظهر، وعظم الورك والمفاصل المختلفة، لتعيش بها الآلام وتنشط نفسها. هذا العمل من الآلام يسبب كل أنواع آلام إلتهاب المفاصل في كل مكان من جسمنا.

231

If they become your friends and ready to show you whatever you want to watch in your dreams, it will be a big success in your entertaining life. New and strange demons will always bring scary, dirty, or at least whatever you do not like to watch to your dreams. When a group of demons control our brain and create a dream for us, those dreams will be more complicated and strange. Demons come out of a lizard, mostly just know about lizards or are just interested in lizards. Demons come out from dog/cat/rat usually know more about those animals. Those demons will be more interested in same kind of breed where they usually like to live or hang out. Then if we have few demons from different areas or families around us, different breed/race around you and you make them your friends, imagine how easily these demons can create and produce such a high class of dreams for you. It is not difficult to convince demons to show you dreams of your desires. One, always act 100 percent confident when you talk to them. You should be very confident that they are around and listening to you. Tell them every night whatever you want to see in your dreams before you go to sleep. If they are still giving you a hard time, so regardless whatever they show you in dreams, do not take any interest in those dreams and keep telling them to listen to you. Otherwise they are wasting their time. Let me tell you one incident. It's a little bit bad, but it will help you understand a little bit the nature of demons.One employee asked me how he can talk to his demons to show him those dreams whatever he wants to see. As usual, I explained to him how. After one week when I got a chance to talk to him, he started telling me about some of his dreams. One dream was interesting.

هذه الأضرار الطفيفة التي تحدثها الآلام عادةً ما تبدأ بها الأمراض الكبرى، فبمجرد أن تكتشف الأمراض/ الحشرات المزيد من تلك الأجزاء التي أصابها ضرر في الجسم، يبدأ تيار لا يتوقف من الحشرات / الأمراض في مهاجمة تلك الأجزاء المتضررة ، ونتيجة لذلك نرى الإلتهابات والسرطانات الرئيسية في أجزاء مختلفة من الجسم. الآن ماذا يأكل الجن؟ بالمقارنة مع الآلام، ليس لدي الجن أي مشاكل في البقاء في الجو المفتوح أيضاً في مجالهم الكهرومغناطيسي.، يحصل الجن علي غذاءهم معظم الوقت أو في الحقيقية ينشطون أنفسهم من المجال الكهرومغناطيسي الموجود بالغلاف الجوي المفتوح. هذا هو السبب الرئيسي في أن الجن لا يدمرونا جسديا لمجرد تنشيط أنفسهم من جسمنا، مثلما تفعل الآلام.

لا شك، أن الجن أكثر قوةً وحيويةً بالمقارنة مع الآلام. إنهم يحتاجون إلى غذاء و طاقة أكثر بالمقارنة مع الآلام. يبقي الجن معظم الوقت، في عقولناو أجسامنا للإستحواذ علينا، و من أجل السيطرة علينا جسدياً وعقلياً. الجن لا يضرونا جسدياً، ولكنهم يحدثون الكثير من المشاكل طوال الوقت، عاطفياً وعقلياً، و عصبياً، و يجعلونا نتصرف بسلبية، تطرف، و كذلك نصاب بأمور فسيولوجية، الخ.

لكن هذا لا يعني أن الجن لا يستطيعون أن يؤذونا أو يضروا بنا. الجن قد يقتلونا في ثواني عن طريق الإضرار بمخنا و قلبنا، أو أي شيء خطير، بمجرد أن يضيقوا بشخص ما أويغضبوا منه أو للإنتقام من شخص ما بسبب شيء ما، ينزعجون بشأنه.

إن إستخدام مكبر الصوت بالهاتف يقلل من فرص الهجوم المباشر من الألم أو الجن علي الجسم من شخص آخر.عادةً ينتشر الجن والآلام مع تلك الإشارات من مكبر الصوت بالهاتف في الجو المفتوح، من المؤكد أن إما الجن أو آلام سيختاروا شخص ما لمجرد أنهم يريدون أن يجعلوا شخص ما ضحية. حتى أتهم قد يأتون إلينا أيضاً.

He said, "Before I went to bed to sleep, I asked demons around me at least for ten minutes that wherever I go every day or every week or every month or every year, take me to all those places tonight. And make sure all beautiful women should be wearing light cloths, wherever I go." Okay, readers, I am sorry, I cannot write his exact wordings. So anyway he said he saw exactly the same dream all night long. He never woke up any single time during night. But the only problem in the dream was that all the women, wherever he went, were wearing proper and nice dresses, but he was just wearing one single underwear only during his entire visit to everywhere all night long. Then he said, he talked to each and every woman, but during the whole dream, he was feeling embarrassed, insulted, ashamed, wherever he was going during all night long in his dream. Well, I do not know what to say. I just told him. Then he asked me again why this happened. I just answer him, maybe your demon wants to give you some message. I further told him that at least now you know that your demon is listening to you or at least your demon is in your contact now. I really don't know if he understands me or not, but he said he will practice more and left me. So maybe, hopefully, you will learn something from this incident too.

Water itself has some demagnetizing qualities. But definitely, holy water is a perfect weapon, tool, and a very good demagnetizing agent. Demons are electromagnetic physical bodies. Demons travel in a naturally available electromagnetic field in the open atmosphere. The spray of holy water in the air or toward where possibly demons are flying or toward our face/ neck/ ear/ head/ chest will create some distortion in the electromagnetic demons and field.

نحن في أمان إلى حد ما عند إستخدام مكبر الصوت بالهاتف، ولكن إذا إستخدمنا سماعة الهاتف مباشرةً علي آذاننا، فسوف نتلقى جميع الجن والآلام يقيناً من الشخص على الطرف الآخر من خط الهاتف أو من الغلاف الجوي المفتوح، لا أعرف ماذا أقول أيضاً عن إستخدام الهواتف؟ ولكن العلم الحديث يحتاج إلى أن يخترع نوعاً من الحماية العازلة لتجنب بمنتهي السهولة، إنتقال الجن والآلام من خلال خطوط الهاتف، أو إشارات الراديو، أوإشارات الإنترنت، أو إشارات التلفزيون من هنا الى هناك و من هناك إلى هنا. بعد كل التعرض لهذا العالم الغير مرئي و القدرة علي رؤية الجن و الإحساس بهم، والتواصل معهم، والسيطرة عليهم، ما رأيك، حياتي هل هي سهلة أم صعبة؟ لا شك، بالتأكيد، أنني أشعر بالثقة الشديدة والأمن الشديد. أنا لا أخاف من الجن. ولدي الكثير من السيطرة لإخراج الآلام بعيداً عن أجسام مختلف البشر كلما أردت ذلك. أستطيع أن أسحب أي جني من شخص ما، كلما طلب مني أي شخص ذلك. أستطيع الوصول إلى أي شخص في أي جزء من العالم لمساعدته ضد الجن والآلام، كما يمكنني إستخدام الكثيرمن الجن الموجودين حول شخص ما في أي جزء من العالم، عن طريق الإتصال بهم بالتوارد التخاطري. أشياء من هذا القبيل. لا يزال من الصعب تصديق أن ذلك يحدث لي، لقد حدث لي. تغيير كبير، أشعر به داخلي طوال الوقت و هو أنني لا أستطيع أن أفكر بأي شيء آخر غير الله.

سوف أعرض علي الجميع مبادئ توجيهية مناسبة للجميع، لماذالا أريد أن أشارك في تلك التجارب؟ أنا خائف قليلاً في الوقت الحالي، وأنا متأكد أنني في الكتاب التالي، سوف أستطيع شرح تفاصيل كاملة عن سرعة الرياح والعواصف الشديدة، و كيفية التعامل معها.

SEE & CONTROL DEMONS & PAIN

The holy water is not a complete or a permanent solution against demon race. Holy water is a problem for demons and their traveling path for sure. If you spray some water on a live electronic circuit, that circuit may have a short circuit. Exactly the same thing or the same relation we have between holy water and demons.

Our brains are perfect machines. Brains can expire or die with the process of death. But any brain will not get psycho or crazy by itself. The operation of a brain just starts malfunctioning or some disorder or problem happens inside it, once the pains damage the brain physically to obtain their food or energy to energize themselves. These minor and initial damages created by pains open doors of invitations for different diseases/insects inside the brain. The second problem which comes to brain is when these demons totally control the mind of a person or a living body and make them crazy, psycho extremist negative, short-tempered, impatient, intolerant, etc., that take a person toward mental sickness. Usually this happens when demons start sending electronic signals of commands and instructions to create new thoughts, desires, wishes, and dreams, or in simple words, we can say when demons start hypnotizing humans to take over their control. So if we have a control on these pains, our brain will not get damage and will not get sick physically eventually. Same way, if we will have control on demons, our minds will not have any psychological illness or problems easily. You will not see any abnormal, psycho, crazy person around you if the demons quit playing with our minds. Everyone will have calm, relax, easygoing brain. As far as someone with some accidental damages to the brain, this can just make him handicapped and unable to use all the brain functions.

رضوان قرشي

يقول مضيف برنامج الساعة السادسة مساءً، علي قناة Fox كل يوم: "عادل ومتوازن". أنا أحب هذا النوع من الناس وسلوكهم. هؤلاء هم الناس الذين سوف ينقذون هذا العالم والجنس البشري. لقد كنت دائماً أفكر ماذا يجنيه الناس السلبيون و المغرضون للغاية،عندما يجلسون معاً و يتصرفون بسلبية طوال الوقت وربما يفعلون كل شيء لتضليل الناس الأبرياء. ، وتفسيري هو أنهم لا يستطيعون رؤية من حولهم. ليس لديهم أي فكرة من الذين يجبرونهم علي عمل بسلبية شديدة و تطرف شديد. ولكني، لا زلت سعيداً أنه يوجد عدد قليل من البشرعادلون ومتوازنون. علي الأقل.

بالنسبة المشاكل بسبب هذا التعرض للعالم الغير مرئي، هناك بالتأكيد العديد من المشاكل، فبمجرد أن يعرف الجن عني بغض النظر في أي جزء من العالم كان، يقوم بزيارتي جني واحد على الأقل من مجموعة من زيارة الجن بالتأكيد للتحقق من معرفتي أو قدراتي. ربما كان ذلك متعة أو مفاجأة للجن، ولكن بالنسبة لي، يجب علي التعامل معهم طوال الوقت. تكون الأربعة و عشرون ساعة الأولى دائماً مشكلة مع الجن الجدد،لانهم يحاولون البقاء على مقربة جداً مني للحصول على مزيد من الإهتمام مني. ثمة مشكلة أخرى هي أنه يكون كل شيئ على ما يرام عندما أري الجن يحلقون هنا وهناك. لا يهم بالنسبة لي بعد الآن حجمهم و عددهم وهم يطيرون من حولي هنا وهناك طوال الوقت، حتى أنني لا أعيرهم إهتماماً، ولكن عندما يقترب مني جني ما، لا يمكن أن أ تجاهل أي جني واحد، و لا حتى لثانية واحدة. ربما هذه نعمة بالنسبة للناس العاديين عندما لا يكنون على علم بإستحواذ الجن عليهم. أو يعلمون عن إستحواذ الجن. ولكن في حالتي، لا أستطيع تجاهل لمستهم و تغلغل جني في جسدي.

The effect of a demon or a pain is more hurtful and more damaging once someone has some accidental damages to his brain as compared to a healthy and fit brain. Undamaged and healthy brains have more resistance for the demons and pains as compared to an accidentally damaged brain.

It is not true that all the demons like to live or stay around dirty places. Demons like to live dark and least-in-use places. Demons do not like cold weather. Demons do not like cold air, cold floor, and cold water at all; all these things have damaging effects for their electromagnetic bodies, due to their electronic nature. Demons like dry and heated atmosphere. No doubt, some demons live around dirty places, but most of the demons really like to live under moderate/ hot weather and very clean places. I think this is just a difference of opinion, about what is dirty for them and what is dirty for us. Same way what is clean for us and what is clean for them. Like bunch of demons like to live in body of a lizard or a black dirty rat. I am sure that these bodies are very comfortable and a good atmosphere for them that is why they are there. I am sure you and I cannot think like this.

So this is just a difference of opinion, what is dirty or what is clean for them or for us. Maybe a few of the demons and few of us have some common ground on this issue. Let me tell you my one incident with a demon which came out of a body of the lizard. I was not ready to take any risk once I already knew that demon came out from a lizard.

لا شك، لم يقم جني بإزعاجي حقاً لفترة طويلة، ولكن ليس لدي قدرة على تحملهم، فإنني أستشيط كالنار بمجرد أن يحاول أي جني الإقتراب مني. نفس المشاكل تحدث مع الجن أيضاً، هذا هو السبب في أنهم يتحركون بعيداً عن. جسمي بمنتهي السرعة. ولكن كل جني جديد يقترب مني حقاً، في المرة لأولى علي الأقل، حتى مجرد لمدة ثلاثين ثانية، حتى لثلاثين ثانية، كانت كافية ليؤذوني. الآن بمجرد أن يأتي لي جني كل ساعة، أشعر أنها ستكون مشكلة أحياناً. أنا لأبقي أي جني من حولي أو في بيتي، و لذلك أطلب من هؤلاء الجن أن يذهبوا هنا وهناك أو يعودوا للشخص الأصلي. أنا لا أتذكر إذا كنت طلبت من أي جني البقاء في بيتي أو حولي أبداً. ولكن تقريبا كل خمسة عشردقيقة يزور ني جني ويريد أن يأخذ تعليمات جديدة، إذا لدي أي تعليمات.

أشعر ربما ليس فوراً، وربما بعد مرور بعض الوقت، ولكن في النهاية فإن معظم الناس في العالم سيكون لديهم فكرة واضحة جداً و الكثير من المعرفة عن الجن بسببي .

و قريباً سيكون الجميع على علم بالجن والآلام. سوف يحصل العلم الحديث على فكرة و توجيه لبدء البحث لمعرفة الجن وسوف يحاول إيجاد سبل لكيفية التعامل معهم. هذا شيء يريحني كثيراً . أنا لا أعرف إلى متى سأعيش، ولكني واثق من أن كتبي ستغيير كل ما له علاقة بأمراض السرطان، و مشاكل الصحة وسوف يكون فيروس نقص المناعة البشرية قابل للعلاج، و ستقل الأمراض العقلية، وفوق كل شيء لن يخاف الناس من الجن أو الأشباح أو الساحرات أو السحر الأسود بعد الآن. الجميع سيعرف كل شيء عن الجن و الآلام، و سوف يتواصل الجميع مع الجن و الآلام لإقناعهما بالبقاء بعيداً عن أجسادهم.

SEE & CONTROL DEMONS & PAIN	رضوان قرشي

I was confident that he was not upset with me anymore because I already communicated with that demon several times before I went to bed.

So by then, he was okay. Now due to my experiences in the past and once I figure out about the powers of that demon, I was already aware that he will be the one who is going to show me the dreams tonight. That was a time when I used to tell demons only not to show me bad dreams. "If you want to show me a dream, just show me good dreams; otherwise, don't worry about me". That day, I asked that demon from the body of the lizard the same thing .I said:" show me good and nice dreams only". All night long, in my dream, I was invited to a party. In that party, they have all kinds of decorations and food for the guests.

That party place was really big and very nice. But the only problem with the dream was that I was the only human who was invited to that party. Rests thousands of guests in that party were all lizards. The party was very nice and well organized. Nobody tried to scare me harass me. It was a very nice atmosphere if you just see the party from my point of view. But God knows how much I am always scared of lizards and dislike them. So this is just not enough for you to tell your demons to do good for you, because you never know what is good in their eyes. So always specify clearly what you like and what you think good is. So your demon friends will have a better idea about your choices of like and dislike. After that day, I always tell them clearly what I want to see in my dreams, if they ask me. As I described, I divided the invisible world into three major parts..

الجميع سوف يسيطرون علي أحلامهم و سيشاهدون أحلاماً عند الطلب في كل ليلة. الله يعلم ماذا سوف تتعلم عن هذا العالم الغير مرئي بسبب مساعدة العلم الحديث في المستقبل القريب.

من الصعب جداً أن تحديد ما إذا كان الناس الحساسون للغاية يستوعبون المزيد من الجن عن غيرهم من الناس أو من الجو، أو أن الجن عندما يستحوذون علي الناس يجعلوهم حساسين وعاطفيين للغاية. لا شك أن الجن يعززون ويضخمون بعض الحالات العاطفية والحساسة. عند هذه النقطة، يمكنني القول أن الناس عاجزون تماماً أمام إستحواذ الجن، ولا يستطيع مقاومة سيطرة الجن عليهم، فالناس لا يستطيعون السيطرة على هجمات الذعر والقلق، والمشاكل الثنائية، والاكتئاب، ومحاولات الانتحار، وما إلى ذلك ولكن الآن يمكنك ببساطة رش الماء المقدس على وجهك و رقبتك ورأسك وأذنيك و صدرك والمناطق المحيطة بك، كما يمكنك شربه أحيانا.

ولابد أن ترفض بإستمرار سيطرة الجن علي عقلك، يمكنك الإستمرار في البقاء حافي القدمين على السيراميك البارد أو أرضية أسمنتية. وسوف تكون على ما يرام. إذا كنت تواجه المزيد من تقلب في المزاج، صعوداً وهبوطاً طوال الوقت، هذا يعني أن عقلك ضعيف جداً و أن الجن يسيطرون سيطرة كاملة على مخك. الثنائي ليس مرضاً، إنها حالة كاملة من سيطرة الجن الشرير جداً على العقل البشري.

إن المزاج المتوازن يعني سيطرة أقل من الجن. الآن إذا لم يكن لديك أي طاقة لتغضب، وكنت صبوراً، و لست مفرطاً أو عاطفياً، وكنت لا تركض وراء رغباتك أو أمنياتك مثل المجنون، و كنت لا تنزعج بسهولة، و كنتن لا تنحاز سياسياً كثيراً، وكنت لا تشعر أيضاً بالحب الشديد أو الكره الشديد لشخص ما، و كنت تستسلم بسهولة، إذا كنت لا تشعر بالتطرف أو السلبية، لم تشاهد أي حلم، إذا كان الجواب بنعم لجميع تلك الأمور الذكورة أعلاه ، إذاً ليس هناك جني من حولك .

I am sure we can subdivide them into thousands of subcategories, but I will leave this for medical science. Now start with the diseases/ insects. They are totally parasites. I wish, if I can say that these diseases/insects share our food with us, but this is not true. These diseases/insects, in actual, eat us, eat our bodies, eat our body parts, and our body organs. Now second, the pains, somehow, they cannot stay in the open atmosphere for a long time.

Pains always need a body to live in or reside in. Pains definitely share food with the living bodies, when they are living inside those living bodies regardless of whether they are human, animal, bird, insect, reptile, etc. As I described several times, pains are the electromagnetic bodies. So which kind of food these pains share with us?. As I said earlier, pains always need a body to live in. Now which kind of food do these pains need and from where can they get that food? Electromagnetic pains need food in shape of energy from our bodies. Energy similar to electric energy. Pains usually damage our nerves or tissues to charge themselves from those kinds of the energies. Pains always target different parts of our body from where they can charge or energize themselves to stay alive. At this point, I will say these pains do not care, when they reside in someone's brain and damage some nerves in the brain, so these pains can suck some energy from those nerves to keep themselves energized and alive. Pains do not care at all if their actions caused a permanent damage in shape of a migraine pain in the head of so many people. Exactly the same way, pains choose different parts of our body with more nerves and tissues like back bone, hip bone, different joints to live and energize themselves. This action of pains causes all kind of arthritis pains everywhere in our body.

رؤية الجن و الآلام السيطرة عليها

معظم الجن، أو أقول تقريباً كل الجن، يكونون إنتقاميون للغاية، فقط إذا أُلحِقَ بهم الضرر بطريقة ما.

بمجرد أن يقتل شخص ما صرصوراً، يخرج جني مستاء جداً من جسم الصرصور الميت، عادة، و يهاجم منطقة العمود الفقري بما في ذلك الكلى للفرد، و بمجرد أن يقتل شخص ما عنكبوتاً، يخرج الجن المنزعج و يهاجموا فوراً الرأس ومنطقة الرقبة، وعلى طول الطريق حتى نحو المخ. بمجرد أن يقتل شخص ما سحلية، يخرج الجن المنزعج و يهاجموا عادة المعدة و منطقة الأمعاء. لأنهم يتسببون في القيء والإسهال وآلام المعدة. هذه هي الهجمات الفورية، ماذا يفعلون في الخطوة التالية، ليس لدي معرفة جيدة حول هذا الموضوع، لأنني أسحبهم دائماً خارج جسدي في غضون دقائق قليلة، لذلك ليس لدي أي فكرة كيف يتصرفون مع الآخرين الشياطين عادة ما يأخذ الجن بالثأر من خلال ثلاث طرق:

(1) الإستحواذ على الجسم، و إحداث المشاكل العقلية والبدنية.

(2) عرض الأحلام المخيفة والسيئة جداً طوال الوقت أثناء النوم، وإظهار صور الأشباح والساحرات في يقظتنا، بشكل غير تام، في المناطق المظلمة من المنزل.

(3) يجلبون المشاكل والعقبات الكثيرة في طريقنا لإيقاع الأذى بنا مالياً، و في الأسرة والصحة امشاكل بإستمرار...

ليس لدي الجن أو أي إنسان أو أي طبيب للجن أي سيطرة على الروح / الروح. لا يستطيع أي جني أو أي إنسان أو أي طبيب أن يأخذ الروح أو إيعيدها في الجسم. في حالة الروح، الجميع بلا حول ولا قوة فيما يتعلق بالروح. لا أحد لديه أي سيطرة على الأرواح داخل أو خارج الجسم. أبداً سواء البشر/الجن. الأرواح ليس لديها أي إرادة حرة، تماماً مثل الملائكة . يجب علي تلك الأرواح أن تتبع توقيتات ومواعيد كما أمر الله.

These minor damages created by the pains usually start major diseases once diseases/insects find out about those damaged parts of the body and a nonstop stream of insects/diseases attack those damaged parts, the result of which we see major infections and cancers in different part of the body. Now demons, what do they eat? As compared to pains, demons do not have any problems in staying in the open atmosphere also within their electromagnetic field. Most of the time, demons eat their food or in real, energize themselves from the electromagnetic field of the open atmosphere. This is the main reason demons do not damage us physically, just to energized themselves from our body, like pains. No doubt, demons are way more powerful and energetic as compared to pains.

Demons need way more food or energy as compared to pains. Demons, most of the time, just stay in our brain and bodies to possess us, to control us physically and mentally.Like pains, demons do not damage us physically, but demons create a lot of problems all the time, emotionally, mentally, temperament wise, extremism, physiological issues, etc .

But it does not mean demons cannot hurt or damage us. Demons can kill us in seconds, by damaging our brain, heart, or anything serious, once they get upset and angry with someone or taking revenge from someone for something, they are upset about.

The use of the speaker of a speaker phone reduces the chances of direct attack of a pain or demon to our body from someone else. Usually with those speaker phone signals, demons and pains will spread in the open atmosphere.

لا تستطيع الأرواح أن تتسكع هنا وهناك كما تفعل الأشباح. الطاقات السلبية الخارجية مثل الجن والآلام لديهم إرادة حرة.، فإنهم يستطيعون أن يدخلوا و يخرجوا من أي جسم معين، وقتما أرادوا. يستطيع الجن والآلام القيام بذلك داخل وخارج الأجسام طوال الوقت. الطاقة الإيجابية، أي الأرواح، ليس لديها هذا الخيار، أما الطاقات السلبية، أي الجن والآلام، وبمجرد أن يخرجوا من الجسم، يشعر بالإسترخاء والصحة أكثر. عادةً لا تدخل الأرواح أو تخرج من أجسام معينة بشكل متكرر.

تذهب الأرواح داخل الجسم لإحيائه عادةً، وبمجرد أن تخرج الروح من الجسم، سيكون جثة. لا تستطيع الجن و الآلام فعل أي شيء جيد لصحتنا بمجرد أن يكونوا داخل أجسامنا، حتى لو كانوا يريدون ذلك . أفضل شيء يمكن للجني أو ألم القيام به للحفاظ على صحتنا جيدة، هو مجرد البقاء بعيداً عن أجسادنا. فمن السهل جداً جعل الشخص المتطرف السلوك أو العنصري أو السريع الإنفعال، من السهل جعله إنساناً متطرِفاً وسلبياً، سواء من خلال إرسال "المزيد من الأوامر ليقوم بها الجن موجودون حول الشخص، أو إستبدالهم بجن أقوى لزيادة مستوى السلبية. كلما زاد إستخدامك للسخان الكهربائي، سيجلب ذلك المزيد من الجن داخلك و من حولك. عادة ما يستحوذ الجن علي منطقة الرأس وهذا مؤشر خطير للغاية. كلما زاد إستخدامك المباشر للهواء البارد سيساعدك ذلك في صد الجن.

يستطيع أي كاتب مبدع كتابة رواية خيالية أو سيناريو لفيلم إذا قرأ كتابي و الكتاب القادم. أنا لا أمانع حتى لو إختاروني كمصدر إلهام لتطوير شخصية ما. يحتاج الكاتب إلى أن يكون لديه فكرة واضحة عن كيفية الوصول إلى عالم الجن و إلقاء الأوامر عليه. الجن موجودون حول كل إنسان والآلات التي بها عقول إلكترونية.

Rizwan Qureshi

For sure, either demons or pains will choose somebody once they want to make someone victim. Even they may come to us too. With speaker phone, we are a little bit safe. But if we are using phone keeping directly to our ears, then for sure we will receive all the demons and the pains from the person at the other end of the phone line or the open atmosphere. I don't know what else to say about the use of phones? But modern science needs to invent some kind of insulation protection to avoid very easily, the traveling and transferring of demons and pains through phone lines, radio signals, Internet signals, or TV signals from here to there and there to here. After all these exposures to the invisible world and the powers to see, sense, communicate, and handling control of them, what do you think, my life is easy or difficult? No doubt, definitely, I feel very confident and secure. I do not get scared of demons. I have a lot of control to take out pains away from the bodies of different humans whenever I want to. I can pull any demon out of someone whenever someone asks me. I can reach any person in any part of the world to help him against demons and pains. I can use a lot of demons around someone in any part of the world by contacting them telepathically. Stuff like this. It is still difficult to believe this happens to me, this is happening to me. I feel a major change all the time inside me, and that is I cannot think about anything else other than God.

I will expose to everyone with proper guidelines for everybody. Why, I don't want to involve in these experiments? I am a little bit scared right now. I am sure, in next book, I will be able to explain complete details about crazy speedy wind and storm and possible cure.

رؤية الجن و الآلام السيطرة عليها

تستطيع هذه الشخصية سحب البيانات من البشر والآلات على حد سواء بواسطة الجن من حولهم، كما يمكنها إنشاء إتصالات توارد خواطر مع أي شخص في أي جزء من العالم لإستخدام الجن الخاص بهم للقيام بأي غرض من الأغراض الإيجابية. يجب علي تلك الشخصية الدخول إلى مجال الإتصالات الكهرومغناطيسي، أو شبكة الجن، لنقل رسالته الى كل الجن في وقت واحد لمتابعة أي من أوامره للتأثير حتى علي السياسة المحلية. لدي صعوبة قليلا في كتابة رواية خيالية أو سيناريو لفيلم لأنه حتى لو كنت سأكتب أي خيال، فإن 90 % من سيكون واقعياً صحيحاً. أنا لا أستطيع كشف نفسي أكثر من ذلك القدر.

لذلك يمكن لأي كاتب مبدع إختياري لإختلاق شخصية خيالية، و إتباع التقنيات الحقيقية للتنويم المغناطيسي، و التخاطر، والسيطرة الكاملة على عالم الجن، كما يمكنني أن أكتب أي شيء عن أي سياسة أو مواضيع ذات صلة. أنا أوافق إذا كان الكاتب يستخدم كل التقنيات والإجراءات الصحيح في التخاطر، التنويم المغناطيسي، أو كان يستخدم الجن من أجل قضية إيجابية. إذا إحتاج أي شخص لبعض المساعدة لفهم هذه التقنيات، أستطيع أن أساعد أكثر ولكن اذا كنت تتبع فقط هذين الكتابين والكتاب المقبل، سيكون ذلك كافياً لتفهم. لقد أجريت إتصال توارد خواطر في كثير من الأوقات، مع ناس رفيعي المستوى جداً، منهم المتعمقون في السياسة، أوبعض اللاعبين غير العاديين، أو الرؤساء، أو أي شخص آخر فقط للتحقق ممن حولهم فقط.

و من وراء كل الأشياء التي يفعلونها. أحصل عادةً، على بعض المعلومات الأساسية و أقوم بإرسال هؤلاء الجن ليعودوا إليهم. المشكلة هي أنني إعتدت علي أن أكون شخصاً بسيطاً جداً، و ما زلت كذلك.

SEE & CONTROL DEMONS & PAIN

On FOX channel at 6 pm, the host of a show says everyday "Fair and balanced". I love that kind of people and behavior. These are the people who will save this world and human race. I always think what too much biased and extreme negative people are getting when they sit together and act so negative all the time and possibly do everything to misguide and mislead innocent people. I am saying because they cannot see who is around them.

They don't have any clue who is compelling them to act so negative and extremist. But, still, I am happy at least few people are fair and balanced. As for the problems due to this exposure of invisible world, there are definitely several problems. Once demons know about me regardless in any part of the world, at least one demon from a group of demons visit me for sure to verify my knowledge or capabilities. Maybe this is a fun or surprise for the demons, but as far as me, I have to deal with them all the time. With new demons, the first twenty-four hours are always a trouble because they try to stay very close to me to get more attention from me. Another problem, it is okay when I see them flying here and there. It does not matter to me anymore how much big and how many demons are flying around me or here and there all the time, even I do not pay attention, but when a demon come close to me, I cannot ignore any single demon, even for one second. Maybe this is blessing in a disguise for the normal people when, they are not aware about the presence of a demon or unaware about the possession of the demons. But in my case, I cannot ignore their touch and the penetration of a demon in my body. No doubt, no demon really bothered me for long time, but I do not have tolerance to tolerate them.

رضوان قرشي

أريد أن أعيش حياة بسيطة جداً مرتاح البال. أنا أواجه الآن كل أنواع التعرض للعالم الغير مرئي القوي وأزداد قوةً كل يوم. ولكن المشكلة هي أن أثناء إستخدامي، و إستخدام كل قواي بشكل صحيح، يحتاج الجن إلى سيطرتي ليقوموا بعمل شيئاً كبيراً. ولكن الوضع ينعكس، عندما لا يكون للجن أي سيطرة علي، ولدي الكثير من السيطرة عليهم. وليس لدي أي نية أو خطة لتغيير هذا العالم أو تغيير كل شيء حولنا. بصراحة، لا تعنيني في كل هذه الامور. وأخيرا كان الأمر كذلك، قررت أنني بحاجة لتدريب العالم كله، كل شخص في هذا العالم للسيطرة على العالم الغير مرئي للجن من حولهم واستخدامهم بشكل إيجابي للتغلب علي التطرف والسلبية في هذا العالم. أنت تقرأ هذا الكتاب. خلال شهر واحد، سيستمع إليك الجن من حولك، وسوف يتبعوك. ستكون مسؤول جزئياً عن التعامل مع الكثير من الأشياء من حولك وحول هذا العالم من بدون إستخدام أي بندقية أو من البشر. شيء آخر، سيكون من الصعب جداً عليك تقدير قدرة وقوة الجن من حولك، ولكني لا أستطيع أن أخبر أي شخص في غضون دقائق قليلة عن قوة و قدرة أي جني، لذلك لا تقلل من شأن نفسك، فأنت لا تعرف أبداً إذا كان أقوي جني في العالم يعيش في المرآب الخاص بك. إذا أصبحت مسؤول عن هذا العالم، إبدأ بتدريب الجن ليصبحوا إيجابيون، ثم قم بإستخدامهم للمساعدة في القضايا الإيجابية في أي مكان في هذا العالم.

بالنسبة لي، لا أعتقد أنه سيكون من السهل بالنسبة لك فهم وممارسة التخاطر. التخاطر به قضية واحدة، إن جعل الجن من حولك أصدقاء لك، و تدريبهم بعد ذلك بشكل إيجابي ثم تقوم بإستخدامهم في مواضيع إيجابية، شيئ سهل جداً.

I catch like fire, once any demon tries to come close to me. The same problems happen to demons too, that's why they move away from my body pretty quick. But every new demon comes really close to me, at least for the first time, even just for thirty seconds, even thirty seconds are enough to hurt me. Now once I am getting a demon every hour, I feel it is a problem sometimes. I don't keep any demon around me or in my house that's why I ask those demons to go here and there or go back to original person. I do not remember if I ever asked any demon to stay in my house or around me ever. I never ask any demon to come back to take more commands from me, ever. But almost every fifteen minutes some demon visits me and wants to take new instructions, if I have any. I feel may be not immediately, maybe after sometime, but eventually most of the people of the world will have very clear and a lot of knowledge about demons due to me.

Soon everyone will be aware about demons and pains. Modern science will get the clue and direction to start research to know about demons and will try to find ways how to handle them. This thing gives me a lot of satisfaction. I don't know for how long I will live, but I am sure my books will change everything related to cancer diseases, health problems, HIV will be curable, less mental diseases, and above all people will not be scared of demons or ghosts or witches or black magic anymore. Everybody will know everything about demons and pains. Everybody will be communicating and convincing pains and demons to stay away from their bodies. Everyone will be controlling their dreams and watching dreams on demand every night. God knows what else you will learn about this invisible world due to the help of modern science in the near future.

يمكن لأي شخص القيام بذلك. ولكن وسائل التخاطر تعني أنك ، بغض النظر عن ما إذا كان الجني صديقك أم لا، تستطيع أن تتصل به و تمرر أوامرك إليه.

إن أقوى الجن متعجرفين جداً، فهم لن يتسامحوا إذا حاولت السيطرة عليهم وإعطائهم أوامر ليتبعوها ويفعلون ما تريد منهم أن يفعلوه. عادةً يعود ذلك النوع من الجن لمهاجمة مخ شخص ما و يؤدي ذلك إلى إتلافه بالكامل. هذا هو السبب في أن99.999999 المئة من الناس الذين يمارسون التخاطر يصبحون غير طبيعيين عقلياً أو مجانين أو مرضي نفسين أو شيء أكثر من ذلك . جميع الجن، بغض النظر عما إذا كانوا أصدقائك أم لا، بغض النظر عن مدى إذا كانوا مخلصين لأي شخص آخر، بغض النظر عن مكان وجودهم في العالم، و بغض النظر عن مدى القوي لديهم، فإنهم سوف يستمعون إليك ويتبعون أوامرك ، عندما تكون أقوى منهم. أنت لا تكون قوياً لأن لديك مجموعة كبيرة من الجن من حولك وكلهم يتبعون كل ما تطلبه منهم القيام به. تأتي قوتك من مخك وعقلك. لابد أن يكون عقلك قوياً جداً لممارسة التخاطر، وينبغي أن تكون قادراً على التعامل مع أي هجوم محتمل من أي جني أ أو ي مجموعة من الجن لإحداث تلف في مخك. يالنسبة للتخاطر، لا أعرف ماذا أقول لك. ولكن إذا كنت تشعر عن طريق الصدفة أن عقلك قوي بما فيه الكفاية للتعامل مع التخاطر و أنك قادراً على ممارسته، سوف تكون قادراً في البداية على الإتصال مع إما الإنسان أو جني واحد فقط، و بمجرد أن تشعر بأنك في حالة جيدة، يمكنك التعامل مع التخاطر بسهولة، ومرة أخرى إذا كنت تشعر بأنك قوي جداً وعقلك قوي جداً، فأنت بحاجة للإنتقال إلى الخطوة الثانية.

241

SEE & CONTROL DEMONS & PAIN

It is very difficult to say whether very sensitive people absorb more demons from other people or from the atmosphere, or when demons get the possession of human bodies, they make them very sensitive and very emotional. No doubt, demons boost and amplify certain emotional and sensitive conditions. At this point, I can say people are totally helpless against the possession of a demon. People cannot resist against the control of a demon. People cannot control their panic attacks, anxiety attacks, bipolar problems, depression, suicide attempts, etc. But now you can simply spray holy water on your face, neck, head, ears, chest, your surrounding and drink it frequently.

Continuously reject the control of the demons on your mind. Stay barefooted on cold ceramic or cement floor. You will be all right. If you are facing more fluctuation in your temperament, too much up and down all the time, it means your mind is very weak and a demon has full control on your brain. Bipolar is not a disease. Bipolar condition is a complete possession of a very evil demon over human mind.

Balance temperament means less under control of a demon. Now if you have no energy to get angry, if you are not impatient, if you are not hyper or emotional, if you are not running behind your desires or wishes like crazy, if you do not get upset easily, if you are not too much biased politically, if you do not feel too much love or hate for someone, if you easily give up, if you do not feel extremism or negativism, if you don't see any dream, if the answer is yes for all the above thing, then trust me, there is no demon around you. Most demons or I will say almost all the demons, are very revengeful, only if you hurt them somehow.

رضوان قرشي

أعتقد حقاً أنني أريد أن أدرب الجميع علي هذا. الخطوة الثانية من التخاطر حتى تتمكن من السيطرة على منطقة معينة من حولك أو في أي جزء من العالم، هي عن طريق إرسال نفس الأمر عدة مرات فقط، لإصلاح مشاكل من حولك. يرجى البقاء دائماً إيجابياً، وإعمل دائماًعلي القضايا الإيجابية. بمجرد أن تصبح خبيراً في التخاطر العادي،عليك أن تبدأ البحث في الإتصالات السلكية واللاسلكية و شبكة إنتقال الجن والمخلوقات الكهرومغناطيسية الأخرى في العالم الغير مرئي. سوف يستغرق الأمر بعض الوقت، و لتكون قادراً على التواصل مع هذا المجال الكهرومغناطيسي، و بمجرد أن تكون قادراً على الإتصال، سوف تواجه الكثير من المشاكل طوال الوقت، القوى الخفية تصيبك أو تضر بك، فتستسلم. إذا كنت لا تزال تشعر بأنك قوي بما فيه الكفاية، فقط قم بالممارسة لوقت طويل لمعالجة المشاكل التي تحدث بمجرد تأسيس إتصال. خذ وقتك؛و الإسوف تؤذي نفسك.

بمجرد أن تشعر بأنك يمكنك تأسيس إتصال تخاطري مع مسار الإتصالات و الإنتقالات في العالم الغير مرئي، يمكنك إذاً ان تعطيهم أوامرك أيضاً، مثل إذا كنت ترغب في إرسال أوامر لجميع الجن في منطقة معينة، لينوموا مغناطيسياً كل الناخبين لقوموا بالتصويت لصالحك في الإنتخابات السياسية أو كل خير تريد أن تفعله. لا يكفي إعطاء الأمر مرة.حدة، عليك أن تعطي هذا الأمر على الأقل مرة واحدة في اليوم حتى تتلقى نتيجة مثالية. بمجرد أن تصل إلى هذا المستوى، حتى العالم الغير مرئي سيتصل بك لتوجيهك لكيفية إستخدام تلك القوى والتعامل معها. حظاً سعيداً.

Once someone kills a cockroach, usually very upset demon comes out of the dead body of cockroach, and attacks the backbone area including the kidneys of an individual. Once someone kills a spider, those upset demons immediately attack the head and neck area, all the way up toward the brain. Once someone kills a lizard, those demons usually attack on stomach and intestine area. They create vomiting, diarrhea, stomachache. These are their immediate attacks, what else they do in next step, I don't have good knowledge about it, because I always pull them out of my body within few minutes. So I have no idea how they act with other people.

Demons usually take revenge in three ways:

(1) Possess the body & then create mental, physical issues and problems.

(2) Show very scary, nasty dreams all the time during sleep, show images of ghosts and witches during, when are up but not too much alert in dark areas of the house.

(3) Bring a lot problems and obstacles in our way to hurt us financially, family and health issues and problems continiously.

Demons or any human or any demon doctor don't have any control on spirit/soul. Spirit/soul cannot be taken out or put back in the bodies by any demon or any human or any demon doctor. In case of spirit, everybody is helpless. Nobody either human/demon will never have any control over spirits in or out of a body. Exactly like angels, spirits do not have any free will. Spirits have to follow their timings and schedules as per order of God,

لا يستطيع الجن البقاء محلقين في الجو أربع وعشرين ساعة، ليكون لها الحياة أو الجاذبية أو الدراما في حياتهم؛ إنهم بحاجة إلى الإستحواذ علي الجسم ليكونوا جزءاً منه، أو يمكنك القول أنهم جزء سلبي منه، وللسيطرة على ذلك الجسم عقلياً وجسدياً. إن الجن أجسام إلكترونية صغيرة جداً، و لهم دماغ إلكترونية أساسية مماثلة تماماً لدماغنا. الجن يشبهوننا عاطفياً، وفي الرغبات، وهم مثلنا يحبون أي أنشطة مادية ممكنة مثل الجنس، الشرب، التدخين، العراك والقتال،وما إلى ذلك، ولكن لا يمتلك الجن أي جسد مادي أو حتى إلكتروني للتمتع بجميع هذه الأنشطة لإرضاء العقل، يبحث الجن عن جسم هادئ يتبعهم بنسبة 100 في المئة بدنياً و عقلياً للقيام بكل الأنشطة الممكنة الممتعة لإستكمال حياة الجني.

الحياة. من السهل جداً علي إستخدَام الجن للأجسام الغير بشرية، كالحيوانات، والطيور والزواحف والحشرات وإستخدامهم لتحقيق جميع أنواع الإستمتاع الجسدي الحقيقي في الحياة والأنشطة البدنية. الجن لا يعنيهم كيف سنعالج مسألة كسب المال لتسديد فواتيرنا. إن إستحواذ الجن علينا، يرتكز علي عقلنا و إستخدامهما وجسمنا لإرضاء أنفسهم . هذا هو نظام الله. الجن لهم عقل يرغب دائماً بعمل شيئاً مادياً مثل الأكل والجنس والقتل والغضب، و الأفعال المتطرفة، وما إلى ذلك، ولكن ليس لديهم جسم للقيام بكل هذه الأشياء. إن الحيوانات والطيور والحشرات والزواحف أسهل في التعامل معها بالمقارنة بالبشر. لأن البشر لديهم الكثير من القيود الإجتماعية و الإلتزامات المادية بالمقارنة مع غير البشر من الحيوانات والطيور، وما إلى ذلك وهذا هو السبب في أن الجن لا يتلقي رفضاً لممارسة أي نشاط بدني من الحيوانات والطيور والزواحف، والحشرات، الخ.

Spirits cannot hang around here and there as ghosts. External negative energies like demons and pains have free will. Whenever they want, they can go in or out from any particular body. Demons and pains can do this in and out all the time. Positive energy, i.e., spirits, do not have that option. Negative energies, i.e., demons and pains, once they come out of a body, that body feels relax and more healthy. Normally spirits do not go in or come out in a particular body repeatedly.

Normally, spirits go inside a body to bring life to that body. Once the spirit comes out of a body, it will be a dead body. Even if they want to, pains and demons cannot do anything good to our health once they are inside our body. The best possible thing a demon or a pain can do to maintain our good health is just stay away from our bodies. It is very easy to make already an extreme behavior or a racist or a short temper person more radical and negative either by sending "do more" commands to the existing demons or replace the existing demons with more powerful demons to increase the level of negativity.

The more you use of electric heater, this will bring more demons in or around you. Usually those demons possess the head area and this is very dangerous sign. The more you use directly cold air, this will help you in repelling demons. By reading both my books and next book, any writer with a creative mind can write a fiction novel or a movie script. I don't mind even if they choose me as an inspiration to develop a character. The writer needs to have a clear idea of how that character has access and command to demon world.

هذا هو سبب في أن يتواجد الجن داخل الأجسام الغير بشرية. ولكن يعيش بعض الجن داخل جسم الإنسان من البداية، وهذا هو السبب في أنهم لا يزالون مع البشر ويبذلون قصارى جهدهم للحصول علي الإستمتاع البدني الجامح الذي يستطيعون الحصول عليه من البشر بقدر الإمكان. ليس مهماً للجن أن يستحوذوا علي شخص جميل جداً وحسن المظهر، أو جسم جميل. لا فرق بالنسبة للجن أن يستحوذوا علي جسم مثير جداً لذكر أو أنثي أو إنسان. إن الجاذبية الجسدية للإنسان أو غيره هي أقل أهمية بالنسبة للجن. أهم شيء بالنسبة للجن هو إيجاد الشياطين أ عقل أو جسم، ربما يمكن أن يقوم بأي نشاط جامح من أجلهم طوال الوقت، مثل الشرب، والكحول، والمخدرات، والتدخين، أيضاً الكثير من العاطفية و الكثير من الحساسية، والغضب، والجنس،، و نفاذ الصبر والصراخ، أي شيء، أي نشاط بدني طوال الوقت مما يجعل هؤلاء الجن أكثر سعادة. إذا كنت لا تفعل أي شيء، سوف تحزن الجن، وتجعلهم بطيئون، و مضطربون، و هم إما سيدفعوك لفعل شيئ أو سوف يبقوك حزيناً، وبطيئاً، و مكتئباً، وما إلى ذلك، حتى تشترك في الأنشطة البدنية الجامحة. هذا هو السبب في أن الجن يبحثون عن عقول ضعيفة أو أقل قوة طوال الوقت، للإستحواذ عليهم و إستخدامهم طوال الوقت لتحقيق أغراضهم دون أي رفض.. اذا سألتني، الذين يعانون أكثر من سيطرة الجن، جسم المرأة أم جسم الرجل؟ بالنسبة لي، وبصراحة، و يبحث الجن عن مزيد من الدراما طوال الوقت. الجن يفضلون أن يستحوذوا علي ضعاف العقول. عادةً يكون الناس العاطفيون أكثر ضعفاً في العقل، بالمقارنة مع الغير عاطفيين يعني، عموماً ضعف العقل يعني سهولة التعامل مع صاحبه. إن الشخصية الضعيفة، مع العقل الضعيف، يعتبر بيئة مناسبة جداً للجن للإستحواذ علي هذا الشخص. حتى إذا كنت سألتني هذا السؤال مرة أخرى، من الأكثر تعرضاً لإسحواذ الجن، المرأة أم الرجل؟ الجواب هو من الذي يكون أكثر عاطفية عادةً ؟ الذي لديه مزيد من هجمات الذعر؟

Rizwan Qureshi

Demon are around each and every human and machines with electronic brains. That character can pull out data from human and machines both by demons around them. That character can establish telepathic contact with anybody in any part of the world to use their demons for any positive purpose.

That character has the access to the electromagnetic communication field or network of the demon to convey his message to all the demons in one time to follow any of his command to establish his influence even on local politics. I have a little bit hard time in writing a fiction novel or a movie script because even if I will write any fiction, the 90 percent of that will be true. I cannot expose of myself as much. So any writer with creative mind can choose me to create a fiction character and follow the true techniques of hypnotism, telepathy, and total control over demon's world and can write anything about any politics or related subjects. I am okay if the writer is using all the true techniques and procedures of telepathy, hypnotism, or the use of demons for any positive cause. If anyone needs some help to understand these techniques, I can help more but if you just follow these two books and the next book, it will be enough for you to understand.

A lot of times, I established telepathic contact with very high-profile people, people too much extreme in politics, some extraordinary players, presidents, or anyone else just to check who is around them. And who is behind all the stuff they do. Usually, I get some basic info and send these demons back to them. The problem is that I used to be and still I am a very simple person.

رؤية الجن و الآلام السيطرة عليها

الذي لديه المزيد من هجمات القلق؟ من يكون ثنائي القطبين؟ هذا الجسم لديه عوامل جذب للجن. إنهم يحبون الدراما طوال الوقت. العواطف جزء من الجذب في الجسم / العقل ولكن الناس الأكثر عاطفية يشكلون مشكلة، فالسلوك الأكثر اطفية يوفر المزيد من السعادة والرضا للجن، فبمجرد أن ينجذب الجن إلي تلك الأجسام، ويقوم الجن بتعزيز و تضخيم تلك السلوكيات العاطفية وتحويلها إلى ثنائية القطبين وإكتئاب، نوبات هلع، وهجمات قلق.

يمكن أن تحبرك أحلامك عن مستوى الحكمة، ومستوى الذكاء، والطبيعة وتركزهم في الجني من حولك. هو صيغة بسيطة إذا كنت تريد أن تبقي الجن الأذكياء و الأقوياء جداً من حولك، عليك البقاء على مقربة وعلى إتصال إما شخصياً أو على الهاتف مع شخص ذكي وناجح جداً. ولكنهم أشخاص أصحاء بالتأكد، بمرور الوقت سوف تمتص إما الجن الخاص بهم، أو أن الجن الخاص بهم، سيقومون بتدريب الجني الخاص بك.

بنفس الطريقة، عليك إذاً الإبتعاد عن هذه الأنواع من الناس. إذا قتلت سحلية اليوم، فلابد ألا يتركك الجني الخاص به وحدك. إذا هاجم جسمك ذلك الجني، سيحدث لك نوع من المرض أو الألم، قد لا تشعر بأي شيء على الفور، لكن ستشعر بالألم لاحقاً. في الخطوة الثانية، سيبدأ ذلك الجني يظهر لك جميع أنواع الأحلام السيئة والمخيفة. ولكن لا تقلق بشأن ذلك الجني أكثر من اللازم. فاجئه بإتصالك به. قل له أنه لابد أن يهدأ و يجد سحلية أخرى., ألا يأتي بأي سحلية داخل منزلك في المرة القادمة تحدث بقدر الإمكان، ثم قم يرش الماء المقدس على نفسك و علي المناطق المحيطة بك، هذا كل ما يجب عليك القيام به للإنتهاء منه. إذا كنت تريد أن تجعل من لك الجني صديق لك، قم بدهن القليل من الزبد أيضاً. سيترك الجني المكان ولكنه سيبقى على إتصال وفي الجوار.

I want to live a very simple life with peace of mind. Now I am experiencing all kind of exposures to the powerful invisible world and getting more and more powerful every day. But the problem in using me and all my powers properly, is that these demons need to have my control to do something big. But the situation is reversed, when demons do not have any control on me, and I have a lot of control on these demons, and I do not have any intention or agenda to change this world or change everything around. Honestly, I am not interested in all these things. So finally, I decided I need to train whole world, each and every person in this world to take control of the invisible world of demons around them and use them positively to defeat the extremism and negativity from this world. You are reading this book. Within one month, demons around you will be listening to you and will be following you. You will be partially in charge of handling a lot of things around you and around this world without using any gun or human army. Another thing, it will be very difficult for you to judge the strength and powers of the demons around you, but I can tell anyone in few minutes about the strength and powers of any demon. So don't underestimate yourself; you never know if the world's most powerful demon lives in your garage. If you become in charge of this world, start training your demons to become positive, and then use your demons to help the good cause anywhere in this world.

As far as I'm concerned, I don't think it will be easy for you understand and practice telepathy. Telepathy has one issue. Making demons around you your friends then train them positively and then use them for positive issues, is very easy.

عندماتكون الحيوانات والزواحف والطيور والحشرات، وما إلى ذلك عادةً، تحت سيطرة الجن تكون هذه المخلوقات حادة جداً ويقظة. بمجرد ألا يكون الجن داخل الجسم، لا تكون هذه الحيوانات ماكرة. الشياطين جعلها أكثر يقظة. إن الجن هم السبب الرئيسي الذي يحافظ عليهم لتأمين أجسامهم من أي خطر محتمل. سواء كانت ذبابة، أوجرذ، أو صرصور، أوعنكبوت، أو سحلية، كم، سيكون من الصعب إعتراضها وقتلهم في بعض الأحيان.

تأتي الرغبة في مشاهدة الأفلام المرعبة و الشريرة، معظم الوقت من الجن الشرير و السيئ للغاية، فهذه الأفلام تعطيهم مزيد من الأفكار والمعرفة، لإظهار المزيد من الأحلام السيئة، والشريرة، ومخيفة. إن الجن العادي بطبعه جبان جداً. لدي العديد من الأمثلة عندما إختبرتهم. فعندما كنت أبحث عن قنوات مختلفة في الليلة الماضية، قمت بإختيار قناة تسمي الفجر بطريق الخطأ. وفجر. قامت تلك القناة بعرض عرض دراما مانو يا نا مانو. و هو عن إمرأة كانت تشعر بالخوف أثناء النوم و حاولت أن تقول شيئا لزوجها. ولكن كان زوجها نائماً نوماً عميقاً، وفجأة، نظرت المرأة نحو دمية صغيرة بجوارنافذة.

كان هذا كل ما شاهدته، لم تكن الدمية مخيفة جداً. هذا كل شيء، وبعد ذلك غيرت القناة إلى شيء آخر. ولكن خلال هذا المعرض، بمجرد أن نظرت المرأة نحو الدمية، قفز كل الجن الموجودين في غرفتي فوقي، وفي خلال ثوان. كان كلهم داخل جسدي.سألتهم: ماذا؟ لماذا القفز على؟ هذه الدراما عنك. تلك المرأة خائفة منك، ممن تخاف؟ على أي حال، كل الجن خرجت من جسدي. في دقيقة واحدة فقط. قبل ذلك، لم أكن على علم بأن هناك الكثير من الجن في غرفتي وأنهم كانوا يشاهدون التلفزيون معي. على أي حال،أستطيع أن أخبرك بأمثلة كثيرة مثل هذه، يمكن أن تثبت أن هؤلاء الجن يشعرون بالخوف من الأفلام المرعبة و الشريرة أيضاً. من الذي يخيفنا في الأفلام المرعبة، الجن الحقيقيون أم، الجن الوهميون؟

Anyone can do it. But telepathy means, regardless of whether a demon is your friend or not, you are going to contact him and will pass your commands to him. Most extremely powerful demons are very arrogant. Those demons will never tolerate if you try to control them and give them commands to follow you and do whatever you want them to do. Usually these kinds of demons come back and attack someone's brain to damage them completely. That's why 99.999999 percent of people who practice telepathy become mentally abnormal or crazy or psycho or something more than these.

All the demons, regardless of whether they are your friends or not, regardless of how much they are sincere with anyone else, regardless of where they are in the world, regardless of how much powers they have, they will listen to you and follow your commands only if you are more powerful than them. You are not powerful because you have a big group of demons around you and all those demons follow you whatever you ask them to do. Your powers come from your brain and mind. As for telepathy your brain needs to be very powerful and should be able to handle any possible attack from any demon or any group of demons to damage your brain. As for telepathy, I don't know what to tell you, but if by chance you feel your brain is strong enough to handle telepathy and you get some command to practice telepathy, initially you will be able to connect yourself with only one either human or demon. Once you feel you are in good shape and you can handle telepathy easily, again if you feel you are very strong and your mind is very, very strong then you need to go to the second step. I really think I want to train everyone about this.

رؤية الجن و الآلام السيطرة عليها

لا تبدأ في إستخدام المناطق المظلمة من المنزل أو أماكن العمل، وإذا لم تكن تستخدمها كثيرا، لا تبدأ بإستخدامها على الفور. لن يترك الجن ذلك المكان بهذه السهولة. إجعل الضوء يظل مضاءً، حتى لو كنت لا تستخدم ذلك المكان كثيراً. ولكن بمجرد ألا يكون لديك أضواء في ذلك المكان وليس قيد الاستخدام لفترة طويلة، بصراحة عليك نسيان تلك الزاوية من منزلك، و السبب هو حتى لو كنت ستبدأ في إستخدامها ، فالجن يعيشون بها، وسيظلوا يصيبوك أنت و عائلتك بمختلف أنواع المرض بدون توقف لإبقائك بعيداً عن ذلك المكان. إذا لم يكن لديك أي خيار فعلى الأقل لا تأكل أي طعام في هذا المكان بالذات لفترة من الوقت حتى تقوم بإصلاح تلك الزاوية. أنا لقول أ ن هذه الزاوية لا يمكن إصلاحها، أنا واثق من أن ذلك يمكنأ، ولكك لن تعرف كم من المتاعب ستلاقيها من الجن.أنا لا أعرف ماذا أقول عنهم. إنهم هكذا في تلك الأنواع من الأماكن، عنيد ون و لا هوادة عندهم معظم الوقت. وأنا واثق من أنني كتبت في مكان ما في هذا الكتاب عن كيفية التعامل مع هذه الأنواع من الحالات. إذا لم يكن لديك خيار، إبدء بإستخدام هذا المكان في بطريقة بطيئة و ثابتة جداً. لا تبدأ بإستخدام ذلك المكان بتلك الطريقة فوراً. وسوف يبقيك ذلك في وضع آمن. لا تأكل أي نوع من المواد الغذائية في تلك الزوايا للحفاظ على نفسك بعيداً عن المرض. إنني أتساءل كل يوم إلى متى سوف أكون قادراً على الحفاظ على السيطرة التامة والعادية على ذهني. وأنا أتعامل مع عدد لا يحصى من الجن من كل مكان في كل وقت كل يوم. دعونا نر, وفقا لتعلمي وخبراتي، لا يستطيع الجن تحريك أي شيء جسدياً من مكان إلى آخر. إذا كان الجن يستطيعون فعل ذلك، فأنا لا أدرك ذلك. وفقا لمعرفتي، حتى الآن، يستطيع الجن الإستحواذ علي الحشرات، أو الزواحف، أو الحيوانات، أو الطيور، أو البشر جسدياً وعقليا، ويجعلوهم يحركون شيئاً من مكان إلى مكان آخر، بغض النظر عن ما إذا كان ذلك يحدث بوعي أو بغير وعي.

The second step of telepathy so you can control certain area around you or in any part of the world is by just sending the same command several times to fix the problems around you. Please always stay positive, always work for positive cause. Once you become an expert of regular telepathy then you need to start searching the telecommunication and traveling network of demons and other electromagnetic creatures of the invisible world. It will take some time to be able to reach and connect with that electromagnetic field. Once you will be able to get connected, you will receive a lot of problems all the time, invisible powers hurt you or damage you, so you give up. If you still feel you are strong enough, just practice for a long time to handle the problems which happens once you establish connection. Take your time; otherwise, you will hurt yourself.

Once you feel you can establish telepathic connection with the communication and traveling path of the invisible world then you can give them your commands also, like if you want to send your commands to all the demons of certain area to hypnotize each and every voter to vote for you in political elections or whatever you want to do for anything good. Only one time command will not be enough. You need to give that command at least once a day until you receive perfect result. Once you will come to that level, even invisible world will come in your contact to guide you on how to use and handle those powers. Good luck.

Demons cannot stay flying in the air for twenty-four hours to have a life or attraction or drama in their lives; demons need a possession of a body to be a part of it or you can say negative part of it and to control that body mentally and physically.

إذا كان الكمبيوتر أو الإنسان الآلي الحديث سيكون لهما عقلاً إلكترونياً يسيطر عليه إشارات إلكترونية أو أوامر أو برمجة كمبيوتر، ويستطيع الجن إعادة برمجة جهاز الكمبيوتر أو الإنسان الآلي لإستخدامه بالطريقة التي يريدونها. يستطيع الجن تنويم أي جسم حي مغناطيسياً لنقل أي شيء من مكان إلى آخر، ولكن لا يستطيع الجن أن يحركوا أي حجر أو ورقة أو صنبور أو سيارة أو مجوهرات وأموال نقدية من مكان إلى آخر. كما هو الحال في حمامي، ليس لدي آلة رش تلقائي للمياه، ولكن فقط في حمام واحد، و يعمل جهاز رش المياه من تلقاء نفسه في كثير من الأحيان، نفس الشيئ، يلاحظ بعض الناس داخل أو خارج منازلهم طوال الوقت يفتح صنبور المياه من تلقاء نفسه. ما زلت أعتقد بشدة أن الجن يستخدمون حيوانات صغيرة أو شيء آخر من حولنا للقيام بهذه الأنواع من الأنشطة. لا يستطيع الجن السيطرة علي أي جسد بلا عقل. قد يكون الجن قادرين على العيش داخل الجسم، ولكن للسيطرة على الجسم، يحتاج الجسم إلي عقل. إن الأجسام التي ليس لها عقل خالية من التنويم المغناطيسي. لست متأكداً حتى الآن. أنت لا تعرف أبداً هوية أي شخص. وإلى أي مدى تصل القوة التي حولهم، لذلك كن حذراً عندما تكون على إستعداد لعدم إحترام أو الإضرار بشخص ما. هذا ليس ضرورياً، حتى لو كان شخص يدرك ما لدي الأشخاص من حولهم لحمايتهم أو للإنتقام ممن يسببون الأذي لهم و لا يحترمونهم. هناك شيء واحد مشترك بين كل الأجسام الحية، و هي الروح / إمداد القوة، بغض النظر عما إذا كان الجسم لإنسان و حيوان أو حشرات وطيور، و زواحف، أو حتى الجن. ليس هناك روح خاصة لنوع معين من السلالات أو الأعراق. يمكن أن تسند أي روح/ إمداد بالقوة إلى أي جسم حي. بمجرد أن يصبح الجسم منتهياً أو ميتاً، نفس الروح تكون حرة وجاهزة للإحالة إلي المهمة المقبلة، أي تنشيط جسم لحي جديد. أن المهمة الجديدة لتنشيط الجسم الحي الجديد هي تنشيط جسم جديد، ربما إنسان أو حيوان أو حديثي الولادة جسم جني جديد.

Demons are very tiny electronic bodies with a mainly electronic brain exactly similar to our brain, they are similar to us emotionally, desire wise, wishes, with love for any possible physical activity like sex, smoking, drinking, fighting, killing etc., but demons do not have any physical or even electronic body to enjoy all these activities to satisfy their brain. So always to satisfy their brain, demons look for an easygoing body that follow them 100 percent physically and mentally to do all possible enjoyable activities to complete the demon's life. It is way easier for demons to use nonhuman bodies like animals, birds, reptiles, insects, to use them to enjoy all kinds of real physical life and physical activities. It is less concern for a demon how we will make money to pay our bills.

Demon's possession is more about controlling and using our brain and body for their satisfaction. This is the system of God. Demons have a brain always desiring to do something physical like eating, sex, killing, angry, extreme, etc., but they don't have a body to do all these. Animals, birds, insects, reptiles are way easygoing as compared to humans. Because human have a lot of social restrictions and financial obligations as compared to nonhuman animals and birds, etc. That's why demons get no rejection of doing any physical activity from animals, birds, reptiles, insects, etc.

This is another reason demons are more into nonhuman bodies. But some demons live within a human body from the very beginning; that's why they continue with humans and try their best to have as much wild physical enjoyment as they can get from a human.

الروح هي مجرد إمداداً بالطاقة لتنشيط أي جسم حي إن المهمة الجديدة هي إمداد الجسم الحي الجديد الذي يكون في الغالب الجسم إنسان جديد، أو حيوان مولود جديد، أو جسم جديد أو جسم جديد لجني. الروح هي الطاقة الإيجابية فقط لتنشيط أي جسم حي. الأرواح لا تنمو مع مرور الوقت. الأرواح لا تشيخ، و لا تموت. مثل إمدادات الطاقة / الكهرباء، الأرواح / النفوس هي المسؤولة فقط عن تنشيط الجسم كي يظل على قيد الحياة. بمجرد أن ينتهي جسم الإنسان أو الجني، تخرج الروح / إمدادات الطاقة من ذلك الجسم. الأرواح لا تنمو مع مرور الوقت. الأرواح لا تشيخ، و لا تموت. مثل إمدادات الطاقة / الكهرباء، الأرواح / النفوس هي المسؤولة فقط عن تنشيط الجسم كي يظل على قيد الحياة. بمجرد أن ينتهي جسم الإنسان أو الجني، تخرج الروح / إمدادات الطاقة من ذلك الجسم.

وهذه الروح / إمدادات الطاقة تخرج فقط من الجثة تكون على إستعداد للذهاب إلى جسم آخر لمولود حديثاً لجعله على قيد الحياة عن طريق تنشيطه. إذا كان البشر/ الجن/ الحشرات، صحيحة الجسم/ عاقلة/ قوية/بكماء/ صغيرة/ مجنونة / طبيعية، ليس لأي من هذه الأشياء أو المشاكل علاقة بالروح/إمدادات الطاقة، فالروح في الجسم تكون مستقلة عن مشاكل جسدية أو عقلية أو تغييرات. إن مخ الإنسان، أو الجني، أو الحيوان، أو الحشرة هو المسؤول أساساً عن وظيفة الجسم، والصفات ذات الصلة، والمؤهلات أو العادات الخاصة بسلالة معينة أو عرق معين.

قد يكون من الصعب على الجميع أن يفهم بسهولة المعلومات التالية، ولكني أحاول أن أصف بنية ومواد جسم الجني. السبب الوحيد لحاجتي لشرح هذا، هو أن ذلك سيساعد العلم الحديث على فهم الجن. في العالم المرئي، تخلق الأجسام الحية من اللحم، بما في ذلك العضلات والعظام. المعالج الرئيسي أو الأساسي هو المخ في جميع الأجسام الحية المرئية. المخ نوع مختلف من اللحوم ولكنه لا يزال لحماً. المخ به كل أنواع الأسلاك داخله. وتنتشر تلك الأسلاك في جميع أنحاء الجسم للحفاظ على إتصال مع الجسم كله.

249

This is not really important for demons to have possession of a very beautiful and good-looking person or a body. This makes no difference for a demon to possess a very sexy male or female body or human. The physical attraction of human or other bodies is less important for the demons. The most important thing for demons is to find a brain or a body that possibly can do any wild and crazy physical activity for them all the time, like drinking, alcohol, drugs, smoking, too much emotional, too much sensitive, anger, sex, yelling, impatient, anything, any physical activity, all the time that make those demons happier. If you are not doing anything, demons will be sad, slow, upset; either they will push you to do something or will keep you sad, slow, depressed, etc., until you get involved in wild physical activities. That's why demons look for less strong or weak minds all the time to possess them to use them all the time for their purposes without any rejections. If you ask me, who suffers more from demon's possession, woman's body or a man's body? To me, honestly, demons look for more drama all the time. So whoever has a weak mind, demons will prefer them to possess. Usually, emotional people have a weak mind as compared to non emotional people. More emotional means easygoing, overall weak personality with a weak brain is very suitable environment for a demon to possess that person. So if you ask me this question again, who is more under the possession of demons, woman or a man?. The answer is who is usually more emotional? Who has more panic attacks? Who has more anxiety attacks? Who is getting more bipolar?

That body has more attractions for the demons. They like drama all the time. Emotions are part and attraction of a body/mind but more emotional is a problem.

السبب في وجود تلك الأسلاك داخل المخ، هو توفير مسار لسفر جميع إشارات / أو الإشاعا ت إلي باقي الجسم. حتى المخ و الأجزاء الأخرى من الجسم المرئي مصنوعة من اللحم، لا تزال جميع الرسائل الواردة من المخ، هي إشعاعات إلكترونية أو إشارات. كل شيء، كل رسالة، كل أمر، كل التعليمات، كل طلب، كل المعلومات التي تنتقل من و إلي المخ، تكون في شكل أشعاعات غير مرئية أو إشارات إلكترونية. الآن قم بمجرد التفكير في بنية المخ، يمكننا أن نرى أن كل المخ مخلوق من اللحم. يمكننا أن نرى كل الأنابيب والأسلاك الموجودة في المخ، كما يمكننا رؤية تدفق الدم و أنابيب الدم الموجودة في المخ. هذه هي الأجزاء المرئية من المخ. لقد إفترضنا بالفعل أن الجسم على قيد الحياة، لذلك نحن لن نتحدث عن الروح / إمدادات الطاقة في الوقت الحالي. لقد وصفت للتو جميع الأجزاء المرئية من مخ الجسم الحي . إذاً ما الذي ينقص المخ في الوقت الحالي؟ ما هو الشيئ الغير مرئي بالنسبة لنا؟. إنها إشارات الإتصالات أو الإشعاعات داخل المخ، هي أجزء غير مرئية في المخ. لدينا أسلاك مرئية داخل المخ ولكن الإشارات الإلكترونية أو الإشعاعات تتحرك داخل الأسلاك الغير مرئية. لقد إفترضنا بالفعل أن المخ على قيد الحياة. الآن نحن بحاجة إلى عكس هذا الوضع. إجعل جميع اللحوم المرئية والأنسجة والدم والأسلاك في المخ إجعلها غير مرئية.

وجميع إشارات الإتصالات الإلكترونية أو الإشعاعات تجعلها مرئية. الآن عندما يكون جزء للحم غير مرئي، يمكننا أن نرى فقط البنية الإلكترونية من المخ، والمصنوعة من الإشارات الإلكترونية أو الإشعاعات. الآن كل ما تراه أمامك من هذه البنية الإلكترونية للمخ المصنوعة من أشعة غير مرئية هي جني. ليس للجن أي لحم أو دم أو أسلاك نحاسية. إن الجن مخلوقون من أشعاعات غير مرئية.

Rizwan Qureshi	رؤية الجن و الآلام السيطرة عليها

More emotional behavior provides more happiness and satisfactions to the demons. Once demons attract to those bodies, demons amplify and boost those emotional behaviors and convert them to bipolar, depressions, panic attacks, and anxiety attacks.

Your dreams can tell you about the wisdom level, intelligent level, nature and their focus in the demon around you. Simple formula is, if you want to keep very intelligent and powerful demons around you, stay close and in contact either in person or by phone with very intelligent and successful but for sure healthy people; with time either you will absorb their demons or their demons will train your demon.

Same way, if you don't want to absorb or attract alcoholic/drug addict, lazy, dumb demons, then stay away from these kinds of people. If you kill a lizard today, there is no way that his demon leaves you alone. If that demon attacks your body to give you some kind of sickness or pain, you may not feel anything immediately but it will happen. In the second step, that demon will start showing you all kinds of nasty and scary dreams. But don't worry about that demon too much. Surprise him by communication. Tell him he needs to calm down and find another lizard. Tell him next time do not bring any lizard inside your house. Talk as much as possible, then spray holy water on yourself and your surroundings, that's all; you are done with him. If you want to make him your friend, then do a little bit buttering too. He will leave but will stay around and in touch.

الإنسان / الحيوان لديهما جسم كامل واقع تحت سيطرة مخ واحد. إن الإنسان لديه قلب و كبد و كلى و يدين و ساقين، و أعضاء التناسلية، هذا هو السبب في وجود أسلاك تنتشر في جميع أنحاء الجسم للتواصل مع المخ، أما الجن فليس لديهم أي أعضاء أ و ساقين، أو ذراعين أو قلب أو كبد أو كلي، لهذا فإن هيكل الجني يتكون من المخ فقط. مخ إلكتروني،و لكنه مصنوع فقط من إشارات إلكترونية و أشعاعات مختلفة.

الجن لا يأكلون أي شيء، إنهم فقط ينشطون أنفسهم. الآن ما هو الفرق بين مخ الإنسان و مخ الجني؟ والفرق الوحيد بين العقلين هو المادة التي إستخدمت لصنع العقل. إن مخ الإنسان مصنوع من اللحم و الدم، والأنابيب، والعظام، والأعصاب، والأنسجة أو التمديدات، بالإضافة إلى الإشعاعات الإلكترونية أو الإشارات، أما مخ الجني فهو مصنوع من إشعاعات و إشارات إلكترونية. لذلك ليس هناك لحم أو دم في كنولوجيا الجن. ولكن العاطفية، والتفكير، والتعليم ، العادات، و الجنس، والغضب، والكراهية والحب، و الغيرة وجميع المزايا الأخرى للعقول البشرية، وكل المواصفات الموجود ةفي العقل البشري، هي نفسها بالضبط الموجودة في عقل الجني أيضاً. الآن يحب الجن لحوم البقر ولكنهم لا يأكلونها. الجن يحبون النشاط الجنسي، ولكنهم لا يملكون أي أجهزة جنسية، والجن يحبون شرب الكحول ولكنهم لا يمكنهم شرب أي شيء، الجن يرغبون في أن يكونوا عاطفيين، لكنهم ليس لديهم أي جسد مادي للشعور أو الإحساس بالعواطف، والجن يرغبون في إستخدام المخدرات، ولكنهم لا يمكنهم أن يدخنوا،الجن يحبون أيلموا الأجسام الأخرى للمس للإنسان / الحيوان، ولكن الجن ليس لديهم يدين، الجن يحبون التقبيل ولكن ليس لديهم أي شفاه. يحب عقل الجني أن يفعل كل نشاط بدني، و عاطفي، ونفسي، أيا كان ما يريد عقل الإنسان/ الحيوان أن يفعله. إن العقل البشري لديه تركيبة مادية، ونفسية، وعقلية للقيام بكل شيء، مهما كان العقل البشري يريد أن يفعله. ولكن عقل الجني ليس لديه أي تركيبة بدنية و عاطفية.

251

SEE & CONTROL DEMONS & PAIN

Usually, animals, reptiles, birds, insects, etc., within the possession of a demon are very sharp and alert. Once demons are not inside the body, these animals are not that much cunning. Demons make them more alert. Demons are the main reason that keep them running to secure their body from any possible danger. A fly, rat, cockroach, spider, lizard, it is difficult to trap them and kill them sometimes. The desire of watching evil and horror movies most of the time comes from very evil and bad demons These movies give them more ideas and knowledge to create more nasty, evil, and scary dreams. Normal demons are very cowardly by nature. I have several examples when I tested them. Even last night, when I was searching for different channels and by wrong, I select a channel called Dawn. Dawn was playing one show or drama *Mano Ya Na Mano*. It was about when a woman gets scared during the sleep and was trying to tell something to her husband. But her husband was in deep sleep. Suddenly, that woman looked towards a small doll by the window. That's all I watched, even that doll was not scary. That's all, and then I changed the channel to something else. But during this show, once that woman looked towards the doll, all the demons in my room jumped over me. And within seconds all of them were inside my body. I asked all of them what? Why jump on me? This drama is about you. That woman is scared of you, who are you getting scared of? Anyway, in one minute all the demons come out of my body. Before that, even, I was not aware that there were many demons were in my room and that they were watching TV with me. Anyway, I can tell you so many examples like this that can prove that demons get scared too from those horror and evil movies. Who scare us in those scary movies, real demons or fake demons?

رضوان قرشي

إن عقل الجني هو مجرد تركيبة لجميع أنواع الرغبات و الأمنيات الجسدية والعاطفية. لقد منح الله الجن قوي لإختراق في أي جسم و قدرة علي الإستحواذ علي جسم آخر، و قدرة علي تحقيق رغباتهم وأمنياتهم عن طريق إستخدام أي جسم حي آخر من لحم و دم، ومثل أي إنسان أو حيوان أو زواحف أو حشرات، وما إلى ذلك الآن هل فهمت لماذا الإنسان هو أرقي عرق أو سلالة على خلقها الله هذه الأرض؟

إسمحوا لي أن أشرح أكثر من ذلك. إذافكرنا بالكثير من الإشعاعات حولنا تتحرك هنا وهناك أو الكثير من الإشارات الإلكترونية للهاتف / الأشعة و إشارات التلفزيون الإلكترونية ، و إشارات الراديو / الإشعاعات، وإشارات الإنترنت،هل نحن قادرون على رؤيتها بالعين المجردة؟ بالتأكيد لا. لكننا نشغل أجهزة التلفزيون، مشغل القيديو و الدي في دي، ، وآلات أخرى بإستخدام جهاز لاسلكي للتشغيل عن بعد.بغض النظر عدم رؤيتنا للإشارات الإكترونية / الإشعاعات التي تخرج من جهاز التشغيل عن بعد وإعطاء الأوامر لتشغيل جهاز التلفزيون. بهذه الطريقة نستطيع تشغيل التلفزبون عن طريق إستخدام الأشعة الغير مرئية المنبعثة من جهاز التشغيل عن بعد الخاص بالتلفزيون. الجن ليسوا إشعاعات، ولكن هيكلهم مصنوع من الإشعاعات فقط. إن جسم جني الكهرومغناطيسي الكامل يتكون أساسا من المخ فقط، ولا توجد أي أجهزة أخرى أو أجزاء أجزاء من الجسم.إن أجهزة التلفزيون، الكمبيوتر، لوحات الدوائر، وآلات إلكترونية أخرى مرئية لنا، بنفس الطريقة التي يكون جسم الإنسان، والجمجمة والدماغ، والقلب مرئية بالنسبة لنا. الآن تتحرك الإشارات الإلكترونية داخل التلفزيون أو الكمبيوتر من زاوية واحدة إلى أخري، لا نستطيع أن نرى تلك الإشارات الإكترونية / الإشعاعات في جهازالتلفزيون أو الكمبيوتر.

252

Don't start using mostly dark areas of the house or workplaces, and if you don't use them more frequently, don't use them immediately. There is no way demons will leave that place that easily. Keep light on, even you are not using that place that much, but once you don't have lights on and that place is not in use for long time, honestly you must forget about those corners of your house.

The reason is that even if you will start using that corner, demons live there, and will keep creating different kinds of nonstop sickness inside you and your family to keep you away from that place. If you don't have any choices then at least don't eat any food in that particular area for a while until you fix that corner. I am not saying that that corner is not fixable. I am sure it is fixable but you never know how much trouble you will get from demons. I don't know what to say about them. They are like this about those kinds of places, hardheaded and uncompromising most of the time. I am sure I wrote somewhere in this book how to handle these kinds of situations. If you don't have choice, then start using that place in a very slow and steady manner. Do not start using that place in that manner immediately. It will keep you in a safe position. And do not eat any kind of food in those corners to keep yourself away from sickness. I wonder every day for how long I will be able to maintain full and normal control over my mind, while I deal with uncountable demons from everywhere all the time every day. Let's see, According to my learning and my experiences, demons cannot move anything physically from one place to other place. If they can, I am still unaware about it.

إننا لا نستطيع أن نرى تلك الإشارات الإلكترونية / الإشعاعات التي تنتقل من دائرة إلى أخرى والتواصل مع بعضهم البعض. ولكن بغض النظر، أننا لا يمكننا أن نرى الاشارات الالكترونية / الإشعاعات، فهي المسؤولة عن الإتصالات في الآلة الإلكترونية، أو الجهاز الإلكتروني، مثل التلفزيون أو جهاز الكمبيوتر. إن الجن عبارة عن أجهزة كمبيوتر غير مرئية أو عقول إلكترونية لديها إرادة حرة. إن الجن الكترونيون الغير مرئيين لهم قوة الاندماج مع الجسم المادي الحي الآخر، كما أن لهم قوي لفرض إرادتهم علي أي جسم حي. الآن كيف يمكن أن تبدأ تنتقل هذه الإشارات الإلكترونية / الأشعاعات من خلال التلفزيون أو الكمبيوتر؟ كيف يمكن لهذه الإشارات الإلكترونية /الإشعاعات أن تبدأ الإتصالات بالدوائر الإلكترونية أو الأجهزة الإلكترونية مثل الكمبيوتر أو التلفزيون؟ كي نبدأ تشغيل التلفزيون أو الكمبيوتر، ونحن بحاجة لجعل هذا الكمبيوتر على قيد الحياة من خلال توفير الروح، أي إمدادات طاقة أو كهرباء. جميع أجزاء أجزاء جهاز الكمبيوتر جاهزة، و كل الأسلاك جاهزة، لكن لا توجد بها حياة، ولا توجد أي رسائل إلكترونية داخل الجهاز حتى نقدم لهذا الكمبيوتر إمدادات الطاقة أو الكهرباء.

فكر الآن، يتم توصيل الكمبيوتربالكهرباء / روح، كيف ستتحرك الإشارات إلكترونية/ الإشعاعات داخل جهاز الكمبيوتر، وتتواصل مع جميع أجزائه؟. لدينا في جهاز الكمبيوتر دائرة و أسلاك نحاسية تربط جميع الأجزاء / الأجهزة مع بعضها البعض. إذا تلك الدوائر والأسلاك النحاسية هي سبيل الإنتقال الوسط الوحيد لتلك الإشارات الإلكترونية / الإشعاعت داخل جهاز الكمبيوتر ليستمر في إستقبال و إرسال الرسائل إلى المخ / معالج الكمبيوتر.

SEE & CONTROL DEMONS & PAIN	رضوان قرشي

According to my knowledge, until right now, demons can possess any insect, reptile, animal, and bird, human physically and mentally and make them move something from one place to another place, regardless of whether it is consciously or unconsciously. If a computer or a modern robot will have electronic brain controlled by electronic signals, commands, or computerized programming, demons can reprogram that computer or robot to use them the way they want it. Demons can hypnotize any living body to move anything from one place to another place, but demons cannot move any stone or paper or faucet or car or jewelry, cash money from one place to any place. Like in my bathroom, I don't have automatic water flushing machine, but only in one bathroom, flushing machine works by itself a lot of times, same way some people observe inside or outside their houses all the time when water faucet come on by itself. I still strongly believe that demons use some small animals or something else around us to do these kinds of activities.

Demons cannot control a body without a brain. Demons may be able to go and live inside that body, but to control a body, that body needs a brain. Bodies without brains are free of demon's hypnotism. I am not sure until now. You never know, who is who, and how much powers they have around them. So always be careful once you are ready to disrespect or hurt someone. This is not necessary, even if someone is aware what they have around them to protect them or to take their revenge to whoever hurt or disrespect them. In all living bodies, one thing is common, i.e., spirit/soul/power supply. Regardless, human, animals, insects, birds, reptiles, or even demons.

تحتاج هذه الإشارات الإلكترونية / الإشعاعات إلي أسلاك و دوائر نحاسية للإنتقال من هنا إلى هناك داخل جهاز الكمبيوتر.حسنا، ماذا عن الإشارات الإلكترونية / الإشعاعات في الغلاف الجوي المفتوح، التي تربط عن بعد جهاز التحكم عن بعد بالتلفزيون لاسلكياً، وتربط الماوس ولوحة المفاتيح لاسلكياً بجهاز الكمبيوتر، أو الإشارة الإلكترونية عن بعد إلى وحدة مكيف الهواء أو الإشارات الإلكترونية اللاسلكية لجهاز التحكم عن بعد الخاص بالسيارة، للتحكم في قفل أو فتح قفل السيارة. لا يمكن توليد كل هذه الإشارات / الإشعاعات إلا إذا كانت جميع الأجهزة الإلكترونية نشطة. إذا لم توجد بطارية / إمدادات الطاقة / كهرباء / روح، لن تعمل جميع هذه الأجهزة الإلكترونية، . لن تكون هناك إتصالات أو حركات أو إشارات للأشعة الإلكترونية داخل الأسلاك أو الدوائر النحاسية، عندما لا توجد كهرباء / روح. تذكر الآن، أن كل الإشارات الإلكترونية / الإشعاعات تعتمد علي وسط، أي دائرة أوالأسلاك نحاسية، ولكن في الجو المفتوح بين التلفزيون وجهاز التحكم عن بعد، لا يكون لدينا وسط مثل الدوائر والأسلاك النحاسية، ولكن لا تزال الإشعاعات أو الإشارات الإلكترونية تنتقل من جهاز التحكم عن بعد الخاص بالتلفاز إلى التلفزيون. إذاً هل ترى تلك الإشعاعات أو الإشارات تنتقل من جهاز التحكم عن بعد الخاص بالتلفزيون إلي التلفزيون عندما تقوم بتشغيله؟

بالتأكيد لا. نفس الطريقة بالضبط، داخل الكمبيوتر، يمكننا أن نرى الدائرة والأسلاك النحاسية، ولكننا لا نستطيع أن نرى الإشعاعات والإشارات الإلكترونية التي تنتقل ذهاباً وإياباً داخل الأسلاك والدوائر النحاسية. بما أننا لا نستطيع أن نرى تلك الإشعاعات أو الإشارات الإلكترونية، هل هذا يعني أنها ليست موجودة؟، هذه الإشعاعات موجودة بالتأكيد. و حركة وإتصالات هذه الإشعاعات أو الإشارات إلكترونية الغير مرئية يشغلون هذا الكمبيوتر و يجعلونه قابل للإستعمال.

254

There is no special spirit/soul for a particular kind of breed or race. Any spirit/power supply can be assigned to any living body Once that body becomes expired or dead, the same spirit will be free and ready for the next assignment, i.e., to energize the new living body.That new assignment is to energize the new living body is possibly a new human body or a newborn animal or a new body of a demon. Spirit is just a power supply to energize any living body. Spirit is a positive energy just to energize any living body. Spirits do not grow with time. Spirits do not get old. Spirits do not die. Like a power supply/electricity, spirits/souls are just responsible of energizing a body to stay alive. Once a body of any human or a demon comes to a position to get expired or dead, spirit/ power supply will come out of that body.

This spirit/power supply just comes out of a dead body will be ready to go to another newly born body to make it alive by energizing it. Human /demons/ animals / insects,if they are healthy /wise/ powerful /dumb/young /old /crazy / normal , any of these things or problems have nothing to do with spirit/soul/power supply. Spirit in a body is independent of physical or mental problems or changes. A brain of a human, a brain of a demon, a brain of an animal, a brain of an insect is mainly responsible for the body function, related qualities, and qualifications or habits of that particular breed or race. The following information may be difficult for everyone to understand easily, but I am trying to describe the body structure and body material of a demon. The only reason I need to explain this, is that it will help modern science to understand demons.

الآن إفترض مجرد إفتراض بطريقة أو بأخرى أنك يمكنك أن ترى تلك الإشعاعت الإلكترونية / الإشارات تتحرك وتتواصل مع أجزاء الكمبيوتر. في الخطوة الثانية إفترض مجرد إفتراض، على نحو ما، و إجعل كل أجزاء الكمبيوتر والدوائر و الأسلاك النحاسية، و لوحة المفاتيح، والماوس غير مرئية تماماً.

إذاً نحن فقط نعكس هذا الوضع. نحن نجعل الأجزاء المرئية غير مرئية، و الأجزاء الغير مرئية أي الإشعاعات/ الإشارات الإلكترونية، ونجعلها مرئية. الآن لدينا شيئين، وإذا كانت أجزاء الكمبيوتر مرئية والإشارات الإلكترونية تتحرك في الأسلاك وأجزاء الكمبيوتر، هذا هو عالمنا المرئي. يمكننا أن نرى جسم الإنسان وأجهزته، ولكننا لا نستطيع أن نرى تحركات الإشعاعات / الإشارات داخل الجسم. فالإشعاعات الغير مرئية تتحرك ذهاباً و إياباً داخل الأعصاب / الأنسجة، وما إلى ذلك، في الجسم المرئي لأي شيء، مثل الإنسان / الحيوان، وما إلى ذلك وهذا قد يكون من الصعب على الجميع أن يفهمه.

هذا موجه أساساً للعلوم الحديثة للحصول على بعض المبادئ التوجيهية لبدء أبحاثهم. الآن عندما نجعل جميع الدوائر النحاسية، و أجزاء الكمبيوتر والأسلاك غير مرئية، ستكون الأشعة الإلكترونية / الإشارات داخل الأسلاك النحاسية مرئية. الآن إفترض مجرد إفتراض أنك قمت بفصل جميع الاشارات الإلكترونية / الإشعاعات عن ذلك الجزء من الكمبيوتر ،سترى جهاز الكمبيوتر الخاص بك بكافة توصيلاته وأجزائه. في الزاوية الثانية، سترى كل الإشعاعات الإلكترونية / الإشارات تتحرك ذهاباً وإياباً، والتواصل مع بعضهم البعض ويؤدون نفس العمل بالضبط، عندما تتحرك هذه الإشعاعات أو الإشارات في الدائرة النحاسية تكون من الجن.

SEE & CONTROL DEMONS & PAIN

In the visible world, living bodies made of meat or flesh, including muscles and bones, the main processor or boss is the brain in all visible living bodies. Brain is a different kind of meat but still meat. Brain has all kinds of wirings inside it. Those wirings are spread all over the body to keep brain connected with whole body. The reason of those wirings inside a brain is to provide a traveling path to all the signals/rays in or to the brain from rest of the body. Even the brain and the other parts of the visible body are made of flesh or meat, still all communications from brain and to the brain are electronic rays or signals. Everything, every message, every command, every instruction, every request, every information to the brain and from the brain is in the shape of electronic invisible rays or signals. Now just think about the brain structure, we can see all the meat portion of the brain. We can see all the tubes and wirings in the brain. We can see all the blood flow and the blood tube of a brain. These are visible parts of a brain. We already assumed the body is alive, so we will not talk about spirit/power supply right now. I just described all the visible parts of a brain of a living body. So what is missing from the brain right now? What is there and invisible to us? Communication signals or rays inside a brain are invisible parts of a brain. We have visible wiring inside the brain but the electronic signals or rays moving inside the wiring are invisible. We already assumed that the brain is alive. Now we need to reverse the situation. All the visible meat, tissues, blood, wiring in the brain make them invisible. And all the electronic communication signals or rays make them visible. Now when the meat part of the brain is invisible, and we can see only an electronic structure of the brain, made of the electronic signals or rays.

رضوان قرشي

في جو مفتوح، و بسبب المجال الكهرومغناطيسي الطبيعي، لا تحتاج هذه الإشعاعات / الإشارات الإلكترونية إلى أي أسلاك نحاسية أو أنسجة للإنتقال من نقطة واحدة إلى أخرى. الشيء نفسه ينطبق في حالة الجن أيضاً. الجن هم مجموعة من الإشارات / الإشعاعات الإلكترونية الغير مرئية، لهم إرادة حرة، و هم على قيد الحياة، و يتنقلون داخل حقل كهرومغناطيسي طبيعي للغلاف الجوي. إن جسم الفيل أو جسم الإنسان كبير جد بالمقارنة بجسم الجني. يتراوح حجم الجني العادي بين حجم الذبابة و الصرصور الصغير. الآن جسم الإنسان أو جسم الفيل كبير جداً، بأجهزة كبيرة جداً، و مخ كبير، للسيطرة على الجسم كله. تستمر كثير من الإتصالات الإلكترونية للإشعاعات والإشارات الإلكترونية في إدارة وظائف الجسم كله.فإذا جعلت جسم الفيل غير مرئي وجعلت جميع الإتصالات و الإشعاعات التي تنتقل من منطقة المخ إلى جسد الفيل، سوف نكون قادرين على رؤية تركيبة كبيرة جداً من الإشعاعات أو الإشارات الإلكترونية. الآن إذا لم يكن هناك جسد مادي للفيل، سوف نكون قادرين على رؤية الجسم الحي فقط كاملة مصنوعاً من الإشعاعات الإلكترونية / الإشارات، ولكن سيكون جسم كبير من الإشعاعات الإلكترونية حقاً ، وذلك بسبب كبر حجم الفيل الحقيقي.

الآن بدلاً من الفيل، فكر في العنكبوت، لا يوجد جسد مادي، مجرد جسد مصنوع من إشعاعات يتحرك داخل جسم العنكبوت لتوصيل المخ بأجزاء الجسم الأخرى . الآن لدينا جسمين، جسم لفيل و جسم لعنكبوت. حتى لو كنا نرى هيكلية إشعاعية، فهي لا تزال كبيرة جداً بالمقارنة بالجن، لأن لديهم جسم كامل وأجهزة كثيرة جداً. الجن لهم تركيبة إلكترونية صغيرة جداً بالمقارنة بالتركيبة الإلكترونية للفيل أو حتى العنكبوت. تتألف تركيبة جسم الجن الإلكترونية أساساً من المخ فقط. إن الجن تركيبة من الإشعاعات الإلكترونية، و الإشعاعات غير مرئية بالنسبة لنا، وهذا هو السبب في أن الجن غير مرئيين بالنسبة لنا.

256

Now whatever you see in front of you this electronic structure of brain made of invisible rays is a demon. Demons do not have any meat or flesh or blood or copper wiring. Demons are just made of invisible rays. Human/animal has a complete body under the control of one brain. Human has heart, liver, kidneys, hands, legs, reproductive organs, that's why wiring to communicate with the brain spread all over the body. Demons do not have any organs, legs, arms, heart, liver, kidneys. That's why the structure of a demon consists of a brain only. Electronic brain and that brain is just made of different electronic signals and rays. Demons do not eat anything. Demons just energize themselves. Now what is the difference between a brain of a human and a brain of a demon? The only difference between two brains is the material used to make the brain. The human brain is made of flesh, blood, tubes, bones, tissue, nerves or wirings, plus electronic rays or signals. The demon brain is just made of electronic rays and electronic signals. So there is no meat/blood or flesh in the demon technology. But emotional wise, thinking wise, education wise, habit wise, sex wise, anger wise, hate and love wise, jealousy wise and all other features of a human brains, are exactly the same for a demon brain also. Now demons like beef but cannot eat beef. Demons like sexual activity but don't have any sex organs, demons like to drink alcohol but cannot drink anything, demons like to get emotional but don't have any physical body to sense or feel emotions, demons like to use drugs but cannot smoke, demons like to touch other human/animal bodies but demons have no hands, demons like to kiss but don't have any lips. The brain of a demon likes to do every physical, emotional, and mental activity, whatever a human/animal brain wants to do.

خلق الله نوعين من الأجسام واحد مثلنا مرئي، و قابل للمس، من لحم / دم وعضلات وغيرها المخلوق الثاني مصنوع من الإشعاعات لتبقيهم مخفيين عن العالم المرئي. بقدر معرفتنا المحدودة، لم نفكر أبدا في أن مزيج الإشعاعات يكون عي شكل جن على قيد الحياة وهذه الإشعاعات لها عقول خاصة بها وقادرة على القيام بنفس ما يقوم به مخ الإنسان و أكثر من ذلك. نحن نعتقد دائماً، أن الإشعاعات دائما تأتي أو تنبعث من مصدر ما بنفس الطريقة التي ينبعث بها الضوء والحرارة، وغيرها من الإشعاعات التي تخرج من الشمس، بنفس الطريقة تنتقل إشارات / إشعاعات التلفزيون، و إشعاعات الهاتف. هناك دائماً مصدر مولد، و محول، ونظام إرسال لتضخيم وتعزيز أو في بعض الأحيان توليد مصطنع لإشارة إلكترونية أو إشعاع إلكتروني. بمجرد أن مصدر المولد الذي يولد نوع معين من الإشعاعات أو الإشارات الإلكترونية يتوقف عن العمل، لن يكون هناك أشعة في الجو المفتوح. مثل الشمس، نحن نستطيع أن نحصل على أشعة الشمس بشكل طبيعي من الشمس، ولكن نحن قادرون على توليد أشعة الضوء لدينا من الكشافات وأضواء السيارات أيضاً بشكل مصطنع. لماذا؟ لأننا في حاجة إليها، ونريدها. الشيء الثاني، لأن لدينا معرفة حول هذا الموضوع.

بنفس الطريقة، إكتشف العلم الحديث مواد توليد يمكن أن ينبعث منها نوع معين من الإشعاعات، و بعد ذلك قام العلم الحديث بتطوير الآلات الحديثة لتضخيم وتعزيز تلك الإشارات و الإشعاعات، لإستخدامها لأغراض معينة، مثل الأشعة السينية وأشعة الليزر، وما إلى ذلك. الآن المشكلة هي أن تلك الإشعاعات السينية أو إشعاعات الليزر ليس لديها مخ أو عقل خاص بهم. هذه الإشعاعات ليست على قيد الحياة، وليست لديها إرادة حرة مثلنا. ولكن النظام الإشعاعي للجي على قيد الحياة، و له إرادة حرة، و مخ خاص به.

Human brain has complete physical, emotional, and mental structure to do everything, whatever human brain wants to do. But a brain of a demon doesn't have any physical, emotional structure. The brain of a demon is just a structure of all kinds of physical and emotional desires and wishes.

God provided demons the powers of penetration in any body or ability of possession of another body, ability of fulfilling their desires and wishes by the use of any other living body of flesh and blood, like any human, animal, bird, reptile, insects, etc. Now do you understand why a human is the most superior race or breed on this earth created by God?

Let me explain more. If we consider a lot of rays around us moving here and there or a lot of electronic phone signals/rays, electronic TV signal, radio signals/rays, Internet signals/rays, are we able to see them by the naked eye? Definitely no. But we operate TV, DVD player, VCR, and other machines with the use of wireless remote. Regardless, we can not see the electronic signals/rays coming out from a remote and give a command to operate a TV. This way we operate TV by the use of invisible rays from TV remote. Demons are not rays. But the structure of demons is made of rays only. The whole body of electromagnetic demon mainly consists of just a brain, no other organs or other body parts. TV, computer, circuit boards, and other electronic machines are visible to us the way human body, skull, brain, and heart are visible to us. Now when within a TV or computer, electronic signal move from one corner to another corner, we cannot see those electronic signals/rays in a electronic TV or computer.

الآن العلم الحديث سيستخدم هؤلاء الجن في المستقبل كسلاح عن طريق زيادة أو تضخيم قوتهم بشكل مصطنع، ولكن كيف سيسيطر العلم الحديث على عقلهم إرادتهم الحرة؟ تنبعث أنواع مختلفة من الإشعاعات من مواد مختلفة . بالنسبة لي خلق الله كل شيء لغرض معين. ربما كان العلم الحديث يتجاهل بعض الأشياء. فربما تساعد تلك المواد التي تنبعث منها الإشعاعات، في حالة الجن في المستقبل. جسم الإنسان يحتوي على بنية من لحم / عضلات / دم. إذا وجدت الروح / إمدادات الطاقة لجسم الإنسان من شأنها تنشيط الجسم كله عن طريق تنشيط جميع أنواع الإشعاعات و الإشارات والإتصالات للحفاظ على حياة المخ والجسم البشري ليستمر في أداء جميع الوظائف اللازمة. إذا تم قطع إمدادات الطاقة/ الروح أو تركت الروح الجسم، ستفقد إشعاعات نظام جميع الإشارات والإتصالات المتاحة كل مصادر الطاقة والتنشيط، و سيكون جسم الإنسان ميتاً. إن إشعاعات نظام الإتصالات والإشارات الإلكترونية في الجسم غير مرئية بالنسبة لنا. سيظل جسمنا مرئيا، حتى ولو خرجت الروح / إمدادات الطاقة من الجسم، و ذلك بسب بتركيبتنا من اللحم/العظام. إن جسم الإنسان مخلوق من دم / لحم بالإضافة إلى إشعاعات. ولكن الجن مصنوعون من الإشارات الإلكترونية أو الإشعاعات. وأنا واثق من أن إذا قرأ لناس هذا الكتاب وفهموه، سوف يقلعون عن التفكير في تطوير أي نوع من التكنولوجيا النووية بغض النظر عن ما إذا كانت لها هدف إيجابي أو سلبي. بالنسبة لي، لن يكون هناك غرض إيجابي للتكنولوجيا النووية عندما تسيطر العقول الإلكترونية للجن على الأسلحة والمفاعلات النووية. آمل ألا أكون على قيد الحياة لرؤية تلك الكارثة. إذا كان هناك أي شخص يقول أن أسلحتنا النووية آمنة ومأمونة 100%، بغض النظر عن ما إذا كان رئيساً أو سياسياً أو أي قائد جيش، ثق بي، أنه ليس لديه أي فكرة عن المستقبل، بالنسبة لتدمير الجنس البشري بمجرد أن يسيطرالجن ذوي العقول الإلكترونية، على كل الأسلحة والمفاعلات النووية. بالنسبة لي، لا تسمح لأي شخص تطوير سلاح نووي.

We cannot see those electronic signals/rays moving from one circuit to other circuit and communicating with each other. But regardless, we can not electronic signals/rays, they are responsible for that communications in an electronic machine or device, i.e., TV or a computer. Demons are invisible computers or electronic brains with a free will. Invisible electronic demons have the power of merging with another living physical body Invisible electronic demons have powers of superimposing their will over the will of any living body. Now how is it possible within a TV or computer to start moving these electronic signals/rays?How these electronic signals/rays will start communications with in the electronic circuits or electronic machines, i.e., computer or TV? To start that TV or computer, we need to make that computer alive by providing the computer a soul or a spirit, i.e., a power supply or electricity. Within a computer, all parts or organs are ready, all wirings are ready, but there is no life, no communications within the electronic machine until we provide that computer a power supply or electricity.

Now think, computer is hooked up with the electricity/spirit, how will electronic signals/rays move and communicate with all parts withina computer ?. In computer we have copper circuit and copper wiring that is interconnecting all the parts/organs with each other. So those copper circuits and copper wires are the travelling path or medium for those electronic signals/rays within the body of the computer to keep receiving and sending messages to the brain/processor of the computer. Within the computer, these electronic signals/rays need copper wiring and copper circuits to move from here to there.

ينبغي أن كل من لديه سلاح نووي يقوم بتدميره على الفور، إذا كان يريد إنقاذ الجنس البشري. ستسيطر هذه العقول الإلكترونية للجن علي التكنولوجيا الروبوتية تماماً من في المستقبل أيضا. في جسم الإنسان، تقوم إمدادات الطاقة / الروح، بتنشيط الجسم وبسبب هذه الطاقة، يقوم الجسم البشري بتنشيط الإشعاعات والإشارات الإلكترونية الموجودة داخل المخ، و كذلك تنشيط بقية الجسم لتطوير الإتصالات والوظائف داخل الجسم والمخ.

إن تركيبة الجن مصنوعة من الإشعاعا ت فقط، عندما يتم توفير إمدادات الطاقة / روح إلى أي جسم كهرومغناطيسي لجني، تقوم الروح / إمدادات الطاقة، بتنشيط الإشعاعات والإشارات الالكترونية في تركيبة أو هيكل الجن لإبقائهم على قيد الحياة. ونتيجة لهذا النوع من التركيبات أو الهياكل، يكون الجن قابلاً للتوسيع عند لمس أي جسم مثل جسم الإنسان، إنهم يعيشون و يبقون على قيد الحياة، ويتنقلون ويتواصلون داخل المجال الكهرومغناطيسي للغلاف الجوي في جميع أنحاء الأرض في كل مكان. إن الجن هياكل إلكترونية، و لهذا فهم لا يحتاجون للأكسجين أو أي ثاني أكسيد الكربون للتنفس.

تتنفس أمراض أو حشرات السرطان / فيروس نقص المناعة البشرية فقط مثلنا. هذا هو السبب في أنها بحاجة للخروج من جسمنا بشكل متكرر للتنفس، ويمكنك تعقبها وقتلها بمتهي السهولة خلال هذا الدخول والخروج.. الآلام لا تتنفس مثل الجن، فهي تحتاج إلي نظام إلكتروني طارد للإشعاعات، لتأخذها بعيداً عن أجسامنا. يحتاج كلا الجن والآلام على حد سواء إلى طاقة للبقاء على قيد الحياة. يحصل الجن علي الطاقة إما من المجال الكهرومغناطيسي للغلاف الجوي أو من أجسادنا عن طريق إتلاف أعصابنا أو أنسجتنا للوصول إلى النظام الكهربائي من أجسامنا.

Okay, what about electronic signals/rays in the open atmosphere, connecting remote to a TV wirelessly, connecting mouse and keyboard wirelessly with a computer, or electronic signal from a remote to a split airconditioner unit or a car remote electronic wireless signal to control car to lock or unlock.All these signals/rays can only be generated when all electronic devices are alive. If no battery/powersupply/electricity /spirit, all of these electronic devices will be dead. There will be no communications or movements of electronic rays or signals within the copper wires or copper circuit, when no electricity/soul/ spirit. Now remember, within the computer all electronic signals/ rays are dependent of a medium, i.e., copper circuit and copper wires but in open atmosphere between a TV remote and TV; we don't have medium like copper circuits and copper wires, still TV electronic rays or signal travel from TV remote to TV. So when we operate the TV, can you see those rays or signals come out from TV remote?

Definitely no. Exactly same way, within a computer, we can see copper circuit and copper wires, but we cannot see rays and electronic signals travelling and moving back and forth within copper wires and circuits. So once we cannot see those electronic rays or signals, does it mean they are not there? For sure these rays are there. And the movement and communications of these invisible rays or electronic signals are making this computer operate able and useable. Now just assume if somehow you can see those electronic rays/signals moving and communicating with the parts of the computer. In the second step just assume, somehow, make all the parts of the computer, copper circuits, copper wires, keyboard, and the mouse are completely invisible.

وهكذا يساعدنا الله لنا في كل وقت بأن يختار أي واحد منا، ويغذيه ببعض المعلومات داخل المخ، والناس استخدام هذا التغذية والمعلومات لإبتكار وإكتشاف مختلف الآلات والتكنولوجيا. مدهش، أليس كذلك؟ آمل ألا يسألني أحد مرة أخرى ماذا يأكل الجن. ولكن لا يزال لديهم عوامل جذب كثيرة للحوم الحمراء، أي لحم البقر. الجن لا يأكلون اللحوم الحمراء، ولكنهم يحبون رائحة لحوم البقر بشدة. إن الجن لديهم رغبة قوية لأكل لحوم البقر، لكنهم لا يستطيعون بسبب تركيبتهم الإلكترونية، ولذلك يستحوذون علي البشر وغيرهم لتحقيق تلك الرغبات طوال الوقت، بنفس الطريقة عندما يستحوذون علي البشر وغيرهم لتحقيق رغباتهم الجامحة الأخرى المتعلقة بالأنشطة البدنية والعقلية.

لدي بعض المعلومات الأساسية عن الملائكة أيضاً، ولكن هذا ليس موضوعنا، ولهذا لن أقوم بمناقشتها هنا. بسبب كثرة عدد الجن، فإن معظمهم يعيشون هنا وهناك بدلا من الحيوانات / البشر، وما إلى ذلك وأنا أعلم أن الأرقام أكثر من هذا، ولكن بسبب كثرة عدد الجن،فإن جني واحد فقط من أصل ألف يكون قادراً على العثور على جسم إنسان / حيوان، لهذا السبب يقتل الجن بعضهم البعض للسيطرة علي جسم مادي مرئي.

الجن لا يحتاجون إلي الأكسجين أو ثاني أكسيد الكربون للعيش. إذاً هل تعتقد أن العلم الحديث سوف يكون قادرأفي المستقبل على إكتشلف جن علي القمر أو أي كواكب أخرى أو أقمار أو اكواكب أخرى؟ هل تعتقد أن الكائنات الفضائية في حقيقتها أجسام روبوتية طورها الجن في الكواكب الأخرى أو الأقمارالأخرى؟ هل تعتقد العلم الحديث سوف يكون قادراً على إستخدام الجن الموجودين حولنا لمعرفة أو تطوير أو إرتباط بالأقمار والكواكب الأخرى؟ ربما سوف أحصل على بعض المعلومات حول هذا الموضوع في وقت ما في المستقبل.

So we just reverse the situation. We made visible parts invisible and invisible parts, i.e., rays/electronic signals, make them visible. Now we have two things; if computer parts are visible and electronic signals are moving within the wires and the parts of a computer.

This is our visible world. We can see human body and organs, but we cannot see the movements of the rays/signals inside the body. Invisible rays move back and forth within the nerves/tissues, etc., in the visible body of anything, i.e., human/animal, etc. This may be difficult for everyone to understand.

This is mainly for modern science to have some guidelines to start their research. Now when we make all computer parts, copper circuits and wires invisible. Only the electronic rays/signals within the copper wires are visible. Now just assume and separate all electronic signals/ rays from that computer part. So what you will see on one side, you will see your computer with all connections and parts. On second corner, you will see all the electronic rays/signals moving back and forth, communicating with each other and performing exactly the same job, when these rays or signals were moving in the copper circuit are demons. In the open atmosphere, due to the natural electromagnetic field, these rays/ electronic signals don't need any copper wiring or tissues wiring to move and travel from one point to the other . The same thing is true in case of demons also.

أو إذا كنت سوف أكون على إستعداد للموت، وسيكون لدي ما يكفي من الشجاعة، حتى أتمكن من توسيع توارد الخواطر الخاص بي لينتشركي يصل إلى الكواكب أو الأقمار الأخرى، كب أقوم بدعوة أو سحب الجن أو مخلوقات أخرى من ذلك العالم إلي أرضنا. أنت لا تعرفني ولكني أعرف نفسي. وأعلم ما يمكنني القيام به.

لذلك لن أحاول الإتصال، إما عندما أشعر أنني مستعد للموت أو عندما أشعرأن العلم الحديث على إستعداد لقتالهم، كما تعلمون، في حال قرروا القتال. سيسمحوا لي أن أعود إلى الأرض. إن الجن يحبون رائحة لحم البقر والليمون / حامض الليمون ، و أوراق النعناع. إن لليمون / حامض الليمون له تأثير مختلف على الجن، لذلك لا تأكل منها ولكن تركها للجن حول الأشجار أو خارج منزلك في مكان ما، حتى يتمكنوا من التمتع بالرائحة أو أكله بإستخدام أجسام أخرى لأي حيوانات أو حشرات الخ ولكن ليس جسمك أنت . يجب أن تشرب النعناع بالماء لتجعل الجن يسترخون، فهو يساعد الجن علي الحد من أنشطتهم السلبية ضدنا، إنه يجلب بعض الإيجابية للجن. قم بشرب ذلك النعناع بالماء كثيراً.

الآن المستوى التالي للجن الإلكترونيين. إن الجن متوافقون جداً مع الكهرباء و الدوائر الكهربائية. إن معظم الجن يعيشون، ويتواصلون، وينتقلون من خلال الأسلاك الكهربائية ويعيشون داخل دوائر إلكترونية حية. إن الجن لهم مخ إلكتروني من تركيبة الإشعاعات الإلكترونية. يشتطيع الجن توليد أي نوع من الإشارات / أشعة مسيطرة، للسيطرة على العقل البشري أو دائرة كهربائية أو آلة إلكترونية بعقل محوسب عن طريق إرسال، والسيطرة على الإشارات الالكترونية / الإشعاعات، أو بلغة سهلة، عن طريق تنويمهم مغناطيسياً. في المستقبل القريب عندما يحتوي الكمبيوترالحديث على معالجات الإلكترونية خارقة / عقول للسيطرة علي الشبكة أجهزة كمبيوتر فائقة بشكل كامل، وسيكون للجن الإلكترونيين سيكونون قادرون على الإستحواذ علي تلك العقول من أجهزة الكمبيوتر الفائقة.

Demons are a group or combination of invisible electronic signals/rays, with free will, alive, travel within a natural electromagnetic field of the atmosphere. The body of an elephant or body of a human is too big compared to the body of a demon. The size of an average demon is usually between the sizes of a fly to a small cockroach. Now human body or the body of an elephant is too big with very big organs and big brain, to control the whole body. A lot of electronic communications of rays and electronic signals keep running the functions of whole body. So if you just make whole body of an elephant invisible and just make all the communication and traveling of rays from the area of the brain to the rest of the body of an elephant, we will be able to see very big structure of rays or electronic signals. Now if there is no physical body of an elephant then we will be able to see only a complete living body made of electronic rays/signals but a real big body of electronic rays, due to the real big size of the elephant.

Now instead of elephant, consider a spider, no physical body, just a body of rays moving inside the body of a spider to connect brain with the other parts of the body. Now we have two bodies, one of an elephant and the second one of a spider. Even we are seeing only structural rays, still these are too big as compared to demons, because they have complete bodies and too many organs. Demons are very small electronic structures as compared to electronic structures of an elephant or even a spider. The body structure of electronic demons mainly comprised of brain only. Demons are structures of electronic rays. Rays are not visible to us; that's why demons are invisible to us.

إن المزيد والمزيد من التكنولوجيا المتقدمة في العقول المحوسبة تجعل من السهل على الجن السيطرة على تلك الآلات الإلكترونية عن طريق الإستحواذ عليها و تنويمها مغناطيسياً. إن ذلك سهلاً بالنسبة لهم، فكما يضيف الجن إشارات إلكترونية / إشعاعات لنظام الإتصالات في عقلنا لإضافة سيطرتهم و أوامرهم، ليتحكموا بنا جسدياً وعقلياً، فمن السهل جداً على الجن إرسال إشاراتهم الإلكترونية / الإشعاعات إلى جهاز ما لتغيير الأوامر أو البرمجة. لكني أشعر أن الجن ينتظرون أجهزة كمبيوتر و روبوتات أحدث حالياً. نحن لدينا إرادة حرة، ويمكننا رفض أوامر أو سيطرة الجني في كثير من الأحيان ، وخصوصاً عندما نكون أكثر وعياً بهم و بأفعالهم. ولكن الروبوتات ليس لديها أي إرادة حرة. سوف تتبع برمجتها وأوامرها فقط. للحصول على قوة بدنية أكثر من الجنس البشري، ستكون الروبوتات من أهم المساعدات للجن. لذلك سوف تكون تكنولوجيا الروبوت في المستقبل ان خطيرة جداً على الجنس البشري لأن العقول الإلكترونية والرقمية والأكثر تقدماً في الروبوتات سيكون لديها المزيد من القبول لسيطرة الجن الإلكترونية . بنفس طريقة تنويمنا مغناطيسياً نحن أو الحشرات أو الحيوانات، بنفس الطريقة بالضبط، يستطيع الجن إرسال رسالة أمر / إشارة / إشعاعات ليسيطرون سيطرة تامة على العقول الروبوتية الحديثة. إن الجن خبراء في العقل الإلكتروني، إن لهم عقول مثالية للسيطرة على أي عقل رقمية محوسب بنسبة 100 في المئة بدون أي مقاومة من الآلات الحديثة. لأن تلك الآلات ليس لديها اي إرادة حرة وهي ليست على قيد الحياة، مثلنا أو مثل الجن. قد يكون هذا حدث فعلاً في مكان ما بالفعل مع بعض الآلات. ولكن بالتأكيد، سوف يستحوذ الجن على العقول الإلكترونية / الرقمية للروبوتات والمعالجات / العقول الإلكترونية لأجهزة الكمبيوتر للتحكم في تلك الآلات, يعيش الجن و يتنقلون بالفعل في الأسلاك والدوائر الكهربائية والإلكترونية.

God created two kinds of bodies. One like us, visible, touchable, with flesh/meat, blood, muscles, etc. The second creature is made of rays to keep them hidden from visible world. As far as our limited knowledge, we never thought there is a combination of rays in the shape of demons that is alive and those rays have their own minds and are capable of doing the same or more whatever a human brain can do. We always think, rays always come out or emit from a source, the same way light, heat, and other kinds of rays come out the sun, the same way TV signals/ rays, phone rays come out. There is always a source generator, transformer, transmitter system to amplify and boost or sometimes artificially generate an electronic signal or a ray. Once the source generator which generates a specific kind of rays or electronic signals, is off, there will be no rays in the open atmosphere. Like the sun, we get light rays from sun naturally, but we are able to generate light rays for our searchlights and car lights artificially too. Why? Because we need it and we want it. The second thing, because we have knowledge about it.

The same way, modern science discovered generating substances that can emit a particular kind of rays, and then developed modern machines to amplify and boost those signals and rays to use for particular purposes, like x-rays, laser rays, etc. Now the problem is that those x-rays or laser rays don't have their own brain or mind. Those rays are not alive. Those rays don't have free will like us. But the rays system of a demon is alive, has free will, and has its own mind.

إن الجن جيدون جداً في إرسال إشارات إلكترونية / إشعاعات لعقولنا، أي التنويم المغناطيسي.. إن لدينا إرادة حرة، وهذا هو السبب في أننا نستطيع أن نرفض هؤلاء الجن في كثير من الأحيان، ولكن أجهزة الكمبيوتر والروبوتات المتقدمة جداً في المستقبل لن تكون ضد الجن، لأنهم ليسوا على قيد الحياة وليس لديهم أي إرادة حرة. فكيف سنقوم بالسيطرة على إستحواذ الجن على الروبوتات الحديثة وأجهزة الكمبيوتر في الوقت الذي لا نستطيع فيه حتى أن نرش الماء المقدس على الروبوتات وأجهزة الكمبيوتر أيضاً؟ نحن بحاجة إلى نتجنب تصنيع الروبوتات و العقول الإلكترونية المتقدمة جداً لإنقاذ الجنس البشري.

.

نحن بحاجة إلى إكتشاف نظام إشعاعي يمكن إستخدامه كسلاح ضد الجن. يجب علي العلم الحديث فقط إكتشاف تلك الإشعاعات وتحويلها إلي شكل آلات حديثة. هذا العلاج ضد الجن موجود دائماً من حولنا من اليوم الأول، نحتاج فقط إلى العمل على ذلك. بمجرد أن يقوم العلم الحديث يدراسة البنية و التركيب الكهرومغناطيسي للجن، سيكون قادراً على إكتشاف تقنية جديدة لكيفية أن نصبح غير مرئيين مثل الجن. والشيء الثاني، هو أن تتعلم العلوم الحديثة، من تكنولوجيا الجن كيفية السفر بسرعة في ثوان من جزء من العالم إلي جزء آخر من العالم. الآن، الجن يرسلون إشارات إلكترونية إلى عقولنا لينومونا مغناطيسياً، لينقلوا لنا الأوامر الخاصة بهم.

ولكن في المستقبل القريب، بمجرد أن يكون الجن قادرون على الإستحواذ علي عقول أجهزة الكمبيوتر الحديثة والروبوتات، سوف يكونون قادرين علي التحدث إلينا بأصوات إلكترونية من للروبوتات والحواسب .

263

Now even modern science will use these demons in future as weapons by boosting or amplifying their powers artificially, but how will modern science control their brains and option of free will? Different substances emit different kinds of rays. To me God has created everything for some purpose. So maybe modern science is ignoring a few things. Maybe those substances and their emitted rays may help in case of demons in the future. Humanbody has a structure of flesh/ meat/ muscles /blood.If spirit/ soul / power supply is provided to a human body that will energize the whole body by energizing and activating all kinds of signals and communication rays to keep a human brain and body alive and to keep performing all the necessary functions. If power supply/spirit will be disconnected or leave the body, all available signals and communication rays system will lose all the energy and activation source, and human body will be dead. The system of communication rays and electronic signals in our body is there, but not visible to us. Our body will still be visible, even spirit/power supply will be taken out from our body due to our structure of flesh/meat/bones. Human body is made of both flesh/blood plus rays. But demons are totally made of electronic signals or rays. I am sure if people will read and understand this book, they will quit thinking about developing any kind of nuclear technology regardless of whether it has a positive or negative purpose. To me, there will be no positive purpose of nuclear technology when electronic brains of demons will control nuclear weapons and reactors. Hopefully, I will not be alive to see that disaster. If anybody says our nuclear weapons are 100 percent secure and safe,

إن عقل الجني قادرة على التعامل مع مزيد من العواطف، ومزيد من التطرف، و مزيد من السلبية، و مزيد من الحب، و مزيد من الكراهية، ومزيد من المنافسة، و مزيد من العنف، وما إلى ذلك، و منجذب إلي كل ذلك. وهكذا فإننا في المستقبل، سوف نتعامل مع روبوتات متطرفة، وأجهزة كمبيوتر سريعة الغضب . سنكون موجودين مع روبوتات عاطفية جداً، بمجرد أن يكونوا تحت سيطرة التنويم المغناطيسي للجن تماماً. في الوقت نفسه، فإن معظم الجن ستستخدم الروبوت وأجهزة الكمبيوتر في قتل وتدمير الجنس البشري. كما أشرح دائماً، ليس كل الجن سيئين. إن الجن مثلنا لهم إرادة حرة أيضاً، يتملهذا فهم يمكنهم الإختيار بين كلا الإتجاهين الخير أو الشر. إن الأمر دائماً هكذا.إن بعض الجن لطفاء وأصدقاء، وبعض الجن شياطين وأشرار. نحن لدينا أداة وميزة الإرادة الحرة. ينبغي لنا أن نحاول تحويلها إلى الجن الطيبين كي يقوموا بتنبيهنا طوال الوقت إذا عرفوا النوايا السيئة للشياطين و الجن الأشرار أو علي الأقل يقوم الجن الطيبون بتوجيه البشر إلي كيفية حماية أنفسهم.

كما وصفت عدة مرات، إن الروح والكهرباء / وإمدادات لطاقة هي نفس الأشياء. الفرق الوحيد هو أن لدينا سيطرة كاملة على إمدادات الطاقة / الكهرباء، ولكن ليس لدينا أي سيطرة على الروح. لقد وصفت بالفعل بالتفصيل أن الجن و الآلام لا يعيشون في الأجسام الغير نشطة أو الميتة. بمجرد أن نموت أو لا توجد روح في الجسم، يخرج الجن من الجثة في ثانية واحدة. السبب هو أن ذلك الجسم الغير نشط أو الميت يمكنه أن يأخذ كل الطاقة من الجن و يجعله غير نشط أيضاً.

regardless of whether he is the president or any politician or any army chief, trust me, even he doesn't have any idea of the future destruction to human race once electronic brains of demons will take over all the nuclear weapons and reactors. To me, do not allow anyone to develop a nuclear weapon and whoever has a nuclear weapon should destroy it immediately, if he wants to save human race. Robotic technology will be totally controlled by these electronic demons brains in the future too. In the human body, a power supply/spirit/soul, energize the body and due to that energy, the human body energizes the electronic rays and signals inside our brain and the rest of the body to develop the communication and functions inside our body and brain.

The structure of demons is just made of rays only, when a power supply/spirit is provided to an electromagnetic body of a demon, the soul/spirit/power supply, energize the rays and electronic signals of demon structure to keep them alive. Due to this kind of structure, demons are expandable when they touch any physical body like humans, they live, survive, travel, and communicate within the electromagnetic field of the atmosphere all around the earth everywhere. Demons are electronic structures; that's why they don't need for breathing any oxygen or carbon dioxide.

Only cancer/HIV diseases or insects breathe like us. That's why they need to come out of our body frequently to breathe. And you can hunt and kill them very easily during this in and out. Pains don't breathe either like demons. So they need electronic repelling system of rays to take them out from our bodies. Demons and pains both need energy to stay alive.

إن الجن ليس لديهم الكثير من الطاقة على أي حال بسبب صغير أحجامهم حقاً. يستطيع الجن العيش وإحداث خلل في أي كائن حي أو جسم نشط بغض النظر عن ما إذا كان تنشيط ذلك الجسم بصورة طبيعية أو صناعية. إن الروح تنشط أجسامنا. يتم تنشيط الكمبيوتر وغيره من الأجهزة الحديثة وأجهزة الإتصالات تحديداً، بشكل مصطنع عن طريق الكهرباء أو الطاقة بنفس الطريقة.

إن اطريقة تعامل الجن والآلام معنا طوال الوقت، من تنويمنا مغناطيسياً ، إحداث الآلام لكل أنواع من المشكلات لنا. بنفس الطريقة بالضبط، فإن الجن والآلام يبذلون كل جهدهم لإحداث خلل في الدوائر الإلكترونية والأجهزة أيضاً، مثل أجهزة الكمبيوتر، والروبوتات، والموجهات، مسجلات الفيديو الرقمية، والأجهزة الإلكترونية الأخرى. الآن الجن يشاركون في إحداث الأعطال في أجسام البشر/ الحيوانات و في الأجسام الإلكترونية. الآن هنا المشكلة أو يمكنك القول حسن الحظ أو سوء الحظ، بمجرد أن يبدأ عطل في جهاز الكمبيوتر الخاص بك، إو الدي في دي ، أو جهاز الراوتر ،فأنت لا تنشط الجهاز أو تجعله ميتاً، إذا قطعنت الكهرباء عن هذه الأجهزة حتى لمجرد ثوان قليلة و أعدت تشغيلها بعد عشر أو عشرين ثانية، فبمجرد عدم تنشيط جهاز الكمبيوتر الخاص بك، و أجهزة الراوتر لبضع ثوان، لا تستطيع الجن و الآلام البقاء في هذه الأجهزة على الإطلاق؛ يجب عليها ترك تلك الأجهزة فوراً لتنشط أو ظل على قيد الحياة. فإذا كنت تريد أن تبقي الأجهزة الخاصة بك خالية من الجن والآلام معظم الوقت، يجب قطع إمدادات الكهرباء أو الطاقة، بمجرد ألا تستخدمهم. فهل هناك أي طريقة نستطيع بها عدم تنشيط الجسم البشري لمدة عشر ثوان مثل الأجهزة الإلكترونية، مرتين في اليوم للتخلص من هذه الآلام والجن في أجسامنا؟ قد تسأل هذا السؤال، إذا تم إعادة تنشيط الجسم ، هل سيعود هؤلاء الجن و الآلام؟ ربما نفس الجن و الآلام أو قد تكون مختلفة، ستعود، نعم، أنها سوف تعود. لهذ نحن بحاجة إلى عدم التنشيط في كثير من الأحيان.

SEE & CONTROL DEMONS & PAIN

Demons charge themselves either from electromagnetic field of the atmosphere or from our bodies by damaging our nerves or tissues to reach the electrical system of our bodies.Demons and pains both need energy to stay alive. Demons charge themselves either from electromagnetic field of the atmosphere or from our bodies by damaging our nerves or tissues to reach the electrical system of our bodies. So this way God helps us all the time by choosing any one of us, and feed some info inside his brain; people use that feeding and information to invent and discover different machines and technology. Amazing, right? Hopefully no one will ask me again what demons eat. But still they have a lot of attractions for red meat, i.e., beef. Demons don't eat red meat, but they like the smell of the beef like crazy. Demons have strong desire to eat beef but they cannot due to their electronic structure, so they possess human and other bodies to fulfill their these desires all the time, the same way when they possess human and other bodies to fulfill their other wild desires related to physical and mental activities. I have some basic feedings and information about angels also, but they are not an issue for us; that's why I am not discussing them here. Due to too much population of demons, most demons live here and there instead of human/animals, etc. I know the figures are more than this, but due to a lot of population of demons, only one demon out of at least one thousands demons is able to find human/ animal bodies. For this reason, demons fight with each other to have a possession of a visible physical living body. Demons don't need oxygen or carbon dioxide to live. So do you think in the future modern science will be able to find out about the population of demons on moon or on other planets or moons of other planets?

رضوان قرشي

أول شيء العلم الحديث عليك القيام به هو لاكتشاف الشياطين في أقرب وقت ممكن. مرة واحدة العلم الحديث سوف تكون قادرة على التواصل مع الشياطين، أن الأمور ستكون مختلفة جدا. لقد خلق الله هذه التكنولوجيا شيطان حتى قبل الإنسان، ولكن العلم الحديث الإنسان لا يزال علم التكنولوجيا شيطان من الله. أنا متأكد من الجميع تقريبا سيكون له الكثير من المعرفة من الشياطين في الأيام القادمة، لذلك أنا واثق من أن الأمور ستكون مختلفة جدا مع الشياطين من حولنا.

حتى أنا أقول لا تتطور الروبوتات الحديثة والعقول الحديثة الرقمية داخل أجهزة الكمبيوتر لحفظ الجنس البشري، ولكن لا يزال الكثير من العلماء تحت تأثير الشياطين الشريرة جدا وقوية ستعمل على تطوير هذا النوع من العقول الإلكترونية وأجهزة الكمبيوتر داخل الروبوتات فائقة. أنا لا أعرف كيف سوف تشعر عندما تعمل آلات سيتم عاطفية أو المتطرفة، غاضب، خفف قصيرة، سوف تذهب مرة واحدة تحت حيازة الشياطين. الشياطين هم من نواح عديدة وفريدة من نوعها التكنولوجيا المتفوقة من الله. العلم الحديث حتى لا يكون أي مسار من الشياطين حتى الآن؟ يمكن الشياطين ينوم أي عالم الإنسان من بناء آلات أكثر وأكثر حداثة مع دفع الدماغ جدا الإلكترونية، والطريقة التي تريد أن يكون لها السيطرة الفعلية من هذه الأرض. يمكن استخدام الشياطين القوة البدنية نفس تلك الأجهزة مع العقول الإلكترونية، والروبوتات ضد الجنس البشري. أنا لا أعرف كم الشياطين تشارك بالفعل في أجهزة الكمبيوتر لدينا والالكترونيات الحديثة الأخرى، ولكن آمل العلم الحديث سوف تجد طريقة أكثر أمانا لجنس البشري. أي شخص أو أي شيطان قادر على الفوز على الإنسان، عندما الإنسان ليست على علم عنهم، ولكن مرة واحدة وأنا واثق الإنسان سوف تحصل على بعض الوعي التكنولوجيا شيطان من الله، وسوف تكون قادرة العلم الحديث لايجاد سبل لتأمين مستقبل الجنس البشري.

266

Demons don't need oxygen or carbon dioxide to live. So do you think in the future modern science will be able to find out about the population of demons on moon or on other planets or moons of other planets? Do you think aliens from other planets are in actual the robotic bodies developed by the demons of other planets or moons? Do you think modern science will be able to use demons around us to find out or to develop a link with other planets or moons? Maybe I will get some feedings about it sometime in the future. Or if I will be ready to die and will have enough courage, so I can expand my telepathic connection to spread up to other planets or moons to invite or pull demons or other creatures from those worlds to our earth. You don't know me but I know myself. I know what I can do.

So I can try to contact, when either I feel I am ready to die or if I feel modern science is ready to fight them, you know, in case they decide to fight, they let me come back to earth. Demons like the smell of beef, lemon/lime, and mint leaves. Lemon/lime has different effect on demons, so don't eat them but them leave for demons, around trees or outside of your house somewhere, so they can enjoy the smell or eat it by using another body of any animal or insect etc but not yours. Mint leaves with water, you need to drink to relax them. It helps demons to reduce their negative activities against us. It brings some positivity to demons. Drink mint leaves with water frequently.

Now the next level of the electronic demons. Demons are very compatible with electricity and electric circuits. Most of the demons live, communicate, and travel through electric wires and live inside the live electronic circuits

الشياطين هم نسبيا أكثر فريدة من نوعها التكنولوجيا بالنسبة لنا لأننا لسنا على علم حول هذا الموضوع، ولكن لا يزال لا يزال الإنسان خلق معظم متفوقة من الله. الآن الشياطين لا تملك السيطرة الفعلية في هذا العالم. لا شك، والشياطين لديهم الكثير من السيطرة على العقول البشرية، ولكن بمجرد الشياطين سوف تحصل على السيطرة على الآلات الحديثة / كمبيوتر / الروبوتات، فإن الشياطين السيطرة بطريقة أكثر مادية من هذا العالم. إذا كان لا أحد يمنعهم، وربما سوف الرؤساء في المستقبل من مختلف البلدان تكون الروبوتات الإلكترونية التي تمتلكها الشياطين. لذلك الاختصار، في المستقبل، أكثر آلات وأجهزة الكمبيوتر والروبوتات يعني المزيد من السيطرة على الشياطين، وربما نهاية الجنس البشري.

كل شيء يبدو مثل الخيال، ولكن ترتكب هذا الخطأ، لا يوجد شيء مثل الخيال في هذا الكتاب، والكتاب الأول. كل شيء في هذا الكتاب صحيح 100 في المئة. عندما لا أريد أن أتعلم شيئاً عن أي شيء، تجبرني الطبيعة علي التعلم. عندما أكون في حالة إنكار لشيئ ما. أقول أنني لست مستعداً للتصديق أو التعلم لقد تم وضعي في مشاكل عميقة أو آلالام لمعرفة الحل. أنا لم أخرج مطلقاً من بعض مواقف معينة حتى أعطي التأكد من أنني فهمت الحل. وهكذا عانيت كثيراً حقاً لمعرفة كل هذه الأسرار، و العلاجات، والحلول. لكني لا زلت أشعر أنني لم أنتهي بعد من معرفة كل شيئ.. ما هو مقدار المعرفة التي سأحصل عليها؟، الله أعلم. لقد كنت أفكر طوال الوقت، كيف يستطيع البشر السيطرة علي الجن والجن الكثيرون، عندما لا يوجد حتى لدي العلم الحديث أي دليل عنهم حتى الآن؟، ولا زالت أشعر أن الأمر سيستغرق وقتأ طويلاً ليقوم العلم الحديث بعمل ضدهم. كيف ستقتال شيئاً لا تعلم أي شيئ عن بنيته و تركيبته، وجوده، وأفعاله؟ أنا لا أعرف كيف سيتم تأمين الجنس البشري في المستقبل عندما...

SEE & CONTROL DEMONS & PAIN

Demons have electronic brain structured by electronic rays. Demons can generate any kind of signals/controlling rays to control a human brain or an electric circuit or an electronic machine with a computerized brain by sending, and controlling electronic signals/rays or, in easy language, by hypnotizing them. In the near future when modern computer will have super electronic processors/brains to control whole network of super computers, electronic demons will be able to have possession of those brains of the super computers. More and more advance technology in computerized brains will make it easier for demons to control those electronic machines by possessing and hypnotizing them. It is easy for them, the way demons add electronic signals/rays with our brain's communication system to add their control and commands, to control us physically and mentally. It is very easy for a demon to send their electronic signals/ rays to a machine to change the commands or programming. But I feel demons are waiting for more modern computers and robots right now. We have free will. We can reject the commands or control of a demon a lot of times, especially when we are more aware about them and their actions. But robots will not have any free will. Robots will follow only their programming and commands. To gain physical strength over the human race, robots will be most important help for demons. So the robot technology of the future will be very dangerous to human race because more advanced and digital electronic brains in robots will have more acceptances for the electronic control of demons. The way demons hypnotize us or insects or animals, exactly the same way, demons can send a signal/rays command message to have complete control over modern robotic brains. Demons are a master piece of electronic brain.

رضوان قرشي

يستطيع هؤلاء الجن تفعيل أي من أو جميع الأسلحة النووية في غضون ثواني . إن السيطرة على أجهزة الكمبيوتر للأسلحة النووية يحتاج فقط إلي بعض الأوامر أو الإشارات الإلكترونية لتفعيلها. الجن أنفسهم إشارات إلكترونية و أوامر. إن الجن عقول إلكترونية، من يستطيع وقفها بمجرد أن تكون جاهزة لتدمير الجنس البشري؟ إذا كنت تقول ذلك، سوف أسألك كيف؟ السبيل الوحيد لأمان الجنس البشري هو ألا يكون لدينا ي سلاح نووي واحد في أي مكان لتدمير الجنس البشري. الشيئ الثاني هو أن تحتفظ بهم، كما هم الآن، في حدود، فقط لا تصنع العقول الإلترونية التي تشغلها الإشارات الإلكترونية أو الأوامر، بغض النظر عما إذا كانت أجهزة كمبيوتر أو روبوتات. جميع الآلات العلمية جداً بعقول إلكترونية قامت بصناعتها العلوم الحديثة اليوم أو في المستقبل، وستكون تحت سيطرة هؤلاء الجن الإلكترونية وسوف تستخدم ضدنا لتدميرنا. بمجرد ألا يكون لدينا سلاح نووي و آلات مادية بعقول إلكترونية، وسنكون في حالة أفضل للتواصل مع الجن. سنكون في وضع أفضل لجعلهم أصدقائنا. ولكن لماذا سبستمع لنا الحن أو حتي بهتمون بأمرنا و هم سيكون جاهزين للتخلص منا من خلال تدميرنا.

يفقد البشر سيطرتهم تحت تأثير الجن، حتى لمجرد بضع دقائق أو ساعات، مثل جلب المسدسات على الطرق أو في العمل أو في المدرسة لقتل أشخاص آخرين، معظم الوقت بدون أي سبب. الناس يقتلون أصدقائهم وعائلاتهم بسبب خلافات طفيفة. إذا سألهم أي شخص لماذا حدث ذلك، أنا واثق من كل منهم سوف يقول أنه فقد السيطرة على عقوله. أراهن إذا كان هناك شخص ما زال يشعر بالفخر من أعماله السابقة المتمثلة في قتل أو تدمير شخص ما. وأنا واثق كل منهم يجب أن يكون لديه شعور بالأسف الشديدا من أعمالهم.

268

Demons are perfect brains to control any digital computerized brain 100 percent without any resistance from modern machines. Because machines don't have any free will and these machines are not alive, like us or demons. This may be already happening somewhere with some machines. But for sure, demons will take possession of electronic/digital brains of the robots and the processors/brains of the computers to control those machines.

Demons already live and travel in electric and electronic wires and circuits. Demons are very good at sending electronic signals/rays to our minds, i.e., hypnotism. We have free will; that's why we can reject these demons a lot of times, but the very advanced computers and the robots of the future will not go against demons as they are not alive and don't have any free will. So how will we control the possession of demons on modern robots and computers when we cannot even spray holy water on robots and computers either? We need to avoid manufacturing robots and very advanced electronic brains to save human race.

We need to discover system of rays that can be used as a weapon against demons. Modern science just has to discover and convert those rays in the shape of modern machines. That cure against demons is always around us from the very first day, just need to work on it. Once modern science will study the electromagnetic structure of a demon, it will be able to discover a new technology of how to become invisible like demons. The second thing is that modern science will learn from demon's technology how to travel so fast in seconds from one part to other part of the world. Right now, demons send electronic signals to our brains to hypnotize us to convey their commands to us.

إذا كان لا يزال هؤلاء الناس لا يشعرون بالأسف لأفعالهم، فهذا يعني أنهم لا يزال جني شرير للغاية يستحوذ عليهم. هذا يحدث طوال الوقت؛ إن الجن يحدثون مثل هذه الأمور من حولنا. إننا لا نسيطر جيداً على أذهاننا نتيجة للضغوط المؤقتة للمشاكل من حولنا . هذا هو الوقت الذي يزيد فيه زيادة سيطرة و ضغط الجن على عقولنا. في ذلك الوقت لا نستطيع أن نرى أي حل إيجابي، فالجن لا يسمحون لنا أن نفكر بإيجابية. الشياطين لحد عقولنا. نحن نفكر في أمرين فقط القتل أو الموت. إنها قضية كبيرة بالنسبة لنا أن نفقد السيطرة ونقتل شخص ما، ولكن بالنسبة للجن، هذه مهمة سهلة للغاية. إن الجن لا يبذلون الكثير من أجل إفساد حياتك و حياة الآخرين. إن الجن يرسلون مجرد إشارات إلكترونية الأمر، إشعاعات لعقولنا. سوف تتقبل عقولنا تلك الإشعاعات / الإشارات كأمر أو أقرار أو فكرة. سيفك المخ الإشارة من الجني في شكل قرار غاضب، و في غضون بضع ثوان، سوف نكون تحت السيطرة الكاملة لتلك الحالة المتوحشة والمجنون، التي أحدثها الجن لنا، لذلك إما سوف نقتل أي شخص أو سنقتل أنفسنا في غضون ثوان قليلة. وهذا الوضع سوف يعطي الجن الكثير من الإرتياح، لأن مهمتهم ستكون قد أنجزت. الآن إنظر فقط إلي الأشياء البسيطة التي لا يمكننا حتى السيطرة عليها، مثل الجشع، والغضب، والكراهية، وإدمان الكحول، والصراخ والسلبية والتحيزات، والغيرة، وغيرها ونحن نفعل كل هذه الأشياء في كل وقت دون إبداء أي مقاومة للجن. ليس لدينا ما يكفي من القوة لرفض سيطرة الجن على عقولنا. فكيف تأتي نستطيع أن نتوقع أن هذه الأجهزة ذات العقول الإلكترونية أن تكون قادرة على رفض أي سيطرة من الجن على عقولهم المحوسبة. حيث أنهم لديهم أي إرادة حرة لإتخاذ قرارات بين الحق والباطل. إن تصميم الجن أعلى بكثير من أجهزة الكمبيوتر لدينا، لذلك لا تعتقد حتى أننا سنكون قادرين على هزيمة الجن بأجهزة الكمبيوتر الحديثة. فإن جميع أجهزة الكمبيوتر الحديثة ستكون بالفعل تحت سيطرة الجن، قبل أن يقرروا التخلص من الجنس البشري.

But in the near future, once demons will be able to possess the brains of modern computers and robots, they will be able to talk to us in the electronic voices of robots and computers. Once demons will be able to possess a brain of modern computer, modern computers will be able to decode the messages of demons and will be able to show them us on computer monitors, under the total possession of demons. Demons are electromagnetic bodies with electronic brains, totally comprised of rays. Human brain is made of flesh/blood/bones and rays. The structure is totally different, but the capabilities and the abilities are plus minus, almost the same. The brain of a demon is more attracted to and capable of handling more emotions, more extremism, more negativism, more love, more hate, more competition, more violence, etc., So in future, we will be dealing with very short-tempered, angry, extremist robots and computers.

We will be around very emotional robots once they will go completely under the possession of demon's hypnotism. At the same time, most demons will be using robots and computers for killing and destroying human race. As I always explain, not all demons are bad. Like us demons have free will too. So they can choose both ways either good or bad. It is always like this. Some demons are nice and friends. Some demons are devil and evil.

إن سيطرة الجن علي العقول الالكترونية أكثر وأفضل ملايين المرات من السيطرة على العقول البشرية. لذلك كل يوم، عندما نصنع روبوتات جديدة وحديثة أو أي آلة يمكن تشغيلها بواسطة أجهزة الكمبيوتر مثل طائرات تجسس جديدة، طائرات مقاتلة جديدة محوسبة، وسائر الآلات سيستخدم الجن تلك الآلات ضدنا لتدميرنا في المستقبل القريب. الآن الأمور تتغير في هذه الأيام، ونحن لا نعتمد على البشر في بناء الآلات الحديثة. الروبوتات هي التي تبني الآلات الحديثة، لذلك سوف يستحوذ الجن علي تلك الروبوتات المصنعة كلما أرادوا لتصنيع وتصنيع روبوتات متقدمة قاتلة، و آلات أخرى لترسيخ قوتهم الجسدية في هذا العالم. لذلك أنا لست متأكداً إذا كان لا يزال لدينا الوقت للعمل و تقييد أنفسنا بتصميم وتصنيع آلات جديدة، تظل خارج نطاق سيطرة الجن. يجب فقط أن نتجنب إعطاء عقول صناعية أو إلكترونية لآلاتنا لإبقائهم تحت سيطرتنا، لأنه إذا كان للجهاز أي نوع من العقل الإلكترونية، هذا الجهاز سوف يعمل مع الجن ضدنا، وربما في وقت قريب جداً.

أحياناً أشعر أنني لست بحاجة لكتابة بعض الأشياء، وليس لأنني لست متأكداً منها؛ السبب الرئيسي وراء ذلك هو لأنني لا أريد تخويف الناس أكثر من اللازم، ولكني أغير رأيي طوال الوقت. على أي حال، كما وصفت عدة مرات، الجن موجودون في كل مكان ولكن قم برش الماء المقدس بشكل منتظم في أماكن قليلة. أنا لا أراهم في تلك المناطق بنفس القدر، ولكنهم لا يزالون هناك. لا مكان خالي تماماً. إذا كنت تعتقد كل أو معظم الجن الشياطين يعيشون في أجسام البشر الحيوانات، فأنت على خطأ هنا، و السبب هو أن عدد الجن أكثر بكثير بالمقارنة بعدد البشر والحيوانات، وما إلى ذلك.

We should try to convert them to good demons so good demons alert us all the time if they find out about the bad intentions of devil and evil demons or at least good demons can guide human race, how to protect themselves.

As I described several times, a spirit/soul and electricity/power supply are same things. The only difference is that we have total control of power supplies/electricity, but we don't have any control of a spirit/soul. I already described in details that demons and pains don't live on de-energized or dead bodies. Once we die, once there is no power or spirit in our body, demons comes out of the dead body in one second, the reason is that the de-energized or the dead body can take all the energy from a demon and make him de-energized too.

Demons don't have as much energy anyway due to their really small sizes. Demons can live and create malfunctions in any living or energized body regardless of whether that body is energized naturally or artificially. Our bodies are energized by the spirit. Modern computer and other devices, specifically communication devices, are energized artificially by electricity or power supplies in the same way.

The way demons and pains work on us all the time, hypnotize us and pains create all kinds of issues for us. Exactly the same way, demons and pains do all their best to create malfunctions in electronic circuits and devices also, like computers, robots, routers, DVRs, and other electronic devices.

إذاً أين يمكن أن يعيش الجن عندما لا يمكنهم العثور على جسم مادي حي مرئي؟، حيث أنها لا تعيش في الغالب؟ عندما يكون لديك منفذ كهربائي، ثم قمت بتوصيل سلك الكهرباء / لوح الكهرباء الذي يحتوي علي منفذ كهربائي، . ثم قمت بتركيب الأجهزة المختلفة مثل التلفزيون، ومشغل الدي في دي ، وواالكمبيوتر، والمروحة، و الشاشة، DVR، وما إلى ذلك، على نحو ما سيتواجد عدد كبير حقاً من الجن حول هذه المنافذ الكهربائية، ولوحات الكهرباء،ء وداخل أو حول المعدات الكهربائية والأجهزة . بطريقة أو بأخرى هؤلاء الجن أكثر تدميراً و أقل تفاهماً.

هؤلاء الجن يؤذون عادةً عندما أكون على مقربة من هذه اللواح ذات المنافذ الكهربائية أو المنافذ الكهربائية أو وراء أي معدات أو أجهزة كهربائية. لقد لاحظت أن هؤلاء الجن ليسوا مهتمين كثيراً بالعيش في الجسم البشري لفترة طويلة. المشكلة حسب تجربتي هي أنني ليس لدي أي فكرة عن كيفية تعامل هؤلاء الجن مع الناس العاديين. إن الآثار السيئة أو الأضرار، هي أن بمجرد أن يدخل الجن داخل جسم الإنسان، يكونون أقوى بكثير من الجن العاديين. أشعرأن منافذ الكهرباء أو اللوحات الكهربائية أو المعدات الكهربائية، هي مصادر الطاقة للجن، لهذا فهم يتجمعون بشكل كبير حولها. أو أن الجن لا يريدون لأحد أن يزعجهم حول مصادر الطاقة الكهربائية تلك . على أي حال، إسمح لي أن ألخص ذلك. عليك أن تكون حذراً جداً لأن وراء جهاز التلفزيون، أو جهاز الكمبيوتر الخاص بك أوأماكن أخرى مماثلة، يجب أن تتوقع وجود عدداً كبيراً من الجن يتجمعون أو يعيشون للتمتع بالطاقة أكثر وأكثر. لذلك عندما تجلس حول هذه المنافذ أو المعدات الكهربائية، وستكون أكثر أمناً إذا أبقيت نفسك على مسافة جيدة من هذه الأماكن. لا تجلس بالقرب من اللوحات أوالمنافذ الكهربائية. وثمة مشكلة أخرى هي أنني حتى لو حاولت تنظيف تلك الأماكن، ...

Now demons are equally involved in creating malfunctions in human/animal bodies and in electronic bodies. Now here is the problem or you can say good luck or bad luck, Once your computer, DVR, or router starts malfunctioning, you de-energize or make them dead, those devices by disconnecting electricity even just for few seconds and if you reset them after ten or twenty seconds. Once your computer, routers will be de-energized for few seconds, demons and pains cannot stay in those devices at all; demons and pains both have to leave those devices immediately to stay energized or to stay alive. So if you want to keep your devices free of demons and pains most of the time keeps them disconnected with electricity or power supplies, once you are not using them. So is there any way if we can de-energize human body for ten seconds like electronic devices, twice a day to get rid of these demons and pains from our bodies?

You may ask this question, If the body is re-energized, will these demons and pains come back? May be the same or may be different pains or demons will come back, yes, they will. That's why we need to be de-energized frequently.

First thing modern science need to do is to discover demons as soon as possible. Once modern science will be able to communicate with the demons, things will be very different. God had created this demon's technology even before human but human's modern science still not aware of demon's technology of the God. I am sure almost everybody will have a lot of knowledge of demons in coming days, so I am sure things will be very different with demons around us.

لفترة طويلة. نظراً للإستهلاك الكثير للطاقة الكهربائية، هؤلاءالجن هم أكثر خطورة و إيذاءً لصحة الإنسان ومزاجه. إن الجن الأشرار و السيئون، والجين الذين يعيشون في مناطق الإشعاع المشعة ومصادر الطاقة الكهربائية يضرون صحة الإنسان. بشدة. الجن ليسوا أجساماً مادية مخلوقة من عضلات وأنسجة، أو معدن، إنهم عقول إلكترونية غير مرئية تتألف من إشعاعات، إنهم عقول إلكترونية بدون جسد مادي مثلنا أو مثل الحيوانات. الشياطين هم العقول الالكترونية لها نفس القدرات، والذكاء، و كل أنواع الرغبات و الأمنيات الجسدية والعقلية طوال الوقت مثلنا.بالنسبة لنا كي نقوم بتلبية أمنياتنا ورغباتنا مثل الشرب والأكل، والعواطف والجنس والتمتع بها، لسنا بحاجة إلى جسم آخر نخترقه ونستخدمه للتمتع بهذه المشاعر والرغبات، ولكن الجن بحاجة إلى جسم يستحوذون عليه، لتحقيق الرغبات. لذلك نحن نتفوق علي . الجن الذين لديهم قوى إلكترونية.

الجن لا يطلبون منا أن نفعل شيئاً، إنهم فقط يرسلون لعقلنا إشارات أو إشعاعات إلكترونية. إن عقلنا لديه خاصية قبول الإشارات الإلكترونية، و تستطيع العقول فك الإشارة بسهولة و تولد فكر قوي أو رغبة قوية في شيء ما. الآن الأمر يعتمد علينا و على قوة عقولنا. كيف يمكننا بسهولة التمييز بين الإشارات الصادرة من الجن أو تلك الصادرة من مخنا. بمجرد أن نبدأ في تفكير كل فكرة يولدها عقلنا وتحليلها، سنقوم برفض الكثير من الأوامر والإشارات الإلكترونية الصادرة من الجن. سيتحقق الوضع المثالي والكامل عندما نكون قادرين على الحد من الجن لأحلامنا أثناء النوم فقط. ليس هناك و لن يكون هناك إمكانية لإبعاد الجن عنا أثناء النوم. الطريقة الوحيدة الممكنة هي عندما ننام في غرفة أو أي مكان حوله سياج مصنوع لإبقاء ...

Even I am saying don't develop modern robots and digital modern brains inside computers to save human race, but still a lot of scientists under the influence of very evil and powerful demons will develop these kind of electronic brains inside robots and super computers. I don't know how it will feel when machines will be acting emotional or extremist, angry, short-tempered, once will go under possession of demons. Demons are in many ways a superior and unique technology of the God. Even modern science doesn't have any track of demons yet? Demons can hypnotize any human scientist to build more and more modern machines with very advance electronic brain, the way they want to have physical control of this earth. The demons can use same physical strength of those machines with electronic brains, robots against human race. I don't know how much demons already involved in our computers and other modern electronics, but I hope modern science will find a safer way for human race. Anybody or any demon can beat human, when human are not aware about them, but once I am sure human will get some awareness about the demon technology of the God, modern science will be able to find ways to secure the future of human race. Demons are relatively more unique technology for us because we are not aware about it, but still human is still most superior creation of the God. Right now demons don't have the physical domination in this world. No doubt, demons have a lot of control on human brains, but once demons will get control on modern machines/computers/robots, the demons will have way more physical control of this world. If nobody stops them, maybe future presidents of different countries will be electronic robots possessed by demons.

المكان خالي من الجن. كل شيء ممكن، يجب علي العلوم الطبية فقط أن تبدأ بشيء بعد نظرية أينشتاين. نحن نعرف سرعة الضوء ولكن الآن نحن بحاجة إلى معرفة من الذي يعيش ويسافر مع هذا الضوء و أنظمة الإشعاعات الأخرى . تحتاج العلوم الطبية لتوسيع أبحاثهم على تكنولوجيا الجن، فهذا البحث والتكنولوجيا سينقل العلم الحديث إلى مستوى مختلف من النجاح والتحديث. الآن تضيع كل طاقاتنا في كيفية علاج السرطان أو فيروس نقص المناعة البشرية. إن العلاج أمامنا فعلاً إلا أننا نسير في الإتجاه الخاطئ. هؤلاء الجن يبقون العلم الحديث بعيداً عنهم لأنهم يعرفون أن بمجرد أن يبدأ العلم الحديث للبشر، في العمل على تكنولوجيا الجن، ستختلف الأمور جداً بالنسبة لكل من البشر والجن. إن الجن يتفوقون في الإستحواذ والسيطرة على عقل آخر، بغض النظر عما إذا كان عقل آلة إلكترونية أو عقل بشري، لأن هذا كل ما يمكنهم القيام به، فهم ينقضون على أي عقل متاحة، و يشرعون في إستخدامه لتحقيق أغراضهم الخاصة. إن الجن مخلوقات ذات عقول إلكترونية متفوقة للغاية، و الإشارات الإكترونية أو الإشعاعات التي تصدر من عقولهم أقوى ولها القدرة على التغلب علي أي إشارات أو إشعاعات أخرى عادية أو غير عادية لأي جهاز إلكتروني أو عقل بشري. إن السبب في أن إشاراتنا و إشعاعاتنا الإكترونية أضعف من إشارات أو إشعاعات الجن، هو أننا لا نعلم الآن أن ماذا يحدث لنا. و بمجرد أن ندرك ما يقوم به الجن معنا، سوف نكون قادرين على زيادة قوة الإشارات والإشعاعات داخل أو خارج عقولنا.

لذلك مشكلتنا يمكن حلها بمجرد أن نبدأ في العمل عليها. بالنسبة للآلات الإلكترونية، لديهم الإرادة الحرة، لذلك يستمر الجن في زيادة قوة الأمر الإكتروني لديهم، لمهاجمة على العقل الإلكتروني للآلات، إلي أن يهزم الجن قوة الإشعاعات الإلكترونية / الإشارات،...

So shortcut, in future, more machines, computers and robots means more control of demons and possibly the end of human race. Everything sounds like fiction, but don't make this mistake. In this book and book 1, there is nothing like fiction. Everything in this book is 100 percent true. When I don't want to learn something about anything, nature compels me to learn. When I am in denial of something, I will say sometimes I was not ready to believe or not ready to learn. I was put in deep problems or pains to learn the solution. I never come out of some particular situations until I give assurance that I got it. So here I really suffered a lot to learn all these secrets, cures, and solutions.

Still I feel I'm not done yet. How much still coming? God knows better. All the time, I think how possibly humans will be able to control demons, so many demons, when modern science does not even have any clue about them yet? And I feel, still, it will take long time to modern science to come in action against them. How will you fight with something once you are not even aware of their existence, structure, and actions? I don't know how the human race will be secured in future when these demons can activate any or all nuclear weapons in a matter of seconds. Controlling computers of nuclear weapons just need some commands or electronic signals to activate them.

Demons are electronic signals and commands by itself. Demons are electronic brains who can stop them once they will be ready to destroy the human race? If you say *you*, then I will ask you *how*? The only possibly way for human race to be safe, is if we will not have any single nuclear weapon anywhere to destroy human race.

و هكذا يمكننا أن نساعد بطريقة ما عقولنا في المستقبل عن طريق زيادة قوة عقولنا، لكننا لن نكون قادرين على السيطرة على أي جهاز إلكتروني من حولنا. وبالتالي فإن الحل البسيط هو تثبيط قدرات الأجهزة التي بها نوعين من القدرات، أي الجسد المادي والعقل الإلكتروني.

نحن بحاجة إلى إيجاد طريقة لجعل التحكم في الآلات بشكل يدوي بدلا من العقول الإلكترونية. إن سيطرة الجن و إستحواذهم على جسم الإنسان ليست دائمة. فيمكننا التغلب على سيطرة الجن علي عقولنا في أي وقت بإستخدام المزيد من المعرفة والمزيد من القوة. سيكون من المستحيل بالنسبة للآلات أن ترفض إستحواذ الجن، و مهما كانت مقاومة أي جهازلإستحواذ الجن، سوف يزيد الجن قوتهم يستمرون في زيادتها و زيادة أعدادهم، للسيطرة على عقل إلكتروني واحد لآي كمبيوتر حديث، أو إنسان آلي. إن أفضل وأسهل طرق إستخدام الجن هي إستخدامهم كجواسيس ضد أي شخص، بغض النظر عن أي شخص عادي أو مجرم أو أي سلاح أو آلة. فإنهم يمكنهم الذهاب في كل مكان، و يمكنهم جلب أي معلومات لأي مهمة سرية. أنا واثق من أن العلم الحديث سيبحث عن سبل للسيطرة علي الجن من الناحية الفنية لإستخدامهم في التجسس لحساب وكالة المخابرات المركزية الأمريكية، على الأقل.

يسيطر البشر علي مختلف الآلات من خلال أجهزة التحكم عن بعد وأجهزة الكمبيوتر، و لكن أجهزة التحكم عن بعد وأجهزة الكمبيوتر هي آلات أيضاً. ترسل أجهزة التحكم عن بعد إشارات إلكترونية و إشعاعات لإرسال الأوامر إلى العقول الإلكترونية لأجهزة مختلفة. إذاً ما الذي ستفعله لو إستحوذ الجن علي جهاز التحكم عن بعد؟ سوف يرسل جهاز التحكم عن بعد تلك الإشارات إلى العقول الإلكترونية لمختلف الآلات ، مهما كان الجن يرسلون من إشارات للآلات للسيطرة عليها.

Rizwan Qureshi

The second thing is to keep them, the way they are right now, within limit, just don't manufacture electronic brains operated by electronic signals or commands, regardless computers or robots. All very scientific machines with electronic brains, modern science is making today or in future, will be under the possession of these electronic demons and will be used against us to destroy us. Once we will have no nuclear weapon and no physical machines with electronic brains, we will be in better condition to communicate with demons. We will be in a better shape to make them our friends. But why these demons will listen to us or even care about us when they will be ready to get rid of us by destroying us.

Under the influence of demons, humans lose their control even just for few minutes or hours, like bringing guns on roads or at work or at school to kill other people, most of the time for no reason. People kill their friends and families due to minor disputes. If someone asks them why this happens, I am sure all of them will say they lost control of their minds. I can bet if there is still someone there who can feel proud of their past actions of killing or destroying someone. I am sure all of them should regret their actions. If still these people don't regret their actions, this means that they are still possessed by an extremely evil demon. This happens all the time; demons create situations like this around us. We don't keep good control of our mind due to temporary pressure of problems around us. This is the time when demons increase the control and pressure on our brains. At that time we cannot see any positive solution. Demons don't allow us to think positive.

رؤية الجن و الآلام السيطرة عليها

إذاً ماذا ستفعل في ذلك الوقت؟ إننا لا نتحدث هنا عن جهاز من صنع الإنسان أو عدو بشري آخر، نحن نتحدث هنا عن الجن أي سلالة أخرى أو عرق آخر أو مخلوق آخر خلقه الله، أقوي في العقل وأكثرفي العدد منا.

لدي إعتقاد قوي أنه بمجرد أن يسيطرالجن فعلياً في هذا العالم، وسوف يقومون بتدمير الجنس البشري تماماً قد لا يدمرون الجنس البشري عن طريق إستخدام الأسلحة النووية إذا كان الجن يريدون أن يبقوا علي الحيوانات والطيور والزواحف، والحشرات على قيد الحياة. بمجرد أن يستخدم الجن الأسلحة النووية لتدمير الجنس البشري، فإن على الأقل كل تلك الحيوانات التي تعيش في تلك المناطق أو في جميع أنحاء تلك المناطق التي يعيش فيها البشر سيموتون أيضاً. بهذه الطريقة، سيذهب الجن في الأدغال إذا كانوا يريدون البقاء في أجسام الحيوانات، و السبب هو تدمير الجنس البشري فقط ، فأينما يستخدم الجن الأسلحة النووية، فإن جميع تلك المناطق ستظل مكاناً جيداً للجن للعيش هناك، ولكن لن يظل البشرالآخرون، والحيوانات، والطيور، والزواحف، والحشرات على قيد الحياة هناك بسبب قتل الإشعاع النووي المستمر. ستعيش آلات والجن فقط في تلك المناطق من الإشعاع. لذلك بصراحة، فإن الجنس البشري لديه إثنين من الأعداء، الأول الجن و الثاني الروبوتات الحديثة وأجهزة الكمبيوتر الواقعة تحت سيطرة . فماذا تريد أن تفعل لإنقاذ الجنس البشري؟ أي شيء؟ أي خطة؟ بغض النظر عن ما إذا كان البشر لهم نفس البنية و التركيب، والقدرات. يختلف البشر فيما بينهم. بعضهم أكثر طموحاً، والبعضهم أقل طموحاً، بعضهم مجرمون، وبعضهم طيبون. البعض يريد أن يصبح رئيس دولة، والبعض الآخر كسول ويحب الحياة السهلة. البعض يؤمن بالمساواة، و البعض إرهابيين. بعضهم علماء، وبعضهم نشطاء. بنفس الطريقة، يمكنك أن تتوقع أن كل الجن سيكونون جزء من هذه الحرب ضد الجنس البشري في المستقبل. إن الجن يعيشون من حولنا أنا واثق من أنهم سيكونون ضد هذه الحرب.

SEE & CONTROL DEMONS & PAIN

Demons limit our minds. We can think of two things only—kill or die. This is a big issue for us to lose control and kill someone, but for demons, it is a very easy assignment. For screwing all your and other lives demons don't have to do a lot. Demons just send an electronic command, signal, or ray to our brain. Our brains will accept those rays/signals as an order or a decision or a thought. The brain will decode that signal from demon as an angry decision. Within a few seconds, we will be under total control of that wild and crazy situation, created by the demon for us. So either we will kill someone or we will kill ourselves within a few seconds. This situation will give demons a lot of satisfaction, as their mission will be accomplished. Now just see the minor things, we cannot even control, like our greed, anger, hate, alcoholism, yelling, negativity, biases, jealousy, etc.

We do all these things all the time without giving any resistance to demons. We don't have enough strength to reject the control of demons on our brains. So how come we can expect that those machines with electronic brains will be able to reject any control of demons on their computerized brain. When even they don't have any free will to make decisions between right and wrong. The design of demons is so much superior then our computers, so don't even think we will be able to defeat demons by modern computers. All modern computers will already be under the possession of demons before demons decide to get rid of human race. Demons will have millions times more and better control on electronic brains than on human brains.

رضوان قرشي

ولكن عدد الجن كثيراً جداً، حتى 1 في المئة من سكان الجن قرروا أن يكونوا ضد البشر، وسوف يستغرق الأمر يوماً واحداً للتخلص من الجنس البشري فوق هذه الأرض. ولكن سيكون من الصعب عملياً علي الجين تدميرنا بسرعة إذا كنا لا نمتلك هذه الأسلحة النووية والروبوتات ذات العقول الإلكترونية لنستخدمها ضد الجن. أعتقد في بعض الأحيان، إذا كنت على قيد الحياة في ذلك الوقت، إذا قرر الجن إستخدام الإشعاع ضد البشر، حيث أعيش بقية حياتي لأن بالصدفة، بلادي لديها قوى نووية.

وثمة مسألة أخرى، وهي عدد الجن. إن حجم وتكوين الجن هي مناسب جداً للجن كي ينموا بسرعة كبيرة في مكان صغير جداً. في غرفة عادية بحجم عادي في منزل صغير، يستطيع ملايين من الجن أن يسكنوا تلك الغرفة بسهولة بالغة. لذلك يمكنك أن تتخيل سكان الجن من حولنا الآن. هناك ميزة واحدة لدينا بسبب الزيادة السكانية للجن، ينقسم الجن إلي مجموعات، و مجموعات فرعية لحماية أماكنهم للعيش وكذلك لحماية الأجسام التي يستحوذون عليها. الجن لا يسمحون لبعضهم البعض للوصول إلى منطقتهم بسهولة. لهذه الأسباب القليلة، يقتال الجن مع بعضهم البعض طوال الوقت. وكما تعلم يستطيع الجن قتل بعضهم البعض بسهولة بالغة. إن الجن متوافقون جداً، مع الغلاف الجوي المشبع بالإشعاع النووي النشط.

تزيد قوة و حيوية الجن أكثر بمجرد أن يزودوا أنفسهم بالطاقة من المجال الكهرومغناطيسي أو الكهربائي أو الإشعاع النووي. إن المناطق التي لا يوجد فيها بشر إما بسبب القصف النووي في تلك المناطق أو أن تلك المناطق قد يكون قد حدث لها أي نوع من مشاكل التسرب الإشعاعي النووي، فإن عدد الجن في تلك المنطقة أكثر من المناطق العادية.

Demons will use these machines against us to destroy us in near future. Now things are changing these days; we are not depending on humans to build modern machines. Robots are building modern machines, so whenever demons want, they can possess those manufacturing robots and manufacture advance killing robots and other machines to establish their physical strength in this world. So I am not sure if still we have time to act and limit ourselves in designing and manufacturing new machines; which somehow stay beyond the control of demons. We just need to avoid giving our machines artificial brains or electronic brains to keep them in our control, because if the machine has any kind of electronic brain, that machine will be working with demons against us, maybe very soon. Sometimes I feel I don't need to write few things, not because I am not sure about them; the main reason behind it is because I don't want to scare people too much, but I change my mind all the time. Anyway, as I described several times, demons are everywhere but usually spray holy water on regular basis in few places. I don't see them in those areas as much, but they are still there. No place is completely clean. If you think all demons or most demons live on human or animal bodies, you are wrong here. The reason is as compared to population of demons, the population of humans, animals, etc., is way less. So when demons cannot find a physical visible living body, where do they live mostly? When you have an electric outlet, and you connect an extension cord/board with the electric outlet, with that extension board you connect different appliances like TV, DVD player, computer, fan, monitor, DVR, etc., somehow there will be a real big population of demons live around these electric outlets, extension boards, and inside or around …

الطاقة النووية المشعة القوية يجعل الجن أكثر تفوقاً و قوة في سلالتهم.. لا يستطيع الجن التعامل مع المواضيع المتعلقة بالمياه بسبب تكوينهم الإلكتروني. خلال المطر، معظم الجن يبحثون عن مكان ما لإنقاذ أنفسهم من خطر المياه المستمر. الجن لا يحبون الطقس البارد, أجواء دافئة خلال الطقس البارد، و سيحتاجون إلي المزيد من الطاقة لتنشيط أنفسهم خلال الطقس البارد، فهم يبقون داخل أو حول السخانات الكهربائية خلال الطقس البارد. إن الجن يحتاجون إلى الكثير من الطاقة لتنشيط أنفسهم، فالجو البارد و الطقس الممطر والثلوج تحد من الطاقة المتاحة الموجودة بشكل طبيعي في المجال الكهرومغناطيسي. يتلقى الجن كميات أقل من الطاقة من الغلاف الجوي خلال الطقس البارد. مع زيادة عدد الجن تزداد درجة حرارة الغلاف الجوي أيضاً. سيمتص الجن المزيد من الطاقة لتنشيط أنفسهم، سوف تتبدد هذه الطاقة في شكل حرارة. لديهم موارد أفضل للطاقة والحرارة قوية، سيبذل الجن كل شيئ ممكن لجلب المزيد والمزيد من الإشعاع المشع في جميع أنحاء العالم لإطعام مثل هذا العدد الكبير من الجن.. إن المناطق ذات درجة الحرارة العالية في جميع أنحاء العالم هي أكثر الأماكن ملاءمةً لنمو الجن وتكاثر عددهم. المزيد من الحرارة يعني مصدر طاقة أفضل ومناخ أفضل للعيش والنمو.

سيبذل الجن قصارى جهدهم لزيادة درجة حرارة هذه الأرض ليكون لديهم ما يكفي من الغذاء / الطاقة لجميع الجن على هذه الأرض. لا بد أن يرفع الجن درجة حرارة هذه الأرض للحصول فقط على المزيد والمزيد من الطاقة لأنفسهم، لهذا، ربما يمكن أن يلعب الجن بالطبقة الواقية حول الأرض لتلقي المزيد والمزيد من الحرارة والطاقة من الشمس. إن الأشعة والحرارة من الكثيرة من الشمس تزيد من قوى الجن.

electric equipments and appliances. Somehow these demons are more damaging and less compromising. So every day, when we make a new and modern robot or any machine that can be operated by computers like new spy aeroplanes, new computerized fighter planes, and all other machines. These demons usually hurt when I am close to these extension boards or electric outlets or behind any electric equipments or appliances. I noticed these demons are not too much interested in living in the human body for a long time. The problem in my experience, is that I have no idea how these demons will behave with normal people. The bad effects or damages are that once these demons come inside the human body, they are way more powerful than regular demons. I feel, because these outlets or electric boards or electric equipments, are energy sources for demons, that's why may be they are hugely populated around them, or demons don't want anyone to bother them around those electric energy sources. Anyway, let me summarize it. You need to be very careful because behind your TV, behind your computer and other similar places, you should expect a huge number of demons gathered or live to enjoy more and more energy. So when you sit around these electric outlets or electric equipments, it will be safer if you maintain a good distance from these places. Don't sit close to electric extension boards or electric outlets. Another problem is that even I tried to clean those places, it is almost impossible to clean these place or at least difficult to keep it clean for long time. So let's see what modern science can do about it. I don't want to misguide anyone, but regardless of whether you use holy water on those places or not, demons don't leave those places for a long time. Due to too much consumption of electric energy,

الجن لا يقومون بممارسة الجنس مثلما يفعل البشر والحيوانات ، و الزواحف، و الطيور، و حتي الحشرات. ليس لدي الجن أي مفهوم للنوع. ليس هناك جني ذكر و جني أنثي. الجن فقط عقول إلكترونية بدون أعضاء مادية، ولكنهم مبرمجون أن تكون لهم أنشطة بدنية وعاطفية طوال الوقت. يمكن الشياطين لا يستطيع الجن ممارسة الجنس مع أي شخص. إن عملية التكاثر عند الجن هي مجرد مجرد إنقسام الجسم إلى قسمين أو ثلاثة، أو أجزاء كثيرة متساوية إما بعد وقت معين أو بعد حجم معين ويبدأ في النمو من جديد بسرعة.

لا تقلل عملية التكاثر هذه من معرفة الجن أو ذاكرتهم. هذا هو السبب الرئيسي لحياة الجن الطويلة. بعد وقت معين، يحول الجني الواحد نفسه إلى مجموعة كبيرة أو عائلة من الجن. يتعلم الجن كل نظام الأسرة والقيم الأسرية من البشر والحيوانات. الجن في حد ذاتهم ليس لديهم أي حياة جنسية بسبب عدم توفر الأعضاء الجنسية ونوع الجنس ذكر أو أنثى. لكن عقولهم مبرمجة لكي يكون لديهم الجنس أو يشعرون به طوال الوقت. لهذا الغرض يستحوذ الجن على أجسام البشر والحيوانات للتمتع بتلك الأنشطة البدنية والعاطفية. لا بد أن يستحوذ الجن علي الجسم خلال النشاط الجنسي بغض النظر عما إذا كان بشراً، أو حيواناً، و غيرهما. ليس هناك فئة معينة أو رأي أو مزاج داخل أي جني عند إستحواذه علي إمرأة أو أي رجل خلال هذا النشاط. الجن هم يعملون لحسابهم الخاص، إنهم جيدون مع كل من الذكر أو اﻷنثى علي حد السواء. نفس الجني الذي يستحوذ علي الرجل أثناء ممارسة الجنس ليس لديه أي مشكلة في الإستحواذ علي جسد المرأة الاليوم التالي أثناء ممارسة الجنس. إنهم غرباء جداً، أليس كذلك؟ ولكن السبب الرئيسي لكتابة هذه التفاصيل هنا هو أن نطمئن الجميع أن الجن أو أي مخلوقات أخرى غير مرئية لا تستطيع ممارسة الجنس مع أي إنسان أو حيوان.

these demons are more dangerous and hurtful for human health and temperament. Other then evil and bad demons, demons living in radioactive radiation areas and around electric energy sources are extremely harmful for human health.Demons are not a body, physically made of muscles, tissues, or a metal. Demons are invisible electronic brains comprised of rays. Demons are electronic brains without a physical body like us or animals. Demons are electronic brains with the same capabilities, intelligence, and full of all kinds of physical and mental desires and wishes all the time like us. To fulfill and enjoy our wishes and desires like drinking, eating, emotions, sex, we don't need another body to penetrate inside it and then use that body to enjoy these feelings and desires, but demons need a body to possess to fulfill all their desires. So we have a plus on demons. Demons are electronic powers. Demons don't request us to do something. Demons just send us an electronic signals or rays as a command to our brain. Our brain has the quality of accepting electronic signals. Brains can decode that signal easily and will generate a strong thought or a strong desire for something. Now it depends on us, it depends on the powers of our brains, how easily we can differentiate between the signals from a demon's brain or that which is coming from our brain. Once we start thinking and analyzing each & every thought generated by our brain, we will be rejecting a lot of commands and electronic signals from demons. The ideal & perfect situation will happen, when we will be able to limit demons just to our dreams during sleep only. There is no and there will be no possibility when we will be able to keep demons away from us during sleep. The only possible way will be if we will sleep in a room or any enclosure, should be made to

إن الإ ستحواذ علي جسم ما   مثل خلط الملح بالماء، لذلك يشعر الجن بالإثارة ويشعرون بنفس ما يشعر به المخ خلال أي نشاط بدني. الطريقة الوحيدة الممكنة للجن للقيام بممارسة الجنس مع أي إنسان لا يمكن تحقيقه إلا في الأحلام، فبمجرد أن يرسل الجن بعض الإشارات الإلكترونية إلى عقولنا، تقوم عقولنا بفك تلك الرسائل الإلكترونية وتحلم بممارسة الجنس مع شخص في مخيلة ذلك الجني . لا يمكن تحقيق مثل ذلك النوع من الأنشطة مع الجن إلا بطريقتين. الأولي، هي أن يصبح الجن جزءاً ظاهرياً و مؤقتاً من الجسم والمخ عن طريق الإستحواذ علي الجسم ليقوموا بإمتصاص نفس المشاعر والإحساس من عقولنا، كل ما تشعربه عقولنا و أجسامنا خلال القيام بهذا النشاط. ليس الجنس هو النشاط الوحيد الذي يتمتع به معنا خلال الإستحواذ علي جسم الإنسان. لا يستطيع الجن شرب الكحول والبيرة والنبيذ، أو أي شيء آخر. لا يستطيع الجن تدخين السجائر أو المخدرات. لكن عقولهم مبرمجة علي أن يكون لديهم هذا الإحساس والتمتع بها، و أن يكون لديهم رغبة قوية للغاية للشرب أو الأكل مثل الإنسان أو الحيوان المادي. ولكن لا يستطيع الحن أن يأكلون أو يشربون أو لا يمكنهم القيام بأي نشاط بدني آخر.

إن الجن يحبون لحوم البقر والليمون بجنون، والجير. ولكن لا يمكنهم أكل أي شيء. وبالتالي إن قوي الجن تمنحهم الخيار الإستحواذ علي أي جسم مادي قوي لأي إنسان أو حيوان، وما إلى ذلك، ويستخدمونهم لتحقيق رغباتهم، بغض النظر عما إذا كانت تلك العادات أو الأنشطة القليلة تضر بنا جسدياً. إن الجن لا يهتمون بصحتنا، إنهم لا يريدون لنا سوى القيام بكل ما يشعرون برغبة فيه. الآن على من جهة ثانية، نحن البشر لدينا إرادة حرة و أقوي عقل في جميع المخلوقات لإتباع الجن في كل شيء يطلبوا منا القيام بعمله أو حصرهم في القيام بالأنشطة والأشياء الخيرية.

keep demon free. Everything is possible, only medical science needs to start a thing after theory of Einstein. We know the speed of light but now we need to know who is living & travelling with this light and other system of rays. Medical science needs to expand their research to demon technology. This research and this technology will take modern science to a different level of success and modernization. Right now all our energies are wasted on how to cure a cancer or HIV. Cure is right in front of us. Only we are moving in the wrong direction. These demons are keeping modern science away from them because they know once modern science of humans will start working on demon technology, things will be very different for both humans and demons. Demons are way more powerful in possessing and controlling another brain, regardless a brain of an electronic machine or a human brain, because that is all they can do. They jump on any available brain and start using it for their own purposes. Demons are superior electronic brains , the electronic signals or rays from their brains are the most powerful and have the ability to overlap or defeat any other ordinary or extraordinary signals or rays of any electronic machine or human brain. The reason why our electronic signals and rays are weaker then the signals or rays of demons, is because we are not aware right now of what is happening with us. Once we will be aware what demons are doing with us, we will be able to increase the strength of the signals & the rays in or out from our brains. So our problem is fixable once we start working on it. As for electronic machines, they don't have free will, so demons keep increasing the strength of electronic command to attack the electronic brain of machines until they defeat the strength of the electronic rays/signals of machines.

سوف يطلب منك الجن أو يدفعوك إلى القيام بالمزيد والمزيد من الأنشطة الممتعة والسلبية مثل شرب الكحول أو الغضب. لاتتوقع الجن أن يطلبوا منك أن تذهب إلى بيت الله والدعاء إلى الله.

إن عقول الجن لا تعمل بسهولة في الأمور الإيجابية. إنهم يجيدون جداً تطوير الذوق والرغبة في القيام بعمل ما أو أكل شيئ ما، لذلك يناضل الجن قليلاً من أجل التمتع بما يريدون. إذا كانت بعض الأجسام البشرية /العقول قررت أن تكون ضد الجن مثل إتخاذ قرار الإقلاع عن التدخين أو الكحول أو تناول المخدرات، وما إلى ذلك، يستمر الجن في دفعنا أكثر فأكثر للعودة للقيام بتلك الأشياء. ليس لدي أي فكرة كيف يمكن للجن جعل هذه الروبوتات و أجهزة الكمبيوتر تشرب الكحول، و تدخن الأعشاب ، وتأكل لحوم البقر من أجلهم. بمجرد أن تنجح في تدمير الجنس البشري.

الفرق الأساسي بين الآلام والأمراض / الحشرات بشكل رئيسي هو أن الآلام أجسام إلكترونية ولا تستخدم الأكسجين أو ثاني أكسيد الكربون للتنفس، أما الأمراض فهي حشرات، و تستخدم الأكسجين و ثاني أكسيد الكربون للتنفس. آلام، لا يمكننا قتل الآلام، لكن يمكننا قتل الأمراض / الحشرات / السرطانات، بسهولة بالغة. إنها تحدث إصابات طفيفة أو كبيرة فقط في جميع أنحاء الجسم داخله أو خارجه، إذ كانت الآلام قوية، تضر بنا. آلام، إذا لم تكن الآلام قوية جداً، فإنها لا تضرنا، لكنها تسيء لنا بهدوء، مثل سد الشرايين، وسد الأنابيب داخل الكلى و كذلك سد شرايين القلب، والغدد الدرقية، أو إنسداد الأنسولين، وما إلى ذلك السبب الرئيسي في ذلك هو تنشيط أنفسهم من هذه المواقع. في الخطوة الثانية، بمجرد أن تحدث الآلام بعض الأضرار هناك، تهاجم الأمراض / الحشرات عادةً تلك المواقع و تحدث إلتهابات وسرطانات هناك من خلال أكل تلك الأعضاء أو أجزاء الجسم.

So even we can help somehow in future our brains by increasing the strength of our brains, but we will not be able to keep control of any electronic machine around us. So the simple solution is to discourage machines with both capabilities, i.e., physical body and electronic brain. To survive, we need to discourage electronic brains. We need to find a way to have manual control of machines instead of electronic brains. Demons control and possession on a human body is not permanent. It will never be permanent. We can defeat that control of demons on our brains any time by using more knowledge and more strength. But it will be impossible for machines to reject the possession of the demons because regardless whatever resistance any machine will show to resist the possession of demons, they will increase and will keep increasing their strength and numbers to control one single electronic brain of any modern computer or a robot. The best and the easiest use of demons are to use them as spies against anyone, regardless of any ordinary person or any criminal or any weapon or machine. They can go everywhere and they can bring any information for any secret service. I am sure modern science will find ways to have some control on demons, technically to use them for spying for CIA, at least.Humans control different machines through remotes and computers, but remotes and computers are machines too. Remotes send electronic signals and rays to send controlling commands to the electronic brains of different machines. So what will you do if demons possess your remote? Then your remote will send those signals to the electronic brains of different machines whatever signals demons will send to those machines to control them. So what you will do at that time?

هناك حالات ومشاكل تحدثها الآلام الإكترونية، و هي آلام الحمى والسعال والأنفلونزا والبرد والجيوب الأنفية، الخ.

بعد مرور بعض الوقت، عندم تنضم الأمراض / الحشرات إلي الآلام، تحدث الأمراض / الحشرات كل أنواع العدوى لجعل الوضع أكثر سوءاً. ولكن الشيء الجيد هو أننا يمكن أن نتعقب ونقتل الأمراض/ الحشرات بمنتهي السهولة . أنا واثق أن في المستقبل ستكون العلوم الحديثة قادرة على ايجاد وسيلة لسحب أو صد هذه الآلام الإلكترونية بعيداً عن جسم الإنسان. لا تبقي هذا الكتاب قريباً منك عندما تكون أنت أو عائلتك على إستعداد للذهاب للنوم، إتركه في مكان بعيداً عنك حيث كنت تعتقد، أن الجن سيقرأونها دون أن يزعجوك. إنهم قادرون على تغيير برمجة مخنا. عندما يقوم الجن بإرسال إشارة إلكترونية إلى المخ، يعلمون بوضوح ماذا يفعلون أو ما يتعين عليهم القيام به لإرسال إشارة إلكترونية إلى المخ،أو يمكنك القول عندما ينومننا مغناطيسياً. مثل عملية إحداث الأحلام الذي هو بمثابة أمر مؤقت أو تنويم مغناطيسي مؤقت يقوم به أي جني. إن الأمر هكذا، نذهب إلي النوم، سنبدأ رؤية نفس الأحلام بنفس الأوامر الإلكترونية أو التنويم المغناطيسي..في الليلة التالية، يأتي جني بأوامر جديدة وأحلام جديدة. إذاً فالتنويم المغناطيسي بالأحلام هو تنويم مغناطيسي مؤقت أو برمجة مؤقتة من الجن. بمجرد أن نفتح عيوننا، سوف نفقد إشارات الجن من عقولهم إلى عقولنا. هذا كل شيء في حالة الأحلام. لا يستطيع الجن إرسال أي أمر أو إشارات دائمة أو تنويم مغناطيسي دائم ، لإنشاء الحلم على أساس دائم. السبب في ذلك هو أننا بمجرد أن نستيقظ، ترفض عقولنا تماماً إشارة /أمرالحلم أو التنويم المغناطيسي ليحل عالمنا الحقيقي محل عالم الأحلام الوهمي.

SEE & CONTROL DEMONS & PAIN

Here we are not talking about a man-made machine or another human enemy; here we are talking about demons, i.e., another breed or race or creature created by God, way more powerful than our brains and way more in numbers than us. I have strong belief once demons will dominate physically in this world, they will completely destroy the human race. They may not destroy human race by the use of nuclear weapons if demons want to keep animals, birds, reptiles, insects still alive. Once demons will use nuclear weapons to destroy human race then at least all those animals live in those areas or around those areas where human live will die too. This way, demons has to go in jungles if they want to stay in the bodies of animals. The reason is just to destroy human race, wherever demons will use nuclear weapons, all those areas will still be good actually very good for demons to live there, but no other human, animal, bird, reptiles, insects will survive there due to the continuous killing of nuclear radiation. Only machines and demons will be living in those areas of radiation. So honestly, human race will have two enemies, one demon and second modern robots and computers under the possession of demons. So what do you want to do to save human race? Anything? Any plan? Regardless of whether humans have the same structure, abilities, or capabilities. Humans are different with each other. Some are more ambitious, and some are less ambitious. Some are criminals, some are good. Some want to become the president of a country, some are lazy and like an easy going life. Some believe in equality, some are terrorists. Some are scientists, and some are activists. The same way, you cannot expect that all demons will be part of this war against human race in future. Demons live around us I am sure will be against this war.

تحتاج عقولنا إلى ذلك الجزء من المخ وآلية إبقائنا في العالم الحقيقي. ولكن الجن يجيدون جداً تغذية أو تغيير الأوامر، أو برمجة عقولنا. مثل لو أنني أرسلت جني واحد إلى شخص ما بأمر لتغيير برمجة عقولهم لبدء كراهية أو حب شخص ما أو شيء ما، سيرسل ذلك الجن إشارة برمجة دائمة للتغير إلى ذلك العقل حتى لمجرد مرة واحدة، و ستكون كافية لفترة طويلة جداً. على سبيل المثال، إذا كنت لا تحب أي سياسي وأرسلت إليك جني لتغيير برمجة عقلك، إذاً ماذا سيحدث؟ حسنا، في الأصل عقلك لا يحب ذلك السياسي، ولكن الجني سيغذيك ببرمجة عكسية في عقلك عن طريق إرسال إشارة إلكترونية لعقلك أو بلغة سهلة، هذا الجني سينومك مغناطيسياً .

الآن كيف ستعمل هذه البرمجة الجديدة الخارجية عليك؟ إذا كنت لا تكره ذلك السياسي كثيراً، فإن البرمجة الخارجية من المخ تبدأ العمل على الفور. حتى أنك لن تعرف أبداً، وفجأة سوف تبدأ في الإعجاب بذلك السياسي. الآن إذا كان كرهك لذلك السياسي بالذات ذومستوى معتدل فإن هذا التنويم المغناطيسي أوالأمر الإلكتروني، سيعمل ضد عقلك طوال الوقت.

كلما فكرت بشكل سيئ بذلك السياسي، ستأتي تلك الإشارة الإلكترونية الخارجية، أو الأمر عبر المخ، ستصر طوال علي تغيير تفكيرك عن ذلك السياسي.. في كل مرة ستفكرفيها بأي شيء سيئ، وسوف يكون لديك دائماً تفكير بالتوازي مع أفكارك الأصلية. هذه الأنواع من الحالات، ستتغير أفكارك بعد حين، أو ستكون محايداً بعد مرور بعض الوقت، مثل عدم وجود كراهية ، ولكن لا يوجد حب أيضاً. هذا النوع من العقول عادة نسميهم "مستقلين".

But the population of demons is so much even 1 percent population of demons decide to go against humans, it will take hardly one day for them to get rid of human race from this earth. But it will be practically difficult for demons to destroy us so fast if we will not have these nuclear weapons and robots with electronic brains for demons to use against them. Sometimes, I think, if I will stay alive for a while and during this time, if demons decide to use radiation against humans, where I am going to live the rest of my life, because by chance my country is a nuclear power.

Another issue which is the population of the demons. The size and configuration of demons is very suitable for demons to grow really fast in a very small place. In a single regular-size room in a small house, millions of demons can fit very easily. So you can imagine the populations of the demons are around us right now. One single advantage we have due to their overpopulation, demons are divided in groups, subgroups to protect their places to live and to protect the bodies they possess from each other. Demons don't allow each other to access their area easily. For these few reasons, they fight with each other all the time. And as you know, demons can kill each other very easily. Demons are compatible, very compatible, with the atmosphere fully covered by the radio active nuclear radiation. They get more and more powerful and more energetic once they can energize themselves from electromagnetic field or electricity or nuclear radiation. Areas where no human can go either due to any nuclear bombing done in those areas or those areas were having any kind of leakage of nuclear radiation problems, the population of demons in those areas is way more than normal areas.

هذه الأنواع من العقول يمكن أن تذهب في اي من الإتجاهين. ولكن إذا تحقق منك نفس الجن مرة أخرى بعد أيام قليلة، وقاموا بإعادة تنشيط أوامره الإلكترونية أو التنويم المغناطيسي، سوف يتغير عقلك على الفور. السبب هو أنه في المرة الثانية، لم زكن هناك معارضة مثل الكراهية ضد أوامر البرمجة الجديدة التي أو الإشارات أو الإشعاعات أو التنويم المغناطيسي. الآن في الحالة الثالثة، عند ما تكره سياسي ما بشدة حقاً. كيف يمكننا إعادة برمجة عقلك؟ عادة، هذا النوع من الكراهية الشديدة تحدث عندما تكون تحت إستحواذ جني شرير حقاً. فإذا لم تكن بتلك الأهمية، سأطلب من مجموعة من الجن الذهاب وركل الجني الشرير أولاً من محيطك. و قد يكون هذا قتالاً بين الجن.

ثم في الخطوة الثانية سيبدأ الجن الجدد في إرسال أوامر جديدة أو إشارات إلكترونية أو تنويم مغناطيسي لعقلك لتحييد برمجة الكراهية في مخك يقوم الجني الشرير من حولك طوال حياتك. بمجرد أن تصبح شخصاً محايداً بمرور الوقت، سيبدأ الجن الجدد في إرسال برمجة جديدة إلى مخك. أعتقد أن الأمر سيستغرق بعض الوقت، ولكن سوف يروق لك ذلك السياسي بالذات في وقت قريب جداً. ليس هذا هو الشيء الوحيد الذي سيتغير فيك. بمرور الوقت سوف تكون أقل تطرفاً و بغضاً في المجالات الأخرى للحياة أيضاً. الآن الحالة الثالثة والأخيرة، عندما تكون شخصاً مهماً حقاً بالنسبة لي، أنا بحاجة إلى تغيير البرمجة المتطرفة الخاصة بك في أقرب وقت ممكن. في هذه الحالة، أولاً سأقوم بإتصال تخاطري مع مخك أو مع الجني الشرير في مخك أو حول مخك.

سوف أعطي أوامري وتعليماتي لذلك الجني، بلطيف أحياناً، وربما بتهديده أحياناً أخري. إما تغيير الأوامر وبرمجة عقلك بالطريقة التي أريدها، أو أن يتركوك وحدك.

SEE & CONTROL DEMONS & PAIN	رضوان قرشي

Demons living in radiation area are more energetic and powerful. So this will be the future. Human population will be reduced due to more and more nuclear radiation all over the world, and demons population will increase more rapidly in those areas due to more availability of area and more energy actually nuclear energy to feed themselves. Demons live inside electric wires and equipments so they can get electric energy easily to energize themselves. Demons energize themselves from the powerful electric energy during the transmissions and distributions of electricity through wires from here to there. Demons will be more powerful, killing each other. The power of demons will be more powerful, the electronic signals of demons to any brain will be more powerful, once demons will be able to energize themselves with more and more powerful source of electromagnetic field, electricity sources, wires, and finally radioactive energy. Radioactive energy is a food for demons like a heaven. Demons love to live an atmosphere where they don't need to go under small wires to absorb electric energy or a weak energy from the atmosphere. They love to live in an open atmosphere where radioactive energy is available everywhere in open surroundings, and demons can energize easily all the time whenever they want to.

More powerful radioactive nuclear energy makes them superior and more powerful in demon race. Due to electronic configuration, demons cannot handle water conditions. During rain, most demons will look for some place to save themselves from continuous water threat

في معظم الحالات، يقبل هؤلاء الجن أوامري بسهولة وعادةً يفعلون ما أطلب منهم القيام به، و إلا سحبت ذلك الجني بعيداً عن ذلك الشخص وإرسله إلى شخص آخر يستحقه أكثر من ذلك الشخص. و في الخطوة التالية أقوم بإرسال بعض الجن اللطيف والهادئون لك أو لذلك الشخص لإعادة برمجة المخ، أو يعيدوا برمجة مخك. ثق بي بعد مرور بعض الوقت، سوف تبدأ في الإعجاب بذلك السياسي.

سوف أعطيك تفاصيل عن كيفية جعل الجن أصدقائك، في هذا الكتاب لاحقاً . لا تحاول التواصل معهم حتى تنتهي من إجراءات رشوتهم لإقناعهم أن يصبحوا لطفاء وودودين معك. هنا،أخبرك بتفاصيل، كيفية يمكنك التواصل مع الجن. يصبح الجن متوحشياً و شريراً جداً ، بمجرد أن يستحوذوا علي جسم الإنسان بنسبة 100 في المئة، وعادةًيستطيعون التحدث في بمثل هذا الصوت البشري ,و لكن ليس كصوت الإنسان العادي، لكن بصوت ثقيل بعض الشيء بالمقارنة مع صوت البشر العاديين. هذه هي الحالة التي لا يتذكر فيها الإنسان أي شيء يحدث من حوله. أنت لست بحاجة إلى ذلك. هذه أسوأ حالة للإنسان، عندما يستحوذ عليه جني شرير أو غاضب للغاية. لذلك أنت لا تحتاج إلى التواصل مع ذلك الجني، فهو يتصرف بجنون في ذلك الوقت. كل ما تحتاجه هو اللتواصل مع جن ودودين ولطفاء. لا يستحق الجن الأشرار والسيئون ☺صداقتك.

إجعل دائماً ذلك قاعدة لك، إذا أراد الجن أن يصبحوا أصدقائك وأرادوا التواصل معك، لابد لهم أن يتصرفوا بشكل صحيح و لطيف، و ودود. بمجرد أن تنفذ هذه القاعدة سوف ترى كيف سيكون هؤلاء الجن لطفاء معك. وسوف تفاجأ عندما تدرك أنهم يتهافتون على التواصل معك.

Demons don't like cold weather. Demons will look for warm atmosphere during cold weather. Demons will need more energy to energize themselves during cold weather. Demons stay inside or around electric heaters during cold weather. Demons need a lot of power to energize them. Cold atmosphere and rainy weather and snow reduce the energy available in the naturally exist electromagnetic field. Demons receive less energy from the atmosphere during cold weather. With the increase of the population of demons the temperature of the atmosphere will increase also. Demons will suck more energy to energize themselves, they will dissipate that energy in the form of heat. To have better resources to powerful energy and heat, demons will do everything to bring more and more radioactive radiation all over the world to feed such a huge population of demons. High-temperature regions all over the world are more suitable for the demons' growth and population. More heat means better source of energy and better atmosphere to live and grow.

Demons will do their best to increase the temperature of this earth to have enough food/energy for the entire population of the demons on this earth. There is no way demons will not raise the temperature of this earth just to have more and more energy for themselves. For this, possibly, demons can play with the protective layer around the earth to receive more and more heat and energy from the sun. More rays and heat from the sun will strengthen the powers of demons. Demons don't do sex as humans, animals, reptiles, birds, or even insects do. Demons don't have any concept of gender. There is no male demon and there is no female demon.

على أي حال، إذا رأيت أي الإنسان في حالة من الحالات المذكورة أعلاه، قم برش الماء المقدس على الدوام برقبته ووجهه وأذنه و رأسه وصدره، وإ طلب منه شرب الماء المقدس أيضاً حتى يخرج ذلك الجني منه أو على الأقل يهدأ.

بمجرد الإنتهاء من إجراءات برشوة الجن، يمكنك أن تطلب منهم دغدغتك في أصابعك إذا كانوا حولك ويستمعون إليك. سوف يبدأون في دغدغتك في غضون ساعات قليلة. إذا لم تستجيب للجن على الفور، سوف يعتقدون أن الدغدغة ليست كافية. وسوف يبدأون في دغدغتك بشكل أشد، لذلك يجب عليك الإستجابة لهم على الفور. تحتاج فقط إلى التحدث إليهم بطريقة طبيعية، و هي نفس الطريقة التي تتحدث بها مع البشر الأخرين. في بعض الأحيان سيقوم الجن بقرصك أو دغدغتك في بعض الأماكن الخطأ حيث سيسببون لك الضرر. يجب أن تخبرهم على الفور أنهم يضروك و لابد لهم التوقف عن التسبب لك بالضرر.و إذا كنت مشغولاً أو لا تستطيع التواصل مع الشياطين، قل لهم فقط أنك سوف تحدث معهم في غضون خمس عشرة دقيقة أو ثلاثين دقيقة، وما إلى ذلك أنا واثق من الجن أنه يمكنهم الإنتظار لبضع دقائق. كلما قام الجن بدغدغتك، لابد أن تتحدث معهم عنك، عن الجدول الزمني الخاص بك، أين أنت ذاهب. ناقش مشاكلك معهم. كلما تحدثت معهم أكثر، كلما إستمعوا إليك. لابد أن تتأكد من أنهم كلما دغدغوك أو قرصوك بلطف في الجسم، لابد أن تستجيب لهم دائماً. إستمر بهذه الطريقة في المحادثة على الأقل لمدة شهر. خلال هذا الشهر الواحد، سوف يكون الجن من حولك أكثر إنسجاماً وتزامناً مع عقلك. لذا يرجى عدم التسرع، خذ وقتك، إذا كنت لا تريد أن تؤذي عقلك.

Demons are just electronic brains without physical organs but programmed to have physical and emotional activities all the time. Demons cannot do any sex with anyone. The reproduction process of demons is just the division of their body into two, three, or more equal parts either after certain time or after certain size and restart growing again rapidly.

This reproduction process does not decrease their knowledge or memory. This is the main reason for the long life of demons. After certain time, one single demon converts himself into a big group or family of demons. Demons learn all family system and family values from humans and animals. By itself demons don't have any sex life because of unavailability of sex organs and male or female gender, but demons' brains are programmed to have or feel sex all the time. For this purpose demons possess the bodies of human and animal to enjoy those physical and emotional activities. There is no way during the activity of sex regardless a human, animal, etc., will not be possessed by the demon. There is no particular class or opinion or temperament inside any demon to possess any woman or any man during this activity. Demons are freelancers; they are okay with both either male or female. The same demon that possesses a body of a man during sex will have no problem in possessing the woman's body the next day during sex. They are so weird, right? But main reason to write these details here is to assure everyone that demons or any other invisible creatures cannot do any sex with human or any animal.

الروبوتات لا تقاوم أي نوع من سيطرة الجن علي عقلهم. ولكن إستحواذ الجن علي الإنسان، بنسبة 100%، فإن ذلك يفسد الحالة العقلية لدى الإنسان. لذلك ليست فكرة جيدة إذا كان الجني يستخدم عقلاً بشرياً للتواصل معك. أنت لا تحتاج إلى السير في هذا الطريق. إبدأ ببساطة بلغة الدغدغة و القرص. إستمر في فعل ذلك ما لا يقل عن لمدة شهر. بمجرد أن تشعر أن الجن الخاص بك مؤهلون بما فيه الكفاية لفهمك والإستجابة لك فوراً، بمجرد أن تتصل بهم، فأنت بحاجة للإنتقال إلى الخطوة التالية. إذا كنت لا تزال تشعر أن الجن لا يستجيبون لندائك على الفور، فأنت تحتاج إلى البقاء على الخطوة الأولى من الإتصالات لفترة من الوقت.

تذكر، سوف يكون هناك العديد من الجن يتواصلون معك في أوقات مختلفة. أفضل طريقة لمعرفة من هو الذي يتواصل معك، هي أن ترشدهم عن إصبع معين أو مكان ليقوموا بدغدغتك فيه. لذلك فالأمر في يدك عندما تريد أن تنتقل إلى الخطوة التاليةمن الإتصال. مرة أخرى، أشعر بقوة الا تنتقل لى الخطوة التالية من الإتصالات حتى أنها يأتوك على الفور بمجرد الإتصال بهم. حسناً، بيجرد أن تصل إلى تلك النقطة عندما كنت تشعر أنك واثق بنسبة 100 في المئة، إنتقل إلى الخطوة التالية. في البداية، تحتاج إلى الإستلقاء أثناء هذه الممارسة. لا تقم برش الماء المقدس من حولك قبل أن تبدأ هذه الممارسة. هذا فقط لغرض الممارسة. بمجرد أن تقوم بهذه الممارسة لمدة لا تقل عن ثلاثة أشهر، ستستمتع إلى الجن و تتواصل معهم في عقلك مثلي. تذكر دائماً أنك تحتاج إلى التحدث معهم، مثلما تتحدث مع البشر الآخرين. ولكنهم سيستجيبون لك عن طريق دغدغتك أو أن الجن سيتحدثون إليك في المخ، فبمجرد الإستلقاء علي سرير ك، وتغمض عينيك إطلب من الجن إرسال الإجابات إلى المخ، والآن إترك عقلك فارغاً. هذا يعني لا تفكر في أي شيء.

The possession of a body is like you mix salt with water. So demons feel same excitement and sensation whatever our brain feel during any physical activity. The only possible way for demons doing sex with any human is in dreams. Once demons send some electronic signals to our brains, our brains will decode those electronic messages as a dream of doing sex with someone in the imagination of that demon. So with demons any activity like this is only possible in two ways. The first is that demons become the virtual and temporary part of our body and brain by the possession of our body to absorb the same feelings and sensation from our brains, whatever our brains and bodies feel during that activity. Sex is not the only activity demons enjoy with us during the possession of human body. Demons cannot drink alcohol, beer, wine, or anything else. Demons cannot smoke cigarettes or drugs. But their brains are programmed to have this sensation, enjoyment, and extremely strong desire to drink or eat like a physical human or animal, but demons cannot eat or drink or cannot perform any other physical activity.

Demons are crazy about beef, lemon, and lime. But they cannot eat anything. So the powers of demons give them option to possess any living physical body of any human, animal, etc., and use them to fulfill their desires, regardless of whether those few habits or activities hurt us physically. Demons don't care about our health. Demons just want us to do whatever they feel desire for to have. Now on the second hand, we humans have free will and the strongest brain in all creatures, to follow everything demons ask us to do or limit them to only good activities and things.

سيكون من الصعب لبضعة أيام، ولكن عندما تقوم بتلك الممارسة، وستكون قادراً على القيام بذلك. تأكد من أنك لا تفكر في أي شيء أو أي شخص على الإطلاق. إبق عقلك خالياً تماماً تماماً. الآن إطرح أي سؤال لديك علي الجن وإطلب منهم إرسال الإجابات إلى عقلك. لا تحاول التفكير في أي جواب. حاول بكل ما لديك ألا تفكر في أي إجابة ممكنة لسؤالك في عقلك. فجأة سوف تتلقى إشارة إلكترونية من الجن الموجودين حولك. سوف تظهر تلك الإشارة في عق ولك علي أنها جواب الجني علي سؤالك. الآن إسأل الجني الخاص بك سؤال آخر أو إقتراح آخر حول أي شيء وإبق عقلك فارغاً تماماً. لا تحاول التفكير في سؤالك أو في الجواب عليه. و في بضع ثوان سيرسل لك الجن إشارة مرة أخرى، وسوف تكون قادراً على قراءة هذا التفكر من الجن في عقلك. هذه ممارسة بسيطة للغاية. قم بهذه الممارسة لبضعة أسابيع بأن ترقد على سريرك في جو هادئ وسلمي. وبمجرد الإنتهاء من الممارسة قليلا.

سيمكنك القيام بذلك في أي مكان أو الإتصال بالجن الخاص بك كلما أردت و أينما كنت، و في وقت لاحق مع أي جني من حولك. تعلمت من تجربتي أن الجن يكونون أكثر راحة عندما نتحدث إليهم بنفس الطريقة التي نتحدث بها مع البشر الأخرين. السبب في ذلك هو أن الجن لا يحتاجون إلى البقاء على إتصال طوال الوقت مع عقلنا لقراءة أفكارنا، إذا نحن حاولنا التواصل معهم.

هذا الشيء يعطي بعض حرية للجن بمجرد تدريب الجن الموجودين حولك تبدأ في التواصل معهم، أنت تحتاج إلى مناقشة مشكلتك معهم، و تحتاج أن تقول لهم إذا كان لديك بعض القضايا المتعلقة بشخص ما، وسوف يوجهوك بشكل صحيح. يستطيع الجن أن يساعدوك بشكل أفضل، والسبب هو أنك لا يمكنك الذهاب الى كل مكان، لا يمكنك قراءة عقول أصدقائك وأعدائك، ولكن الجن الخاص بك يمكنهم الذهاب في كل مكان، كما يمكنهم قراءة أي عقل في ثوان قليلة فقط .

Demons will always ask you or push you to do more and more enjoyable and negative activities like drinking alcohol or getting angry. Don't expect demons will ask you to go to the house of God and pray to God.

Demons' brains do not work easily for positive things. Demons are very good in developing the taste and desire to do or to eat something whatever they want us to do or eat, so demons has to do less struggle to enjoy whatever they want. If some human bodies/brains decide to go against them like decide to quit smoking or quit alcohol or quit drugs, etc., demons keep pushing and punishing us to restart those things. I have no idea how these demons will make robots and computers drink alcohol, smoke weed, and eat beef for them, once they will be successful of destroying human race.

The basic difference between the pains and the diseases/insects mainly is that pains are electronic bodies and don't use oxygen or carbon dioxide for breathing. Diseases are insects, use oxygen carbon dioxide for breathing. Pains, we cannot kill them. Diseases/insects/cancers, we can kill them very easily. Insects/ diseases /cancers just create minor or major infections all over the body regardless inside or outside. Pains, if powerful, hurt us.

Pains, if not too much powerful, do not hurt us, but it damage us quietly, like block arteries, blocking tubes inside kidneys, block heart's vessels, thyroids, or insulin blockage, etc.

قبل أن يعطيك الجن أي إقتراح أو فكرة أو معلومات، فإنهم يستيقنون، ويتحققون من الأمر أولاً، ثم يعطوك المشورة الصحيحة. إستمر في إجراء هذه الممارسة، فهذه الممارسة القليلة تفتح عينيك و عقلك إلى عوالم عدة لم تكتشف. بمجرد أن تعلم شيئاً يجب أن تنشره بين الآخرين لمساعدتهم. تذكر دائماً أن المعرفة والتنوير، والتعلم، والتعليم يزيد دائماً بمجرد أن ت. إقوم بنشره، فإذا كنت تتعلم مني اليوم، قم بمحاولة تعليم شخص ما غداً.

إن أدوات الدفاع أو إحداث الضرر بين الجن و البشر، هي إستخدام الإشعاع ضد البشر، والبشر يستخدمون الماء المقدس ضد الجن. عندما يقوم العلم الحديث بالعمل على تطويرسائل يزيل الطاقة أو يزيل المغناطيسية، و يكون معادلاً للمياه المقدسة، و سيكون أيضاً ذو مستوى معادل للإشعاع.. فإذا إستخدم الجن الإشعاع المشع ضد البشر، سيستخدم ا البشر سائل إ زالة الطاقة ضد الجن.

تكون سيطرة الجن علي البشر والتواصل معهم من خلال إستخدام التنويم المغناطيسي، ويمكن للبشر إستخدام التخاطر للتواصل مع الجن والتحكم فيهم. إن الجن لديهم بعض الأشياء ضدنا، بنفس الطريقة البشر لديهم بعض الأشياء ضد الجن أيضاً. ولكن البشرليس لديهم ما يكفي من المعرفة عن الجن، وهذا هو السبب في أن البشر يحتاجون إلى أن يأهبوا أنفسهم في حالة أن تكون في حاجة إلي للدفاع عن أنفسهم ضد الجن في المستقبل. إن البشر يحبون بعض الإيقاعات أو الأغاني، وبنفس الطريقة يحب الجن.بعض القراءات والصلوات و السحر السيئ؛ و السبب هو عمر الجن.

The main reason for that is to energize themselves from these locations. In second step, once pains create some damages there, usually diseases/ insects attack those locations and create infections and cancers there by eating those organs or body parts. Other situations and problems created by the electronic pains are fever, cough, flu, cold, sinus, etc.

After some time, when diseases/insects join the pains, diseases/insects create all kinds of infections to make the situation worse, but the good thing is that we can hunt and kill very easily diseases/insects. I am sure in the future modern science will be able to find a way to pull out or repel these electronic pains away from the human body. Don't keep this book close to you when you or your family is ready to go to sleep. Leave it in a place far from you, where you think, it will be easy for your demons to read it without bothering you.

Demons are capable of changing the programming of our brain. When demons send an electronic signal to our brain, demons clearly know what they are doing or what they need to do to send an electronic signal to our brain or you can say when they hypnotize us. Like the process of dreams creation which is a temporary command or a temporary hypnotism by any demon. So it is like this, whenever we will sleep we will start seeing the same dreams under the same electronic command or hypnotism. The next night, the next demon with new commands and new dreams. So dream hypnotism is temporary hypnotism or temporary programming from demons.

اذا كان الجني يعيش منذ عدة آلاف من السنين الماضية، وخلال فترة حياته، إذا قام شخص ما بربط ذلك الجني تحت سيطرة أي كلام مقدس معين أو تحت أي سحر شرير، سيظل ذلك الجني بمثابة العبد لذلك الكلام المقدس أو تلك القراءات السحرية الشريرة. ولا شك أن الكلام المقدس يوجه إلي الجن الطيب، بينما توجه القراءات السحرية الشريرة للجن الشرير. إسمح لي أن أشرح لك. إذا كان هناك جني حول إنسان ما، و أصبح صديقاً ذلك الإنسان. إذا قام ذلك الإنسان بربط لك الجني أو إعطاءه أمرما، فبمجرد أن يقوم شخص ما بقراءة ذلك الكلام المقدس أو السحر الشرير، سيقوم الجني بمتابعة ذلك الشخص. لا يزال جميع أطباء الجن هؤلاء لديهم هؤلاء الجن القدماء من معلميهم أو أساتذتهم السابقين ، لا يزال جميع أطباء الجن هؤلاء يستخدمون نفس الكلام المقدس لإستخدام / السيطرة على الجن الطيب والسحر الشرير، للسيطرة على الجن الشرير. ولكن لا تقلق، هذا هو عصرنا وزماننا. قم بإتباع إجراءاتي وتعليماتي وسيكون لديك المزيد من السيطرة على العالم الغير مرئي، أكثر من أي طبيب للجن.

الآن متى وكيف نستخدم الماء المقدس لصد الجن. هناك أربع حالات. معظم الأوقات توجد الآلام بعمق في الجسم حيث لن يستطيع رذاذ الماء المقدس لمس هذا الألم. في هذه الحالة، قد يساعد شرب الماء المقدس إذا كانت المياه ستصل إلى مكان المشكلة في غضون ثلاثين ثانية. الحالة الثانية هي عندما يوجد الجني في مكان عميق داخل الجسم حيث لا يمكن للمياه المقدسة الوصول أو لمس الجني بسهولة. ولكن في حالة الجن، أنه من غير المألوف جداً أن يبقى الجن في مكان عميق جداً داخل جسم الإنسان خلال إستحواذ الجني علي عقل الإنسان. الجن أكبر نسبيا وأكثر إهتماما بالإستحواذ علي عقل الإنسان.

Once we open our eyes, we will lose the signals of demons from their brains to our brains. That's it in case of dreams. Demons are not capable of sending any permanent command or signal or hypnotism to create a dream on permanent basis. The reason is that once we wake up, our brain completely rejects that dream signal/ command or hypnotism to replace the imaginary world of dreams to our real world.

Our brains need that part of them and mechanism to keep us in real world. But demons are very good in feeding or changing commands or programming of our brains. Like if I will even send one demon to someone with a command to change the programming of their brains to start to hate or like someone or something, that demon will send a permanent programming change signal to that brain even just one time, it will be enough for a long, long time. For example, if you don't like any politician and I send a demon to change the programming of your brain, then what will happen? Okay, originally your brain don't like that politician but the demon will feed an opposite programming in your brain by sending an electronic signal to your brain or in a easy language, that demon hypnotize you.

Now how these new external programmings work on you? If you don't hate that politician too much, the external programming of your brain will start working immediately. Even you will never figure out, and suddenly you will start liking that politician. Now if your hate for that particular politician is of moderate level then this hypnotism or electronic command will work against your brain all the time.

لهذه الأسباب هم يتواجدون داخل الجسم معظم الوقت، ولكن منطقة كبيرة من أجسادهم تبقي علي سطح الجلد أو الرأس أو الرقبة أو الأذنين، خلال إمتدادهم للإستحواذ علي جسم الإنسان . الحالة الثالثة، عندما يبقي الألم داخل الجسم بالإضافة إلى بعض المناطق من الجسم فوق الرأس أو الجلد أو في مكان ما حول الجسم.. في مثل تلك الظروف عادةً، إذا كان الماء المقدس أقل فعالية، نكون بحاجة إلى إستخدام بعض المراهم العلاجية مع الكلام المقدس. سأشرح ذلك في الصفحات القليلة القادمة. الآن الحالة الرابعة عندما يكون الجن حولنا للإستحواذ أساساً علي عقلنا لينومونا مغناطيسياً. في هذه الحالة، يكون 50 في المئة من الجن داخل جسمنا و50 في المئة حول أجسادنا و عقولنا. لا يستخدم الجن جسمنا كمصدر للغذاء أو الطاقة، وهذا هو السبب في أنهم لا يدخلون بعمق في جسمنا.

يوجد الجن بنسبة50-50 % داخل / خارج الجسم . هذا يكفي بالنسبة لهم للإستحواذ علي الجسم تماماً، بغض النظرعما إذا كان الجسم أو العقل. ولكن هذه نقطة في صالحنا، ففي كل مرة تشرب الماء المقدس أو ترشه، تضطرللهرب لإنقاذ الدوائر الخاصة بهم. لذلك سوف يأتي الجن العنيدون جداً بإستمرار مراراً وتكراراً عدة مرات للإحتفاظ بإستحواذهم علي جسمك. ولكن إذا ظللت ترش الماء المقدس عدة. أشياء محتملة قد تحدث. لن يضيع الجن الأقوياء جداً والأشرار وقتهم حولك، لأن أمر خطير جداً بالنسبة لقوتهم وصحتهم، اذا واصلت رش الماء المقدس عليهم و ظللت تجردهم من طاقتهم بإستمرار طوال الوقت. أنا متأكد من أنهم سوف يبحثون عن شخص لن يلعب معهم بهذا الماء المقدس. إذا كان الجن الموجودون حولك مرتبطون بك حقاً أو بذلك البيت أو المكان، و لم يكونواعلى إستعداد لتركك أنت أو المكان، سيلعب هؤلاء الجن مع الأضواء .

Rizwan Qureshi

Whenever you will think bad about that politician, this external electronic signal or command comes across your brain and will insist all the time that you change your thinking about that politician. Every time you will think anything bad, you will always have a parallel thought, arguing with your original thoughts. So in these kinds of conditions, your thoughts will change after some time, or you will be natural after some time, like no more hate but no like either. We call these kinds of brains usually "independents." These kinds of brains can go either way. But if same demons will check you again after few days and reenergize his electronic commands or hypnotism, your brain will change immediately. The reason is because at the second time, there was no opposition like hate against that new programming commands or signals or rays or hypnotism. Now the third case, is when you really extremely hate a politician.

How we can reprogram your brain? Usually, this kind of extreme hate occurs when you are under the possession of a really evil demon. So if you are not that important, I will ask a group of demons to go and first kick out that evil demon from your surroundings. This may be a fight between demons. Then in the second step new demons will start sending new commands or electronic signals or hypnotism to your brain to neutralize the hate programming from your brain, this is done by the evil demon around you all your life. Once with time, when you will become a neutral person, new demons will start sending new programming to your brain. I think it will take some time, but you will start liking that particular politician very soon.

سيختار هؤلاء الجن زوايا منزلك حيث لن تكون قادراً على إزعاجهم طوال الوقت عن طريق رش الماء المقدس، ولكن بمجرد أن تنام، سوف يكون الجن قادرين على الوصول إليك. معظم الجن، إذا لم يكونوا عنيدين للغية حقاً، لن يجازفوا بالوجود حولك عندما لا يعلمون في أي وقت سوف تبدأ برش الماء المقدس هنا وهناك. لذلك بدلاً من البقاء في ذلك الجو الغير مريح، وسوف يبحثون عن مكان أفضل حيث يمكنهم العيش والقيام بإستحواذهم علي أجسام البشر.براحة بال ومع مزيد من الحرية، لذلك سيكون من المجبذ بالنسبة للجن، سوف يكون رش الماء المقدس على نفسك و علي محيطك فعال دائماً. كلما زاد رش الماء المقدس، كلما قل عدد الجن الموجودين من حولك. الآن بمجرد أن ترش الماء المقدس، سيظل عدد قليل من الجن حولك. هؤلاء الجن ليس لهم جدول أعمال مجنون.

حتي لو رششت الماء المقدس بشكل متكررطوال الوقت الذي سوف يتجردون من طاقتهم نتيجة لذلك العمل، سوف يغادرون المنزل. لا شك في أن الجن سيكونون أكثر يقظةً، وسوف يحاولون جعل أنفسهم بعيداً عنك أو عن رذاذ الماء المقدس. الشيء الثاني الذي سيفعله الجن هو أنهم لن يزعجوك بنفس ا لقدر، لذلك ستشعر بأنك بحاجة إلى رش الماء المقدس بإستمرار. كما قلت عن آلام المياه المقدسة عندما يكون عدد الجن قليلاً حتي فوق سطح الجلد، وإلا، سأخبرك بمزيد من الإجراءات لمحاربتهم، حتى تستخدم العلوم الطبية آلات إلكترونية لصد هم بعيداً عن أجسامنا.

قم برش المياه المقدسة داخل منزلك فقط دائماً . لا تقلق بشأن خارج البيت، والسبب هو أنك إذا بدأت برش الماء المقدس خارج المنزل، سيبدأ الجن من أماكن خارج المنزل في المجيئ داخل بيوتكم. لا تحاول أبداً إفتعال إشتباك مع أي جني.

This is not the only thing that will change in you. With time you will be less extremist and less hateful in other areas of life too. Now the third and the last condition, when you are really an important person to me and I need to change your extreme programming as soon as possible, in that case, first I will contact your brain or the evil demon in your brain or around your brain telepathically.

I will give my commands and instructions to that demon, sometimes nicely, may be sometimes threaten him to either change the commands and the programming of your brain the way I want it or to leave you alone. In most cases, those demons accept my commands easily and they usually do as I ask them to do. Otherwise usually, I pull that demon away from that person and send him to someone else who deserves him more, and in the next step I will send some nice and easygoing demons to you or to that person to reprogram or rehypnotize your brain. Trust me after sometime, you will start liking that politician.

Later in this book, I will give you details on how to make demons your friends. Don't try to communicate with them until you finish the procedure of bribing them to convince them to become nice and friendly with you. Here, I am giving you details, how you can communicate with them. Demons, become very wild and evil, once they possess any human brain 100 percent, and they are usually able to talk in that human voice, not in a normal human voice, like how humans talk, but in a little bit heavy voice as compared to their normal voices. This is the condition, when that human will not remember anything happening around him. You don't need this....

انها ليست فكرة جيدة. بقدر ما تفعله بفسك وبيتك، لديك سبباً وجيهاً جداً لهذا. أنت تريد حماية نفسك بالتأكيد ذلك جيد ولكن لا ترش الماء المقدس خارج المنزل. حتى داخل المنزل، لا تقم برش الماء المقدس في المرآب أو في الحجرات القليلة الإستخدام و الزوايا الأخرى القليلة الإستخدام من منزلك. تحتاج إلى ترك بعض المساحة لهم في مكان ما بالتأكيد. بسبب الرش المستمر للمياه المقدسة، والآن سيظل الجن حول المنزل أو حولك أو ستكون نوعاً ما محاطاً بالجن، سيكونون لطيفاء وودودين للغاية معك بمرور الوقت. تذكر دائماً، أنت لا تحتاج أن تجعل الجن أعداءً لك بشكل متع. ما عليك القيام به كل ما تحتاجه للمحافظة علي سلامتك، يجب أن تخبرهم أن يصبحوا أصدقائك و تصرعلي ذلك. هذا من واقع تجربتي الخاصة. الجن لا يستمعون لك حتى يعرفون أنك شخص على الأقل يمكنك إستخدام شيء ضد أنشطتهم لحماية نفسك. سوف يكون الجن أكثر حذراً وأقل خطورةً بمجرد أن يعرفوا أنك على علم بوجودهم من حولك ، و أنك تستطيع أن تدافع عن نفسك لصد هم بعيداً عنك. في تلك الحالة سيكون الجن أقل إزعاجاً، وسوف يحاولون أن يكونوا أكثر ودأً معك، و بمجرد أن صبحوا أصدقائك، ثق بي، سوف تستمتع حقاً بصداقة حقيقية ونقية.

الخطوة التالية هي كيفية تحضير المياه المقدسة. جميع الأدعية و الكلمات المقدسة في الكتب المقدسة ليس لديها نفس التأثيرات. كل دعاء أو كلام مقدس له تأثيرخاص به، وفوائد، و إستخداما.ت خاصة بها. هناك بعض الأدعية الخاصة جداً جداً، بغض النظر عن معانيها، و القوي الحارقة التي تصد قوى الجن بعيداً عنا. كل دين به هذه الأنواع من الآدعية. لذلك بدلاً من إضاعة وقتك، فقط إتصل برجال الدين وإطلب منهم إرشادك إلي تلك الأدعية الطارد.ة للجن. إذا لم يكن لديك الشجاعة لتسأل شخص ما عن ذلك، إذهب الى مواقع الويب الدينية الخاصة بك على شبكة الإنترنت و إبحث عنهم، وسوف تجدهم بمنتهي السهولة.

رؤية الجن و الآلام السيطرة عليها

This is the worst condition of a human, when possessed by an evil or extremely angry demon. So you don't need to communicate with that demon. That demon is acting crazy at that time. You just need to communicate with friendly and nice demons. Evil and bad demons don't deserve your friendship.

So always make your rule if demons want to become your friend and want to communicate with you, they need to behave right, nice, and friendly. Once you will make this rule you will see how nicely these demons will behave with you. You will be surprised when you will figure out these demons are dying to communicate with you.

Anyway, if you ever see any human in the above-mentioned condition, always spray holy water on his face, neck, ear, head, and chest, and ask him to drink holy water also until that demon comes out of him or at least calms down.

Once you finish my procedure of bribing demons then you can ask them to tickle you on your fingers if they are around you and listening to you. They will start tickling you within few hours. If you will not respond to demons immediately, they will think that the tickling is not enough. They will start tickling you harder. So you better respond to them immediately. You just need to talk in a normal way, the way you talk to other humans. Sometimes they pinch or tickle you at some wrong places where it will hurt you. You should tell them immediately that they are hurting you and they need to quit hurting you. If you are busy or not in a position of communicating with demons, just tell them that you will talk to them in fifteen minutes or thirty minutes, etc..

الآن سأخبرك كيف تستخدمهم . يكون الدعاء المقدس أو الكلمات المقدسة فعالة دائماً، عند قراءتها باللغة الأصلية بدلاً من ترجمتها لأي لغة أخرى. جميع الأدعية أو الكلمات المقدسة، بمجرد أن نقوم بقراءتها مراراً وتكراراً، فإنها تولد موجات و إشعاعات تصد وتحرق . كلما قرأت تلك الكلمات مراراً وتكراراً، كلما تولدت موجات و إشعاعات أكثر في فمك. إقرأ بالحد الأدنى مراراً وتكراراً على الأقل دون توقف إحدى عشرة مرة بدون التحدث أو قول شيئا آخر. في الخطوة التالية، وعلى الفور بعد الإنتهاء من القراءة، إما في الماء في زجاجة رذاذ أو في كوب ماء أو كليهما، قم بضخ أو نفخ الهواء من فمك ست مرات ليخلط أو يضاف لتلك الموجات أو الإشعاعات من الفم إلى الماء العادي. حسناً، بمجرد قراءة الآدعية أوكلمات المقدسة إحدى عشرة مرة وتنفخ تلك الأشعة من فمك ست مرات، فهذا يعني أنك تخلط / تضيف هذه الموجات الإشعاعية الحارقة أو الصادة في الماء العادي. ذلك الماء هو الماء المقدس الخاص بك الآن. ستبقي هذه الموجات و الإشعاعات الصادة داخل المياه لمدة 40-50 ثانية كحد أقصى، وهذا يعني أن الماء العادي هو الماء المقدس الخاص بك وسوف يكون فعالاً للأربعين ثانية المقبلة. بدون إضاعة ثانية واحدة، لابد أن تقوم برش الماء المقدس أن على نفسك، وأطفالك، والمناطق المحيطة بكم وما إلي ذلك، إذا كان الأمر يحتاج إلى أكثر من أربعين ثانية، قم بقراءة اللأدعية أو الكلام المقدس مرة أخرى لإعادة تنشيط الماء. في البداية، تحتاج إلى رش الماء المقدس بإستمرار. مع مرور الوقت، إذا قمت بعمل ذلك مرتين في اليوم ستبقى في أمان. قم برش الماء دائماً قبل الذهاب إلى النوم. الآن للتخلص من الآلام والجن العنيد، يمكنك إستخدام نفس الإجراءات من قراءة اللأدعية أو الكلمات المقدسة في الشراب أو مع علاج المراهم العلاج لصد الآلام من جسمك.

SEE & CONTROL DEMONS & PAIN

I am sure demons can wait for few minutes. Whenever demons tickle you, you need to talk to them about you, about your schedule, and where you are going. Discuss your problems with them; the more you will talk to them, the more they will listen to you. You need to make sure whenever they tickle you or give you a nice pinch on your body, always respond to them. Keep this way of conversation at least for one month. During this one month, demons around you will be more harmonious and synchronize with your brain. So please don't rush, take your time, if you don't want to hurt your brain. Learn slow and steady; otherwise demons will try to put more pressure on your brain to convey messages to you. It may hurt you, so go easy.

In the future, it will be easy when demons will have possession of modern computers and robots and will use their electronic brain's communication system of making voices or noises. Robots are not like humans. Robots don't resist any kind of possession of their brain from demons. But demons' possession of human brain, 100 percent screw up the brain condition of a human. So it is not a good idea if a demon uses a human brain to communicate with you. You don't need to go this way. Simply start with tickling and pinching language with demons. Keep doing for at least for a month. Once you feel your demons are good enough to understand you and respond to you immediately once you call them, then you need to move to the next step. If still you feel demons don't respond to your call immediately then you need to stay on first step of communication for a while.

رضوان قرشي

المراهم العلاجية والشراب العلاجي بشكل رئيسي يتم تناوله بغرض الشفاء، ولكن بمجرد إضافة/ خلط الكلمات أو الأدعية المقدسةالخاصة بك مع الشراب العلاجي أو المراهم العلاجية، سوف تكون فعالة بنفس الدواء لصد أو طرد الآلام الإلكترونية من الجسم. ولكن لا ننسى. أن هذه الموجات و الإشعاعات الناتجة من الأدعية أو الكلمات المقدسة ستبقي داخل ذلك الشراب العلاجي أو المراهم لأربعين ثانية فقط كحد أقصى. يكون ذلك عادةً وقتاً كافياً للعمل ضد أي ألم، وإلا، كرر العملية. فقط تأكد من أن تلك المياه أو الشراب أو المرهم وصل إلى المكان الذي يوجد به هذا الألم. أحياناً تكون تلك الآلام والجن قليلا أقوياء / قاسين، لذلك قد تضطر إلى إستخدام هذه الإجراءات في كثير من الأحيان حتى تهزمهم.أن أقوم بكل هذه الممارسات المقدسة بشكل نمطي، حتى معظم الوقت، وأنا لا أحتاج ذلك. إن ذلك فعال جداً ويبقينا بصحة وأمان كافي طوال الوقت. هذه الإجراءات فعالة وتعالج الجن و الآلام فقط، و لكنها ليست فعالة أو مفيدة بنفس القدر في حالة عدوى الإصابة / أو السرطان / أو فيروس نقص المناعة البشرية.

لقد قمت بتوجيه بالفعل لكيفية تعقب وقتل تلك الأمراض / السرطان / الحشرات في بداية هذا الكتاب. قم بإستخدام كل الأفكار والإجراءات المقدسة للحفاظ على نفسك محمياً و بصحة. تقوم الأدعية و الكلمات المقدسة بتحويل الماء العادي إلي ماء مقدس فقط لبضع ثوان، ولكن كن علي ثقة أن تلك المياه المقدسة ستؤدي الغرض منها حتى ولو لبضع ثوان! و هذا أكثر من كافي لآي جني أو ألم لترك الجسم.

اسمح لي أن أذكر مرة أخرى أي طبيب أو أي عالم بحث طبي، لا يزال لديه بعض الشكوك في عقولهم عن وجود مادي للجن و الآلام، إذا كانت على إستعداد لبدء البحث لإكتشاف الأشعة لإستخدامها ضد الجن والآلام لمساعدة البشرية ، وأنا على إستعداد لإثبات وجود الألم الجسدي أو المادي أمامهم في أي وقت.

Remember, there will be several demons communicating with you at different times. The best way to find out who is who is to tell them which particular finger or place to tickle you in. So it is in your hand when you want to go to next step of communication. Again, I strongly feel don't go to next step of communication until they come to you immediately once you call them. Okay, once you come to that point when you feel 100 percent confident then go to next step. In beginning, you need to lie down during this practice. Don't spray holy water around you before you start this practice. This is just for practice purpose. Once you will do this practice for at least three months, you will be listening to demons in your brain and communicating with them in your brain like me. Always remember you need to talk to them the way you talk to other humans, but they will respond to you by tickling you or demons will talk to you in your brain. Once you lie down in your bed, close your eyes and ask anything of your demons. Ask demons to send answers to your brain. Now leave your brain empty. It means don't think about anything. It will be difficult for a few days, but when you will practice, you will be able to do it. Make sure you are not thinking about anyone or anything at all. Keep your brain completely blank. Now ask any question to your demons and tell them to send answers to your brain. Don't try to think about any answer. Try your best not to think about any possible answer of your question in your brain. Suddenly you will receive an electronic signal from the demons around you. That signal will appear in your brain as the answer from that demon to your question. Now ask another question or suggestion about anything from your demon and keep your brain completely blank.

رؤية الجن و الآلام السيطرة عليها

جميع الإجراءات المذكورة أعلاه، وجميع الأساليب، عادةً ما تكون للناس العاديين، حتى يتمكنوا من مساعدة أنفسهم ضد هؤلاء الجن والآلام. أنا لست بحاجة إلى أي وسيلة لمحاربة هؤلاء الجن والآلام 99.99 في المئة من الوقت. أستطيع أن يثبت لآي طبيب أو عالم بحث طبي وجود الآلام في بضع دقائق . حتى أنني لا أحتاج إلي رؤية هؤلاء الأطباء و العلماء، إنني أحتاجهم فقط أن يكونوا على الهاتف معي، وأنا سوف أقوم بتحريك آلامهم الطبيعية مثل الصداع، آلام الظهر، آلام الركبة، وآلام الرقبة وغيرها، بعيداً عنهم. إذا كانوا يريدون مني أن أثبت أكثر، يمكنني أن أحرك آلامهم من جزء واحد من الجسم إلى جزء آخر من الجسم. اذا كانوا يريدون مني أن يثبت أكثر من ذلك، يمكني أن أنقل الألم شخص آخر لأجسامهم، سوف أبذل قصارى جهدي لإثبات الوجود المادي للألم لهم لإقناعهم، إذا وعدوا بالبدء في البحث الجدي للغاية لإكتشاف وتضخيم جميع أنواع الأشعة والموجات إلكترونياً لمحاربة الآلام والحن لمساعدة البشرية.

لا يستطيع الجن تحمل الماء المقدس على الإطلاق. فإنهم يتركون ذلك الجسم و المكان فوراً، ولكنهم قد يعودون بسرعة. لذلك تحتاج إلى إستخدام هذه الإجراءات بشكل متكرر. أفضل وسيلة لمحاربة أي ألم هي تناول الدواء المعالج، لعلاج الضرر أولاً، ثم إستخدم الماء المقدس أو المرهم مع أي أدعية أو كلمات مقدسة لطرد الألم الإلكتروني من جسمك. ليس هناك أي آثار جانبية لإستخدام الماء المقدس علي الإنسان.

ولكن هناك الكثير من المشاكل للجن حين يتصلون بالماء المقدس. الشياطين لا تحب الطريقة الماء المقدس. الجن لا يحبون الماء المقدس، بنفس الطريقة تماماً لا يحب الإنسان الذي إستحوذ عليه الجن، الماء المقدس أيضاً بسبب تأثير الجن.

Don't try to think about your question or about its answer. In a few seconds demons will send you a signal again and you will be able to read that thought of the demon in your brain. This is a very simple practice.

Do this practice for few weeks by lying in your bed in a quiet and peaceful atmosphere. Once you have a little bit practice. Then you can do this communication wherever or whenever with your demons and then later on with any demon around you. I learn from my experience that demons are more comfortable when we talk to them in the same manner we talk to other humans. The reason for that is that demons don't need to stay in touch all the time with our brain to read our mind if we are trying to communicate with them.

This thing gives some freedom to demons. Once you train demons around you and start communication with them, you need to discuss your problem with them. You need to tell them if you have some issues with someone. They will guide you right. Demons can help you better. The reason is that you cannot go everywhere, you cannot read the brains of your friends and enemies, but your demons can go everywhere and can read any brain just in few seconds. So before demons will give you any suggestion or idea or information, for sure, they will check around first, and then demons will give you the right advice. Keep doing this practice, this little practice will open your eyes and your brain to several undiscovered worlds. Once you learn something spread it to others to help them. Always remember, knowledge, enlightenment, learning, and education always increases once you spread it. If you are learning from me today, try to teach someone tomorrow.

ولكن بغض النظر عن مدى إنزعاج هؤلاء الناس، إذا كنت ترغب في علاجهم، إستمر برش الماء المقدس عليهم حتى يخرجوا من إستحواذ الجن عليهم. يجب عليك البقاء بلا حذاء على أرضية خرسانية أو سيراميك عندما يرش عليك شخص ما رذاذ الماء المقدس، و ذلك لطرد الجن. إن وجود أرض مسار أسمنتي، سيسهل جداً علي الجن والآلام الخروج من الجسم.

الآن سوف أقول لك كيف تبدأ في جعل الجن أصدقائك. لم يكن الأمر سهلاً بالنسبة للجن. هذا شيء جديد حقاً بالنسبة لهم، أن أعطيك مبادئ توجيهية لتقرب الجن منك قليلا، كأصدقاء لك. يشعر الجن دائماً بثقة من أن البشر يستطيعون التحدث عن الجن، كما أنهم يستطيعون تقديم مجموعة من الإفتراضات حول الجن ولكنهم دائماً في شك من وجود الجن. حسناً، سأ غير ذلك، سأعطي كل إنسان ثقة كبيرة و طريقة للوصول للجن، حتى و لو إستغرق الأمر أكثر من بضعة أشهر كي يستطيع الإنسان التواصل مع الجن علنا. إذا لم يكن الجن لطفاء وودودين مع هؤلاء البشر من حولهم، سيكون من الصعب على الجن البقاء حول هؤلاء الناس لفترة طويلة. لذلك هذا هو الوقت الذي يحتاج الجن فيه إلي التخلي عن جميع أنشطتها السرية ضد البشر و أن يصبحوا أكثر انفتاحاً و تعاوناً معهم يجب علي الجن الكف عن مضايقة وتخويف البشر و أن يتعرضوا فوراً لجميع البشر. حتى الآن، يمكنني تغيير الكثير من الأمور بيني وبين الجن منذ أن بدأت أشعربهم و بدأت رؤيتهم، وفي الخطوة التالية، بدأت الإتصال بهم. في البداية، كان من الصعب جداً إقناع أي جني بالإستماع إليك أو الإنتباه بك، لأن الجن يشعرون دائماً بثقة تامة بأن البشر لن يكونوا على يقين إذا كان الجن حولهم أم لا. الخطوة الأولى هي مستوى الثقة.

Rizwan Qureshi

The defending or damaging tools between demons and humans are that demons will use radiation against humans and humans will use holy water against demons. When modern science will develop deenergizing or demagnetizing liquid equivalent to holy water, that liquid will be of equivalent level to radiation. So if demons use radioactive radiation against humans, humans will use de-energizing liquid against demons.

Demons control humans and communicate with them by the use of hypnotism; humans can use telepathy to communicate and control demons. The way demons have some stuff against us, the same way humans have some stuff against demons too. But humans do not have enough knowledge of demons; that's why humans need to prepare themselves in case they will need to defend themselves against demons in the future. The way humans like some tunes or songs, the same way there are some prayers and some bad witchcraft readings that demons like. The reason is the age of demons.

If a demon is living since the last several thousand years, during his life span, if somewhere someone bind that demon under any particular pray or under any evil witchcraft readings, still this demon will act like a slave for those prayers or evil witchcraft readings. No doubt, prayer goes for good demons and evil reading for evil demons. Let me explain to you. If a demon was around a human and became a friend of that human, and If he binds that demon or gives him a command to, once anybody reads this prayer or evil witchcraft, that demons has to follow that person.

رؤية الجن و الآلام السيطرة عليها

قبل أن أبدأ رؤيتهم، كان يختلط علي الأمر ما إذا كان الجن موجودون حولي أم لا، إلي أن يأتي أي جني بالقرب مني، لذلك بدأت أشعر بهم. في ذلك الوقت، كنت أفترض دائماً أنه يوجد بإستمرار جني واحد أو إثنين من حولي. إنهم أ ذكياء، ولم يكن يأتي إلي الكثير من الجن بالقرب مني.

ولكن فوجئت بعدد الجن عندما بدأت رؤيتهم. لم يقترب مني حتى ولو جني واحد، في وقت من الأوقات، لأنني سبق أن إختبرت على نفسي استخدام الماء المقدس. كان كل الجن من حولي على علم الشياطين أنه كلما شعرت بأي جني من حولي، سوف أقوم برش المياه المقدسة لدفعهم أو طردهم بعيداً عني. لهذا السبب كانت معظم الشياطين البقاء بعيدا عني. ولكن بمجرد أن بدأت رؤيتهم، فاجأني كم الجن الذي ينتشر في كل مكان في هذا العالم. في منزل صغير مكون من غرفتين / ثلاثة غرف نوم، يجب أن تتوقع عدة آلاف من الجن في منزلك، من حولك طوال الوقت. لذلك فثقتكم الكلية وإعتقادكم بأن هناك عدد لا يحصى من الجن من حولك طوال الوقت، هذه هي الخطوة الأولى والرئيسية نحو الصداقة مع الجن. لا يمكنك الإنتقال إلى الخطوة الثانية حتى تصبح ممتازاً في الخطوة الأولى، و السبب هو أنك تستمطيع تفادي الإنسان ولكنك لا تستطيع تفادي الجني. سيقرأ الجن عقلك للحكم على مستوى ثقتك في حضورهم و وجودهم من حولك.

هل لديك مشكلة في ذلك؟ حسناً، ثق بي. الآن لا تشعر أو تشك في وجود الجن من حولك. كن دائماً على يقين أن لديك عدد لا يحصى من الجن من حولك، في المرآب الخاص بك، في المقاعد الخلفية من السيارات الخاصة بك، و في الغرف المظلمة في منزلك، وهنا وهناك، وفي كل مكان. خذ وقتك، مهما طال، ولكن لا تنتقل إلى الخطوة الثانية حتى تكون ناجحاً تماماً في الخطوة الأولى.

297

Still all these demon doctors have those old demons from their ex-teachers or masters, still all these demon doctors are using the same prayers to use/control good demons and evil witchcraft to control evil demons. But don't worry; this is our age and our time. Follow my procedures and instructions, and you will have more control of the invisible world, more than any demon doctor. Now when and how to use holy water to repel demons. There are four situations. Most of the times pains are deep inside the body where spray of the holy water will not be able to touch that pain. In that case, drinking holy water may help if the water reaches the spot of problem within thirty seconds. The second situation is when a demon is way deep inside the body where holy water cannot reach or touch that demon easily. But in case of demons, it is very unusual if demons will stay so much deep inside the human body during the possession of human brain. Demons are relatively bigger and very much more interested in possessing the brain of a human. For these reasons most of the time they are inside the body but a lot of area of their bodies during their expansion to possess a human body stay on the surface of our skin or head or neck or ears. The third situation is when a pain is staying inside the body plus some area of their body is above the skin or head or somewhere around our body. In those kinds of conditions usually, if holy water is less effective then, we need to use some medicated ointments with prayers. I will explain this in a few pages. Now the fourth condition is when demons are around us to possess mainly our brain to hypnotize us. In this situation, 50 percent demons are inside and 50 percent are around our bodies and brains. Demons don't use our body as a source for their food or energy; that's why demons don't go deep inside our body.

إذا لم تكن تشعر بثقة تامة و إنتقلت إلى الخطوة الثانية، ثق بي، إنك فقط تضيع وقتك. في الخطوة الثانية، يجب أن يكون لديك صورة واضحة جداً لهم. أنهم يطيرون هنا وهناك في كل في منزلك، إنهم يستمعون لك و يراقبونك بإستمرار، ومشاهدة باستمرار لك. يجب أن يكون لديك صورة صحيحة عنهم في خيالك. لا تفكر بأشباح أو سحرة أو أي اجني كبير مثل الصورة التي يصورها الناس لهم في الأفلام. فكر وتصور فقط في أحجامهم الحقيقية و كيف يبدون في عقلك، لأن الجن سوف يقرأون عقلك، إنهم مخلوقات طائرة و صغيرة جداً، إما شفافة اللون أو لون الدخان الأسود الخفيف جداً. إن أشكال صغيرة و مدورة. يبدو بعضهم وكأنهم خيوط تطير. كما يبدو البعض الآخر مثل الفقاعات الشفافة الصغيرة الجوفاء. بعضها يشبه شكل عنكبوت صغير.

تتراوح أحجامهم كلهم تقريباً بين حجم صرصور صغير إلي نملة صغيرة. ولكن معظمهم يساوي حجمه حجم ذبابة. فعندما تشعر أنك تفهم مظهرهم وهيكلهم أو بنيتهم وتشعر بثقة تامة من وجودهم حولك في كل مكان، قمر بإختيار وقت في المساء، الساعة:5:00 مساءً، خذ حوالي نصف رطل من اللحم المفروم في يدك، وإنشرها في يدك أمامك حتى يتمكن الجميع من رؤية اللحم المفروم في يدك. إبدأ الآن في المشي ببطء في كل غرفة، المرحاض، وجميع الزوايا داخل المنزل فقط. يجب عليك أثناء كل ذلك الوقت، أن تتكلم مع الجن وتناديهم بطريقة لطيفة للغاية ورشوتهم مثل هذا، " يا كل أصدقائي من الجن، أرجو أن تأتوا ورائي. سأطعمكم اللحم حتى تتمتعوا بلحم البقر ".

إمشي في كل مكان في منزلك وكرر هذه الجمل على الأقل 15 إلي20 مرة. الآن مع تكرار نفس الجملة أو شيئاً من هذا القبيل لطيف جداً وبطريقة الرشوة، ...

Rizwan Qureshi	**رؤية الجن و الآلام السيطرة عليها**

Most of the time they are 50-50% inside/outside the body. This is enough for them to possess a body completely regardless body or brain. But this is a plus point for us. Every time you will drink or spray holy water, demons have to run to save their circuits. So very hardheaded demons will keep coming again and again several times to still maintain their possession on your body. But if you will keep spraying holy water several things are possible. Very powerful and evil demons will not waste their time around you. Because it is risky for their powers and health, if you keep spraying Holy water on them and keep de-energizing them continuously all the time. I am sure they will look for somebody who is not going to play with them with this holy water. If demons around you are really attached to you or they are attached to that house or place and they are not willing to leave either you or that place; those demons will play with low profile. Those demons will choose those corners of your house where you will not be able to bother them all the time by spraying the holy water, but once you sleep, still they will be able to access to you. Most demons, if they are not really, really hardheaded, will not take risk around you when they never know at what time you will start spraying holy water here and there. So instead of staying in that uncomfortable atmosphere, they will look for some better place where they can live and do their possessions of human bodies with peace of mind and with more freedom. So with demons, it will be always effective to spray holy water on yourself and your surroundings. The more frequently you spray, the fewer demons you will have around you. Now even once you are spraying holy water, few demons will still stay around you.

إمشي باتجاه خارج المنزل وإترك لحم البقر في بعض الزوايا بعيداً عن الأشجار. أنت بحاجة إلي أن تبقي على لحم البقر بعيداً عن الأشجار حتى يتمكن الجن من الوصول إليه. إذا تركت لحم البقرقرب الشجرة، فإن الجن الموجودين حول شجرة لا يسمحوا للجن الآخرين من هنا وهناك من الحصول على لحم البقر. الجن لا يأكلون لحم البقر.

في الواقع الجن لا يأكلون أي شيء. ولكن برمجة عقلهم الإلكترونية، تجعل لديهم رغبة شديدة لتناول لحم البقر. بمجرد أن نعرض علي الجن تناول لحم البقر في الجو المفتوح، سيصل الجن إلى هناك من كل مكان، عن طريق الإستحواذ علي الحيوانات المختلفة والطيور والزواحف، والحشرات، وسوف تتمتع بلحم البقر بمجرد أن تأكله الحيوانات. هذه رشوة مفتوحة للسيطرة علي الجن. على أي حال، عندما يمتع الجن بالأنشطة البدنية الأخرى، بمجرد أن يستحوذوا علي أجسام الحيوانات، الإنسان، وما إلى ذلك، بنفس الطريقة بالضبط، يتمتع الجن بلحم البقر وبمجرد أن تأكل الحيوانات الأخرى لحوم البقر، من خلال إستحواذ الجن علي تلك الأجسام. لا تحاول إطعامهم لحم البقر داخل منزلك. قم بفعل ذلك دائماً بالخارج و في الجو المفتوح. سيكون ذلك أكثر أماناً، كما ستكون دعوة مفتوحة لأي مجموعة أو أي جني. الآن تقريباً في نفس الوقت، كرر هذه العملية لسبعة أيام على الأقل. الآن من يوم 8، عندما يكون جميع الجن على علم بك و بالفعل الذي تقوم به، سوف ينتظروك لتأتيهم وتطعمهم لحم البقر. تحتاج إلى إضافة صياغات أكثر مع الصياغات السابقة الخاصة بك، مثل، " أرجو أن تكونوا لطفاء معي أيها الأصدقاء من الجن، من فضلكم لا تؤذوني أو تؤذوا عائلتي. أريد أن أصبح صديقكم، لذا أرجو أن تصبحوا أصدقائي" .خلال المشي في منزلك، كرر هذه الأنواع من الجمل ما لا يقل عن خمسة عشرة مرة، بمجرد أن يستمع الجن إلي هذا منك، سوف يستميتون في التحدث إليهم، ولكن عليك أن تكون صبوراً جداً على الأقل لمدة أسبوع.

These are very low-profile demons with no crazy agenda. Even you spray holy water on them frequently, all the time they will de-energize due to this action. Still they will leave the house. No doubt demons will be more alert and will try to keep themselves away from you or holy water spray. The second thing is those demons will do is they will not bother you as much, so you feel you need to spray holy water more frequently. As I said on pains, holy water works when the demons will be even a little bit above the surface of our skin; otherwise, I am going to tell to more procedures to fight against them, until medical science uses electronic machines to repel them away from our bodies.

Always spray holy water only inside your house. Don't worry about outside. The reason is, if you will start spraying holy water outside the house, demons from outside places will start coming inside your houses. Don't ever try to pick a fight with any demon. It is not a good idea. As far as whatever you do for yourself and your house, you have a very genuine reason for this. Definitely you want to protect yourself. It's okay. But don't spray holy water outside the house. Even inside the house, don't spray holy water in garage or few not in use closets and few other corners of your house. You need to leave some space/room for them, somewhere for sure. Due to continuous spray of holy water, now demons will still be around your house or you will be kind a tamped, they will be a little bit easygoing and with time definitely very nice and friendly with you. Always keep one thing in your mind—you don't need to make demons your enemies on purpose. You need to do whatever you need to do for your safety, but keep telling them and keep insisting them to become your friends.

حافظ على إطعامهم لحم البقر كل يوم، ويمكنك تقليل كمية اللحم البقري الآن، ولكن لا تسقط أي يوم. لأنهم ينتظروك أن تتمكن من إطعامهم كل يوم. الآن يجب إطعامهم لحم البقر بالفعل لمدة خمسة عشر يوماً، و خلال تلك الأيام سوف تلاحظ الكثير من الأشياء تحدث من حولك، ولكن فقط تجاهل كل شيء، و كأنك لا تعلم أي شيء. الآن اليوم 16، عند إطعامك لحم البقر للجن الخاص بك، قل كل شيء كالمعتاد، مهما كنت تقول لهم أو نطلب منهم روتينياً. الآن تحتاج في ذلك اليم أن تطلب منهم الإتصال بك عن طريق إعطائك بعض الإشارات، حتى تتمكن من معرفة أن الجن من حولك يريدون أن يجعلوك صديقاً لهم. الآن من ذلك اليوم، وسيحاول الجن أن يعطوك بعض أو عدة علامات أو إشارات ليقولوا لك أنهم أصدقائك، حاول أن تفهم علاماتهم وإشاراتهم.

يجب أن تسمح لهم بالمحاولة أولاً. الآن في اليوم التالي، و أثناء إطعامك الجن لحم البقر، أخبرهم بوضوح أنه يجب عليهم دغدغة أصابعك بمجرد أن يرغبوا في التواصل معك. أخبر كل الجن أنه يجب علي كل جني أن يختار إصبع مختلف لكل جني ليدغدغه. ثق بي، لن يستغرق ذلك وقتاً طويلاً، حتي يبدأوا جميعهم بدغدغتك، الواحدا تلو الآخر،ليظهروا لك إهتمامهم بالحديث معك، وأنهم يرغبون في أن يصبحوا أصدقائك. يجب أن ترد عليهم. وتتحدث معهم بطريقة طبيعية مثل الطريقة التي تتواصل بها مع البشر. إذا كانوا يدغدغوك بق أو فيوة شديدة أو في المكان الخطأ، أخبرهم بذلك على الفور. إذاً هذه هي بداية إتصالاتك بالجن. الآن سوف يبدأ مختلف الجن في زيارتك طوال الوقت، وخلال زيارتهم لك، سوف يقوموا بدغدغتك في مكان معين ليخبروك أنهم حولك و أنهم يريدون التحدث إليك.

This is my own experience. Demons don't listen to you until they know you are somebody or at least you can use something against their activities to protect yourself. Demons will be more careful and less dangerous once they will know that you are aware about their existence and presence around, and that you can defend yourself to repel them away from yourself. In that condition, demons will bother you less and will try to be friendlier with you. Once they will become your friends, trust me, you will really enjoy a true and pure friendship.

The next step is how to make holy water. All the prayers in holy books don't have the same effects. Every prayer has its own effects, benefits, and use. There are some particular, very particular prayers, regardless of their meanings, have burning and repelling poweörs to demons away from us. Every religion has these kinds of prayers. So instead of wasting your time, just contact your religious leaders and ask them to guide you about those demon-repelling prayers. If you don't have courage to ask someone about it then just go to your religious websites on the Internet and search for them; you will find them very easily.

Now I am going to tell you how to use them. Holy prayers are always effective when you read them in the original language instead of their translations in any other language. All the holy prayers, once we read them repeatedly, will generate repelling and burning waves and rays. The more repeatedly you read, the more waves and rays will be generated in your mouth. Minimum repeatedly read at least eleven times nonstop without talking or saying something else.

رؤية الجن و الآلام السيطرة عليها

الآن عليك أن تبدأ بالتحدث معهم، مثل مرحباً، كيف حالكم؟، أو أشكركم على إتصالكم بي، أو أي شيء لطيف. هذه لا تزال جلسة الممارسة، لذلك لا تطلب منهم فعل أي شيء من أجلك. لأنهم بمجرد أن ي، وسوف تركوك لن يكون لديك أي شخص آخر للقيام بممارسة إتصالاتك. الآن سوف يقوم الجن بدغدغتك طوال الوقت، لأنهم يصبحون سعداء جداً بمجرد أن يصبح البشر أصدقائهم. لذلك هذا هو وقت تدريبهم، يجب أن نشرح لهم متي يمكنك التواصل معهم ومتي يصعب عليك التواصل معهم، الخ.

يمكنك أثناء ذلك أن تبدأ تطلب منهم كل ما تريد أن تراه في أحلامك علي الأقل. أخبرهم كل يوم ماذا تريد أن ترى مراراً وتكراراً. تأتي الآن إلي المرحلة الثانية من الإتصالات مع بالحن. ولقد وصفت بالفعل ذلك في مكان ما أن في هذا الكتاب، في إطار كيفية التواصل مع الجن. الآن بمجرد أن تبدأ ممارسة المزيد والمزيد من كيفية التواصل مع الجن، سيبدأوا في التحدث معك بكل وسيلة ممكنة. خلال ذلك، سيكون بعض الجن لطفاء جداً، وسوف يظهروا لك أحلام لطيفة جداً، ولكن بعض الجن سوف يستمرون في محاولة اللعب معك من خلال عرض بعض الأشباح أو الكوابيس.، ولكن تحتاج إلى البقاء على ثقة وتخبرهم بالضبط ما يحاولون القيام به معك. من هذه هي ممارستك الأساسية وتدريبك الأساسي. من هناك سوف تبذل المزيد من الجهد والممارسة، وسوف تتعلم أكثر وسيكون لديك المزيد من الثقة والقوة مع الجن.

في هذه المرحلة، لديك مجموعة من الجن من حولك وجميعهم أصدقائك. الآن تواصل معهم أكثر وأكثر، سوف يصبح هؤلاء الجن أصدقاء مقربين لك جداً. تذكر، أنه من الصعب جداً الحصول على جني جيد ومخلص جداً. بمجرد أن ترسلهم هنا وهناك، تذكر أنك قد تفقدهم.

SEE & CONTROL DEMONS & PAIN

In the next step, immediately you finish reading, either in a water in a spray bottle or in a glass of water or both, blow air from your mouth six times to mix or add those waves or rays from your mouth into plain water. Okay, once you read holy prayers eleven times and blow those rays from your mouth six times, it means you mix/add those demons burning or repelling waves or rays in the plain water. This water is your holy water now. These demons repelling waves or rays will stay inside the water for maximum forty to fifty seconds. This means that plain water is your holy water and will be effective for the next forty seconds. Without wasting a single second, you need to spray that holy water on yourself, your kids, and surroundings, etc. If it takes more than forty seconds then read prayers again to reenergize the water. In beginning, you need to spray holy water more frequently. Then with time, if you do this twice a day, this will keep you on the safe side. Always spray before go to bed. Now to get rid of pains and hardheaded demons, you can use the same procedures of reading prayers with any medicated syrups or with medicated ointments to repel the pains out of your body. Medicated ointments and medicated syrups are mainly taken for the healing purpose, but once you will add/mix your holy prayers with medicated syrups or ointments, the same medicine will be effective to repel or kick out the electronic pains from your body. But don't forget. These waves and rays of prayers will stay inside those medicated syrups or ointments only for maximum forty seconds. Usually this is enough time to work against any pain; otherwise, repeat the process. Just make sure either water or syrup or ointment should reach at the point where this pain is sitting.

بعد مرور بعض الوقت يمكنك أن تبدأ أن تطلب من أصدقائك من الجن ما تريد منهم أن يفعلوه لك. الآن سأقول لك ما يستطيع الجن أن يفعله لك وماذا يمكنك أن تطلب منهم أن يفعلوه.

يجب أن تعرف أن الجن يمكنهم قتل بعضهم البعض بسهولة بالغة. بمجرد أن تطلب من الجن عمل أي شيء لك، أنت لا تعرف أبداً إذا كان الجن سيتقاتلوا مع الجن الموجودين حول أشخاص آخرين.، فقد تفقد الجن الخاص بك خلال تلك المعركة. إن مجموعة الجن الباقين في منزلك أو من حولك منذ فترة طويلة، و الذين أصبحوا أصدقائك، هم الأكثر إرتباطاً و إخلاصاً من حولك. بمجرد وضع الجن في مأزق من خلال إرسالهم للقيام بشيء صعب من أجلك، إذا مات الجن الطيبون جداً، فهذا يعني أنك تفقد الكثير. بمرور الوقت، سوف تحصل علي جن جدد كل يوم، أو حتى مجموعات من الجن من حولك، ولكنها قد لا تكون مخلصة ومتعلقة بك بنفس القدر. حسنا، يمكنك أن تطلب من الجن الخاص بك الذهاب لآي شخص و تنويمه مغناطيسياً لجعله في صالحك أو في صالح شخص آخر أو ضد شخص ما.

يمكنك أن تطلب من الجني الخاص بك إ حداث شجار بين إثنين آخرين من الناس، كما يمكنك أن تطلب منهم زرع الحب أو الكراهية بين شخصين أو أكثر. يمكنك أن تطلب من الجني الخاص الذهاب وقتل شخص ما، الذهاب والتسبب في أزمة قلبية لشخص ما، أو جعل شخصا ما مريضاً، ويمكنك نطلب منها ان تعطي أي مرض لأحد. إن الجن لديهم القدرة علي القيام بهذه الأنواع من الأشياء في ثوان. في الواقع إنهم يحبون كل هذه السلبية. يمكنك أن تطلب من االجن الخاص بك الذهاب و التسبب في حادث سيارة لشخص ما عن طريق فعل أي شيء. قد يستغرق ذلك بعض الوقت، ولكن في نهاية المطاف سوف يحدث.

Sometimes pains or demons are a little robust/ tough, so you may have to use these procedures frequently until you defeat them.I do all these holy practices in routine, even most of the time, I don't need it. It's very effective and keeps us healthy and safe all the time.These procedures are effective and treat only demons and pains. It is not as much effective or useful in case of infections/cancers/HIV infections.

I have already guided you how to hunt and kill those diseases/ cancers/insects in the beginning of this book. Use both ideas and holy procedures to keep yourself healthy and protected. Holy prayers convert plain water to holy water just for few seconds, but trust that holy water even for few seconds does the job!And it is even more than enough for any demon or pain to leave a body.

Let me remind any doctor or any medical scientist again, who still has some doubts in their minds about the physical existence of pains or demons if they are ready to start research to discover the rays to use against demons and pains to help mankind, I am ready to prove the physical existence of pain in front of them any time. All the above procedures, all the methods, are normally for normal people, so they can help themselves against these demons and pains. I don't need any tools to fight against these demons and pains 99.99 percent of the time. I can prove to any doctor or medical scientist in few minutes the existence of pains. Even I don't need to see those doctors or scientists, they just need to stay on the phone with me, and I will move their normal pains like headache, back pain, knee pain, neck pain, etc., away from them.

رؤية الجن و الآلام السيطرة عليها

يمكنك ان تطلب من الجن الخاص بك لتخويف شخص ما أو إظهار أحلام مخيفة أو أحلام جميلة له، أو كل ما تطلب منهم القيام به. يمكنك أن تطلب من الجن الخاص بك إحداث إنجذاب لك في نقس رجل ما أو امرأة ما، أو تجميد عقل شخص ما، أو ذاكرته، أو فكاره. يمكنك كذلك أن تطلب منهم الذهاب وإتلاف عقل و ذاكرة من شخص ما، أو التجسس لك، أو قراءة أفكار شخص ما وإبلاغك بها، أو الحفاظ على سلامته منزلك من الشر و من الجن الآخرين . يمكنك أن تطلب منهم كذلك ترك كل الأشياء السيئة والشريرة و أن يصبحوا جن طيبون وايجابيون جداً . يمكنك أن تطلب منهم الذهاب داخل الآلات الإكترونية وتدميرها. إذا كان لديك جهاز التحكم عن بعد للروبوت، يمكنك أن تطلب الجن الخاص بك السيطرة على الروبوت بدون جهاز التحكم غن بعد. يمكنك أن تطلب من الجن الخاص بك الذهاب داخل دوائر الحاسوب وإحداث بعض العطل داخل تلك الدوائر.

يمكنك أن تطلب منهم جعل أي شخص يشعر بالدوار خلال قيادة السيارة أو في وقت آخر. إن الجن يحبون القيام بكل الأنشطة السلبية والمتطرفة. أعتقد أنني بعد الإنتهاء من هذا الكتاب، سوف أحاول الإسترخاء قليلاً. بعد ذلك ربما، حتى بالرغم من خوفي الشديد ، ولكني ما زلت لا أعرف إلى متى سوف أكون قادراً على السيطرة على نفسي حتي لا أقوم بأي تجارب جديدة، أو إحداث إتصال تخاطري من بعض المناطق الغير عادية / أو المخلوقات في العالم؟ دعونا نرى. من الصعب أن نحصل علي بعض الأعمال الإيجابية من الجن، على الأقل لفترة طويلة. لا يستطيع الجن إنتاج أو بناء أي بيت لك، إنهم لا بستطيعون جعلك فائزاً في ورق اليانصيب. إنهم لا يستطيعون أيضاً جلب الأموال النقدية أوالذهب لك بالسحر أو بدون سحر. لا يستطيع الجن تغيير أرقامك في نسخ الفحص أو الإختبار الخاص بك.

SEE & CONTROL DEMONS & PAIN

If they want me to prove more, I can move their pain from one part of the body to other part of the body. If they want me to prove more, I can move someone else's pain to their body. I will do my best to prove the physical existence of the pain to them to convince them, if they promise to start a very serious research to discover and amplify electronically all kinds of rays and waves to fight against the pains and demons to help mankind.

Demons cannot withstand holy water at all. They leave immediately from that particular body or that place, but they may come back quickly. So you need to use these procedures frequently. The best way to fight against any pain is take healing medication first to heal the damage then use holy water or any ointment with holy prayers to kick out electronic pain from your body. There are no side effects of the use of holy water for humans.

But there are a lot of problems for demons to come in contact with holy water. The way demons don't like holy water, the same way a human totally possessed by a demon does not like holy water either, due to the influence of demons. But regardless of how much those people get upset, if you want to fix them, keep spraying holy water on them until they come out from the possession of that demon. To kick out a demon or pain from your body, stay barefooted on concrete or ceramic floor during someone spray holy water on you.Grounding with cement floor give very easy path to demons and pains to leave the body.

رضوان قرشي

يستطيع الجن تنويمك مغناطيسياً لتصوير شكل إنسان ما حولك في مخيلتك طوال الوقت. ولكن في الواقع، لا يستطيعون تحويل أو تغيير أنفسهم في أي حيوان، أو إنسان، أو أي شيء آخر. يستطيع الجن إنشاء أي صورة مؤقتة أو دائمة لآي شبح أو ساحرة أو إنسان أو حيوان من حولك، ولكنهم لا يستطيعون تغيير أنفسهم. لأي شيء في الواقع.، و لا يستطيعون تحريك أي شيء مادياً من مكان إلى آخر. كذلك لا يستطيعون القيام بأي وظيفة مادية لك، مثل نقل الأشياء من مكان إلى مكان، بغض النظر عما إذا كانت صغيرة جداً أم كبيرة جداً. كما أنهم لا يستطيعون مساعدتك في القيام بأي عمل بناء في منزلك، و لا يستطيعون جلب أي سيارة جديدة أو أي هدية لنا. ولا يستطيعون تنظيف البيت لك، ولا يستطيعون سرقة المال من جيوبك، إنهم حتى لا يستطيعون تحريك قرش واحد من مكان إلى آخر. يستطيع الجن تنويم شخص ما مغناطيسيا ليسرق لك، ولكن لا يستطيع الجن فعل ذلك بأنفسهم. لا يستطيع الجن قيادة سيارتك، أو أن يصبح جني ما صديق أو صديقة لك في الحياة المادية الحقيقية. يستطيع الجن أن يظهروا لك أي شيء حتى و إن كان رجل حسن المظهر أو إمرأة جميلة في أحلامك طوال الوقت ولكن فقط في الأحلام أو في خيالك، و ليس في الحقيقة على الإطلاق. يستطيع الجن أن يقوموا بتنويم أي رجل أو إمرأة بمنتهي السهولة لتقع في حبك، وحتي مختلف البشر طوال الوقت.

يستطيع الجن جلب أي إنسان في أحلامك طوال الوقت وبالطريقة التي تريدها. إنهم يستطيعون أن يأخذوك في رحلة إلي أي مكان في العالم، أي فندق، أي شاطئ، أي مسرح، أي بارك، في أحلامك طوال الوقت مراراً وتكراراً. تجنب تدريب الجن الخاص بك على القيام بأشياء شريرة.

304

Now I am going to tell you how to start making demons your friends. Demons don't ever take it easy. This is something really new for demons, when I am giving you guidelines to bring demons a little close to you as your friends. Demons always feel confident that humans can talk about demons. They can make a bunch of assumptions about demons, but humans will always be in limbo and in doubts about the existence of the demons. Okay, I am going to change this. I am going to give each and every human so much confidence and access to demons; even it will not take more than few months when all human will be communicating with demons openly. And if demons will not become nice and friendly with those human around them, it will be difficult for demons to stay around those people for a long time. So it's time when demons need to give up all their secret activities against humans and become more open and cooperative with them.Demons need to quit harassing and scaring humans immediately and expose themselves to all humans. Until now, I change a lot of things between me and demons since I started sensing them and then started seeing them, and in the next step, I started communication with them. In the beginning, it is very difficult to convince any demon to listen to you or pay attention to you, because demons always feel totally confident that humans will never be sure that demons are around or not. So the very initial and first step is your confidence level. Before I started seeing them, I was always confused that any demons are around me or not, until any demons come close to me, so I started sensing them. At that time, I always assumed that always one or two demons were around me. They are smart; not too many of demons were not coming close to me.

حاول تدريب الجن الخاص بك على القيام بالأشياء الجيدة لأنهم سوف يعيشون ربما لمائة سنة، ولكن الجن الخاص بك سوف يعيش عدة آلاف من السنين مع الأجيال القادمة الخاصة بك. لا تتورط مع أي طبيب للجن. السبب هو بمجرد أن يرسل أي طبيب للجن، جن شرير و قوي جداً من حولك، في الخطوة الأولى تلك سيقتل الجن الشرير، أصدقائك من الجن الخاص بك لإفساح المجال لأنفسهم حولك. هؤلاء الجن من أطباء الجن يعملون دائماً من أجل أطباء الجن هؤلاء. وسيسيطرون عليك، و علي عائلتك، وشؤونك الخاصة، و عملك، وفقاً لأوامر أطباء الجن. لن يكون هؤلاء الجن أصدقائك المخلصين أبداً. لذلك أفضل شيء هو الحفاظ على الشياطين المخلص الخاص بك حولك طوال الوقت. لا تسيئ إستخدامهم، حتي يظلواعلى قيد الحياة لوقت طويل ويقوموا برعايتك.

قبل بضعة أيام، كنت أقرأ الأخبار على الإنترنت MSN عن إمكانية إكتشاف نحو عشرة عوالم جديدة مماثلة للأرض. إسمح لي أن أقدم لك فكرة قليلة. هذا هو كل شيء عن، E= 2MC2. لقد ترك أعظم عقل هذه النظرية لنا ولكن العلم الحديث لا يزال غير قادر على الغوص في أعماق هذه النظرية. على أي حال، ذهني يلي قليلا من هذه النظرية. أنا خائف جداً من زيارة تلك الأماكن مثل الشمس، قد تقتلني و تقتل عقلي في ثانية واحدة. لكنني متفتح كثيراً لتأسيس إتصال تخاطري مع تلك العوالم العشرة الجديدة المماثلة للأرض. المشكلة هي ماذا سوف أجد هناك؟ إذا كان هناك أي شيء مماثل للجن أو العقول الإلكترونية في تلك العوالم الجديدة / الآراضي، بغض النظر عما إذا كانوا في أجسام الحيوانات أو الروبوتات أو الأسلحة، أو داخل الأجسام الغريبة، أو داخل أجهزة الكمبيوتر، سوف أكون قادراً على تقديمهم في عالمك/عالمي.

But when I started seeing demons, it surprised me about their population. In one time, sometimes, even no single demon was coming close to me because I already tested on myself the use of holy water. All demons around me were aware that whenever I will sense any demon around me, I will spray holy water to push or repel them away from me. For that reason most demons were staying away from me. But once I started seeing them, it surprised me how much population demons have everywhere in this world. In a small house of two/three bedrooms, you should expect several of thousand demons in your house around you all the time. So your total confidence and believe that all the time uncountable demons are around you, is the first and the major step towards friendship with demons. You cannot go to the second step until you become perfect in the first step.

The reason is that you can dodge a human but you cannot dodge a demon. Demons will read your mind to judge your confidence level about their presence and existence around you. Do you have problem in that? Okay, just trust me. Now never feel or think doubtful about demons' presence around you. Always be sure you have uncountable demons around you in your garage, backseats of your cars, dark rooms in your house, and here and there, everywhere. Take your time, regardless of how long, but don't move to second step until you are totally successful in step one. If you are not feeling total confidence and you move to step two, trust me, you are just wasting your time.

إلى متى سيبقون هنا أو يغادرون على الفور من هنا، لست متأكداً من ذلك. لا أعتقد أنهم سيكونوا قادرين على العثور على طريق العودة إلى كوكبهم الأصلي/عالمهم. ولكن إذا كنت سأستطيع القيام بذلك. إذا قمت بتقديمهم إلى عالمك/عالمي هنا وعن طريق الصدفة، إذا كانوا متقدمين للغاية علمياً، كيف ستسيطر العلوم الحديثة أو تتنافس معهم، إذا ما قرروا التوحد وإستخدام الجن المحليين الموجودين في مجتمعاتنا في عالمنا لأغراضهم؟ ما هوالحد الأقصى الذي يمكنني القيام به ، أعتقد، إذا لم ينسحبوا على الفور مني، إذا لم يقتلوني على الفور، وقرروا البقاء حولي لبعض الوقت، يمكنني الحصول على كل المعلومات الممكنة منهم عن مناطق أخرى من الكون و خاصة المعلومات حول كوكبهم أو عالمهم الخاص بهم . أنا لا أعتقد أنني يمكنني أن أفعل أكثر من ذلك.

سوف أشارك الجميع كل ما لدي من المعرفة بالتأكيد ، في الكتاب المقبل، ولكن هذه ليست وجهة نظري. وجهة نظري هي عندما لا يكون العلم الحديث على علم بالعوالم الموازية غير المرئية من حولنا هنا، كيف ستستطيع العلوم الحديثة التعامل مع مخلوقات غير مرئية من عوالم أخرى في الأشهر القليلة القادمة؟ دعونا نرى ما ذا سيحدث.

شكراً ونتمنى لك التوفيق!

In the second step, you should have very clear picture of them. They are all flying here and there in your house, they are continuously listening to you, and watching you. You should have their right picture in your imagination. Don't think about ghosts or witches or any big demons as people portrait in movies. Only think and imagine about their real sizes and looks in your mind, because at that time demons will be reading your mind. Demons are very small flying creatures. Either clear or very light black smoky color. Small round shapes. Some look like flying threads. Some look like small clear hollow bubbles. Some look similar to a small spider shape. Their sizes are almost between a small cockroach to a small ant. But most of them are equal to the size of a fly. So once you feel you understand their looks and structure and you feel total confidence about their presence around you everywhere, choose a time around evening, like 5:00 p.m, take around half pound of ground beef in your hand, and spread your hand in front of you so everyone can see ground beef in your hand. Now start walking slowly in each and every room, restroom, and all the corners inside the house only. All that time, you need to call demons in a very nice and bribing way like this, "All my demons friends, please come behind me. I am going to feed you beef so you can enjoy the beef." Walk everywhere in your house and repeat these sentences at least fifteen to twenty times. Now by saying the same sentence or something similar in a very nice and bribing way, walk towards outside your house and leave that beef in some corners away from the trees. You need to keep that beef away from the trees so any demons can access it. If you leave it by the tree, then demons around tree will not allow other demons from here and there to have access to that beef. Demons don't eat beef.

Actually demons cannot eat anything. But in the programming of their electronic brain, makes demons have crazy desire to eat beef. So once you offer demons to eat beef in an open atmosphere, they will reach there from everywhere by possessing the bodies of different animals, birds, reptiles, and insects and will enjoy the beef once other animals eat it. This is open bribing to control them. Anyway, when demons enjoy other physical activities once they possess the bodies of human, animal, etc., exactly the same way demons enjoy beef once the other animals eat beef during their possession of those bodies. Don't try to feed them beef inside your house. Always do this outside and in the open atmosphere. This will be secure and will be an open invitation and open party for any demon. Now almost at the same time, repeat this process for at least seven days. Now from day 8, when all demons will be aware about you and your action already, will be waiting for you to come and feed them beef, you need to add some more wordings with your previous wordings, like, "All my demons friends, please be nice with me. Please don't hurt me or my family. I want to become your friend, so please become my friend." During your walk in your house, repeat these kinds of sentences at least fifteen times. Once demons hear this from you, they will be dying to talk to you, but you need to be very patient at least for one week. Keep feeding them beef every day; you can reduce the quantity of beef now but don't skip any day, because they wait for you every day, so you can feed them. Now altogether you should have to feed them the beef for fifteen days. During these days, you will observe a lot of things happening around you, but just ignore everything, and act as if you are not aware of anything.

Now day 16, when you feed beef to your demons, as usual say everything whatever you tell them or ask them in routine. Now this day you need to ask them to contact you by giving you some signals, so you can figure out that demons around you want to make you their friend. Now from this day, demons will try to give you some or several signs or signals to tell you that they are your friends. Try to understand their signs and signals. You need to let them try first. Now the next day, as you feed demons beef, tell them clearly that they need to tickle on your fingers once they want to communicate with you. Tell all demons to choose a different finger for each demon to tickle. Trust me, it will not take a long time, and all of them, one by one, will start tickling you to show you their interest in talking to you and in becoming your friend. You need to respond to them.

You need to talk to them in a normal way the way you communicate with humans. If they are tickling you too hard or at the wrong place, tell them immediately. So this is your start of communications with demons. Now different demons will start visiting you all the time and during their visit to you, they will tickle you at a particular place to tell you that they are around and want to talk to you. Now you need to start talking to them, like hello, how are you doing? Or I am very thankful to you once you are communicating with me or anything nice. This is still your practice session, so don't ask them to do anything for you, because once they leave, you will not have anyone else to do your communication practice.

Now demons will tickle you all the time, because they become so happy once humans become their friends. So this is time to train them. You need to explain to them when you can communicate with them and when it is difficult for you to communicate with them, etc.

During this you can start asking them at least whatever you want to see in your dreams. Tell them repeatedly and every day what do you want to see. Now come to second stage of communications with demons. I described that somewhere already in this book, under how to communicate with demons. Now once you start practicing more and more how to communicate with demons, demons will be talking to you in every possible way. During this, some demons will be very nice and will show you very nice dreams, but some demons still try to play with you by showing you some ghosts or nightmares. But you need to stay confident and tell them exactly whatever they are trying to do with you. This is your basic practice and training. From there you will put more effort and practice, you will learn more and you will have more confidence and strength with demons.

At this point, for sure you have a bunch of demons around you and all of them are your friends. Now more and more you communicate with them, these demons will become your very close friends. Always remember, it is very difficult to get a very good and sincere demon. Once you send them here and there, remember, you may lose them. After some time you can start asking your demon friends whatever you want them to do for you. Now I will tell you what possibly demons can do for you and what you can ask them to do.

You should know that demons can kill each other very easily. So once you ask your demons to do something for you, you never know if your demons have to fight with the demons around other people. During that fight, you may lose your demons. The groups of demons staying in your house or around you since long time and become your friend are the most attached and most sincere demons around you. Once you put these demons in trouble by sending them to do something difficult for you, if somehow during the fight with other demons, if you're nice and very good demons die, it means you lose a lot. With time, every day, you will get new demons or even groups of demons around you, but they may not be as much sincere and attached with you. Okay, you can ask your demons to go and hypnotize anyone to bring them in your favor or someone else's favor or against someone. You can ask your demon to set a fight between two more people. You can ask them to create love or hate between two or more people. You can ask your demons to go and kill someone, go and give a heart attack to someone, make someone sick; you can ask them to give any sickness to anyone. Demons are capable of doing these kinds of things in seconds. Actually demons love all these negativity. You can ask your demons to go and give car accident to anyone by doing anything. This thing may take some time, but eventually it will happen. You can ask your demons to scare someone or show them scary dreams or nice dreams or whatever you ask them to do. You can ask your demons to create attraction for you inside some man or some woman. You can ask your demons to freeze someone's mind, memory, or thoughts.

You can ask your demons to go and damage the mind and memory of someone, or to spy for you, or to read someone's thoughts and inform you about them, or to keep your house safe from evil and other demons. You can ask them also to leave all bad and evil things and become very good and positive demons.

You can ask them to go inside electronic machines and destroy them. If you have a remote control robot, you can ask your demons to control that robot without remote. You can ask your demons to go inside computer circuits and create some malfunction inside those circuits. You can ask them to make anyone dizzy during driving or any another time. Demons love to do all negative and extreme activities. I think, after finishing this book, I will try to relax a little bit. Then may be, even I am scared to death, but still I don't know for how long I will be able to control myself not to do any new experiments or not to establish telepathic contact from some unusual areas/worlds or creatures? Let's see. It is difficult to take some positive work from demons, at least for a long time. Demons cannot do or perform any magic for you or for anyone else. Demons cannot bring or build any house for you; they cannot make you a lottery winner, they cannot also bring cash money or gold for you by magic or without magic. Demons cannot change your numbers in your examination copies. Demons can hypnotize you to create an imagination of a human around you all the time. But in actual, they cannot convert or change themselves in any human, animal, or anything else.

SEE & CONTROL DEMONS & PAIN

Demons can create any temporary or permanent image of any ghost or witch or human or animal around you, but in actual they cannot change themselves to anything. They cannot move anything physically from one place to another. They cannot do any physical job for you, like moving things from one place to another, regardless of whether it is very small or very big. They cannot help you in doing any construction work in your house. They cannot bring any new car or any gift for us, or clean your house for you, or steal money from your pockets, they even can not move a single penny from one place to another. Demons can hypnotize someone to steal for you, but demons cannot do it by themselves. Demons cannot drive your car, or become your boyfriend or girlfriend in real physical life. Demons can show you anything even a good-looking man or a beautiful woman in your dreams all the time but only in dreams or in your imagination, not in reality at all. Demons can hypnotize any man or woman very easily to fall in love with you, even different people all the time. Demons can bring any human in your dreams all the time the way you want. They can take you to a trip anywhere in the world, any hotel, any beach, any theater, any park, in your dreams all the time again and again. Avoid training your demons to do evil things. Try to train your demons for good things because you will live maybe for one hundred years, but your demons will live several thousand years with your next generations. Don't get involved with any demon doctor, the reason is that once any demon doctor send his very powerful evil demons around you, the first step of those evil demons is that they will kill your demon friends to make some room around you.

Those demons from demon doctors always work for those demon doctors. They will control you, your family, your affairs, and your business, according to the commands of demon doctors. Those demons will never be your sincere friends ever. So the best thing is to keep your sincere demon friends around you all the time. Don't misuse them, so they stay alive for long time and take care of you.

Few days ago, I was reading on MSN Internet news about the possible discovery of around ten new worlds similar to earth. Let me give you a little bit of clue. This is all about, $E = mc2$. The greatest brain left this theory for us but still modern science is unable to go deep inside that theory. Anyway, my brain follows a little bit of this theory. I am very much scared to visit places like the sun; it may kill me and my brain in one second. But I am very much open to establish a telepathicconnection to those ten new worlds similar to Earth. The problem is what will I find there? If there is anything similar to demons or electronic brains on those new worlds/earths, regardless of whether they are in bodies of animals or robots or inside weapons or in aliens or inside computers, I will be able to bring them in your/my world. For how long they will stay here or will leave immediately from here, I am not sure about it. I don't think they will be able to find the route to go back to their original planet/world.

But If I will be able to to do it. If I bring them to your/my world right here and by chance, if they are extremely modern scientifically, how our modern science will control or compete with them, if they decided to unite and use our local demons of our world for their purposes?

What maximum I can do, I think, if they will not leave me immediately, if they will not kill me immediately and decided to stay around me for some time, I can obtain every possible information from them about other areas of the universe and especially information about their planet or their world. I don't think I can do more than this. For sure, I will share all my knowledge with everyone, in the next book, but this is not my point.

My point is when modern science is not aware about invisible parallel worlds around us, right here, how come our modern science will be able to handle the invisible creatures of the other worlds in the next few months? Let's see what happens.

Thanks and good luck!